DATE DUE

APR	1 1996		
GAYLORD			PRINTED IN U.S.A.

fragments of
Redemption

Jewish Literature and Culture
Series Editor, Alvin Rosenfeld

fragments of Redemption

JEWISH THOUGHT AND LITERARY THEORY IN BENJAMIN, SCHOLEM, AND LEVINAS

Susan A. Handelman

INDIANA UNIVERSITY PRESS
Bloomington and Indianapolis

The paper used in this publication meets the minimum requirements of American
National Standard for Information Sciences—Permanence of Paper for Printed
Library Materials, ANSI Z39.48-1984.

Manufactured in the United States of America

Library of Congress Cataloging-in-Publication Data

Handelman, Susan A.
    Fragments of redemption : Jewish thought and literary theory in
  Benjamin, Scholem, and Levinas / Susan A. Handelman.
        p.   cm. — (Jewish literature and culture)
    Includes bibliographical references and index.
    ISBN 0-253-32695-8 (cloth)
    1. Judaism—20th century. 2. Jews—Germany—Cultural
  assimilation. 3. Benjamin, Walter, 1892–1940. 4. Scholem, Gershom
  Gerhard, 1897– . 5. Lévinas, Emmanuel—Views on Judaism.
  I. Title. II. Series.
  BM565.H26   1991
  296.3′092′2—dc20   90-26795

1 2 3 4 5   95 94 93 92 91

Idea for an Arcanum:

To present history as a trial in which man as advocate for mute nature makes a complaint against the nonappearance of the promised Messiah. The court, however, decides to hear witnesses for the future. There appear the poet who senses it, the sculptor who sees it, the musician who hears it, and the philosopher who knows it. Their testimony thus diverges, though all of them testify to his coming. The court does not dare admit its indecision. Hence there is no end of new complaints or new witnesses. There is torture and martyrdom. The jury benches are occupied by the living, who listen to the human prosecutor and the witnesses with equal mistrust. The jurors' seats are inherited by their sons. At length they grow afraid they may be driven from their benches. Finally all the jurors take flight, and only the prosecutor and the witnesses remain. (Walter Benjamin)

The only philosophy which can be responsibly practiced in the face of despair is the attempt to contemplate all things as they would present themselves from the standpoint of redemption. Knowledge has no light but that shed on the world by redemption: all else is reconstruction, mere technique. Perspectives must be fashioned that displace and estrange the world, reveal it to be with its rifts and crevices as indigent and distorted as it will appear one day in the messianic light. To gain such perspectives without velleity or violence, entirely from felt contact with its objects—this alone is the task of thought. It is the simplest of all things, because the situation calls imperatively for such knowledge, indeed because consummate negativity, once squarely faced, delineates the mirror image of its opposite. But it is also the utterly impossible thing, because it presupposes a standpoint removed, even though by a hair's breadth, from the scope of existence, whereas we well know that any possible knowledge must not only first be wrested from what is, if it shall hold good, but is also marked, for this very reason, by the same distortion and indigence which it seeks to escape. The more passionately thought denies its conditionality for the sake of the unconditional, the more unconsciously, and so calamitously, it is delivered up to the world. Even its own impossibility it must at last comprehend for the sake of the possible. But beside the demand thus placed on thought, the question of the reality or unreality of redemption itself hardly matters. (Theodor Adorno)

Contents

Acknowledgments

The support and generosity of many people and institutions have made this work possible. A Howard Foundation Fellowship administered by Brown University for the year 1982–83 enabled me to begin the project. The General Research Board of the University of Maryland enabled me to continue it with grants for the summers of 1982 and 1985 and the spring semester of 1987. Publication of this book has been subsidized by the office of the Dean of the College of Arts and Humanities of the University of Maryland, College Park (special thanks to Dr. Robert Griffith), and by the Littauer Judaica Publication Fund through the Joseph and Rebecca Meyerhoff Center for Jewish Studies at the University of Maryland, College Park. The Meyerhoff Center also awarded me a Samuel Ivry Fellowship for support during the summer of 1987.

I have also benefited immensely from conversations with many scholars whom I personally contacted during the long years of work on this book. I was first inspired to read Levinas over fifteen years ago by Geoffrey Hartman, who—as innumerable other scholars can attest—is one of the most generous and supportive senior scholars in the field of literary studies. Warren Zev Harvey also gave me encouragement and guidance in the initial stages of my work. Annette Aronowicz shared her superb translations of nine of Levinas's talmudic lectures before they were published, as well as her energy, enthusiasm, and support for the difficult task of understanding Levinas's philosophical works. Robert Gibbs kindly sent me a large chunk of his work in progress on Levinas, which I found to be among the best studies I have read on the topic. Richard Cohen gave me numerous essays of his own and inspired me to think more deeply about the relation of Levinas and Rosenzweig. And final thanks to Mr. Mark Pedreira for his intellectual support and indispensable help in tracking down lost references and proofreading the manuscript. My other innumerable intellectual inspirations and debts are listed in the footnotes and bibliography.

An early version of chapter 7 was published in *Poetics Today* 9:2 (1988) under the title "Parodic Play and Prophetic Reason: Two Interpretations of Interpretation" and is reprinted by permission of Duke University Press. Portions of chapters 7 and 8 appeared in *Religion and Literature* 22:2 (1990). Reprint permission has been granted by *Religion and Literature*, University of Notre Dame, Notre Dame, IN 46556. I have also used many excerpts from *The Correspondence of Walter Benjamin and Gershom Scholem*, 1932–1940, edited with a preface by Gershom Scholem, translated by Gary Smith and Andre Lefevere. English translation and Introduction copyrighted © 1989 by Schocken Books, Inc. Reprinted by permission of Schocken Books, published by Pantheon Books, a division of Random House, Inc. The many excerpts from Scholem's memoir of Benjamin, *Wal-

ter Benjamin: The Story of a Friendship, are reprinted with permission of the Jewish Publication Society. Permission to quote at length from Levinas's talmudic lectures in *Difficile liberté* has been given by Editions Albin Michel, Paris. My thanks to all.

The Hebrew noun for the dedication to a book is *hakdashah*, from the verb *hikdish*, meaning "to consecrate, devote, sanctify, designate." I dedicate this book to Rabbi Menachem Mendel Schneerson, the Lubavitcher Rebbe, in honor of his life's work of dedication and devotion to the entire Jewish people and the sanctification of the world.

Note on Documentation and Style

The system of references, endnotes, and bibliography in this book follows the format recommended by the Modern Language Association (MLA). Citations within the text are keyed to a list of research materials I have used. This list is compiled alphabetically at the back of the book under the title "Works Consulted." Within the body of the text itself, parenthetical documentation is used. When the list of works consulted contains only *one* work by an author, the parenthetical reference in the text then cites only the author's last name and the page number of the quotation: e.g., (Aarsleff 99). When the list of works consulted contains more than one work by an author, the parenthetical reference gives the title of the book or article (or a shortened version of it) in addition to the author's last name and page number: e.g., (Rosenzweig, "The New Thinking" 204–205). For further readability and conciseness, when the author's name or the title has already been mentioned within the sentence or in the preceding paragraph of the text, it is not repeated again in the parenthetical reference at the end of the sentence; only the page number is given: e.g., (204–205).

Footnotes at the end of each chapter are used for information, evaluation, and comments that the text cannot accommodate, or to give alternative bibliographic references and cross-references.

For additional conciseness, I have abbreviated the titles of the most frequently cited major primary works of the three major authors I study here. These extra abbreviations are listed below. Full citation and complete bibliography for these titles can be found in the "Works Consulted" list at the end of this book.

When I began this book in 1982, only a few small essays from Levinas's several volumes of Jewish writings had been translated into English, although his main philosophical works were available. By the time I completed this manuscript, translations into English of many of his important Jewish essays and lectures were in press. See Annette Aronowicz's *Nine Talmudic Readings by Emmanuel Levinas* and Sean Hand's translation of *Difficile liberté*. I have used the published English translations of his philosophical works; for his Jewish writings, I employ my own translations from the French except where otherwise specified.

List of Abbreviations

Works of Walter Benjamin:

GS	*Gesammelte Schriften*
Illum	*Illuminations*
OGTD	*The Origin of German Tragic Drama*
Refl	*Reflections*

Works of Emmanuel Levinas:

ADV	*L'au-delà du verset*
DL	*Difficile liberté*
DSS	*Du sacré au saint*
EE	*Existence and Existents*
OTB	*Otherwise Than Being*
QLT	*Quatre lectures talmudiques*
TI	*Totality and Infinity*

Works of Gershom Scholem:

Corr	*The Correspondence of Walter Benjamin and Gershom Scholem, 1932–1940*
JJC	*On Jews and Judaism in Crisis*
KS	*On the Kabbalah and Its Symbolism*
Mess Idea	*The Messianic Idea in Judaism*
MT	*Major Trends in Jewish Mysticism*
SF	*Walter Benjamin: The Story of a Friendship*

Preface

> All criticism follows upon performance.
> The drama critic will have little to say *be-*
> *fore* it, no matter how clever he may be, for
> his criticism is not supposed to testify to
> what cleverness he had prior to the perfor-
> mance but to that which the performance
> evokes in him. Similarly, a theory of
> knowledge that precedes knowledge has no
> meaning. For all knowing—whenever any-
> thing is really known—is a unique act, and
> has its own method. (Rosenzweig, "The
> New Thinking" 204–205)

> A book is interrupted discourse catching up
> with its own breaks. But books have their
> fate; they belong to a world they do not in-
> clude, but recognize by being written and
> printed, and by being prefaced and getting
> themselves preceded by forewords. They
> are interpreted and call for other books and
> in the end are interpreted in a saying dis-
> tinct from the said. (Levinas, *OTB* 171)

A preface is the first thing a reader of a book encounters, but it is often the last thing the author writes. After the first drafts have been laboriously produced and repeatedly revised, all questions have been settled about what to include and what to leave out, and every other task has been finished, the closure of the work is delayed by the author's need to explain a critical question: to whom is this book addressed and for what purpose? That this question takes priority over and orients all of the book's actual contents is signified by the fact that the preface is placed at the very beginning of the text, even though chronologically it may be written last.

There is much to be learned from this anachronism. Levinas finds in it a confirmation of one of his most fundamental theses about the essence of language: that language is always *to* and *for* someone before it signifies any specific content. And the nature of this primary relation to the other as the structure of ethics which is always prior to logic, ontology, epistemology, and politics is a main preoccupation of his philosophical work. Rosenzweig, a key influence on Levinas, writes in a similar fashion when he argues that criticism *follows* performance, that there is no theory of knowledge prior to the actual experience of coming to know, and so all real acts of knowledge are unique and have their own methods.

These thoughts help me both frame and answer the questions of audi-

ence, purpose, and method that a preface entails. I wrote this book for
several reasons and several audiences. On one level, I wrote for myself—
because I wanted to understand more about Walter Benjamin (1892–
1940), Gershom Scholem (1897–1982), and Emmanuel Levinas (b. 1906).
I chose these three figures because each is a Jew engaged in mediating the
Jewish and modern worlds, as I am. More specifically, each has had enormous influence on contemporary ideas about language, history, and interpretation in a variety of fields from literary criticism to religious studies,
philosophy, and social theory.

Thus this book is also a continuation of a work I published in 1982, *The
Slayers of Moses*, which was a result of my interest in the relations between
contemporary literary theory and theological interpretation. In that work, I
examined the historical foundations of interpretation theory in traditions
of biblical exegesis, surveyed the early schism between Jews and Christians
over proper interpretation of the Bible, and traced the reemergence of that
interpretive conflict in modern literary criticism. I subtitled that book *The
Emergence of Rabbinic Interpretation in Modern Literary Theory* because I
perceived striking affinities between ancient modes of rabbinic exegesis
and recent trends in modern literary criticism, especially as practiced by
secularized Jewish thinkers such as Freud, Derrida, and Harold Bloom.

I was gratified by the response to that book, and also stimulated by the
many questions subsequently put to me by reviewers, lecture audiences,
and those who wrote to me after reading it. I also found that there was a far
broader audience for the kind of interdisciplinary discussion I was attempting than I had realized. In this book, I have tried to keep all those
audiences in mind: scholars of literary criticism who are well versed in
postmodern linguistic theory and cultural studies but who have little background in Jewish history or theology; those in the field of religious studies
who are well trained in theology and hermeneutics but not literary history
and theory; students and teachers in rabbinical seminaries and Christian
divinity schools connected with universities and seeking to link their own
work with recent developments in the humanities; rabbis and ministers,
architects, legal scholars, historians of science, philosophers, and psycholo-
gists who have become interested in the ways contemporary literary theory
has elaborated upon the nature of reading, meaning, and signification; and
contemporary Jews in search of a way to understand Jewish tradition in
relation to modern thought.

Had I chosen to address only one specific audience or one group of
specialists, this book could have been shorter. Needless to say, it is no easy
task to write for several audiences of varying levels of knowledge. Information that can be taken for granted among one audience has to be presented
and explained for another. Readers from various backgrounds will no
doubt find certain sections somewhat esoteric and others somewhat elementary. In providing background for nonspecialists, I have sometimes
had to simplify extraordinarily complex and contentious issues. The phi-

losopher, for example, may be looking for a more intricate reading of Levinas in light of technical issues in contemporary phenomenology or analytic philosophy. My goal, however, is to explain the fundamentals of Levinas's thought to a broad audience unfamiliar with his work, to use some of his insights as a critique of contemporary literary theory, and to relate his philosophical to his overtly Jewish writings. I hope each reader of this book will make the necessary allowances for the others to whose needs I have tried to respond.

On another level, this mixture of audiences and fields is embedded in the heart of the work of the three writers I have chosen to study here, and that is one of the primary reasons I was attracted to each of them. Each lived and wrote on the border of several areas. Benjamin is not just a "German literary critic," Scholem an "Israeli historian," or Levinas a "French philosopher." Benjamin wrote a highly philosophical form of criticism which became increasingly "historicized" under the pressure of the collapsing Weimar Republic, the challenge of Marxism, and the rise of Nazism. Scholem was a historian of religion, an emigrant to Palestine from Germany, and the creator of the modern field of the academic study of Jewish mysticism at the Hebrew University. He was also an intimate and lifelong friend of Benjamin, with whom he shared and debated ideas about language, commentary, philosophy, history, politics, and modern Judaism. Levinas is a Russian Jew who went to study philosophy in Freiburg and Strasbourg as a young man, eventually became a French citizen, then director of a Jewish school in Paris as well as a philosophy professor.

Each was caught up in the most catastrophic events of the twentieth century. Benjamin committed suicide when he could find no escape from Nazi Europe. Levinas survived the war in a French prisoner-of-war camp but lost all his family, who had remained in Russia. Scholem escaped the Nazis through his early emigration to Palestine in 1923 but also lost close family members in the Holocaust, and suffered the agonizing and endless Arab-Jewish conflicts in Palestine.

The intellectual, historical, and personal conflicts each of these writers endured as both a European and a Jew gave rise to their extraordinary works of criticism, commentary, history, and philosophy—to meditations on language and interpretation, messianism and materialism, Judaism and secular thought. There is still an intense ongoing debate about whether Benjamin was at heart a Marxist theoretician, or an aesthete, or a covert Jewish mystic. Scholem's work on Kabbalah (the Jewish mystical tradition) continues to inspire innumerable secular writers and critics from Celan to Borges to Harold Bloom, and has created a revolution in modern Jewish scholarship. Levinas introduced phenomenology to France and is well known and highly esteemed by continental philosophers. But he also wrote extensively on Judaism and Jewish life, trained Jewish teachers for the Alliance Israélite Orientale, gave lectures on the Talmud, and has been a major figure in French-Jewish cultural life. Yet despite the great interest

of contemporary literary theorists in French philosophy and the phenomenological tradition, Levinas is infrequently mentioned, even though Derrida has acknowledged his profound debt to Levinas's critique of
Heidegger and Husserl.

Each of these thinker's writings have influenced and continue to have
much to say to current debates in literary theory. In the many years I have
been working on this book, the focus of literary theory has shifted from
debates about the abstract nature of linguistic signification to issues of how
language and literary texts affect and are affected by political and cultural
contexts, i.e., to an increasing recognition of the way questions of language
and questions of history and power are inextricably intertwined. Scholem,
Benjamin, and Levinas were deeply preoccupied with all these issues. The
problems of history, historicism, and historical method—and the relation
of history to the language which creates and narrates history—are major
themes in much of their work. In different ways, they each wrote out of a
deep frustration with the academic and "scientific" nineteenth-century
historical method and its Enlightenment heritage.

Benjamin formulated an idea of explosive messianic time which he allied to a revolutionary Marxism. Denied a teaching position in the German university, he abandoned the conventional academic forms of literary
criticism. As the situation in Germany deteriorated and he finally was
forced into exile, he had to make his living by his pen. It was a precarious
existence in which he moved from one drab inexpensive lodging to another. He wrote book reviews for newspapers, radio scripts, and luminous
and extraordinary commissioned essays, and worked on a massive private
project for years—a cultural history of the Paris Arcades which dealt with
the origins of modernity and remained unfinished and fragmentary at the
time of his death.[1]

Scholem attempted to practice a rigorous kind of academic, philological,
and historical study of Jewish mysticism, and he published scores of books
and essays which were widely acclaimed in his lifetime. Many of his speculations about kabbalistic linguistics were indebted to Benjamin. Benjamin
in turn, despite his later turn to "dialectical materialism," was called the
"Marxist rabbi" because of the continuing influence of Scholem. But
Scholem and Benjamin came to differ strongly on political questions.
Scholem was intensely anti-Marxist, fervently embraced a cultural form of
Zionism, and strove to keep messianic and apocalyptic thought out of
actual Zionist politics in Palestine. It was almost as if his critical and
distanced mode of academic history writing was a kind of dam to contain
the explosive forces in the mystical texts he had brought to the fore, and
with which he often intuitively identified. At the same time, his relation
with Benjamin sharply influenced his philosophy of history.

In Levinas's view, apocalyptic ecstasies (political or theological), mystical fusions, the seductions of the irrational, were not only dangerous but
also allied with the egoism and violence which he perceived at the very

foundation of Western philosophy. His task would be to reveal that violence and create an "ethical metaphysics," a philosophy for both Jew and non-Jew in the wake of the Holocaust and its horrors. Like Benjamin and Scholem, Levinas was also in search of a solution to the problems of the modern Jew whose ties to Jewish tradition and Jewish faith had been strained by the Enlightenment and the culture of modernity. And like them, he argued that there could be no retreat to a pre-Enlightenment faith, nor any simple casting off of Western thought and its challenges.

But he also brings this culture to judgment, an imperative judgment in which both Jew and non-Jew partake. Nor will he completely abandon the Enlightenment vision of reason and universalism. Instead, he tries to formulate a "second" type of reason which is neither autonomous and imperialistic nor slavish and mindless. Ethics, as the binding of the self to the other, constitutes "the 'rationality' of a reason less hard on itself than the reasons of the philosophical tradition"—not a diminished but a fuller rationality (*ADV* 176).

Whereas Scholem set out to make respectable the body of Jewish mystical literature which had been in academic disrepute, and so to transform the image of Jewish thought and history, Levinas defends the inspiration, grandeur, and philosophical depth of what had been denigrated as dry, pharisaic legalism. In this philosophical and ethical rationalism of the rabbis he finds a "reason prior to reason" and the power to judge, transform, and redeem history. For Levinas, a renewed relation to classical talmudic texts, not to Jewish mysticism, is what is required for the revival of both modern Judaism and modern philosophy. In his view, a purely historical approach to classical Jewish texts is essentially meaningless for contemporary Jewish life. The modern Jewish intellectual needs both philosophy and Judaism, the university and the Talmud.

While the work of Scholem is well known and accessible, Benjamin and Levinas are far more difficult and opaque writers, even for specialists. Benjamin's work does not have the logical rigor or consistency of systematic philosophy, though it is deeply philosophical. Levinas's work assumes a sophisticated knowledge of Hegel, Heidegger, and Husserl, but it, too, is not systematic in any purely logical sense. Because I have chosen not to write solely for specialists, and because of the difficulty of many of the texts I examine, I have taken extra space to outline and explain some of the backgrounds and basics before adding my own interpretations, analyses, and comparisons.

This leads to the question of my method. If, as Rosenzweig writes, "all knowing—whenever anything is really known—is a unique act, and has its own method," then this book also had to evolve its own method. Indeed, my method evolved much as Rosenzweig describes—following upon performance. I did not set out to "apply" any specific literary theory to a set of given texts, or to have literary criticism "instruct" Jewish Studies or philosophy or history from a position of superiority. The historically lived personal relation of Benjamin and Scholem itself provided a kind of frame-work for the way I discuss the interrelations among literary criticism, the-ology, and philosophy in part I. Scholem and Benjamin were interlocutors who at times were quite intimate and at other times quite alienated from each other; at times allies and at times antagonists; friends who at times supported and at other times deeply disappointed each other. Scholem wrote in his diary in 1918,

> Of late I have been getting along with Walter very well again—probably be-cause I now have found the locus from which I can tacitly resist him in my inner affairs. This way everything is all right; those scenes were, in the final analysis, nothing but moments in which he glimpsed a sphere of my condition that was not destined for him. After all, he did not reveal such things to me either, and our community consists precisely in each of us understanding the other man's reticence *without words* and respecting it. (*SF* 71)

As time passed, however, Scholem respected that reticence less and less, and he caused great strains in their relationship by aggressively criticizing the paths Benjamin's later work took, and accused him of abandoning his true genius and mission.

In part I of this book, I discuss Benjamin and Scholem by continuously juxtaposing, interweaving, and alternating their ideas about language, re-demption, messianism, politics, and history, by reading one in light of the other. The dialogue between the two men itself enacted and modeled a complex relation among criticism, theology, and politics. The Benjamin-Scholem relationship shows, for example, what a cultural materialist could learn from theology, and what a theologian or historian could learn from a literary critic—and also some of the stresses and strains of such an engagement.

In part II of this book, which is devoted entirely to Levinas, the issues and method are framed by Levinas's own dual career as a philosopher and theologian, as a "Greek" and a "Hebrew." Yet Levinas himself is often uncomfortable with this admixture, its tensions and problems, and claims to write a philosophy which has no theological starting point or any sectar-ian orientation. I am interested, however, in the way his philosophical and Jewish concerns intermingle. Thus I examine both Levinas's philosophical and his Jewish writings together, again reading "one in light of the other." Levinas's insistence on the priority of ethics has also inspired me to re-think and reevaluate much that is going on in contemporary literary stud-ies, and to realize how this important issue was missing from my first book.

The broader framework of this study, then, is the relation of Jews such as Levinas, Benjamin, and Scholem to modernism and postmodernism in general. Their works and lives demonstrate that sacred and secular inter-mingle far more than we have admitted, and show us ways in which criticism and theology might again vigorously engage each other. Especially if the practitioners of those fields would be willing to rethink those hard questions that a book's preface poses: *to* whom and *for* what purpose is the work done?

Winston Churchill, an enormously prolific author, once commented that writing a book "is like an adventure. To begin with it is a toy and amusement. Then it becomes a mistress, then it becomes a master, then it becomes a tyrant. The last phase is that just as you are about to be reconciled to your servitude, you kill the monster and fling him to the public." I herewith fling the monster to the public.

Part One

GERSHOM SCHOLEM AND
WALTER BENJAMIN

Introduction

The Story of a Friendship: Germans and Jews

> If there were not extant a German-Jewish
> tradition, we would have to discover one
> for our own sakes. (Habermas, "German
> Idealism" 42)

In 1941, Gershom Scholem published what was to become one of the classics of contemporary Jewish scholarship, *Major Trends in Jewish Mysticism*, the fruit of his twenty years of research into the Kabbalah—the Jewish mystical tradition. In the epigraph, he dedicated the book as follows: "To the Memory of Walter Benjamin (1892–1940). The friend of a lifetime whose genius united the insight of the Metaphysician, the interpretive power of the Critic and the erudition of the Scholar. Died at Port Bou (Spain) on his way into freedom." Scholem had made his own way to freedom in 1923 when he had emigrated from Germany to Palestine, although he was unable to convince his friend to do so as well. Benjamin, later trapped in Nazi Europe, died desperate and destitute after an abortive attempt to escape by crossing the Pyrenees at the border between France and Spain. He had been prepared for the worst and committed suicide. The next day, however, the border was reopened, and the other members of his party were allowed out. Benjamin was buried somewhere near the border town of Port Bou; no one knows the exact location of the grave.[1]

At the time of his death, Benjamin had published several books and numerous articles in newspapers and literary journals, and he was affiliated with the Institute for Social Research (otherwise known as the Frankfurt School of Critical Theory), whose stipends helped him survive. He was well known to a small circle of the intellectual elite, but the ambition he had confessed to Scholem in 1930 to become "the premier critic of German literature (*Briefe* II:505) was unfulfilled. Much of his work remained unpublished in his lifetime, nor was he able to attain any academic appointment. His second doctoral thesis (two were required to obtain a German university position), *The Origin of German Tragic Drama* (1924), was rejected by the examiners, who claimed not to understand it.

Through the efforts of Scholem and another close student and friend,

Theodor W. Adorno, a leading member of the Institute for Social Research, Benjamin's writings and papers began to be collected and published in 1955.[2] In the succeeding decades, Benjamin's ambition posthumously has been fulfilled. With the rise of the New Left in the late 1960s, Benjamin's works could be found in paperback in railway stations in Germany. In the 1970s and 1980s analyses of his work proliferated in the most important journals of literary criticism and theory in America. Today he is indeed recognized as the most eminent critic of his era.

As for Scholem, in the years after Benjamin's death, he continued his prodigious research on Jewish mysticism and attained a reputation as one of the greatest Jewish scholars of our time. He established the academic study of Jewish mysticism and sought to legitimate Kabbalah as a vibrant aspect of Jewish thought. In so doing, he aimed to radically alter the study and image of Judaism that his predecessors, the practitioners of *Wissenchaft des Judentums* (the "Scientific Study of Judaism"), had developed. He argued that they had tried to excise the mystical strand from Judaism, and that their excessive rationalism had biased them against the esoteric lore of the Kabbalah. He castigated what he thought was their apologetic attempt to define Judaism as a purely rational religion through which Jews could take part in European culture through universal human brotherhood.[3]

Scholem insisted upon the centrality of Kabbalah to Judaism; moreover, he claimed to have found in Kabbalah a resurgence and transformation of mythical ideas at the very heart of Jewish monotheism, ideas which were, he thought, a secret source of its vitality. This line of thinking led to his massive study of the notorious "false messiah" of the seventeenth century, Sabbatai Sevi, and Scholem's controversial argument that Sabbatianism (a heretical antinomian extension of certain kabbalistic ideas) played a much larger role in Jewish life and in the formation of modern Judaism than had previously been acknowledged.

Scholem first met Benjamin in Berlin in 1915, when Scholem was seventeen years old and Benjamin five years his senior. From 1915 until Scholem's departure for Palestine in 1923, they spent a great deal of time together. During 1918 and 1919, Scholem joined Benjamin in Switzerland, where Benjamin was working on his doctoral thesis. Both were adamantly opposed to World War I and had received medical discharges. Scholem's friendship with Benjamin became strained, however, after Scholem emigrated to Palestine in 1923. They met again only twice, in Paris in 1927 and 1938, although they carried on an intensive correspondence and continually exchanged and debated copies of each new work from their pens. Scholem was particularly fastidious in recording all his conversations with Benjamin in his diary. After settling in Palestine, Scholem maintained there a private "archive" of all the essays, reviews, postcards, notes, and approximately three hundred letters Benjamin sent to him. These letters, Scholem wrote, were among his most precious possessions (*Corr.* 5). About ten years before he died, Scholem wrote a book-length memoir about his relationship with Benjamin using all the material he had accumulated: *Walter Benjamin: The Story of a Friendship* (1975). In sum, as he said, their friendship was "the most important of my life" (*From Berlin* 70), and "what thinking really means I have experienced through his living example" (*JJC* 174). Benjamin in turn wrote to Scholem in a letter, "Living Judaism I have certainly encountered in no other form than you" (*SF* 161).

After Scholem's departure, however, Benjamin's thinking turned in new directions. As the situation in Europe worsened, and Germany suffered devastating inflation and political strain, Benjamin intensified his interest in "historical materialism," especially through a love affair with Asja Lacis, a Soviet revolutionary he met in Capri in 1924, a visit to her in Moscow in 1926–27, a reading of Georg Lukács's *History and Class Consciousness*, and a growing friendship with Bertolt Brecht, whom he met in 1929. Scholem thought these developments were ominous and tried to combat the growing influence of Marxism on his friend by admonishing him and trying to persuade him to come to Palestine and study Hebrew. He even succeeded in arranging a meeting between Benjamin and Judah Magnes, then head of the newly created Hebrew University in Jerusalem. Magnes, persuaded of Benjamin's professed desire to devote himself to the study of Jewish texts, sent him a stipend for the purpose of studying Hebrew in Palestine. But Benjamin used up the stipend in Europe and never came to Jerusalem.

Yet despite Brecht's influence, and even at the height of his "Marxist phase" in the 1930s, Benjamin's writing was permeated with theological ideas. In his draft for his uncompleted magnum opus, the Paris Arcades project (*Das Passagen-Werk*), which he worked on from 1927 until his death, he wrote: "My thinking relates to theology the way a blotter does to ink. It is soaked through with it. If one were merely to go by the blotter, though, nothing of what has been written would remain" ("Theory of Knowledge" [N 7a, 7]).[4] The theological and materialist ideas were in uneasy, almost impossible, juxtaposition, and Brecht complained in his diary about Benjamin's "mysticism in spite of an antimystical attitude" and his perennial "judaisms" (*SF* 176). But upon hearing of Benjamin's suicide in 1940, Brecht remarked that it was the first loss Hitler had caused German literature.

Needless to say, Scholem detested Brecht's influence and wrote Benjamin two especially harsh letters from Palestine in 1931 informing Benjamin that his brand of dialectical materialism was "a self-deception" that even the Communist party itself would reject as counterrevolutionary and bourgeois. He criticized the "stupendous incompatibility and lack of relation between your *real* and *alleged* process of thinking" and described Benjamin's connection of theology and materialism as an "illegitimate association" (*SF* 228). Benjamin's real insights, Scholem claimed, grew out of his early metaphysics of language and were gained in the theological process. If Benjamin persisted in the attempt to combine economic materialism with dialectical metaphysics, Scholem warned, "You would not be the last but perhaps the most *incomprehensible* victim of the very confusion between religion and politics, the true relation of which you could have been expected to bring out more clearly than anyone else" (*SF* 130).

Benjamin wrote back admitting the ambiguities of his position and disavowing any illusions about the infallibility of his work or its reception by the Communist party, which he never agreed to join (although his brother Georg, a doctor, had done so and had worked with the poor in Berlin): "All right, I am going to extremes. A castaway who drifts on a wreck by climbing to the top of an already crumbling mast. But from there he has a chance to give a signal leading to his rescue" (*SF* 233).

The question of Judaism was central to the relationship between Scholem and Benjamin, especially in the years 1915–23, the period of their closest contact. In the first part of this book, I propose to read Benjamin and Scholem in light of each other's thinking. I want to study the ways in which their relationship affected each of their philosophies of language and history as part of a larger project of trying to understand the relation of theology and literary criticism in contemporary literary debates. To what extent might Scholem's theories of the meaning of language in Jewish mysticism have been influenced by Benjamin's early aesthetic and metaphysical theory? What significance would that have for the evaluation and reception of Scholem's work in the field of Jewish Studies, and for the relation of contemporary Jewish Studies to literary criticism?[5] And how do secular materialist theories of language and history relate to theology, a situation which Benjamin in his last work described through a remarkable parable:

> The story is told of an automaton constructed in such a way that it could play a winning game of chess, answering each move of an opponent with a countermove. A puppet in Turkish attire and with a hookah in its mouth sat before a chessboard placed on a large table. A system of mirrors created the illusion that this table was transparent from all sides. Actually, a little hunchback who was an expert chess player sat inside and guided the puppet's hand by means of strings. One can imagine a philosophical counter-part to this device. The puppet called "historical materialism" is to win all the time. It can easily be a match for anyone if it enlists the services of theology, which today, as we know, is wizened and has to keep out of sight. (*Illum* 253)

Deconstructionist critics, Marxist theorists, and cultural materialists have been somewhat uncomfortable with that concealed little hunchback and have claimed Benjamin as one of their own; they view Scholem as a pernicious influence and ideological misinterpreter of Benjamin's work. Scholem countered that Benjamin's true genius and real mode of thought was as a metaphysician of language, an esoteric theologian who probed the nature of revelation and redemption in a secular world.

In another complication, other literary writers and critics from Borges to Harold Bloom have claimed Scholem as one of *their* own, as a visionary theorist of literary language and texts. Bloom has even asserted that there are only three figures who represent strong Jewish culture today—Freud, Kafka, and Scholem—and that for the contemporary Jewish intellectual, this trio "are already larger figures in the ongoing tradition of spirituality than are, say, Leo Baeck, Franz Rosenzweig and Martin Buber . . . because the former grouping far surpasses the latter in *cultural achievement*" ("Masks" 14). In this cultural achievement, moreover, Bloom finds the seeds of a postmodern Jewish spirituality, a "prolepsis of a still hidden form of Judaism, one that is necessarily still unapparent to us" (16).

All of which is to say that between them, Benjamin and Scholem played out so many of the possibilities of modern thought—from aestheticism, to linguistic philosophy, textual criticism, anarchism, Marxism, mysticism, radical cultural critique, and revisionary historicism. They have both deeply influenced the way we think about language, interpretation, history, and sacred texts. Philosophy of language and philosophy of history, mysticism and materialism, Judaism and the problematic of modern Jewish identity are all interwoven here. And here, too, are all the critical elements in current arguments about the nature of literary criticism, the meanings of texts, and the relation of history and ideology to language.

THE CATASTROPHES OF PROGRESS

Benjamin once made the comment that "a major work will either establish the genre or abolish it; and the perfect work will do both" (*OGTD* 45). In a way, Scholem's work on Kabbalah did precisely that; it is a long discourse on the often subtle line between orthodoxy and heresy, "establishing and abolishing." Like Benjamin, Scholem characterized his own thought as "dialectical," although they each used that term quite differently. Scholem's dialectic involved a struggle between creative and destructive forces which paradoxically establish and abolish at once. Benjamin would develop a "dialectics at a standstill" in his "historical materialism," where clashing images crystallized in moments of powerful shock and recognition.

> It isn't that the past casts its light on the present or the present casts its light on the past; rather, an image is that in which the Then and the Now come into a constellation like a flash of lightning. In other words: image is dialectics at a standstill. For while the relation of the present to the past is a purely temporal, continuous one, the relation of the Then to the Now is dialectical—not development but image, leaping forth.—Only dialectical images are genuine (i.e. not archaic) images; and the place one happens upon them is language. ("Theory of Knowledge" [N 2a, 3])

On another level, the dialectical attitudes of these thinkers came from an ambivalent attitude toward what has come before, to what has been transmitted. Such ambivalence, of course, is a characteristically modern attitude, and to Benjamin we owe some of the most penetrating studies of "the modern"—especially in the Arcades project, in which he sought to comprehend the "prehistory" of modernity.

Both Benjamin and Scholem were passionately concerned with the problem of origins, the origins of religious, literary, and historical phenomena, and this concern reflected their troubled relation to the historical past. What remains when the authority of tradition has broken down? How does one cope with the violence of that break, with the darker catastrophic forces which erupt and destroy? How does one live amid the ruins? Neither of their philosophies of history was merely academic. They both were intensively concerned with "rescuing" and redeeming history, hearing the voices which have been muffled, and exploiting the radical potential in those lost images and cries. Writes Benjamin:

> . . . history is not just a science but also a form of memoration (*eine Form des Eingedenkens*). What science has "established," memoration can modify. Memoration can make the incomplete (happiness) into something complete, and the complete (suffering) into something incomplete. That is theology; but in memoration we discover the experience (*Erfahrung*) that forbids us to conceive of history as thoroughly a-theological, even though we barely dare not attempt to write it according to literally theological concepts. ("Theory of Knowledge" [N 8, 1])

> The concept of progress should be grounded on the idea of catastrophe. That things "just keep on going" *is* the catastrophe. Not something that is impending at any particular time ahead, but something that is always given. ([N 9a, 1])

The critique of liberal notions of "progress," the pains and powers of memory, the tortured relation to theology, the awkward conjunction of sacred and profane—these themes also reflect Benjamin and Scholem's experiences as German Jews coming to maturity around World War I, when the promises of Jewish emancipation were beginning to fade, and rabid nationalism led Europe into catastrophe. Both Benjamin and Scholem took the highly unpopular stance of opposing World War I despite the general "patriotic" consensus of their friends and families, and even such distinguished intellectuals as Freud, Buber, and Hermann Cohen. Scholem's opposition to the war led to his expulsion from school in 1915.

The families into which both were born were comfortable, assimilated, and bourgeois. Scholem's father was in the printing business; Benjamin's father was an antique dealer. These families were typical of the large segment of German Jewry who had benefited from the emancipation of the Jews from the onerous restrictions and humiliations of the medieval ghettoes. When these ghettoes were torn down after the French Revolution and the Jews enfranchised, Jewish society underwent an upheaval and transformation that affected every aspect of Jewish life.[6]

When the French gave equal civic rights to the Jews in 1791, however, Count Clermont Tonnerre declared to the National Assembly in a now-famous statement: "To the Jew as an individual—everything: to the Jews as a nation—nothing." Jewish entrance into Western society seemed to demand the abandonment of Jewish distinctiveness. The invitation to join the non-Jewish world as equals thus posed an excruciating dilemma. Although some Jews were ready to forsake entirely any distinctive Jewish identity, others could not relinquish their heritage so easily. Emancipation politically freed the Jews but left many, especially among the intelligentsia, with an inner torment and divided identity. The entire notion of Jewish identity was put into question. What did it mean to be a Jew, and how could one justify remaining a Jew? How could one live in two worlds? And in the wake of the Enlightenment's challenge to religion, how could Judaism be defended in the age of universal reason? Could one be a Jew if one no longer believed in the absoluteness of divine revelation and the authority of "Torah from Heaven"?

There were various responses to these dilemmas. One could, for instance, solve the problem by converting to Christianity, or one could identify oneself preeminently as French or German. Or one could attempt to justify Judaism in terms of the surrounding European cultural values. Or one could try to redefine Judaism as a religion and not a nationality; or as a nationality and not a religion; or as a historical tradition that could be the object of critical and scientific study. One could also try to solve "the Jewish question" by becoming a Marxist, as did Scholem's brother Werner and Benjamin's brother Georg. (Werner Scholem was the youngest Communist deputy to the Reichstag. He was arrested on the night of the Reichstag fire in 1933, again at the end of April 1933, and never released. He died in Buchenwald in 1940; Georg Benjamin died in Mauthhausen in 1942.) Or one could become a Zionist, as did Scholem, or a German Nationalist, as did Scholem's father, or a cultural Jew, or a Socialist, or a Yiddishist. Or one could despair entirely. In any case, the Jewish world broke apart and has yet to be put back together. In 1921, around the time when Benjamin and Scholem's friendship was at its peak, Jakob Wasserman expressed his anguish thus:

> Apostasy is, for the self-respecting, out of the question on principle. Secret assimilation bears fruit only for those who are suited to assimilation, which is to say, the weakest individuals. Persisting in old ways means torpor. What remains? Self-destruction? A life in twilight, anxiety, and misery? . . . It is better not to think about it. Yet I am German and I am a Jew, one as much and as completely as the other; one cannot be separated from the other. (Qtd. in Gay 150)

In the space of a few generations, Jewish families often underwent rapid transformation. As restrictions on where Jews were allowed to live were lifted, many moved from the poorer provinces of the cities, engaged in small business, and attained the life of the comfortable middle class. Often much of their Jewish observance was left behind as well, although the consciousness of being Jewish remained. Even if they tried to escape it completely through conversion, they were again reminded of the pains of Jewish identity by the rise of antisemitism, especially in the 1880s and 1890s as the promises of emancipation began to fade.

Scholem's family had followed the typical pattern, and by the time he was born, they had little use for most Jewish observance, although they maintained a sense of vague "Jewishness." It was this "self-deception" that so disgusted Scholem, Kafka, Benjamin, Freud, and other writers who were the children of these families. Kafka's famous *Letter to His Father* is a classic statement of the ensuing conflicts between parents and children. Scholem and Benjamin, like many others, disavowed their father's middle-class complacency, would have nothing to do with their father's businesses, and sought ways to live differently—as artists, critics, writers, Communists, Socialists, Zionists. Some, such as the great German-Jewish philosopher Franz Rosenzweig, even rediscovered and returned to the world of Jewish religious thought and observance cast off by their parents.

Faced with his son's passionate attachment to Zionism and Judaism, Scholem's father angrily asked him: "Do you want to return to the ghetto?" He eventually solved the problem in 1917 by giving his then twenty-year-old son a small sum and a registered letter ordering him to leave the house (*JJC* 6, 15). Benjamin's father supported his son's studies for several years and finally, frustrated by the failure of his son to earn any kind of living, also discontinued support when Benjamin was thirty-two.

But for Scholem, the revolt against the assimilationist bourgeois culture of his father was also something else: a rejection of the entire "German-Jewish" symbiosis. Unlike Jakob Wasserman, Scholem had no compunctions about separating his Jewishness from his Germanness. Zionism for him as a youth was not preeminently a *political* but a "moral decision, an emotional one, an honesty-seeking response. The honesty did not express itself in the desire for a state, but in a revolt against the lie that Jewish existence was" (*JJC* 2). He was intent on retaining a separation between religion and politics to the end of his life, adamantly refusing to identify contemporary political Zionism with apocalyptic and Jewish messianic dreams, and harshly rebuking Benjamin for confusing politics and theology.

To Scholem, the "love affair" between Germans and Jews was a "lurid and tragic illusion" (*JJC* 190) made worse by the fact that it was one-sided and unreciprocated (86). As Moritz Goldstein wrote in 1912: "We Jews administer the intellectual property of a people which denies us the right and ability to do so. . . . Our relation to Germany is one of unrequited love" (qtd. in Arendt 30). Scholem even denied that such a thing as a German-Jewish dialogue ever existed. The supposed golden age of German

Jewry, the fruitful interweaving of two cultures which produced the brilliance of fin-de-siècle Vienna and the Weimar Republic, was, in his view, a fraud. The German discussion with Jews was "always based on the expressed or unexpressed self-denial of the Jews, on the progressive atomization of the Jews as a *community*. . . . [No one] addressed them with regard to what they had to *give as* Jews, and not what they had to *give up* as Jews" (62–63).

In reality, Scholem argued, Jews spoke only to themselves in that German-Jewish "dialogue." He further extended his indictment to what he saw as the eager willingness of the Jews themselves to liquidate their traditions and identity, to deny themselves and their peoplehood, and to rupture their historical consciousness. This was what the Germans demanded of them; yet when it was accomplished so quickly and easily, it aroused German suspicion and contempt. For what could a heritage be worth if it was so readily abandoned?

Thus assimilation proved no solution to the dilemma; it did not ease but only displaced the tension between Jew and non-Jew. Scholem describes the result as the "double disorder of the Jews": they were disordered by the humiliating social conditions under which they had previously been forced to live, and they were disordered again by the insecurity and duplicity that plagued them when they left the ghetto to assimilate (*JJC* 77). The worst disorder, perhaps, was their very refusal to recognize their condition, and the result, says Scholem, was the terrible emotional confusion of German Jews between 1890 and 1920, the years of his young manhood.

Nevertheless, for Scholem this tension was "dialectical": a creative potential was released from this negativity, and this creativity of the Jews fortuitously converged with that of the Germans at the very moment when German bourgeois culture reached its own zenith. Despite their submission to the Germans, there remained some kernel of Jewishness:

> Even in their complete estrangement of their awareness from everything "Jewish," something is evident in many of them that was felt to be substantially Jewish by Jews as well as Germans—by everyone except themselves!—and that is true of a whole galaxy of illustrious minds from Karl Marx and Lassalle to Karl Kraus, Gustav Mahler and George Simmel. (*JJC* 82)

Yet what was this indefinable "Jewishness"? How could those who had little Jewish background, whose interests were not identifiably Jewish in the traditional sense, and who in fact are known for their stunning contributions to secular European culture still be called "Jewish"? And what is the relation between these Jews and modernity?

Needless to say, this question has been endlessly debated. In his *Freud, Jews, and Other Germans*, Peter Gay has tried to debunk any notion of the Jew as paradigmatic modernist. He argues that although Jews such as Marx, Freud, Einstein, and so many others were well represented in the cultural elite, modernism was by no means a "Jewish movement." It had roots in German romanticism, the Paris of Baudelaire, French impressionism, and the work of many non-Jews (21). Many Jews, furthermore, were quite reactionary and unmodern: "Germany's Jews were woven into the very texture of German culture and Germany dyed its Jews through and through" (102).

Gay admits to only three ways for a writer to be Jewish: by choice of audience, choice of language, or choice of subject matter (142). Most of those Jews thought to be archetypal modernists wrote to a non-Jewish audience, in the European languages (not Hebrew or Yiddish), and did not write about particularly Jewish matters. But one might respond to Gay's three criteria with Kafka's comments in a letter to Max Brod about the "three impossibilities" faced by the German-Jewish writer, whose problem "was not really a German one": "the impossibility of not writing, the impossibility of writing German, the impossibility of writing differently" (*Letters* 288–89).

Thus despite his consummate mastery of German, Kafka considered the Jews' use of that language to be a "bumptious, tacit, or self-pitying appropriation of someone else's property . . . [which] remains someone else's property, even though there is no evidence of a single solecism" (288). Yet this generation of Jews, having lost Jewish tradition, had no other language available to it. Hence Kafka is tempted to add a "fourth impossibility," "the impossibility of writing."[7] As we shall see, Kafka's work was of deep interest to both Benjamin and Scholem, and each found in Kafka a kind of emblem for his own respective project. At a time of great tension in their relationship due to Benjamin's increasing involvement with communism, the subject of Kafka revitalized their exchange of letters. As Benjamin wrote Scholem in July 1934, "I see no subject more perfectly suited to our correspondence" (*Corr* 120), and in the letters of that summer and fall, they argued about the meaning of revelation, law, commentary, nihilism, redemption, and messianism in Kafka. These letters, and another exchange in 1938, are the intellectual highlight of the entire correspondence and among the most brilliant Kafka criticism ever written. As Anson Rabinbach aptly describes it:

> In all its esoteric splendor and subtlety, the Kafka discussion is an inner-messianic dispute about the "tradition" of Judaism and the meaning of commentary in exile and in catastrophe. Expressed through their Prague connection, it is a debate between a Zionist whose nihilistic impulse and admiration for heretics and mystics did not fully abandon the tradition of the commentators, and an exiled "student" whose messianic commentary had lost its original text, its Holy Writ. (*Corr* xxxii)

In any case, the point is that one cannot so easily disregard Jewish tradition, religion, or culture as important influences on modern Jewish identity and writing simply because these elements do not appear in a clearly and overtly expressed way. Since Jewish identity became problematic in the aftermath of the Enlightenment and emancipation of the Jews, Jewishness could no longer be expressed as it once had been—within the parameters Jewish tradition had set forth—through performance of the ritual commandments, or devotion to the Jewish sacred texts. Jews were indeed now writing for non-Jews, in German or French, or other languages, and their subjects may not have been typically "Jewish," but that does not mean that the question of their Jewishness was not critical for them or their work. Precisely because it was a *question*, their expressions of it were far more tentative, indirect, oblique, and tortured. And often "impossible." Such was the case with Kafka, and such was the case with Benjamin. This indirection has spawned intense scholarly arguments about whether Benjamin was "really" a Jewish mystic and metaphysician *or* a secular Marxist materialist.[8] Or whether Scholem was obliquely writing a covert modern Jewish theology in the guise of critical historical philology, as David Biale, Eliezer Schweid, and Baruch Kurzweil argue, *or* whether he was simply a ruthlessly honest seeker after objective historical truth, as Joseph Dan has insisted—a Jewish nationalist but no theologian. Indeed, Benjamin and Scholem, each in his own way, sought the truth in the esoteric, the neglected, the obscure detail. For Scholem, it was the intentionally obscure texts of Jewish mysticism that required study and mediation through academic critical historiography; for Benjamin, it was the obscured "dialectical images" of history buried in the ruins of time and traced obliquely in cultural objects, in the very detritus of industrial society. As Michael Jennings writes, the structure of Benjamin's Arcades project, its concentration on fragments of social experience and its focus on cultural objects ripped from their historical context and rearranged via montage in a new "constellation,"

> reflects the two major themes of Benjamin's theory of criticism: the conviction that truth, the hint of redemption, is present to the modern world in hidden and fragmentary form and the corresponding conviction that this truth can be revealed only by a destructive process that purges the cultural object of its mythical or dehumanized character. (12)

Similarly, the Jewishness of a Benjamin or Kafka is present in often fragmentary and esoteric form, revealed only negatively, through its "impossibilities." But their greatness lay in the way these writers lived and wrote out of these very impossibilities, conjoining their despair with a strange utopian hope. Benjamin's historical methodology of collage, of the juxtaposition of disparate fragments and quotes, was just such a way of living out the impossible tensions between materialism and theology. As Irving Wohlfarth writes, however, the central question is whether the inconsistencies in Benjamin's thought are "*avoidable internal contradictions,* or whether, on the contrary, they correspond to *unavoidable external* ones" ("Re-fusing Theology" 10). Do they signify a highly idiosyncratic and ulti- mately unsuccessful personal journey, or were they "intended as the sub- jective correlative to what Benjamin took to be the objective revolutionary possibilities of his time" (11)?

To Scholem, Benjamin's attempt to fuse theology and Marxism was en- tirely avoidable, a deluded endeavor just like the rest of the "German- Jewish" symbiosis. Nevertheless, Scholem continued to think that even in Benjamin's materialist phase, Benjamin's "insights are in all essentials still those of the metaphysician who, it is true, has evolved a dialectic of in- quiry, yet one that is worlds apart from the materialistic dialectic. His insights are those of a theologian marooned in the realm of the profane. But they no longer appear plainly as such" (*JJC* 187).

Scholem ultimately numbers Benjamin among those few who did not succumb to the illusion of being a part of German culture and tradition and so became writers of the highest rank:

> Freud, Kafka, and Benjamin belonged to those few. . . . they wrote in full awareness of the distance separating them from their German readers. They are the most distinguished of the so-called German-Jewish authors, and it is as much their lives that bear witness to that distance, its pathos and creative quality of potentiality, as their writings in which things Jewish figure rarely if at all.
>
> They did not fool themselves. They knew they were German writers—but no Germans. They never cut loose from that experience and the clear aware- ness of being aliens, even exiles. . . . Closely as they knew themselves tied to the German language and its intellectual world, they never succumbed to the illusion of being at home. . . . (*JJC* 191).

ONE

Language and Redemption

There are times like our own in which tradition can no longer be handed down, in which tradition falls silent. This, then, is the great crisis of language in which we find ourselves. We are no longer able to grasp the last summit of that mystery that once dwelt in it. The fact that language can be spoken is, in the opinion of the Kabbalists, owed to the name, which is present in language. What the value and worth of language will be—the language from which God will have withdrawn—is the question which must be posed by those who still believe that they can hear the echo of the vanished word of the creation in the immanence of the world. This is a question to which, in our times, only the poets presumably have the answer. For poets do not share the doubt that most mystics have in regard to language. And poets have one link with the masters of the Kabbalah, even when they reject Kabbalistic theological formulation as being still too emphatic. This link is their belief in language as an absolute, which is as if constantly flung open by dialectics. It is their belief in the mystery of language which has to become audible. (Scholem, "The Name of God and the Linguistic Theory of the Kabbalah" 194)

The conviction which guides me in my literary attempts . . . [is] that each truth has its home, its ancestral palace in language, that this palace was built with the oldest *logoi*, and that to a truth thus founded, the insights of the sciences will remain inferior for as long as they make do here and there in the area of language like nomads . . . in the conviction of the sign character of language which produces the irresponsible arbitrariness of their terminology. (Benjamin, *Briefe* I: 329)

LANGUAGE CRITIQUE

One of the distinguishing characteristics of the period in which Benjamin and Scholem formed their friendship was that the crisis of tradition which permeated Jewish and non-Jewish society became formulated as a crisis of language. George Steiner has observed how the catastrophe of World War I led to a particular crisis of spirit; in the succeeding decade in Germany it spawned the utopian, apocalyptic, and "violent" works of Bloch, Spengler, Barth, Rosenzweig, Heidegger, and Hitler: "It was as if the urgent prolixity of these writers sought to build a capacious house of words where that of German cultural and imperial hegemony had collapsed. . . . The language itself must be made new. It must be purged of the obstinate remnants of a ruined past" ("Heidegger" 32, 34).

Yet in the decades before the war, this urge to purify language was equally intense. Allan Janik and Stephen Toulmin have elegantly described in their *Wittgenstein's Vienna*, for example, how the critique of language was a key factor in the radical transformations that Viennese culture underwent from 1890 through the 1930s. Language critique was central to the very development of modernism as it emerged in architecture, non-representational painting, twelve-tone music, Wittgenstein's philosophy, Freudian psychoanalysis, journalism, and radical politics. This obsessive concern with language was partly related to the general corruption of late Hapsburg society, wherein "all established means of expression from the language of politics to the principles of architectural design had seemingly lost touch with their intended 'messages' and were robbed of their capacity to perform their proper function" (30).

Despite the liberal ideals and attempts at political reforms in the 1860s and 1870s, by the 1890s regressive politics had again appeared, and anti-semitism was on the rise in Vienna.[1] Karl Kraus, born of a comfortable middle-class Jewish family, and aptly described by Peter Demetz as a combination of "H. L. Mencken, Soren Kierkegaard, and a demonic Woody Allen" (xxxv), called Vienna a "proving ground for world destruction" in his famed satirical journal *Die Fackel* (Janik 67). Kraus called for the critique of language as a means to purify the corruption of a duplicitous and hypocritical society, and to restore integrity to the social debate. His influence was acknowledged by figures as disparate as Arnold Schönberg, the modernist architect Adolf Loos, and Wittgenstein.

In a 1931 essay on Kraus, Benjamin (though already well into his so-called Marxist phase) wrote that Kraus's criterion for and concept of creation are theological, but "a transformation has taken place that has caused it, quite without constraint, to coincide with the cosmopolitan credo of Austrian worldliness, which made creation into a church in which nothing remained to recall the rite except an occasional whiff of incense in the mists" (*Refl* 244). Kraus in fact had converted to Catholicism—albeit without passion and only for twelve years; the passion was reserved for the

Catholic aristocrat he had fallen in love with, Sidonie Nadherny. But the important point is that despite what appeared to be the lack of an identifiable Jewish content in Kraus's writing, Benjamin finds a core Jewishness precisely in Kraus's conception of language:

> Nothing is understood about this man until it has been perceived that, of necessity and without exception, everything—language and fact—falls for him within the sphere of justice. . . . It has been said of Kraus that he has to "suppress the Jewishness in himself," even that he "travels the road from Jewishness to freedom"; nothing better refutes this than the fact that, for him, too, justice and language remain founded in each other. To worship the image of divine justice in language—even in the German language—that is the genuinely Jewish somersault by which he tries to break the spell of the demon. For this is the last official act of this zealot: to place the legal system itself under accusation. (254–55)

Benjamin describes Kraus's work as a Jewish "theater of a sanctification of the name" (265) and concludes the essay by comparing the figure who might emerge at the end of Kraus's destructive purifying work to one of the evanescent talmudic angels "who, according to the Talmud, are at each moment created anew in countless throngs, and who, once they have raised their voices before God, cease and pass into nothingness. Lamenting, chastising, or rejoicing?" (273). As with many of his other Judaic references, Benjamin had been informed about talmudic angels by Scholem, and the image of an apocalyptic but horrified "angel of history" haunted Benjamin's own last work as a kind of allegorical emblem for himself. As Peter Demetz notes, Benjamin's comments on Kraus are also an ambivalent critique of Benjamin's own metaphysics of language (xxxviii).

Both Benjamin and Scholem shared an intense interest in the philosophy of language, and it was the focus of many of their discussions and letters. In May of 1919, while still in Switzerland with Benjamin, Scholem decided to radically change his academic goals and pursue graduate work in Jewish mysticism instead of mathematics; he aimed to write his doctoral dissertation on the linguistic theory of the Kabbalah (*SF* 83). But by 1920, immersed in the study of kabbalistic manuscripts in Munich, he decided he needed a "less pretentious subject" (92). It was not until 1970, when he was in his seventies, that Scholem addressed the topic in depth in lectures he gave at the Eranos conferences and later published as "The Name of God and the Linguistic Theory of the Kabbalah."

Scholem had shared with Benjamin his budding discoveries about kabbalistic texts in their time together in Switzerland. In his memoirs of Benjamin, Scholem writes that in their years together during World War I and afterward, Judaism occupied Benjamin a great deal, and with Scholem's guidance he read much on the subject. Molitor's four-volume work on Kabbalah was especially important to him, as was the work of Franz Rosenzweig. In Rosenzweig's *The Star of Redemption* and in the "kabbalistic

writings, he experienced that profound attachment of genuine Jewish theological thinking to the medium of language that became so marked a feature of his own work" (*JJC* 192). In 1929, six years after Scholem had
departed for Palestine, Benjamin wrote a review called "Books That Have
Remained Alive," in which he listed the four most important German-
language scholarly works of the twentieth century; these included Rosenzweig's *Star* along with Lukács's Marxist classic *History and Class Consciousness* plus a work on art history and another on iron construction (*GS*
III: 169–71). This melange epitomizes the disparate sources which inspired
Benjamin and which he tried to bring together: Jewish theology, Marxism,
aesthetics, and the brutal cultural realities of modern urban-industrial life.

For Scholem as well, Kabbalah was not just another theory of language
but an extraordinary opening up *within* Jewish tradition of the notion of
revelation. Scholem's entire reading of Kabbalah as a mythic renewal of
Judaism, a radical reinterpretation of tradition, an upsurge of a kind of
anarchic vitality, is, of course, a reading which finds values in the kabbalistic tradition that are strikingly similar to the values of Scholem's generation of German-Jewish intellectuals. Michael Lowy calls this an "elective
affinity" between the traditions of Jewish messianism and the secular,
revolutionary, anarchist utopianism of German-Jewish intellectuals: "The
two are rooted in the same ground, the two develop in the same spiritual
climate—that of the anti-capitalist romanticism of the German intelligentsia"; this ties together figures such as Landauer, Bloch, Benjamin,
Scholem, Lukács, Toller, Buber, Rosenzweig, et al. ("Jewish Messianism"
110). Lowy presents an excellent analysis but uncritically accepts
Scholem's "anarchistic" version of Jewish messianism for the thing itself.
Scholem's views have not gone unchallenged, and my purpose here is not
to decide how correct or incorrect was Scholem's reading of Kabbalah.
What is important, rather, are the assumptions which lie behind his very
method of interpretation itself. For it is Scholem's *interpretation of* Kabbalah that has so influenced contemporary writers and critics.

And it is the Benjamin-Scholem relationship, their mutual attractions
and disaffections, their discussions and continuing debates, which itself is
a kind of model colloquy of religious, political, and literary studies. Benjamin's idiosyncratic views of language and politics were stimulated by the
theological insights of Scholem; and Scholem's historical and linguistic
interpretations of Kabbalah were stimulated by Benjamin's philosophical
reflections. Both men mingled the theological and secular in extraordinarily fruitful ways, and in extraordinarily awkward ways that were not always
successful. By the late 1930s their early idealism had been tempered by
painful disillusioning experiences: for Benjamin, the lack of an outlet for
publishing his work and any means of adequate financial support, the degradations of communism in Stalinist Russia, and the 1939 Hitler-Stalin
nonaggression pact; for Scholem, the Arab riots in Palestine and splits in
the Zionist movement over how to negotiate for a state and peace.[2] In one

of his final letters to Benjamin, on June 30, 1939, Scholem discouraged Benjamin from coming to Palestine because of the threat of impending civil war between Jews and Arabs. He expressed his depression at the situation. He writes of the "unmitigated despondency and paralysis, which have gripped me for months in the face of the state of things here. . . . And the future of Judaism is totally cloaked in darkness. . . . In this darkness I only know how to be silent" (*Corr* 255). Despite the severe tensions about their respective intellectual and political alliances, in the last letter Benjamin wrote to Scholem, in January 1940, he spoke poignantly of how "the arrangements made by the *Zeitgeist*" had led to a safeguarding of the common ground between them, such that it was even stronger than it had been twenty-five years earlier: That *Zeitgeist*

> has set up markers in the desert landscape of the present that cannot be over-looked by old Bedouins like us. Even though it is a sad thing that we cannot converse with one another, I still have the feeling that the circumstances in no way deprive me of such heated debates as we used to indulge in now and then. There is no longer any need for those today. And it may well be fitting to have a small ocean between us when the moment comes to fall into each other's arms *spiritualiter*. (262–63)

But nine months later Benjamin was dead. What we are left with is not the record of their reconciliation but their debates and dialogues in all their intensity and brilliance.

In the end, it would be inaccurate to describe as "influences" the friend-ships Benjamin carried on with Scholem and Brecht, or his readings of Lukács, Rosenzweig, German aesthetic theory, Baudelaire, the surrealists, Kafka, and the endless other writers and ideas he absorbed. Scholem had a strong interest in promoting the influence of Jewish sources, and his por-trait of Benjamin has to be read with caution. Arthur Cohen is probably correct when he characterizes Scholem's memoir of Benjamin as exuding "Scholem's desire to maintain decisive influence over a friend dead 40 years and . . . another sustained battle in Scholem's long war with those who would claim for Germany and German culture anyone or any idea to which Scholem has staked a prior to Jewish claim" ("Short Life" 35). When they were together in Switzerland, some of their ambivalent feelings toward each other were disguised in an exchange of letters that Scholem and Benjamin's infant son Stefan (written in the hand of Benjamin's wife, Dora) would leave for each other. "Stefan" once wrote: "You are wrong in what you write, dear Uncle Gerhardt. I believe you really know very little about my Papa. There are very few people who know anything about him" (*SF* 68). That is good cautionary advice for anyone who desires to write about him.

In an apologetic moment, Benjamin did say to Scholem once, "If I ever have a philosophy of my own . . . it somehow will be a philosophy of Judaism" (*SF* 32). But Scholem also wrote elsewhere in his diary: "The word *irgendwie* ['somehow'] is the stamp of a point of view in the making. I never have heard anyone use this word more frequently than Benjamin" (31). Benjamin's philosophy was always "in the making," and his Marxist friends were as frustrated and critical of his heterodox and idiosyncratic uses of dialectical materialism as was Scholem of his theology. Despite the stipend from the Institute for Social Research which helped keep Benjamin afloat in the 1930s, his relations with its members were tense, and his contributions to its journal were subject to painful critique on account of his non-orthodox Marxist analyses.[3]

Benjamin in the end has the best comment on the subject of influence: "Only the indolent are really 'influenced,' while he who really learns sooner or later comes to the point of appropriating that part of the work of another which is of use to him, in order to assimilate it into his work as technique" (*GS* IV: 502).

THE PHILOSOPHICAL QUEST FOR LANGUAGE AS KNOWLEDGE

Benjamin's early linguistic theory was worked out in his essays "On Language as Such and on the Language of Man" (1916), "The Task of the Translator" (1923), and the "Epistemo-Critical Prologue" to *The Origin of German Tragic Drama*, written in 1924–25; these are among the writings which influenced and excited Scholem the most. In his memoirs, Scholem describes his intense discussions with Benjamin about the special relation of Jews to language, and whether or not that might be traced to their thousands of years of occupation with sacred texts (*SF* 106).

Firstly, the relations among language, signification, and history in Benjamin's and Scholem's work must be understood in the context of their polemics against contemporary *Lebensphilosophie* ("philosophy of life"), especially as it had influenced the German youth movements to which both had belonged and which both then repudiated. Benjamin and Scholem both strongly opposed any cult of pure immediate experience, including Buber's *Erlebnismystik* theology, which proclaimed the superiority of intuitive ecstatic experience (*Erlebnis*) to the truths mediated through language.

Benjamin strongly criticized Buber and the youth movements for supporting the nationalistic and proto-fascist ideologies of "blood and soil," and for enthusiastically supporting German involvement in World War I. Benjamin's "longstanding, insurmountable mistrust of that man [Buber]" (*Corr* 187) continued throughout his life. Scholem's own debates with Buber and his later critique of Buber's interpretations of Hassidism sources dovetailed with Benjamin's. We shall see later that Levinas shares with Benjamin and Scholem this disapproval of Buber; like them, he has a negative attitude toward desires for immediate experience, and a positive attitude toward language as mediation and medium of revelation through time. For Levinas, World War II explicitly showed the dangers of this kind of emotional and intuitive mysticism, and his target was Heidegger.[4] Distrust of personal subjectivity was one reason Scholem adopted the distancing and mediating method of historical scholarship and critical-philological method, which he nevertheless combined with a romantic dialectical philosophy of history. Benjamin, in turn, refused to identify the meaning of art with "personal experience," as in his famous line from the translation essay: "No poem is intended for the reader, no picture for the beholder, no symphony for the listener" ("Task" 69).

But neither should Benjamin's position on subjectivity be confused with Barthes and Foucault's poststructuralist "Death of the Author." Benjamin's attempt to define the core "mode of intention" of the work of art came from his philosophical search for a realm of knowledge and experience beyond the traditional "subject/object antinomy." In 1917, in an essay Scholem admired entitled "Program of the Coming Philosophy," Benjamin wrote positively of Kant's attempts to ground and justify philosophy; but he criticized Kant for basing his Enlightenment notion of certain reality and knowledge on "a reality of a low, perhaps the lowest order," and for neglecting experience that was not based on the experience of the sciences, physics, and mathematics, or pure empirical consciousness ("Program" 41). The future philosophy would need to "undertake the epistemological foundations of a higher concept of experience" (43), a "deeper, more metaphysically fulfilled experience" (44). Benjamin described as a "mythology" the entire idea of knowledge as a relation between a subject and an object where an individual ego receives sensations. The reconception of knowledge and experience and their relation to subject and object required a "purification of epistemology" which would make metaphysics and religious experience logically possible (45).

Yet how was this to be done? Benjamin argued that transformation and correction of Kant's concept of experience "oriented so one-sidedly along mathematical-mechanical lines, can only be attained by relating knowledge to language, such as was attempted by Hamann during Kant's lifetime." The decisive fact that "all philosophical knowledge has its unique expression in language" was neglected by Kant, and it is only by virtue of this linguistic character that philosophy can assert supremacy over science and mathematics. And this would lead to "theology": "A concept of knowledge gained from reflection on the linguistic nature of knowledge will create a corresponding concept of experience which will encompass realms Kant failed truly to systematize. The realm of religion should be mentioned as the foremost of these" (49).

In other words, where could a "positive objectivity" be found that was not of the Kantian kind, that was not defined by Enlightenment rationalism or intuitive ecstasy? Was it in "history" or "language" or "epistemology" or "theology" or some new relation among them? This quest led Benjamin later to explore disparate realms—from surrealism, to the effects of hashish, to the architectural arcades of urbanized Paris in the nineteenth century, to Kafka, children's literature, Brecht's "crude thinking," talmudic angels, "the work of art in the age of mechanical reproduction," and so forth. And to find ways of relating them in new "constellations."

Benjamin insisted above all in his early essays that language was not merely a conventional instrument of communication or an arbitrary system of signs (contra Saussure and the Saussurean legacy to recent semiotics and poststructuralist literary theory). Its main function was not to impart information; rather, language was a superior mode of knowledge. The precedents for this high estimation of language came from German romanticism and philosophy—from Hamann, Mauthner, Humboldt—and from the French romantic poets and critics such as Mallarmé, all figures whom Benjamin had intensively studied. He and Scholem read Humboldt, Kant, and Mauthner together, and Benjamin had plans for an anthology of Humboldt's writings on the philosophy of language, although they never came to fruition (*SF* 139).[5] But this high estimation of language also had deep roots in the Jewish tradition's belief in the creative, revelatory Word of God and the infinite meanings of the Torah. Benjamin mingled these Jewish, philosophical, and literary sources together, but the question then becomes, "Exactly what kind of truth and knowledge does language give forth?" Does language give knowledge of itself alone, or of something hidden within its depths, of something entirely Other as transcendent and redemptive, or inhuman and monstrous—or all at once? A pure form, or some concrete content? And if a content, how is it to be specified? Doctrinally? Poetically? Philosophically? Theologically? Historically? Needless to say, these questions still remain vexing in the discourse of modern literary theory and contemporary theological reflection.

Before we embark upon a more detailed discussion of Benjamin's writings, however, some prefatory remarks are needed precisely about the relation of Benjamin's own linguistic style to his thought. The experience of reading Benjamin often parallels Scholem's description of listening to him in conversation. Benjamin could never remain seated or quiet but paced back and forth as he spoke: "At some point, he would stop before me and in the most intense voice deliver his opinion on the matter. Or he might offer several viewpoints in turn, as if he were conducting an experiment" (*SF* 8).

Benjamin's essays are also often so filled with twists, turns, qualifications, and ambiguous references that one can plausibly infer several differing positions from them. This is characteristic of his entire mode of juxtaposing contradictory positions, or fragments of positions, and weaving them together—albeit with so many loose threads that the pattern or design of the argument appears, disappears, and shifts from one reading to the next. Benjamin wrote—perhaps ironically—in a letter of March 1931 to Max Rychner about this characteristic of his thought: "I have never been able to inquire and think otherwise than, if I may so put it, in a theological sense—namely, in conformity with the talmudic prescription regarding the forty-nine levels of meaning in every passage of the Torah" (*Briefe* II: 524). But as Benjamin wrote to Scholem in 1932, there were also external reasons—his precarious financial and personal existence: "The literary forms of expression that my thought has forged for itself over the last decade have been utterly conditioned by the preventive measures and antidotes with which I had to counter the disintegration constantly threatening my thought as a result of such contingencies" (*Corr* 14); "The real miracle is that I can still sum up the concentration to work" (18).

The early essays, like much of Benjamin's work, have the effect of intense compression, aphoristic density, revelatory pronouncement, and hidden meaning. Scholem describes this characteristic well: "His sentences often enough have the authoritarian stance of words of revelation . . . lending themselves to quotation and interpretation. What is illuminating in them is meshed with the thoroughly enigmatic. . . . They are sentences from the Holy Writ of an initiate, scarcely and scantily disguised, at once rational and mystical, as is becoming to sentences of this kind" (*JJC* 198–99).

These stylistic characteristics do not invoke the esoteric simply for its own sake but reflect Benjamin's early search for an alternative epistemology and concept of experience. In a passage that might also be used to describe the very problems of reading him, Benjamin writes that "another relation between thesis and antithesis is possible beside synthesis," and that would be the "non-synthesis of two concepts in another" ("Program" 47). Like so many other nineteenth- and twentieth-century thinkers who criticized the great "systems" of German philosophy—the epistemology of Kant and the idealism and historicism of Hegel—Benjamin found in literary criticism, in commentary, the fragment, the collage, and the aphorism modes of exploring alternate kinds of truth, modes which embodied the linguistic density of all knowledge. In his later writing, he radicalized these earlier literary and philosophical tendencies and applied the method of collage to history writing in order to produce a "shock effect"—to awaken the reader from ideological sleep. In that same 1931 letter to Rychner, Benjamin explained that he associated with Brecht, "not because I am a 'believer' in the materialistic 'Weltanschauung,' but rather because I am laboring to direct my thinking toward such subjects where the truth always appears most densely concentrated" (*Briefe* II: 523).

Michael Jennings astutely notes that "many of his essays can be only understood as experiments," and warns against the tendency of so many of his interpreters to efface "the tension inherent in his work and enlist him in the service of an intellectual cause or critical direction" (8). For this reason, it is deceptive and almost impossible to try to paraphrase Benjamin's "arguments"—to "translate" him. So in discussing him here, I must quote him at far greater length than is usual. Indeed, Benjamin's ideal in the Arcades project was a montage of quotations which raised "the art of quoting without quotation marks to the very highest level" ("Theory of Knowledge" [1, 10]). In effect, he forces one to read and write about him in the very mode in which he wrote, and to grasp and formulate those "constellations" of meaning he sought to elicit.

The elusiveness of Benjamin's prose is related to the key idea he puts forth in his essay on translation—that the best translation seeks that which is "untranslatable," the pure language which is beyond communication of information or content. This "pure language" is elusive, concealed, glimmering. Perhaps this is one reason why Scholem, with his interest and expertise in Jewish esoteric texts, was so sympathetic to Benjamin's difficult work: he reads Benjamin as an esoteric thinker, parallel to the way Scholem spent an entire career patiently deciphering enigmatic kabbalistic texts:

> Two categories, above all, especially in their Jewish version, assume a central place in his writings: Revelation, the idea of the Torah and of sacred texts in general, and on the other hand the messianic idea and Redemption. Their significance as regulative ideas governing his thought cannot be overrated. . . . later when he turned to historical materialism, out of those two categories of Revelation and Redemption, only the latter was preserved *expressi verbis*, but not the former, closely though it was bound up with his basic method of commenting on great and authoritative texts. In the process of transformation of his thought, the notion of Revelation vanished—or rather, I am inclined to suspect, remained unsaid, having become truly esoteric knowledge. (*JJC* 193–94)

Some reviewers have criticized the impersonality of Scholem's memoir of Benjamin, *The Story of a Friendship*, failing to make the connection between the way in which Scholem wrote about Kabbalah and the way in which he interpreted Benjamin. His book on Benjamin is "impersonal" in the manner of his kabbalistic researches, a meticulous bibliographic assemblage of manuscripts, dates, meetings, reports of conversations, diary extracts. As Scholem realized, there was a deep paradox in the very idea of a "public esoteric" tradition: how, after all, can one "communicate the incommunicable"? A similar irony, he saw, shadowed the attempt of the academic historian to grasp the meanings of that literature through an impersonal critical-philological technique. Yet this very distance may give access to esoteric writings in a way that attempts at personal immediacy, emotion, and identification may not.

In Benjamin, too, there is a distrust of subjective and personal immediacy as the grounds for truth. His own writings, from the highly abstract early essays to the collages of quotations and studies of the cultural objects of modernism, have an air of impersonality. Yet in his great later essays— such as those on Proust, Baudelaire, Kafka, and Kraus—he seems to be talking intimately about himself through the mask of these others—that is, allegorically, emblematically. And as we shall see, his theory of allegory, especially in *The Origin of German Tragic Drama*, was one of the keys to his work, and one of his greatest legacies to contemporary literary criticism, deeply influential on Paul deMan and Fredric Jameson.

Yet Benjamin's allegories were not "allegories of reading" in the deManian sense of deconstructive aporias. Benjamin's experimental method allowed contradictions to clash, and he sought illumination in the resulting sparks and flashes, as well as from the intense concentration or crystallization of fragments, and the "reconstellation" of the relations among them. Benjamin's "somehow" was positive action and search, a way of dealing with "impossibilities" that was skeptical, engaged, and utopian all at once. Benjamin's compression of expression and aphoristic brilliance seem to evoke and allude to a larger whole hidden just beyond their horizon—the "somehow"—but his essays intentionally resist the coherence of "system" and refuse any organic reassembly of their fragments.

Scholem notes Benjamin's attraction to the minute: "to create, or discover, perfection on the small and very smallest scale was one of his strongest urges." One of the problems for his editors has been his intensely compressed handwriting. "It was his never-realized ambition," writes Scholem, "to get a hundred lines onto an ordinary sheet of notepaper. In August 1927 he dragged me to the Musée Cluny in Paris, where in a collection of Jewish ritual objects, he showed me with true rapture two grains of wheat on which a kindred soul had inscribed the complete *Shema Israel*" (*JJC* 176–77).

Perhaps it was not so much "perfection" that Benjamin sought as the very power, force, or transfiguration that comes from compression itself. For the ordinary becomes extraordinary through compression. (Freud, for example, recognized this power in the mechanisms of the dream-work.) There is also a strong parallel in the kabbalistic idea that God created the world not through expansion but through *contraction*, or *tzimtzum*. "Voiding" the world of God's presence was necessary to create a "place" for the finite and material world. Benjamin's compressed and aphoristic style is the counterpart of his later idea of the historical image as a "monad." The monad, of course, is also a form of compression. Since any larger "organic" whole or Hegelian "totality" is what Benjamin resists as false, mythical, or ideological, the monad or the miniature, the fragment or the detail, becomes a mode of obtaining a certain "wholeness" in the very fragments themselves. What is unavailable as a larger whole or by any power of expansion is available instead in the compressed, in the miniature.

"THE TASK OF THE TRANSLATOR"

During their 1927 reunion in Paris, Scholem arranged a meeting for Benjamin with Judah Magnes, the first chancellor of the newly established Hebrew University in Jerusalem. Benjamin discussed with Magnes the possibility of coming to Jerusalem to learn Hebrew in order to become a critic of Hebrew literature, and he remarked that his work as a translator of Proust and Baudelaire had led him to the philosophical and theological reflections that made him more clearly conscious of his Jewish identity (*SF* 137–38). In "The Task of the Translator," the preface to his own translation into German of Baudelaire's *Tableaux parisiens*, Benjamin wrote:

> If there is a language of truth, the tensionless and even silent depository of the ultimate truth which all thought strives for, then this language of truth is—the true language and this very language, whose divination and description is the only perfection a philosopher can hope for, is concealed in concentrated fashion in translation. (*Illum* 77)

Benjamin, like Rosenzweig and Buber, was a serious and active translator, and like Rosenzweig, Benjamin connected translation to the utopian and redemptive elements of language. As early as the 1916 essay "On Language," Benjamin wrote that the relation between the language of humans and that of things is precisely "translation," and that "translation" redeems nature from its muteness. In the 1923 essay "The Task of the Translator," these utopian elements become even more pronounced. But whereas for Rosenzweig translation was redemptive because it enabled communication, made a bridge between humans and among different tongues, for Benjamin, the ultimate aim of translation is *not* human communicability but that "pure language" of ultimate meaning which is finally incommunicable—that is, where all particular meaning is extinguished, a realm which is less a content than a pure form.[6]

Commentators on Benjamin trace his idea of "pure language" to different sources—from the French symbolist tradition, to Mallarmé's perfect texts about "nothing," to sources in German philosophy, especially Humboldt and Hamann. In one of his curricula vitae, Benjamin noted that his interest in the philosophy of language began with a reading of Humboldt and continued with Mallarmé. Scholem wrote Benjamin that if he would repudiate the attempt to integrate dialectical materialism into his thought and return to his original base in the metaphysics of language, Benjamin could become "a very important figure in the history of critical thought, the legitimate bearer of the most fruitful and most genuine ongoing traditions of a Hamann and a Humboldt" (*SF* 228). And indeed it is Hamann's famous phrase "Language, the mother of reason and revelation, its alpha and omega," that Benjamin cites (*Refl* 321) in the essay "On Language"— and not any kabbalistic source.

Other interpreters place more or less emphasis on Benjamin's relation to Scholem and the kabbalistic ideas he might have absorbed from their discussions. Charles Rosen puts it best: Benjamin "found much that was congenial to him in mystical writings, particularly those of the seventeenth century. Nevertheless, the little that Benjamin found in the Kabbalah was only what he had already been looking for" ("Ruins of Walter Benjamin" 158). Yet most of these critics take Scholem's explications of Kabbalah as the "real thing itself," unmediated by Scholem's own ideologies and philosophies.[7] David Biale and Michael Jennings astutely note that the reverse might be equally likely—that Benjamin in fact influenced Scholem's philosophy of language. They do not, however, engage in any extensive analysis of the relation between Benjamin's linguistic theory and Scholem's interpretations of kabbalistic linguistics and ideas about revelation and tradition.

In 1937, Scholem wrote a remarkable letter to his publisher Zalman Schocken about the motives for his kabbalistic studies:

> Three years, 1916–1918, which were decisive for my entire life, lay behind me: many exciting thoughts had led me as much to the most rationalist skepticism about my fields of study as to intuitive affirmation of mystical theses which walked the fine line between religion and nihilism.
>
> I later [found in Kafka] the most perfect and unsurpassed expression of this fine line, an expression which, as a secular statement of the Kabbalistic world-feeling in a modern spirit, seems to me to wrap Kafka's writings in the halo of the canonical. (Qtd. in Biale, *Scholem* 75)

Those three decisive years which Scholem mentions in his letter to Schocken, 1916–1918, were also the years Scholem spent most intensively with Benjamin. For although he had been interested in Kabbalah since 1915, Scholem did not decide to transfer his field of doctoral study from mathematics and philosophy to Kabbalah until 1919, after spending time with Benjamin in Switzerland.[8]

In his rediscovery of Jewish identity, Scholem had participated in and been dissatisfied with the various possibilities of German-Jewish life—from the youth movements, to religious orthodoxy, to the bourgeois forms of Zionism. Ironically, the association with Benjamin was the least "overtly" Jewish option of all the others. In 1916, shortly after they first met, Scholem wrote in his diary with anticipation about forthcoming discussions with Benjamin on Plato and the philosophy of mathematics:

> When one has been reflecting about certain matters for a long time, one cannot help but be uplifted by the prospect of such inspiring and reverent company. I cannot talk about these things with . . . anyone else, for that matter; nor can I discuss my Zionist interests with the Zionists. . . . Instead I have to go to the non-Zionist and nonmathematician Benjamin, who has sensibility where most of the others no longer respond. (*SF* 19)

One of the attractions was their mutual "anarchism," which seemed to reinforce Scholem's disappointment with all the traditional sources of authority—or at least the current corrupted "concrete expressions" of them: "To our way of thinking, theocratic anarchism was still the most sensible

answer to politics" (*SF* 84). As Biale notes, Scholem was a thinker who
quite early on made his basic choices, developed his key ideas, and spent a
lifetime pursuing them. Biale also aptly specifies what he thinks "anarchism" meant for Scholem—not a nihilistic denial of all authority but
rather a belief in the lack of any central authority. That is, instead of
affirming any one dogma or tradition as ultimately authoritative, Scholem
posited in his work a conflicting plurality of authorities and traditions, the
historical and dialectical totality of which defined Judaism. I would add
that this view also has roots in Benjamin's idea of pure language as the
totality of conflicting languages—utopian, perhaps unreachable, "without
specific content," but nevertheless the "intention" of each.

In another sense, Benjamin's "pure language" was also a kind of "lost
Holy Writ" analogous to Scholem's pursuit of a lost esoteric tradition. In
the essay "The Name of God and the Linguistic Theory of the Kabbalah"
(1972), in which Scholem finally fulfilled his early aim to explore that
topic, he stressed the importance of the link between the idea of revealed
truth and language that Judaism forged. Central in all of Scholem's writings about the kabbalistic concept of revelation and language are the key
ideas also put forth by Benjamin in his essay on translation: *the highest
sphere of language is "beyond communication," the pure language "no
longer means or expresses anything," and the ultimate creative Word extinguishes all information and sense.*

That this seminal idea of "pure language" should be the focus of an
essay on the topic of translation is no accident. For thinkers such as Benjamin and Scholem, the question of translation itself was highly charged—
philosophically, politically, and personally. Translation was also intimately
linked with the problems of emancipation, assimilation, and the relation of
German and Jewish cultures. Moses Mendelssohn, the first great German-
Jewish philosopher of the Enlightenment, took a momentous step when in
the late eighteenth century he translated the Hebrew Bible into German in
accord with his belief that Jewish rationalism was compatible with German culture. Buber and Rosenzweig were also both eminent translators
who collaborated for many years on a new German translation of the entire Hebrew Bible closer to the idioms of the original.[9] Translation of the
Bible has always been an explosive issue linked to beliefs about the nature
of revelation, the "real" meaning of the text, the authority and power of
the interpreter, and the constitution of the faithful community. In the Renaissance, for example, English Bible translators who were unauthorized
by the ecclesiastical authorities paid for their work with their lives.

In the Buber-Rosenzweig translation of the Bible, or in Buber's translations of Hassidic tales, in Scholem's work on Kabbalah, and in Benjamin's
reflections on language, translation was intertwined with the most painful
and penetrating theological questions: How does the word of God speak,
and how is it heard? Is the voice direct or indirect? In what sense is it
commanding or imperative, abstract or concrete? How does the spiritual

"word" relate to the materiality of human language? Is revelation immediate or mediated—in the past or in the present tense? How is it "transmissible," and is it transmissible any longer? What is the relation of the divine word to the multiplicity of human tongues? Does translation repair the ruins of Babel, overcome alienation from God's word, and bring redemption? Yet what might be lost in the translation? What might be preserved in the translation? What is "true" understanding of the text? What is the relation of the original language to the history of its interpretations?

Whether working with the Bible or Baudelaire, the translator is inevitably a kind of literary theorist and scribal exegete, and translation a form of literary criticism and transmission of tradition. For even a translator of secular texts has to deal with critical questions about the way language means, and what constitutes the "intention of the author" or the text's "original" meaning, with problems of linguistic multiplicity and the historical transformation of meanings, with the relation between different languages, form and content, structure and idea.[10]

For both Benjamin and Scholem, these questions linked philosophy of language and philosophy of history. In another sense, they each "translated" their respective philosophy of language into a philosophy of history. For "translation" involves a relation between two objects which is intimate but not mimetic, which always involves some displacement of the original into another realm—as Benjamin "translated" theology into materialism and vice versa, and Scholem translated Kabbalah into the language of historical philology. In sum, Benjamin's early abstract and theological essays should not be thought of as ultimately separate from or disavowed by his later materialist work. Nor should Scholem, that eager young German student of mathematics and philosophy of language, be entirely separated from Scholem the Hebrew University professor, bibliographer, and historian.

Benjamin's essay on translation is characteristically difficult and elusive and has been read in any number of contradictory ways—from being a theological affirmation of the ultimate spiritual wholeness of language, to a deconstructive denial that language is anything other than a fragmented play of differences prohibiting any stable meaning, to a seminal source for the "reception theory" of historical meaning.

The key question in the debate about "The Task of the Translator" is just what Benjamin means by the "pure language." Does he mean a divine *ursprach*, the ground and goal of all human language and meaning, or is this "purity" the purity of a pure vacuum, an absolute meaning which requires the extinguishing of all concrete meanings, one so "silent" that in this abyss all our own language hears is its own reverberating echoes?

In the long quotation from "The Task of the Translator" cited at the beginning of this section, the qualifier *if* in the sentence "If there is a language of truth" could also lead one to argue that the "pure language" is only a heuristic, a hypothesis, or a "utopian absolute that can be approached but never reached" (Biale, *Scholem* 107). Paul deMan, on the other hand, argues against any utopian theological or political interpretations of Benjamin's "pure language," and characteristically asserts that for Benjamin, pure language "does not exist except as a permanent disjunction which inhibits all languages as such" (*Resistance to Theory* 92). But even as subtle a reader as deMan is forced to qualify his own interpretation of the essay: "Whenever I go back to this text, I think I have it more or less, then I read it again, and again I don't understand it" (103). No matter what one thinks of deMan's interpretation, almost every reader of Benjamin can identify with deMan's perplexity.

The "fragment" becomes in Benjamin's essay on translation a key figure for the relation of the original language of the text to its translation, and to the totality of languages supplementing each other and intending the "pure language" of truth:

> Fragments of a vessel which are to be glued together must match one another in the smallest details, although they need not be like one another. In the same way, a translation, instead of resembling the meaning [*Sinn*] of the original, must lovingly and in detail incorporate the original's mode of signification [*Art des Meinens*], thus making both the original and the translation recognizable as fragments of a greater language, just as fragments are part of a vessel. ("Task" 78)

For Benjamin, this "mode of signification" of the original is to be identified with neither the "objective" contents of the work nor any "subjective" effect it might have on a receiver. Although translation is part of what Benjamin calls the "afterlife" or "posthistory" (*Nachgeschichte*) of the original (thus anticipating "reception theory"), this should not be confused with any individual's personal experience. The definition of "life" in the phrase "afterlife" of an artwork as an aspect of the "translatability" of the original, is not "life" defined by notions such as "soul" or physical "sensation." It is not an organic, "natural" life but is "determined by history rather than by nature": "The philosopher's task consists in comprehending all of natural life through the more encompassing life of history" (71).

By these criteria, a translation which aimed primarily at imparting the content or "information" of the original would be a bad translation. There is a larger issue involved, of course, for the purpose of "life" is not, as in *Lebensphilosophie*, an immediate "expression of its nature" but something higher, the "representation of its significance." This is done through, in, by, and for languages: "Translation thus ultimately serves the purpose of expressing the central reciprocal relationship between languages . . . in embryonic or intensive form" (72). "Embryonic," that is, as a kind of compression expression.

In other words, the kinship of languages and the aim of translation is not any mimetic content of translation to original but something higher, the higher aim of all languages. Even the historical process as the afterlife and continuous renewal of a work and the continuing changes and transformations in its meanings and language are signs of this "beyond." This "superhistorical kinship of languages rests in the very intention underlying each language as a whole—an intention, however, which no single language can attain by itself and which is realized only by the totality of their intentions supplementing each other: pure language" (74). The "referent" of words is not the same as their "mode of intention." Charles Rosen explains that by "mode of intention," Benjamin means something more than the connotations of words. Rather, each word has a "range of significance . . . which, when followed to its limits, to the extreme, will mirror the whole civilization and history governed" by a given language. "The total range of significance, *represented objectively*, and as a structure of its most distant relationships, is the Idea in Benjamin's sense" ("Ruins" 159). But even a good translation cannot be a direct, immediate, or final grasp of the words' ultimate meaning, although its "goal is undeniably a final, conclusive, decisive stage of all linguistic creation," i.e., that higher pure language, or that realm of complete reconciliation and fulfillment of all languages. Although ultimately inaccessible, Benjamin argues, there is in translation an element that points to this "beyond" of pure language— when the translation goes "beyond" merely conveying the subject of the original.

   That element, he paradoxically adds, is what is "untranslatable" in the original—that is, what remains after its contents, information, or subject matter is stripped away. Translation, then, has a different relation and task in regard to language than does the original poem. In a translation, there is no close unity of content and language such as exists in the original, "for it signifies a more exalted language than its own and remains unsuited to its content, overpowering, and alien" to the original. (The stripping away of contents and the alienness of the translation to the original are also the structures that Benjamin emphasizes in his work on allegory in the book on the German tragic drama. "Stripping away" is also related to Benjamin's interest in miniaturization and compression.) The task of the translator, then, is entirely different from the task of the poet and more akin to the task of the critic, a task directed toward "language as such, at its totality," at "integrating many tongues into one true language" ("Task" 76; 77).

   But this pure language is unattainable, or is silent. And if it can be glimpsed only when a translator moves beyond communicating the content or sense of the original, how indeed can it be "communicated"? "Faithfulness" to the original would instead mean orientation toward its "longing for linguistic complementation," by refracting the light of the pure language onto the original. In this sense, faithfulness to the original becomes inverted into *freedom* from sense, as the movement toward "some ultimate, decisive element remain[ing] beyond communication—quite close and yet infinitely remote, concealed or distinguishable, fragmented or powerful" (79). Note the characteristic juxtaposition of opposites in this last phrase. The brilliant metaphor which Benjamin uses to describe this inverted relation of fidelity and freedom is that of a tangent which touches a circle (i.e., the sense or content) lightly and at one point, "with this touch rather than the point setting the law according to which it is to continue on its path to infinity" (80).

Yet Benjamin also maintains that the nucleus or seed of pure language is not simply the unattainable object of a utopian yearning but is found as an "active force" (79) in all languages and their historical evolution, which translation also involves. For a good translation also lets its own language be affected by the alien language of the original, and it is in turn expanded and deepened toward the pure language.

As Benjamin notes in the conclusion of the essay, however, there is a risk that in such a vastly opened language, in the trajectory toward infinity, the translator will literally go off on a tangent where "meaning plunges from abyss to abyss until it threatens to become lost in the bottomless depths of language," enclosing the translator in silence. Only in Holy Scripture, he adds, where the text in all its literality is "the true language," that is, where revelation and language are entirely one without any tension, can this fall be "halted"—or, as Carol Jacobs argues, "held, retained," depending upon how one translates Benjamin's own phrase *Halten*. In an interlinear version of Scripture, the original sacred text contains its own translation. And this, Benjamin concludes, is true to some degree of all great texts, ending the essay with the sentence: "The interlinear version of the Scriptures is the prototype or ideal of all translation" (82).

THE "PURE LANGUAGE"

But how does this newly invoked Holy Word relate to the "pure language" Benjamin has been discussing throughout? Is the Word of "In the beginning was the Word," which Benjamin cites in Greek (78) (perhaps to retain its foreignness or "otherness" to German), is this Word "identical" to the "pure language"? Yet how could this be, since "in this pure language—which no longer means or expresses anything but is, as expressionless and creative Word, that which is meant in all languages—all information, all sense, and all intention finally encounter a stratum in which they are destined to be extinguished" (80)?

The pure realm of language is held out as a kind of transcendent otherness, yet it extinguishes all meaning and sense and commonality. Is the pure word an empty abyss or creative plenitude? divine or radically profane? the redeeming Word of holiness or the nihilistic word of the relentlessly inhuman? Is the "abyss" the nonhuman emptiness of language's own immanent self-critique, or its "depth" as divine plenitude? Is the abyss God's catastrophic withdrawal, or the hidden dimensions of God's abundant and beneficent presence? Is this very ambiguity what Scholem meant when he wrote to Schocken of his "intuitive affirmation of mystical theses which walked the fine line between religion and nihilism"?

Has Benjamin put forth a disguised theological version of language, or an immanent critique where there is no divine anchor to the abysses of language? Although one can ask this question of all of Benjamin's work, any "answer," I believe, is not to be found in phrasing the question in an either/or mode. In Benjamin's characteristic fashion, seemingly opposite positions are thrust together, and the force of this thrusting generates a dialectical relationship, which does not consummate in any resolving synthesis of the opposing terms—what he would later call "dialectics at a standstill." As Benjamin wrote with some pique to Scholem in 1934, one should not attempt to extract some "credo" from his writings: "You know very well that I have always written according to my convictions—save perhaps a few minor exceptions—but that I have never made the attempt to express the contradictory and mobile whole that my convictions represent in their multiplicity, except in very extraordinary cases and then never other than orally" (*Corr* 108–109).

HERMETIC AND ORPHIC LANGUAGE

Moreover, the question about the nature of "pure language" in the essay on translation has to do with the most difficult issues of linguistic meaning, and with the ontological status of language—the being of language and the being of the world, and the relation between those two. As Gerald Bruns has put it, there is a "Janus-like character of the linguistic sign":

> The sign appears to derive its power of signification from the formal principles that determine its relative position within a semiotic system; at the same time, however, it claims for itself its ancient power to transcend the system and to announce a meaning on the basis of its unity with a world of things. (*Modern Poetry* 234)

Bruns correlates these two aspects of signification with two basic concepts of literary language that have alternated, clashed, and interpenetrated since ancient times: the "hermetic" and the "orphic." The hermetic attitude defines the essence of literary language by its deviation from ordinary social and communicative discourse. It turns language away from the world and back upon itself into a pure realm of forms, that is, a world of solely interlinguistic structural relations analogous to music. The less "content"—or reference to practical, ordinary worldly communication—the more "pure" and essential, the "higher" the apprehensions to which language gives rise. Language becomes its own transcendence, its own intransitive world. In the nineteenth century, paradigmatic expressions of the hermetic attitude are found in the French symbolist tradition, especially in

Mallarmé's idea of poetic language as a purifying word which seeks to return to an original pure void apart from all external meaning and human expression (*le Neant*), a Nothing which constituted the highest Beauty.

Both the hermetic and orphic attitudes are found in the most ancient speculations about language. Contemporary exponents of the hermetic position in literary criticism would include the many varieties of formalism, from the New Criticism to structuralism, semiotics, and deconstruction. The orphic tradition, by contrast (named after the ancient mythical figure, the singer Orpheus), exalts poetic speech as a creative power based on an ideal unity of word and being that establishes the human and natural world—like the creative Word of God—and thus makes all signification and knowing possible. Heidegger and the phenomenological tradition would be recent exponents.

While hermetic language turns away from the world, "voids it" for the work of art, and orphic language turns toward the world, grounds and establishes the world for human meaning, both these modes assert the primacy of language (*Modern Poetry* 1–2). Words in the hermetic tradition become realities in themselves—constitute their own transcendental world; words in the orphic tradition aspire to a primal condition where word and world were one. Both traditions, that is, aim at some primal identity of word and reality, though that "reality" is defined differently. And the world of human and inanimate nature can be seen as either an obstacle to and fall from that higher reality, or its very matrix and goal. For example, Bruns writes, in Coleridge's romanticism, the word is a locus of power, which we grasp in

> an act or moment of "intuitive knowledge," in which "reality" is encountered *mediately*, but with all the force and energy of an "immediate presence." . . . the function of the word is clear: it is to mediate between mind and world, not simply to correlate the one to the other but fabricate an *immediate* relationship between the two. It does so, moreover, by appearing to become the reality: the word is elevated into a thing. . . . (55)

We shall also find that Benjamin was intrigued by this magical "mediated immediacy of language" and sought to understand and exploit it throughout his work. And Benjamin, with his own self-described "Janus-face," interwove both these conceptions of language. Unlike many other twentieth-century literary theorists, he did not sacrifice one for the other, or polemically oppose them. They are both used in complicated and often idiosyncratic ways in all his work from the earlier, more "idealist" reflections on language to his later political "historical materialist" writings. One consistent principle in all his work, though, is that language cannot be reduced to its ordinary, communicative functions. In the early essays, he invoked ideas of "pure language," of intentionless, silent, expressionless ultimate meaning, and constructed a theory of the Name as the essence of all language—that which linked the divine, human, and natural worlds of expression.

In the translation essay, his own language is obliquely theological, but it is important to note that there is no reference to a divine guarantor of pure language, or to the certainty of its eventual disclosure. "Pure language" seems to operate as a hopeful assumption or semiutopian vision gained through evanescent glimmers, i.e., as something almost "messianic." A kind of secularized messianism or messianic secularity is another key theme in Benjamin from his early writing to the very last paragraph of his last work, the "Theses on the Philosophy of History." That piece, which juxtaposes political revolution with Jewish remembrance, concludes by describing "every second of time" as the "strait gate through which the Messiah might enter" (*Illum* 264).

This "messianism" elicits an "other" history beyond/behind the catastrophes of present history, and points to a redemption that demands action even if its goal is invisible or unrealizable. It was one important source for Benjamin's conjoining of politics, theology, and literary criticism. In a letter to Scholem of May 29, 1926, Benjamin defended his new political orientation and wrote, "I am not ashamed of my 'earlier' anarchism; . . . I consider anarchist methods unserviceable and Communist goals meaningless and non-existent. Which does not detract from the value of Communist action one iota, because it is the corrective of Communist goals—and because meaningful *political* goals are non-existent." Judaism and radical politics, he maintained, could serve each other (*Briefe* I: 426).

Perhaps this particularly Jewish brand of messianism, which involved a historical thrust, a "rupturing" of Being by history, saved him from the dangers of completely "hypostatizing" language, dangers to which both "hermetic" and "orphic" traditions are subject, and to which much twentieth-century literary theory has fallen prey—i.e., making language a being or universe in and of itself, with no "outside." This hypostatizing, as Bruns notes, has a certain theological substratum: "language makes a claim to divine definition as a circle whose center is everywhere and whose circumference is nowhere. . . . [This] divine circle . . . becomes transcendent in its own right, an over arching horizon beyond which we need not and perhaps cannot go in search of what is real" (98). Consequently, *L*anguage becomes the very being of literature.

Needless to say, the loss of religious belief in the modern era meant the loss of the divine connection between words and things, language and reality. As Fredric Jameson, citing Nietzsche, put it in the title of his book on Russian formalism and French structuralism, we are trapped in the "Prison-house of Language." "Structure," "system," "langue" are the ghostly fictions which take the place that God would have had. In the New Criticism, for example, the text itself was invested with this divine power of autonomy, self-containment, and immanent meaning. One should not confuse a work's meaning, so this argument went, with its historical background, the author's intentions or biography, or the reader's response, and so forth. Language was emptied and formalized.

Another way of putting it is that Language with a capital L takes the place of God—or becomes what Kenneth Burke would call a "God-term," an explanatory principle, a ground, a self-reflexive entity. Moreover, as the Bible was being desacralized by historical and critical scholarship in the nineteenth century, literature, through the efforts of critics such as Matthew Arnold, was becoming a substitute religion and "sacralized."[11] Language becomes "autonomous," and autonomy as the engendering of the ground of one's own being, as the creation of one's own origin, is the classical attribute of divinity as totally self-contained, self-related, autonomous. This drive to recapture the autonomy of origins is part of the pathos of modernism. And Levinas will argue that a theology based on autonomous ontology, on God as ultimate and independent "Being," is violent and idolatrous. Like Rosenzweig, Levinas is inspired in this argument by a particularly Jewish sense of God as "otherwise than Being," of God as "passing" (*se passer*, instead of "coming into being" or "appearing") through a distinctively nonontological but ethical relation between humans, a relation oriented by and toward a "messianic" redemption of the violence of immanent history. History, then, is messianic insofar as it can escape total enclosure within the circles of autonomous "Being."

Levinas's immediate polemic is directed against Heidegger and Hegel, figures whom Benjamin also detested. Benjamin's "messianism" is in many ways quite different from that of Levinas and Rosenzweig, but he shares with them the key Jewish notion of possibilities in history that can break open the circular and mythical patterns of destruction, fate, and violence. I am arguing, in other words, that this "messianism" is one of the factors that prevented Benjamin's absorption in a symbolist ahistorical world of "pure language."

Charles Rosen has argued that Benjamin's technique of writing and representation, in which the discontinuous arrangements of sentences and quotations produce a "shock" effect and different contextual resonances, was derived in large part from Mallarmé and French symbolism: what Mallarmé defined for poetry, Benjamin adapted to philology. In Rosen's apt phrase, Benjamin "created a poetry of philology": "As Mallarmé treats words, Benjamin treats ideas: he names them, juxtaposes them, and lets them reflect one off the other. . . . his arrangements are material for contemplation, they force the reader himself to draw the meaning from the resonances of the ideas" ("Ruins" 163, 165). That was a transformation of philology that Scholem, however, would not make in his own work. For both Benjamin and Scholem, philology was bound up with their critiques of positivist historicism and their constructions of different kinds of historical narrative. Yet Benjamin, unlike Scholem, also saw the mythical elements in philology itself: "Philology," he wrote, "is the examination of a text which proceeds by details and so magically fixates the reader on it," a magic which needs to be exorcised but whose exorcism involves the philological effort itself, preserved and surpassed (*Aesthetics* 136–37).

For Benjamin's Marxist critics, however, his method was not "dialectical enough"—not mediated through the "total social process" as Adorno wrote to him about the Arcades study: "your dialectic lacks one thing: mediation. . . . your study is located at the crossroads of magic and positivism. That spot is bewitched. Only theory could break the spell—your own resolute, salutarily speculative theory" (*Aesthetics* 128–29). The objections which Adorno made to Benjamin are similar to charges often made against the contemporary genre of literary criticism known as the "New Historicism"—that its "materialism" and its presentation of empirical evidence are undialectical and incoherent. Benjamin could be seen as one of the great precursors of the New Historian, but unlike most of its practitioners, he never accepted the premise of the arbitrariness of the linguistic sign. In other words, Benjamin's Arcades project is what a New Historicist work might look like without the burdens of poststructuralist linguistic theory and the rigid polemical opposition between materialism and idealism.[12]

Truth, Benjamin wrote in his study of the German tragic drama, belonged to the realm of Ideas, not "knowledge," i.e., ordinary, "profane," communicative instrumental meanings that one could master and possess. Charles Rosen also notes that Benjamin's idea of the "autonomy" of truth and of the work of art, and Benjamin's discussion of the relation between what he called in his essay on Goethe the "truth content" and "material content" of the work, appropriated the image of the autonomy of the sacred text. But Benjamin also understood "autonomy" to mean that the work of art revealed its "transcendence" or its "truth content" only as it was projected through history—its tradition of meanings, or "afterlife," its material content ("Ruins" 137).[13] History is a process of both stripping off what was inessential in the work, and revealing among the ruins its philosophical idea; at the same time, the work's history preserves these ruins and the remnants of the time from which it originated. Benjamin understood that both these aspects needed attending, and so he termed the study of a work's truth content "criticism," which is philosophical, and the study of the material content "commentary," which uses the method of philology. He refers to his Goethe essay and these two terms in his defense to Adorno of his "undialectical" use of philology (*Aesthetics* 137).

In other words, despite the symbolist influence, for Benjamin "truth content," or philosophical Idea, or pure language, or autonomy of the work did not mean abandoning "History" for "Language"; nor did it express the wish to dissolve history into "pure language," as his deconstructive readers claim. Rosen evokes Benjamin to counter Harold Bloom's assertion that poems refer primarily to other poems within the realm of *literary* language; rather, "it is into the *whole* of language that each work is absorbed," i.e., the entire cultural context which includes ordinary language—and even beyond the past cultural totality that produced the work, but "as it moves through time it reveals the capacity to refer to the future as well" ("Ruins" 171–72).

This capacity to refer to the future, I would add, is another one of the Jewish-messianic aspects of Benjamin's criticism. In his later work, this future lends a retrospective power to Benjamin's "historical materialist" to redeem the past, to revolutionize the present, and to break open the realms of myth and fate. Without it, there is paralysis between the extremes of an abstract, empty, ahistorical pure language and the unredeemable, inert material content of philology or historical artifact, or what he called the "trash of history." Both of these realms, as Benjamin recognized, then threaten to return to the realm of myth. This danger, one might add, also exists in the problematic relations between poststructuralist linguistic theory and the material cultural object in the New Historicism. To save the terms *language, history, power, ideology,* etc. from "hypostatization," many New Historicists resort to tropes such as *oscillation, network, negotiation* to describe the continuously fluctuating relations among these forces. Yet these catchall terms do little to solve the theoretical problem.

To use Rosen's words one final time, philology as "the painstaking study of the fragmentary documents of the past" becomes in Benjamin "an act of transforming memory, of translation" (170).

"PLENTY OF HOPE, BUT NOT FOR US"

Given this background and the trajectory of Benjamin's work, the interpretation of his essay "The Task of the Translator" by deconstructive critics calls for some comment. Like Paul deMan, Carol Jacobs argues that Benjamin's essay is ironic, deceptive, and disorienting—that its subject is the very "Monstrosity of Translation," the fall into the groundless abyss of language, and not any apotheosis of reconciling harmony. By pure language, Benjamin does not mean "the materialization of truth in the form of a supreme language . . . but signifies rather that which is purely language—nothing but language" ("Monstrosity" 761).[14] And language, in her deconstructive reading, is nothing but the play of difference. Benjamin's own essay, like the ideal translation, Jacobs argues, would "say nothing."

Along with Paul deMan, she reads the word *Aufgabe* or "Task" in the title in its literal sense: "surrender, giving up, failure" ("Monstrosity" 765; deMan, *Resistance* 80). DeMan, in a characteristic deconstructive reading, maintains that the essay's critique of the communicative elements of language indicates that Benjamin is really talking about the "impossibility" of translation. By the "extinguishing" of meaning in the pure language, Benjamin intends a nihilistic view of language and history wherein purity means mortification, disarticulation, and destruction, "killing the original" (*Resistance* 84). Benjamin's idea of translation, then, is of "desacralization, de-canonization" (96–98). All this refers, moreover, to the formal structure of *language itself,* not to any kind of human, personal, or historical pathos. For deMan this signifies the unbridgeable gap between meaning and reference, language and the world, hermeneutics and poetics, symbol and symbolized.

I shall have occasion in my later chapters on Levinas to discuss the strange intensity of deMan's insistence on the utter inhumanity and indifference of language, an assumption taken up by many of his followers as a key element in the poststructuralist view of language in literary theory, as well as in much of the New Historicism's intense hostility to "bourgeois humanism and individualism." Here, deMan is equally intent on denying any possible theological meaning to Benjamin's "pure language," and argues that the messianic reading of Benjamin is all the fault of Scholem, whom deMan harshly criticizes as "the man who bears the strong responsibility in this unhappy misinterpretation of Benjamin . . . who deliberately tried to make Benjamin say the opposite of what he said for ends of his own" (103).

Without entering here into the difficult debate about deMan's own controversial political actions and writings during World War II in relation to Jews, his refusal of the theological element in this text is a kind of blindness to and obliteration of the Jewishness of Benjamin.[15] To deMan, the essay is all about the impossibilities of meaning, and about language as something purely formal and inhuman: "in a very radical sense [there is] no such thing as the human" (96). But to cite Kafka once again, German-Jewish writers dealt with many kinds of "impossibilities." And these impossibilities, like so many other of the impossibilities of Jewish history, nevertheless had to be lived out in a way to which deMan is entirely insensitive, for these "impossibilities" were not *purely epistemological* dilemmas, as they are for deMan.

DeMan reduces language to a mode of abstract "knowing," which always points to the impossibility of making any ontological claim, and which thus excludes any enactment of "modes of being." Language, therefore, has nothing personal, human, or "historical" about it. But Benjamin, in his attempt to revise Kantianism by reconnecting thought to language, intended to incorporate *many* alternate kinds of experience and subjectivity. And Benjamin sharply disagreed with Saussure's concept of language as a set of signs whose meanings are arbitrary. For Benjamin, language and the "literary" were repositories of truth, even though that truth might be at present inaccessible; this was a "theological" messianic component, nowhere to be found in semiotics and structuralism.

Benjamin's attraction to communism, despite what he characterized as its crude and faulty metaphysics, and his attempt to juxtapose historical materialism with theology, and philosophy of language with philosophy of history, were part of his larger program—but also came from his recognition of the need for action despite the epistemological or theoretical "impossibilities." In a letter he wrote to Scholem in 1926, Benjamin defended the political and materialist turn of his thought, and the need he felt "to

take leave of the purely theoretical sphere." There were, he asserted, only
two ways to accomplish this:

> through religious or political conduct. Essentially I would not admit to a dif-
> ference between these two types of conduct. But neither is there an overlap
> between them. I am speaking of an identity which, paradoxically, manifests
> itself in transformations of one into the other (in both directions); and the
> essential consideration is that every instance of action proceed ruthlessly, and,
> in its own self-understanding, radically. Therefore, the task plainly is not to
> decide once and for all, but rather at every moment. But what is essential is to
> *decide.* . . . whoever amongst our generation seriously feels and understands
> the present historical moment as a struggle cannot reject the study and praxis
> of that mechanism whereby things (and relations) and masses affect one an-
> other. It may be that such a struggle, viewed from the standpoint of Judaism,
> proceeds altogether differently, disparately (but never hostilely). That cannot
> be helped: "justified," radical politics will always be serviceable for Judaism
> and, what is infinitely more important, will find Judaism serviceable for itself.
> (*Briefe* I: 425–26)

In that "present historical moment," writers such as Scholem and Benjamin experienced "impossibilities" in forms other than pure epistemology.
There were the quite concrete impossibilities of living as flesh-and-blood
Jews in Germany, and also of living as Jews in traditional Judaism, but
which nevertheless had to be lived anyway, lived "somehow." Benjamin's
"somehow" was the counterpoint to these impossibilities. It was a utopian
aspect of his thought, the echoes of which confuse deMan and which he
blames upon Scholem. Kafka had written in that famous letter to Max
Brod about the problems of the German-Jewish writers who wanted to
break with Judaism with the vague approval of their fathers, but "with
their posterior legs they were still glued to their father's Jewishness and
with their waving anterior legs they found no new ground. The ensuing
despair became their inspiration" (*Letters* 289). Benjamin well understood
this Jewish element in Kafka, and wrote eloquently of it. The disparity
between the long-delayed utopian redemption promised by Jewish messianism and the seeming abandonment and endlessness of the fallen present,
between hope and hopelessness, is one of the keys to his brilliant essay on
Kafka and the later letter (1938) he wrote to Scholem about it:

> This much Kafka was absolutely sure of: First, that someone must be a fool if
> he is to help; second, that only a fool's help is real help. The only uncertain
> thing is: can such help still do a human being any good? It is more likely to
> help the angels who could do without help. Thus as Kafka puts it, there is an
> infinite amount of hope, but not for us. This statement really contains Kafka's
> hope; it is the source of his radiant serenity. (*Corr* 225)

As Adorno once wrote, that Kafka quote "there is an infinite amount of
hope, but not for us" could also have served as the "motto of Benjamin's

metaphysic" (*Prisms* 321). But for Brecht, the Kafka essay was simply another of Benjamin's regressive "Jewish fascisms" (*Refl* 208). In the end, though, it was not "Jewish" fascism that made it *literally*, not just linguistically or epistemologically, impossible for Benjamin to live in Europe. It was another kind. The rise of Nazism denied Benjamin outlets for publishing his work and making a living. He was exiled from Germany in 1933 and lived a hand-to-mouth existence in Paris, and in Denmark with Brecht. In a poignant letter to Scholem from Ibiza after he had left Germany in 1933, he noted, "My constitution is frail. The absolute impossibility of having anything at all to draw on threatens a person's equilibrium in the long run, even one as unassuming and as used to living in precarious circumstances as I am" (*Corr* 51). A year later, writing from Paris while living on a small stipend from the Alliance Israélite Universelle, he noted, "In my situation, one can only give oneself up to the feeling of hope with great dietary precaution" (100). The next six years were spent moving from one cheap hotel room to the next: "There are places where I could earn a minimal income, and places where I could live on a minimal income, but not a single place where these two conditions coincide" (28). He was interned with other German émigrés in a detention camp in 1940 after the Nazis invaded France. Finally, when completely trapped, when impossibility reached its ultimate extreme, he committed suicide. Yet the last words of his "Theses on the Philosophy of History," written in 1940, still evoke political revolution, Jewish remembrance, and "every second of time" as the "strait gate through which the Messiah might enter" (*Illum* 264).

Irving Wohlfarth has argued, moreover, that the self-conscious fragmentation and incompleteness of Benjamin's work, especially in the Arcades project, alludes to the Work to come, from which all work at present is separated. Benjamin's writing and his project itself, his messianism, are "the very opposite of defeatism" ("Re-fusing" 8). Stanley Corngold and Michael Jennings also note that there was a "messianism" in the very act of "Benjamin's will to read and write" ("Benjamin/Scholem" 363), an inspired despair to go on under such difficult circumstances of poverty, exile, and uncertainty. In his very last letter to Scholem, in January 1940, Benjamin wrote: "Every line we succeed in publishing today—no matter how uncertain the future—is a victory wrenched from the powers of darkness" (*Corr* 262).

There are echoes in the ironies, tensions, displacements in Benjamin's text, and in his allusions to redemption and messianism, which neither deMan's nor Brecht's ear can hear. These echoes sound forth from the depths of the German-Jewish experience: "My thinking relates to theology the way a blotter does to ink. It is soaked through with it. If one were to go by the blotter, though, nothing of what has been written would remain" ("Theory of Knowledge" [N 7a, 7]). Perhaps Benjamin's image of the fragments of a broken vessel to signify the relation of languages to each other and to the pure language might also be applied to the relation of German and Jewish, theological and material elements in his work. The relation is not mimetic; the fragments are quite different, but in running up against each other at the broken places they "somehow" are of a piece.This strange fraternal asymmetry has its counterpart in Benjamin's image of the off-sided way the line tangentially touches the circle on its trajectory to infinity. Similarly, Jews touched German culture, and the trajectory of Jewish thought was altered on its way to the "beyond" of "theological" infinity. But in the process, Jewish thought and theology were also "translated" into "German." The question is: Was this a poor translation, mere apologetics, as Scholem argued, or a secularization and extinction of the Jewish content, as Gay argues? Was that translation necessary for the expansion of the translating language? In this asymmetrical supplementarity were Jewish thought and theology deepened, redirected in their own trajectory? Did the "translation"—especially as worked by writers such as Kafka and Benjamin—purify and expand the German original, redeem it? Or was this asymmetry an illusory love affair which became a monstrous hybrid? Did the tangent lose itself in the abysses of language and become unreadable and unhearable?

As Carol Jacobs asks, "who pieces the vase together?" ("Monstrosity" 764). Are its shattered parts always broken, its default lines always shaky and visible? She finds in the metaphor an allusion to Scholem and the kabbalistic doctrine of the "breaking of the vessels" (*shevirat ha-kelim*), part of the mystical theory of creation. The goal of humanity in the kabbalistic view is to redeem the sparks of holiness still attached to these vessels as they fell and became embedded into the material world, to repair and redeem (*tikkun*) the world by restoring the sparks to their source and so bring about the final redemption. But like deMan, Jacobs thinks that Benjamin refers to the redemptive aspect only to negate it. We shall see, though, that messianic redemption in Jewish thought is no simple matter, nor can "negation" in Benjamin be understood either in its traditional logical sense (as complete cancellation or opposition) or in a dialectical sense (as part of a dynamic process of ultimate resolution). In his preface to his book on the German tragic drama, Benjamin writes again about fragmentation when he discusses the digressive method that belongs to treatises which do not attempt to be systematic representations of truth. The treatise constantly digresses, begins again, pauses, pursues different levels of meaning in an irregular rhythm:

> Just as mosaics preserve their majesty despite their fragmentation into capricious particles, so philosophical contemplation is not lacking in momentum. Both are made up of the distinct and the disparate; and nothing could bear more powerful testimony to the transcendent force of the sacred image and the truth itself. The value of fragments of thought is all the greater the less direct their relationship to the underlying idea, and the brilliance of the representation depends as much on this value as the brilliance of the mosaic does on the quality of the glass paste. (*OGTD* 29)

Truth content is thus grasped only through immersion in the minute. All this well characterizes Benjamin's own work, from his early essays to his last writings.

Scholem was at great pains in all his work to stress the apocalyptic and destructive as well as restorative and utopian elements in Jewish messianism. In his view, it contained explosive tensions between a vision of history as teleologically meaningful, moving toward a redeemed future, and that same redemption as a negation and destructive purgation of that very history. The destruction is a prelude for redemption. In this schema, the tensions can lead to many positions, depending upon how the balance of these forces turns and is crystallized in any given moment. Messianism can involve a defense of revolutionary destruction, or furnish consolatory images of a lost and future paradise, or attempt to repair the ruins of the present by healing the wounds of the oppressed, or spawn heretical efforts to precipitate and make immediate the End—and thus range from political activism to meditative quietism, from theological conservatism to heretical radicalism.

One finds in Benjamin almost all of these "messianic" positions in one form or another—sometimes "translated" into historical materialism or advocacy of revolutionary nihilism, or into utopian images tinged with nostalgia and yearning in his literary essays on Proust and Kafka, or into meditations about ironic hunchbacks, dwarfs, and angels. Irony, which Scholem does not discuss, is another classic Jewish expression of delayed messianism, especially in Eastern European Jewish folklore. In deMan, irony becomes the paradigmatic deconstructive mode, the acknowledgment of the impossibility of ever making reference and meaning, or language and reality, coincide, the expression of impotence in the face of the abyss of signification. But in Jewish irony, the conditions of impotence and broken reality took a different turn—a turn in which the very delays and disparities between utopian promise and historical reality were charged and turned into messianic anticipation. Benjamin well understood the irony of this position, and that is why he understood the deep affinity between Kafka's tales, Yiddish folklore, and Hassidic stories (*Illum* 126, 134–36).

The painful disparity between ideal and real, fulfilled and unfulfilled time, hope and loss of hope is ironically expressed in a Yiddish folktale neither he nor Scholem cites about the fictitious town of Chelm.

It was once rumored that the Messiah was about to appear. So the Chelmites, fearing that he might bypass their town, engaged a watchman, who was to be on the lookout for the divine guest and welcome him if he should happen along.

The watchman in the meanwhile bethought himself that his weekly salary of ten gulden was mighty little with which to support a wife and children, and so he applied to the town elders for an increase.

The rabbi turned down his request. "True enough," he argued, "that ten gulden a week is an inadequate salary. But one must take into account that this is a permanent job." (Qtd. in Howe and Greenberg, *Treasury* 626)

The ironic melancholy of deferral and disparity is combined here, as in Kafka, with a "radiant serenity" and a comic-satiric counterassertion against all those forces, human *or* divine, which delay the Messiah. The innocence of hope is castigated and affirmed at once. Hope, plenty of hope—but not for us. This irony, though, is no futile resignation but retains its sharp edge, its caustic critique, a critique which in Jewish thought is tied to messianic hopes, as deferred as they might be. In his final comment about Kafka in the correspondence with Scholem of February 4, 1939, Benjamin astutely wrote: "I think the key to Kafka's work is likely to fall into the hands of the person who *is able to extract the comic aspects from Jewish theology* [italics his]. Has there been such a man? Or would you be man enough to be that man?" (*Corr* 243).

SCHOLEM AND MESSIANIC DELAY

There is something grand about living in hope, but at the same time there is something profoundly unreal about it. . . . Thus in Judaism, the Messianic idea has compelled a *life lived in deferment* in which nothing can be done definitively, nothing can be irrevocably accomplished. . . . the Messianic idea is the real anti-existentialist idea. Precisely understood, there is nothing concrete that can be accomplished by the unredeemed. This makes for the greatness of Messianism, but also for its constitutional weakness. Jewish so-called *Existens* possesses a tension that never finds true release; it never burns itself out. And when in our history it does discharge, it is foolishly decried as . . . "pseudo-Messianism." . . . Little wonder that overtones of Messianism have accompanied the modern Jewish readiness for irrevocable action in the concrete realm, when it set out on the utopian return to Zion. (*Mess Idea* 34–35)

In this oft-cited passage, Scholem stressed that the messianic idea, although it was the promise of happiness, was also the deferral of that happiness. Messianism, from Scholem's adamant Zionist perspective, also extracted a great price: his underlying claim is that messianism made Jew-ish history provisional and Jews ultimately powerless on the stage of world history. Yet this analysis is itself highly ideological and reflects Scholem's concept of Zionism as the Jews' determination to abandon suprahistorical hope, end deferral, and reenter world history by the construction of a homeland in Palestine. (Scholem's politics led to an equally flawed evalua-tion of Kafka: he wrote to Benjamin in 1931 that Kafka has no place in the continuum of German literature, "something that he himself did not have the least doubt about; as you probably know, he was a Zionist" [*SF* 170].)[16] It is as if Scholem is once again decrying diaspora culture, connecting its messianic religious hopes to political impotence. The argument, however, that Messianism means that "nothing concrete" can be accomplished by the unredeemed is a distorted one. Jewish messianism and eschatology do not result, as Scholem wants to argue, in the devaluation of all historical concrete action. Rather, one can also argue, to use the philosopher Steven Schwarzschild's words, that Jewish messianism makes humanity's "ethical (and, indeed, scientific) tasks not an interim obligation but his perpetual (if you please, his metaphysical) destiny" ("On Eschatology" 174); "Jewish eschatology is the metaphysical as well as ethical absolutization of moral-ity" (182) which found its concrete expression in Jewish law and in a set of rational norms. This aspect of Jewish messianism is neglected in Scholem's historiography. The deferral is the gap between the messianic perfection or "ought" of the world, and the way it actually "is." The bridge between ought and is in Judaism is ethics—willed concrete acts in the imitation of God to perfect the world in the direction of the messianic future, or the eternity and infinity of moral striving.

Schwarzschild's interpretation allies Jewish messianism with a legacy in German philosophy that Scholem devalued and often scorned—the ratio-nalism of Kant and Hermann Cohen. This gap between ought and is here generates an ethical struggle against the "idolatry" of a "pagan naturalism" or the representation and being of things as they are. As Schwarzschild astutely notes, in the Jewish members of the Frankfurt School from Adorno to Benjamin, "art is action that envisions and suffers from the unattainability of Utopia; it is not a state of being. . . . Or as Hermann Cohen has put it, art depicts the Messiah; that is, art is man's anticipatory construction of the world as it ought to be, as God wants it to be."[17] Art is subordinated to ethics. This gap between ought and is is also the source of a certain irony, the irony in the folktale about the Messiah and the humor Benjamin recognized in Kafka; indeed, "Kant and Hermann Cohen stipu-lated that humor and irony be among the chief elements of art, inasmuch as these administer aesthetic-ethical criticism to the actual world for its evils" (Schwarzschild, "Aesthetics" 4).

Contra Scholem, Schwarzschild argues that Jewish messianism is not inevitably caught between the impossible extremes of passive impotence and the unreality of any action in the present versus apocalyptic destruction of the present in order to realize the messianic future. "Far from implying a bracketing of messianism ('utopianism') as irrelevant to the daily historical occurrences of moral problems . . . messianism in fact operates, therefore, as a direct producer of moral values and as an intermediate criterion of proper action in any and every situation" ("On Eschatology" 183). That is the messianic function of Jewish law, or *halakah*, as the set of norms and actions that attempt to bridge the gap between ought and is.[18] Because of Scholem's stated theological anarchism, his antipathy to Jewish law, and to rational Enlightenment utopianism, he "overstates the dichotomy between rabbinism (e.g. Maimonides) and messianism as well as between ethical messianism and apocalypticism" (195), whereas these four factors are inseparably linked with one another in Judaism (we shall see this linkage in chapter 9 in Levinas's analysis of talmudic texts on messianism).

The same holds true, I would add, for Scholem's adoption of the rigid romantic opposition symbol/allegory, his dichotomizing of mysticism/philosophy, apocalyptic/normative, "conservative" rational/"vital" anarchic forces, dualisms which reflect his own ideological agenda. Unfortunately, most of the literary critics who discuss the relation of Benjamin and Scholem accept at face value Scholem's depictions of the catastrophic and apocalyptic aspect of Jewish messianism. But Scholem's overemphasis on these factors reflected much of the ambience and ambivalence of German-Jewish thought around the turn of the century, *despite* Scholem's attempt to repudiate the notion of any German-Jewish symbiosis. Clearly, his relation with Benjamin, despite their differences, reflected and reinforced these tendencies. As I shall argue later, Scholem ultimately retained much more of a German romantic aesthetic ideology than did Benjamin. That, perhaps, is one main reason why Scholem's work has been embraced so enthusiastically and uncritically by many contemporary literary critics, themselves inheritors of the same legacy.

In the field of religious studies, as Moshe Idel has written in his brilliant reexamination of Scholem's work, there has also been a "basically conformist tendency characteristic of the academic study of the Kabbalah" (*Kabbalah* 13). Many scholars

> have tended to the notion that his [Scholem's] views on Kabbalah are tantamount to Kabbalah itself. . . . There is a widespread failure to distinguish between the authentic material and the opinions of scholars on the content of this material. Far more than in other fields, we encounter references to the view of the Kabbalah that are based solely upon Scholem's own assertions. (17)

Idel argues that one of the major problems in Scholem's approach was precisely its overemphasis on the "philological-historical," i.e., "textual," approach, which neglected comparative study, larger concepts and systems. This philological approach diminished the "practical-experiential" aspects of mysticism and tended to portray Kabbalah more as a form of speculative theory, "theosophical conceptions, various beliefs, and hermeneutic devices. . . . more a gnosis than a practical or experiential attitude towards reality" (22–27).

Benjamin, however, well understood the limits of philology, and wrote in his Arcades project of the need to "keep reminding oneself that the commentary on reality (since it is a question of commentary, a construing of details) calls for a method completely different from that required for a text. In the one case theology is the basic science, in the other philology" ("Theory of Knowledge" [N 2, 1]).

In this sense, Benjamin, who was ostensibly the literary and political critic, had a more radical view of the relation of commentary and theology. And Scholem, ostensibly the historian and Zionist, was more "literary." The key, perhaps, is that Scholem was also a far more conservative thinker than Benjamin. He viewed discharges of the messianic tension as dangerous flash points in Jewish history; every attempt to concretely and immediately realize the messianic hope, he thought, had unleashed self-destructive forces. And so Scholem warned that present-day Zionism was equally susceptible to the crisis of the messianic claim that had been conjured up (*Mess Idea* 36). Scholem's own Zionism was "utopian" but not apocalyptic, and he fiercely warned Benjamin against confusing politics and religion. Yet his attraction to Benjamin was also based on an affinity for the radicalism of Benjamin's way of thinking, and the darker currents of their mutual anarchism. In the final paragraph of his now-classic work *Major Trends in Jewish Mysticism* (1946), Scholem wrote that the story of Jewish mysticism "is not ended, it has not yet become history, and the secret life it holds can break out tomorrow in you or in me"; but "to speak of the mystical course which, in the great cataclysm now stirring the Jewish people more deeply than in the entire history of Exile, destiny may still have in store for us—and I for one believe that there is such a course—is the task of prophets, not of professors" (350).

KAFKA

> I plan to write on religious nihilism. And
> just to be on the safe side, I acquired a seat
> in the synagogue "for life"; judge from that
> how delicate the topic is. (Scholem to Ben-
> jamin, June 20, 1934)

Scholem's scorn for the intrusions of historical materialism into Benjamin's thought was a constant source of tension in their relationship. In a letter of April 19, 1934, after reading a review essay Benjamin wrote for the journal of the Frankfurt School, the *Zeitschrift für Sozialforschung*, Scholem wrote back claiming not to have understood the piece and sarcastically queried, "Is it intended to be a Communist credo? And if not, then what actually is it?" (*Corr* 107). Benjamin angrily responded on May 6 that "such questions, it seems to me, tend to absorb salt on their way across the ocean and then taste somewhat bitter to the person who has been questioned," and he reminded Scholem of the necessary "circumspection" that a correspondence such as theirs required (109). "A credo," he added,

> is the last thing my communism resorts to . . . it is a drastic, not infertile expression of the fact that the present intellectual industry finds it impossible to make room for my thinking, just as the present economic order finds it impossible to accommodate my life. . . . [It is] nothing but the lesser evil. . . . The evil—compared to those that surround us—is of so much less that it should be affirmed in every practical, productive form, except for the unpractical, unproductive form of a credo. (110)

What saved the correspondence at this point was a discussion of Kafka—the one figure with whom they could both deeply identify. For they both found in Kafka an uncanny expression of their own struggles with the philosophical and theological tensions between mediation and immediacy, nature and history, nihilism and redemption, revelation and tradition, ultimate pure Word and finite human language, Scripture and commentary, the secular modern Jew and the remnants of Jewish tradition. Scholem was fond of telling his students in the 1930s "that in order to understand the Kabbalah, nowadays one has to read Franz Kafka's writings first, particularly *The Trial*" (*SF* 125).

In 1927, Benjamin was reading *The Trial* and making preparations for an essay on the novel which was to be dedicated to Scholem (*GS* II: 1190); he wanted to develop Scholem's idea of the category of deferral as constitutive for Judaism.[19] Comments Scholem, "Thus from 1927 on our thoughts on at least one central subject approached a single point" (*SF* 145). Yet they would later differ in their interpretation of what this deferral was all about. Was it the nonfulfillment and nondecipherability of the Law or its absence?

In 1931 Benjamin planned a review of Kafka's *Great Wall of China* and asked Scholem for some "hints" about Kafka, to which Scholem responded with a long letter in August (*SF* 169–74). Scholem advised Benjamin to begin his thinking about Kafka's linguistic world with the Book of Job, and to focus it around the possibility of divine judgment. In Kafka, Scholem found an affinity to the language of the Last Judgment.

> It would be an enigma to me how you as a critic would go about saying something about this man's world without placing the *Lehre* [the teaching], called *Gesetz* [law] in Kafka's works, at the center. I suppose this is what the moral reflection—if it were possible (and this is the hypothesis of presumptu-

ousness!)—of a halakhist who attempted a *linguistic* paraphrase of a divine judgment would be like. Here, for once a world is expressed in which redemption cannot be anticipated—go and explain this to the goyim! (171)

In 1934, at a time of great financial distress for Benjamin, Scholem obtained from Robert Weltsch, the editor of the *Jüdische Rundschau* (the journal of the umbrella organization that encompassed all political branches of the Zionist movement in Germany), a commission for Benjamin to write an essay to commemorate the tenth anniversary of Kafka's death. Benjamin wrote the piece (translated in *Illuminations* 111–40) and once again asked for Scholem's reflections on the subject. Scholem replied on July 9 with an unpublished "theological didactic poem" he had written on *The Trial* for Kitty Marx and had then given to Weltsch to be printed together with Benjamin's essay. Despite their mutual dislike for the simplistic theological interpretations given to Kafka's work by critics such as Max Brod and Hans Schoeps, Scholem wrote that he was "still firmly convinced that a theological aspect of this world, in which God does not appear, is the most legitimate of such interpretations" (*Corr* 122). While Benjamin's "portrayal of the preanimistic age as Kafka's seeming present" was insightful and made "98%" sense, "the *existence* of secret law foils your interpretation"; Benjamin had gone too far in eliminating theology, "throwing the baby out with the bathwater" (123).

Yet what kind of theology? The poem Scholem enclosed with the letter is a meditation on just that question. It begins:

> Are we totally separated from you?
> Is there not a breath of your peace,
> Lord, or your message
> Intended for us in such a night?
>
> Can the sound of your words
> Have so faded in Zion's emptiness.
> Or has it not even entered
> This magic realm of appearance?

The poem essentially answers with a theology of religious nihilism:

> Give then, Lord, that he may wake
> Who was struck through by your nothingness.
>
> Only so does revelation
> Shine in the time that rejected you.
> Only your nothingness is the experience
> It is entitled to have of you.

This nothingness is also the realm of "hidden judgment," and the following stanzas of the poem (7–13) reflect on the implications of this situation for redemption.

> Nobody knows the way completely
> And each part of it makes us blind
> Nobody can benefit from redemption.
> The star stands far too high.

This seems to be a negative allusion to Rosenzweig's *Star of Redemption*, and Scholem continues that, although a ray sometimes breaks through "from the center of destruction," "None shows the direction / The Law ordered us to take." This absence also becomes a trial of God: "Who is the accused here? / The creature or yourself?" (*Corr* 123–25).

In a letter written to Benjamin a week later, on July 17, Scholem elaborated on his views, asserting that Benjamin mistakenly viewed the Law only from its profane side and that

> Kafka's world is the world of revelation, but of revelation seen of course from that perspective in which it is returned to its own nothingness. . . . The *nonfulfillability* of what has been revealed is the point where a *correctly* understood theology (as I immersed in my Kabbalah, think . . .) coincides most perfectly with that which offers the key to Kafka's work. Its problem is not, dear Walter, its *absence* in a preanimistic world, but the fact that it cannot *be fulfilled*. (126)

Benjamin wrote back to Scholem on July 20 "unhesitatingly recognizing" the possibility of the more complex theological interpretation in Scholem's poem and pointing to a "broad—though admittedly shrouded—theological side" to his own essay. He expressed his "unreserved identification" with stanzas "7 to 13. And several that precede those" and asked whether Scholem's final stanzas on the Last Judgment's projection into world history turn the judge into the accused, the proceedings into a punishment, elevate the Law, or bury it? Kafka, he thinks, had no answer to these questions but created a gestural world in which the questions no longer had any place because "their answers, far from being instructive, make the questions superfluous" (128). Relating the core of his essay to the verse from Scholem's poem "Only your nothingness is the experience, / It is entitled to have of you," Benjamin writes, "I endeavored to show how Kafka sought—on the nether side of that 'nothingness,' in its inside lining so to speak—to feel his way towards redemption" (129).

In another letter a few weeks later he continued to elaborate his differences with Scholem. To Benjamin, the existence of secret law was not the crucial category: "I consider Kafka's constant insistence on the Law to be the point where his work comes to a standstill, which means only that it seems to me that the work cannot be moved in any interpretive direction whatsoever from there" (*Corr* 134–35). Moreover,

> you take the "nothingness of revelation" as your point of departure, the salvific-historical perspective of the established proceedings of the trial. I take

as my starting point the small, nonsensical hope, as well as the creatures for whom this hope is intended and yet who on the other hand are also the creatures in which this absurdity is mirrored. (135)

Four years later, in 1938, on a trip to Europe and New York, Scholem met with Zalman Schocken, Kafka's publisher, and tried to obtain another commission for Benjamin for a book about Kafka. Scholem asked Benjamin to write a letter containing his views of Kafka, which Scholem might then use to help persuade Schocken to issue the contract. Benjamin then wrote the extraordinary letter of June 12, 1938, in which he described the sickness of tradition at the heart of Kafka's work. In a brilliant passage which itself characterized the dilemmas faced by Benjamin, Scholem, and many of their generation of Jews, Benjamin wrote that Kafka listened to tradition, but only indistinct sounds reached him.

> There is no doctrine that one could learn and no knowledge that one could preserve. The things one wishes to catch as they rush by are not meant for anyone's ears. . . . Kafka's work presents a tradition falling ill. Wisdom has sometimes been defined as the epic side of truth. Such a definition marks wisdom as a property of tradition; it is truth in its aggadic consistency.
> It is this consistency of truth that has been lost. Kafka was far from being the first to face this situation. Many had accommodated themselves to it, clinging to truth or what they happened to regard as such, and, with a more or less heavy heart, had renounced its transmissibility. Kafka's real genius was that he tried something entirely new: he sacrificed truth for the sake of clinging to its transmissibility, its aggadic element. Kafka's writings are by their nature parables. But it is their misery and their beauty that they had to become *more* than parables. They do not modestly lie at the feet of doctrine, as aggadah lies at the feet of *halakah*. When they have crouched down, they unexpectedly raise a mighty paw against it. (*Corr* 224–25; *Illum* 143)

But how can one have transmissibility without content? What does one transmit? This again is another form of the question raised by Benjamin's essay on translation and by Scholem's idea of the "nothingness of revelation." Does the pure language toward which translation as transmission aims have any concrete meaning, or is it an abyss, an empty, silent, but pure form? And how could that contentless truth be itself transmitted? Unfortunately, as Scholem writes in his memoirs, Zalman Schocken, for whom the essay was written, "had absolutely no appreciation of Benjamin. . . . [He] made fun of these writings and gave me a lecture in which he declined to support Benjamin, concluding that Benjamin was something like a bogeyman of my own invention" (*SF* 217). At this time, sadly, Benjamin's only other source of support, his stipend from the Horkheimer and the Institute for Social Research, was also in doubt, and the institute had refused to publish his essay on Baudelaire which Adorno had sharply critiqued. Benjamin wrote to Scholem on March 14, 1939, "While you still have a sundry cargo of ideas from my last letter lying at anchor waiting to be unloaded, this new barge is setting out to sea freighted far beyond the load line with much heavier cargo—my heavy heart" (*Corr* 248).

HALAKAH AND *AGGADAH*: ANARCHIC SUSPENSION AND HISTORICAL CONCRETION

The *aggadah* to which Benjamin relates the notion of "transmissibility" in the 1938 letter on Kafka refers to the vast body of *nonlegal* and non-prescriptive Jewish narrative and exegetic tradition found in the Talmud, Midrash, and oral traditions—containing stories, legends, parables, folklore, imaginative speculations about the meanings of the text, supplementary accounts of events in the lives of biblical and talmudic figures, etc. The word *aggadah* is the noun form of the verbal root *higgid*, meaning "to say, tell, narrate." *Halakah*, from the root *halakh*, meaning "to walk, go," refers to the body of discourse about *legal* and binding prescriptions, commandments, ritual ordinates, directives, i.e., the concrete "path" of behavior one is to follow.

Aggadah and *halakah* together roughly constitute the basic elements of Jewish tradition, the so-called Oral Torah (though it has long been written down) which comments upon, expands, and applies the Written Torah, i.e., the documents of sacred Scripture and revelation. Through *aggadah* and *halakah*, the word of revelation is passed down, transmitted in time, translated, and renewed for new generations. This dialectical interplay of *aggadah* and *halakah* conceived broadly as different modes of thought that could be universalized was the subject of a famous essay written in 1917 by Hayyim Nahman Bialik, the great Hebrew poet and contemporary of Benjamin and Scholem. Scholem had translated this essay into German for Buber's journal *Der Jude* in 1919, and Benjamin had read it and regarded it as "quite extraordinary" (*SF* 82). He requested a copy of it again from Scholem in 1934 during the writing of the Kafka essay.

Bialik had asserted in this essay the necessity and complementarity of these two modes of thought: "They are related to each other as words are related to thought and impulse, or as a deed and its material form are to expression. *Halakah* is the concretization, the necessary end product of *Aggadah; Aggadah* is *Halakah* become fluid again" (56). When either was lost, the power and will of a people were weakened. Bialik described the current generation as "completely *Aggadah*," no longer knowing the *halakah* and hence weak in its literature and life, promulgating "a kind of arbitrary Judaism" with "strident slogans: nationalism, renascence, literature, creation, Hebrew education"—all with an ethereal and fragile love but without duty and durable deeds (63).

There is a parallel between Benjamin's comments about the relation of *halakah* and *aggadah* in Kafka and the relation of translation to original in his translation essay. In this schema, *aggadah* would be to *halakah* as the translation is to the original—tangentially attached to it, but faithful only by freely pursuing its own course, "unexpectedly raising a mighty paw against it." In Benjamin's reading of Kafka, the sickness of tradition, the loss of authoritative ground and truth mean that only a detached *aggadah* is left. As Robert Alter comments on this passage in Benjamin, what remains is "lore in quest of Law, yet so painfully estranged from what it seeks that the pursuit can end in a pounce of destruction, the fictional rending the doctrinal" (60). That "power of destruction" reconnects backward to Benjamin and Scholem's mutual early anarchism and forward to Benjamin's engagement with revolutionary politics as another way to attach *aggadah* to a material concrete base.

To carry the analogy further, if *aggadah* is like the language of translation, then what Benjamin sees in Kafka is an "allegory" for Benjamin's own work as well. "Translation" becomes again here a key theological category—related, as in Benjamin, to something inarticulate, something as yet inexpressible, yet something objective, some other realm of experience for which we have no words, and which may be of no help. Translation, in these quasi-secularized terms, is the question of revelation, the relation of the divine and human languages when there is no direct access to the divine, when only indistinct echoes of the Torah from Heaven are heard. When Kafka sacrificed truth for the sake of clinging to its transmissibility, to its *aggadic* element, then, as Benjamin wrote in the 1938 letter to Scholem,

> we can no longer speak of wisdom. Only the products of its decay remain. These are two: One is the rumor about the true things (a sort of theology passed on by whispers dealing with matters discredited and obsolete); the other product of this diathesis is folly—which, to be sure, has utterly squandered the substance of wisdom but preserves its attractiveness and assurance, which rumor invariably lacks. Folly lies at the heart of Kafka's favorites. . . . This much Kafka was absolutely sure of: First, that someone must be a fool if he is to help; second, that only a fool's help is real help. The only uncertain thing is: Can such help still do a human being any good? It is more likely to help the angels who could do without help. (*Corr* 225)

In a similar vein, Scholem had written at the end of his late essay on the linguistic theory of the Kabbalah that when every direct approach to the divine was gone, when the mysteries had been demystified and secularized, in language remained "the echo of the vanished word of the creation in the immanence of the world" ("Name of God" 194). These echoes, however, were also indistinct—not the commanding voice of Sinai. Thus in both Benjamin and Scholem, the focus turned away from any attempt to immediately "fuse" with that pure language and instead to intensifying one's gaze on its fragments, remnants, ruins, echoes, traces, in the "concrete," i.e., in history, tradition, manuscripts—in all their physicality and minutiae in the immanence of the world. In Benjamin's work, especially in the

Arcades project, there is the most intense attention to detail, to minutiae, to the debris of history; this was paralleled by Scholem's meticulous and awesome compilations of bibliographic research, his collection of kabbalistic manuscripts, and his attempt to reconstruct the history of Jewish mysticism. These, too, were forms of "translation" which, of course, required the most minute attention to the particulars of language.

Kafka spoke deeply to Benjamin and Scholem's temperaments and to their preoccupation with the meanings of those fragments and traces, those obscure scriptures. Or to use Benjamin's descriptions of Kafka's characters:

> The gate to justice is learning. And yet Kafka does not dare attach to this learning the promises which tradition has attached to the story of the Torah. His assistants are sextons who have lost their house of prayer, his students are pupils who have lost the Holy Writ. Now there is nothing to support them on their "untrammeled, happy journey." (*Illum* 139)

This passage became one of the "prooftexts" for their debate over Kafka. Argued Scholem, these pupils "are not so much those who have lost the Scripture . . . but rather those students who cannot decipher it" (*Corr* 127). Responded Benjamin, "Whether the pupils have lost it or whether they are unable to decipher it comes down to the same thing, because without the key that belongs to it, the Scripture is not Scripture, but life. Life as it is lived in the village at the foot of the hill on which the castle is built" (135). Countered Scholem: to say that it doesn't matter whether the disciples have lost the Scriptures or whether they can't decipher them is "one of the greatest mistakes you could have made." The distinction is that between revelation having *validity* but *no significance*, as explained in Scholem's own definition of the "nothingness of revelation:"

> a state in which revelation appears to be without meaning, in which it still asserts itself, in which it has *validity* but *no significance*. A state in which the wealth of meaning is lost and what is in the process of appearing (for revelation is such a process) still does not disappear, even though it is reduced to the zero point of its own content so to speak. (142)

Scholem further placed that negativity inside the tradition itself and argued that the antinomy of the *aggadic* which Benjamin saw in Kafka was not specific to Kafka alone; "rather it is grounded in the nature of the aggadic itself. Does this opus really represent 'tradition falling ill' in your sense? I would say such enfeebling is rooted in the nature of the mystical tradition itself: it is only natural that the *capacity* of tradition to be transmitted remains as its sole living feature when it decays" (236). It then takes the form of commentary. As to Kafka, "This commentator does indeed have Holy Scriptures, but he has lost them. Thus the question is: What can he comment upon?" And why did Benjamin think that Kafka had failed, "since he really did comment, if only on the nothingness of truth or whatever might emerge there?" (237).

This debate over Kafka was obviously at bottom a debate over what Scholem and Benjamin had personally come to think about revelation, Scripture, redemption, and commentary—and the paths their own lives had taken. Benjamin and Scholem were also sextons who had lost their house of prayer and students who had lost their Holy Writ, and the question of whether Kafka ultimately succeeded or failed was a judgment implicitly made upon their own labors, their own commentaries, as well. If "hope, plenty of hope, but not for us" might serve as Benjamin's motto, then "he *really* did comment, if only on the nothingness of truth" might serve as Scholem's.

There was a shared sensibility in those two mottoes. In a letter to Scholem of September 15, 1934, Benjamin quoted approvingly a definition of revelation Scholem had written in 1932: "Nothing ever . . . is, with reference to historical time, more in need of concretization than . . . the . . . 'absolute concreteness' of the word of revelation. The absolutely concrete can never be fulfilled at all." That applied to Kafka, Benjamin argued, and helps make "the historical aspect of his failure obvious." Although his Kafka essay had been published and he had ended his preoccupation with "purely literary subjects," he wanted to continue his reflections and work on Kafka, especially in light of this remark of Scholem's: "This topic is ideally suited to become the crossroads of the different paths my thought has taken" (*Corr* 139).

Scholem's statement had come from a critique he had written of a book by Hans Joachim Schoeps on the contemporary possibilities for Jewish faith. In Schoeps's critique of liberal rationalist theology, Schoeps had taken up a kind of Barthian-Kierkegaardian "Protestant" attitude, condemning the talmudic traditions of Judaism as outmoded and artificial, and redefining Judaism as essentially a biblical religion of nonrational and immediate revelation without need of any mediating historical traditions. Revelation, Scholem countered, was a *medium*, "absolute, meaning-bestowing, but itself meaningless that becomes explicable only through the relation to time, to the Tradition." The absolute word of God would be "destructive" if it were undialectical and unmediated; there is no concrete unmediated Word.[20]

Yet what, then, were the consequences for *halakah*, which was, as Bialik put it, the "concretization of *aggadah*"? In his essay, Bialik had written of *halakah* and *aggadah* as modes of thinking but cautioned that his paean to the greatness of *halakah* did not exactly mean "a return to the *Shulhan Arukh*" (61). The *Shulhan Arukh* is the authoritative code of Jewish law compiled in the sixteenth century by R. Yosef Caro, which even today remains for the Orthodox Jew the all-encompassing set of prescriptions for daily behavior in the concrete world and guide to the minutiae of ritual practice. Although Scholem was passionately interested in all aspects of Jewish tradition and history, he was adamantly non-Orthodox and antipathetic toward the authority of *halakah* (despite a brief fling with Orthodoxy in his adolescence). Scholem relates that his conversations with Benjamin often centered around Jewish theology and ethics, "but hardly on concrete matters and situations." In a discussion with Benjamin and his wife, Dora, in their early years in Switzerland about the *halakah*, the validity of the Ten Commandments, and whether one may transgress them, Scholem defended his refusal of an Orthodox way of life by arguing that "for me that manner of life was connected with the concretization of the Torah in a false, premature sphere. . . . I said I had to maintain the anarchic suspension." The problem was later solved for him, he adds, through a change in his historical perspective, "for my understanding of the sense in which one may speak of revelation had changed" through "kabbalistic considerations" (*SF* 72). Scholem attributes to his study of Kabbalah, in other words, the discovery of a more appealing notion of revelation, one more in harmony with his affinity for the "nothingness of revelation" and the impossibility of concretely fulfilling any absolute word.

He would later define this "anarchic suspension" as a fundamental category of the mystical concept of revelation, as somehow rooted deep within Jewish tradition itself. But the question is to what extent Scholem was reading the antinomian and anarchistic proclivities he shared with Benjamin and their circle of German-Jewish intellectuals back onto the Kabbalah. When Benjamin was beginning his work on the Arcades project in the late 1920s, Scholem was discovering the Sabbatian heresy, which he described as "a messianic antinomianism that had developed within Judaism in strictly Jewish concepts." At their meeting in Paris in 1927, Benjamin became the first person Scholem told about his discovery in Oxford of the Sabbatian Abraham Miguel Cardozo's manuscripts. This discovery, Scholem wrote, had "given an entirely new turn" to his studies and to the "perennial question of what Judaism was all about" and whether it was "still alive as a heritage or an experience, even as something constantly evolving, or did it exist only as an object of cognition," a question he grappled with for years (*SF* 136).

Scholem consequently argued that the messianic idea in Judaism was itself double-edged in regard to *halakah*. On the one hand, the restorative aspect of messianism meant the creation of ideal conditions for the complete fulfillment of the law; on the other, the radical utopian apocalyptic elements hinted at a new heaven and earth wherein the law's fulfillment would be its supersession, where the *halakah* would no longer be necessary. (That was also the messianic argument of Paul and early Christianity.) Scholem again labels this an "anarchic" element which, along with the restorative element, "appears in Messianism again and again with dialectical necessity," and can be joined as well by entirely antinomian possibilities—such as the case of Sabbatai Sevi and the Frankists.

> From the point of view of the *Halakah* to be sure, Judaism appears as a well-ordered house, and it is a profound truth that a well-ordered house is a dangerous thing. Something of Messianic apocalypticism penetrates into this house; perhaps I can best describe it as a kind of anarchic breeze. . . . [a] vital . . . anarchic airing. . . . (*Mess Idea* 21)

Of course, it is by no means a universal "profound truth" that a well-ordered house is dangerous. Scholem's polemic here is directed toward what he saw as the degenerate, bourgeois, and shallow Judaism of his own era, but he extends it to the entire *halakhic* tradition in Judaism. His framing of the issue in such either/or terms implies that there were few vital forces within *halakah* itself, or that the only way to expand *halakah* was to engage some sort of "dialectical opposite" which could only be anarchism.[21]

The distaste for "concretion" in Scholem paralleled the early Benjamin's identification of the concrete communicative meanings of language as "inferior." Yet both these highly abstract and idealistic thinkers would seek "concretion" not through immersing themselves in the immediacies of any personal experience, or through adherence to any particular credo, but through constructing revisionary histories filled with esoteric and hidden forces, forces which were disruptive and violent but which opened the space for redemption as well.

Scholem wrote that in 1927 he had expected the solution to the question of whether Judaism was still alive to come "only from my new life in Eretz Yisrael" (*SF* 136). But Zionism did not mean a concrete political credo for him. In an extraordinary letter to Benjamin of August 1, 1931, Scholem described his alienation from other members of the Zionist Congress and "the split between my conception of Zionism, which I heard characterized as a religious-mystical quest for a regeneration of Judaism (a characterization I agree with), and empirical Zionism, whose point of departure is an impossible and provocative distortion of an alleged political 'solution to the Jewish question'" (171). He despairs that Zionism "has triumphed itself to death" and, using a kind of kabbalistic terminology, says it had "been victorious too early" in the "visible realm before it had been decided in the invisible realm—that is, the regeneration of language": "Our catastrophe started where the vocation did not maintain itself in its profanation, where community was not developed in its legitimate concealment, but where instead the betrayal of the secret values that lured us here became transformed into a positive side of the demonic propaganda. By becoming visible our cause was destroyed" (173). These sentiments reflect once more his distaste for "concretion," his idea that somehow language and revelation are purer in their "nothingness" than in any specific concrete revelation in the "visible" world of common public speech and reality.

In the second half of this book, I shall examine the ways in which

Levinas, following Rosenzweig, formulates entirely different relations among history, philosophy of language, theology, and Jewish law. In his work, the "purity,"the "depth," or "otherwise" of language is not meaningless and beyond all interhuman communication; on the contrary, it is manifest precisely *within* the interhuman relation as ethical call and imperative, as the ethical order to the Other—Other both as God and as neighbor. And in Levinas and Rosenzweig, *halakah*, the set of concrete imperatives regulating human behavior, do not constitute what Scholem describes as "the stony wall of the law." Kabbalah, argued Scholem, "dissolves" this wall by making it "transparent," i.e., a "symbol" of a deeper reality, and this symbolic dissolution culminates in Reform Judaism's retention of the law only as a mere abstract remnant (Biale, "Ten Aphorisms" 82). In Rosenzweig and Levinas, by contrast, *halakah* becomes the way of connecting and concretizing God's word in the human word and world.

Rosenzweig came to understand *halakah* not as a set of dry and constraining rules but as something much deeper. He wrote several famous letters to Buber, urging him not to adopt an antinomian position but to recognize the possibilities for teaching within the *halakhic* tradition: moreover, Rosenzweig argued that the form *kalakah* had taken in Western European Jewish Orthodoxy of the nineteenth century was by no means its essence: "For me, too, God is not a Law-giver. But He commands. It is only by the manner of his observance that a man in his inertia changes the commandments into Law . . . without the realization of the 'I am the Lord,' without 'fear and trembling,' without the awareness that the man stands under God's commandment" (*Jewish Learning* 116).[22]

Scholem taught in Rosenzweig's *Lehrhaus*, the center for Jewish Studies and adult education Rosenzweig founded in Frankfurt. Scholem also delivered an eloquent address on Rosenzweig at a memorial service at the Hebrew University on the tenth anniversary of his death in 1930, but he published a far less complimentary reevaluation of *The Star* a year later. One of the reasons for the difference in tone of these two essays is their respective audiences—a community of Jews already in Israel, and one in diaspora. In the memorial address, Scholem called the great chapter of the second part of *The Star of Redemption* "Revelation, or the Ever-Renewed Birth of the Soul" "one of what may be called Judaism's 'definitive statements' on religious questions" ("Rosenzweig" 36–37). In the 1931 piece, though, Scholem takes Rosenzweig to task for the way in which he deduced "the two possibilities for theocratic modes of life in Judaism and Christianity from the dialectics of the concept of redemption" (*Mess Idea* 322). Here he is referring to the third part of *The Star*, which is a phenomenological analysis of the liturgical structures of each religion, and the ways in which "religious time" relates to the historical existence of each religion.

For Scholem, *theocratic* is a term of opprobrium here, referring to Rosenzweig's reaffirmation of the authoritative classical ritual, liturgical, and communal structures of Jewish religious tradition. To reduce Rosenzweig's complex argument to a crude summary, these are "messianic" structures in that they *already* partake of the suprahistorical, eternal reality of redemption; and the existence of the Jewish peoplehood is *already* rooted in this "eternal life." Christianity, by contrast, is the religion of the "eternal way"—on through history toward salvation. For Scholem the committed Zionist, this "ahistorical" view of Judaism was regressive and politically impotent, and it served to further solidify that bourgeois "very neatly ordered house of Judaism. He [Rosenzweig] opposed the theory of catastrophe contained in Messianic apocalypticism which might be considered the point at which even today theocratic and bourgeois modes of life stand irreconcilably opposed" (323).

Scholem's focus, then, is not the *halakhic* concretions, or the community and continuity of this word, but the abyss and catastrophe of its apocalyptic manifestations in Jewish history. Indeed, like Benjamin, Scholem takes catastrophe and disruption as the perspective from which to construct a revisionary history. Otto Pöggeler well sums up Rosenzweig's response to Scholem:

> Rosenzweig was of the opinion that Scholem combined scientific and "nihilistic" asceticism with his "central dogma" that Judaism was in a deathlike trance and could be revived only "beyond," that is, after its reconstruction in the land of Israel. "Judaism is for him [Scholem] only a cloister. . . . Perhaps he is the only one who has truly come home. But he has come home *alone*." (Qtd. in Pöggeler, "Between Enlightenment" 111)[23]

Zionism instead of *halakah* had represented for Scholem that communal, public, and national endeavor which was the contemporary legitimate Jewish mode of "material and historical concretization." Historical materialism played a somewhat similar role for Benjamin, though both had to cope with far more uncertain results than they had anticipated. Benjamin belonged temperamentally to no group, and would not join the Communist party; he continued to mingle theology and messianism into his materialism to the very end.

Scholem, of course, also recognized that one of the distinguishing characteristics of Jewish mysticism was its acceptance of the discipline of *halakah* and that many of the great kabbalists were also great halakhists (R. Yosef Caro himself was both). Yet he argued that there was an unconscious tension between the world of law and mysticism that these thinkers did not recognize or masked. For Scholem, the mythical, anarchic inspiration of the mystics had resulted in a situation where "the lives and actions of the Kabbalists were a revolt against a world which they never wearied of affirming. And this of course led to deep-seated ambiguities" (*KS* 98).

But it could be argued against Scholem that the kabbalists' attitude toward *halakah* was due less to ambivalence or unconscious revolt, or

immersion in the "formless" or "symbolic" theosophical realm where revelation became "meaningless," than to a belief in *halakah* as a valid form
of *concretization* of God's word, and link between the human and divine
realms—as the presence of God reachable through the specific concrete
actions embodied in the commandments and prescriptions of Jewish law.

Moshe Idel has written the most recent learned and sophisticated critique of Scholem's work and methodology, and this issue is crucial in Idel's
work. Idel proposes to revise and supplement Scholem's "historical" methodology with a more "phenomenological" type of analysis, an "inner history" of the Kabbalah and its forms of religious expression (*Kabbalah* xiii).
Idel defines two major trends in Kabbalah: the "theosophical-theurgical"
and the "ecstatic." The first deals with the structure of the divine world,
and its aim is not simply contemplation or *gnosis* but a "ritualistic and
experiential way of relation to the divinity in order to induce a harmony"
in the cosmos (xi). Theurgy, as the attempt to influence this divine realm,
was intimately connected to performance of the traditional exoteric and
communal commandments of Jewish law and explanations of their rationale (*ta'amey mitzvot*), their deeper meanings. Human activity centered on
halakah was thought to affect the harmony of the divine realm, a notion
which was quite ancient and implicit in traditional Jewish thought about
the commandments. Kabbalah was by no means a revolution or upsurge of
"myth" into some abstract "rabbinic legalism."

In contrast to this "nomian" and "theocentrically" centered type of
Kabbalah, ecstatic Kabbalah (whose most well known representative is
Abulafia) focused on the mystical experiences of the individual uncon-
nected to any impact on the divine realm. Practically and anthropomor-
phically oriented, it used "anomian" techniques to achieve paranormal
states (xii). Anomian but not *anti*nomian. Idel characterizes nomian techniques as those which "spiritualized" or "interiorized" the practice of the
law through "intention" or *kavvanah*—i.e., meditating on the effect of
these performances on the supernal realm with the ultimate goal of
devekut, or unifying oneself with God. On the other hand, "*anomian* refers
to those forms of mystical activity that did not involve *halakhic* practice,"
though they were far from alien (75). Practice of these extraordinary and
sometimes dangerous techniques was limited to an elite. Theosophical-
theurgic kabbalah was centered in Spain, ecstatic Kabbalah in Italy and the
Orient.

In both types of Kabbalah, however, the predominant aim was not *theoretical* but *practical* and *experiential*, a point missed by Scholem, who, Idel
writes, "overstressed the importance of the speculative over the mystical.
Kabbalistic symbolism is envisaged as a way to penetrate the texts and to
understand the divine structure, rather than as a path towards experiencing the divinely revealed texts" (14). In this sense, Scholem followed the
trend of other nineteenth-century pioneering academic scholars of Kabbalah and their earlier Christian counterparts in the Renaissance. These

Christian thinkers interested in Kabbalah were under the influence of Neo-Platonism, and they "philosophized" Kabbalah, which they saw primarily as one more kind of occult and speculative lore rather than an essentially religious phenomenon. But as Idel so well puts it: "Being for the most part a topography of the divine realm, this theoretical literature served more as a map than a speculative description. Maps, as we know, are intended to enable a person to fulfill a journey; for the Kabbalists, the mystical experience was such a journey" (29).

Of course, for Christian commentators, kabbalistic speculations on the efficacy of Jewish law would be philosophically and theologically irrelevant. The same was true for Jewish academic scholarship in the nineteenth century, an offspring of the secularization and modernization of Western European Jewry. This scholarship similarly reflected the break with traditional modes of study and belief. It presented Judaism in Western categories as an abstract system of thought and held a similarly negative attitude toward *halakah*. As a result, the extensive kabbalistic literature concerning the rationale for the commandments is a "major genre . . . that has passed nearly unnoticed by scholars" (28).[24]

The key question for Benjamin and Scholem was: Where could an authentic mode of concretion be found, and one that was not dangerous like the simplistic immediacy of *Lebensphilosophie*? Given the alternatives available, Benjamin's turn to historical materialism and his attraction to Brecht's "crude thinking" are not mysterious. "Language itself" had supplied one form of "mediated" immediacy, something that allowed a kind of *aggadic* freedom; historical materialism supplied the concretion, the *halakah*, the ethic of action in the crude world, the directives for justice between humans.

In different ways, Benjamin and Scholem each sought in the forces of negation and rupture, profanization and secularization, some hidden path to an as-yet-unforeseen redemption. Scholem depended on cultural Zionism and an almost romantic-Hegelian dialectic of history to somehow bring this about. Benjamin trusted to "totality" or any of the traditional powers of "dialectical synthesis." Faithful to the ruins, he would seek other ways to salvage them.

TWO

Suspended over the Abyss

"ON LANGUAGE AS SUCH"

For Scholem, mysticism made a vertiginous opening in the language of tradition and revelation, boring back to an ultimate source in the Divine Name. This Name was itself ultimately meaningless, without any specific meaning, but nevertheless the dialectical source of all meaning—just as in Benjamin's pure language, the ultimate creative Word was without any concrete or communicable signification. We can more clearly see the inter-relation of Benjamin and Scholem's ideas about language by comparing Benjamin's 1916 essay "On Language as Such and on the Language of Man" with Scholem's essay on the linguistic theory of the Kabbalah.

Long before Scholem had begun his advanced research into Kabbalah, Benjamin's early notion of a contentless pure language had strongly at-tracted him. When Scholem met Benjamin in 1915, Scholem was a student of mathematics and planned a dissertation on the philosophical founda-tions of mathematics: "attempts to attain a pure language of thought greatly fired my imagination. . . . In those days I fluctuated between the two poles of mathematical and mystical symbolism—much more so than Benjamin whose mathematical talent was slight" (*SF* 49).

During 1916, Scholem had written Benjamin a long letter about the relationship of language and mathematics, and Benjamin wrote an exten-sive reply, which he later reworked as his essay "On Language as Such and on the Language of Man" (34). This essay remained unpublished in Benja-min's lifetime, but it has become one of the most discussed of his works in current literary and theological criticism. The essay is dated 1916—the height of World War I and also the year in which Saussure's *Course in General Linguistics* appeared. Scholem tried to translate portions of this essay into Hebrew, for it was "very close to my heart" (38). Benjamin's essay is in part a reaction to the corruption of language for political pur-poses in the war, and a refutation of the Buberian position that language cannot communicate the essence of revelatory experiences, that these are ultimately intuitive, ecstatic, ahistorical, and individual. The essay also continued Benjamin's early aesthetic and philosophical projects, especially his program to transform the legacy of Kantianism through an encounter with language and other forms of experience and knowledge.

The argument is subtle and difficult, and Benjamin's style in this essay is characteristic of his early work at its most "esoteric." In his preface to

an equally difficult text, *The Origin of German Tragic Drama,* Benjamin
wrote about his ideal of a contemplative mode of representation where the
writer forces the reader to pause, stop, and restart every sentence: "truth is
not a process of exposure which destroys the secret, but a revelation which
does justice to it" (*OGTD* 31). Thus a true philosophical style will exercise
the "art of the interruption in contrast to the chain of deduction" (32). The
essay "On Language" operates in this fashion, and Benjamin's own language here seems to aspire to some of the "immanent magic" of language it
describes. It certainly does not "convey information" easily and clearly;
the essay becomes its own kind of self-reflexive medium of revelatory but
esoteric pronouncement. Each sentence of the essay is put forth as an
almost inscrutable axiom, and the links of the argument are not deductive
in any simple sense. Each sentence, moreover, presents an extraordinary
compression of thought.

My summary here is a rough paraphrase, and even with this simplification, I fear that it will be hard for the reader to follow. Nevertheless, I think
it important to try to examine the essay in some detail. It gives the reader
some sense of the texture of Benjamin's writing. Moreover, the summaries
of it one often finds in critical essays tend to neglect its nuances. As is
always the case with Benjamin, these nuances are all the difference; they
are pressure points where the complexity of his thought resists systematiza-
tion and ideological simplification. They are especially crucial in any attempt at deciphering the relation of theology and criticism in his work.

Benjamin begins by asserting that the existence of language is coexten-
sive with and inherent in absolutely everything. "There is no event or thing
in either animate or inanimate nature that does not in some way partake of
language, for it is in the nature of all to communicate their mental meanings" [*geistiges Wesen*—this term could also be translated as "spiritual
being" or "spiritual nature"] (*Refl* 314). Here "language" is understood as
a broad phenomenon of "expressibility," of which human verbal language
is but particular instance. The "mental entity" or "spiritual nature" is also
distinguished from the linguistic entity *in* which it communicates. Benjamin wants to stress that language is not merely a transparent instrument
through which something is communicated, but a medium in a quite different sense. He is trying to work out a different schema of relations among
mind, language, and nature.

Although language expresses and communicates mental meanings, "the
view that the mental essence of a thing consists precisely in its language—
this view, taken as a hypothesis, is the great abyss into which all linguistic
theory threatens to fall, and to survive suspended precisely over this abyss
is its task" (315). This statement would foreclose any premature deconstructive readings such as those deMan, Jacobs, and Miller made concerning the "Task of the Translator" essay. Moreover, it runs against the
current of poststructuralist linguistic theory, for Benjamin argues in this
essay that the semiotic view of language as an arbitrary system of signs is a

result of the "Fall" from an original pure nonsignifying language of names. He identifies the "semiotic" view with the position that the purpose of language is simply to convey "information."

Nevertheless, he continues, the paradox of the identity of mental and linguistic being (logos) does have a place "as a solution, at the center of linguistic theory, but remains a paradox, and insoluble if placed at the beginning" (315). Benjamin will propose that only in human language are mental and linguistic being identical, and he will construct a kind of hierarchy of linguistic expression beginning with the absolute creative and cognizing Word of God, and successively descending to a pure Adamic and paradisiacal language of names, then to a fallen historical human language of instrumental communication, and finally to a mute language of nature seeking redemption through translation into human language.

The first stage in any linguistic theory, he claims, must be this very *distinction* between mental and linguistic entity. What, then, is the relation between these two terms? While language communicates the mental being "corresponding" to it, "it is fundamental that this mental being communicates itself *in* language and not *through* language" (315). It is not the result of a speaker who speaks through the language. Linguistic being, then, is defined as the aspect of *communicability,* the capacity for communication of the mental being—but this does not comprehend the whole of mental being or its expression.

This "communicable" aspect of the linguistic being of things (in distinction from their mental being) is language itself. So if one asks, "What does language communicate?" the answer is, "All language communicates itself," and this is *not* a tautology. "What is communicable *of* a mental entity, *in* this it communicates itself. Which signifies: all language communicates itself. Or more precisely: all language communicates itself *in* itself; it is in the purest sense the 'medium' of communication" (316).

Benjamin is at pains to italicize the preposition *in* to distinguish it from *through*. The medium, that is, becomes the very "immediacy" of mental communication, and "mediation, which is the immediacy of all mental communication, is the fundamental problem of linguistic theory, and if one chooses to call this immediacy magic, then the primary problem of language is its magic" (317). What all these intricate distinctions amount to is an attempt to refute any philosophy which views language as a derivative and inferior "mediation" of a higher truth—a truth to which direct and immediate access can be gained through nonlinguistic experiences. The very "mediation" of language, Benjamin seems to be saying, is a magical kind of immediacy.

As Winfried Menninghaus writes, Benjamin's idea is "that a medium is not merely a space of instrumental mediation between existent extremes—for example, the mediation of a nonverbally conceived 'content' between two speakers. He would argue that, what is more, the medium first *produces* what it seemingly 'mediates. . . . ' " He had formulated this idea in his theory of the medium of reflection in Novalis and Schlegel. This concept of a medium as a "mediating betweenness," Menninghaus adds, is a kind of threshold or passage between two realms which in a sense "creates" them, and a figure which threads through all of Benjamin's work, culminating in his study of the literal architecture of "passages," the Arcades project or *Passagen-Werk.* This entire project was concerned with the threshold or passage between "sleeping and awakening" from the nineteenth century (310). Menninghaus also points to the figure of the narrow temporal threshold in that last image in the "Theses on the Philosophy of History," where every second of time is "the strait gate through which the Messiah might enter" (*Illum* 266).

In retaining the distinction between mental and linguistic being, Benjamin also clearly *refutes* what he calls a "mystical view of language," wherein the *essence* of the thing is the word. Human language is related not to things in and of themselves but to the "language of things." Moreover, this "immediacy" of language is not tied to its ability to communicate pieces of finite information, but is the very essence of communicability itself—a kind of contentless potential of all meaning. I will later note the parallel to this idea in Scholem's notion of the ultimate meaningless word and in Rosenzweig's idea that the original content of revelation is revelation itself.

But this immediacy is not an empty self-reflexivity. That is, what is communicated *in* and not *through* language "cannot be externally limited or measured" (*Refl* 317); it is infinite, incommensurable, and in this sense "magical." Here again the phrase "linguistic being" is to be distinguished from any particular "verbal meanings."

This argument for the magic, immediacy, and infinity of language leads Benjamin to a connection of language with theology. The crucial link is made when Benjamin next proceeds to examine the distinctive nature of *human* language, the language of words. For Benjamin, human language is distinguished both from "language as such," which he has been discussing up until now, and from other nonhuman languages. The reason: human language is a *naming* language; "it is therefore the linguistic being of man to name things" (317). The name, however, is not a factual piece of information about some object *through* which a person communicates his or her mental being to an addressee (or, what Benjamin here calls the "bourgeois conception of language"). The name, rather, is that *in* which s/he communicates and "in naming the mental being of man communicates itself to God" (318).

Naming is the innermost nature of language: "Naming is that by which nothing beyond it is communicated, and *in* which language itself communicates itself absolutely." Only in human language is the mental being equivalent to *language as such,* and here only is the mental being of man (as opposed to all other kinds of mental beings) "communicable without residue" (318). That is, pure language speaks through the human as namer.

Hence there is a marked difference between human language and the language of inanimate or natural things. But the fact that there is also another "language of nature" allows the human as knower to name things, and something more: "God's creation is completed when things receive their names from man, from whom in name language alone speaks" (319). Name, then, is the very "language of language," and in this sense the human is the only speaker of language, and human language the only complete language.

Through name, mental being and linguistic being become identified and equated, and language becomes equivalent to mental being.

> The equation of mental and linguistic being is of great metaphysical moment to linguistic theory because it leads to the concept that has again and again, as if of its own accord, elevated itself to the center of linguistic philosophy and constituted its most intimate connection with the philosophy of religion. That is the concept of revelation.

In revelation, as the "inviolability of the word," "the most expressed is at the same time the purely mental." That is, the concept of revelation, which for Benjamin is the highest mental (or "spiritual") region of religion, means the utterly expressible, not the inexpressible. But this ultimate mental being of religion as revelation of name "rests solely on man and on the language in him"; whereas art and poetry rest on "language-mind confined to things" (320).

INTERPRETING GENESIS

Benjamin finds these relations among language, nature, human speech, and revelation expressed in the first chapter of Genesis. He prefaces his exposition of the scriptural text with the caveat that he does so not because the Bible is "objectively revealed truth" but because "the present argument broadly follows it in presupposing language as an ultimate reality, perceptible only in its manifestation, inexplicable and mystical. The Bible, in regarding itself as a revelation, must necessarily evolve the fundamental linguistic facts" (322).

In other words, Benjamin uses the religious text as a parallel or correspondence with his own meditations on the infinity and magic of the word, which he claims to reach through analysis of the immanent facts of linguistic being as given in the world. This approach is similar to the way he later described the very nature of truth: as a kind of "constellation." Biblical, philosophical, and linguistic ideas are drawn together into a kind of constellation; truth lies in the lines drawn between the various points of reference, not behind or within any of them—or in any collapse of these relations into identity. We shall see that this idea of truth as "constellation" may indeed be influenced by Rosenzweig's astronomical metaphor for truth, the constellation which is the "truth" of the "Star" of Redemption. (The concept of reading as a kind of tracing of surfaces of the lines of constellation was also to be important in all of Benjamin's work.)

What, then, is Benjamin's view of this relation of this divine creative language to the language of humanity? In the second creation story (Gen. 2:3) the human, unlike the other creatures, is not created from God's word but is given the gift of language and elevated above nature. There is a special relationship between humanity and language due to the act of creation, for the creative act itself is intimately tied to language. In Genesis 1, the first creation story, Benjamin notices a distinct rhythm: God says "Let there be," then God makes, and then God names: "With the creative omnipotence of language it begins, and at the end language as it were assimilates the created, names it. Language is therefore both creative and finished creation, it is word and name. In God name is creative because it is word, and God's word is cognizant because it is name" (*Refl* 323). This absolute relation of name to knowledge, though, exists only in God; only there is name identical to the creative word and so can be the pure medium of knowledge.

Benjamin notes that in the second creation story (Gen. 2:3 ff.), the creation of humanity is described differently, and the rhythm of Let There Be—He Made—He Named is changed. In contrast to Genesis 1:27, in this passage God neither names nor creates the human from the word:

> He did not wish to subject him to language, but in man God set language, which had served *Him* as a medium of creation, free. God rested when he had left his creative power to itself in man. This creativity, relieved of its divine actuality, became knowledge. Man is the knower in the same language in which God is creator. God created him in his image, he created the knower in the image of the creator. (*Refl* 323)

But human language remains only a limited reflection of this utterly unlimited and creative infinity of the divine word. There is still, however, a powerful point of intersection between the divine infinity of the pure word and the human word: the name. "The theory of proper names is the theory of the frontier between finite and infinite language." The human is the only creature who names him- or herself, and "the proper name is the word of God in human sounds. By it each man is guaranteed his creation by God, and in this sense, he is himself creative. . . . the proper name is the communion of humanity with the *creative* word of God" (324).

Moreover, through this word, the human names and is bound to the language of things. This relation of divine, human, and natural object languages stands in opposition to what Benjamin calls the "bourgeois" concept of language—language as an arbitrary system of *mere* signs, where words relate to their objects arbitrarily or only by convention.

Most commentators on Benjamin characterize his theory as a "mystical view of language." Benjamin is at pains to point out, however, that the correct alternative to the bourgeois conception is *not* a mystical linguistic theory wherein the word is considered to be simply the *essence* of the thing. This position misses a critical distinction: the thing in itself may have "language," but it has no *word;* it is created from God's word and known through the human word, the name given it. And this human name as knowledge of the thing is no longer *equivalent* to the spontaneous, un-limited, creative word of God; human language "cognizes" and "elevates" nature—but is not equivalent to the absolute creative, cognizing word of God.

Instead, the relation between human words and the language of things is one of "translation," which is found "at the deepest level of linguistic theory" (325). Humanity, that is, translates the mute language of things into the articulate human language of words; and this is not merely a process of articulation into sound but also the translation of an imperfect language into a more perfect one. The guarantor of the objectivity of this translation, of the correspondence between the name-language of human-ity and the nameless language of things, is God, from whose creative word both proceed. The human being translates and thereby transforms the mute nameless language of things into articulate sonic name. Humanity's naming language can be related to matter's nameless language because both emanate from the creative word of God.

The important point here is to notice the fine distinctions and hierarchy Benjamin constructs among the terms *God's creative word,* the *naming language of man,* and the unspoken *language of things.* The ultimate in-equality of these terms and the fall from the paradisal state of one language results in the multiplicity of human languages, or several different "trans-lations" of the languages of things into the language of human words. And that is Benjamin's version of the Fall in Eden, which occurs *before* the fall into linguistic multiplicity described in the Tower of Babel episode. The Fall of Adam in Eden is now interpreted as a linguistic fall, and that leads to an entirely different understanding of the "sin" of Eden, and its relation to the tree of the knowledge of good and evil.

In Benjamin's interpretation, the original language of paradise was one of perfect unified and undifferentiated knowledge; the differentiated knowledge of good and evil which Adam and Eve obtain through their sin in Benjamin's view is an "external, vain" knowledge. "Name steps outside itself in this knowledge: the Fall marks the birth of the *human word*" in which name becomes externalized and loses its immanent magic, and now "the word must communicate *something* (other than itself). That is really the Fall of language-mind" (327).

The sign-theory of language (language as a *sign* for something else) then would be a result of this Fall from a pure language of names: language now becomes a means, and a mere sign. In the Fall, "man abandoned immedi-acy in the communication of the concrete, name, and fell into the abyss of mediateness of all communication, of the word as means, of the empty word, into the abyss of prattle." The purity of names is injured, and the name is no longer immediate but becomes external and thus a word of judgment. The tree of the knowledge of good and evil in the Garden does not dispense information but is the "emblem of judgement over the questioner. This immense irony marks the mythical origin of law" (328). "Purity" and "sin" are thus redefined here in linguistic and epistemological terms—not as a personal relation between humans and God, or between humans and humans, but between languages. Scholem's description of Kafka might well be applied here to Benjamin: "This is what the moral reflection of a halakhist who attempted a *linguistic* paraphrase of divine judgement would be like" (*SF* 171).

In sum, the "purity" of the name-language was injured, and this fall from the pure language of names into a mediated empty system of signs is also the origin of judgment, abstraction, and "prattle," which results in a further fall into linguistic confusion and the Tower of Babel episode. "The enslavement of language in prattle is joined by the enslavement of things in folly almost as its inevitable consequence." The muteness of nature, after the fall, now becomes a deep melancholy and a mourning, "and for the sake of her redemption the life and language of *man*—not only, as is supposed, of the poet—are in nature" (*Refl* 329).

The "enslavement of things," the distorted relation of humanity to the world, and the need for redemption are the themes of both theology and politics. Irving Wohlfarth, in his perceptive reading of this essay, notes that "Benjamin's reading of Genesis already contains the seeds of a certain Marxism." The interpretation of the Fall as the fall of the divine name into the human word implies a fall from being to having, a distorted and disrupted relation with nature. In the pure paradisal language of names, nature called to humanity and humanity communicated with nature; the relation of name to thing was interior. After the Fall, when the word became an arbitrary sign, its relation to the thing changed. The word became instrumental, i.e., exploitative, exterior, reifying. Subject and object split; abstraction, judgment, law ensue. Subject becomes subjectivity and enforces subjection ("Jewish Motifs" 14). That is why Benjamin calls the sign-theory of language "bourgeois." Wohlfarth notes that

> the "bourgeois concept of language" would thus be with its insistence on the arbitrary nature of the sign, supremely oblivious to the Fall. For it conceals *how* arbitrary the sign really is. Instead of comprehending the fall from names into signs, such a theory merely legitimates its effects. Thus the sign becomes the fetish of the bourgeoisie, its transcendental commodity, the *a priori* condition of its traffic. Modern semiology would have the same status for Benjamin as the classical bourgeois theories of political economy had for Marx. In each case a double reification would be at work. For language should not be said to *be* arbitrary, but to have *become* so. . . . Structural linguistics would, it seems, be a "fallen," "inappropriate" "subjective" form of knowledge. (5–6)

In becoming an arbitrary instrument, the sign is connected to technology and capitalism. Thus Wohlfarth sees in Benjamin's reading of Genesis a "prehistory of Marxism" recounted as a philosophy of language: "the fall is made to coincide with the advent of bourgeois society," for the fall into the arbitrary human word is also the fall into history; "such full-blown theology represents, paradoxically, the deep structure of Benjamin's later Marxism. But it will, in turn, be profoundly altered by the naturalism it anticipates. It is difficult to tell which is the 'substructure' of the other" (7). Here already is the little hunchback of theology manipulating the puppet of historical materialism in Benjamin's 1940 parable from his "Theses on the Philosophy of History."

As deeply as he immersed himself in historical materialism, however, Benjamin never abandoned his attachment to language as a mode of redemption and revelation. He shared with Rosenzweig and Levinas the belief that language is the medium of truth and redemption. But there also is a strong point of disagreement among them. As Stéphane Mosès writes,

> The communicative function of language, which for Benjamin represents the main symptom of its degeneracy, is for Rosenzweig identical with its quality of revelation, precisely because it mediates between individuals, because the act of speaking means the opening-up of the subject, previously locked in himself, to the Other. Language is revelation in so far as it is the "language of souls," the self-revelation of human inwardness. ("Walter Benjamin" 198)

Mosès's essay contains an excellent summary and comparison of Benjamin's 1916 essay "On Language" with some of Rosenzweig's main ideas on language and drama in *The Star of Redemption*. Mosès notes that Benjamin anticipates some of Rosenzweig's important thoughts, although there are also important differences and different sources of inspiration:

> Basic experience for Benjamin as a young man was that of a devalued and degenerate reality, whose desolation was even more obvious against the background of an original, but now lost, perfection. The religious categories of creation and revelation are experienced here in their negativity, while for Rosenzweig, precisely in their religious positivity, they are two cornerstones of the experience of reality. (199)

We shall see that Levinas follows Rosenzweig in viewing language as preeminently the medium of human relationship, and characterizes this relationship as inherently and primordially ethical before it is epistemological or political; ethics is defined precisely as this opening up, as giving oneself over to the Other. Levinas will also follow Rosenzweig in viewing this revelatory capacity of language as available *now*, in the *present,* and not lost in some mythic past from which we have fallen. The ethical nature of language will then be affirmed for both Rosenzweig and Levinas through the concrete contents of Jewish law. But for Benjamin and Scholem, *halakah* was a premature concretion or inauthentic expression of that pure word.

HIDDEN IDEOLOGIES IN DEBATES OVER
THEORIES OF LANGUAGE

Despite the mystical overtones, Benjamin nowhere overtly cites any kabbalistic thinkers or sources in this essay. There was a subterranean connection to Kabbalah, however, in the long historical precedent for using the biblical text to formulate linguistic theory. Hans Aarsleff reminds us that theories of language in Germany in the nineteenth century were rooted in older debates in which Enlightenment and eighteenth-century theories of language played a considerable role; and the texts of Genesis 2 and 11 were extremely influential in the history of linguistic theory in the West. During the Renaissance, kabbalistic doctrines became known among Christian writers and thinkers and were intermingled with views about the origins of language. The notion of an Adamic language of paradise was also reinforced by the mystics and visionaries of the seventeenth century and strengthened by the influence of the Christian Kabbalah—especially through the writings of Jacob Boehme, whose ideas were widely known in England (Aarsleff, *From Locke* 60).

In other words, Benjamin followed a long tradition when he interpreted Adam's name giving as some primal prelapsarian language where name was the magical link between word and thing. In the seventeenth century, in fact, the biblical Adam was considered to be the greatest philosopher and etymologist. The story of Babel was not interpreted as a fall into complete arbitrariness of meaning; rather, it was thought that remnants of the Adamic language remained and might be recaptured through comparative etymological study. Boehme went so far as to claim that moments of divine inspiration enabled him to comprehend the essence of things, and so to understand the Adamic language. Where the word was thought of as the essence of the thing, language became a kind of formula for understanding the secrets of nature (*From Locke* 281–82).

Indeed, as Aarsleff recounts, the concept of "Adamic language," the perfect language of naming, was the "most widely held seventeenth-century view of the nature of language" (25). This doctrine was resurrected by the romantics in the nineteenth century even after Locke sharply critiqued it in his *Essay* and maintained that language was human and conventional, not divine and natural. Language, Locke argued, was about "ideas," not "things," and he thus laid the groundwork for the modern philosophy of language—i.e., for the conception of language as a social institution and for the Saussurean idea of the arbitrary relation between signifier and signified.

Locke's critique was thus also related to the rise of the "New Science" in the seventeenth century and the question of the best way to understand nature. The New Science sought to examine God's revelations in the "Book of Nature" by means of the peaceful and orderly processes of self-sufficient reason, not via disputatious and confusing interpretations of the "Book of Scripture." Now if the object of study were to be nature, the question then became whether language itself was a phenomenon within nature, or whether it had an existence *apart from* nature. To what sort of knowledge did it give rise: a direct, clear knowledge of things, or only to ideas about things? (43). In other words, did language yield any authoritative knowledge of nature, of the relation of creation and creator through remnants of some Adamic naming language? Or did it inhibit such knowledge? Such questions led to intense speculation about the origins of language in the search for basic principles, and these speculations also led to the development of the genetic method in the attempt to distinguish between what was natural and what was artificial (147–48).

What is especially interesting for the Benjamin-Scholem discussion is Aarsleff's demonstration of how the model of "comparative-historical philology" created in Germany in the nineteenth century (largely due to Humboldt's educational program and related to Humboldt's own philosophy of language, which made philology the model humanistic discipline) was, in fact, "a revival of the Adamic doctrine in new terms." This would form another link between Scholem's adherence to this method, which he absorbed in his academic training in Germany and then used in his analyses of Kabbalah, and his attachment to Benjamin's linguistic theory. It also illumines a covert relation of this "scientific-critical" method to theology.

The comparative historical-philological view presupposed some common origin or *Ursprache* behind the variety of languages and significations that might be glimpsed from comparative study. But there was more. Aarsleff argues that the kind of science with which nineteenth-century historical philology allied itself—"factual, descriptive, classificatory, empirical, and comparative"—had several aims. One was to defuse leftist political ideology, which was identified with the dangers of the French Revolution; another was to "sustain the argument for final causes and for assurances of the Creator's presence in creation" (32). The underlying theology in this science was revealed in the debate over the essentialist view of nature versus the Darwinian developmental evolutionary theory. The link was the comparative anatomy formulated by Cuvier around 1800, which also became the model for language study and anthropology. Cuvier insisted on the fixity of species since the time of Creation; the key to understanding anatomy was therefore the correlation of parts, not any historical evolution.

To understand this structural correlation, the argument went, one need only observe, describe, and classify; speculation was unnecessary (34). In other words, the final cause is found in the structure of each part, and that precisely is what made all cognition of nature possible. Max Müller thought that *language* illustrated this theory perfectly, and that language was subject to the same kind of science because it was a fixed natural object. In this view, the historical changes in language were not due to any human intervention; the proper methods for a science of language were description, classification, and arrangements of facts which led back to its roots, which were names of concepts—implying an Adamic language.

These ideas, of course, were also meant to oppose utilitarian theory, and they were taken up in the nineteenth century by figures from Carlyle to Coleridge who, like Benjamin and Scholem, sharply rejected any attempt to define the essence of language via its common social and communicative functions. Like Scholem, Coleridge and Carlyle were especially interested in the symbol and the symbolic aspects of language as giving access to these deeper divine realms. These philosophers and poets also sought to recover the remnants of the Adamic language, the mystery of its deeper meanings, and etymology and philology were means of eliciting these deeper natural meanings, or ways of "remembering" these original meanings. The nineteenth century, that is, rejected Locke. Aarsleff adds that the critique of this German philological tradition thus had to come from outside—from France—because comparative philology was so entrenched in the German university (289–92). Michel Bréal, a French linguist, harshly criticized German comparative philology, and his critique deeply influenced Saussure, resulting in a revival of the neglected linguistic philosophy of the Lockean tradition.[1]

As we have seen, the young Benjamin, under the sway of German romanticism and French symbolism, opposed this new conception of language as an arbitrary system of signs—a mere human and social institution—calling it "bourgeois" and identifying it with a linguistic fall. And Scholem, even in his late work, still appealed to the "mystery of language," to which he claimed only poets now have access. He and the early Benjamin were very much a part of the German tradition and its romanticist legacy—the view of language as a natural organism with its own life, independent of its speakers, transcending any human social use. Language, that is, held some original mysterious perfection and had been subject to a subsequent decadence (*From Locke* 295–96). Aarsleff aptly sums up the central principle of the French critics, which, by contrast, was that

> language does not have independent existence as a product of nature, but is the expression of human activity. It is an institution. Its function is communication, its being is social, and the linguistic sign is arbitrary. Since historical study alone cannot take account of these factors, it provides an insufficient basis for the understanding of the system or structure of language at any given moment. (299)

Aarsleff does not carry this analysis further into contemporary literary theory, but strangely enough, certain strains of contemporary poststructuralist literary theory, neglecting this intellectual background, have virtually "reromanticized" Saussure. That is, the distinction in Saussure between language as an ahistorical synchronous system, and language in its diachronic evolution over time was originally a critique of German romanticist notions. In much poststructuralist theory, however, "Language" (the synchronic *langue* as opposed to the diachronic *parole* or "speech") becomes "hypostatized" once again into a kind of self-reflexive, self-engendering world of pure signifiers or forms. Or "Language" becomes personified as if it were an autonomous entity that knows and does things independently of human will or subjectivity—as if it were an impersonal fact of nature rather than a social and human institution, as if a person or society were an "effect" of linguistic and textual forces, not vice versa. Harold Bloom, himself a great scholar of romanticism, puts it well when he writes that language became a kind of "Demiurge replacing the self-as-Abyss or even self-as-Jehovah" in modern thought *(Agon* 19).[2] But the original social and human thrust of the French critique was to deny that language has its cause, aim, and end in itself.

The *social* and political aspects of Saussure's legacy, however, have recently been revived in poststructuralist theory through a new engagement with Marxist criticism, with the work of Foucault, with cultural anthropology, and in the "New Historicism." Marxist critics such as Fredric Jameson and Terry Eagleton, in turn, have helped revive interest in Walter Benjamin, who then appeared to be a remarkably prescient critic because he brought together an awareness of the deconstructive abyss of pure language with a sense of language as a force marked by history and ideology. But Marxist critics and New Historicists are often uncomfortable with the theological element in Benjamin; and deconstructionists are more sensitive to the romantic and theological elements, even as they proceed to subvert them. All of these theories, however, continue to wrestle with the romantic legacy of the problem of "the subject," along with questions about the relation between the social and the individual, and the nature of the knowing and speaking consciousness.

In America, it is no accident that those critics who were the earliest proponents of structuralism and deconstruction were scholars of romantic literature. In fact, the main thesis of Aarsleff's book is that the eighteenth-century contribution to the theory of language and the French connection to Locke have been completely ignored in histories written about linguistics because of this nineteenth-century romantic ideology under which we *still* labor, and which had denigrated the Lockean tradition. In words that also might well be applied to debates about Scholem, his historiography, and its relation to the fields of Jewish Studies and literary criticism, Aarsleff writes,

> No purely internal history of a science or a discipline can achieve coherence and lead to the sort of understanding that yields a sense of explanation. It is only by inclusion of external factors that genuine intellectual history becomes

possible. The prerequisite is disengagement from conventional patterns and from subservience to the institutional bias of folk-history. (318)

Philippe Lacoue-Labarthe and Jean-Luc Nancy have also argued that "we still belong to the era it [romanticism] opened up. . . . A veritable romantic *unconscious* is discernible today, in most of the motifs of our 'modernity' " (*Literary Absolute* 15). Yet what romanticism has passed down is often unrecognized as such, even though the legacy of "literature" devoting itself to the search for its own identity (theory) comes to us precisely from romanticism, especially in the form of the "literary absolute." In other words, romanticism was the birthplace of the concept of "literature" as such and of the theoretical project in literature where "theory itself is literature," and literature becomes an "absolute" (3–5).

Put this way, the various "formalisms" often linked with modernism belie romantic preoccupations with the relation of form and the formless, the contingent and the absolute, and the problem of the nature of the subject. The question of "form" is a legacy from Kant, for whom the mind, with its analytic and synthesizing powers of imagination and understanding, builds up and structures the "formless" flow of our experience of the world. These forms make the world intelligible, although we can never know if they correspond to the world as it is in itself. In post-Kantian romantic aesthetics, as Gerald Bruns well puts it, there is a "transformation of Kant's account of mental activity into a theory of poetic activity" (*Modern Poetry* 209), wherein Kant's critical idealism becomes aesthetic idealism. The mind's capacity to form objects merges with the artistic power of formation; poetry becomes philosophy and vice versa; art creates and structures reality. Language then becomes viewed as above all a world-creating *formative activity,* a cognitive process where the mind builds the world out of the chaos of sensation. This was the keynote of Benjamin's critique of Kant—that Kant had neglected this aspect of language and had too narrowly restricted what counted as "experience." This was also the "mystery" in language to which Scholem appealed, the mystery to which he thought only the *poets* have the key now that the divine voice has been stilled.

Lacoue-Labarthe and Nancy remind us that romanticism still marks all of the humanities:

> From the idea of a possible formalization of literature (or of cultural productions in general) to the use of linguistic models (and a model based on the auto-structuration of language); from an analytic approach to works based on the hypothesis of auto-engendering to the aggravation of the problematic of a subject permanently rejecting subjectivism . . . to a general theory of the historical or social subject; from a belief that the work's conditions of production or fabrication are inscribed within it to the thesis of a dissolution of all processes of production in the abyss of the subject. (16)

Literary theories from Russian Formalism, Prague and Parisian structuralism, to the New Criticism, Marxist structuralism, deconstruction, and New Historicism would all carry the latent problematic of romanticism.

What I have been hinting at and will argue extensively in the next chapter is that there is a certain uncritical and aesthetic "romantic unconscious" in Scholem's phenomenology of religion and in his understanding of religious language, especially in his concept of the symbol as the distinctive form of mystical expression. Scholem's interpretation of the mystical meaning of the absolute word of God as "contentless" and "meaningless" but the source of all meaning, for example, borrows from Benjamin's adaptation of French symbolist and German romantic theories of language and art. Schlegel, for instance, thought of the individual work of art in relation to the "absolute artwork," a transcendent form-giving idea which guaranteed the infinity and unity of art. There was a dialectical relation between the individual forms of the works of art and the ultimate form of the absolute artwork in which they are comprehended, a tension of form and formlessness. In the case of the French symbolists, especially Mallarmé, in whom Benjamin was so interested, the pure form of language attained to the absolute through dissolution of all concrete meaning into *le Néant* or Nothingness.

In yet another twist, "the true aesthetic," Schlegel wrote, "is the Kabbalah."[3] German romanticism and French symbolism themselves in turn had absorbed, via the Christian Kabbalah, currents from various esoteric philosophies. The matter is quite complex, but suffice it to say here that Jewish kabbalistic ideas about language and symbol were themselves transformed and radically changed in the process of mediation through the Christian Kabbalah, and those changes were then absorbed and perpetuated in Scholem's attempts to reconstruct Jewish mysticism. As Moshe Idel has brilliantly shown, the distinctively Jewish *halakhic*-theurgic elements were dropped, and Kabbalah was translated into a primarily speculative and symbolic theosophical system. To take it a step further than Idel, this symbolic theosophy then was "aestheticized" in German romantic thought. Kabbalah then emerges in Scholem conceived as a great work of "art," a great revitalizing upsurge of "creative myth" and "symbol" in the heart of "sterile" rabbinic-*halakhic* Judaism and the "dry empty" rationalism of Jewish philosophy. In sum, the question here is not so much what precise historical influence mysticism itself had upon romanticism (for it was certainly a component) but the ways in which that romantic aesthetic itself influenced both Scholem and Benjamin's interpretation of Judaism and theology, and the reception of their work in modern literary criticism.

Scholem finds three basic themes in the kabbalistic view of language:

1. That creation and revelation are essentially autorepresentations of God; the relation of the infinite and finite can be expressed only symbolically, and language is this symbolic expression, and thus the essence of the universe.

2. The "Name of God" is the metaphysical origin of all language, and

language is the explanation of this name. The language of God which constitutes the sacred text is itself crystallized in the "Name of God." As in Benjamin's linguistic theory, this primal language of names is a higher realm beyond "communicative" language. For the kabbalists, the various Divine Names or—in other accounts—the singular Divine Name is the basis of all language and is manifested not directly but symbolically. Only those who know the correct formulas and secrets of interpretation can decipher it.

3. Since the Divine Names are a concentration of divine power, Scholem perceives a dialectical tension between "magic" and "mysticism" which carries over into a belief in the extraordinary powers of the human word as well. Names come to represent the "magic" of the word, some intrinsic immediate connection to things, a creative power language has over the world of things (Scholem, "Linguistic Theory" 62–63).

There is an obvious parallel here to Benjamin's idea of the name as the quintessence of human language. Name in Benjamin, however, is more of a mediating link between the human naming language, God's absolute creative word, and the mute world of nature. Benjamin does not directly refer to a language of Divine Names of God; human naming language is more of a lower reflection of the divine word, and "the proper name is the word of God in human sound," but it can never be *equivalent* to the divine creative word. There already is loss, decline, and little hope to reunite these spheres.

The central point which Scholem and Benjamin consistently agreed upon was that the creative word of God is not a word of *concrete* revelation which directly or immediately materializes in a sacred written (or in the aesthetic) text. The materiality of the text is already a "translation." Benjamin's analysis in "On Language" does not take as its starting point the language of a written sacred text as does Kabbalah. The text his human name-giver has to interpret and translate instead is *nature.* Humanity translates the language of nature into the language of names and thus redeems nature's muteness and connects it to God. So despite the idealist tendencies in his early thought, Benjamin is as concerned here with the obdurate world, the life of things, as in his later materialist phase.

What needs to be given voice, then, is the language of nature and names—which are not necessarily coincident with the words of Scripture. In Benjamin's schema, there is something impotent and passive about the remnants of human language and the unavailability of the divine language. In making any comparisons of Benjamin's ideas to those found in Jewish mysticism, it is important to bear in mind that any knowledge which Benjamin had of Kabbalah was entirely second-hand and elementary, obtained through his association with Scholem. As he wrote to Scholem in a letter of January 15, 1933, thanking Scholem for a copy of an encyclopedia article on Kabbalah which Scholem had written: "Though no judgment can arise out of the abyss of my ignorance in this area, you should still know that the rays of your article did force their way even down here. Otherwise, however, I have to content myself with cobweb-thin esoteric knowledge" (*Corr* 26).

I would also argue that even if Benjamin had never met Scholem, he would have incorporated these "mystical" notions from the traditions of German romanticism and the linguistic theories of Humboldt and Hamann. To reiterate his justification for using the Genesis text in the 1916 essay, the Bible is employed not because it is "objectively revealed truth" but because "the present argument broadly follows it in presupposing language as an ultimate reality, perceptible only in its manifestation, inexplicable and mystical. The Bible, in regarding itself as a revelation, must necessarily evolve the fundamental linguistic facts" (*Refl* 322).

The problem for Benjamin, however, becomes how to relate the epistemological thesis—that language is a form of redemptive knowledge—to its actual power in the brute world of nature. If the ultimate language is contentless, noncommunicative or pure word, and the relation of language as sign to things outside itself is a fallen relationship, then what indeed is the efficacy of the language of names in the mute material world?

Benjamin's disgust with the propagandistic uses of language in World War I was one of the motives which had led him to assert the contentlessness of the "pure language" as a purifying instrument. Interpreters such as Michael Jennings connect this to his nihilism: i.e., redemption can come only through destructive purgation. But as Benjamin's thought progresses and the situation in Germany drastically declines in the 1920s and 1930s, he tries to rework this relation of language to the *material* world. In this sense, preoccupations with the pure language of names are not the opposite of, but in clear *continuity* with, his later historical materialism—linked through the idea of redemption, a redemption which he sometimes treated ironically, sometimes apocalyptically, sometimes with nihilistic despair, sometimes with hope. In other words, Benjamin's materialism and idealism are mirror images—inextricably linked.

LANGUAGE, MATERIALISM, AND THE MIMETIC FACULTY

In 1933, well into his "Marxist" phase, Benjamin wrote two other closely related essays on language in which he tried to apply to his earlier theological insights a more immanent, anthropological, and historical analysis. The "Doctrine of the Similar" was composed in Berlin in early 1933, revised in exile in Paris later that year, and retitled "On the Mimetic Faculty." It is again striking that these pieces were written at a moment of supreme personal and historical crisis, the victory of the Nazi party in the elections and the ascendancy of Hitler to the chancellorship. In a letter to Scholem of February 28, 1933, Benjamin wrote, "The little composure that people in my circles were able to muster in the face of the new regime was rapidly spent, and one realizes the air is hardly fit to breathe anymore—a condition which of course loses its significance as one is being strangled anyway" (*Corr* 27). The Nazis had purged the media of Jewish editors, producers, and writers, and the journals and newspapers from which Benjamin had made a living as a contributor could no longer publish his work. From his exile later, however, he wrote and successfully published some pieces in the German press under the pseudonym "Detlef Holtz."

Benjamin continues in this 1933 letter that he has no idea "how I will be able to make it" through the next few months, "whether inside or outside Germany. . . . If I report that, despite such circumstances, a new theory of language—encompassing four handwritten pages—has resulted, you will not deny me due homage" (28). He had no intention, though, of publishing these reflections. Scholem wrote back that he was very keen to receive a copy of this new text, but Benjamin delayed sending it. In May, now in exile on the island of Ibiza and separated from his books and papers, Benjamin wrote Scholem to request a copy of his 1916 essay "On Language" from Scholem's "archive" in order to compare it to his new "jottings on language" (52). Scholem sent a copy and wrote back on June 15, "It won't have escaped you that I'm looking forward to the second text on language with the unfeigned interest of the Black Magician who expects a theory to shore up his formulae" (55).

Benjamin still had not sent the new piece when he wrote to Scholem in late June that the notes on language were only "an addendum to the larger essay. . . . If hints serve any purpose here, the text deals with a new turn in our old tendency to show the ways in which magic has been vanquished" (61). Benjamin probably had other reasons for not wanting to send these new notes to Scholem, for they were very much influenced by the materialist shift in his thinking of which Scholem so strongly disapproved. In January of 1934, Benjamin had the Institute for Social Research commission him to do a review-survey on the philosophy of language, a piece which Scholem claimed not to understand (the comment he made about most of Benjamin's more "Marxist" writings) and over which he incurred Benjamin's wrath by asking whether it was a communist credo.

When Scholem finally received the text of "On the Mimetic Faculty" within the year, he did not comment on it in writing, but when he met Benjamin in Paris in 1938, they took up the subject. Scholem describes the encounter and writes that the essay on the mimetic faculty, "which he considered important, was the subject of his repeated complaints that I had not reacted to it" (*SF* 205–206). At this reunion, Scholem and Benjamin fiercely argued over his Marxist orientation, and their discussions were marked by "an emotionally rather charged atmosphere and even included two or three downright dramatic moments" relating to Benjamin's relation with the Institute for Social Research, Brecht, and the Stalinist trials in Russia. Scholem thought that Benjamin's view of language had become "polarized" between a materialistic attempt to abolish the magic of language that conflicted with "all his earlier reflections on language, reflections under theological, mystical inspirations that he still maintained . . . as in his essay on the mimetic faculty." Scholem, however, badly misreads this piece when he concludes the account by remarking that "his essay on the mimetic faculty still lacks even the slightest hint of a materialistic view of language. On the contrary, matter appeared here only in a purely magical connection" (209).

In the brief essay "On the Mimetic Faculty," Benjamin attempted to attribute the "magic of language" to the human ability to perceive similarities; language is now described as the repository of "nonsensuous similarities." The central issue in the essay is how to retain his view that language is far more than an arbitrary system of signs, and yet find a less theological guarantee for its objectivity and cognitive possibilities. In other words, from a more anthropological or naturalistic perspective, is there a way to anchor human language or have it correspond in any way to things? Benjamin turns to the human mimetic faculty, defined as the desire to become similar or identical to things or persons, and the capacity to produce similarities, to behave mimetically. This capacity, he notes, is found in children, in play, and in the very highest mental functions. The ancient world was far more filled with these "magical correspondences" than the modern, but the faculty has not been lost, only historically transformed and directed into other realms.

This interest in "correspondences" extends Benjamin's earlier examination of the "magical immediacy" of human language and again follows his program of revising the Kantian model of perception. As he said to Scholem, "A philosophy that does not include the possibility of soothsaying from *coffee grounds* and cannot explicate it cannot be a true philosophy" (*SF* 59). Benjamin here also shares the general interest in "primitive thought" of many writers and artists of his time, from Jung and Lévy-Bruhl to Cassirer to Scholem himself. For Scholem, the category of "myth" was to be critical in understanding the Kabbalah and its symbolism, and Baudelaire's famous "correspondences" would be a later subject for Benjamin in his analysis of modernity.

Yet this shift toward a more naturalistic perspective is offset by Benjamin's resort to astrology and graphology for clarifying examples. Astrology, he argues, is a human "imitation" of a perceived characteristic unity of the stars, and astrology then becomes Benjamin's metaphor for the cognitive act of perceiving similarity: "The perception of similarity which occurs is in every case bound to an instantaneous flash. . . . It offers itself to the eye as fleetingly and transitorily as a constellation of stars" ("Doctrine" 66). The similarities are glimpsed in a fleeting instant which cannot be fixed, in contrast to the more determinate methods of astronomy and the mode of scientific observation.

This model of the "instantaneous flash" and the "constellation" will be at the center of his later materialist historiography. The instantaneous flash is also a *temporal* form of compression or miniaturization. As he writes in the Arcades project, "In the fields with which we are concerned, knowledge (*Erkenntnis*) exists only in lightning flashes. The text is the thunder rolling long afterward" ("Theory of Knowledge" [N 1, 1]). The flash, in other words, is a moment of shock or awakening, and the moment of true historical understanding. The constellation as configuration of past and present becomes both here and in the "Theses on the Philosophy of History" an interruption, a way of releasing revolutionary energies and infusing the present "with chips of Messianic time" (*Illum* 263). It is encountered not in static images of "nature" or "matter" per se but in language as cognition and perception.

In the 1933 essays on the mimetic faculty, language is defined as the great repository of nonsensuous similarities; it makes both these more ancient and these alternative revolutionary perceptions available to us today.

> Language is the highest application of the mimetic faculty: a medium into which the earlier perceptive capabilities for recognizing the similar had entered without residue, so that it is now language which represents the medium in which objects meet and enter into relationship with each other, no longer directly, as once in the mind of the augur or priest, but in their essences, in their most volatile and delicate substances, even in their aromata. In other words: it is to writing and language that clairvoyance has, over the course of history, yielded its old powers. ("Doctrine" 68)

The question for both "empirical philology" and "mystical and theological theories of language" (67) is how all the words meaning the same thing in different languages are "similar" to that thing. This is not adequately answered, he maintains, by reference to *sensuous* similarity (onomatopoeia).

But here Benjamin no longer has recourse to "the pure language" as he did in the translation essay, or to "God's" ultimate creative word and an Adamic language of names. "Graphology" provides a (rather unconvincing) possible link. Written language, especially, through the graphic image is an archive of "nonsensuous" similarity—and graphology, he thinks, is one indication of this faculty. Reading is thus "profane and magical"; the pupil reading his ABC's is analogous to the astrologer reading his stars. Reading originated, Benjamin argues, in tracing constellations of meaning from stars, entrails, hieroglyphs, and evolved into the finding of nonsensuous similarities in written and spoken language "so that it is now language which represents the medium in which objects meet and enter into relationship with each other" (68). The very swiftness of reading is required for these similarities to flash up fleetingly.

This magical aspect of language, however, also requires the "semiotic" side—the ordinary communicative meaning of words. "The mimetic element in language can, like a flame, manifest itself only through a bearer. This bearer is the semiotic element." The coherence of ordinary communicative meaning "is the bearer through which, like a flash, similarity appears" (*Refl* 335).

The differences between the two versions of the essay are that in the second version ("On the Mimetic Faculty") many of the same points are made, but the magical and mystical elements are diminished—or, as Scholem would have it, recede into an esoteric, hidden background—and Benjamin tries to make his analysis of the mimetic faculty more naturalistic and historical. Overt references to mystical and theological analysis of language have been taken out; reading is no longer said to have both magical and profane elements, and the essay is considerably shortened by these elisions. In the last paragraph, the mimetic element in writing and language represents the highest level of mimetic behavior; it has transformed the earlier powers of mimetic production "to the point where they have liquidated those of magic" (336).

Anson Rabinbach, in his introduction to the "Doctrine of the Similar," argues against the idea that the move to a more historical-anthropological view in the second version of the piece was due to Benjamin's increasing Marxism. He claims that both pieces should be seen more in the light of Benjamin's critique of Kant's theory of knowledge and his estimation of the Enlightenment in general as an "epistemological mythology." Benjamin was interested in the capacity to perceive similarities as a prerationalistic way of thinking which had its own validity—a validity denied to it by Enlightenment thought. This paralleled his fascination with children's books, the world of the insane, and the realm of the occult as alternate ways of viewing the world, as different modes of perception in which subject and object were not clearly differentiated.

Benjamin was trying "somehow" to work out a more naturalistic account of language, but one which was not crudely material or purely immanent, one which yet retained language's cognitive powers. At their meeting in Paris in 1938, Scholem told Benjamin that he seemed "torn between his predilection for a mystical theory of language and an equally strong need to struggle against it in the context of a Marxist view of the world." Benjamin admitted this contradiction "and said it was simply a matter of a task that he had not yet mastered but for which he had high hopes." He was attracted to Brecht, he explained, because Brecht was writing a totally unmagical language. Yet, the perplexed Scholem writes, Benjamin still spoke in their discussions of "God's words," in contrast to human words as the foundation of all linguistic theory (SF 209).

THE MEANINGLESS WORD AND THE DIVINE NOTHING

For Scholem, the writings of the young Benjamin on language such as the 1916 essay and "The Task of the Translator" had expressed his true genius before it had become corrupted by historical materialism. But Benjamin disagreed and

emphatically defended his orientation. He said that his Marxism still was not dogmatic but heuristic and experimental in nature, and that his transposition into Marxist perspectives of the metaphysical and even theological ideas he had developed in the years we had spent together was in fact meritorious, because in that sphere they could become more active, at least in our time, than in the sphere originally suited to them. (*SF* 207)

In any case, the revolution, he added sharply, would supply the missing philosophical link better than he could. Comments Scholem: "Someone who did not believe in *that* revolution hardly could make any response to this statement." But Scholem did believe in other forms of "revolution," the cultural revolution and regeneration that he hoped Zionism could effect, along with the revolution in the scholarly history of Judaism and Jewish thought that he was effecting with his studies of Kabbalah.

Scholem retained throughout his life the early "theocratic anarchism" he had shared with Benjamin, and he remained faithful to those early thoughts about "pure language" and religious nihilism. In his famous later essays when Scholem discussed the linguistic theory of the Kabbalah, and revelation and tradition as religious ideas in Judaism, he framed the key issues precisely in terms of Benjamin's earlier thoughts about the communicative and noncommunicative aspects of language—and in terms solely of epistemology of language.

The first few pages of Scholem's 1972 essay "The Name of God and the Linguistic Theory of the Kabbalah" are filled with reflections about language in general and mystical theories of language as a whole. His central assertion is

> the conviction that the language—the medium—in which the spiritual life of man is accomplished, or consummated, includes an inner property, an aspect which does not altogether merge or disappear in the relationship of communication between men. . . . [There is] something else vibrating, which is not merely communication, meaning, and expression . . . beyond our understanding. (60)

The basis of *any* linguistic research, claims Scholem, is exactly this assumption that "language is something more than communication and expression" and not a conventional arrangement of signs.

Mystics of all the religious traditions, he continues, view language as the point of intersection between the divine and human, the point where "the language of God infiltrates the spoken language and because of this infiltration lays itself open to discovery" (62). They sense and solicit a hidden dimension in language beyond its uses for intrahuman communication, meaning, and expression:

> The original concern of the mystics was that they departed from the language used by mortal men, in order to discover within it the language of revelation, or even discover language *as* revelation. . . . From time immemorial they

> have sensed an abyss, a depth in language. . . . the point at which language
> should be at once the language of revelation and the language of human rea-
> son. (61–62)

The "Name of God" was a key aspect of kabbalistic linguistics, and
Scholem's description of the name/word relation in Kabbalah parallels
central passages in Benjamin's linguistics—especially Benjamin's description in his translation essay of the relation of finite languages to the pure
silent language where all communication and meaning are extinguished,
and his elaboration in the 1916 essay "On Language" of the dual character
of the paradisal Adamic naming language, a language which likewise communicated no "information."

Scholem argues that whereas in the Bible there had been a basic distinction between the *name* of God and the *creative word* of God, in the Kabbalah they became identified. The name of God becomes a quintessence of
the sacred, and the agent of creation.

> From the coincidence of word and name two important consequences
> emerged which were instrumental for the development of the mystique of
> language in Judaism. On the one hand, by virtue of this identification, the
> word which communicates something, even if the communication takes the
> form of an imperative ("Let there be light!"), the word which imparts infor-
> mation of some kind becomes a name which issues no information save itself.
> (70)

Another consequence of this identification of word and name is the importance given to the very letters which constitute language. For the kabbalists, Hebrew is the original divine language, and so the Hebrew letters
themselves are carriers or concentrations of divine energies. Their various
combination and recombination are, as it were, the formulas of creation. The written image acquires a magic connection with the sounds it
represents, part of the magic of the divine language ("Linguistic Theory"
72–75).

Contrast this with Benjamin's attempts to analyze the "magical" practices behind reading and writing in the two 1933 essays on language. In a
letter of October 24, 1935, Benjamin thanked Scholem for sending him a
copy of translations of some parts of the *Zohar* (one of the most well
known kabbalistic texts) that Scholem had done:

> You won't be surprised to learn that this is a matter still close to my heart,
> even if you probably didn't read the short paper in which it found its expres-
> sion on Ibiza ("On the Mimetic Faculty") in quite that way. Whatever the
> case, the concept of nonsensuous similarity developed there finds manifold
> illustration in the way in which the author of the Zohar conceives of the
> formations of sounds—and written signs to an even greater extent, most
> likely—as the deposits of cosmic connections. Yet he seems to be thinking of a

correspondence that is not ascribed to any mimetic origin. This may well follow from his commitment to the doctrine of emanation, to which my theory of mimesis presents the strongest possible opposition. (*Corr* 170)[4]

But the critical question one can ask about both Scholem and Benjamin's linguistic categories is just what is meant by that "something more," that "something else," that "abyss" or "depth" in language that both mystics and poets sense and explore—a nihilistic void or a depth of divine mystery? Is the "beyond" the negative abyss of all meaning and expression (as deMan and Jacobs argued) or a higher, fuller realm of meaning? And how does the negative relate to the positive? Can an "abyss," a realm utterly beyond all human grasp and articulation, nevertheless contain traces and powers of redemption? Moreover, why does Scholem identify that which is beyond *expression* as that which is beyond all *meaning,* and not only certain kinds of human meaning? Perhaps he does so because the idea of the ultimate meaningless word is connected to another one of Scholem's fundamental assumptions: that mystical *experience* is amorphous, and that precisely because of its formlessness, it can be clothed in an unlimited number of different forms (*KS* 8). This characteristic necessitates what Scholem calls a "symbolic" mode of thought: The mystic reinterprets the traditional materials in light of this amorphous experience through *symbolic* representations, which, according to Scholem, are the *only* means to describe an indescribable reality.

Scholem recognizes, however, that this characterization of an ultimately meaningless divine word and amorphous experience opens another "abyss" at the heart of revelation and a displacement of authority. For in Scholem's schema, the symbolic dimension revealed by the mystic radically transforms even as it confirms religious authority. This tension is volatile; the mystical experience can result in a conflict with the given forms of tradition. In some historical circumstances, when the mystic is unable to find communal acceptance or unable to use the forms of the tradition to express his or her experiences, an open clash of authority ensues.

Mysticism can then take a quite radical direction if the mystics attempt to establish a new authority based on their own experience, and nihilistic mysticism is the extreme result when the formless impulse overwhelms the concomitant attempt to build new forms (*KS* 11). In this case, the dissolution of all forms at the base of the mystical experience becomes the goal; the nihilistic mystic no longer returns to the forms of tradition but, as Scholem puts it, "descends into the abyss in which the freedom of living things is born" (29), committed to no form and rejecting all, immersed deeply into the "Source of Life," "the anarchic promiscuity of all living things" (28).

So in Scholem's view, the mystic exists in a "dialectical" tension between conservative and revolutionary attitudes toward the tradition in

which she or he is located; and it is this very tension between the reinterpretation of traditional authority and the establishment of an entirely new
authority that gives mysticism its vitality. Scholem's use of rhetorical figures such as "Source of Life," "anarchic promiscuity," and "vitality" is
quite telling, for they echo the ideas of the *Lebensphilosophie* which
Scholem and Benjamin so adamantly opposed. Benjamin and Scholem had
insisted that there was no unmediated pure experience of truth; language,
rather, mediated experience. But there remained in each of their work a
counterdrive, a nostalgia, a desire for some kind of "immediacy" or
"Source of Life" which took different forms. Zionism as the concrete and
immediate entry of Jews into history was one such form for Scholem;
intimations of the "abyss" in language or the "anarchic promiscuity of
life" were another. *Language itself* also became a kind of ontological substitute for immediate experience, for language was said to contain other
forms of "knowledge" and "experience."

In Scholem's own historiography, one could say, there is a romantic
fascination with the "amorphous" world of mystical experience and symbolic representation, combined with a postromantic skepticism, a recognition and insistence that these experiences can be approached only through
the critical tools of historical and philological research. "Certainly," he
wrote to Zalman Schocken,

> history may seem to be fundamentally an illusion, but an illusion without
> which in temporal reality no insight into the essence of things is possible. For
> today's man, that mystical totality of "truth" [*des Systems*], whose existence
> disappears particularly when it is projected into historical time, can only be-
> come visible in the purest way in the legitimate discipline of commentary and
> in the singular mirror of philological criticism. Today, as at the very beginning
> of my work, my work lives in this paradox, in the hope of a true communica-
> tion from the mountain, of that most invisible, smallest fluctuation of history
> which causes truth to break forth from the illusions of "development." (Qtd.
> in Biale, *Scholem* 76)

The relation of Scholem's attitude toward history and his attitude toward language can be seen in another of his more personal writings, the
ninth of his "Ten Unhistorical Theses on the Kabbalah":

> Totalities can only be conveyed [*tradierbar*] in an occult manner. God's name
> is capable of being addressed in language but not of being uttered in language.
> For only its fragmentariness renders language utterable. The "true" language
> cannot be uttered, just as the absolutely concrete cannot be realized. (Biale,
> "Ten Aphorisms" 86)

This last sentence cites again the line from Scholem's polemic against Hans
Schoeps of which Benjamin so highly approved, and the whole paragraph
is reminiscent of Benjamin's words in "The Task of the Translator" about

the "language of truth, the tensionless and even silent depository of the ultimate truth which all thought strives for . . . whose divination and description is the only perfection a philosopher can hope for, [and which] is concealed in concentrated fashion in translation" ("Task" 77). As Stéphane Mosès puts it, the early Benjamin "sees language as a system of signs that conceals itself as a secret but ideal center behind the endless multiplicity of concrete utterances" ("Walter Benjamin" 199). Human language is imperfect and fragmentary on account of the breakdown of the original correspondence of word and thing, but translation is a function within language that can help redeem it: "The utopian function of translation is in no way that it aids communication, but that it attempts to recreate the original essence of language as magic. Behind every concrete text is an ideal meaning which is hidden by the linguistic utterance. It is the duty of the translator to free this hidden meaning" (200). That is the "pure language," which is ultimately that "silent depository of the ultimate truth." Scholem shares with Benjamin the idea that ultimate truth is "beyond" all human finite attempts to grasp it, but language may address and evoke it, for language has a special status: its source is the divine, and it is the intersection of the divine and human. Nevertheless, human language as human is "fragmentary" and cannot grasp the whole or the divine infinity. As the *medium* of truth, however, it is also the very *mediation* of this truth.

Benjamin and Scholem ultimately diverged in their estimation of what kinds of "mediation" were possible and necessary. Benjamin would take up those very "fragments" of language, intensifying and concentrating them, compressing them as if by doing so they would then release their secrets. He would also extend the realm of "Language" far beyond verbal texts into the language of things, and into the images of history, as if one could glimpse the "absolutely concrete" through making the limited concrete fragments of the material world more "concrete," i.e., "monads," miniature whole worlds. Or as if by employing and activating esoteric language oneself, some of this truth might be mediated and expressed. In his own way, Benjamin tried to bring together philosophy of language and philosophy of history, absolute and concrete, spiritual and material, theology and politics.

Scholem, like Benjamin, considered the liberal progressive idea of historical development an illusion (as he writes above), and the only legitimate ways to approach the "mountain" were for him through careful historical textual commentary and philology, and the nonapocalyptic cultural action of Zionism in the historical realm. Yet he became disillusioned with the way the Zionist ideal had been "concretized" in contemporary empirical politics: "We were victorious too early"—victorious in the "visible realm" before victory "had been decided in the invisible realm—that is, the regeneration of language." "Secret values" had been betrayed in their public propaganda (*SF* 173); and "between London and Moscow we strayed into the desert of Araby on our way to Zion, and our own hubris blocked the path that leads to our people" (174). Nevertheless, Scholem retained his allegiance to the project. Writing to Benjamin on July 26, 1933, he affirmed: "My life here is only possible . . . because I feel devoted to this cause, even if in the face of despair and ruination. Otherwise, the suspect nature of a renewal that tends to manifest itself mostly as hubris and linguistic decay would have torn me apart long ago" (*Corr* 66).

Scholem's adherence to Zionism despite its "vulgar" concretizations was matched by Benjamin's adherence to Marxism despite its cruder manifestations, but Scholem could not see this parallel. He was unwilling to grant any validity to Benjamin's highly unorthodox brand of Marxism or Benjamin's desire, as he expressed it in a 1924 letter to Scholem, "no longer to represent the topical and political elements in my ideas in an outmoded disguise but to develop them by way of experiment, in extreme form" (*SF* 124). Instead, Scholem thought of Benjamin's historical materialism as a kind of awkward and ill-fitting clothing, incompatible with Benjamin's true genius and insights as a metaphysician of language. Benjamin, he claimed in a stinging letter of March 1931, did not truly practice but only played with "the ambiguities and dissonances" of materialistic method, a "completely alien formal element that any intelligent reader can easily detach, which stamps your output of this period as the work of an adventurer, a purveyor of ambiguities, and a cardsharper" (228).

In reply, Benjamin tried to explain to Scholem what the difference in their respective physical and historical circumstances implied, and the necessity for the complexities and ambiguities of his thought: "If I were in Palestine, it is entirely possible that things would be quite different. Your position on the Arab question proves that you have quite different methods of unambiguous differentiation from the bourgeoisie. Here there are no such methods. Here there is not even this method. For with a certain justification you could call what I call unambiguous the height of ambiguity" (*SF* 233). As a member of the small group of intellectuals in Palestine who belonged to "Brit Shalom" ("Peace Alliance"), Scholem advocated joint Jewish-Arab sovereignty in the whole of Palestine. But as he wrote Benjamin on July 10, 1937, after the British government had proposed partition into two separate states, one Jewish and one Arab, realistically there was little choice: "The question of the day is only whether something better can be gained by rejecting partition . . . and, unfortunately, this can scarcely be answered in the affirmative" (*Corr* 200).

Scholem, however, retained to the end his belief that Benjamin's thought, even in its most Marxist phase, was determined by its attachment to the Jewish categories of revelation and redemption; the latter was openly retained, but the former, "closely though it was bound up with his basic method of commenting on great and authoritative texts . . . remained unsaid . . . having become truly esoteric knowledge" (*JJC* 194). In another and more personal "parable" that he included in an essay on Rosenzweig, Scholem employed kabbalistic metaphors to reflect about what this concealment of the theological and the modern power of historical materialism might mean:

> The divinity, banished from man by psychology and from the world by sociology, no longer wanting to reside in the heavens, has handed over the throne of justice to dialectical materialism and the seat of mercy to psychoanalysis and has withdrawn to some hidden place and does not disclose Himself. Is He truly undisclosed? Perhaps this last withdrawal is His revelation. Perhaps God's removal to the point of nothingness was a higher need, and He will reveal His kingship only to a world that has been emptied. . . . ("Franz Rosenzweig" 27–28)

If "the absolutely concrete cannot be fulfilled," and "revelation returned to its own nothingness," then who could search within or speak from that nothingness? In another highly romantic gesture, Scholem designated *poets* and *artists* as the legitimate heirs of mystical experience in the modern world. He noted that with the decline of religious authority after the Enlightenment, nihilistic or secularized mystics such as Blake or Rimbaud have become prominent. Although their source of authority is themselves, they nevertheless are unable to do away with the traditional religious imagery of the church or the esoteric tradition. Scholem does not exclude these secular mystics from the realm of authentic mystical experience; on the contrary, he argues that "mystical experience is essentially amorphous and can therefore be interpreted in any number of ways," even "in a purely immanent, naturalistic way without the slightest reference to religious authority" (*KS* 17). What is ultimately formless can take on an infinite number of forms.

The comment is telling and itself parallels the kabbalistic hermeneutic of the infinity of meaning of the sacred text. When a mystic does return to the forms of his own tradition, Scholem writes, he or she metamorphoses the sacred texts by symbolically reinterpreting them, opening them up to this realm of infinite meaning: "The holiness of the texts resides precisely in their capacity for such metamorphosis. The word of God must be infinite, or, to put it in a different way, the absolute word as such is meaningless, but it is *pregnant* with meaning. . . . Authority no longer resides in a single unmistakable 'meaning' of the divine communication, but in its infinite capacity for taking on new form" (*KS* 12–13).

One of Scholem's best illustrations is the classic Hassidic master R. Mendel of Rymanov, who elaborated upon the talmudic debate about what words the Israelites actually heard at Sinai. All they really heard, R. Mendel said, was the first letter of the first word of the Ten Commandments, the aleph of the word *anokhi* (*anokhi* = "I" of "I am the Lord your God"). This aleph, Scholem comments, which is also the first letter of the Hebrew alphabet, is the simple opening of the larynx and is

nothing more than the possibility taken by the larynx when a word begins with a vowel. Thus the *aleph* may be said to denote the source of all articulate sound. The Kabbalists regarded it as the spiritual root of all other letters, encompassing in its essence the whole alphabet and hence all other elements of human discourse. To hear the *aleph* is to hear next to nothing; it is the preparation for all audible language, but in itself conveys no determinate, specific meaning. (*KS* 29–30)

To Scholem, the rabbi of Rymanov's interpretation was a daring transformation of the meaning of the revelation on Sinai into a "mystical revelation pregnant with infinite meaning, but without specific meaning" (30). This implied that only through translation into human language could it become the foundation of religious authority; thus the statements on which religious authority are grounded would ultimately be human interpretations of this other transcendent inarticulate sound (31).

The key point is that Scholem's explanation makes the concrete particulars of revelation (e.g., legislation, ritual, commandments, narrative description) already mediated and derivative—human interpretations. The "imperative" aspect to language or the Word of God would not then constitute any direct prescription for action but would rather imply the endless solicitation of that inarticulate voice or pure language. In another late essay, "Reflections on Jewish Theology," Scholem discussed the freedom of interpretation this position implies: "Only through the medium of infinite refraction can the infinite turn into the finite word, and even then it lends to such a word a depth which goes far beyond anything representing a specific meaning, a communication with other beings" (*JJC* 278).

But if the holiness of a text is its *capacity* to be opened up symbolically to infinite interpretation rather than any concrete positive content, then what is the difference between certain secular texts which have a similar capacity by virtue of the nature of language itself, and sacred scriptures? Or what would invalidate Benjamin's mode of naturalizing these capacities in language or searching for what Benjamin called "profane illuminations," or exploiting this potential in an analysis of profane rather than sacred texts? As Adorno so perceptively wrote of Benjamin:

> He transposed the idea of the sacred text into the sphere of the Enlightenment, into which, according to Scholem, Jewish mysticism itself tends to culminate dialectically. His "essayism" consists in reading profane texts as though they were sacred. This does not mean that he clung to theological relics, or as the religious socialists, endowed the profane with transcendent significance. Rather, he looked to radical defenseless profanation as the only chance for the theological heritage which squandered itself in profanity. (*Prisms* 234)

Adorno is referring here to Scholem's famous and controversial thesis that the Sabbatian heresy, which exacerbated the tensions between concrete law and the amorphous dissolution of all meaning, and which took certain kabbalistic ideas to radical antinomian extremes, was itself a covert source of the Jewish Enlightenment and Reform movement.[5] Some critics have claimed that Scholem's own intense interest in Sabbatianism and the antinomian aspects of Kabbalah "expressed an essential aspect of his relation to Judaism's historical predicament in his own day. Perhaps he found in Kabbalistic antinomianism an internal echo, or even an internal affirmation, of the modern Jew's rebellion against diasporic Judaism" (Schweid 31).

Nevertheless, Scholem's portrayal of the kabbalistic view of language has become an attractive model for many contemporary writers and poets, especially those in search of alternate and revolutionary traditions. The concept of revelation as a kind of contentless transparency that does not consist of concrete communications, but instead legitimates an infinite number of different interpretations, has certain parallels with the post-structuralist insistence on the noncentered play of signifiers, the endlessness of interpretation, the mediation of all reality through language, and the deep antinomian strain in writers such as Barthes, Derrida, and Foucault. The idea of a text open to endless human mediations, no one of which could claim authority over the others, and all of which are only fragmentary, also allows for an "anarchic" potential of meaning. "Infinite refraction" is the ongoing tradition of interpretation, of which Scholem's own historical-philological criticism becomes a secular equivalent.

At the end of his essay on the linguistic theory of the Kabbalah, Scholem again summarizes the central point of his entire review: for the kabbalists, the name of God, the original source of all language, "has no 'meaning' in the traditional understanding of the term. It has no concrete signification."[6] What, then, does this conclusion imply about the idea of revelation when the Torah is taken to be the manifestation of the name of God? Although without meaning, this name is that which "enables meaning to be given. It is this element which endows every other form of meaning, though it has no meaning itself." Scholem describes the consequence in a highly speculative and poetic manner which echoes certain elegiac phrases from Benjamin's essay on Kafka:

> The word of God is infinitely liable to interpretation, and it is reflected in our own language. Its radiation or sounds, which we catch, are not so much communications as appeals. That which has meaning—sense and form—is not this word itself, but the tradition behind this word, its communication and reflection in time. This tradition, which has its own dialectic, goes through certain changes and is eventually delivered in a soft, panting whisper. (194)

The essay concludes with the quotation which is the epigraph of the previous chapter, describing the hollowness of our present time in which this tradition has fallen silent. This, he claims, is *our* crisis of language, a language from which God has withdrawn, and the only ones able to find an answer about the worth of this language, to "hear the echo of that vanished word of the creation in the immanence of the world," are the poets—for it is they who still "believe in language as an absolute, which is as if constantly flung open by dialectics," and it is their belief in the mystery of language which must now be heard (194). In these final words, Scholem departs from his role as magisterial, objective historian, and his own implicit theology appears via a linguistic theory strongly marked by his relationship with Benjamin and romantic philosophy.

In sum, Scholem's overall schema of linguistic explanation and description comes not so much from a "critical-historical philology" but from a philosophic framework rooted in German romanticism, aesthetics, and Benjamin's formulations on philosophy of language. Or, one could look at it in another way: Benjamin and Scholem "secularized" a kabbalistic or mystical theory of language (as did other German romantic writers), then established it as a philosophical critical category, then applied that category as the criterion by which to interpret *all* other manifestations of language.

THREE

The Legacy of German Idealism

The purely material and this absolute spiritual are the poles of the satanic realm.
(Benjamin, *OGTD* 230)

What made for this "elective affinity" between Kabbalah and the traditions of German idealism and romanticism? Moshe Idel points out that Nachman Krochmal and M. Landauer, Scholem's early nineteenth-century Jewish predecessors in academic kabbalistic scholarship, actually became interested in the study of the Kabbalah "under the aegis of German idealism, which, as we now know, was sometimes influenced by Kabbalistic thought via the Swabian Pietists" (*Kabbalah* 8). Jürgen Habermas has also noted how the Kabbalah was itself a covert source of German idealism where the "spirit of Jewish mysticism lives in a hidden way." Transmitted through the Christian Kabbalah and thinkers such as Boehme and Schelling, Jewish mysticism was absorbed into Protestant German idealism (*Philosophical Profiles* 21, 38).[1]

Benjamin and Scholem's problems in relating the absolute and the concrete, the totality and the fragment, the spiritual and material, and the very terms which they used to frame their discussions came from the legacy of German philosophic idealism. In another of Scholem's "Unhistorical Aphorisms" on the Kabbalah, he wrote: "the conception of the Kabbalists as mystical materialists with a dialectical tendency would certainly be thoroughly unhistorical, yet anything but meaningless" (Biale, "Ten Aphorisms" 76). This statement refers especially to the concept of *tzimtzum* developed by the great sixteenth-century kabbalist R. Isaac Luria. Lurianic Kabbalah proposes that God created the universe not through an expansion but through "contraction" (*tzimtzum*). In order for there to be "room" for a finite universe, God had to "withdraw," so to speak, into Himself, "contract" His infinity. In the empty space which then resulted, God created the universe from this contracted "point." The material world thus results from a "dialectical" process of divine withdrawal and return.

In Lurianic Kabbalah, the idea of creation through the divine self-contraction or self-exile of God effectively explained the power and impenetrability of matter. Yet it also showed how matter retained a divine potency and claimed that humanity's role was to redeem the material realm by reuniting it with its divine source. Habermas sees here a source for the key idea from Benjamin through Bloch that "matter is in need of redemption" through human praxis ("German Idealism" 39). The Jewish brand of German idealism from Rosenzweig to Adorno thus "produces the ferment of a critical utopia" (42), and the varying interpretations of the creative or apocalyptic role of the negative lead in several possible directions: to a materialistic dialectic of nature as in Schelling, Hegel, and Marx; to a revolutionary theory of history; and to the nihilism of a postrevolutionary enlightenment (*Philosophical Profiles* 209). Moreover, Habermas argues, many of the great German-Jewish philosophers of the late nineteenth and early twentieth centuries (such as Benjamin and Rosenzweig) elaborated and critiqued idealism from the standpoint of language, for idealism had condemned language and "elevated a divinized art as its substitute" ("German Idealism" 24).

To "translate" kabbalistic schemas into philosophical terms: If creation occurs through God's "self-negation" or withdrawal, the Becoming of the world would result from the passage of Being through Nothing. The nature of this "nothing" is the critical issue: Is it an absence which, as total emptiness, is a source of evil, a self-division in God, and so the source of all rupture in the world? Or is it merely a "veiling" or "hiding" of God's unbroken plenitude and goodness? Was it "literal" or "metaphorical?" What would God's "absence" imply? Was Luria really anticipating Hegel by several centuries? And what is the role of language in all this? What is the relation of the human language to the Names of God or the divine language which is an expression of God's essence? What role does the Nothing have in the connection or disconnection between God's language and human language?

To quote once again the ninth of Scholem's "Ten Unhistorical Aphorisms": Scholem writes, "Totalities [*Ganzheiten*] can be communicated only in occult fashion. The Name of God can be pronounced but cannot be expressed, for only that which is fragmentary makes language expressible. The 'true' language cannot be spoken, just as the absolutely concrete cannot be realized" (86–87). This statement is again reminiscent of Benjamin's early philosophy of language, and of his continued "philosophy of fragmentation" later applied through "historical materialism" to the "language" of the ruins of history and cultural objects. In the later Benjamin, one way to deal with these forces of fragmentation was to adopt them, try to use them against themselves, and so break through and release the energies of redemption.

We return to the contradictory meanings of "pure language." Is this realm "beyond" all concrete meaning a nihilistic voiding or messianic redemption? Are these indeed the only alternatives? And why does Scholem insist on defining this otherness or "beyond" or depth in language as "meaningless," using Benjaminian language such as the "extinguishing" of all meaning to imply a nihilistic propensity at the heart of kabbalistic theology? Is this a projection of anachronistic philosophical and literary categories onto the theology of the Jewish mystics?

The idea of a "negation" within God has also been attractive to certain contemporary writers such as Derrida and Jabès who take this idea to mean a literal withdrawal of God—a negativity or rupture in God that engenders the free play of language.[2] The "abyss" becomes a nonhuman emptiness—language's own immanent self-critique rather than its "depth" as divine plenitude in Jabès. "God's questioning of God" becomes identified with the linguistic self-reflexivity of the poet, an empty space which produces the space of literature, of words suspended in a void, questions without answers.

For Scholem, this question about the nature of the material world and its dialectical relation to the spiritual also involved at bottom the question of language—or what under the sway of romantic philosophy he calls the "symbolic" nature of language. On one level, he notes that Kabbalah uses quite "materialistic language" such as "contraction" to speak about God. And there are also the complex kabbalistic descriptions of God's *sefirot*, i.e., God's instruments, attributes, manifestations, creative powers, which are thought to form the very structure of the universe as macrocosm to microcosm. These *sefirot* are often described in highly anthropomorphic terms as the "body of the King." In another of his unhistorical aphorisms, Scholem writes: "The materialist language of the Lurianic Kabbalah, especially in its deduction of the *tzimtzum* (the self-contraction of God), gives rise to the thought as to whether the symbolism that uses such imagery and modes of discourse could not be the reality itself" (76–77). David Biale aptly sums up the issue here: "Does a mystical, symbolic language merely 'represent' its subject or is the language an essential part of the 'thing itself'? (77). In other words, what is the ontological status of this language, and what is the ontological status of the empty space, the Nothing?

Moshe Idel notes, however, that the "central theme characterizing the history of the *sefirotic* concepts is the vacillation between infradivine and extradivine theories, just as the history of philosophy is marked by the philosophical theories on the existence of ideas *within* or *outside* of the divine mind" (*Kabbalah* 137). In other words, there were several alternative descriptions and definitions of the *sefirot*: one was that they were part of the divine nature and partook of the divine essence; another was that they were nondivine in essence but the immediate *instruments* of God in creating and maintaining the world—or the *vessel* for transmitting the divine influence; another was that they were the immanent element of divinity's emanation within created reality; and still another was that they were a process taking place within the individual being and psychology of the human person (137).

But Idel stresses that the *sefirot*, above all, were aspects of a dynamic process of God's relation to the world and the reciprocal human activity of relating the world to the divine through various theurgic or contemplative

actions. The goal in all of these discussions of the *sefirot* was not meditation on the "symbol" itself but rather the deciphering and experiencing
of the ever-changing configurations of divine dynamic processes and relations. In theosophical-theurgic Kabbalah, the gap between humanity and
God was breached through ritual and commandment, through *halakah*.
For the Spanish kabbalist Abulafia, the *sefirot* were internalized and psy-
chologized, and the aim of interpreting the *sefirot* was to achieve divine
union and ecstatic experience.

In sum, the key question was not the ontological status of the *symbol*,
definable either as the static "essence" of the thing *or* as its "representation." That very way of framing the question assumes a Platonic Western
metaphysics. Idel argues that such a distorted view of Kabbalah as primarily a "speculative theosophy" in harmony with other ancient esoteric
philosophies was a result of the mediation of Kabbalah through the Neo-
Platonism of Renaissance hermetic thought, and then again through the
Christian Kabbalah. These adaptations focused solely on the *speculative*
aspects of Jewish mysticism and detached it from its intrinsic connections
to Jewish law and ritual, and only this detached speculative theosophy was
passed on and of interest to later German idealism—which likewise denigrated Jewish law.

Scholem also wrote about Kabbalah as primarily a theosophy, and that
is reflected especially in his view of Kabbalah as preeminently the expression of a "symbolic" mode of thinking. As we have seen, diminishing the
theurgic and ecstatic components of Kabbalah and the role of the commandments then led to a loss of content, or set of active referents of this
"symbolic" language. In Scholem's view, the ultimate word was "meaningless" though giving rise to infinite meaning; the "Nothing" led to an
anarchic plurality of interpretation, to an upsurge of myth, and religious
vitality, and so forth.

Moreover, although the Kabbalah might at times have adopted some of
the vocabulary of Western metaphysics, the terms were applied to quite
different processes. The "Nothing" in Luria's idea of the *tzimtzum* (the
contraction of God in the process of creation) was not the negation of
the finite world but its *activation*. In other words, if the central issue is the
ontological status of the *sefira* itself, and not the *sefira as symbol*, the key
question is not whether language is *either* representation *or* reality. It is,
instead, whether reality is to be defined as relational and dynamic or as
fixed and static. A Western philosophical vocabulary of "essence" and
"existence," of "dialectic" and "negation" applied to Kabbalah is inadequate and misleading. The problematic of "translating" Western spirituality into Western conceptuality is also at the heart of Levinas's work, and I
will discuss it in part II of this book.

Benjamin also struggled with the question of how to employ the vocabulary of German idealism in the preface to his book on the German tragic
drama. There Benjamin defined truth as a "constellation" of ideas, a rela-

tional configuration—analogous to Rosenzweig's great figure in *The Star of Redemption*. It is interesting to note that Luria also used the astronomical image to describe a dynamic, relational reality. This figure governs his image of interpretation of the *Zohar*, a preeminent kabbalistic book. Writes Luria:

> The worlds change each and every hour, and there is no hour which is similar to another. And whoever contemplates the movements of the planets and stars, and the changes of their positions and constellation and how their stand changes in a moment . . . will understand the changes of the constellations and the position of the [supernal] worlds, which are the garments of *Eiyn Sof* . . . and in accordance with these changes are the aspects of the sayings of the book of the *Zohar* changing, and all are words of the living God. (*Etz Hayyim* I, I, 5, 15a, qtd. in Idel, *Kabbalah* 248)

The supernal worlds are no static essences but are constantly in flux and in a reciprocal relation with human activity; and this continuous flux reciprocally affects human interpretation of the Kabbalah itself—the *Zohar*. As Idel puts it, "Thus, even theoretically, the possibility of attaining its 'ultimate' significance is nil; each moment brings its own novel understanding" (248). The plurality of meaning, then, comes not from any inherent fragmentary nature of language, nor from its ultimate emptiness, nor from its symbolic nature, but from the infinitely changing dynamic process of the divine life and the human active relation to it.[3]

JEWISH LAW AND GERMAN IDEALISM

Another important effect of the legacy of German idealism in the relation between Benjamin and Scholem was the way in which Jewish law had been perceived in the great systems of Kant and Hegel. Nathan Rotenstreich has well described how the evaluation of Jewish thought by German philosophers took place in the context of the heated debate over Jewish emancipation and the political and social status of Jews in Germany. This "evaluation" of Judaism was related to the question of whether or not Jews "merited" citizenship (*Jews and German* vii). Jewish philosophers, in turn, often presented Judaism in such a way as to bolster the argument for their inclusion in the modern state; these were part of the apologetics Scholem so detested.

The attitudes of Kant and Hegel laid the basic groundwork for the successive debates. Kant's distinction between legality and morality assigned an inferior role to the observance of duties due to an externally commanded law (i.e., to authority and heteronomy), as opposed to those observed out of inner conviction (i.e., reason and autonomy), or for their "own sake." Kant viewed Judaism as an inferior and purely statutory religion of heteronomous law. The problem for Kant's philosophy, then, was how to find an ethical system grounded in the autonomy of reason, but one that still allowed room for God. How could free, self-guided reason relate to divine revelation or command?

As Rotenstreich aptly puts it, reason for Kant is "an equivalent or transformed version of grace" (58). Protestant Christianity, with its emphasis on inner grace and illumination, would be the philosophically "superior" religion in this schema, and so Kant fully accepted Christianity's proclamation that it had superseded Judaism. He thought that the establishment of the moral system of his philosophy would likewise inevitably bring about the dissolution of Judaism, or its "euthanasia," as Kant so unfelicitously put it (3–5).[4]

In Hegel's philosophy, universal history was conceived as the "dialectic of the Spirit," alienated from itself on its long journey, and then ultimately returning to itself in the consummation of Absolute Knowledge. For Hegel, Judaism represented a partial and antithetical stage in the dialectic, a negative moment, that of the *separation* or alienation between God and humanity, and between the spiritual principle and nature. On the one hand, Hegel recognized in this separation the source of a certain religious "sublime" in the contemplation of the vast gulf between divine infinity and human finitude. Such contemplation motivates a deep religious experience of fear, trust, and obedience to the law in great figures such as Abraham and Job. On the other hand, Hegel asserts that Judaism, unlike Christianity, is not a "universal religion" and so is rightfully historically "sublated" into Christianity. Christianity brings about a new stage of the reconciliation of the spirit and world, mediating through the figure of Jesus the divine and human realms, concretizing divine infinity within finite human particularity, and transforming human finitude. The continuing existence of the Jews after Christianity again becomes an anachronism and a puzzle.

Hegel and Kant, of course, had highly distorted views of Judaism and little direct access to the wealth of Jewish tradition, especially in its postbiblical phases, but their discourse set the terms of the discussion. Kant and Hegel never understood Judaism "from the inside" in its positive forms. As thinkers immersed in German Protestant culture, they implicitly accepted the Pauline theology of Judaism as a religion of harsh and untenable law, and Christianity as the consummation of grace, freedom, and salvation—even when they were engaged in transforming Christian theology into Enlightenment or phenomenological philosophy. Ongoing, living, Jewish historical existence had no place in their systems. The Jews' continuing presence on the world stage could be explained only as an expression of a primitive tribal consciousness, or of stubbornness, or the remnants of an inferior, anachronistic, rigid, and sterile religion frozen in time.[5]

The literal Jew in the flesh and in history, with a concrete text, *present*, willing, existing, continuing, surviving, was a problem for traditional Christian theology and the philosophies which emanated from it. A standard ancient Christian theological response to the puzzle of the continued existence of the Jews after the arrival of Christ was to make the Jews into a sign and witness—an allegory—to the perils and punishments of those who would reject salvation. In Kant and Hegel as well, there were philosophical "allegories" of the Jew as another figure of negativity. Allegorizing the figure of the Jew can be another way to deny the Jew any positive existence.

Even today, one finds in many of the most "postmodern" anti-Hegelian thinkers such as Blanchot, Derrida, Jabès, or Kristeva an identification of the Jew with the principle of "negativity." In much of this contemporary literary theory, the Jew often comes to represent an ahistorical "textual principle" of gap, abyss, negativity in God, external exile, wandering meaning, self-reflexive and endless questioning without any living, concrete, historical presence or inheritance of a physical homeland.

Scholem well recognized the danger of "allegorizing the Jews" in the last letter he ever wrote to Benjamin. Benjamin had asked Scholem's opinion of Frankfurt School theorist Max Horkheimer's essay "The Jews and Europe," which had been written as an exhortation addressed to the Jews in the Second World War. Scholem wrote a scathing critique:

> . . . the Jews interest him not *as Jews*, but only from the standpoint of the fate of the economic category they represent for him—as "agents of circulation." . . . he has no *answer* of any kind [to the question of what Europe would be like after the expulsion and destruction of the Jews] to give to the Jews on whose behalf he does not even *ask*—except for the facile final phase with the horrible allegorization of monotheism, which has nothing to say to the *unallegorizable* Jew and *his* concerns with mankind [italics his]. (February 1940; Corr 265)

One reason the Jewish reformers in the nineteenth century had insisted on a *historical* approach to Judaism had been to demonstrate Judaism's continuing positive validity by showing how it, too, was "historical" in the Hegelian way; by showing that Judaism also welcomed change and had been transformed. This capacity for change would now make it convertible into a modern and acceptable religion, one which did not conflict with the goals of social emancipation for the Jews (Rotenstreich, *Jews* 89–91). Scholem's polemic against the "Science of Judaism" was a reaction to the excesses of this historicism and the implicit liquidation of Jewish existence in the German-Jewish "symbiosis." Yet he had internalized much of this German culture as well, and his critique of rationalistic historiography and of Jewish apologetics never led him to abandon in his scholarship—as did Benjamin—the critical-historical method he absorbed from the German university. For Scholem, autonomous positive Jewish self-understanding could be guaranteed only by the rebuilding of an independent cultural identity in the land of Israel, and by the Jews' regaining control of their own history.

There remain, however, strong echoes of German romanticism and a certain broad Hegelianism in Scholem's "dialectical" conception of history and his schema of a three-stage historical development of religion—a schema which contrasts strongly with and has no basis in his meticulous critical-philological method of amassing bibliographic facts and excavating the textual history of Jewish mysticism. Mysticism itself can arise only, writes Scholem, at a particular stage in religious consciousness when the "abyss" between humanity and God is felt as an intimate fact of inner consciousness. He then proposes a three-stage theory of religion: "mythical," "classical," and "mystical" (*MT* 7–9). In the first, "mythical," era, humanity is in harmony with the world, and nature is filled with the presence of gods. In this "innocent" stage, the argument goes, there is a sense of the unity of all things, of the directly accessible and immediate presence of the divine prior to the subject-object distinctions of abstract knowledge.

In the second, or "classical," stage, myth is rejected, and humanity's dream of a primary harmony between itself and the universe is shattered. Religion functions to "destroy the dream harmony of Man, Universe, and God," to isolate humanity, and to create a vast abyss between the infinite divinity and the finite creature. The supreme function of religion in its classical stage is to make humanity aware of the otherness and transcendence of God. Scholem identifies this stage with "institutional" religion and the great monotheistic religions in which History instead of Nature becomes the scene of the divine-human relation. Only the commanding voice of God in law-giving revelation and the voice of humanity in prayer cross the abyss.

The third stage is mysticism, which Scholem calls the "romantic period of religion." Mysticism seeks to bridge the abyss between humanity and God without denying or repressing that gap, but searches for a secret path to the old unity. Old mythological elements from the first stage combine with the awareness of the revelations of the second stage and are united "on a new plane," in an experiential but self-reflexive religion. Scholem's schema is similar to Hegel's, wherein a primary unity has moved through alienating division and multiplicity and then returned to a higher unity-in-multiplicity. Compare the following quotation from Hegel's *Logic*:

> In its instinctive and natural stage, spiritual life wears the garb of innocence and confiding simplicity: but the very essence of spirit implies the absorption of this immediate condition in something higher. The spiritual . . . sunders itself to self-realization. But this position of severed life has in its turn to be suppressed, and the spirit has by its own act to win its way to concord again. (Qtd. in Abrams 221)

In Scholem's schema, mysticism effects that reconciliation. It infuses creation, revelation, and redemption with new meanings that revitalize but often strain the limits of the old beliefs, and when these strains push the old forms and beliefs farther than institutional religion allows, mysticism often is transformed into heresy (*MT* 7–9). As in Hegel, this tripartite schema identifies the classic formulations of Jewish monotheism and law with a stage of alienation and priestly institutionalism; mysticism, by contrast, transforms God "from an object of dogmatic knowledge into a novel and living experience and intuition" (10). Rabbinic Judaism, the "creation of the diaspora," implicitly becomes an inferior stage; Zionism and mystical reinterpretation implicitly become its dialectical sublations.

Eliezer Schweid has pointed out the schema's many historical inaccuracies and philosophical difficulties and argues that Scholem employs "such general concepts as 'dialectic' and 'paradox' to resolve the tensions that emerge between his historical findings and his presuppositions regarding the essence of mysticism and its role in Judaism" (89, n. 72). David Biale puts Scholem's three-stage schema in the context of debates in Jewish historiography and Scholem's disputes with the historian Heinrich Graetz and with Leo Baeck, who had coined the term *romantic religion* but used it negatively. Biale also writes that Scholem comes close here to accepting the Christian assumptions about the repressive nature of Jewish legal institutions, and argues that Scholem's three-stage schema might also have a source in Molitor, the great Christian kabbalist whom Scholem and Benjamin both greatly admired; Molitor saw Kabbalah as the "third stage" in Jewish history (*Scholem* 119–27).[6]

Idel adds to the controversy by arguing that Scholem's assumptions of a rabbinic Judaism which at first triumphed over and freed itself of myth and mysticism, and then was later penetrated and overcome by an alien nonrabbinical and gnostic Kabbalah all remain to be proved:

> . . . Scholem created a simplistic division between a defeated mythical Gnosticism and a triumphant nonmythical rabbinism . . . one can propose an alternative picture according to which the need to understand the meaning of the central Jewish activity—the commandments—moved the Kabbalists to elaborate upon and reconstruct the implicit myths or theosophies that had once motivated and offered an organic significance to the commandments. In other words, there is no need to divorce *halakhah* from myth in a fundamental way nor to presuppose basic tensions between them. (*Kabbalah* 156–57)

In other words, ancient biblical and rabbinic Judaism preserved many theurgical, theosophical, and mythical motifs in its perception of the commandments which Kabbalah then more intensively elaborated and combined with other philosophic terminologies. The central notion of a *reciprocal* divine-human relation, of the conditioning of divine activity by human acts, is found throughout the Talmud and Midrash, and "the performance of the divine will via the commandments is therefore the means by which man participates in the divine process" (166). The Torah and its commandments are precisely what mediates between the divine and the human realms, and the Torah's "singular nature stems from its capacity to change human acts into theurgical influence" (177). Rosenzweig's intense anti-Hegelianism led him—in contrast to Scholem—to perceive the strength of Jewish thought within the seemingly "ahistorical" world of Jewish ritual life, *halakah*, Talmud, and Midrash. He saw in Judaism a positive and autonomous alternate *philosophical option*, an alternate epistemology.

GERMAN ROMANTICISM AND "SPILT RELIGION": THE SYMBOL

David Biale has also perceptively written that Scholem never systematically articulated his "philosophy of history," but he was essentially "the product of the romantic revision of the *Wissenschaft des Judentums*" that took place in the early twentieth century (*Scholem* 35). Romanticism is an endlessly complex and continuously debated phenomenon, and it is far beyond my scope here to enter into those debates. Yet the overall intermingling of theology, philosophy, materialism, and politics we have been tracing throughout cannot really be considered without some further discussion of the legacy of German romanticism. It plays a great role not only in the thought of Benjamin and Scholem but in the very creation of modernism, of which romanticism is a main undercurrent. In the very thinkers who provided the philosophical matrix of the culture in which Benjamin and Scholem intellectually matured, theology, philosophy of history, aesthetics, and criticism were intensively intermingled.

Benjamin knew the philosophy of the German romantics quite well. His first doctoral dissertation was titled "The Concept of Art Criticism in German Romanticism" (*Der Begriff der Kunskritik in der deutschen Romantik*, 1919). Goethe, Schlegel, Novalis, Fichte, and Hölderlin figure prominently in his work, and he wrote important essays devoted to Goethe and Hölderlin as well.[7] When Benjamin confessed to Scholem that his ambition was "to be considered the preeminent German literary critic" (*Briefe* II: 505), the model of criticism he probably had in mind was initiated by romantic writers for whom criticism had the highest philosophical status.

Benjamin's study of German romanticism was linked to his attempt in his early "Program for the Coming Philosophy" to expand the Kantian ideas of intuition and experience. Romantic notions of art could contribute to his exploration of language as a *cognitive* medium wherein one might glimpse truth, and art as a form of experiencing a higher truth; criticism, as the philosophical apprehension of the art, was a fundamental link. We have also seen, however, that Benjamin was highly critical of those tendencies in romantic thought which had led to the proto-fascist politics of the German Youth movement, and like Scholem he was wary of any attempt at ecstatic direct fusion with the "absolute." Schlegel had propounded the theory of the fragment as a miniature version of the whole, and Benjamin's obsession with truth as a monad, with collage, fragmentation, and rubble, found a precursor there. Despite his intense studies and conversations with Benjamin, Scholem wrote, however, "We hardly ever discussed aesthetic theory, which I had no interest in" (*SF* 67). This may help explain Scholem's seemingly uncritical and naive application of certain German romantic aesthetic categories to his studies of Kabbalah. Indeed, Scholem's invocation of "dialectic" and "paradox" as explanatory *historical* categories is directly linked to this romanticism. These are not the categories of "objective science" but modes of thinking which come from the realm of philosophy, literature, myth, and religion. Scholem's three-stage schema is itself reminiscent of the biblical myth of a fall from a paradisal unity with God into exile, albeit with the promise of future return and redemption in a transfigured heaven and earth, a new unity.

M. H. Abrams has argued that it was this very Judaeo-Christian myth which became displaced and transfigured in romantic literature. Traditional religious categories such as the relation of "creator and creation" were now reformulated as the relation of "subject and object" or "ego and non-ego" or "human consciousness and nature" (*Natural* 12–13). Romanticism, that is, at its heart assimilated and reinterpreted theological ideas and ways of thinking into a secular world-view.[8] (Fichte, Schelling, Hegel, and Hölderlin had all been university students of theology.) Just as Benjamin had interpreted the Genesis text to be a tale about the fall from a primal unity of the pure language of names into alienated human language, Hegel and Schelling used it to illustrate the fall into the alienating separation of subjective consciousness from nature and the objective world.

In Hegel's philosophy of history, the biblical plot of creation, fall, and redemption is transformed into the theodicy of the Spirit. Or as Abrams puts it, "This retention of traditional Christian concepts and the traditional Christian plot, but demythologized, conceptualized, and with all-Controlling Providence converted into a 'logic' or dialectic that controls all the interactions of subject and object, gives its distinctive character and design to what we call 'Romantic Philosophy' "(91). Evil, suffering and alienation are a necessary part of what Hegel calls in the *Phenomenology* the "Golgotha of the absolute Spirit." History is the painful process of the Spirit's self-education and coming to self-knowledge, a spiraling journey which ends by recovering in maturity an earlier stage of unity with itself and the world. But the teleology is now *immanent*, not aimed at an external goal or driven by a God who is "outside" history and nature, but by the self-moving, self-sustaining "system," the manifestation of the "Idea," which generates its own opposites out of itself. For Hegel, the culmination of this journey of self-knowledge lies in his own philosophy—which thus marks the "end of philosophy," philosophy completed and fulfilled in German Idealism and the Prussian state, which he identifies with the manifestation of universal history and reason.[9]

The artist and art were paradigmatic models for this "organic" auto-formation. *Poiesis* was the process of making, of "formative" power, or the power of form (*Bilden*), and thus the artist becomes the "educator" of humanity, and philosophy a *Bildungsroman*, a story of self-education. Art and philosophy become mutually identified. Or as David Miles writes, Hegel "anticipated a time when literature would become so inner and self-conscious that it would actually be absorbed into philosophy, in an act of self-transcendence (something already transpiring among those herme-neuts [*sic*] and deconstructors who would totally absorb literature into their own philosophical texts)" (24).

In the corresponding aesthetic, the poet now became the visionary seer and assumed the role of the prophet in proclaiming and envisioning the new redeemed world—art took over the role religion had played in provid-ing a means to regenerate humanity and the world. Aesthetic cognition (via imagination and symbol) would enable a new merger of mind and nature. Schiller introduced the central romantic concept of art as that which can heal the divisions and fragments of a broken civilization; the aesthetic became the principle of integration, harmony, and reconciling unity in beauty. Nietzsche and Schopenhauer, of course, followed this trend of as-signing a redemptive role to art. T. E. Hulme, in a famous phrase, summed it up well when he defined romanticism as "spilt religion."

It is important to add that this transformation in the relation of philoso-phy to art, literature, and criticism was also a response to the problems Kant had opened in his work about the conditions of possibility of philo-sophical knowledge. Like Benjamin, the romantics were attempting to deal with the legacy of Kant's critique of philosophy, and his separation of the "phenomenal" realm from the ultimately unknowable "noumenal" realm, and the gap left between the bounded individual's subjectivity and the apprehension of the unity of the whole. The work of art and aesthetic judgment might be a bridge between these realms where other modes of cognition were bound to fail. Art might be a locus wherein the absolute manifested itself in the world, and in this sense it became a kind of substi-tute religion.

We have seen the *romantic sublime*, the sense of the infinite and abso-lute as the unbounded and unattainable but necessary aim of finite human-ity's endless strivings, echoed in the early Benjamin and Scholem's ideas about the "pure language" as contentless, formless, unbounded, and unat-tainable. We have seen it as well in Scholem's descriptions of the absolute revelation as beyond all expression—meaningless yet the source of all fi-nite meaning. When the "absolute" is definable only by its lack of all forms and concretion, it can then be articulated only through fragments, or "symbols."

SCHOLEM AND SYMBOL

> If we had to condense the romantic aes-
> thetic into a single word, it would certainly
> be the word "symbol." (Todorov 199)

Eliezer Schweid has astutely noted that the allegory/symbol distinction runs throughout Scholem's work and "has the status of a methodological principle" (43, n. 41). Nathan Rotenstreich likewise has observed that "symbolism, on the one hand, and the denial of the *unio mystica* and pantheism, on the other, seem to be the two correlated axes, comprising as it were, the epistemological and ontological components, respectively, of Scholem's interpretive work" ("Symbolism" 605). Idel adds that Scholem was far too categorical in his assertions about the pervasiveness of kabbalistic symbolism and, moreover, that *unio mystica* was in fact an aim of the ecstatic mode of Kabbalah (*Kabbalah* 201–202). Symbolism was important for the nonunitive theosophical Kabbalah, but ecstatic Kabbalah was interested in direct unitive experience of God through possession of the human intellect by the divine. In Abulafia, for example, these unitive experiences were expressed in *allegorical* rather than symbolic modes. Abulafia himself was opposed to the theosophical form of Kabbalah and its doctrine of the ten *sefirot*, or divine potencies which were aspects of God's essence and instruments in creation, and whose reality was expressed through symbols. For a more philosophically inclined kabbalist such as Abulafia, "symbols substituted for precise definitions" and showed lack of clear thought and experience rather than any mysterious communication of the incommunicable (201–202).

When Scholem defines kabbalistic linguistics preeminently as an expression of the "*symbolic* nature of language," and identifies the symbol as that which paradoxically tries to communicate the incommunicable, he implicitly adopts the romantic ideology of the symbol, which is by no means a "scientific critical-philological category." The symbol is a literary term of variable meaning; in Scholem's use, it contains the very *theology* of German romantic criticism. Scholem applies it, however, as if it were some "objective" category in his historiography.

The strict opposition of allegory and symbol was invented by the romantics as one way of legitimating their own philosophy. Again, we must go back to Kant, whose *Critique of Pure Reason* had pointed to the necessity of some third term to reconcile reason and sensibility, for the ideas of reason are not presentable in intuitive form. For Kant, the symbol could be a partial link between reason and sensibility, because symbolic apprehension was intuitive and sense-based; a symbol was not merely a sign of mathematical or abstract reason. In the *Critique of Judgement*, Kant thus gave a new meaning to the "symbolic." Prior to that, *symbol* had no special status and was often interchangeable with words such as *sign, allegory, emblem*, and so forth.

In the further development of this notion, the infinite was said to appear "symbolically," in images, in signs, in poetic language, but not directly through logic. Romantic aesthetics was permeated with a nostalgia for some lost, prior organic unity or "totality" of being [*ganzheit*] which would be restored dialectically after a process of self-division, alienation, and fragmentation; the symbol was the means to repair the breach. Artistic

representation, particularly the symbol, becomes the form wherein the absolute could be experienced and realized in some unmediated way. To the
symbol was attributed the power to overcome the gap between the noumenal and phenomenal realms, the finite and the infinite, the material and
the spiritual, sensibility and reason.

Whereas Kant's "thing in-itself" was ultimately unknowable, the "symbol" acquired the property of being a thing-in-itself, autonomous, self-
contained in its own existence, yet at the same pointing to something else.
As Lacoue-Labarthe and Nancy put it, for Schelling and Schlegel,

> art, the work, and the artist are in this perspective what the System, the Con-
> cept, and the philosopher himself . . . are in the Hegelian perspective. . . . the
> religion in question here is not "religion within the limits of reason alone,"
> but rather *religion within the limits of art.* . . . For this reason, the great ques-
> tion of religion understood in this manner is that of the *formation of form.* (77)

Of course, form and formlessness are the categories Scholem uses to describe mystical experience—part of this romantic legacy in which the symbol is that which places the finite in immediate relation to formless
absolute truth.

We shall see later how Benjamin, in an antiromantic reaction, attacked
the ideology of the symbol (which he called "bad theology") and the organic whole so prevalent in German idealist aesthetics. Benjamin instead
resurrected "allegory" as a fundamental epistemological and linguistic category for this "otherness" in language. Allegory was faithful to the ruins,
the losses, the pains of mortality; it did not disguise or repress them in a
"symbolic transformation." David Miles observes that Adorno, like Benjamin, recognized the relation of these myths of organicism to irrational and
reactionary political forces, and refused the optimistic Hegelian synthesis
for a "negative dialectics" which the Marxist critic Georg Lukács sardoni-
cally called the "Grand Hotel Abyss" (Miles 30).[10]

Goethe's speculations on the difference between allegory and symbol
were the locus classicus for what became the conventional romantic notion. Roughly speaking, the symbol was characterized as natural, intransitive, immediately intuitable, existing in and for itself as well as for what it
signifies; it was an indirect expression of the inexpressible, a passage from
the particular to the general via *participation* of the ideal in the object.
Allegory, by contrast, was characterized as mechanical, external, arbitrary,
utilitarian, and rational, a transmission of an intellectual meaning which
dispenses with the object once it has been used to convey the meaning; a
mode which seeks the general *through* the particular rather than *in* the
particular. This distinction reflects the older debate over the nature of
language: whether language was conventional and arbitrary, or natural and
organic—a mechanism or a medium, directly connected to the knowledge
of things, or only to ideas the mind has about things.

Goethe thought of the symbol as a higher mode of knowledge and defined it as that which constitutes the properly poetic—an immediate intuitive grasp of the particular which unconsciously yields the general as well. The idea of the general thus becomes conscious after the fact. Allegory, by contrast, was said to begin with the general idea and search for a particular to embody it. Goethe further differentiated between the "concept" imaged in allegory and the "idea" imaged in the symbol. Whereas the concept is "bounded" within the allegorical image (i.e., allegorical meaning is finite, complete, dead), the idea is "unbounded" in the symbol; meaning is infinite and inexpressible, ever active and living. An infinite, inexpressible, and unbounded meaning generates endless interpretation. Writes Goethe, "Symbolism transforms the phenomenon into an idea, the idea into an image, and in such a way that the idea remains always infinitely active and unapproachable in the image, and even if expressed in all languages, still would remain inexpressible" (*Maxims and Reflections* no. 1113, qtd. in Todorov 204–205).

This romanticist distinction between allegory and symbol is wholly taken over by Scholem, becoming in his analysis a further contrast between rationalist Jewish *philosophy*, which he identifies with an allegorical mode of thought, and Jewish *mysticism*, which he maintains is essentially *symbolic*. In his definitions of allegory and symbolism, allegory and philosophy are clearly devalued as modes of apprehending truth. Jewish philosophers, he writes, discovered truths of metaphysics or ethics "outside the sphere of religion" and projected them back upon the older Holy Scriptures. The philosopher converts "the concrete realities of Judaism into a bundle of abstractions. . . . By contrast, the mystic refrains from destroying the living texture of religious narrative by allegorizing it" and instead thinks symbolically (*MT* 26). Allegory is associated with the "death" of the text, symbolism with its life and vitality. Allegory, continues Scholem, arises from the *gap* between form and meaning; in allegory everything can represent everything else—that which is allegorized loses its own meaning and becomes a vehicle of another meaning. Although this lack of inherent connection between form and meaning does lead to a certain "infinity of meaning" as an infinite network of correlations, Scholem characterizes allegory as "immanent" in contrast to the kind of "transcendence" glimpsed in the symbol. (We shall see that precisely these characteristics of allegory are valorized by deMan and used to define his mode of deconstructive reading; in this, he was inspired by Benjamin and followed Benjamin's *inversion* of the priority of symbol over allegory.)

One of Scholem's central assumptions is that in essence the mystical experience is formless; as such, it can take on limitless forms through symbolic representations. The symbol is "the means of expressing an experience that is in itself expressionless" (*KS* 22), and so becomes a kind of magical mediator between form and formlessness, finite and infinite, the manifest and the indistinct, private experience and public expression. Yet

Scholem notes that Jewish mysticism contrasts strikingly with other forms of religious mysticism in its reticence to use descriptions of personal mystical experience; and despite its immersion in "formless experience," it retains a metaphysically positive attitude toward language as the instrument of God (*MT* 15). Through symbolic reinterpretation of the Torah, the mystic is able to transcend history and reach toward the absolute:

> It is one of the main functions of religious symbols to preserve the vitality of religious experience in a traditional, conservative milieu. The richness of meaning they seem to emanate lends new life to tradition, which is always in danger of freezing into dead forms—and this process continues until the symbols themselves die or change. (*KS* 22)

The symbol, he asserts, is "a form of expression which radically transcends the sphere of allegory," for in the mystical symbol that ultimate reality which is formless and shapeless "becomes transparent and, as it were, visible, through the medium of another reality which clothes its content with visible and expressible meaning, as for example the cross for the Christian."[11] Whereas allegory treats the object it allegorizes as if it were an "empty shell," the object which becomes a symbol "retains its original form and its original content. . . . in itself, through its own existence, it makes another reality transparent which cannot appear in any other form" (27). So Scholem is making a clear *metaphysical* and *ontological* distinction between allegory and symbol, and an ontological claim about symbols which is a corollary of his view of the ontological status of language. This distinction reflects the romantic ideology which itself had theologized the symbol to try to repair the breach opened by Kant's theory of knowledge. Allegory, he adds, is the "representation of an expressible something by another expressible something"; the mystical symbol is the "expressible representation for something which lies beyond the sphere of expression and communication, something which comes from a sphere whose face is, as it were, turned inward and away from us." The symbol, in other words, reflects "true transcendence"; allegory does not. Thus the symbol/allegory distinction is a crucial element in Scholem's three stages of religion theory wherein mysticism, via symbolic reinterpretation, is the healing third stage which bridges the abyss or gap between humanity and the divine.

Yet what is the nature of the "beyond" or transcendence to which symbols give access? In words which again echo the idea of the meaninglessness of the ultimate pure word, Scholem writes, "The symbol 'signifies' nothing and communicates nothing, but makes something transparent which is beyond all expression." In describing the symbol as "transparent," as signifying nothing, Scholem, like Coleridge, inadvertently blurs the distinction with allegory. For it was in allegory that the material object is "emptied" of its natural meaning, whereas in the symbol, the very materiality of the figure retained its independence. Scholem then appeals to the category of time to distinguish the two modes: whereas allegory arduously uncovers different layers of meaning, the symbol can be apprehended only instantaneously and completely, or not at all; it is a "momentary totality," perceived intuitively in a "mystical now" in which subject and object merge (*MT* 27). The symbol thus allows the inexpressible and infinite to shine through the finite without demolishing it.

In effect, the symbol itself has here become an agent of redemption, itself theologized in that high romantic displacement of philosophy and theology into aesthetics. This notion of a fluctuating relation between the form of the symbol and the formless, infinite, inexpressible reality it conveys mirrored the romantic idea that aesthetic activity and aesthetic form are the compensatory realms in which the absolute might be experienced or actualized. For Schelling, the symbol can fuse contraries: "the symbol does not simply signify, but also *is*: in other words by the intransitivity of that which symbolizes. In the symbol, 'the finite is at the same time the infinite itself, and does not merely signify it'" (Todorov 209). The symbol both is, and at the same time signifies. Art and myth are privileged realms where an image can be concrete and abstract, general and particular at the same time—autonomously "for itself" and signifying something else.

This underlying assumption leads to Scholem's interpretation of Kabbalah as a "great living myth" that revitalized monotheism. And symbolism is a key to this revitalizing power. In an interview, Scholem confessed that he was interested in Kabbalah because of "its power to transmute things into symbols. And the symbols are not subjective. They are an objective projection of the inner. . . . they did not speak only to the private individual—they displayed a symbolic dimension to the whole world." The problem of modern humanity, he claims, is that our symbols are now merely private and subjective, and technology has repressed the symbolic dimension. It is that symbolic, mysterious dimension which must somehow be found again in the secular (*JJC* 48).

In sum, for Scholem to assert not only that the kabbalists *used* or manipulated symbols and allegories, but that the kabbalists' "essential mode of thinking is . . . symbolical in the strictest sense" (*MT* 26) is already to take a certain philosophical and aesthetic approach to the problems of religious truth, an approach somewhat at variance with Scholem's historical method. Scholem's definition of the symbol as saying and communicating "nothing," but only making transparent what is beyond expression, is itself an aesthetic-mystical rather than a "historical-critical" definition. Perhaps this underlying romantic ideology is what has made Scholem's work so attractive to so many contemporary writers, artists, critics, and various modern "myth makers." Via Scholem, Kabbalah now emerges as great "myth making," a grand symbolic construct, a heroic act of imagination to be placed alongside other great modern artistic visions. We have art, Nietzsche once said, in order not to die of the truth.

THE SYMBOL AS STATIC OR DYNAMIC

What other ways are there to speak about Kabbalah, then? Idel has explored the issue in depth and also finds Scholem's philosophy-allegory/ Kabbalah-symbol opposition oversimplified because

> it underrates the unique contribution of allegory to the expression of psychological processes or the description of the relationship between the human and the Divine. Allegory was not merely an adoption of philosophical forms of thinking but, in some important cases, an inherent need of Kabbalah itself in its primarily mystical rather than theosophical modes. (*Kabbalah* 218)

To the ecstatic mystic, philosophy offered a model for a certain kind of intellectual union with God—the absorption of the knower and known in the act of cognition—and also a vocabulary to describe it. In Idel's view, Scholem's neglect of allegory was a result of his overemphasis on Kabbalah as a theosophical system. The alternate mode of Kabbalah, ecstatic Kabbalah, aimed at personal experience of God but rarely presented these personal experiences directly in its written accounts. Instead, the ecstatic kabbalist used allegorical language to describe these experiences as if "he felt his language was adequate to convey mystical feelings" (219). The use of symbolic or allegorical language was not due to any difficulty in "describing the ineffable," as was indeed the case for the Christian mystic attempting to portray his or her experience.[12]

Idel proposes that the symbol/allegory distinction in Kabbalah ought to represent more of a "functional" rather than a hierarchical division between two distinct modes of apprehension. And even here, the notion of the kabbalistic symbol needs to be revised. One important difference between the kabbalistic notion of the symbol and the Christian notion in the Middle Ages, Idel argues, is that in Christian thought, influenced by Platonism, the relation of symbol and the object symbolized—i.e., the divine archetype present in a lower manifestation in matter—was essentially static. Yet "for most of the kabbalists, symbolism was more than the representation of divine manifestations in texts or nature. . . . They wished to realize the process taking place between these entities" (222).

For this reason, the unit of kabbalistic exegesis in theosophical Kabbalah was less the individual word than the verse or set of verses. Symbolism was part of a hermeneutic that sought to capture "the dynamics of divine forces":

> Interactions, relationships, union, or separation of the *Sefirot* from one another were the syntax of Kabbalistic hermeneutics. The divine manifestations therefore were seen not as ideas existing in frozen perfection within the divine thought but as living entities whose dynamism often attained imperfect states, to be repaired through human activity. A Kabbalistic symbol invited one to act rather than to think. (223)

The key point Idel is making here, contra Scholem, is that the kabbalistic symbol was not preeminently a romantic sublime or attempt "to express the inexpressible" but an attempt to express and enact relationships, i.e., to act appropriately, to change the condition of God, humanity, and world (ecstatic Kabbalah aimed as well at an active human experience, not a detached speculation). Idel's definition returns to Jewish mysticism its ethical imperatives and its continuity with more traditional Jewish thought, whereas the romantic ideology by which Scholem interprets Kabbalah turns Jewish mysticism into more of a contemplative aesthetics and radical rupture with the past. This latter mode of interpretation was clearly influenced by the climate of German-Jewish thought in the first two decades of the twentieth century.

In sum, in Idel's analysis kabbalistic symbolism is inducement to action rather than contemplation of static meaning; it is not essentially epistemological but experiential: "it implies a radical change in the perception of the Torah, as well as the personality and the status of the Kabbalist himself" (229). Symbols were necessary to describe the divine realm of the *sefirot* "because several aspects of the ever-changing system need to be expressed, not because the revealed facet of divinity is beyond expression in conceptual terms owing to its transcendence" (231–32). The aim of understanding of these relationships is precisely *participation* in the divine life and human world, not through "faith and enlightenment, but primarily by an *imitatio* of the dynamics. The transparency of the divine world through symbols is secondary to the pedagogic role of bringing someone to action" through the Torah's commandments (232). There is no static ontology in this theosophy; rather, the divine worlds are incessantly changing and reciprocally related to human action. The infinity of meanings in the biblical text result from its reflection of these incessantly changing supernal relationships. The various "worlds" and ceaselessly changing *sefirotic* patterns prevent any permanently fixed link between the symbol and what it symbolizes; one word in the Bible can signify several different ontological and supernal structures: "Hence, the assumption that there is an immanent relationship between the symbol and the symbolized becomes more difficult—the more polysemous the nature of the symbol, the less organic its affinity to the symbolized" (231).

The fixing of kabbalistic symbols into a static code, and the view of Kabbalah primarily as a "hermeneutic" or theosophical speculation originated in the Christian version of the Kabbalah in the Renaissance. Christian Kabbalah detached and neutralized the theurgic component, the component which was so essential to the dynamic vision of the *sefirot* and their connections to the world of Jewish law and commandment, the human actions influencing and repairing the world and the divine realms. The disregard of the theurgic component was necessary for a Christian perspective in which classical Jewish law had been abrogated with the arrival of Jesus, and also for the assimilation of Kabbalah into the Renaissance "Platonic-Pythagorean-Hermetic synthesis" (262). Ficino, Pico, and Reuchlin assumed that Christian truth was affirmed through the various garbs of ancient philosophies, and read Kabbalah accordingly.

The historian of science Steven Goldman has shown how this *ontologizing* of images and symbols in Renaissance Christian thought was also connected to the rise of modern science, when the images and symbols of the nature philosophers were interpreted *"literally* as depicting what they stood for, as being icons of a reality existing external to the mind and beyond the senses" ("Christian Origins" 1). Modern science similarly depends to a great extent on "just such iconic interpretations of the mathematical modeling of natural phenomena"—what Whitehead in his critique of this view called "the fallacy of misplaced concreteness" (1). In other words, science's own theoretical constructions were often ontologically identified with the external reality conceived to be their object, a trend later opposed by such quantum physicists as Heisenberg and Bohr.

What is especially relevant for our purposes is Goldman's thesis that this Renaissance and Christian ontologizing of symbols contrasts to "an intensely aniconic, deliberately nonpictorial and consequently positivistic attitude towards metaphors and symbols in the contemporary Judaic thought," including the Kabbalah, which was part of the Jewish nature philosophy that became known to Christian thinkers in the Renaissance (2).

Ficino, for example, was one of those Christian thinkers who mediated Kabbalah, but he based his interpretation of symbols on the "Platonic and Neoplatonic attribution of ontological significance to the relation between the ideal 'original' and their 'copies' in matter. The reality of the latter derives from their participation in their ideal original form" (3). Similarly, the symbol "participates" in the original and is a conduit for its potency. This led to the development of talismanic magic, and to the idea that contemplation of the symbol led to a more perfect knowledge of the symbolized object.

The difference is whether symbols are thought of as actual "embodiments" of the powers and virtues of the original or mere "representations" of them. As Goldman shows, the ontologizing of formal relations was especially critical to the development of Western rationalism in Descartes, Spinoza, and Leibniz. This attribution of *ontological significance* to *logical necessity* means that "the order and connection of ideas is the same as the order and connection of things," that logically necessary truths were privileged candidates for absolute truth (10). Goldman argues that there was a nonontological interpretation of images and symbols in Jewish thought, even among those Jewish thinkers who heavily used and relied upon them—the rabbis of the Midrash with their extensive parables and metaphors, and, of course, the Jewish mystics. But the relationship between the content of the parable or metaphor and the subject it purports to discuss (i.e., the nature of God, prayer, etc.) is not one of ontological participation and identification but mere formal comparison, a correlation. "The elements of the parable have nothing to tell us about the elements of the problem" (14); the hearer must construct relationships that suggest correlation between the contents of the parable and the object or issue to which it refers. (Benjamin's idea of truth as the "constellation" or "configuration" of "Ideas" well describes this sensibility.)

Goldman observes that the kabbalists constantly warned their readers not to take literally their descriptions of the divine realms and *sefirot*, for there can be no ontological identity or comparison between God and humanity. The pictorial descriptions are meant rather "as so many vehicles for conveying to the mind certain functional, and not structural features of the divine nature" (15). This would support Idel's central assertion that kabbalistic theosophy was understood in terms of theurgy, i.e., in terms of the *functions* and *effects* the Torah's commandments and human action could have upon them and the world. (I would call this a "rhetorical" understanding of the symbol rather than a "hermeneutic" one.) In sum, Goldman writes,

> the Judaic attitude towards symbols has a distinctly positivistic aim to it, in its rejection of identity between the elements of theoretical constructs and their objects and in its acceptance of relationships as the sole aim of those constructs. But there is no concomitant Judaic rejection of the *possibility* of illuminating the real by way of such constructs, no positivistic rejection of the value of metaphysics in Judaic philosophy. (18)[13]

Bergson is the example Goldman gives of such Judaic tendencies in modern philosophy. For our purposes, it is interesting that Bergson was one of the important early influences on Levinas. As I will discuss at length in part II of this book, Levinas's critique of ontology, of the foundational idea of "being" in the history of Western metaphysics, is tied to a critique of the notion of transcendence as any kind of "participation" in the Being of beings. Instead, Levinas will try to articulate the sphere of what is totally "otherwise" or "beyond" being—a nonontological *relationship* which he finds "embodied" in the *ethical* relation with the Other—not as participation but as imperative and turning to the human other. Like Rosenzweig, Levinas will affirm the realm of Jewish law as a special affirmation and concretization of this ethical relation. For Levinas, ethics is prior to and founds metaphysics, and the attempt to grasp the totality of being through "knowing" is *not* the foundational act of philosophy. When taken as such, philosophy is violent.

What I have argued so far, then, is that whereas Scholem's mode of distancing from his kabbalistic texts was effected through his adherence to historical-philological method, his literary-philosophical assumptions "smuggled in" his own personal and modern theological reconstruction of Jewish mysticism via the categories of a symbolic-mythical hermeneutic.

The priority of theoretical "knowing," that legacy of classical Western philosophy, is another source of the Renaissance transformation of Kabbalah into what Idel calls a "gnosis" (*Kabbalah* 263), a transformation which was critical for the later reception of Kabbalah in Western scholarship. Idel argues that Scholem's overemphasis of the theosophical and neglect of the theurgic-*halakhic* and ecstatic aspects of Kabbalah perpetuated the idea of Kabbalah as a form of gnosis.[14]

In this light, I would add, one can further understand why Scholem's work on Kabbalah has affected so many contemporary literary critics, poets, and modern writers: Kabbalah and Scholem's work itself come to represent the possibility for a kind of *modern gnosis*. Harold Bloom has gone so far as to define Scholem as essentially a gnostic in a historian's disguise, and identified himself as a "Jewish gnostic" as well. One could also say that in much recent poststructuralist theory, literature and criticism, specifically "literary *language*," are also conceived as a kind of gnosis—a special form of esoteric *knowledge* unavailable in any other way. "Language" with a capital *L*, from the Russian formalists to deMan, is conceived as a set of signs, detached from "personal experience" and "ethical or moral prescription." The human arena is an intersection of linguistic and semiotic forces; the human is the subject of language. Understanding language proceeds independently of individual human selfhood and is a matter of deciphering codes or hidden meanings, or the modes in which texts subvert meanings, or the hidden intersection of social forces and literary codes—a gnosis.[15]

Yet there has also been a strong reaction against the view that the text is a thing constituted of, by, and for Language. In recent literary theory, feminist, political, and cultural criticism have recognized that the model of language on which earlier structuralism and semiotics had been based is inadequate; there is much more to "language" and especially "literary language" than epistemological problems and skeptical aporias. Benjamin once more seems to have marked the path ahead of everyone else when he turned from his earlier, more "esoteric" epistemological work toward a more exoteric, politically engaged criticism. Yet this was continuous with—and not at all a repudiation of—Benjamin's early project to revise Kant; language itself was a form of knowledge, but also a form of alternate "experience" and a mode of "redemption" of nature and history. In Benjamin, the need for action led from speculation on "pure language" to a "Marxist theology," a venture into political criticism as part of the active reconstruction and redemption of the world. Scholem also recognized the continuity of Benjamin's Marxism with his previous thought; and what Scholem writes about Benjamin's fascination with surrealism could equally well describe the nature of Scholem's own interest in the Kabbalah:

> Benjamin read those periodicals in which Aragon and Breton proclaimed things that coincided somewhere with his own deepest experiences. What hap-

pened here was similar to his encounter with what he called "extreme communism." Benjamin was not an ecstatic, but the ecstasies of revolutionary utopias and the surrealist immersion in the unconscious were to him, so to speak, keys for the opening of his own world, for which he was seeking altogether different, strict, and disciplined forms of expression. (*SF* 135)

Benjamin and Scholem ultimately chose different "disciplined forms of expression" which necessitated a different politics.

FOUR

Allegory and Redemption

BENJAMIN AND SCHOLEM: THE POLITICS OF HISTORIOGRAPHY

Benjamin, who had been so thoroughly immersed in the thought of romanticism, would try to break the "organic" link between ontology and structure. This was necessary, he thought, to break the dangerous spell of "symbol" and myth and move into history—and so he tried to construct in his Arcades project a history that would be an awakening from the "dream of the nineteenth century." As he wrote to Scholem about this project in August 1935,

> I believe that its conception, however personal in origin, addresses our generation's most decisive historical interests. . . . The work represents both the philosophical application of surrealism—and thereby its sublation [*Aufhebung*]—as well as the attempt to retain the image of history in the most inconspicuous corners of existence—the detritus of history, as it were. (*Corr* 165)

Despite his interest in alternate modes of experience and "noncommunicative" modes of language, Benjamin also clearly differentiated himself from the traditions of symbolism and surrealism. Louis Aragon's *Le paysan de Paris* (1926) had given him the impetus for the study of the Paris Arcades. Benjamin demurred, however:

> Whereas Aragon persistently remains in the realm of dreams, here it is a question of finding the constellation of awakening. . . . what matters here is the dissolution of "mythology" into the space of history. Of course, that can only happen through the awakening of a knowledge not yet conscious of what has gone before. ("Theory of Knowledge" [N 1, 9])

Benjamin saw allegory as the form in which the sharp pains of time, history, and finitude were recognized—and as the key to understanding modernism, its history, and aesthetics. In one sense, "modernism" is a "negative" strain of romanticism, a recognition of the irremediable gaps between mind and nature, and the underside of the "imagination" where prophetic vision becomes destructive apocalypse. The creative perceptions of the New Heaven become the shock of phantasmagoria in the new urban hell. Benjamin emphasized this strain in his characterization of Baudelaire, whom he portrayed as the archetypal modern poet-as-allegorist. One of Benjamin's great contributions, we shall see, was his philosophical re-definition and reconstruction of allegory as the vision of the irremediable ruins of time and history in opposition to the unified, seamless, romantic theological realm of the symbol. For Benjamin, the use of the "Symbol" in an attempt to cover the breach or repair the ruins was illegitimate.

Benjamin, consequently, has a different notion of "dialectic" than Scholem, who employed "dialectic" in a more organic Hegelian-theological way. Benjamin, unlike Hegel, did not grant to history any "totality." In 1918, he wrote to Scholem that what he had read of Hegel had repelled him, and he called Hegel's "mental physiognomy . . . that of an intellectual brute, a mystic of violence, the worst kind there is: but a mystic for all that" (*SF* 30). Benjamin's "dialectic" avoided any mediation whereby opposing forces could be related to each other, or synthesized in any integral narrative. Allegory preserved the gap, the disparity, the difference between this world and redemption. History was the site of ruin, and only out of an "unfaithful leap" or moment of reversal comes redemption. This moment of reversal is not continuous with any prior "organic development." Scholem was also attracted to that position insofar as it was a critique of liberal Enlightenment notions of progress. Yet he also retained a more romantic notion of a dialectical mediation and synthesis of opposites within a "totality"—"totality" conceived as Jewish history itself as the very scene of an ongoing and open creative interplay and synthesis of opposites.

Yet just as Benjamin tried to link the politics of historical materialism to his linguistic theory and historiography in the search for some objective deliverance, so Scholem linked the politics of Zionism to his historiography. The establishment of the Jews with political autonomy in their own land, Scholem thought, would enable Jewish history to be written without political apologetics or theological dogmas, i.e., "autonomously" and "objectively." In 1925, when Benjamin was forced to abandon his hopes for a university appointment, Scholem was unexpectedly appointed lecturer in Jewish mysticism at the newly founded Institute for Judaic Studies, the nucleus of the School of Humanities of the Hebrew University in Jerusalem. He had come to Palestine intending to make his living as a high school teacher of mathematics; academic appointments in kabbalistic studies were nonexistent. The Hebrew University was opened in April 1925, just about a year after his arrival. This newly founded Institute for Jewish Studies, he writes,

> was an important step toward the establishment of a center that would be free from any fixed theological orientation but devoted to a living historical-critical investigation of Judaism. Such a center would give rise to great expectations for a regeneration of the *Wissenschaft des Judentums* ["Science of Judaism"] (about whose state I had considerable misgivings . . .). (*SF* 128)

As Biale notes, "For Scholem, objective historiography is guaranteed by

Zionism because Zionism is by definition anti-dogmatic: it stands above all particular interpretations of Judaism and is the one common denominator which unites all Jews" (*Scholem* 8). Zionism, that is, enables Jews to assume the totality of their history and is an "immanent" interpretation of Jewish history, one not centered around a transcendent God.

Benjamin, however, did not have Zionism to guarantee a totality to history, and Benjamin did not write his history of "Paris, Capital of the Nineteenth Century" in his Arcades project in the form of a coherent narrative but only as a collection of fragments. He would not—or he could not. As he wrote to Scholem on May 20, 1935, after about nine years of work on the project, the work would "mobilize its own theory of knowledge,"

> though I can foresee neither whether it will find a form of representation of its own, nor to what extent I may succeed in such a representation. . . . In the midst of the incredible difficulties I am faced with, I sometimes enjoy dwelling on the following thought: how much of a dialectical synthesis of misery and exuberance lies in this research, which has been continually interrupted and repeatedly revised over the course of a decade, and which has been driven to the remotest of regions. Should the book's dialectic prove to be just as sound, then it would find my approval. (*Corr* 159)

In his later work, Benjamin brings "dialectics" to what he calls a "standstill" in a "messianic cessation of happening" (*Illum* 263). The colliding images of past and present are brought by the radical historian into a momentary "constellation," pregnant with meaning and "now-time," which can break open the continuum of "bourgeois" linear history in the service of redemption and revolution.[1] There is no ontological integration of positive and negative forces into a unified whole. To awaken humanity from its benighted illusory sense of history, Benjamin thought, a shock effect is needed, and history written as a smooth narrative whole is but one more soporific, one more contribution to oppression, to the lull of ideological sleep. Scholem, however, interpreted this "standstill" as a symptom of what Benjamin himself described in a letter to Scholem as his own "pathological vacillation" (*SF* 156): "it took me some time to understand that at bottom that clarification was not possible for him. His later work proved that he was incapable of making a decision between metaphysics and materialism (as he conceived of the latter)" (169).

Unlike Benjamin, Scholem would not go so far as to identify his own politics with messianism, for he was fearful of the dangers that the release of the apocalyptic impulse had wrought in Jewish history. He defined Zionism instead as "a utopian retreat of the Jews into their own history" (*Judaica* II:49, qtd. in Biale 186), using a "backward metaphor" for redemption as Benjamin often also did. For Scholem, that meant a "retreat" from the Jews' engagement with European culture, a critique and rebellion against that culture, but not an apocalyptic or nihilistic call for a complete end to history in order to bring about the redemption or the revolution. Scholem's Zionism turns the utopian drive into an immediate constructive engagement of Jews with their own concrete past history through the process of rebuilding their ancient land and nation, and a simultaneously purified Jewish historiography. Through Zionism, Scholem thought, the Jew could take hold of and act responsibly in history. Scholem was clearly a radical "culture critic" in his own way. He, too, left the cloisters of German academic life and acted upon his convictions about what were the necessary Jewish concrete material actions in history. Zionism, he maintained, not political revolution or class struggle, would enact that judgment on the distorted life of the Jew in Europe and make possible another, more authentic Jewish life.

Scholem was by no means a pure Hegelian, for in his view Jewish history is not brought to any consummation, nor is it subject to any grand overarching "Idea." It remains open, undetermined. David Biale has remarked upon the strong strains of Nietzschean counterhistory in Scholem, although these were not as radically employed as in Benjamin. Nietzsche was one of the main inspirations for the more skeptical and radical historical visions of other modern Jewish thinkers such as Berdichevsky and Buber, but "counterhistory" could take conservative forms as well. Scholem opposed Nietzsche's nihilism and identified himself as a follower of Ahad Ha'am's cultural Zionism, but Scholem's rejection of Nietzsche was only partial, and there is "a certain affinity between some of Scholem's radical historical categories and Nietzsche's" as well (*Scholem* 38). Scholem identified Kabbalah and Sabbatianism as revolutionary traditions hidden *within* Jewish history itself and, like Benjamin, he sought revitalization through examining realms of experience and understanding that Kantianism and liberal rationalism had neglected and devalued.

Scholem thought he had found in Kabbalah a "mythical reaction in realms which monotheistic thinking had with the utmost difficulty wrested from myth . . . foreign mythical worlds are at work in the great archetypal images of the Kabbalists, even though they sprang from the depths of an authentic and productive Jewish religious feeling" (*KS* 98). In the 1937 letter Scholem wrote to Zalman Schocken, he explained that originally he had wanted to write not the history but the "metaphysics of the Kabbalah." But what kind of metaphysics? He claimed that he was particularly incensed by the rationalistic bias of Jewish philosophers such as Saadia, Maimonides, and Hermann Cohen, who had tried to separate monotheism and myth instead of "elevating them to a higher level." (The Hegelianism of this statement is obvious.)

> I sensed such a higher level in the Kabbalah. . . . It seemed to me that here, beyond the perceptions of my generation, existed a realm of associations which had to touch our own most human experiences. To be sure, the key

to the understanding of these things seemed to have been lost, if one is to
judge according to the obtuse standards of the Enlightenment. (Qtd. in Biale,
Scholem 75)

Critique of Enlightenment ideals was one thrust of Benjamin and
Scholem's attack on the bourgeois, rationalistic, liberal culture into which
they were born and against which they were always firmly allied. This
attack was carried into Scholem's angry critique of the "Science of Judaism," which he thought had attempted to present Judaism as a pure, spiritualized, rationalistic monotheism in conformity with the liberal bourgeois
standards of contemporary society. Yet, for Scholem, any *direct* return to
Jewish belief or *immediate* reimmersion in myth or mysticism was impossible because of the very ruptures in Jewish tradition and the undermining
of any literal notion of revelation which the Enlightenment itself had
effected.

Like Benjamin, Scholem severely criticized the Enlightenment's over-
rationalistic and progressive philosophy of history, but he nevertheless
adapted the historical-philological *methods* of the "scientific" study of Judaism. In Biale's words, Scholem's "counterhistory" was not so much a
negation of the "Science of Judaism" as its "dialectical neutralization"
(*Scholem* 206) and the "completion of its program under reordered priorities," priorities which valorized the irrational and heretical forces that
had been depreciated. Thus for Scholem, Kabbalah itself as "a counter-
historical interpretation of normative Judaism becomes a suggestive model
for the modern historian seeking to rejuvenate Jewish historiography in a
secular age" (191).

Rejuvenation of historiography was also Benjamin's goal, but Benjamin
severely criticized the methods of rationalist scholarly historicism. As Irving Wohlfarth puts it, like the more radical Nietzscheans, Benjamin
thought of the historicist as one who "painstakingly reconstructs some
bygone era out of a tell-tale need to *forget* the present. . . . Unable to seize
the day, they indiscriminately embrace any old past, passing off their
promiscuity as so much empathy. The historicist is a culture-vulture. He
scavenges off the garbage of other times and places" in search of the "soul"
he is losing—motivated by urgent but unacknowledged present needs, "his
claim to historical objectivity masking a flagrant subjectivism" ("Et Cetera?" 157). Benjamin would survey this garbage, which he called the "trash
of history," in a different kind of salvage attempt. Here is another stark
historical contrast with Scholem: while Benjamin was forced to live literally like a rag picker among the ruins, denied an academic appointment
and any steady income, Scholem rose to prominence and financial security
at the Hebrew University from his first appointment in 1925 to his death
in 1982. His writing conformed to academic style and is a tour de force of
lucidity, scholarly exposition, and meticulous bibliography.

This difference in style was partially a result of the different goals toward which each man adapted those early mutual reflections on the philosophy of language and history. Scholem had his "material base" settled in Palestine at the Hebrew University, and also in the collections of kabbalistic manuscripts he devoted his life to interpreting. He would decipher their language by trying to understand the "paradoxes" (a key trope in his thought) by which these texts attempted to "communicate the incommunicable." This hidden depth could also open up an "abyss," an amorphous and anarchic world of nihilism and antinomianism—as was the case in the apostasy of Sabbatai Sevi, the infamous false messiah of the seventeenth century, whose life and legacy Scholem elevated into a critical phase of modern Jewish history. Benjamin, with almost no material base and barely the means to support himself, an exile in a collapsing Europe with no Promised Land, tried to use those hidden depths in language to open history to redemption through a "tiger's leap," to release the revolutionary energy of dialectical images, to redeem the past and flash a new constellation for the future.

Although Scholem would never write history in the form of montage as did Benjamin in the Arcades project, he was certainly no benighted, unconscious historicist. His association with Benjamin perhaps helped prevent that. He knew well his motives and the ambiguity of his position as a historian. Benjamin's "Theses on the Philosophy of History" were an obvious model and inspiration for Scholem's "Ten Unhistorical Aphorisms on Kabbalah" (published in 1958), where he allowed himself to muse "unhistorically" (i.e., free from the constraints of critical-philological method) on the relations among modern historiography, Kabbalah, modern philosophy, and linguistic theory. In the first aphorism, Scholem writes that "the philology of a mystical discipline such as the Kabbalah has something ironic about it." The kabbalist attempts to transmit a truth that "can be known, but not transmitted," or transmitted only in a decayed form. Similarly, "Does there remain for the philologian something visible of the law of the thing itself or does the essential disappear in the projection of the historical?" There is no certain answer, he continues, and the irony of the philologist's attempt to understand the Kabbalah parallels the ironic nature of the kabbalistic project itself: both the historian-philologist and the kabbalist attempt to describe the indescribable, to know the unknowable, to transmit a truth beyond all expression.

Idel adds an interesting commentary to Scholem's 1937 letter to Zalman Schocken in which Scholem professed that he originally wanted to discover the "metaphysics" of the Kabbalah. Scholem assumed, Idel writes, that "on a deeper level, Kabbalah expresses a metaphysical reality that can be grasped by a proper hermeneutics, using historical, philological, and philosophical tools"; and the academic discipline of studying Kabbalah could therefore encompass the kabbalistic quest. But he also hoped for something more, to approach the "mountain," the *core* of that reality. That was something that could not be accomplished through academic methods.

One had to passively await a "hint" emanating or calling forth from it. Asks Idel: what, then, for Scholem was the relationship between the historical-philological search and the mystical quest, between the "metaphysical core of the Kabbalah and the 'mountain,' the core of reality"? The answer was unclear, though Scholem recognized the dangers of an academic "spiritual death." In any case, "The common perceptions of his personality either solely as a historian or as a historiosopher unnecessarily reduce his spiritual physiognomy to his obvious and manifest activity, blatantly ignoring his own statements." Idel characterizes him as a "theoretical mystic or a mystic in theory, as well as a theorist of Kabbalah" (*Kabbalah* 12).

When Scholem wrote in the 1937 letter to Schocken that his work lived "in this paradox, in the hope of a true communication from the mountain, of that most invisible, smallest fluctuation of history which causes truth to break forth from the illusion of "development" (qtd. in Biale, *Scholem* 76), he is describing truth in a manner similar to Benjamin: as a breaking forth, a leaping out, an *ur-sprung* that does not come from any rational, progressive, historical development. What Scholem patiently waits for, in the paradox of his work, is what Benjamin aggressively solicits in his history writing. Scholem's "paradox," in other words, is Benjamin's "dialectics at a standstill," the flashing up of the dialectical image, the constellation between past and present that appears at the moment of danger. For Benjamin, that reading of reality cannot remain confined to philology. It is radical political/theological action, the messianic "now-time" that blasts open the continuum of history. For Scholem, the "tiger's leap" into history is instead the Zionist endeavor of the Jewish people to become politically autonomous actors in history through rebuilding their ancient land. Yet it is also clear that Scholem's academic historical-philological study of Kabbalah was itself a direct response to a "moment of danger," the degeneration, hypocrisy, and decay of Jewish life in Europe. And it was also a kind of "memory"—a remembering of the forgotten strata of Jewish mysticism and myth.[2]

On the whole, however, Scholem was a more conservative thinker than Benjamin. His emigration to Israel and affirmation of cultural Zionism provided him with a way to avoid what he perceived to be the stifling ahistorical forces of *halakhic* Judaism, on the one hand, and the dangerous tendencies of messianism, on the other, to escape oscillating between the extremes of a passive "life lived in deferment" and an apocalyptic, catastrophic, and therefore equally "impotent" way of acting in history. But in holding this position, as Steven Schwarzschild perceptively writes, Scholem also put "out of operation all those forces in Judaism which preserve the wide gap between what is and what ought to be or will be— *halakah*, messianism, philosophical ethics, and W. Benjamin's sense of tragedy" ("On Eschatology" 195). It is to Benjamin's book on tragedy that we now turn.

BENJAMIN: THE CRITIC AS ALLEGORIST AND
THE GERMAN TRAGIC DRAMA

> Allegories, are, in the realm of thoughts,
> what ruins are in the realm of things.
> (*OGTD* 178)

> Tout autor de moi devient allégorie.
> (Baudelaire, "Le Cygne")

Benjamin and Scholem were both deeply engaged in the politics of historiography, but Benjamin, strangely, was more the radical "theologian" when it came to history writing; and the notion of allegory in the baroque German tragic drama would be key to his historiography. Benjamin's great work on allegory begins with his book on the German tragic drama, which he wrote as his second habilitation thesis. Like Scholem, Benjamin was studying a literature that was esoteric, disparaged, difficult, extreme—the baroque German *Trauerspiel*, literally "mourning play," from the era of the Thirty Years War. He worked on this project for several years and completed it in 1925; it constituted Benjamin's final attempt to secure an academic post and attain some financial stability. Unfortunately, it was rejected by the professors on his review committee, who claimed that they did not understand it. As Charles Rosen aptly writes, though, "If they had understood it, they would have turned it down anyway" ("Ruins" 135), for it attacked all the forms of criticism then prevalent in the German university. Benjamin finally succeeded in publishing the book in 1928. It greatly influenced Adorno, who did attain an academic position in Germany and taught semester-long seminars on the book. Scholem poignantly notes, however, "Thus the beginning of my university career, which opened up so unexpectedly, coincided with the miscarriage of the career that Benjamin had pursued now for six years. I simply had better luck." (*SF* 129).

In the years during which the book was composed, the German economy was collapsing, and Benjamin began his serious interest in communism. He pondered joining the German Communist party but in 1927 decided against doing so. Scholem, however, again badly misreads Benjamin when he claims that

> his book on tragic drama, during the incubation period of which his new Communist perspective worked only as an inhibiting factor, contains no references or allusions to that perspective. The philosophical background he gave to this book and the theses he developed there on the dialectics of the phenomenon of the *Trauerspiel*, remained rooted in the physical realm from which they derive their execution as well. Marxist categories do not figure in this work. (*SF* 123)

Despite his expertise in reading esoteric texts and in deciphering Benjamin's highly abstract early works, Scholem practices a kind of deaf-and-dumb literalism when he reads any of Benjamin's texts with Marxist undertones or explicit Marxist categories. I would argue instead that the category of allegory was one of the ways Benjamin tried to connect his earlier idealistic reflections on language and philosophy back somehow to the material conditions of the world, an attempt to repair the ruins of history. In fact, the discussion of allegory in the tragic drama book is the beginning of his deep engagement with materialist political thinking. Allegory becomes in Benjamin's hands that very mode of philosophical contemplation which strives for the salvation of phenomena by the ruthless unmasking of their fallenness—a melancholy science. Whereas for Scholem, the Kabbalah was important because of its power to transmute *things into symbols*, for Benjamin the German *Trauerspiel* was compelling because it transmuted *things into allegories*. Allegory for Benjamin is the vision of the world which expresses the pains of history, transience, death, and it is allegory rather than symbol that draws Benjamin's inner empathy. Benjamin's thought as a whole, Fredric Jameson has astutely written, itself is "best grasped as an allegorical one, as a set of parallel, discontinuous levels of meditation" (*Marxism* 60).

In writing about the allegorical nature of *Trauerspiel*, Benjamin intensely criticized the influence of the romantic concept of the symbol on aesthetics: this concept lacks what he calls "dialectical rigor" and does not do justice to content in formal analysis and to form in the aesthetics of content:

> For this abuse occurs wherever in the work of art the "manifestation" of an "idea" is declared a symbol. The unity of the material and transcendental object, which constitutes the paradox of the theological symbol, is distorted into a relation between appearance and essence. The introduction of this distorted conception of the symbol into aesthetics was a romantic and destructive extravagance which preceded the desolation of modern art criticism. (*OGTD* 160)

In the romantic symbol, the beautiful merges with the divine in an unbroken whole. Benjamin argues that this is a false totality. It means that the moral world is purely immanent in the world of beauty, and so the ethical subject is lost in the beautiful soul. (Rosenzweig and Levinas make this same critique.) The eccentric, dialectical extremes of allegory disrupt these false totalities: "In the field of allegorical intuition, the image is a fragment, a ruin" (*OGTD* 176). Needless to say, Benjamin himself ultimately remained in the ruins of history; he found no redemption as did Scholem in a homeland in Palestine or anywhere else.[3] "Allegories," Benjamin writes, "are, in the realm of thoughts, what ruins are in the realm of things" (178). The ruin is the decay, the transience of nature where "history has physically merged into the setting" (177–78). As such, history is the process not of an eternal life but of irresistible decay. Allegory thereby declares itself to be beyond beauty and the symbol.

One of the decisive categories for understanding the difference between allegory and symbol, then, is *time*. Benjamin discusses at length Friedrich Creuzer's theories of allegory and symbol. Although he criticizes Creuzer for repeating many of the old romantic clichés about the inferiority of allegory, he thinks Creuzer indirectly opens the path to a better epistemological understanding of allegory through a recognition of the very temporality of allegory. In the symbol, Creuzer had written, there is momentary and total apprehension, like a flash of illuminating lightning or a force seizing hold of one's being. In his later work, Benjamin would transfer this power from the realm of myth and symbol to that of materialist history, and use the figure of momentary flashing illuminations to define his "dialectical images," which flash up at moments of danger as revolutionary energies: "The dialectical image is a lightning flash. The Then must be held fast as it flashes its lightning image in the Now of recognizability. The rescue that is thus—and only thus—achieved, can only take place for that which, in the next moment, is already irretrievably lost" ("Theory of Knowledge" [N 9, 7]).

The moment when past and present flash into a constellation is the dialectical image at a standstill, a kind of *nunc stans*, or in Benjamin's later term, *Jetztzeit* [now-time], which is defined as genuinely historical time as opposed to the empty time of historicism. And this "image" is not found in nature but in language. When he later worked out his idea of the dialectical image in the Arcades project, Benjamin wrote reflectively about his earlier book *The Origin of German Tragic Drama* and recognized that he had transferred Goethe's concept of truth and *Urphänomen* ("origins") "from the realm of nature to that of history. Origins—the concept of the primal phenomenon, carried over from the pagan context of nature into the Jewish contexts of history" ("Theory of Knowledge" [N 2a, 4]).

So his early search for the "origins" of the German tragic drama and his later quest for the "origins" of modernity in the Arcades project were linked; Benjamin's critique of the romantic idea of the symbol in the *Trauerspiel* book was a crucial move in historicizing his idealism. This defense of allegory was a move away from the pseudotheology of the romantic symbol toward materialism, and toward the definition of a different kind of redemption, a "profane" theology. Allegory would be a model of the salvation of phenomena by means of their very profanation.

Scholem and Benjamin discussed the ideas of the *Trauerspiel* book when they met in Paris in 1927, and Scholem was especially interested in Benjamin's ideas about allegory and symbol (*SF* 140). It is quite interesting that Scholem concludes his discussion of the symbol in his *Major Trends in Jewish Mysticism* with a quote from Friedrich Creuzer's *Symbolik und Mythologie der alten Völker* (1810), from the very same passage Benjamin cites in his own discussion of allegory and symbol in the *Trauerspiel* book.

Creuzer makes the symbol/allegory distinction to legitimate his revalorization of myth. The symbol, Creuzer wrote, is "a beam of light which, from
the dark and abysmal depth of existence and cognition, falls into our eye
and penetrates our whole being." The symbol, Scholem adds, thus yields
an "instantaneous totality," whereas allegory requires a successive progression of thought through time, and lacks this instantaneous character (*MT*
27; *OGTD* 163–64).

This notion of a temporal delay in allegory was central to Benjamin's
elevation of allegory as a superior epistemological mode.[4] The symbol is
self-contained, momentary, and analogous to the silent, natural world; allegory is fluid, historical, subject to a violent dialectic.

> Whereas in the symbol destruction is idealized and the transfigured face of
> nature is fleetingly revealed in the light of redemption, in allegory the observer
> is confronted with the *facies hippocratica* of a history as a petrified, primordial
> landscape. Everything about history that, from the very beginning, has been
> untimely, sorrowful, unsuccessful, is expressed in a face—or rather in a
> death's head. And although such a thing lacks all "symbolic" freedom of ex-
> pression, all classical proportion, all humanity—nevertheless, this is the form
> in which man's subjection to nature is most obvious and it significantly gives
> rise not only to the enigmatic question of the nature of human existence as
> such, but also of the biographical historicity of the individual. This is the heart
> of the allegorical way of seeing, of the baroque, secular explanation of history
> as the Passion of the world; its importance resides solely in the stations of its
> decline. (*OGTD* 166)

From these early meditations until his last "Theses on the Philosophy of
History," Benjamin was haunted by this sorrowful catastrophic view of
history. Whereas Scholem found in both Zionism and the study of Kabbalah positive responses to the tortures of Jewish history and exile, Benjamin could not, in the end, come to Jerusalem; he remained as Europe
collapsed around him until it was too late—like the angel of history he
envisions in his parable (which has a poem by Scholem as its epigraph) in
Thesis IX,

> his face is turned toward the past. Where we perceive a chain of events, he sees
> one single catastrophe which keeps piling wreckage upon wreckage and hurls it
> in front of his feet. The angel would like to stay, awaken the dead, and make
> whole what has been smashed. But a storm is blowing from Paradise; it has got
> caught in his wings with such violence that the angel can no longer close them.
> This storm irresistibly propels him into the future to which his back is turned,
> while the pile of debris before him grows skyward. This storm is what we call
> progress. (*Illum* 256–57)

So, too, in the allegory of the *Trauerspiel*, the relations among history,
redemption, and destruction are torturous. Allegory is born of "a strange
combination of nature and history" (*OGTD* 167). Like the angel, the alle-

gorist contemplates the ruins of history, but allegory does not "idealize" destruction, nor does it transfigure nature in the light of redemption. In allegory, "any person, object, relation can mean absolutely anything else. With this possibility a destructive, but just verdict is passed on the profane world: it is characterized as a world in which the detail is of no importance." Yet this does not reduce allegorical objects to mere empty shells, irrevocably dead. Here Benjamin turns allegory back toward redemption: for in allegory "all of the things which are used to signify derive, from the very fact of their pointing to something else, a power which no longer makes them commensurable with profane things, which raises them onto a higher plane, and which can, indeed, sanctify them. Considered in allegorical terms then, the profane world is both elevated and devalued" in a religious dialectic (175). This is one of the links between allegory and criticism, and the critic and allegorist: "Criticism means the mortification of the works. By their very essence these works confirm this more readily than any others. Mortification of the works; not then—as the romantics have it—awakening of the consciousness in living works, but the settlement of knowledge in dead ones" (182).

Philosophical criticism explicates artistic form differently from romantic aesthetics:

> to make historical content, such as provides the basis of every important work of art, into a philosophical truth. This transformation of material content into truth content marks the decrease in effectiveness, whereby the attraction of earlier charms diminishes decade by decade, into the basis for a rebirth, in which all ephemeral beauty is completely stripped off, and the work stands as a ruin. (182)

This definition clearly contests the romantic notion of the seamless unity of the transcendental and the material in the symbol, or of the beautiful as expression of the absolute. In place of an organic unity of material content and truth content, Benjamin elicits the temporal dissolution of this link. It occurs in the historical "afterlife" of the work, as a decomposition; rebirth of the truth content of the work is possible only through (or as) its fragmentation and ruin. There is no immediate apprehension of truth in a symbol, no translucent penetration of nature, but the disjunction between the natural and the human, form and meaning.

In allegory, nature is transience, subjection to death: "death digs most deeply the jagged line of demarcation between physical nature and its significance . . . significance and death both come to fruition in historical development" (166). Hence the baroque allegory has an "endlessly preparatory, circumlocutious, self-indulgently hesitant manner . . . of giving form" (183)—a description that could well be applied to Benjamin's own thought, which is perhaps the allegory of allegory. The gaze of the allegorist (or the critic who "mortifies works") is a melancholy one which strips, drains, and empties the innate life of the object to the point where, unlike the symbol, it can no longer have any meaning of its own. The allegorist then has the object in his or her power: "In his hands the object becomes something different; through it he speaks of something different and for him it becomes the key to the realm of hidden knowledge; and he reveres it as an emblem of this. This is what determines the character of allegory as a form of writing" (183–84).

In allegory, nature becomes "other," a "writing," a realm of proliferating signs and hieroglyphs. Needless to say, Benjamin's emphasis on fragmentation, ruin, "difference," "writing," "otherness" has been very appealing to deconstructive critics, but a definition of allegory which focuses only on the empty, mortifying aspect of this otherness does not go far enough.[5] For Benjamin, the stripping or mortification of the works was only one part of the dialectic of allegory; in making things "other," there is a countermovement toward redeeming them as well. On another level, Benjamin could be said to be endeavoring to relate the sacred and profane, theology and materialism "allegorically." These allegorical images become his later "dialectical images," which crystallize at moments of historical danger, linking past and present in a pregnant moment of now-time, a "dialectics at a standstill."

FAITHFULNESS AND BETRAYAL: SACRED AND PROFANE

The profaning, mortifying work of the critic-allegorist reduces the work to ruins, and breaks down history "into images, not stories" ("Theory of Knowledge" [N 11, 4]) in order to effect a rescue, to find an "other" meaning. (Politically, this translates into a hope for the oppressed.) But this "other meaning" (the etymology of *allegoresis*) does not rest easy in itself, as does that of the symbol. The otherness always retains the sense of gap, discontinuity, between allegorical object and its meaning.

In this sense, baroque allegory itself becomes an allegory of Benjamin's own criticism, and what Benjamin finds in the baroque era of allegory is a kind of prehistory and emblematic image of his own time. He does indeed note the parallels between the baroque and modern expressionist art; more broadly, though, many of Benjamin's most incisive comments and characterizations of the baroque describe his own dilemmas, especially the problematic relations of immanence and transcendence, materialism and metaphysics, Marxism and theology. The *Trauerspiel*, in his view, is a secularized form of the medieval mystery play wherein history is no longer the story of redemption and where there is no longer any fulfilling eschatology. As such, it is a play of mourning and despair, filled with visions of death and catastrophe. Yet

> for all that the increasing worldliness of the Counter-Reformation prevailed
> . . . religious aspirations did not lose their importance: it was just that this

century denied them a religious fulfillment, demanding of them, or imposing upon them, a secular solution instead. These generations enacted their conflicts under the yoke of this compulsion or the spur of this demand. (*OGTD* 79)

Needless to say, this paragraph also describes quite well the dilemma of Jewish thinkers such as Benjamin, Scholem, and Kafka, and there are certain parallels between the situation of these German Jews in the early twentieth century and the German Christians in the seventeenth century. In Benjamin's interpretation, however, the authority of Christianity remained unshaken in the baroque era, and heresy was not an option. Hence "all the energy of the age was concentrated on a complete revolution of the content of life, while orthodox ecclesiastical forms were preserved" (*OGTD* 79). While a problematic relation to the Orthodox forms of religious life is a major preoccupation in Benjamin, Scholem, Kafka, Buber, and other modern Jewish intellectuals, the external "institutional authority" had little to do with the power of these forms. For two thousand years, Judaism of the diaspora—unlike Christianity—had not been completely merged with any state power; the modes in which it compelled its adherents, especially after the breakdown of the ghetto and the enfranchisement of the Jews after the Enlightenment, were more internal. One was also "externally" reminded of one's Judaism by the declining situation in Europe. Like the writers of the *Trauerspiel*, these Jews had lost faith in the traditional eschatology and were driven to seek modes of redemption within fallen nature and history itself. The *Trauerspiel*, Benjamin notes, "is taken up entirely with the hopelessness of the earthly condition. Such redemption as it knows resides in the depths of this destiny itself rather than in the fulfillment of a divine plan of salvation. . . . [It is a] rash flight into a nature deprived of grace" (81). How to redeem a history that was a pile of ruin, how to find an eschatology within the profane, how to express religious yearnings through the secular would be part of Benjamin's and Scholem's task, too.

As Benjamin also points out, however, there is not only mourning [*Trauer*] in the *Trauerspiel* but also *Spiel*, play. Art, in both the romantic and baroque eras, takes on a "playful form only when life, too, in the face of intense preoccupation with the absolute, has lost its ultimate seriousness." Thus in the baroque drama, "the play-element was demonstratively emphasized and transcendence was allowed its final word in the worldly disguise of a play within a play" (82). One might well extend Benjamin's insights here to the "playful" aspects of postmodernism, which itself displays a kind of baroque allegorical sensibility, often exhibited in elaborate self-conscious displays of artifice, in plays of surface and self-reflexivity. In a deconstructionist textual interpretation, for instance, the arbitrary free play of signs is foregrounded and the target text is reduced to fragments. In postmodernism, the modernist mourning and nostalgia is attenuated; there is little of the sad desire or anguished yearning for the transcendent in the secular that marks modernism and the baroque. And there is little sense either of the fall or of any coming apocalypse. Instead of the drive toward redemption, an ironic pleasure is taken in the very transience and emptiness.

Benjamin's allegory, however, is filled with the pain of the fall, "for an appreciation of the transience of things and a concern to rescue them for all eternity, is one of the strongest impulses in allegory." Benjamin here applies to allegory his ideas from his earlier essay "On Language" about the linguistic fall of the creature and nature; nature mourns this fall into muteness, and the allegorist as a fallen Adam attempts to redeem nature by knowing it and giving it voice, though only uncertainly (225). In so doing the allegorist speaks the very language of the fall, striving for "knowledge," not truth. As in the essay "On Language," "knowledge" is distinguished from "truth," and knowledge itself is occasioned by and signifies the fall. Allegory now becomes the knowledge of the fall wherein "the unity of guilt and signifying emerges as an abstraction," a language of abstraction, uprooted from things, unattached and arbitrary, a language of judgment (234). This notion of a fall from the paradisal language of names into a language of judgment is again familiar from Benjamin's earlier work.

The result is that the allegorist guiltily "betrays the world for the sake of knowledge" (224). And when the allegorical contemplation of objects is "not so much patiently devoted to truth, as unconditionally and compulsively, in direct meditation, bent on absolute knowledge, then it is eluded by things, in the simplicity of their essence, and they lie before it as enigmatic allegorical references, they continue to be dust" (229). (There is an interesting parallel between this analysis and Scholem's recognition that the "mountain," or core of metaphysical truth in the Kabbalah, may disappear when the historian tries to grasp and acquire it through the critical-philological method and projection into historical time, the methods of acquisitive "knowledge" with which he as historian tried to penetrate the mist around the "mountain.") Underlying Benjamin's distinction between "knowledge" and "truth" is the critique of philosophical idealism—of Hegel's "absolute knowledge" as the redemptive unity of knowing and being. This same critique is also a focal point of Rosenzweig's *Star* and of Levinas's ethical metaphysics.

Yet Benjamin notes that the allegorist's "conscious degradation of the object . . . [also] keeps faith with its own quality as a thing in an incomparable way" (225). Absorbed in contemplating things, "in its tenacious self-absorption it embraces dead objects in its contemplation, in order to redeem them" (157). Allegory seeks some kind of magical knowledge which will transform all the things it touches into significance, like the alchemist who converts dirt to gold. However, this desire for an absolute knowledge, for the illusion of freedom and independence, also connects to the realm of evil because the experience and basis of evil is "the realm of absolute, that is to say, godless, spirituality, bound to the material as its counterpart" and dominated by a mood or mourning.

Thus there is a dialectic of faithfulness and betrayal in allegory. In seeking some absolute knowledge or significance in things, it also "kindles the rebellious, penetrating gaze of Satan in the contemplative man" (229), and Satan is absolute spirituality "destroying itself in emancipation from the sacred" and so falling into soulless materiality. "The purely material and this absolute spiritual are the poles of the satanic realm" (230). One might also say that these were the extreme poles of the contemporary philosophies with which Benjamin struggled: idealism and materialism; esoteric philosophy and cultural commentary; intentionless truth and revolutionary praxis (Marx turning Hegel on his head). With the sacred lost, abandoned, unavailable, or betrayed, the material became a home for the spiritual, though the home was a ruin.

How, then, to mediate these extremes? The words Benjamin uses to describe the baroque allegory pertain aptly to his own work, his attempt to relate historical materialism and Jewish messianism; it is this very fall, taken to its final extreme, that in the end reverses its movement: "As those who lose their footing turn somersaults in their fall, so would the allegorical intention fall from emblem to emblem into the dizziness of its bottomless depths, were it not that, even in the most extreme of them, it had so to turn about that all its darkness, vain glory, and godlessness seems to be nothing but self-delusion" (232). The turn to salvation and redemption, however, is not different from the very visions of destruction, ruin, and catastrophe, for finally *these visions too* become allegories—the allegory of the resurrection. "Ultimately in the death-signs of the baroque, the direction of allegorical reflection is reversed: on the second part of its wide arc it returns, to redeem" (230). This reversal is the final extreme of allegory: that it undoes itself by its own devices. The allegorist loses everything that is its own and awakens in God's world:

> And this is the essence of melancholy immersion: that its ultimate objects, in which it believes it can most fully secure for itself that which is vile, turn into allegories, and that these allegories fill out and deny the void in which they are represented, just as, ultimately the intention does not faithfully rest in the contemplation of bones, but faithlessly leaps forward to the idea of resurrection.

So that at its end, even evil becomes allegorical "and means something different from what it is. It means precisely the non-existence of what it presents" (233). It discovers itself to be ultimately subjective and unreal.

BENJAMIN'S BAROQUE ALLEGORY AND DEMAN'S DECONSTRUCTIONIST CRITICISM

What gods will be able to rescue us from
all these ironies? (F. Schlegel)

This description of allegorical meaning as difference, as an undoing of itself by its own devices, has obvious parallels with recent deconstructive ideas about the nature of meaning. Benjamin's book on the *Trauerspiel* was, in fact, one of the main inspirations for Paul deMan's immensely influential essay "The Rhetoric of Temporality," a classic deconstructive study of allegory, symbol, and irony.[6] Like Benjamin, deMan harshly attacks the elevation of symbol over allegory, describing it as "an act of ontological bad faith" (*Blindness* 211). Allegory as the mode of discontinuity, fragmentation, self-reflexiveness, and temporality is no longer a subordinate "rhetorical figure," but it constitutes for deMan the epistemological modality of rhetoric itself. Allegory cannot ultimately eradicate the dialectical play between allegorical temporality and the mystified symbolic forms of language, and the interplays between the two "make up what is called literary history" (226). Allegory becomes the authentic figure for all interpretation for deMan, and he accordingly titles one of his later books *Allegories of Reading*.

In deMan's analysis, the aesthetic elevation of the symbol "refuses to distinguish between experience and the representation of this experience," and assumes that poetic language can transcend this distinction and have direct access to the infinite truth as some total and universal meaning— that there is a unity between sensory image and suprasensory totality, incarnate and ideal beauty. This "unity between the representative and the semantic function of language" is the latent romantic assumption behind so much other contemporary literary criticism and history (*Blindness* 189). DeMan's critique of the symbol is effected through a philosophical revalorization of allegory now defined as that mode which recognizes the "disjunction between the way in which the world appears in reality and the way it appears in language" (191). The symbol, he argues, cannot be relied upon to resolve philosophical antinomies, nor can it be granted the kind of priority over all other rhetorical figures attributed to it in romantic and postromantic thought. Allegorical tendencies are found "in all European literature between 1760 and 1800 . . . at the most original and profound moments in the works, when an authentic voice becomes audible" (205). Allegorical apprehension was not simply superseded by symbolism in the development of romantic literature and theory; it is rediscovered in moments of renunciation and sacrifice and "always corresponds to the unveiling of an authentically temporal destiny" (206).

Following Benjamin, deMan asserts that time is the essential category of allegory; there is no simultaneous coincidence of the representation and its substance. In allegory, temporality intervenes between signs and their meanings, and the sign refers to other preceding signs: "The meaning constituted by the allegorical can then consist only in the *repetition* . . . of a previous sign with which it can never coincide, since it is of the essence of this previous sign to be pure anteriority" (207).

Allegory is thus for deMan the negative moment in early romanticism; and since in this period allegory has been secularized, there can be no recourse to divine will, redemption, or transcendence. In the later development of romanticism in the nineteenth century, the aggressive assertion of the superiority of symbol over allegory becomes, in deMan's phrase, "a defensive strategy that tries to hide from this negative self-knowledge"— i.e., knowledge of the way the self is inextricably implicated in the temporal relations of a system of allegorical signs instead of being directly related to natural objects. The exaltation of the symbol is thus a regressive but "tenacious self-mystification" (208) which permeates broad areas of nineteenth- and twentieth-century European literature and criticism.

Allegorical representation is the more "authentic" and painful knowledge of difference, disjunction, nonidentity. But in contrast to the melancholy of Benjamin's allegory, deMan's allegory has renounced "the nostalgia and desire to coincide, [and] it establishes its language in the void of this temporal difference" (207). It prevents an illusory identification with the object world, or the nonself, and thus avoids the extreme identifications of subjective idealism (the object is ultimately the same as the subject) or materialistic naturalism (the subject is the same as the object).

It is not difficult to see, then, why allegory in deMan's analysis comes to represent the archetypal model of deconstructive reading. DeMan displaces the interpersonal dialectic of a subject's relation to an object (or mind to nature) for the impersonal relations of "signs in a system." That is the structuralist move drawing on Saussurean linguistics; the deconstructive step is to then make temporality the central category so that the relation of signs is one of noncoincidence and nonidentity, and signs are inevitably distant from their origin. Benjamin, however, did not exalt a semiotic conception of language as an arbitrary system of signs. He considered that conception to be a *fall* from a purer language of truth, and he never broke the connection between his language theory and the search for redemption—even in his most political phase.

It has been argued that deMan's continuous polemic against the delusions of those who confuse representation and experience is a covert critique of his own early political errors as a Nazi sympathizer, and that his own language theory is a radical political allegory. If so, he would be recognizing very belatedly what Benjamin and Scholem already knew in 1916 when they opposed contemporary *Lebensphilosophie* and its direct connection to the horrors of World War I. DeMan is simply retrofitting Benjamin with a poststructuralist vocabulary, and drawing on the pessimistic side of

Benjamin's thought while neglecting Benjamin's recognition of the need for both a politics and a theology. He replaces these with the elevation of "irony" as another figure of discontinuity and a form of "saying one thing in terms of another," and connects irony to allegory, symbol, and developments in philosophy and literature from Kierkegaard and Baudelaire to Nietzsche and Derrida. Irony becomes for deMan the doubled and disinterested self-reflexivity characteristic of dry laughter. Indeed the entire tenor of all of deMan's own interpretive work is characterized precisely by this disinterested, self-reflexive irony that calmly and chillingly presides over the discontinuities, aporias, and endless deferrals of meaning in literature.

DeMan employs Baudelaire's analysis of the comic to redefine the ironic as the perception of the nonidentity of the self, of its duplication into many discontinuous selves through differentiation from what it is not. The relation between these selves is *not interpersonal or intersubjective* but one of reflective distance from the nonhuman world. Following Baudelaire, he attributes this power of ironic redoubling, or "reflective disjunction," to artists and philosophers—those for whom language is an autonomous material, not a secondary tool. In this interpretation, language is not only the "privileged category, but it transfers the self out of the empirical world into a world constituted out of, and in, language" (213). DeMan is here making the characteristic deconstructive move: language, the argument goes, is found in the world but is unique because it is the very entity by which the self is differentiated from the world, divided between an empirical self and the self as differentiating sign.

In Baudelaire, the recognition of this division is connected to the fall, but the fall is now "comical and ultimately ironical" (214). This notion of the fall is quite different from Benjamin's.[7] For deMan, the language-determined man or "linguistic self" laughs at his own mystifications and mistaken assumptions about himself, recognizing "difference" instead of an intersubjective relation to nature. "The Fall, in the literal as well as the theological sense, reminds him of the purely instrumental, reified character of his relationship to nature" (214), a nature which he cannot dominate or transform into something human, but which can treat him as a thing. The linguistically constituted self is thus the ironic knower of the mystifications of the empirical self—to which it relates in detachment and disinterestedness. Yet this ironic knowledge is not comforting; it threatens to become a dizzy vertigo, a mad laughter undermining everything.

The "irony of irony" which for deMan is engendered in all true irony comes to the rescue: it is the act of not becoming the dupe of one's own irony, of maintaining that detachment, that continuing statement of the impossibility of "reconciling the world of fiction with the actual world," or of reconciling self and world, ideal and real via art. There is no vision of ultimate unity or synthesis but an infinite and endless sequence of temporal acts of consciousness "endlessly caught in the impossibility of making this knowledge applicable to the empirical world" and dissolving into the spiral of a linguistic sign becoming ever more remote from its meaning (222). (In view of deMan's political past, it has been asked to what extent this theory reflects an extreme and obsessive reaction of one who had indeed been "duped" and had witnessed the dire political consequences of those illusions.)

These discrete temporal acts cannot be synthesized into a totality; allegory and irony share the same fundamental consciousness of temporality which forbids a totality. The ironic "moment" is the "instant at which the two selves, the empirical as well as the ironic, are simultaneously present, juxtaposed within the same moment but as two irreconcilable and disjointed beings" (226), the reverse image of the instantaneous apprehension of a totality in the symbol.

This temporality, however, makes for an unhappy consciousness, and also has led some writers to try to rescue themselves from irony by what deMan characterizes as "a leap out of language into faith" (223). DeMan thus implies that "faith" is a realm opposite to language and irony, a realm where an apocalyptic sensibility tries to overcome the temporality of language. This opposition "faith/irony," as Benjamin knew, is too facile. What, then, does Benjamin mean when he writes of that final faithful/ faithless leap of allegory? Bainard Cowan, using deconstructive categories, claims that the final leap or reversal of allegory in the *Trauerspiel* book is ultimately a kind of "desperate faith," as is the intrusion of the awkward *deus ex machina* to solve the plot in the baroque *Trauerspiel*. The resolution is difficult and unnatural; the ultimate fulfillment is deferred beyond life and history, and "this unfaithful leap constitutes the essential discontinuity of allegory" ("Theory of Allegory" 119).

Redemption does not come through any inevitable progression or logical chain of cause and effect:

> The leap is one of desperation, out of history into eschatology, out of statement into parable and out of the indicative mood into the subjunctive. The rhetoricity of allegory is this something that does not drop away once its object is unveiled, but rather forms its inner structure. Whatever unveiling of eschatology allegory may accomplish, it does not efface the negativity of the discourse out of which it leapt: the trace of the leap remains with it even in its most mystical moment. (119)

This interpretation would characterize Benjamin as the kind of writer deMan admires but who he thinks is rare: one who has transcended irony without regressing into myths of organic totality or evading the temporality of language.

Certainly the negativity within allegory is significant for Benjamin—as a movement of resistance, a kind of countertheology within theology, a movement of radical profanation and ruin which becomes the way back to redemption. Yet Benjamin's irony, unlike deMan's, is what Leo Baeck termed "messianic irony" and connected to a deeply Jewish sensibility: "Only those who are imbued with this pessimism, this mockery, this protest and this irony are the really great optimists who hold fast to the future and lead the world a step further towards it" (*Essence* 232). Schwarzschild noted this characteristic in his comments on the messianic idea in Judaism: the disparity between the ideal and real worlds founds messianic activism; it is not a life lived in impossible and impotent deferral, nor is it transformed into an epistemology of impotence and impossibility.

DeMan does not perceive this side of negativity, caught as he is in the extreme abstract formalism of the Saussurean and Derridean schemas where language is an impersonal system of arbitrary signs detached from all referents, and where *all* signs are to be understood on the model of the *linguistic* sign. DeMan's assertion that there is a special character in the language perceived by artists and philosophers that "transfers the self out of the empirical world into a world constituted out of, and in, language" ("Rhetoric" 213) itself comes from the romantic notion of an intransitive, autonomous poetic language, and this very notion is a secularized theology, "religion within the limits of art." Again the influence of Mallarmé is apparent—deMan's doctoral dissertation was about Yeats and Mallarmé, and deMan is one of the most recent avatars of hermetic traditions about language.

Tzvetan Todorov has perceptively written that "men have described their symbols for centuries but they have done so by claiming to be observing the signs of others" (*Theories* 223)—others who are supposedly more "primitive" or mystified than they. "In the belief that they were discovering the *other* sign, they have often described *our own* symbol" (226). Symbols and signs, in fact, are always being transformed into each other, and Todorov argues that theoreticians who "assert that everything is sign, that the symbol does not, or should not exist" (223), and that language is solely made up of signs have a highly reductive and defensive view of language. Todorov adeptly notes the connections between latent romantic ideas of language and their seeming opposites, among which are "scientific" structuralisms. Roman Jakobson, the great proponent of Russian formalism, was himself influenced by Novalis and Mallarmé, and by romantic ideas of intransitivity which are at the heart of the notion of autotelic poetic language (272). Multiple systems function within language, and "we have to stop identifying language with the part of it we know best" (282).

In this sense, deMan would himself be acting out another form of "mystification," the mystification of the "abyss" and negativity which he wants to find at the heart of language. The distancing ironic laughter and "irony of irony" would be a defensive strategy to ward off the threat of any symbolic element in language. Benjamin knew better. His linguistic revision of Kantianism was meant to include *many other* kinds of meaning, and was not restricted to a pure logical formalism of signs, which in his view was a fallen language to which one ought *not* be reconciled. As he wrote to Scholem, "A philosophy that does not include the possibility of soothsaying from coffee-grounds cannot be true philosophy" (*SF* 59)—thus his passionate interest in phenomena such as children's books, writing by the insane, surrealism, his astrological metaphors of truth as a constellation, and his attempt to fuse esoteric linguistics with historical materialism.

THE RETURN OF THE SYMBOLIC:
HOPE FOR THE HOPELESS

Benjamin advised Max Rychner, a Swiss critic and editor of the *Neue Schweizer Rundschau*, that one should not read the *Trauerspiel* book from beginning to end, but instead read its "Epistemo-Critical Prologue" only at the conclusion. If one takes Benjamin's advice, one finds a reevaluation of the symbolic elements in language then after working through the analysis of allegory. In the prologue, he seems to attempt a "rescue" of this symbolic character (as deMan, Saussure, and Derrida do not). Benjamin's critique is of the "romantic" symbolic, not the "symbolic" dimension of *all* language. (One of the main problems in deMan's criticism in general is his generalization of local deconstructive readings of selected literary texts to apply to *all* language—itself a kind of "totalizing" movement.)

George Steiner has called Benjamin's prologue to the *Trauerspiel* book "one of the more impenetrable pieces of prose in German, or, for that matter, in any modern language" ("Introduction," *OGTD* 13). Benjamin himself characterized the introduction in a letter to Scholem as an "enormous chutzpa" (*Briefe* I: 372). Around 1930, Benjamin told Max Rychner and Theodor Adorno that it could be understood only by someone familiar with Kabbalah, and on the copy he gave to Scholem, Benjamin inscribed "To Gershom Scholem, donated to the *ultima Thule* of his kabbalistic library." Scholem speculates that Benjamin's remark might have referred to the study's incomprehensibility, or to its esoteric nature, or perhaps to the relation of kabbalistic ideas to the linguistic theory put forth in this prologue. Or perhaps Benjamin was "playing hide-and-seek with me" (*SF* 125). Irving Wohlfarth hits just the right note in describing it as "an attempt to face academic regalia and turn the concomitant *Wissenschaft* against itself" ("Et Cetera?" 150).

"Truth," Benjamin writes in a now-famous statement, is "the death of intention" (*OGTD* 36), beyond the grasp of acquisitive, systematic, methodical knowledge. In other words, there is a sharp distinction to be made between the "object of knowledge" and "truth." Knowledge is an act of intention, appropriation, communication, but "truth is an intentionless state of being, made up of ideas. The proper approach to it is not therefore one of intention and knowledge, but rather a total immersion and absorption in it" (36). Yet one cannot approach truth by any kind of intellectual "vision," as one approaches the world of appearance. There is no immediate direct vision of truth, nor does contemplation yield images. On the contrary, the realm of the ideas is *linguistic*:

> Truth is not an intent which realizes itself in empirical reality; it is the power which determines the essence of this empirical reality. The state of being, beyond all phenomenality, to which alone this power belongs, is that of the name. This determines the manner in which ideas are given. But they are not so much given in a primordial language as in a primordial form of perception, in which words possess their own nobility as names, unimpaired by cognitive meaning. (36)

These thoughts are familiar from Benjamin's earlier works on language. The "name" is a primordial form of perception which represents this truth; that is, the name is the symbolic essence of the word. The ideas of truth are linguistic; they constitute the "symbolic" in the essence of any word. In empirical perception, however, this symbolic essence is obscured, for words have fallen into the realm of arbitrary signification and have acquired an "obvious profane meaning," i.e., when they act as signs. The task of the philosopher is to "effect the salvation of phenomena by means of ideas": to

> restore the primacy of the symbolic character of the word, in which the idea is given self-consciousness, and that is the opposite of all outwardly directed communication. Since philosophy may not presume to speak in the tones of revelation, this can only be achieved by recalling in memory the primordial form of perception. (34, 36)

In contrast to the spontaneous intuition of the romantic aesthetic symbol, then, the philosopher requires memory. Memory begins to play a central redemptive role as in Benjamin's later work, where historical materialism will itself be reconstructed as a form of memory. In the *Trauerspiel* book, remembering is a form of contemplation in which "the idea is released from the heart of reality as the word, reclaiming its name-giving rights" (37). So Adam the name-giver and not Plato is the real father of philosophy, a position which recalls Benjamin's analysis in the 1916 essay "On Language." The names which Adam gives are paradisal without the struggle involved in the communicative signifying aspects of language: "Ideas are displayed, without intention, in the act of naming, and they have to be renewed in philosophical contemplation" (*OGTD* 37). The name as a primordial form of perception beyond all specific meaning is the linguistic carrier.

But neither does the linguistic nature of ideas reduce truth to the impossibility of truth. In the 1916 essay, Benjamin had clearly recognized the abyss at the heart of linguistic theory (the abyss that deMan's deconstruction dwells on and in) but warned that one must remain "suspended over" it, not fallen into it. In a description of truth similar to that which Rosenzweig lays out in the first part of *The Star of Redemption*, Benjamin maintains that the ideas or essences of the real or truth are not a totality but exist in complete independence from each other, like orbiting stars of a constellation. While the distance between ideas is unbridgeable, their configurations and relations constitute truth (37). Despite this variety of configuration, the realm of ideas is a "discontinuous finitude" (38), and philosophy has been and should be "a struggle for a limited number of words which always remain the same—a struggle for the representation of ideas" (38).

Charles Rosen, in one of the best explications of this prologue, locates possible sources for Benjamin's use of the word *Idea* in Kant and the early romantics, particularly Schlegel and Novalis. In Novalis, the Idea within an artwork means that which cannot be contained in any proposition but is an "infinite series" in a continuous process of realization, something incommensurable and untranslatable. From Kant as well comes the distinction between Idea and concept—the former cannot be defined by a simple proposition; the latter can. Benjamin, however, adds the notion of "configuration" and "constellation" to describe Ideas (Rosen, "Ruins" 155–56). "Ideas are to things as constellations are to stars" (*OGTD* 34). Or as Rosen summarizes: "the concept defines a class of phenomena, the Idea determines the relation of the phenomena in the different classes to each other." The "concept" of tragedy defines a set of plays; the Idea of tragedy is the broad configuration of relations of the plays to history ("Ruins" 156).

Consistent with his earlier thought, Benjamin maintains that there is no immediate or intuitive perception of Ideas; rather, they are linguistic. The word in its "symbolic sense" names an Idea, and it is the philosopher's task not to "intuit" but to *restore and represent* this aspect of the word, which is not found in any of the word's ordinary, profane meanings. The term *representation* is critical here, for as Rosen writes, it means that "the symbolic aspect of the word has not been perceived until its representation has been constructed" (158).

This emphasis on representation distinguishes Benjamin from Heidegger and from many mystical theories of language, and it derives in part from Benjamin's reading of Humboldt and Mallarmé. From the former he takes the idea of language as an independent system apart from our subjective intentions, but one which is nevertheless a repository of our experiences and history through its ranges of associations, connotations, and cultural constructs. From the latter comes the emphasis on the noncommunicative or esoteric aspects of language as the modes which preserve this "symbolic" dimension. Mallarmé's technique—like Benjamin's—involves isolation of words, acontextual and juxtaposed quotations, indirect allusiveness, and the idea of an illumination which appears from the interrelations of words themselves. In this sense, Rosen argues, Benjamin was the first to apply symbolist poetics to historical criticism (165).

So the "representation of Ideas" does not occur directly, and the "symbolic" character does not mean any immediate fusion with a transcendant object, or any organic, natural, instantaneous connection between particular and general, or symbol and symbolized. The representations of Idea are configurations, a set of relations between meanings or things which retains the separation, where there is no unity or collapse into an identity. In sum, there is no ontologizing of the symbolic (as discussed above in relation to Goldman and Idel's ideas of the difference between Jewish and Christian modes of symbolism) but a recognition of the discontinuity that yet obtains in the coherence of the relationships.

Rosen also aptly clarifies how Benjamin proceeds to employ the theory of the "Epistemo-Critical Prologue" to his analysis of the German tragic drama: a "concept" such as "the baroque" finds a set of similarities, norms, or identities common among phenomena and puts them together in a class or definition. The "Idea," however, does not construct a unity by abstracting what is common to historical formulations; rather, it searches for the coherence or configuration among the extremes, among the disparate realms of the politics, theology, art, science of a period (161). Benjamin's study of the seventeenth century and the baroque tragic drama "is Benjamin's synthesis of extremes, a dialectical method but not a Hegelian one. It does not resolve the contradictions in a false unity but represents their relationship as part of a much larger, total pattern" (163).

This search for a configuration among the extremes is part of Benjamin's attempt at the "rescue of phenomena," and a continuing messianic undercurrent of his thought which helps bind together the philosophical opacity of the Prologue with the later development of his historical materialism. "Only for the sake of the hopeless one have we been given hope," Benjamin wrote in his essay on Goethe. So finally for Benjamin, the allegorical ruin is a special mode of beauty which remains faithful to the profane as well as the spiritual, to the suffering of history and the flesh. Like the ruin of a great building, Benjamin says, in which "the idea of the plan speaks more impressively than in lesser buildings, however well preserved they are," the *Trauerspiel* and the spirit of allegory deserve attention. From the beginning it is conceived as a fragment and ruin, and so Benjamin concludes the book with the words: "Others may shine resplendently as on the first day; this form preserves the image of beauty to the very last" (*OGTD* 235).

Hope for the hopeless: another fitting epigraph to Benjamin's own life. In a letter of 1916, he wrote, "I learned that he who fights against the night must move its deepest darkness so that it gives out its light" (*Briefe* I: 131).

ALLEGORY AND MODERNITY

Benjamin began his work on the Arcades project around 1927, a few years after the completion of the *Trauerspiel* book. The new turn in his thinking in those years did not mean a disavowal of his earlier writings and philosophical speculations; allegory now became the foundation for his study of the culture of modernity and his reinterpretation of historical materialsim. The Arcades project was a prehistory of modernity, and his study of Baudelaire a key part of it. Benjamin asserts that "Baudelaire's genius, which is fed on melancholy, is an allegorical genius" (*Refl* 156), but here, allegory has turned its vision from the ruins of the outer world to those of the inner. It has gone underground, so to speak, to reemerge in sudden terrible moments: "Its technique is the technique of the *putsch*" (*Charles Baudelaire* 100). Allegory reappears as the profound moment of shock, disorientation, and discontinuity in Baudelaire.

Benjamin subtitled his study of Baudelaire *A Lyric Poet in the Era of High Capitalism*. The grim theological background of the Counter-Reformation of the *Trauerspiel* now finds its counterpart in the modern capitalist economy. He wrote to Scholem in 1935 that both the baroque book and the Paris Arcades project "focus on the unfolding of a handed-down concept. Whereas in the former it was the concept of the *Trauerspiel*, here it is likely to be the fetish character of commodities. . . . just as the Baroque book dealt with the seventeenth century from the perspective of Germany, this book will unravel the nineteenth century from France's perspective" (*Corr* 159). In Lutheranism, belief had been set apart from works; this emptied meaning from the realm of the everyday and resulted in a certain melancholy. The same disjunction, Benjamin notes, underlies the capitalist world-view: the human is alienated from labor, and life in the process becomes reified. Objects are turned into dead things; they become commodities. Torn from their original contexts, manipulated, given alien meanings, they become the "ruins" of the modern world. This "fetish character" of commodities is discussed in the famous first chapter of the first part of Marx's *Capital*.

And that is the very movement of the allegorical, found also in Baudelaire's dreamlike visions of the ruins of the modern urban landscape. Fredric Jameson puts it well: "Benjamin's sensitivity is for those moments in which human beings find themselves given over into the power of things. . . . For allegory is precisely the dominant mode of expression of a world in which things have been for whatever reason utterly sundered from meanings, from spirit, from genuine human existence" (*Marxism* 71). By this definition, baroque allegory and Baudelaire, Babel and Golgotha, the German *Trauerspiel* and modern capitalism share a similar structure. Benjamin restores allegory to us, in Jameson's phrase, as a kind of modern "pathology" (72). Or as Benjamin wrote, it both "denies and fills out the void." Jameson astutely observes that Benjamin's own analyses of modernity are "in reality an exercise in allegorical meditation, in the locating of some fitting emblem in which to anchor the peculiar and nervous modern state of mind which was Benjamin's subject matter" (76).

Indeed, a 1931 essay by Benjamin, "Unpacking My Library," also becomes a kind of allegorical meditation on one's relation to objects, to the past, and to the transmission of truth. Like Scholem, Benjamin was a bibliophile and obsessive book collector. The book collector's relation to his objects, Benjamin writes, is nonutilitarian. He locks them "within a magic circle" of his own making, and in discriminating among them and contemplating their history, he becomes a physiognomist, an "interpreter of fate" (*Illum* 60). Like the baroque allegorist, he deciphers the ruins and emblems with which he is surrounded. "To a true collector the acquisition of an old book is its rebirth" (61). "To renew the old world—that is the collector's deepest desire when he is driven to acquire new things" (61); that is the "childlike" element in the collector. The highest value of a collection is as a heritage: "the most distinguished trait of a collection will always be its transmissibility" (66). Here again lifeless objects enclose secret worlds, but they need to be redeemed, made alive again, transmissible—that great theme of Benjamin and Scholem's meditations on Kafka. But in a book collection, the mode of redemption is static collection, a freezing of objects—just as allegorical contemplation fixes, freezes, and frames its objects, or the gaze of the hypothetical historical materialist freezes the progress of history to redeem an image from the past and flash it in the present.

Benjamin's allegorist is not only the chronicler of the spectacle of catastrophe and ruin but its profane redeemer. Perhaps by pushing allegory to its extreme, Benjamin as modern secular allegorist hoped also to effect its "reversal"—so that things become illuminated in a new way, in what he calls "profane illumination" in his 1929 essay on surrealism. To recall his words to Scholem in a letter of April 1931 in defense of his turn to historical materialism: "All right, I am going to extremes. A castaway who drifts on a wreck by climbing to the top of an already crumbling mast. But from there he has a chance to give a signal leading to his rescue" (*SF* 233).

Adorno thought that by reworking his theological insights through a naturalistic framework, Benjamin tried to save the idea of redemption by making it profane. Similarly, Benjamin was inspired by the surrealists' attempts to transfigure everyday profane reality through the dream image—a kind of counterpart to the allegorist's gaze at the ruins of history. The surrealists dealt with the detritus of everyday life, and by integrating the fragments of mundane bourgeois reality into art, they narrowed the gap between art and life in a way that might supposedly also serve the purpose of political revolution. Adorno again best describes Benjamin's use of the dream elements of surrealism: "The absurd is presented as if it were self-evident, in order to strip the self-evident of its power" (qtd. in Wolin, "Aesthetic" 98). Stripping the self-evident becomes part of the overthrow of common bourgeois realism, part of ideology critique.

Both allegory and surrealism try to overcome alienation by employing that alienation to the extreme—that is, by estranging objects, taking them from their mundane contexts, displacing and disordering them so that they could be invested with a radically new meaning. This kind of illumination was not grasped by the romantics, Benjamin writes, because they stressed only the mysterious side of mysterious phenomena. To comprehend surrealism, occult experience, dreams, to profane illumination, one must instead, like the critic-allegorist, "mortify" the work. As he puts it in his 1929 essay on surrealism:

> We penetrate the mystery only to the degree that we recognize it in the everyday world, by virtue of a dialectical optics that perceives the everyday as impenetrable, the impenetrable as everyday. The most passionate investigation of telepathic phenomena, for example, will not teach us half as much about reading (which is an eminently telepathic process) as the profane illumination of reading about telepathic phenomena. . . . The reader, the thinker, the loiterer, the flaneur are types of illumination just as much as the opium eater, the dreamer, the ecstatic. And more profane. Not to mention that most terrible drug—ourselves—which we take in solitude. (*Refl* 190).

The profane does not *merge* with the mysterious in a unity of form and content in a seamless symbol. The relation between profane and sacred in Benjamin's thought is less "dialectical" in the pure Hegelian or Marxist sense than it is "allegorical," i.e., discontinuous. His "dialectical optic" holds the two extremes in focus, freezes them in juxtaposition, in a new "constellation," and this moment of condensation or crystallization, Benjamin thinks, contains the potential energy for a revolutionary release of truth. By destroying the natural contexts of things, by alienating and estranging them, a shock effect is produced in the manner of surrealist montage; and this notion of the "profane illumination" becomes the later "dialectical image" of his materialist and revolutionary historiography.

CITING THE PAST

Benjamin employs these ideas about alienation and estrangement from natural context in his own literary technique—especially through his use of quotation. "Quotations in my work are like robbers by the roadside who make an armed attack and relieve an idler of his convictions" (*GS* I: 571). Quotations are another way of "mortifying" the work. As in allegorical or surrealist technique, citation can fragment, tear out of context, interrupt, and so illumine in a new way. In the Arcades project, Benjamin envisioned an ideal work which would be entirely composed of quotations without any accompanying text. Quotations are piled up, juxtaposed in a kind of montage which disrupts any linear progression of logical cause-and-effect.

This idea of quotation is a kind of counterpart to his earlier notion of the name as the base of language. (The idea of the text as a montage of quotations is also somewhat analogous to the kabbalistic idea of the Torah as a montage of the names of God.) In Benjamin's later thought, this theological power of the name becomes accessible through the profane power of citation. In his 1931 essay on Karl Kraus, Benjamin observes that Kraus's polemical essays worked precisely by the method of quotation, and he connects citation and naming:

> To quote a word is to call it by its name. . . . In the quotation that both saves and chastises, language proves the matrix of justice. It summons the word by its name, wrenches it destructively from its context, but precisely thereby calls it back to its origin. It appears now with rhyme and reason, sonorously, congruously in the structure of a new text. As rhyme it gathers the similar into its aura; as name it stands alone and expressionless. In quotation the two realms—of origin and destruction—justify themselves before language. And conversely, only where they interpenetrate—in quotation—is language consummated. In it is mirrored the angelic tongue in which all words, startled from the idyllic context of meaning, have become mottoes in the book of Creation. (*Refl* 268–69)

This calling and wrenching back to origin is a mode of redemption in which preservation and destruction are inextricably related. In Benjamin's schema, quotation involves a destructive moment; quotation brings the word back to its origin by an act of violence—like the degradations and elevations of allegory. In this essay, as in so many of his others, the authors about whom Benjamin writes serve as allegorical emblems for himself. One could write about him just what he writes of Kraus: "Only in despair did he discover in quotation the power not to preserve but to purify, to tear from context, to destroy; the only power in which hope still resides that something might survive the age—because it was wrenched from it" (270).[8]

In his late "Theses on the Philosophy of History," Benjamin again quotes Kraus: "Origin is the goal." Origin (*Ursprung*) here as in the *Trauerspiel* book does not mean an empirical cause traceable in a linear historical chain but, as Rainer Nägele aptly puts it, a "point from which something leaps out and from which it escapes and that escapes it at the same time" ("Benjamin's Ground" 22). The problematic relation to origin is, of course, at the heart of Benjamin's philosophy of history. Hannah Arendt puts it well: "Benjamin knew that the break in tradition and the loss of authority which occurred in his lifetime was irreparable and concluded he had to discover new ways of dealing with the past. In this he became a master when he discovered that the transmissibility of the past had been replaced by its citability" ("Introduction," *Illum* 38).

Benjamin tried to transform citability from a merely "literary" technique into a political and revolutionary act in relation to the past. For him, political revolution meant redemption of the *past* as well as the present, for "*even the dead* will not be safe from the enemy if he wins. And this enemy [fascism] has not ceased to be victorious" (*Illum* 255). "To be sure, only a redeemed mankind receives the fullness of its past—which is to say, only for a redeemed mankind has its past become citable in all its moments. Each moment it has lived becomes a *citation à l'ordre du jour*—and that day is Judgement Day" (254).

Benjamin's own mode of citing the past is itself a "judgment day," an explosive action aimed at disrupting the linear, chronological, ordered procession of events—or what Benjamin calls "historicism." Historicism tries to establish a logical chain of cause-and-effect between various moments in history, "telling the sequence of events like the beads of a rosary" (263). The "historical materialist," by contrast, has an entirely different relation to the past and struggles against the historicist's view of history as a conformist, progressive tradition. "The past can be seized only as an image which flashes up at the instant when it can be recognized and never seen again. . . . To articulate the past historically does not mean to recognize it 'the way it really was' (Ranke). It means to seize hold of a memory as it flashes up at a moment of danger" (255).

This flashing memory image is not the "homogenous, empty time" of the historicist "but time filled by the presence of the now (*Jetztzeit*)" which disrupts the long, empty continuum of traditional bourgeois history and its idea of "progress": "Thus, to Robespierre ancient Rome was a past charged with the time of the now which he blasted out of the continuum of history. The French Revolution viewed itself as Rome incarnate. It evoked ancient Rome the way fashion evoked costumes of the past" (261).

Benjamin intends this evocation to be a revolutionary action, a "tiger's leap into the past" (261) through which the present can become filled "now-time," a point where time stands still in a kind of mystical *nunc stans*. This now-time is the moment when the empty flow of time is stopped: "When thinking suddenly stops in a configuration pregnant with tensions, it gives that configuration a shock, by which it crystallizes into a monad" (262–63). This moment of cessation is recognized and used by the historical materialist to "blast a specific era out of the homogenous course of history" to redeem both past and present.

The question, of course, is to what extent the configuration or "dialectical" image is "subjectively" constructed by the historian. Is the constellation or correspondence between past and present intrinsic, objective, and material—or a subjective and ideal relation? Benjamin was clearly and consistently opposed to pure subjectivity as a path to truth, but since the dialectical image depends on the cognition of the historical materialist as it flashes up at political moments of danger, how is it to be characterized? Michael Jennings thinks that "Benjamin's sense of revolution has more in common with an act of inspired reading than it does with seizing railroads," and describes the relational structure of Benjamin's historical "constellations" as "mystical." Mysticism then would be the "link between Benjamin's epistemological and political convictions" (*Dialectical* 37).

But this is a mysticism turned very much toward the world in the service of a materialist ideology critique. For it attempts to unmask the historicist tradition as a kind of false consciousness, and a violent "triumphal procession in which the present rulers step over those who are lying prostrate." The spoils carried off in this victory parade, Benjamin asserts, "are called cultural treasures." And these cultural treasures are built on the "anonymous toil" of those who are the oppressed contemporaries of the great minds who have created these cultural icons. Thus follows Benjamin's famous statement, "There is no document of civilization which is not at the same time a document of barbarism" (*Illum* 256). From this kind of history, Benjamin's historical materialist must dissociate himself; he must instead "brush history against the grain" (257), a phrase which David Biale aptly uses as his epigraph to his study of Scholem's historiography.

The view of truth as a constellation is familiar from Benjamin's earliest works, and the image of the "tiger's leap into the past" is reminiscent of the "leap" of allegory toward transcendence—the leap as *Ur-sprung*, an attempt at "springing out," and somehow connecting two discontinuous realms—here the past and the present, materialism and messianism. But the realm of fallen history which Benjamin elaborated fifteen years earlier in his study of the *Trauerspiel* has now literally become the petrified landscape in which he himself is trapped in 1940. The "Theses on the Philosophy of History" were written after his release from the Vernuche internment camp near Nevers in France where he and other German refugees had been confined after the outbreak of the war. Hitler and Stalin had signed their notorious nonaggression pact, and Europe was crumbling into ruins around him. A few months later, in September 1940, he committed suicide at the Spanish border after his unsuccessful attempt to cross into freedom.

Lisa Fittko was the woman who led Benjamin over the Pyrenees in his failed attempt to escape Nazi Europe. She tells a story about Benjamin's behavior in the camp that illumines his propensity for concentration and concentrated images. In his theoretical writing, the ideas of the "monad," "dialectical image," "fragment," "ruin" represent concentrated and compressed objects which by their very compression had a power to encompass/release or redeem a larger realm. Fittko relates that her husband had been in the internment camp with Benjamin. Benjamin was a heavy smoker but had decided to give it up in the camp, and he was enduring the agony of withdrawal. Her husband told Benjamin that to survive in the face of their adversity, he ought to look instead for gratification and not for more hardship. Benjamin replied: "I can bear conditions in this camp only if I am forced to concentrate my mind entirely on one great effort. To quit smoking requires such effort, and so it will save me" "(Last Days" 53–54). Another desperate attempt at redemption.

Whereas Christian allegory had leaped toward the transcendence of another future world, Benjamin's "tiger's leap" into the past as a mode of redemption was another desperate leap into political messianism: "A historical materialist approaches a historical subject only where he encounters it as a monad. In this structure he recognizes the sign of a Messianic cessation of happening, or, to put it differently, a revolutionary chance in the fight for the oppressed past" (*Illum* 263). "To put it differently"—that is, to translate it into other terms. But what is the relation between politics and theology in this translation? Historical memory in this late essay now becomes openly allied with the Jewish mode of remembrance as the "little hunchback" of theology inside the puppet of historical materialism who reemerges in the final paragraph:

> The soothsayers who found out from time what it had in store certainly did not experience time as either homogenous or empty. Anyone who keeps this in mind will perhaps get an idea of how past times were experienced in remembrance—namely, in just the same way. We know that the Jews were prohibited from investigating the future. The Torah and the prayers instruct them in remembrance, however. This stripped the future of its magic, to which all those succumb who turn to the soothsayers for enlightenment. This does not imply, however, that for the Jews the future turned into homogenous, empty time. For every second of time was the strait gate through which the Messiah might enter. (264)

What, however, is the mechanism that energizes and drives the messianic arrival? How does one link memory of the past and what Benjamin describes as messianic "cessation" of happening to a political transformation? The little hunchback of theology hidden in the puppet of historical materialism may win all chess games, but can this baroque contraption fuel a revolution or bring real redemption, for either politics or theology? The "baroque" and mechanical aspects of the contraption are in the parable which he chose to place at the very *beginning* of the "Theses" and also refer back to Benjamin's study of baroque allegory in the *Trauerspiel*. It is as if here, too, an allegorical stripping, mortification, freezing could release a hidden life in history. This historical materialism was not "dialectical" in any classical Hegelian or Marxist sense; it was more of an allegorical philosophy of history. Benjamin seems again to have anticipated aspects of the "New Historicism" in current literary criticism. New Historicists attempt to construct a nonidealist and nondialectical relation of the historical and the literary, the aesthetic and the social, but rely on a postmodern sense of fragmentation and discontinuity and poststructuralist theories of language. Their difficulty is to find an adequate theory of language to describe the "mediation" between the aesthetic and the social. Benjamin, however, recognized the inadequacy of any theory of language that reduced language to an arbitrary system of signs. Because of these problems with "mediation" and "dialectics," questions constantly arise about the compatibility of "real" Marxism with the work of both Benjamin and the New Historicists. T. W. Adorno and Benjamin's other colleagues at the Institute for Social Research chastised Benjamin for the inadequate mediation in his own "dialectic," and Jurgen Habermas (the most eminent contemporary representative of the Frankfurt School) has argued that Benjamin propounds an intensely "anti-evolutionary concept of history." The idea of redemption and revolution as instants of a mystical messianic now which interrupt linear historical time and form "constellations" with images of the past finally cannot be fitted, Habermas asserts, into a genuinely Marxist view of history: "An anti-evolutionary conception of history can't be tacked onto historical materialism as if it were a monk's cowl" ("Consciousness-Raising" 51).

FIVE

Memory Is the Secret of Redemption

Messianism and Modernity

> Memory is the Secret of Redemption. (The
> Ba'al Shem Tov)

It would be more fitting, though, to say that Benjamin attaches the power of memory to dialectical materialism not so much like a monk's cowl as a Jewish *tallith* or "prayer shawl." While Habermas has also described the "Theses on the Philosophy of History" as "among the most moving testimonies of the Jewish spirit" (*Profiles* 34), he cannot understand how memory can be progressive. I return, therefore, in this chapter to the interplay of historiography, literary theory, and Jewish messianism in Benjamin and Scholem. The historian Yosef Haim Yerushalmi has written at length of the special relation in Judaism between history and memory. Memory, of course, has to do not so much with the pure chronicling or recording of historical facts as with their latent meanings. And the idea that there was a moral and theological meaning to history, that God intervenes and can be known in history, that history and not nature is the realm of divine action, was specifically Jewish:

> If Herodotus was the father of history, the fathers of meaning in history were the Jews. . . . Only in Israel and nowhere else is the injunction to remember felt as a religious imperative to an entire people. Its reverberations are everywhere, but they reach a crescendo in the Deuteronomic history and in the prophets. "Remember the days of old, consider the years of ages past" (Deut 32:7). . . . And, with a hammering insistence: "Remember that you were a slave in Egypt." (*Zakhor* 9–11)

This memory, effected through command, recital, and ritual, is selective; recorded and evoked are God's acts and the human responses—a history considered more "real" than that of the rise and fall of empires. This has little to do with modern historiography, or what Benjamin critiqued as "historicism": "Historicism gives the 'eternal' image of the past; historical materialism supplies a unique experience with the past" (*Illum* 262). As David Roskies, in a more psychological interpretation, puts in his book on the responses of Jews to catastrophe in history: "Memory is an aggressive act" (*Against* 10)—a kind of preexistent pattern or grid, a context through which to filter responses to individual and collective crises.

Thus memory is also the prime agent in the recontextualization, citability, and "transmissibility" of the past, and figures prominently in Baudelaire, Proust, and Kafka, writers who were also so painfully aware of the break in tradition, the shocks and ruptures of modern life. These were the authors who were the subjects of Benjamin's great essays of the 1930s. Memory, in Benjamin's unorthodox Marxism, is a way of mediating the material base and the ideological superstructure, and a different way of conceiving the dialectical progression of history.

At the height of his "Marxist" period, in 1937, Benjamin wrote that hope and memory are the "genuinely epic experiences of time" (*Illum* 98). He takes from Georg Lukács the notion of the novel as a particularly modern genre, "the form of transcendental homelessness," and the only form of art in which *time* is a crucial constitutive principle. Time becomes central when the transcendent has been lost; that is, when the relations between meaning and life, the essential and the temporal, have been disrupted. In this sense, the "novel is nothing else but a struggle against time. . . . " In the novel, creative memory tries to overcome the gap between inner and outer worlds by an act which "transfixes the object and transforms it." The unity of a life grasped by compression in memory becomes insight into "the unattained and inexpressible meaning of life" (98). The parallels to Benjamin's study of allegory are clear, for essentially he conceives of the allegorist in much the same way Lukács conceives of the novelist—one faced with the dilemma of entrapment in a decayed and transient world with little access to the beyond except through extreme contortions and manipulations of objects.

The novelist, like the philosopher, then, practices the art of memory as a way of transforming objects. Memory, like Benjamin's dialectical image or historical monad, is an act of *compression* which releases an otherwise unavailable meaning. In Jewish historiography, similarly, the ancient rabbis used the interpretive technique of compression and anachronistic simultaneity to construct their own species of dialectical images, to give meaning to a history in which God seemed to have abandoned them, in which the holy Temple had been destroyed, and the Jews sent into a painful exile. As Yerushalmi puts it, the rabbis "seem to play with Time as though with an accordion, expanding and collapsing it at will. . . . [with] rampant and seemingly unselfconscious anachronism" (19).

In fact, Benjamin's theory of quotation could well be applied to Midrash, to explain the seeming "distortions" and "misreadings" of the rabbinic reinterpretations of Scripture. Like Benjamin's baroque counter-reformation period and modern Europe between the world wars, the world in which the ancient midrash reached its greatest development was one of exile, historical catastrophe, and ruin, where the presence of God seemed withdrawn, and where redemption had to be sought elsewhere, more immanently—through remembrance, citation, a "tiger's leap into the past," new organizations of social and political power: until the Messiah comes. Benjamin understood the purgative and redemptive power of citation as a way of calling the word back to origin and to justice, and one could also apply Benjamin's analysis of Kraus's mode of citation to what appear to be arbitrary and violent rabbinic misreadings and acontextual quotations from the Scriptures: "In it is mirrored the angelic tongue in which all words, startled from the idyllic context of meaning, have become mottoes in the book of Creation" (*Refl* 269). Benjamin's theory of quotation would grant a theological depth and profound "philosophy of history" to this rabbinic material that traditional historicist readings do not.[1]

For Judaism, history as the scene of the divine-human drama was neither the linear flow of empty time nor the mythical sphere of eternal fate and repetition. To use Benjamin's terminology, the ancient rabbis constructed "constellations" of meanings between past and present historical events. For example, several distinct catastrophic events were said to have all occurred on the same date: "Five calamities befell our ancestors on the seventeenth of Tammuz and five on the ninth of Av. On the seventeenth of Tammuz, the Tablets of the Law were broken, the daily burnt offering ceased, the walls of Jerusalem were breached, wicked Apostomos burned the law and set up an idol in the Temple" (*Mishnah Tanith* 4:6). Roskies comments that the intent here is not to recall a coincidence of factual historical anniversaries "but to set the time of the first event, the primal act of a broken covenant that anticipated all the shattered stone down through the ages. The law had been defiled once, and yet again, always on the same day." The date becomes "transtemporal, reaching across the millennia" (17). Thus the devastation of the event is subsumed into collective memory for redemption. Benjamin's theory of dialectical image, constellation, and "now-time" as the relation of past and present sketches out a somewhat similar memory in the service of redemption.

In Benjamin, one way to deal with the forces of disaster and fragmentation is to use them to release the energies of redemption. Roskies also locates this strategy, which he calls a "survivor's tactic," in rabbinic thought:

> They can take the supreme act of profanity [e.g., destruction of the Temple] and convert it to sacred use, creating their own "sacred parody." . . . This technique of imitating the breach of God's promise in the parody of Scripture has been variously called "symbolic inversion" and "countercommentary" by those who recognize its use only in the modern age. It is in fact one of the two basic forms of Jewish response to catastrophe. (*Against* 20)[2]

In other words, by imitating the sacrilege or destruction, one mimics God's disruption of His promises and so enacts a "defiant affirmation," expanding the meaning of the text to allow for the suffering and negation experienced by the victims. What, however, is the difference between defiant affirmation and heretical negation? The sufferer's willingness "to accept the covenantal framework of guilt, punishment, and restitution" limits the parodic inversion (20). Thus parodic countercommentary, on the one hand, and the relocation of the catastrophe in the continuity of memory, on the other, are for Roskies the two sides of the Jewish response to catastrophe.

"Acceptance of the covenantal framework" meant not only adherence to a set of abstract concepts but accepting the covenant as law and concrete command—something which the ancient rabbis or the medieval and renaissance kabbalists never abrogated. Benjamin and Scholem, however, sought the concrete almost everywhere but in the covenantal aspect of Jewish law. In different ways, they each sought in the forces of negation and rupture, profanization and secularization, some hidden path to an as yet unforeseen redemption. Scholem depended on Zionism and a quasi-romantic-Hegelian dialectic of history to somehow bring this about, as he hints in his essay on Rosenzweig: "Perhaps God's last withdrawal is His revelation. Perhaps God's removal to the point of nothingness was a higher need, and He will reveal His kingship only to a world that has been emptied" ("Rosenzweig" 27–28).

Benjamin, faithful to the ruins, sought other ways to salvage them. A different kind of memory was one of these ways. Hope is turned backward, like the face of Benjamin's "angel of history." Benjamin sought that transtemporal moment of "now-time" in the finite world as both a utopian hope and a "revoluntionary chance for the oppressed." This exploration of memory was also part of his reaction against the bourgeois notion of time as a commodity, linear, objectified, measurable; and it is a critique of the modern—of the desperate search for novelty, the separation of information from experience, the pursuit of the sensations of the moment. But the kind of memory Benjamin evokes here is no simplistic nostalgia but a memory which reaches to an archaic, almost transpersonal level. He refers to it as Proust's *mémoire involontaire,* which is distinct from any subjective, conscious *mémoire volontaire.* In other words, it is a nonsubjective memory, emanating from a realm other than active personal cognition or chronological narrations of past events. As in Proust's famous scene of the *petite madeleine,* this involuntary memory is released in a sudden moment of recognition from an encounter with an object.

Proust is one of the best readers of Baudelaire, says Benjamin, because he saw in Baudelaire's *correspondances* moments of completion of memory apart from the shock time of consciousness:

> What Baudelaire meant by *correspondances* may be described as an experience which seeks to establish itself in crisis-proof form. This is only possible within the realm of ritual. . . . The *correspondances* are the data of remembrance— not historical data, but data of prehistory. What makes festive days great and significant is the encounter with an earlier life. (*Illum* 182)

Baudelaire's ability to appropriate these *correspondances* enabled him "to fathom the full meaning of the breakdown which he, a modern man, was witnessing" (181).

In Proust, memory is the last realm where experience undergoes a transformation, a profane illumination. Underlying all of Proust's labors of memory is "the quest for happiness" that is the key to his work:

> There is a dual will to happiness, a dialectics of happiness: a hymnic and an elegiac form. The one is the unheard of, the unprecedented, the height of bliss; the other, the eternal repetition, the eternal restoration of the original, the first happiness. It is this elegiac idea of happiness—it could also be called Eleatic— which for Proust transforms existence into a preserve of memory. (203)

Adorno locates this same desire in Benjamin himself, "the promise of happiness" as the center of Benjamin's thought and the source of its allure: "Everything that Benjamin said or wrote sounded as if thought, instead of rejecting the promises of fairy tales and children's books with its usual disgraceful 'maturity,' took them so literally that real fulfillment itself was now within sight of knowledge. In his philosophical topography renunciation is totally repudiated." And just as in Proust, where this desire for happiness has to bear up under painful disillusion, so too in Benjamin, "the devotion to happiness which has been denied is won only through a regretful sorrow" (*Prisms* 230). His work contains a dialectic between this will for a utopian, unprecedented future and the will for return to a blissful, lost Edenic past. The vaguely remembered paradise of the naming language in the early essays is not abandoned even in the Marxist phase.

HISTORY, MODERNITY, AND MESSIANISM

The contradictory nature of this dialectic of happiness also characterizes the painful "modernity" of Proust and Benjamin. Modernity itself is characterized in part, of course, by a changed sense of *time* in which the "modern," the present, is set against the ancient, the past—and past loses its authority, power, and value. The term *modern* was first used in the fifth century to distinguish the Christian present from the pagan past: it expresses the consciousness of a new relation to what had gone before. As Jurgen Habermas points out, "the term 'modern' appeared and reappeared exactly during those periods in Europe when the consciousness of a new epoch formed itself through a renewed relation to the ancients" ("Modernity" 3). With the French Enlightenment, the relation between ancient and modern became antagonistic, with the assumed superiority of the moderns. The belief in science and progress led to a devaluation of the past and orientation toward the future. In the nineteenth century, the consciousness of modernity became radicalized, and the past and present bitterly opposed. The search for the new now valorizes transitory phenomena and represents a desire for a kind of fulfilled present moment (as in Benjamin's "now-time"). This present is a subversive force which seeks to explode the continuum of tradition and history.

Paul deMan, in his discussion of literary modernity, aptly summarizes the contradictions of this position in a commentary on Nietzsche and Baudelaire, both archetypal "moderns." On the one hand, Nietzsche (in his *The Use and Abuse of History*) rigidly opposes history to modernity, and defines life as the ability to forget the past and live spontaneously in a nonhistorical way, to overcome anteriority. The true present thus achieved would then become a point of origin for a new departure. Or as deMan puts it, "The combined interplay of a deliberate forgetting with an action that is also a new origin reaches the full power of the idea of modernity" (*Blindness* 148).

Yet as Nietzsche discovers, history cannot be disposed of so easily. For the present is always experienced as transient, as something that passes away, into a past that becomes irrevocable and maintains claims on the present. To sever oneself from the past means also to cut oneself off from the present; and the present, moreover, is formed and determined by the past in many unalterable ways. Thus Nietzsche's writing, like that of so many other modernists including Freud and Kafka, is filled with parricidal imagery, with the revolt of sons against fathers whose strength is fearful and domineering. Still, each son becomes father in turn; modernity generates its own history, and it becomes impossible to overcome history. History and modernity conflict with each other yet are dependent upon one another. History needs modernity to keep it from becoming regressive and paralyzed, but modernity is always absorbed back into history. Like Nietzsche, deMan finds no escape from this predicament, which in his view is the mode of our contemporary modernity. History and modernity are locked in self-destroying union. Characteristically, the only consolation deMan can offer is that in this sense "modernity" has *always* been a feature of literature. In the end, "the assertions of literary modernity often end up by putting the possibility of being modern seriously into question" (*Blindness* 161–65).

However, as Matei Calinescu notes, there have been since the nineteenth century in effect two conflicting modernities: an aesthetic modernity, the kind defined by deMan and represented by thinkers such as Nietzsche, Baudelaire, and the surrealists, and a scientific bourgeois modernity which secularizes the notion of a forward movement of history toward a future redemption, with a concomitant belief in progress and technology (*Faces* 41). The emergence of utopianism, in this view, is the "single most important event in the modern intellectual history of the West," and the most significant legacy that the eighteenth century bequeathed to our modernity. It is the source of modern ideas of revolution, the "rage for utopia which pervades modernity" (63), and our orientation toward the future.

On the other hand, this secularized eschatology is also caught in self-contradictions. Secular utopianism is a critique of the Christian eternity and desires a totally new future, but it contains at the same time an anti-utopian drive. Utopianism defines itself as a future different from the past and imperfect present. Yet a final future perfection would mean a stasis, a repetition, a fulfillment infinitely repeating itself:

> Modernity, rendered possible by the consciousness of an irreversible time (which critical reason has purified of all transcendent or sacred memory), engenders the utopia of a radiant instant of invention that can suppress time by repeating itself endlessly—as the central element of a new and final tradition (no matter how antitraditionally conceived).

Thus modernity "perpetuates the past it tries to negate and opposes the notion of the future it tries to promote" (68). It is, to use Octavio Paz's phrase, a "tradition against itself" (78).

Scholem would argue contra Calinescu that secular utopianism is not solely a legacy of the rationalist eighteenth century but also has roots in the theology of Jewish messianism and its modern transformations. Scholem argues that the distinguishing characteristic of Jewish messianism is that its activist stirrings are directed *outward*, in contrast to the Christian tendency to make redemption first and foremost an *inward* affair. This radical activist element in Jewish messianism influenced "the political and chiliastic Messianism of important religious movements with Christianity" (*Mess Idea* 15–16). And though Jewish messianism was itself reciprocally influenced by Christianity's tendency to make messianism an inner condition of the spiritual life, it is distinguished from Christian messianism by not ultimately differentiating between internal and external salvation: "An inwardness which does not present itself in the most external realm and is not bound up with it in every way, was regarded here as of no value. According to the dialectics of Jewish mysticism, the drive to the essence was at the same time the drive outward" (17).[3]

Scholem also fiercely argued against what he considered to be the distortion of Jewish intellectual history by scholars and philosophers (e.g., Hermann Cohen) who presented Jewish messianism as a purely rational, progressive, utopian concept in harmony with Enlightenment ideals: "Jewish Messianism is in its origins and by its nature—this cannot be sufficiently emphasized—a theory of catastrophe—this theory stresses the revolutionary cataclysmic element in the transition from every historical present to the Messianic future" (7). The dialectic of positive and negative forces, of apocalyptic transformation and restoration of a lost past, characterized for Scholem the essence of Jewish messianism, and made it particularly susceptible to powerful secular reinterpretations in the modern era.

In his analysis, of the three central theological concepts of Judaism, "creation, revelation, and redemption," only the *last*, in the form of messianism, remains vital and powerful today. The messianic idea, despite being attenuated, "has proved itself of highest effectiveness and relevance—even in its secularized forms. It was better able to stand a reinterpretation into the secular realm than the other two ideas . . . it has become the center of great visions in the present age" (*JJC* 284). For Scholem, the sources of Jewish tradition were such that they could be extrapolated in a variety of contradictory ways, for the "Jewish tradition preserves a constant conflict—never ending and never settled—among opposing elements in Messianism. . . . between apocalypic tendencies and those aiming at their abolition, as well as between restorative and Utopian ones" (284). The messianic idea crystallizes from both the apocalyptic and restorative tendencies, but these two factors are never in harmony and fluctuate wildly throughout Jewish history (*Mess Idea* 3).

The restorative tendency in the messianic idea envisions the return of a past condition remembered as ideal, the time of the First Temple and the Davidic Kingdom. As Scholem puts it, "Here hope is turned backwards" (3). But the utopian tendency presses forward to the vision of a future state, a condition which has never yet existed. Moreover, the restorative force itself contains a utopian impulse which is projected back on the past: and the utopian force contains the image of an ideal past projected onto the future—along with entirely new elements. These extravagant apocalyptic and utopian elements come to the fore in "the writings of the most important ideologists of revolutionary Messianism, such as Ernst Bloch, Walter Benjamin, Theodor Adorno, and Herbert Marcuse, whose acknowledged or unacknowledged ties to their Jewish heritage are evident" (*JJC* 287). In these thinkers, he argues, the rationalist utopian idea of history as gradually progressive is rejected for an apocalyptic sense that the era of redeemed life is entirely antithetical to this era. These secularized thinkers similarly adopt the radicalized theological idea that there can be no smooth transition between the present era and the messianic idea: catastrophe, destruction, upheavel must occur before the utopian view of realized redemption can be fulfilled.

In ancient Jewish theology, these extravagant aspects of apocalyptic thinking were partially a response to the terrors and catastrophes of Jewish history, particularly the destruction of the Second Temple in the first century of the Common Era. But in one of his most controversial theses, Scholem argues that historical trauma also precipitated the development of the Lurianic school of Kabbalah in the sixteenth century. The Lurianic idea that creation occurred through a primordial act of God's "withdrawal" or self-contraction (*tzimtzum*) had a corollary doctrine called the "Breaking of the Vessels." In the process of creation, the divine forces "shattered" their containing "vessels"; the fragments of those vessels "fell" and became "embedded" in the lowest material worlds. Humanity's task is to repair those vessels and so bring about redemption of the cosmos itself. Scholem argued that Lurianic Kabbalah was a *historical reaction* to the catastrophe of the Jews' expulsion from Spain in 1492. In other words,

Lurianic Kabbalah itself became a way of explaining and redeeming *historical* catastrophe through a myth of *cosmic* catastrophe at the heart of creation. Scholem theorizes that Luria and his followers transposed the historical catastrophes suffered by the Spanish Jews into the intradivine life of God, thereby absorbing the apocalyptic expectations these historical catastrophes had ignited, and providing an answer to the great problems of the time. The historical sufferings of the Jews became symbols and enactments of a larger cosmic drama, a great mythic story. The meaning of Jewish exile and redemption was now a reflection of a cosmic cataclysm that affected the very life of God. The vitality of these symbols and their appeal for popular religion made them adaptable to a social ideology, made Kabbalah popular among the masses, and provided "a new myth for Judaism," though this was not Luria's original intent (*Sevi* 27).[4]

Moshe Idel has argued contrary to Scholem, however, that Lurianic Kabbalah was a complex system that was inaccessible to the masses, and its "widespread dissemination . . . in the wake of Sabbantianism, assumed by modern scholarship has yet to be demonstrated by detailed studies" (*Kabbalah* 257). The messianism of Lurianic Kabbalah was no greater than that of earlier Kabbalah, and like earlier theurgic Kabbalah

> perceived human activity to be capable of restoring the primeval harmony to the divine world, but such activity, although it might carry eschatological overtones, certainly did not constitute messianic activism. Luria, like the *Zohar,* envisioned the achievement of a perfect state in the divine world as a cumulative process requiring collective theurgical activity. . . . The individual Messiah was emblematic of the attainment of the messianic age rather than its initiation. (259)

Idel thus takes issue with Scholem's central thesis that Sabbatianism, focused on the person of Sabbatai Sevi as the Messiah, was a result of the spread of Lurianic Kabbalah among the masses. Idel argues, moreover, that Scholem's misperceptions of the relations between Lurianism and Sabbatianism, the expulsion of the Jews from Spain, and Lurianic Kabbalah are due to flaws in his historiosophy—his assumption that "a given cultural or religious phenomenon is closely intertwined with or dependent upon its immediate historical predecessors. *Historia non facit saltus*" (264). Benjamin, of course, advocated precisely the opposite: that history does make jumps, and that the role of the historical materialist was to trace the constellations of these jumps, to activate new ones, and so to release the redemptive energies within history.

Idel also argues that Kabbalah itself was more interested in primordial and eschatological rather than historical processes, and so needs also to be interpreted in this light. Lurianic texts never even mention the Expulsion, nor can one posit, as did Scholem, that a historical event such as the expulsion of the Jews from Spain was a necessary and dominant causal factor in the subsequent evolution of all of kabbalistic thought. Rather, innovations in Lurianic Kabbalah were due to inner developments (265). Yet the "impact of the Expulsion is a cornerstone of Scholem's historiosophy." In Scholem's grand schema, the expulsion of the Jews from Spain generated messianic expectations that Lurianic Kabbalah articulated, and which in turn were taken up by Sabbatianism and the even more heretical messianic movement of Jacob Frank's "redemption through sin"; a counterreaction supposedly led to the neutralization of these messianic tendencies in Hassidism and their dialectical reappropriation in the Jewish Enlightenment. But Idel demurs:

> The conviction that characterizes Scholem's statements and the uncritical way in which they have been accepted by both the larger public and the scholars who deal with Jewish mysticism and history, have had little to do with the historical facts as I know them. No elaborate discussions based upon detailed analysis of all the pertinent material underpin these far-reaching historical visions. (266)

Idel does not speculate on the reasons for this uncritical acceptance or for the grandiosity of Scholem's historiosophic vision. Perhaps we can say that while claiming to write the history of the Kabbalah, Scholem was actually also writing that "metaphysic" to which he had so early aspired—that Scholem, like Benjamin, was writing history as a "constellation," sighting the "dialectical" images which flashed up at a moment of danger, the relations between present and past charged with "now-time." The moment of danger was a dying German and Jewish culture in Europe, the catastrophes of World War I, Nazism, and fascism, and the need for some apocalyptic change—be it removal to Palestine or political revolution to break clear a path to new life. Like other members of the German-Jewish intelligentsia, Benjamin and Scholem devalued the historical present as inauthentic and repressive, and thought it required a radical transformation or some destructive purgation. Scholem indeed makes the parallel between Germany in 1933 and Spain in 1492 in some chilling remarks contained in a letter of April 13, 1933, to Benjamin, now exiled in Ibiza:

> The horrible thing about it, though, if one dares to say so, is that the human cause of the Jews in Germany only stands to benefit if a real pogrom were to take place, instead of the "cold" pogrom that they will be trying to restrict themselves to. It represents almost the only chance of bringing about something positive from such an eruption. For although the extent of the catastrophe is of historic proportions, and it can teach us something about 1492, the stuff of which resistance is made has reduced in German Jewry to a very small fraction of what existed in those days. (*Corr* 39)

Scholem thought that the idea of a catastrophic and destructive transition from the historical present to the messianic future had been transposed into the language of political revolution through dialectical materialism. Authentic human experience and true history were now placed in an eschatological postrevolutionary future (*JJC* 285–87). Since these utopian visions of redemption required destructive purgation of a degenerate culture, they also tended to be antinomian and anarchic. This strain was found in Scholem and Benjamin's early philosophy of language, in which the "pure word" could not be concretized; so, too, in Benjamin and the Frankfurt School's later political philosophy, and Scholem's later disillusioned Zionism, the future utopia could not be grasped concretely.[5] Nevertheless, it still could be used to enact a negative judgment on the corruption of the past and present. Adorno expressed that sensibility magnificently in the final paragraph of his *Minima Moralia*:

> The only philosophy which can be responsibly practiced in the face of despair is the attempt to contemplate all things as they would present themselves from the standpoint of redemption. Knowledge has no light but that shed on the world by redemption: all else is reconstruction, mere technique. Perspectives must be fashioned that displace and estrange the world, reveal it to be, with its rifts and crevices, as indigent and distorted as it will appear one day in the messianic light. To gain such perspectives without velleity or violence, entirely from felt contact with its objects—this alone is the task of thought. It is the simplest of all things, because the situation calls imperatively for such knowledge, indeed because consummate negativity, once squarely faced, delineates the mirror image of its opposite. But it is also the utterly impossible thing, because it presupposes a standpoint removed, even though by a hair's breadth, from the scope of existence, whereas we well know that any possible knowledge must not only first be wrested from what is, if it shall hold good, but is also marked, for this very reason, by the same distortion and indigence which it seeks to escape. The more passionately thought denies its conditionality for the sake of the unconditional, the more unconsciously, and so calamitously, it is delivered up to the world. Even its own impossibility it must at last comprehend for the sake of the possible. But beside the demand thus placed on thought, the question of the reality or unreality of redemption itself hardly matters. (247)

Similarly, the memory of the irremediably lost pure language of naming in Benjamin's early essays had served as a judgment on the fallenness of our present language of arbitrary signification. While Scholem and Benjamin shared a belief that language was ultimately the repository of truth, neither thought it provided direct access—or explicit direct meaning. For Scholem and the early Benjamin, the truths hidden in the depths of language had to be elicited indirectly, through commentary, critique, through an examination of the traditions of interpretations of that truth. The pure language or ultimate Word did not give forth any positive, concrete, determinate meaning, but rather was the potential for infinite meanings. For the later Benjamin, the "open air of history" became the arena of interpretation—of the constellations of historical objects in dialectical images which released the energies of redemption and revolution. Nevertheless, these "images" still did not embody any concrete, positive description of what the transformed future would look like. As Anson Rabinbach aptly puts it, "Language is the medium of redemption, but history is the showplace of catastrophe," and in Benjamin and the Frankfurt School, the sense of the catastrophic collapse of European culture subsumed Jewish messianism into radical cultural criticism ("Between Enlightenment" 121, 123). This modern Jewish messianism was a kind of "ethos" of radical Jewish intellectuals combined with a libertarian anarchism, a romantic anticapitalism, and a conviction that the world as it was had to be repudiated and the old order destroyed (83). But it was, finally, a "Jewishness without Judaism" (82).

Scholem was aware that the revolutionary nihilism of the German Jews was quite distant from the traditional Jewish ideal of utopia as the realization of ethical values. Morality appears in the work of this avant-garde "only as a distant frontier. It escapes the relativism of empirical moral concepts in an imperfect world by jettisoning them and by their nihilistic disavowal" (*JJC* 276). But as Michael Jennings writes, Benjamin's radical historiography, his assertion that one must "brush history against the grain" to oppose the barbarism and violence masked by historicism, is also an attempt "to reintroduce an explicit and conscious ethical element in history writing . . . to rewrite history in such a way that a purgative and redemptive political action ensues" (*Dialectical* 51). Richard Wolin adds that Benjamin suppressed his early abstract metaphysics for his later materialist theory of knowledge in order to open phenomena to redemption "*exoterically* rather than *esoterically*" (*Benjamin* 203). While this is quite true, Benjamin still was faithful to his earlier thought in maintaining that dialectical images were encountered only in *language,* and had to be read; in this sense, he maintained, they were "historical" rather than "archaic." He had transferred Goethe's *Urphänomen* from the "pagan context of nature into the Jewish contexts of history" ("Theory of Knowledge" [N 2a, 4]). "Jewish" because for the Jews, history was the scene of divine redemption.

HISTORY WILL NOT BRING THE MESSIAH

Yet Benjamin's "Theological-Political Fragment," which Scholem ascribes to the early 1920s, though others date it to the late 1930s, stresses the disjunction between the messianic and the historical, and denies to the messianic any concrete ethical imperatives for the present. Nature of itself is not complete, nor is history, he writes. "Only the Messiah himself consummates all history, in the sense that he alone redeems, completes, creates its relation to the Messianic. For this reason nothing historical can relate itself on its own account to anything Messianic." The messianic is what *ends* history; it is not a progressive "goal," and the Divine Kingdom cannot serve as a guide to build the political order of the profane. But in his characteristic way, Benjamin correlates these two opposite orders through their very opposition and collision:

> The order of the profane should be erected on the idea of happiness. The relation of this order to the Messianic is one of the essential teachings of the philosophy of history. It is the precondition for a mystical conception of history, containing a problem that can be represented figuratively. If one arrow points to the goal toward which the profane dynamic acts, and another marks the direction of Messianic intensity, then certainly the quest of free humanity for happiness runs counter to the Messianic direction; but just as a force can, through acting, increase another that is acting in the opposite direction, so the order of the profane assists, through being profane, the coming of the Messianic kingdom. (*Refl* 312)

Needless to say, this relation of opposing forces runs counter to the Hegelian style of dialectics, wherein the two opposites are generated out of each other and ultimately synthesized in a higher order. Again, there is no mediating force or "totality" into which they are absorbed. The analogy is to a kind of physical law of nature, of pressure and counterpressure. Again, it is as if the very force of compression could release a counterforce of redemption and truth.

The order of the profane "should be erected on the idea of happiness," yet Benjamin also defines profane redemption and profane happiness in this fragment in a "backwards" way as the "eternal downfall of wordly existence," and "the rhythm of this eternal transient world existence, transient in its totality, in its spatial but also in its temporal totality, the rhythm of Messianic nature, is happiness. For nature is Messianic by reason of its eternal and total passing away" (*Refl* 313). Corngold and Jennings interpret this to mean that "the coming of the messianic order is hastened precisely by the movement of human history towards it own extinction (even in bliss)." This is a paradigmatic expression of Benjamin's nihilism and apocalypticism,

> his sense of history as an irreversible process of continuous deterioration [which] will remain a cornerstone of his political thought. . . . He can tolerate the mood of historical optimism only as it arises from a reflection of the process of decline. There is strictly speaking no idea of progress in Benjamin's thought except through political action which accelerates the rate of decline. ("Benjamin/Scholem" 359–60)

Writes Benjamin, profane happiness is found "only in good fortune" as a "wordly restitution" that leads to the eternity of downfall. Yet "restitution" is a kind of return or making whole what was lost in transience and natural decay. Benjamin seems to be saying that the eternal falling of nature, eternal transience, in the very "eternity" or repetition of its tran-

sience allows for a "return" (like some Nietzschean "eternal return")[6]—
and also for a transience of the very loss as well.

The "eternity of downfall" also is a kind of profane, inverted counterpart to the "eternal delay" of the Messiah in classical Jewish religious
thought. Maimonides's classic formulation of the Jewish belief in the coming of the Messiah is usually translated as "and though he may tarry, I
anticipate him, nonetheless, on every day, when he may come." Steven
Schwarzschild follows Hermann Cohen in interpreting this phrase to mean
that not only has the Messiah not yet come, but "he will always not yet
have come, into all historical eternality" ("On Eschatology" 172). There is
an ambiguity in the grammar of the Hebrew phrase *ahakeh lo bekhol yom
sheyavo*—"I will anticipate him on every day, when he may come." "On
every day, when he may come" also can mean "on every day that he
comes," i.e., "that he does come, conditionally, on every day, on all days,
into all eternity," as numerous talmudic legends assert. Schwarzschild
notes the connection between Jewish doctrines of resurrection of the dead
and immortality connected with messianism and eschatology, and similar
ideas in Adorno, Marx, and Benjamin. The postmessianic is what occurs
after the coming of the Messiah, after the completion of the spiritualiza-
tion of history, and what finally resolves the dichotomy of matter/spirit or
body/soul. Adorno in *Negative Dialectics* writes, "Hope clings, as in Mi-
gnon's song, to the transfigured body" ("On Eschatology" 179–82). He
cites Adorno's statement that "the center of Benjamin's philosophy is the
idea of the salvation of the dead as the restitution of deformed life through
the perfection of its objectification" (205, n. 58).

Benjamin writes that profane wordly restitution corresponds in its own
way to the spiritual restitution of theological immortality—just as he elsewhere cites the role of "memory" in history writing as one form of this
worldly restitution. This eternally transient worldly existence is "the
rhythm of Messianic nature" as happiness. In its eternal passing away and
transience, nature points back toward the messianic, which is the apocalyptic end and complete (i.e., eternal) downfall of the profane. In Benjamin, "progress" is often imaged as a kind of abrupt inversion, a being
forced forward by going backward. Redemption is a kind of a "backside"
which cannot be seen—as in the metaphor in Benjamin's letter to Scholem
about Kafka's search "on the nether side of that 'nothingness,' in its inside
lining, so speak—to feel his way towards redemption," a quest for which
there was not any traditional theological victory (*Corr* 129). This backside
was also the position of Benjamin's "angel of history," facing and trans-
fixed by the piles of ruin which constitute the past, but being blown "backward" toward the future, propelled almost against his will by the winds of
paradise.

Since there is a disjunction between the profane and the messianic, or
history and redemption, the present and the revolutionary future, the task
of world politics, Benjamin concludes in the "Theological-Political Frag-

ment," is to strive after this eternal and total passing away of nature (thus allying itself with the messianic aspect of nature), and its "method must be called nihilism" (*Refl* 313). Needless to say, this "fragment" is an argument of intense compression and enigma, in which politics and theology, redemption and nihilism are mixed in complicated and unorthodox ways. "Eternity," on the one hand, is the "spiritual always" as the "forever" where the moment is not lost, and, conversely, the "profane always" of nature as the "always" passing away of transience. The secular, in its very secularism, points back to the theological. Or, as Irving Wohlfarth puts it in describing the messianic aspect of the Arcades project, for Benjamin it is the "task of the profane to be profane, to ignore theology, and *thereby* rejoin it" ("Re-fusing" 6). DeMan once again misreads the "Theological-Political Fragment" as a complete denial of messianism and theology ("Task of the Translator").

"MY SECULARISM IS NOT SECULAR"

The movement "backward" is also evoked in Benjamin's description of the radical historical materialist's role in the "Theses on the Philosophy of History": "He regards it as his task to brush history against the grain" (*Illum* 257). This phrase is aptly used by David Biale for the epigraph to his study of Scholem's own historiography. Biale's thesis is that Scholem, like the other thinkers of his era, wrote his own form of "counterhistory"—defined as "the theory that there is a continuing dialectic between an exoteric and subterranean tradition. The true history lies beneath the surfaces and often contradicts the assumptions of the normative tradition" (*Scholem* 195).

Yosef Haim Yerushalmi in his own reflections on "history" and "memory" notes that modern Jewish historiography was an ideology which was itself precipitated by the crisis of Jewish emancipation:

> The modern effort to reconstruct the Jewish past begins at a time that witnesses a sharp break in the continuity of Jewish living and hence also an ever-growing decay of Jewish group memory. In this sense, if for no other, history becomes what it had never been before—the faith of fallen Jews. For the first time history, not a sacred text, becomes the arbiter of Judaism. (*Zakhor* 86)

In the modern era, unlike the medieval world, there is little mutual interaction between Jewish philosophy and general philosophy, and so, Yerushalmi adds, historicism has become the primary channel between Jewish and modern culture. Yet that modern vision of "history" also stood in tension with its subject matter, for it repudiated the main premises on which Jewish history had been built—divine providence as the central causal force, and the uniqueness of Jewish history (89). The modern sense of historical time as a fluid medium meant, moreover, that Judaism could not be defined by any a priori form but was subject to open-ended evolution.

Yerushalmi, however, does not think that modern historiography can heal the wounds of memory or halt or replace the decay of Jewish collective memory, for it is an entirely different kind of recollection. In any case, "It is not modern Jewish historiography that has shaped modern Jewish conceptions of the past. Literature and ideology have been far more decisive. . . . Jews . . . seem to await a new, metahistorical myth, for which the novel provides at least a temporary modern surrogate" (96, 98). Myth and memory are what generate and condition action.

Certainly Benjamin understood that, and so tried to write a different kind of history, but one which opposed the regressive and reactionary nature of "myth," and one in which the dialectical image allowed for a different kind of remembering tied to the redemptive needs of the present. Scholem discovered what he thought was a subterranean world of "myth" in the Kabbalah and Sabbatianism, but he warned that while those documents from the past changed our understanding of the potentials of Jewish life, there could be no immediate application of them to the present. Cultural Zionism, instead, was the guide to immediate action in the present. Scholem's historian had to approach the "mist that hangs around the mountain" with the tools of philology. Yet it is no accident that Scholem's historiographical work has itself become the source material for poets, novelists, and literary critics in search of "a new myth." In the aftermath of the catastrophes of World War II, Scholem's own writings on the Kabbalah seemed to provide materials for a new postmodern "myth" for alienated Jews who, like their historical precursors in medieval Spain and modern Germany, had lost their faith in rational philosophy, progressive history, and the covenant. The literary critic Harold Bloom goes so far as to say that "Scholem's Gnosticism, masking as historical scholarship, is somehow more available as an emergent Jewish theology than is Rosenzweig's *The Star of Redemption* or Buber. . . . many of us shape a still inchoate and perhaps heretical new Torah out of the writings of Freud, Kafka, and Scholem" ("Masks" 23).

Bloom is elaborating upon the romantic and revisionist aspects of Scholem's historiography. What Bloom thinks he finds in Scholem's studies of the heretical tendencies in kabbalistic gnosticism are the ways in which Jewish identity, always changing, "conceals its changes under the masks of the normative. The authority of identity is not constancy-in-change, but the *originality* that usurps tradition and becomes a fresh authority, strangely in the name of continuity" ("Masks" 9). Bloom is attempting to effect, via Scholem, an identification of secular modernist Nietzschean counterhistory with the traditional modes of constructing Jewish identity throughout Jewish history. Judaism itself becomes interpreted along the lines of Bloom's literary theory of revisionism and poetic influence as a Nietzschean struggle to overcome the past and become one's own origin. Counterhistory had been defined by Nietzsche as the "attempt to gain a past *a posteriori* from which we might spring, as against that from which we do spring" (*Use and Abuse* 21)[7] Scholem's studies of the past ruptures and latent heresies in Jewish theory would thus become models for a new Jewish theology in our own age, an age fractured, broken, and alienated from much of the normative Jewish past. In light of Scholem's work, says Bloom, "who can say, or ever could say, what is heretical in regard to our traditions" (23).

But even though the problem of "heresy" and "profanation" is complex, is it so impossible to distinguish between the heretical and the nonheretical? Scholem's uses of the Kabbalah to blur these lines was part of his affirmation of the "nothingness of revelation." The inaccessible, completely transcendent aspect of God is called by the kabbalists the *ein sof* ("without end, limitless, infinite"), and the first *sefira* or divine emanation is often referred to as *ayin* ("nothingness"). Philosophically, a problem for the kabbalists was how to maintain a distance between the *Ein Sof* and *ayin* to retain the fundamental Jewish belief in God's absolute transcendence and difference from the world. Luria's idea of the *tzimtzum* helped to supply the mechanism to retain this distance between the "nothing" of God and the "something" of the world so that pantheism—the emanation of the world out of God's essence—would be prevented.

In Aphorism 5 of his "Unhistorical Aphorisms," Scholem describes the relationship as follows: God's transcendent plenitude beyond all knowledge "becomes Nothingness in the primal act of emanation" as the beginning of creation: "This is that Nothingness of God which necessarily had to seem to the mystics, from the basic perspective of their path, to be the ultimate stage in the process of 'profanation' " (78–79). Scholem puts the word *profanation* in quotation marks. Why the passage through "nothing" should mean "profanation" is not clear, especially if *nothing* is the adaptation of a philosophical term to describe the traditional Jewish refusal to identify God with any natural Being. If "nothing" in this sense meant the affirmation of God's transcendence, and God's transcendence for both Kabbalah and traditional Jewish thought was never disconnected from the realm of the commandments and ethics (as Idel has shown), there was no necessary "profanation" involved but rather ethical "purification."

Steven Schwarzschild, proceeding from the philosophical legacy of Kant and Hermann Cohen, makes a similar critique of Scholem. The notion of a divine emptying or withdrawal was not at all a "profanation," or an antirationalistic or anti-*halakhic* move. In classical Jewish thought, the absolutely transcendent God related to the world through imperatives. History was the enactment of those imperatives toward the messianic goal. Kabbalah and Hassidic thought shared the same body of values and thought, especially regarding the *ta'amei ha mitzvot,* the theurgic contemplations of the meanings and efficacy of the commandments. The elimination of any "divine essence" through the divine imperatives was a structure similarly effected in the negative withdrawal of the divine name from the empirical world, and the ethical purification of the world in preparation for the total and universal return of God in the world ("R. Hutner" 260). *Halakah* is then the way to the goal of the eschaton: the "*eschaton* is in its very nature law-ruled, and history is the law-ruled road to the law-ruled *eschaton*" (245). Scholem then would also be incorrect to oppose Jewish mysticism to Jewish philosophy; Jewish mysticism would be but another form of Jewish philosophy analogous to the relation of Neo-Platonism and Platonism: "Rationalism tends to use Platonic ideas as constructionalistic concepts; mysticism tends to hypostatize them as ontological claims" (258). They regularly come together and can be translated into one another (260).

But Bloom and Scholem's entire interpretation depends on a definition of "normative" Judaism as a sterile, empty legalism with which we have little in common, and to which is opposed a "vitalizing" high romantic and poetic passion for creating new "myth" and autonomous self-generation—albeit tempered by a postmodern awareness of our "belatedness" and the impossibility of being completely original. As Biale puts it, the historical study of the sources of Judaism provided Scholem with a way to return to Judaism without Orthodoxy as "his personal solution to the problem of Judaism in a secular age" (*Scholem* 207). Like Benjamin's solution, this answer was idiosyncratic and mandarin, yet it was uneasily conjoined with a broad political movement—Zionism for Scholem, communism for Benjamin. Both indeed were "theologians marooned in the profane."

In personal interviews, Scholem affirmed that "the transition through secularism [is] necessary, unavoidable. But I don't think that Zionism's secular vision is the ultimate vision" (*JJC* 33). Out of secularization, he believed, a new spirituality will "dialectically" emerge, a new manifestation of God, and a new flourishing of life for the Jewish people in Zion: "I am sure of my belief in God. My secularism is not secular" (46). As to the possibility of Jewish mysticism in our time, Scholem was more circumspect and had no clear answer. Our age, he noted, is one of crisis and disaster, conditions ripe for the production of such mysticism. But the communal bases of Jewish life have been weakened, and the faith in an absolute revelation of God's word and the authority of Jewish law have been questioned. In his view, anyone who does not accept the great fundamental principle of "Torah from Heaven" or the revelation of Sinai "may be considered to be an anarchist"; among these he includes those who have been "diverted into historical criticism." And "as far as religion is concerned, we are all of us, to some extent anarchists" ("Reflections" 50). This anarchism offers little hope, Scholem realizes, for any kind of new mysticism to have broad communal and public significance.

Zionism, however, did have that communal, public, and material significance for the entire Jewish people. At the same time Scholem realized that the needs of building the nation in Zion and secularization had diverted energies. These energies might in other times have been poured into more traditional forms of Jewish spirituality, or into mysticism. Yet, he concludes, "who knows the limits of sanctity? . . . Perhaps a double way is possible, secular and holy, toward which we are evolving? Perhaps this holiness will be revealed at the heart of the secular, and the mystical is not recognized because it appears in forms which are new to the concepts of tradition" and will be of secular significance. The poet Walt Whitman is the example he offers—a writer whose song of America emanated from "a feeling of the absolute holiness of the completely secular." Whitman represents for Scholem the whole class of recent visionaries in which mystical experiences took on "the forms of higher naturalistic consciousness . . . only outwardly devoid of traditional religiosity" (52). Here, as at the end of his essay on the linguistic theory of the Kabbalah, Scholem again turns to the poet to be the modern carrier of the mystical impulse—and to a high romantic poet at that.

THE ANGEL OF HISTORY

Benjamin, too, wondered what illumination and what redemption might come out of the ruins of the secular. But at the end of his life, he did not turn to the poets for answers. In the "Theses on the Philosophy of History," written after his release from the internment camp in France and just before his suicide, Benjamin wrote perhaps his most poignant allegory about the "angel of history." In the final moment of allegory, Benjamin had written in the *Trauerspiel* study, the death's head turns into an angel's countenance (*OGTD* 232). But it is the distressed face of an angel he contemplates here.

He prefaces his description of the angel of history with an excerpt from a poem Scholem had written as a birthday present for Benjamin in 1921, entitled "Greetings from Angelus." The poem was about a Paul Klee painting, *Angelus Novus,* that Benjamin had purchased. Scholem reports that "Benjamin always considered the picture his most important possession" (*JJC* 219). When Benjamin made out a will in 1932, he directed that the painting be bequeathed to Scholem as a special personal gift.[8] Eight years later, in 1940, when Benjamin escaped Nazi-occupied Paris, he cut the picture from its frame and packed it in one of the two suitcases with his papers that he entrusted to George Bataille, who hid them in the Bibliotheque Nationale (210). The excerpt from Scholem's poem which Benjamin used as an epigraph for the "Theses" reads: "My wing is ready for flight, / I would like to turn back. / If I stayed timeless time / I would have little luck." Benjamin then writes:

> A Klee painting named "Angelus Novus" shows an angel looking as though he is about to move away from something he is fixedly contemplating. His eyes are staring, his mouth is open, his wings are spread. This is how one pictures

the angel of history. His face is turned toward the past. Where we perceive a chain of events, he sees one single catastrophe which keeps piling wreckage upon wreckage and hurls it in front of his feet. The angel would like to stay, awaken the dead, and make whole what has been smashed. But a storm is blowing from Paradise; it has got caught in his wings with such violence that the angel can no longer close them. This storm irresistibly propels him into the future to which his back is turned, while the pile of debris before him grows skyward. This storm is what we call progress. (*Illum* 257–58)

The image of angels appears throughout Benjamin's work. In the early 1920s he had plans to found his own journal and intended to call it *Angelus Novus*. In the 1931 essay on Kraus, Benjamin also refers to Klee's *New Angel*, "who preferred to free men by taking from them, rather than make them happy by giving to them," as an image for Karl Kraus's mission of purifying language and society through destructive critique. The Kraus essay concludes with the image of the new angel:

Perhaps one of those who, according to the Talmud, are at each moment created anew in countless throngs, and who, once they have raised their voices before God, cease and pass into nothingness. Lamenting, chastising, rejoicing? No matter—on this evanescent voice the ephemeral work of Kraus is modeled. Angelus—that is the messenger of the old engravings. (*Refl* 273)

Benjamin's knowledge of these talmudic angels came, of course, from Scholem, with whom he had conversed about Jewish angelology (*SF* 100–101). But the angel is also the final allegorical emblem that concentrates within itself all the ruins of Benjamin's life. Scholem writes that Klee's painting literally served Benjamin "as a picture for meditation and as a moment of a spiritual vocation" (*JJC* 210). The gaze of the angel seems to encompass horror, blessing, melancholy, and hope; its eyes are both averted and staring; the drawing itself is at once childlike and fragmentary, enigmatic and emblematic. The angel's shape, Geoffrey Hartman also notes, is like Torah scrolls unraveling (*Criticism* 79).

In Hebrew, the word for angel (*malach*) literally means "messenger"; yet this messenger's tidings are unclear and his power is limited. He is an angel being exiled and is impotent to halt his flight, caught between hope and catastrophe. In the Karl Kraus essay, Benjamin had associated Klee's angel with the evanescence of the beings described in the Talmud; their song of praise, their truth, was one of the moment—a full present but a transient one. The voices raised in lament, hope, horror, chastisement were those of beings living in a precarious instant and soon to vanish into nothing, yet also to be followed by the instantaneous creation of another angelic horde.

This transience is reminiscent of the dialectic of happiness Benjamin had described in the Proust essay, the moment of bliss which, however, is evanescent and disappears—countered by the repetition of the experience which had dissolved into the past, the "yet again." In the "Theological-

Political Fragment," the eternal transience of nature was a force of both downfall and redemption—the profane counterpart of a messianic redemption, the messianic kingdom which will transfigure and consummate nature. Until that ever-delayed occurrence, however, the profane search for happiness and a political nihilism points back/forward toward the messianic. There is an apocalyptic disjunctive link—not one of linear causality—from profane to messianic.

Just as the profane connects with the messianic by a seemingly backward move, a move in the opposite direction, similarly Benjamin's angel of history in the "Theses" is blown backward into the future, fixing his gaze on the past as a catastrophe, not a chain of events, and gazing in pain as ruins and wreckage are piled at his feet. But this angel does not sing praises or hymns; he is impotent. He would like to stay, resurrect the dead, heal, redeem, but he cannot. The storm from paradise is pushing him in the opposite direction, back into the future.[9] Paradise here is the source of a "storm," not a peaceful idyll. The storm is a violent force which catches the angel and propels him against his will. This storm also seems to represent the destructive aspects of a revolution, whose purgation alone can bring any "progress" to the ruins of history. Scholem again misreads by completely depoliticizing the text; he claims it propounds a cyclic conception of history rather than disjunctive allegory: "paradise is at once the origin and the primal past of man as well as the utopian image of the future of his redemption—a conception of the historical process that is really cyclical rather than dialectical" (*JJC* 232).

In some fragments written in 1933 on the island of Ibiza after he had fled Nazi Germany, Benjamin had also written of the new angel, calling it "Agesilaus Santander." Scholem decodes this name as an anagram of *Der Angelus Satanas*, "The Angel Satan," who represents a combination of angelic and satanic elements. Another part of Benjamin's vision of this angel was taken from a Jewish tradition he had discussed with Scholem, a tradition "about the personal angel of each human being who represents the latter's secret self, and whose name nevertheless remains hidden from him" (*JJC* 213). Benjamin writes in "Agesilaus Santander" that his own personal angel was interrupted in his moment of praise to God and "made me pay for having disturbed him at his work" (205). In the second version of the piece, Benjamin, with all the poignancy of the exile refugee, writes that the angel "resembles all from which I have had to part: persons and above all things. In the things I no longer have, he resides. He makes them transparent, and behind all of them there appears to me the one for whom they are intended" (207). Fixing his glance on Benjamin, the angel tries to

> pull him along with himself on that way into the future from which he came. . . . He wants happiness: the conflict in which lies the ecstasy of the unique, new, as yet unlived with that bliss of the "once more," the having again, the lived. This is why he can hope for the new on no way except on the way of the return home, when he takes a new human being along with him. (207–208)

Yet this is a happiness without fulfillment; it is a conflict, a dialectic without resolution, a constant oscillation between a moment that cannot last and a repetition in search of home. The "yet again," the repetition, seeks to grasp the evanescent moment of the "not yet" and the unique.

The angel wants happiness, yet the very definition of happiness prevents him from attaining it. Repetition seeks to hold fast an original moment which by definition cannot be held fast but is evanescent; and the evanescent seeks to repeat itself but cannot. The future moments are lost as they dissolve into an unredeemed past, and the past consists of empty repetitive unfulfilled moments—the anguish of modernity. The only way into the past is via the utopian future, and the only way into the future is via the past. The storm which pushes the angel of history toward the future keeps him from fulfilling his desires. He is not allowed to stay. Yet the storm blows from paradise, paradise as origin, as the realm from which humanity has been expelled yet to which it desires to return. But this origin as *Ursprung* is also new world as well, entirely other—both political revolution and theological redemption.

Perhaps here, too, the line of the profane nevertheless is connected to the messianic. The angel of history is stuck, his wings are immobilized, he can't close them to halt his flight. The future to which he is driven is undefined, and the angel's back is toward it. Yet the storm of "progress," the destructiveness of linear empty time, pushes the angel even as it inhibits him. The forces of destruction and catastrophe somehow both contain within themselves and propel movement toward the future redemption.

Scholem stressed that in Jewish messianic thinking, catastrophe and redemption are intertwined. A famous talmudic legend relates that on the day the Temple was destroyed—the saddest day in Jewish history, and the catastrophe that began the long exile—the Messiah was born. The forces of the redemption come not only from a transcendent intercession but from the very depths of the catastrophe itself, from the ruins (*JJC* 245). Geoffrey Hartman notes in his commentary on the "angel of history" that "catastrophe, instead of remaining fixed in the past, and hope, instead of being an eschatological or future-directed principle, reverse places. Catastrophe becomes proleptic. . . . it ruins time and blocks, even as it propels, the angel. As for hope, that is located mysteriously *in* the past, a defeated potentiality of retroactive force. . . . " This chiasma of hope and catastrophe saves hope from being unmasked only as catastrophe: as an illusion or unsatisfied movement of desire that wrecks everything. The foundation of hope becomes remembrance, which confirms the function, even the duty, of the historian and critic (*Criticism* 78–79).

In any case, this angel is both Marxist and talmudic. Benjamin has secularized the Jewish apocalyptic even as he has theologized historical materialism. The moment of writing the "Theses" was bitter: there was the aftermath of the Hitler-Stalin pact, the betrayal of the revolution, a Europe in ruins, and Benjamin himself "frozen in flight." The "Theses" open not with an angel but with a hunchback:

> The story is told of an automaton constructed in such a way that it could play a winning game of chess, answering each move of an opponent with a counter-move. A puppet in Turkish attire and with a hookah in its mouth sat before a chessboard placed on a large table. A system of mirrors created the illusion that this table was transparent from all sides. Actually, a little hunchback who was an expert chess player sat inside and guided the puppet's hand by means of strings. One can imagine a philosophical counter-part to this device. The puppet called "historical materialism" is to win all the time. It can easily be a match for anyone if it enlists the services of theology, which today, as we know, is wizened and has to keep out of sight. (*Illum* 253)

Yet how comfortably does this hunchback sit within the automaton? He is concealed within the automaton of historical materialism in an artificial and uncomfortable position. He is wizened and unattractive but joined to the brainless puppet of historical materialism in order to win all games. Yet how long can the games be played? For the coexistence of the hunch-back and the puppet in Benjamin's parable depends on a ruse; it is a baroque contraption with a system of mirrors creating the illusion that the chess table was transparent—a baroque contraption in which modern history has become a *Trauerspiel*. Perhaps these parable-theses were Benja-min's ironic version of baroque allegory for his own age, in which he gathered all the threads, fragments, and ruins of his life in a pessimistic messianism caught between catastrophe and hope. As in allegory, the ruins are heaped together, and these fragments do not attain a unity or an "iden-tity" in any traditional kind of way. Benjamin would have opposed such a unity in any case. But they somehow are all connected in the field of vision of the allegorist, and the angel of history who, as Scholem puts it, is "the occult reality" of Benjamin's inner self (*JJC* 229).

Although the theses begin with the baroque puppet game, they conclude with a vision of Jewish memory in which redeemed time opens the future so that "every second of time was the strait gate through which the Mes-siah might enter" (*Illum* 264). Through remembrance comes redemption; by going back one also moves toward the future—like the angel of history who faces the past and is blown forward. In his essay on Kafka, Benjamin referred to memory as the heart of Judaism, and he cited a theological interpretation of *The Trial* which maintains that the real object of the trial is "forgetting, whose main characteristic is the forgetting of itself," and agrees that "this mysterious center . . . derives from the Jewish religion" where memory is intimately involved with piety (131).[10] In forgetting and oblivion, he continues, things become distorted, and in Kafka all the fig-ures of distortion are connected with the prototype of distortion, the hunchback. Quoting a folksong called "The Little Hunchback," Benjamin writes, "This little man is at home in distorted life; he will disappear with the coming of the Messiah" (134).

In the "Theses" the little hunchback of theology, like the angel of his-tory, is also caught, and in need of redemption. Benjamin's messianic time is brought about by a revolutionary "tiger's leap into the past" which uses the power of memory to burst the historical continuum and realize the "time of now." This leap is similar to the faithless leap of allegory when, at the depths of its fall, it turns round toward redemption, and where its own ultimate objects turn into allegories which "fill out and deny the void in which they are represented" (*OGTD* 233). Politics here is a kind of allegory of religion, and religion an allegory of politics. As Scholem comments:

> It is matter of dispute whether one can speak here—as I am rather inclined to do—of a melancholy, indeed desperate view of history for which the hope that the latter might be burst asunder, by an act like redemption or revolution, continues to have about it something of that leap into transcendence which these theses seem to deny but which is even then implied in the materialistic formulation as their secret care. (*JJC* 235)

Or, one might ask, are these theses more like the parables of Kafka, which Benjamin described so beautifully as "fairy tales for dialecticians" (*Illum* 117)? Kafka, Benjamin wrote, struggled with the prehistoric world, the world of myth, and tried to rewrite legends as fairy tales. He "inserted little tricks into them; then he used them as proof 'that inadequate, even childish measures may also serve to rescue one' " (117–18) "The wisest thing—so the fairy tale taught mankind in olden times, and teaches children to this day—is to meet the forces of the mythical world with cunning and high spirits." The fairy tale thus has a "liberating magic" pointing to the complicity of nature with liberated man: "A mature man feels this complicity only occasionally, that is, when he is happy; but the child first meets it in fairy tales, and it makes him happy" (102).

But there was to be no happy ending to Benjamin's life, and no arrival of the Messiah amid the ever-increasing pile of ruins. Today, Benjamin's image is so fractured, Jürgen Habermas maintains, because Benjamin combined all kinds of diverging motifs without actually unifying them. Those who so desire can create a Marxist Benjamin, a kabbalistic Benjamin, a neo-conservative aesthetic Benjamin, and so forth: "Benjamin belongs to those authors who cannot be summarized and whose work is disposed to a history of disparate efforts" ("Consciousness-Raising" 32). Habermas asserts that finally the hunchback theology and the puppet of materialism cannot come together because Benjamin's idea of anarchic now-time cannot be integrated into a materialist theory of social development. Benjamin's project was ultimately unsuccessful "because the theologian in him couldn't accept the idea of making his messianic theory of experience serviceable to historical materialism." Yet Benjamin also "sacrificed theology by accepting mystical illumination only as secular, i.e. universalizable exoteric experience" (52).

Yet Benjamin said of Kafka: "To do justice to the figure of Kafka in its purity and its peculiar beauty one must never lose sight of one thing: it is the purity and beauty of a failure. . . . There is nothing more memorable than the fervor with which Kafka emphasized his failure" (*Illum* 144–45). Ought one to say the same of Benjamin? That he, too, ultimately failed in his project to bring together the hunchback and the puppet? Or is it simply a matter of patience, of the hope and redemption that are there—but not for us? For despite his anguished self-contradictions, Benjamin, like Kafka, with whom he so identified, seems to preside over these fragments, parables, and paradoxes with patience and serenity. As he wrote in the first version of "Agesilaus Santander": "For nothing can overcome my patience. Its wings resemble those of the angel in that very few pushes are enough for them to preserve themselves immovably in the face of her who my patience is resolved to await" (*JJC* 204). Adds Scholem, "Benjamin was the most patient human being I ever came to know, and the decisiveness and radicalism of his thinking stood in vehement contrast to his infinitely patient and only very slowly opening nature. And to deal with Benjamin one had to have the greatest patience oneself. Only very patient people could gain deeper contact with him" (222).

There is, finally, the image of him left by the last person who saw him, the woman who guided him over the Pyrenees to the border of Spain. Lisa Fittko describes his unfailing courtesy in the midst of the worst dangers. The arduous trek over the mountains was made worse by his heart condition, and Benjamin was also lugging a briefcase with which he refused to part, and in which he had what he described as his new manuscript. He told her, "This briefcase is the most important thing I have. I mustn't lose it. My manuscript *must* be saved. It is more important than I am" ("Last Days" 52). But it, too, was lost after his suicide. Because of his ill health Benjamin walked slowly, but the night before he had calculated a precise walking pace that would allow him to survive the journey. He also knew that he would not have enough strength to cross the border again if the first attempt failed and if he were to be returned to France "Here, too, he had calculated everything in advance, taking enough morphine with him for a fatal dose" (58). He planned his crossing carefully, and "at regular intervals—about ten minutes, I think—he would stop and rest for perhaps a minute." He told her, "With this method I'll be able to go all the way. I rest at regular intervals—*before* I become exhausted. Never spend yourself entirely" (54). Her reaction:

> What a strange man, I thought. A crystal-clear mind, unbending inner strength, yet hopelessly clumsy. *Walter Benjamin once wrote about the nature of his strength that "my patience is unconquerable." Reading that phrase years later, I saw him before me once again, walking slowly and measuredly along the mountain path. And his inner contradictions suddenly seemed less absurd* [italics hers]. (55)

Part Two

EMMANUEL LEVINAS

SIX

The Rupture of the Good

Marx knows what is evil, but he does not describe the good. (Max Horkheimer)

Idealism completely carried out reduces all ethics to politics. (Levinas, *Totality and Infinity* 216)

That which imparts truth to the known and the power of knowing to the knower is what I would have you term the idea of the good, and this you will deem to be the cause of science, and of truth in so far as the latter becomes the subject of knowledge. . . . The good may be said to be not only the author of knowledge to all things known, but of their being and essence, and yet the good is not essence, but far exceeds essence (*epekeina tes ousias*) in dignity and power. (Plato, *The Republic* 508e–509b)

The place of the Good above every essence is the most profound teaching, the definitive teaching, not of theology, but of philosophy. (Levinas, *Totality and Infinity* 103)

Unlike the truth of the philosophers, which is not allowed to know anything but itself, this truth must be truth for someone. (Franz Rosenzweig, "The New Thinking" 205–206)

LEVINAS'S BACKGROUND

"History itself," wrote Hegel, "is the final judge of history": *Die Weltgeschichte ist die Weltgericht.* For Emmanuel Levinas as for Walter Benjamin, this "universal history" was a grotesque spectacle of suffering and brutality. As Benjamin was desperately seeking a way to escape Nazi Europe, Levinas was drafted into the French army. Captured by the German forces, he ultimately survived in a prisoner-of-war camp. He writes in an autobiographical essay that his biography is "dominated by the presentiment and the memory of the Nazi horror" ("Signature" 177). One of his later philosophical masterworks, *Otherwise Than Being* (1974), is dedicated to the memory of those killed by Nazis, to those "closest" among the six million Jews, and to the "millions of all confessions and all nations, victims of the same hatred of the other man, the same anti-semitism."

In his philosophical writings, Levinas, like Benjamin, revolts against the immanent and impersonal laws of nineteenth-century historicism and constructs a theory of "messianic time" to open history to redemption. Unlike Benjamin, however, Levinas had little admiration for either Jewish mysticism or dialectical materialism. As a Jewish child born in Russia in 1906, Levinas had witnessed the chaos and violence of the Bolshevik revolution and subsequent civil war.[1] Levinas found his critique of history and philosophy elsewhere. Like Gershom Scholem, he too would return to the sources of Judaism, but he would locate the authentic and creative core of Judaism not in the Kabbalah but in the Talmud, that massive compilation of rabbinic law and commentary.

Levinas left Russia in 1923 for philosophical studies in Strasbourg and then later in Freiburg with Husserl and Heidegger. Like Benjamin, he became enamored of French culture, and in 1930 he became a French citizen. When he was mobilized as a citizen into the French army at the beginning of the war and later captured by the Germans, that French uniform saved him from deportation to the gas chambers. During his internment in the prisoner-of-war camp, his wife was hidden and saved with the help of a friend from his Strasbourg University days, Maurice Blanchot. All his family remaining in Russia were murdered by the Nazis.

Emerging from the camp after the war, Levinas wrote of his "profound need to leave the climate of that [Heidegger's] philosophy" (*EE* 19). Yet in the same sentence he also writes that we nevertheless "cannot leave it for a philosophy that would be pre-Heideggerian." He proceeded to rethink the work of Husserl and Heidegger he had studied in the 1920s and 1930s and inverted phenomenological thought in a new way: his philosophical critique now made ethics prior to and the condition of metaphysics. In 1947, at the same time he began writing his philosophical masterpieces, Levinas also became the director of the École Normale Israélite Orientale, a Jewish school which was part of the Alliance Israélite Orientale. The Alliance, founded in 1860, was an organization dedicated to spreading French and Jewish culture throughout Jewish communities in France and its former Mediterranean empire.[2] The Alliance was formed to respond to the problems of the emancipation and assimilation of Jews in France, protect their interests, help defend them from persecution, and increase Jewish solidarity.

Levinas was also writing prolifically on Judaism and Jewish life. His first collection of lectures on the Talmud, *Quatre lectures talmudiques,* appeared in 1968 in the Critique series by Éditions de Minuit—the same series in which Derrida published *De la grammatologie, Marges de la philosophie,* and *Positions,* and which also includes the key works of the intellectual avant-garde of France: Bataille, Deleuze, Andre Green, Irigaray, Lyotard, Robbe-Grillet, Marin, Serres. What all his writing shares with the works in the Critique series is the question of the "other"—the other of philosophy, the disruption of the logic of identity by the irruption of the heterogeneous other. As Vincent Descombes lucidly outlines in his *Modern French Philosophy* (titled in French *La même et l'autre*), this attempt to absorb and then break free of the philosophy of the "three H's"—Hegel, Heidegger, and Husserl—and to redefine the relation of same and other is a central aim of all modern French philosophy, from phenomenology through poststructuralism. Like Derrida and many other contemporary French thinkers, Levinas has worked at the very limits of philosophy, pondered the "end of metaphysics," and above all solicited the breakup of philosophical "totality" by the "other."

Despite his celebrity and influence in France, however, Levinas has not been as well known in America, especially in literary circles. But it was Levinas who introduced phenomenology to France with his translation of Husserl's *Cartesian Meditations* in 1931, and who became one of the first great interpreters of Heidegger and Husserl beginning with his first book in 1930, *The Theory of Intuition in Husserl's Phenomenology.* He has continued to produce widely read books and essays up to the present.[3] "But it was Sartre," as he wryly notes in an interview, "who guaranteed my place in eternity when stating in his famous obituary essay on Merleau-Ponty that he, Sartre, 'was introduced to phenomenology by Levinas'" ("Dialogue" 16). Levinas did not only introduce phenomenology, he radically critiqued it. Blanchot, his long-time friend, has written: "When Levinas asked if ontology were fundamental . . . [the question] was unexpected and unheard of, because it broke with what seemed to have renewed philosophy [Heidegger], and also because he was the first to have contributed to understanding and transmitting this thought" ("Clandestine" 43).[4] Levinas is also one of the thinkers who made Derrida and deconstruction possible, and Derrida in turn made possible a renewed appreciation of Levinas. As Derrida wrote in his 1967 essay on Levinas entitled "Violence and Metaphysics," "the thought of Emmanual Levinas can make us tremble. At the heart of the desert, in the growing wasteland, this thought, which fundamentally no longer seeks to be a thought of Being and phenomenality, makes us dream of an inconceivable process of dismantling and dispossession" ("Violence" 82).

Because Levinas's work is unfamiliar to many American readers, I will spend considerable time in this chapter outlining the major themes of his philosophical works in the context of contemporary literary theory, and I will often use Derrida's work and reflections on Levinas as a convenient point of orientation. As in the case of Benjamin, my outline of some basic ideas of Levinas's thought crudely reduces its complexity to a set of propositions, and inevitably betrays its subtlety. To offset this reductiveness, I will quote liberally from Levinas's writings, since many of his arguments depend more on nuances of expression and an accumulating network of associations than on axiomatic definitions and theses. Although this material is difficult, my hope is that it will inspire the reader to engage Levinas's work on her or his own.

The reader also will find in this reductive outline a certain repetitiveness. But as Derrida perceptively notes, Levinas's first masterwork, *Totality and Infinity,* is not a philosophical treatise; Derrida calls it a work of *art* because its thematic development "is neither purely descriptive nor purely deductive. It proceeds with the infinite insistence of waves on a beach, return and repetition of the same wave against the same shore" ("Violence" 312, n. 7) Over and over again, the ideas of the other, proximity, substitution, responsibility, exposure, signification are examined. But when waves break again and again, they repeat each time with a difference. In Derrida, repetition is a part of parodic doubling, an off-centering displacement; in Levinas, stylistic repetitiveness perhaps attempts to express the overflow of the infinite of which he writes.[5]

I will argue that Levinas's work is less "art" than a kind of "prophetic appeal," for Levinas's repetitive writing style reflects that insistent call and appeal from the other which for him defines the essence of language. That is, his prose itself embodies this sense of otherness—not as what is irrational or playful or ecstatic or flamboyant but as a grave call, insistent, unavoidable, inescapable, the call he wants us to hear as the summons to inescapable responsibility. The "coherence" of his prose and his "argument" is an effect of a recursiveness, a continuous coming back and circling around. Levinas's repetitive prose style is thus not "disclosure" but the constant "exposure" and reexposure of philosophical language to the intrusions of the other. The subject (both the philosophical "knowing subject" and the "subject" as the "contents" or object of his philosophy) recurs to itself not as a self-coincidence but as a constant exposure and reexposure to the other, a going back again and again, insistently, restlessly, relentlessly. It has the structure of an "insomnia," a figure he often uses to characterize the putting into question of consciousness. Yet each time, it somewhat differently bears down on the "themes" of responsibility, exposure, vulnerability, substitution for the other.

A style which would try to em-body this exposure to alterity would not be able to advance rigorously forward with thesis, evidence, proof, conclusion, complete comprehension with no remainder. So repetitive recurrence, a continuous holding open, replaces a style which argues and "thematizes" through logical deduction and hierarchical ordering. The overall rhetorical effect of Levinas's prose, in sum, is like a battering, an "obsession"; it is the very demand of the alterity Levinas is trying to elicit—as an object of not aesthetic contemplation but ethical conscience. In this sense, as a vocative mode, it parallels the language (and aim) of the biblical prophets—as urgent appeal, imperative demand, anguished rhetorical questioning.[6] After surveying the main themes of Levinas's philosophical work, I will proceed in the subsequent chapters to consider their relation to this prophetic appeal in his specifically Jewish writings.

REASON-FOR-THE OTHER: SOURCES FOR
LEVINAS'S CRITIQUE OF PHILOSOPHY

> If we retain one trait from a philosophical
> system . . . we would think of Kantism,
> which finds a meaning to the human with-
> out measuring it by ontology . . . and out-
> side of the immortality and death which
> ontologies run up against. (*OTB* 129)

Neither Derrida nor Levinas, of course, was the first to critique metaphysics—Kant did that decisively for modern philosophy and laid out its subsequent course. In post-Kantian thought, aesthetics and ethics become possible alternatives to the end of metaphysics. Whereas romantic aesthetic theory took one road, as we saw in the previous chapters, Levinas pursues the other branch of the Kantian legacy: ethics. Levinas's conception of the other culminates in an "otherwise than being" whose structure is radically ethical and leads to the "infinite" and "transcendent." Ethics here is not conceived as a determinate set of beliefs or practices; rather, it is the origin prior to every origin. In Levinas's analysis, the "a priori" of every "ontological" structure is, in fact, the very "relation to the other."

This relation to the other is the "meta" of metaphysics, which Levinas makes prior (rather than subordinate) to ontology. "Meta" as what is "behind" or "beyond" is redefined as the desire for this other, a nonnostalgic desire for that which overflows or is "outside" thought. "Thought" connotes here the phenomenological adequation of idea and thing, or reason and being, i.e., what can be "re-presented," brought to light, disclosed, reabsorbed, and possessed in the knowledge of the knower, an act which Levinas criticizes for reducing otherness to what is the same. By contrast, "the metaphysical desire aims toward *something else entirely,* toward the *absolutely other.* . . . The metaphysical desire does not long to return. . . . [It] has another intention; it desires beyond everything that can simply complete it" (*TI* 34–35).

This beyond or otherness is not, however, either a *negation* or complement of thought as in the Hegelian dialectic, i.e., a movement of thesis and antithesis into a synthesis which effectively reabsorbs the negation back into the consciousness of the subject. Like Benjamin and Rosenzweig, Levinas proposes an assault on all philosophical idealisms and Hegelian dialectics which claim to encompass the All in thought. For other contemporary French theorists of alterity such as Lacan, Kristeva, Barthes, *desire* is also a key term, but they accept and draw upon the Hegelian notion of the negation at the heart of desire, of desire-as-lack and need to overcome the other. Levinas is unique in postulating a desire that is not a lack but an independent positivity. Levinas's alterity is not the *negative* of identity but its positive surplus, an overflow of the structures of thought. This "infinity," "exteriority," or "transcendence" is "invisible" to thought, for it cannot be seen in the light of the cognition which brings objects to representation in the play of appearances. But "invisibility does not denote an absence of relation; it implies relations with what is not given, of which there is no idea" (*TI* 34). (There is a parallel here to Benjamin's idea in his prologue to the *trauerspiel* book that "truth is the death of intention," beyond the grasp of cognizing consciousness.)

In defining this relation to alterity, moreover, Levinas differs from many other contemporary critics of metaphysics and philosophy, by not abandoning reason. Ethics as the relation of obligation and responsibility *to* and *for* the other is the relation and revelation of this otherness, an-other reason. "Already *of itself* ethics is an 'optics' " (*TI* 29). The subject now is redefined as "for-*the-other*," not a consciousness bringing objects to representation "for *itself*." In other words, subjectivity as for-the-other involves not a "plural reason" commanded by the logic of identity, which itself is the return of difference to the same—a "for itself"—but instead a reason commanded and penetrated by the other, heteronomous instead of autonomous. And "plural" because it is a relation with an other which escapes (is before and beyond) all absorption into autonomous system and identity.

In other words, Levinas opens reason to the command of the Other, in a prophetic and ethical call that comes prior to but itself makes possible consciousness, representation, knowing, will: "We think that existence *for itself* is not the ultimate meaning of knowing. . . . The essence of reason does not mean securing foundations and powers for man, but calling him into question and inviting him to justice" (*TI* 88). "We name this calling into question of my spontaneity by the presence of the other ethics" (43). Steven Schwarzschild has characterized this viewpoint as the "one perennial differentia of all Jewish philosophical thought—what Kant calls 'the primacy of practical reason,' i.e., the metaphysical ultimacy of ethics and its constitutive and functional decisiveness even for the cognitive world" ("Introduction" 252). Since Levinas views "philosophical systems" as oppressive and totalitarian, however, he does not categorize this obligation to the other as a universal law; the imperative is not categorical as it is for Kant.

Levinas's great attack on "totality" in Hegel, Heidegger, and phenomenology in his *Totality and Infinity,* and his inversion of consciousness *of* and *for itself* into the ethics of *for the other,* has another strong Jewish influence: the work of Franz Rosenzweig. Like Levinas, Benjamin, and Scholem, Rosenzweig was also a Jew at first far more familiar and comfortable with Western philosophical thought and culture than Jewish study and practice. He, too, came from an assimilated and well-to-do German-Jewish bourgeois household, but after a spiritual search which led him to the brink of converting to Christianity, he returned to Judaism and proceeded to revitalize Jewish thought and life for his generation.

And like Levinas, Benjamin, and Scholem, Rosenzweig early on was immersed in the traditions of German philosophy, and had to contend with the imposing legacy of German idealism and the influence of Hegel. Rosenzweig's doctoral dissertation and first major philosophical work was *Hegel and the State* (1920). His philosophical masterwork, *The Star of Redemption,* was begun in 1918 when he was a soldier on the Balkan front in World War I, and initially was written on postcards he sent home. Here he tried to work through the problematic relations of religion and philosophy, Judaism and Christianity, and elaborated what he called his "new thinking." This was a "working through" that also led him to abandon what would have been a brilliant career in the university. Instead, he founded the Frankfurt Free Jewish House of Studies (*Freies jüdisches Lehrhaus*), a center for Jewish Studies and adult education. Scholem and Benjamin knew Rosenzweig during this time, and Scholem, before his departure for Palestine, taught in Rosenzweig's *Lehrhaus.*

At age thirty-four, soon after completion of *The Star* in 1920, Rosenzweig came down with amyotrophic lateral sclerosis and became paralyzed. He lost virtually all movement and finally even his capacity for speech, and died nine years later in 1929. During his illness and in spite of his debilitating paralysis, he continued to write and publish, and also translated the Hebrew Bible into German with Martin Buber. At his death, he was one of the luminaries of European Jewry.

Rosenzweig is a complex and extraordinary thinker, and his role in shaping modern philosophy is still underacknowledged. Benjamin, astute critic that he was, cited Rosenzweig's *Star of Redemption* as one of the most important books of the century. In her account of the Benjamin-Adorno relationship in *The Origin of Negative Dialectics,* Susan Buck-Morss notes the influence of Rosenzweig on Adorno via Benjamin, especially Rosenzweig's critique of Hegelian totality and closed system, his notion of a fragmented reality composed of individual phenomena in "constellation," his ideas of redemption and of knowledge of the object bound to the "name" which cannot be absorbed into a "category," and of knowledge as revelation and redemption of past and present:

> Specifically, it was Benjamin's ability to scrutinize the concrete and conceptless details of which, as Rosenzweig had argued, reality was composed, in a way which released a transcendent meaning, without ever leaving the empirical realm. Benjamin thus achieved insights which paralleled mystical revelation, while adhering to the Kantian anti-metaphysical role of staying within the data of experience. (*Origin* 6)

At the beginning of *Totality and Infinity* Levinas writes, "We were impressed by the opposition to the idea of totality in Franz Rosenzweig's *Stern der Erlösung,* a work too often present in this book to be cited" (*TI* 28).[7] Rosenzweig's great undoing of "totality" in *The Star of Redemption* was a critique of the epistemological pretensions of Western philosophy "from the Ionean Islands to Iena"—that is, from Thales to Hegel—to "know the All." This project culminates in Hegelian idealism where philosophy seeks to construct out of itself a completely autonomous totality, identifying the self-fulfillment of thought with the very consummation of world history. This purported apotheosis brought all things, including God and theology, into the unified totality of the autonomous philosophical system, finally uniting thought and being.

For Rosenzweig, the main aim of philosophical thought is to reduce the heterogeneity of the truth of experience to a statement of what reality is at bottom. "All is . . . X": water, the Idea, Spirit, mind, self, matter, etc. The meaning of phenomena thus comes from their inclusion in this whole, culminating in the totalization of philosophy in Hegel wherein history encompasses and judges all states, all thought, all beings. As Levinas writes, Rosenzweig wants to bring to philosophy the irreducibility of experience, a project which Levinas describes as "an empiricism which has nothing of the positivist" ("Entre" 126).

Or as Rosenzweig puts it in the very first sentence of his book, "All cognition of the All originates in death, in the fear of death" (*Star* 3). Such attempts at universal cognition are a kind of defense mechanism which deals with the terrors of individual mortality and life by ridding the world of what is singular, by dissolving it into comprehensive concepts and systems which identify reason and being. In the first part of *The Star,* Rosenzweig defines the "meta" of metaphysics (as well as what he calls "meta-ethics" and "meta-logic") as that which is beyond, outside, irreducible, resistant to the "All." The realm of the "meta" is the space of the nonidentity of being and reason (12–13, 19, 52), and for Rosenzweig here, too, is the place of the singular person in her or his individuality, unique life and death. This particularity is denied and dissolved into the "universal" in all systems of philosophical idealism where truth is identified with an impersonal reason capable of cognizing the All. This resistant singular life of the singular person is part of all that Rosenzweig calls "irreducible" or the "indigestible actuality outside the great intellectually mastered factual wealth of the cognitive world" (11).[8]

For Rosenzweig, the "irreducible realities" always encountered in human experience are God, humanity, and world. That is, they are the "poles or constellation" of thought and experience between which that experience constantly moves. "God" may be defined not only as a "fact" but as a set of the values, concepts, ideas from which human existence proceeds. "Constellation" is the great trope of "Star" which guides *The Star of Redemption.* ("Constellation," we remember, was also a critical figure in

Benjamin's philosophy of history—a way of expressing a nonhistoricist relation between historical events.) In Rosenzweig, as Scholem put it using kabbalistic terminology, there was a " 'breaking of the vessels' of idealism" ("Rosenzweig" 26), the shattering of the All and its autonomous totality, and these broken vessels are what Rosenzweig repaired anew through the philosophical reemergence of theology. Rosenzweig redefined the relations of the three shattered concepts of the philosophical All (God, human, world) through the concepts of creation, revelation, and redemption, and constructed among them a new set of relations, a new "constellation," a Star of Redemption.

In sum, there is a clear line from Rosenzweig's critique of Hegelian thought in *The Star* to Levinas's critique of totality, and also to his conceptions of language, the face, alterity, messianism, eschatology, history, and the relation of Jewish to non-Jewish thought—and from Levinas on to Derrida's critique of Western metaphysics. Levinas proceeds to apply Rosenzweig's critique of totality to the contemporary forms of impersonal reason which deprive the known being of its alterity "through a third term, a neutral term, which itself is not a being" (*TI* 42).[9] He finds this move repeated in the phenomenology of his mentors Husserl and Heidegger. Heidegger's "Being," postulated as both distinct from and the source of illumination of individual existents, is just such a neutral third term.

Richard Cohen observes that although Levinas adapts the phenomenological *method* from these mentors, he also "finds within phenomenology itself the resources for its own undoing." From phenomenological method, he takes "1) the turn to the concrete, 2) the break-up of the formal structures of representation, and 3) the recognition that the formal structures of representation 'live from' and are 'endowed' with significance by horizons unsuspected by intentional thought" ("Phenomenologies" 175). But with the help of Heideggerian ontology, he rejects Husserl's idea of the intentionality of consciousness, of a consciousness always adequate to its objects and correlated with them in a luminous disclosure. Cohen argues that it is a reading of Rosenzweig in 1935 that then enables Levinas to critique Heidegger's ontology as another totalizing movement which forecloses alterity, and to then develop the notion of philosophy as ethics.

Although some of these moves may imply an existentialist slant, Levinas did not view the cry of protest of the personal subject to be the answer. "It is not I who resist the system, as Kierkegaard thought; it is the Other" (*TI* 40). In both Rosenzweig and Levinas, the first move is the protection of the singular separate self from the impersonal totality—but the analysis does not end there, and the aim is not to revel in the glories of free subjectivity. This self is opened up, its isolation is broken up; it is turned to and bound over to the other in ethics and love and obligation. The idea of the subject who is defined by the other yet also unique and singular distinguishes Levinas and Rosenzweig from traditional humanist or existentialist notions of the individual self. Existentialism, of course, was superseded in France in the 1960s by structuralism, which then destroyed the freedom and identity of the personal self as a locus of meaning and defined it instead as the locus of impersonal structures and codes. In much literary theory of the 1970s and 1980s, the abstract concept "Language" took up, one could say, the role of the impersonal term through which all is mediated or known. The alterity of the singular, personal human other is then defined only as a subordinate function or "site" of impersonal significations. The "author" is dead, in Barthes's famous phrase.

Levinas contested this move as well, condemning the "structures" of structuralism as neutral, anonymous, indifferent, and oppressive. "Structuralism," he writes, "is the primacy of theoretical reason" (*OTB* 58), another form of totalizing idealism. Unlike many other critics of structuralism, however, he did not make this critique to uphold the personal ego; for him, the ego in its natural state is narcissistic and violent. A reason founded on an autonomous subjectivity, free and above all constraints, denies the other, knows and is bound only to itself, and is an egoism. Levinas instead defines the self by its relation with the other, a relation which is not, as we have seen, a subject/object relation. The "other" is disproportionate to all "the power and freedom of the I," and precisely this disproportion between the other and the I is "moral consciousness." Moral consciousness, then, is not "an experience of values" but an access to exteriority, to Being as other, and finally beyond ontology to the otherwise than being ("Signature" 183).

> Modern antihumanism, denying the primacy of human reason, free and for itself is true over and beyond the reason it gives itself. It clears the place for subjectivity positing itself in abnegation, in sacrifice, in a substitution preceding the will. Its inspired intuition is to have abandoned the idea of person, goal, and origin of itself, in which the ego is still a thing because it is still a being. . . . Humanism has to be denounced only because it is not sufficiently human. (*OTB* 127)

The key phrase here is "of itself." Rosenzweig shows Levinas the path through which cognition of the All is shattered, and how the subsequent autonomous fragments—each isolated in and for themselves—then can be opened up to and for-the-other. In an essay on Rosenzweig, Levinas makes the crucial comment that the conjunction *and* to designate the reconnections made in *The Star* among God, humanity, and world as creation, revelation, and redemption means *for*: God for humanity, humanity for world, etc. The unity Rosenzweig constructs is not any formal unity of philosophical logic but "is in the sense that they are one for the other, when one is placed in these elements themselves" ("Entre" 128). "One for the other" is a "living" relation, not a philosophical category or a Hegelian dialectical synthesis which empties the terms of their irreducible individuality, or perceives them from the "outside" in the all-seeing gaze of the philosopher. This one for the other becomes in Levinas's own philosophy the very essence of signification as saying, as ethics, and as revelation.

I will further discuss Levinas's connections with Rosenzweig in later chapters dealing with Levinas's specifically Jewish writings, but we should also note here the importance for Levinas of Rosenzweig's ideas about the relation between philosophy and theology. While there is not space here to examine Rosenzweig's position in depth, Rosenzweig asserts that what he calls his "new thinking" is not theological in any classical sense, nor is it any form of "apologetics":

> If this is theology, it is, at any rate, no less new as theology than as philosophy. . . . Theology must not debase philosophy to play the part of a handmaid, yet the role of charwoman which philosophy has recently assigned to theology is just as humiliating. The true relationship of these two regenerated sciences is a sisterly one. . . . Theological problems must be translated into human terms, and human problems brought into the pale of theology. (In Glatzer, *Rosenzweig* 201)

Or as he writes in *The Star*:

> The theologian whom philosophy requires for the sake of its scientific status is himself a theologian who requires philosophy—for the sake of his integrity. What was for philosophy a demand in the interests of objectivity, will turn out to be a demand in the interests of subjectivity for theology. They are dependent on each other and so generate jointly a new type, be it a philosopher or theologian, situated between theology and philosophy. (106)

"Creation, revelation, and redemption" are the bridges Rosenzweig builds between theology and philosophy in *The Star* through linguistic analysis, "speech-thinking," sociological analysis, "common sense," and "absolute empiricism"—through a different notion of truth from that posited by abstract conceptual idealism. Truth is not defined by the illusions of timeless self-enclosed, self-absorbed, self-generated idealist thought, but is generated out of a relation with the other in language, life, and time; it is a truth "beyond the book"—a relation *with* and *for* someone like the relation of speech.

Like Rosenzweig, Levinas claims not to base his philosophical writings a priori on any traditional "theology." He firmly maintains that he does not use the Bible or theology as his starting point, nor does he rely on or intend any orthodox theology. His "other than being," he asserts, is not theological—"of the logos," or any "ology"—i.e., any identification of logos and being or assertion of a God who is the Being behind or beyond things. It does not refer to another world behind the scenes. Although the other "resembles God," the relation to the other and the assignation from the Good survive the death of God (*OTB* 123). Yet he does clearly use the name "God" as a name outside essence: "It precedes all divinity" (190,

n. 38). And in the very first pages of *Otherwise Than Being,* he states that "to hear a God not contaminated by Being is a human possibility no less important and no less precarious than to bring Being out of the oblivion in which it is said to have fallen in metaphysics and in onto-theology" [which was Heidegger's project] (xlii).

In his philosophical works, however, Levinas mainly avoids overtly mentioning or depending on classical Jewish sources for his arguments. Metaphysics is redefined as the realm of what cannot be thought in ontology, as the "nonphilosophical" which is prior to and founds philosophy, and also what follows its breakdown. In this sense, Levinas, Rosenzweig, and Derrida are all anti-Hegelian "philosophers of the nonphilosophical," thinkers who struggle with the end of metaphysics, with questions about what has been excluded or repressed by philosophy, with what "succeeds" it and into what philosophy is now to be transformed. "A community of the question," as Derrida puts it at the very beginning of his first essay on Levinas, "about the possibility of the question" ("Violence" 80). The very question of whether and how philosophy might have died, Derrida adds, might be unanswerable and perhaps not even philosophy's questions, but they are "the only questions today capable of founding the community, within the world, of those who are still called philosophers" (79).[10]

Yet what kind of philosophy? Writing of the relation between philosophy and life in Rosenzweig's work, and the "end of philosophy" which is "perhaps the very meaning of our age," Levinas emphasizes: "The end of philosophy is not the return to an epoch where it had not begun, where one could not philosophize; the end of philosophy is the beginning of an era where all is philosophy, because philosophy is not revealed through philosophers" ("Entre" 124). "Theoretical man has ceased to reign" (125)—that is, theory, as enchaining, totalizing system. But the result cannot be simple spontaneity or anarchic protest. Aristotle's "it is necessary to philosophize to not be a philosopher" defines the extreme possibility of philosophy in the twentieth century, a statement with which Derrida agrees and which he cites in his own essay on Levinas ("Violence" 152).

But Levinas also finds sources for his key idea of the otherwise than being *within* the history of Western philosophy, most paradigmatically in Plato's "Good beyond Being" in the *Republic,* in Plotinus's *Enneads,* and in the very founder of the cogito Descartes's "idea of the infinite" in the *Third Meditation.* In Descartes, the idea of the infinite is a "beyond being" as an excess, surplus, overflow in the finite mind as it conceives of "infinity." It is an idea that comes from "beyond" the finite mind, and one that the mind cannot contain. In sum, as Levinas writes, "The Place of the Good above every essence is the most profound teaching, the definitive teaching, not of theology, but of philosophy" (*TI* 103).

ONTOLOGY AND VIOLENCE: ETHICS AND POLITICS

For Levinas, then, the critique of metaphysics, reason, and theory does not become an intoxication with excess as the irrational, a fascination with the abyss or schizophrenic and psychotic states, a paralytic self-reflexivity, or a political ideology—as is the case with many other modern French literary critics. Yet Levinas clearly saw that political totalitarianism and violence (from which he had so personally suffered) were inseparable from the "ontological totalitarianism" of Western philosophy, a connection both he and Rosenzweig made long before it became a tenet of contemporary literary theory. Before Foucault discussed the relation of knowledge and power, and prior to Derrida's "deconstruction of metaphysics," Levinas wrote in 1961 in his first major masterwork, *Totality and Infinity*:

> Ontology as first philosophy is a philosophy of power. It issues in the State and in the nonviolence of the totality, without securing itself against the violence from which this non-violence lives, and which appears in the tyranny of the State. Truth, which should reconcile persons, here exists anonymously. Universality presents itself as impersonal; and this is another inhumanity. . . . A philosophy of power, ontology is, as first philosophy which does not call into question the same, a philosophy of injustice" (*TI* 46)

Like Heidegger and Derrida, Levinas views Western philosophy as primarily ontology. But Heidegger and Husserl are also indicted as participants in this "ontological imperialism." Husserl's idealist pure consciousness, for instance, represents the object to itself as a pure present, proceeding from the same and foreclosing alterity and temporality (*TI* 122–26). And Heidegger's paeans to Being held little appeal for one who saw even Heidegger and the German university capitulate to Nazism. Although Levinas does not overtly mention his personal wartime experience in his philosophical writings, in his Jewish writings he is quite sharp: "It is difficult to forgive Heidegger" (*QLT* 56). Heidegger "inundates the pagan corners of the western soul" (*DL* 256); his fascination with the mystery of place and Being is the "eternal seduction of paganism, beyond all the infantilism of idolatry, long surmounted . . . of the sacred filtering through the world. . . . Judaism is perhaps the negation of that. . . . The mystery of things is the source of every cruelty in relation to humanity" (*QLT* 257).

In another pointed reference to the Heideggerian idea of *es gibt* (the "generosity" of being, the way it "gives itself"), Levinas writes in an autobiographical essay: "No generosity which the German *'es gibt'* is said to express showed itself between 1933 and 1945. This must be said! Illumination and sense dawn only with the existing beings' rising up and establishing themselves in this horrible neutrality of the *there is*" ("Signature" 181). This attack on what he calls the neutral impersonal realm of the *il y a* ("There is") is part of his critique of Heidegger's subordination of individual existents to existence, or being to anonymous Being. "To affirm the priority of *Being* over *existents* is to already decide the essence of philosophy; it is to subordinate the relation with *someone*, who is an existent, (the ethical relation) to a relation with the *Being of existents*, which, imper-

sonal, permits the apprehension, the domination of existents (a relationship of knowing), subordinates justice to freedom" (*TI* 45).

The connection between the historical horrors of the Nazi period and
the philosophical idea of a neutral, impersonal "Being" is direct. For as
Levinas writes, ontology as the attempt to reduce the other to the same, or
"beings" to "Being," is ultimately an egoism. "Philosophy is an egology"
(*TI* 44), and "Heideggerian ontology, which subordinates the relationship
with the Other to the relation with Being in general, remains under obedience to the anonymous, and leads inevitably to another power, to imperial-
ist domination, to tyranny" (47). As I shall argue later, Levinas's critique
of Heidegger and his connection of Heideggerian ontology to political violence may also be applied to Paul deMan's linguistic theory, the key to
which is the impersonality and autonomy of language; and this critique
would shed some light on deMan's own problematic relation to Nazism.

For Levinas, Western philosophy has "mainly remained at home in saying being, that is, inwardness to itself, the being at home with oneself, of
which European history itself has been the conquest and jealous defense."
Like Benjamin, Levinas also notes that this history of the West nevertheless bears "in its margins, the traces of events carrying another signification" in which "the victims of the triumphs which entitle the eras of
history [are not] separate from its meaning" (*OTB* 178). The distinctive
mark of Levinas's philosophy, I would say, is the passionate search for a
way out of this violence, this "multiplicity of allergic egoisms" as he calls it
in the opening pages of *Otherwise Than Being*. In his interpretation of
etymology, Being or essence—the Latin *esse*—is rooted in *interesse* or "interest," egoism, usurpation. "War is the deed or drama of the essence's
interest. . . . Essence is the extreme synchronism of war" (4). Even when
these conflicting interests and egoisms are transformed into the unstable
"peace" of commerce, exchange, calculation, or politics, they assemble
themselves into a totality without "fissures"—that is, with no room for the
gratuitous, for real peace:

> The true problem for us Westerners is not so much to refuse violence as to
> question ourselves about a struggle against violence which, without blanching
> in non-resistance to evil, could avoid the institution of violence out of this
> very struggle. . . . One has to find for man another kinship than that which
> ties him to being, one that will perhaps enable us to conceive of this difference
> between me and the other, this inequality, in a sense absolutely opposed to
> oppression. (177)

Levinas tries in all his major works to articulate a philosophy of the
other that is based not on war, even as a game, but on justice and peace—
peace as that very moment of renunciation, welcome, and vulnerable exposure to the other. Hence he formulates a philosophy in which the judgment
of history and the critique of philosophy's modes of intelligibility come

through ethics, ethics as relation between *separated* beings in discourse, and not an ecstatic fusion, a relation which is that of justification, appeal, command, and obligation.

In contemporary debates in literary theory, "reason" and "ethics" have often been associated with conservative attacks on poststructuralism as nihilistic, self-indulgent, and elitist. Frustrated by these polemics, J. Hillis Miller, Wayne Booth, and other critics have tried to recoup and articulate an "ethics of reading."[11] Yet most poststructuralist critics, be they Lacanians, semioticians, New Historicists, feminists, or cultural materialists, still suspect any call to ethics and reason to be a mask for a "discredited bourgeois humanism." Not only are God and the author dead, but so too, they would argue, is the "subject" (or self)—especially as some kind of unified, autonomous center. So what are the choices but anarchic dissemination of signs, or analysis of the "codes" determining meaning, or demystification of oppressive ideologies by revealing their status as constructs?

For Levinas the role of critique itself, of "calling into question," leads neither to self-reflexive undecidability nor to ideology. Critique is indeed the questioning of all foundations as in deconstruction, but the calling into question of the same (that is, of the repressive logic of identity) is neither produced by nor results in any free play, or arbitrariness of signs. It comes, rather, from the demanding appeal, order, call of the other. In another key difference from most poststructuralist thought, Levinas maintains that the "call" from the other resounds through the personal human other, through whom the "other" of the "other than being" passes: "*L'absolument Autre, c'est Autrui*" (*TI* 39)—"The absolutely other is the Other." (Translators generally employ the word *Other* with a capital *O* for Levinas's term *autrui*, which designates the personal other. This term is distinguished from his use of *autre*, "other," rendered with a small *o*. This translation and capitalization is somewhat problematic.)

The otherwise than being is precisely the *for-the-other* of the ethical and interpersonal relation (a Rosenzweigian influence) and not another form of anonymous and impersonal linguistic effect. When "otherness" and "alterity" themselves are recuperated back into impersonal linguistic categories and principles (even in the guise of Foucaultian "discursive practices"), they become totalizing and repressive of the human other. This point is missed in much contemporary poststructuralist thought, including the New Historicism, whose adherents claim to have rescued the study of literature from an idealizing and ahistorical focus on language itself. The underlying claim is that such "subversion," "demystification," and "calling into question" serve the cause of "empowerment," justice, and freedom by making us more "conscious of" covert ideologies and the complicit relations of knowledge and power.[12] Argues Levinas, however, "The call to question is not a matter of turning around and becoming conscious of the calling to question. The absolutely other is not reflected in consciousness.

... We are concerned with questioning a consciousness, and not with the consciousness of questioning" ("Trial" 41).

In French, "consciousness" and "conscience" are denoted by the same word, and for Levinas, the consciousness of questioning is the question of conscience. This means an overturning of the egoism and narcissism of consciousness, of its autonomy and self-coincidence, its identity and repose. But the exile of the self through the demand of the other is not the "consciousness of this exile"; that is, the movement of questioning is not negative but "precisely the welcome reception of the absolutely other" which summons me to reply. Calling into question means "binding me to the other in an incomparable and unique fashion" ("Trail" 41), as if the whole of creation rested on me. (This move beyond the "consciousness of questioning" also distinguishes Levinas's thought from that of Edmond Jabès, another contemporary French Jew who interprets Judaism in the light of postmodernism and vice versa.)

The other is neither hostile (Sartre's famous "Hell is other people" in *No Exit*), nor a scandal, nor a plaything, but "the first rational teaching, the condition for all teaching" (*TI* 203). To welcome the other leads to a knowledge beyond that of the cogito; it means to be conscious of my own injustice. Philosophy as a critical knowing thus begins with conscience. (86). Calling into question is not "the representation of questions raised in a naive act of cognition," in the infinite regress of a futile search for ultimate origin or foundation. It is calling into question of freedom itself, for "to welcome the other is to put in question my freedom" (85), and the "freedom that can be ashamed of itself founds truth. . . . Morality begins when freedom, instead of being justified by itself, feels itself to be arbitrary and violent" (83–84). Calling into question then becomes a calling to account for the other as neighbor in personal responsibility.

Again, the urgency of the question of the other comes not only from intellectual problems in the legacy of Hegel and Husserl and Western thought, but from Levinas's attempt to combat the catastrophic hatred and violence in European history resulting from these philosophical systems. "Political totalitarianism rests on ontological totalitarianism" (*DL* 257), for there is an "implicit metaphysics in the political thought of the West" (221). Levinas, however, did not follow the intellectual trends of postwar France in another respect as well; he was never attracted to Marxism. For him, ethics is irreducible and *prior* to politics, just as it is prior to ontology. As Derrida puts it so well, Levinas's work is a "non-Marxist reading of philosophy as ideology" ("Violence" 97). Nevertheless, Levinas also recognizes the "ethical" intent and importance of

Marx's critique of Western idealism as a project to understand the world rather than to transform it. In Marx's critique we find an ethical conscience cutting through the ontological identification of truth with an ideal intelligibility and demanding that theory be converted into a concrete praxis of concern for the other. It is this revelatory and prophetic cry that explains the extraordinary attraction that the Marxist utopia exerted over numerous generations. (Kearney, "Dialogue" 33)

This prophetic cry and quasi-Marxist perspective underlie much of the recent "cultural materialism" in literary studies. J. Hillis Miller perceptively notes that despite differences in their reasons for attacking the ahistoricism of deconstructive linguistic theory, both the political left and the right "resort to moral or moralistic denunciation." The left claims it is immoral not to be concerned with history and society, and only to indulge in the contemplation of language playing with itself; the right claims that the skepticism about language and humanistic tradition is immoral and nihilistic ("Presidential Address" 283–84).

Levinas would not differ with the New Historicists or political critics about the need for political analysis or action, but rather about the position given the political and material vis-à-vis the ethical. He defines the political as the realm of the "moral" as distinct from the "ethical." The moral realm contains the rules of social organization, of distribution and exchange of power, of legislation, and mediation of various "interests." Ethics, as the realm of extreme disinterestedness, vulnerability, and sensitivity to the other, becomes "morality" when it moves into the political world of the "impersonal 'third,' " the other of the other—institutions, government. The key point: "But the norm that must continue to inspire and direct the moral order is the ethical norm of the interhuman" ("Dialogue" 29–30). "Politics left within itself bears a tyranny within itself" (*TI* 300).

In other words, the realm of politics cannot be separated from its origin in ethics, or else one justifies a "State delivered over to its own necessities" (*TI* 159). This is not an authentic justice but another kind of manipulation of the masses. Without ethics as *first* philosophy, there is not even any way to discriminate among political systems. Moreover, "equality of all is born by my inequality, the surplus of my duties over my rights" (*OTB* 159). And since responsibility is for what is precisely "other," i.e., nonencompassable, these obligations can never be satisfied but grow in proportion to their fulfillment; duty is infinite.

Levinas would then pose a question to all *materially based* movements for human freedom and justice: "The forgetting of self moves justice. [One must then know] if the egalitarian and just State in which man is fulfilled . . . proceeds from a war of all against all, or from the irreducible responsibility of the one for the all, and if it can do without friendship and faces?" (*OTB* 159–60). In other words, without some primary act of withholding, of self-abnegation, heteronomy, "passivity," "otherwise than being," all the alternatives still partake of the violent impersonal realm of being; they are "egoisms struggling with one another, each against all, in the multiplicity of allergic egoisms which are at war with one another," whether the context is politics, psychology, sociology, or linguistics (4).

It is not fortuitous that Levinas begins and ends both his great works, *Totality and Infinity* and *Otherwise Than Being,* with meditations on war and peace. The very first sentence in the preface to *Totality and Infinity* is, "Are we duped by morality?" Isn't war the very "truth of the real," as Heraclitus long ago argued when he said, "War is king of all"? If so, politics as the art of foreseeing and winning war would be the "very exercise of reason" (*TI* 21), and moral consciousness would have no recourse against "the mocking gaze of the political man." Harold Durfee points out that the philosophical or ontological foundations of war and peace and the philosophical status of politics have been much-neglected topics despite the vast literature of political and social theory. And despite interest in intersubjectivity, few phenomenologists have attended to this except Levinas. In Levinas's thought, Harold Durfee finds original and important suggestions for social philosophy that challenge the Anglo-Saxon tradition of empirical individualism and those of social contract and rationalism ("War" 549–50).

The political turn of poststructuralist criticism bears out Levinas's assertion that "idealism completely carried out reduces all ethics to politics" (*TI* 216). As literary theory (especially under the influence of Foucault) has turned to consider more deeply the relations between knowledge and power, force and signification, the old "pleasures of the text" have turned into the "war of discourses." Politics as manuever intersects with the strategic play of signifying forces. Deconstructionist "textual strategies" have been transformed into "cultural criticism." These debates involve the question of "legitimation," and in Jean-François Lyotard's view, postmodernism itself is defined precisely by the crisis in the various modern "narratives of legitimation." In his anti-Habermas polemic, Lyotard claims that the great narratives such as the Hegelian "dialectics of the Spirit," the hermeneutics of meaning, or the emancipation of the rational subject are no longer operative (*Postmodern* xxiii). These total systems have dispersed into fragmented and heterogeneous Wittgensteinian "language games."

What Levinas calls "the mocking gaze of the political man" appears as the key principle in Lyotard's understanding of language: "to speak is to fight, in the sense of playing, and speech acts fall within the domain of a general agonistics" (*Postmodern* 10). In Lyotard's schema one can, of course, make moves for pleasure and not just to win, but these agonistic language "moves" also constitute the social bond itself, and every move involves a displacement and a countermove (16). Like many other postmodern theorists, Lyotard condemns "consensus" as an "outmoded and suspect value," an implicit repression of difference, otherness, and heterogeneity. "But," he observes, "justice as a value is neither outmoded nor suspect," and an idea of justice separate from consensus is needed. The very recognition of "heteromorphous language games" is the first step and "implies a renunciation of terror which assumes they are isomorphic and tries to make them so" (66). Lyotard's model of agonistic language games also makes any contract between players local and subject to cancellation.

What is interesting about this argument from a "Levinasian" point of view is that despite Lyotard's argument that we are all subjects of language, positioned in and by a communication system which precedes and shapes us, and that our life and freedom come in knowing how to play and disorient the game, Lyotard nevertheless ultimately appeals to "justice" and defends "values" which are here identified with otherness and irreducible heterogeneity. Yet he gives no explanation of *why* or *how* a player would make that very first act of "renunciation of terror," or subdue that desire to overpower the game and obliterate the opposition. Nor does he explain what conditions would allow the agonistic players to first even *agree* to the contract that sets up the rules. If language is agon, conflict, and war game, how could any player ever step "outside" it to appeal to justice, or to agree to a set of constraining rules? At bottom, this model ultimately continues to pit one form of aggression against another, one violence against the next. Is the game ultimately judge of the game, to paraphrase Hegel?

This question involves the central issue of locating an "outside" or "exterior," a "transcendence" or "ex-cendence" of being or Hegelian history or language game. For Lyotard and other theorists such as Barthes, Bataille, Kristeva, or Derrida, there is an "outside" insofar as there is the "excess" of alterity to rupture the system. The key question, which is also at the heart of Benjamin, Scholem, and Levinas's critical projects, then is: "What is the relation of this excess to language and/or to a utopian (*u-topos* or nonsite) eschatology or "other" history?

EXTERIORITY AND ESCHATOLOGY

Levinas wants to question at the very beginning of *Otherwise Than Being* whether even the difference between "essence" in war and the unstable peace of politics and commerce "does not presuppose that *breathlessness of the spirit,* or the spirit holding its breath, in which since Plato what is beyond the essence is conceived and expressed? And ask if this breathlessness or holding back is not the extreme possibility of the Spirit, bearing a sense of what is beyond essence?" (*OTB* 5). For the realm of the game with which he is concerned is the killing fields of history, which must be judged from an "outside," an "exteriority" (thus the subtitle of *Totality and Infinity: An Essay on Exteriority*). Levinas's phrasing of this sentence as a question is characteristic of his style. At critical points in his work, assertions are formulated as questions. The very nature of his philosophical project, and of philosophy working on the boundary of nonphilosophy and seeking a mode of intelligibility other than classical philosophical reason, requires that assertions be proposed as questions. The question, as interruption of thought, opens a space for an "exterior" to thought.

Yet how is this "outside" possible? From where can one contest the philosophy of being and its concomitant warfare and imperialism since this philosophy itself has determined the very conditions of intelligibility in the West? For Levinas, as for Benjamin and Rosenzweig, the judgments of universal history and universal reason are cruel, destroying singularity for totality. They stifle speech and are the history made by the survivors, not the victims (*TI* 242–33). Another judgment "has to be made against the evidence of history, and against philosophy as well, if philosophy coincides with the evidence of history" (243). "Evidence" is here defined as what is produced by the kind of reason and thought which permits no outside, which always returns consciousness to itself and identity, and so is the history of the victors. "The verdict of history is pronounced by the survivor who no longer speaks to the being he judges. . . . The judgment of history is always pronounced in absentia" (240, 242).

But "under the visible that is history, there is the invisible that is judgment. The invisible must manifest itself if history is to lose its right to the last word, necessarily unjust for subjectivity, inevitably cruel" (246). Like Benjamin, Levinas is seeking an explosive force available to "experience," and like his phenomenological mentors he is searching for "the overflowing of objectifying thought by a forgotten experience from which it lives" (28). But in his search for the "other" than being, the "beyond" being, he must also fracture the synthesizing totality of phenomenology's intentional subject, the "transcendental ego" whose "consciousness of" acts to grasp, know, unify, totalize—and thus obliterates the other. Pure cognition will never lead beyond universal history to the other than being, or to peace. It can never bring history to judgment, never preside at the trial of the subject, nor can it be the ultimate tribunal before which philosophy justifies itself. And this Benjamin also understood—from his early critiques of Kant to his later extreme juxtapositions of messianism and materialism.

Philosophical "justification" for Levinas does not mean only the logical intelligibility of an argument but—quite *literally*—justification as the very rationale or "goodness" of philosophy itself. The critical point here is that Levinas will try to neither *substitute* eschatology for philosophy nor *disavow* philosophy, but rather find a reference *within* philosophy and totality itself to this *beyond* by moving back from the experience of totality "to a situation where totality breaks up, a situation that conditions totality itself." This is the "nonknowing" where philosophy begins and which makes philosophy possible. And this he finds in the "gleam of exteriority or of transcendence in the face of the Other [*le visage de autrui*]" (*TI* 24), an alterity which is personal, not an anonymous, impersonal force but a command and call to responsibility.

The manifestation of this "invisible" judgment would depend on no miraculous epiphany, no supernatural magic, no irrational passion, no dialectical law. It would be produced *within* history as the very goodness of Levinasian subjectivity. The very subjectivity which Levinas will construct as the "for-the-other" itself is produced as judgment: "when it [subjectivity] looks at me and accuses me in the face of the Other—whose very epiphany is brought about by this offense suffered, by this status of being stranger, widow, and orphan" (*TI* 244).

In other words, the "face" of the other would make existential subjectivity and fear of death convert into ethical subjectivity: the fear of murder. This kind of judgment not only accuses but also exalts subjectivity by calling it to infinite responsibility for the other. "Judgment is pronounced upon me in the measure it summons me to respond. Truth takes form in this presence to a summons" (244); the I is therefore "elected" and summoned to trial (245). As Derrida again puts it so well, *Totality and Infinity* is a great trial of philosophy itself ("Violence" 84).

However, this is a trial clearer in its demands than the one to which Joseph K. was subjected in Kafka's novel, and in Benjamin and Scholem's interpretations of that work. The trial in Levinas becomes a forum of judgment for the victims and against the murderers in this century of catastrophic slaughter. It is a trial of history. But it is a trial "which requires all the resources of subjectivity . . . to be able to see, beyond the universal judgements of history, the offense of the offended" (*TI* 246–47), an offense which "universal" Hegelian history itself reproduces in its dissolution of particulars. The ultimate principle of this judgment is Goodness, which "consists in taking up a position in being such that the Other counts more than myself" (247).

Needless to say, the metaphor of the trial is deeply rooted in Jewish thought and literature from Abraham's great argument with God about justice for the righteous people of Sodom (Genesis 18) to Job's anguished request for a fair trial with God.[13] His trial of philosophy which Levinas conducts is connected to an "outside" or "exteriority" which he solicits by such terms as the Other, the idea of the infinite, the trace, the Good beyond being. This trial is also related to what he calls at the beginning of *Totality and Infinity* a "prophetic eschatology" and "eschatology of messianic peace." He articulates it as a relation with a "beyond" that is not a being *behind* being, or some invisible truer world, or the "void" where completely free and arbitrary subjectivity reigns (or the negativity of Scholem's "Nothingness of Revelation"). This beyond is an "excess, a surplus and overflow" of totality (*TI* 22), not a *via negativa* but a *via superlativa.*

Levinas finds a precursor in Descartes's "idea of the infinite," which is defined as an overflow of the thought that thinks it. Thus while the relation with infinity is not enclosed within "experience," its "infinition" is produced in the very overflow of experience. And it would be the very "condition of possibility" of experience: "if experience precisely means a relation with the absolutely other, that is, with what always overflows thought, the relation with infinity accomplishes experience in the fullest sense of the word." It fully accomplishes experience by being both "within" and "without" experience, and so *can* bring history to judgment, can redeem it, at every instant: "We oppose to the objectivism of war a subjectivity born from the eschatological vision" (25)—a subjectivity not of personal egoism but one founded in the idea of infinity and itself called to judgment, to justify itself, and to participate in this judgment.

Why, however, call this excess a "messianic" or "prophetic" eschatology? In what sense is this a utopian, idealistic dream, and what significance do these "theological" connotations have? A being behind being would still belong to the realm of ontology—and a negation is still tied to what it negates, as the Hegelian dialectic demonstrates. But an excess, or ex-cendence, is a different kind of beyond, an "otherwise" than being which also is "reflected *within* the totality and history, *within* experience":

> The eschatological, as the "beyond" of history draws beings out of the jurisdiction of history and the future; it arouses them in and calls them forth to their full responsibility. Submitting history as a whole to judgement, exterior to the very wars that mark its ends, it restores to each instant its full significance in that very instant: all the causes are ready to be heard. It is not the last judgment that is decisive, but the judgment of all the instants in time, when the living are judged. (23)

Like Benjamin's messianic moments of now-time, this eschatological beyond is an explosion of linear, empty time, a disruption of a self-enclosed historicist system, a judgment that redeems the instant. Although the judgment disrupts history, it is no simple negation. Levinas seeks a positive moment of redemption for individual beings to be freed from the domination of totality, and to be affirmed as personal and individual "existents" who can now *speak in history,* whose voices are not muted. But this judgment also calls them to responsibility; it does not liberate them for arbitrary freedom, or dionysiac ecstasy, or passive listening to Being, or the revolt of the masses.

Rosenzweig is again a key influence here; his meditations on history, theology, philosophy, politics, and redemption forged an opening for this judgment upon history. Rosenzweig's critique of philosophy was also inextricably connected to the critique of politics, especially to Hegelian notions of state and history. Like Benjamin and Scholem, he was profoundly affected by the catastrophic nationalism and vicious slaughter of World War I. How could this utter collapse of Christian European civilization support the Hegelian pretension that this culture itself constituted the "realization of universal history"? Stéphane Mosès, one of the most brilliant contemporary readers of Rosenzweig, notes that these bloody catastrophes at once confirmed and condemned "the Hegelian vision of history as the scene where, across the confrontation of States, the constitution of universal Spirit is accomplished" ("Hegel" 329). Confirmed and condemned at once—for the political realities of war, violence, and catastrophe *themselves* effectively enact judgment upon this Hegelian history. In other words, as Mosès subtly points out, for Rosenzweig the Hegelian system is all too true—it encompasses everything; and ironically it is verified in contemporary history. But this verification shows only its horror. The condemnation of this unraveling of history "has a moral character, thus is exterior to the system, to the extent it refuses the system's axioms" (332)—especially the primary Hegelian axiom from *The Philosophy of Right* that war is itself the expression of morality. (We remember that Levinas, too, begins *Totality and Infinity* precisely with this question of the morality of war.)

Like Benjamin and Scholem, Rosenzweig struggled with received notions of history, and could no longer accept the views of his teacher Meinecke and the German historiographical school that history was the progressive judgment of Reason through the development of the Spirit. Levinas also notes that Rosenzweig's thought does not refer only to the events of his own time; it was also a "presentiment" of the catastrophe of modern history and a "rupture with the ways of thinking which bore responsibility" for them, a "*presentiment of the dangers which menace Europe, of which Hegelian philosophy remains a remarkable expression*" [italics his]. ("Une pensée" 211, 209). What World War I was for Rosenzweig, Benjamin, and Scholem, World War II and the Holocaust would be for Levinas. In Rosenzweig, Levinas finds a resource for an "other" history, a "counterhistory" in some ways similar to but in other ways quite different from those Benjamin and Scholem also tried to construct.

Rosenzweig's analyses of the nature of redemption, time, eternity, and history are too complex to discuss at length here. I will elaborate a bit more on them in later chapters. Suffice it to say that for Rosenzweig, the lived collective liturgies, practices, rituals, and histories of the Jewish and Christian communities respectively embody the way in which eternity and redemption are brought into time and the moment. Rosenzweig also maintained that both paths of Judaism and Christianity are essential to truth and redemption, but each must be lived independently if it is to complete the other. Rosenzweig, however, reverses the conventional notion of the relation between Judaism and Christianity. In his schema, the "wandering Jew" already partakes of eternity ("Eternal Life") within the closed circle of Jewish peoplehood and the liturgical year. The Christian, by contrast, lives the "Eternal Way"—the course of the Church as it progresses through and encompasses history, and engages in the politics of statehood and power in its conquering mission to transform pagan society while awaiting the return of Jesus. The Christian is continually concerned about the need to be reborn and original sin, whereas the Jew is *born* Jewish, needs no conversion, and already lives an "eternal life" through the countless generations of the Jewish people. These generations constitute a transhistorical Jewish community which transmits the anticipation and perpetuation of the End through Jewish liturgical and social forms of life.[14]

From one point of view, Rosenzweig appears to be putting the Jews in a position essentially "beyond history," and of course this aspect of thought is one of the most controversial, for if the Jews live already in eternity, then in what way is Jewish collective existence tied to land, to Zion, state, law, or politics? Scholem, as we have seen, severely criticized Rosenzweig for opposing the apocalyptic and catastrophic strands of Jewish messianism and taming their anarchic potential. Scholem, moreover, thought this view of Judaism was politically impotent and too conservative, too affirmative of traditional rabbinic Jewish law and practice. But Rosenzweig's position, like that of Levinas, is that this "withholding," this "beyond" the brutalities of politics, is at the heart of Jewish power and is the secret of Jewish survival and eternity. The Jews defy secular history, a history defined by the machinations of politics, war, rootedness in land. The violence of the state, the wars and revolutions which create and transform nations and peoples, would not affect the eternity of the Jewish people, for this eternity is created in the specific modes of Jewish time—in its ritual patterns of law and practice, and so forth.[15]

Obviously, though, the Jews have been all too painfully subject to the violence of universal history, tragic victims of its merciless cruelty and passions. When Rosenzweig describes the Jews as being "outside" history, he means to again cite Stéphane Mosès that the temporality of Jewish collective existence is entirely different from that of Western historical consciousness. Or in the terms I have been using, this temporality constitutes what Benjamin or Levinas might call an "other history" running "underneath" or "over against" it—a "time of the other" or "another time." The very marginality of the Jews to "universal history" is their "being otherwise" and thus the *confirmation* of their role for history. Jewish existence "apart" from history, living from eternity, would then be the symbol which guides the rest of history and the nations toward the goal of redemption. In place of Hegelian history, Rosenzweig would

> sketch the idea of a discontinuous, non-accumulative history, punctuated not by the succession of great civilizations and major political events, but by the each time unique occurrence of qualitatively significant facts, endowed with a symbolic value, whose succession designates, beneath the records of apparent history (and sometimes against it), the invisible coming of Redemption in the world. ("Hegel" 330)

Or, to use the Levinasian phrase, "the invisible that is judgment"—or to use Benjamin's phrase, "now-time." This vision of a discontinuous history coincides with certain characteristics of history as reconceived in poststructuralist thought from Foucault to the New Historicism. A Levinasian position would hold, however, that the "subversiveness" of the poststructuralist histories or their "otherness" does not leave the immanent realm of politics, its war of forces, strategies, machinations. Rosenzweig and Levinas stress that without an "elsewhere," an "other" to politics itself, there can be no judgment, reversal, or even subversion of the violence and repressiveness of history, but only the repetition of its cruelties.

Perhaps Benjamin also realized this by his entangling materialist counterhistory with a messianic eschatology. Levinas writes that what Rosenzweig elicits is not an eschatology somehow added onto reality or instituted by decree; rather, "it delineates the primary coordinates of Being" ("Une pensée" 212). In other words, Levinas, Rosenzweig, and Benjamin all retain the idea of a judgment possible through a time that interrupts the immanence of universal history. At every moment, Levinas writes in an essay on Rosenzweig, the world is ripe for judgment "before the end of history and independently of this end": "the trauma of the real is religious history. It commands political history. This is Rosenzweig's anti-Hegelian position" ("Entre" 137).

It must be said, though, that while Levinas's philosophical writings are inspired by Rosenzweig, in his philosophical works Levinas does not identify the "otherwise than being" with Jewish existence or with any phenomenology of religion. He does not even mention these topics. He is trying to find this opening, this possibility for judgment, within experience itself as a possibility for all persons. Or, as he writes in one of his essays on Rosenzweig, "Israel, beyond carnal Israel, includes all persons who refuse the purely authoritarian verdict of History" ("Entre" 221). Levinas's messianic eschatology, like Benjamin's, attempts to be neither a religion, a dogma, a morality, nor a mysticism. As Derrida writes, "It can even be understood as the trial of theology and mysticism"; it is a "space or hollow within naked experience where this eschatology can be understood, and where it must resonate. . . . It is opening itself, the opening of opening" that can't be enclosed in any totality ("Violence" 83).

In sum, eschatology is the relation with infinity that breaks up totality, war, and empire. As such, this eschatology cannot be conceived within a history that is the "history of being" as war and totality—either as the end of that war or as the end of that history (*TI* 24). Levinas does not intend some kind of "teleology," nor does he want this eschatology to "equal the revealed opinions of positive religions" whose theologies are subject to ontology. In the next chapter, we shall see how this eschatology of peace, a "non-allergic relation with alterity," is for Levinas imbedded in the heart of language which is precisely this call to responsibility, to justice: "Peace is produced as this aptitude for speech" (23). The very temporality of time itself also breaks up totality; in time, in the "trace," in fecundity, language, the "face," in daily life and experience, and at every moment, Levinas finds, there can be judgment.

SEVEN

The Trace, The Face, and the Word of the Other

TIME AND THE OTHER

> To require time means that we cannot an-
> ticipate, that we must wait for everything,
> that what is ours depends on what is an-
> other's. (Rosenzweig, "The New Thinking"
> 199)

In *Of Grammatology* (1967), one of his first major works, Derrida acknowledged his debt to Levinas for the idea of the "trace": "Thus I relate
this concept of trace to what is at the center of the latest work of Emmanuel Levinas and his critique of ontology" (70); this was a reference to
Levinas's essay "The Trace of the Other," published in 1963. Levinas had
developed the idea of the "trace" and the *nonsynchronous* temporality of
the other in order to help explain how "experience" of the other than
Being is possible without having to give up philosophy or resort to a blind
faith in transcendence.

Levinas's notion of encounter with the other as separation—otherness is
that which is beyond all identification or any fusion with it—and of separation as opening or rupture of totality is also the opening of *time*. Fusion
with the other would mean ecstatic timelessness; time arises only with the
separated other. In other words, the "otherwise than being" does not occur
in some atemporal eternal order but in the very temporalization of time.
Yet this time is outside "history" when history is defined in a Hegelian
manner as a closed universal system which ultimately recuperates everything back to the subject. The temporality of the other and the otherwise
than being are precisely what interrupt that universal history; they are
what it cannot homogenize and recuperate.

There would then be two aspects to time: (1) an irreducible diachrony
where time is a succession of instants, and where the intervals between
instants each allow for distinction and difference, and (2) the time of universal history and memory, wherein the instants are synthesized and syn-
chronized into a whole, "recuperated."[1] Needless to say, this problem of
time and its recuperability or reconstruction through memory, myth, historiography, consciousness, or imagination is a central preoccupation of

modernism and postmodernism. Benjamin's "historical materialist" constructs new revolutionary and redemptive constellations of these irreducible instants to disrupt the continuities of "historicism." Levinas's attack on universal history must also be understood in this context: when he speaks of "history" and "memory" he is referring to that universal history which he wants to oppose with a nonrecuperable moment, a diachrony, an "anachronism"—something that does not get taken up in the Hegelian dialectic or the phenomenological consciousness and so lose its otherness in the totality of sameness or synchrony.

In this analysis, "representation," the "concept," "logic," "history," "memory," all ultimately return the other back to the same, and thus when Levinas elicits their other, he will speak of a "past more ancient than every representable origin, a pre-original and anarchical past" (*OTB* 8). This endeavor again parallels Benjamin's idea of a disjunctive messianic instant which disrupts the flow of historicist time. Like Levinas, Derrida also conceives temporality in terms of deferral, disruption of identity, nonrecuperable lapse, but Levinas's analyses of temporality are also made in terms of aging, passivity, patience, the body, sensibility, exposure.

To reiterate, Levinas's time of the other as future and opening is not "otherworldly." Or as Derrida writes of Levinas's notion: "It is present at the heart of experience. Present not as a total presence but as a trace." This idea is important, Derrida continues, because it means that "experience itself is eschatological at its origin" prior to all dogmas or articles of faith about eschatology ("Violence" 95). When asked by Richard Kearney whether his own search for a nonsite or *u-topos* other than that of Western metaphysics can be construed as a prophetic utopianism, Derrida himself answers by affirming a positive moment in deconstruction as a response to the call of alterity. Although he interrogates the classical ideas of *eschaton* or *telos*, "that does not mean I dismiss all forms of Messianic or prophetic eschatology. I think that all genuine questioning is summoned by a certain type of eschatology." Although he does not feel the kind of "hope" that would allow deconstruction to have a prophetic function, as "exodus and dissemination in the desert" it does have, he admits, certain "prophetic resonances"—but as a search without hope for hope (Kearney, *Dialogues* 118–19). Echoes again of Kafka and Benjamin: "Hope, plenty of hope, but not for us."[2]

In his essay "On the Trail of the Other," Levinas uses the same images of exile and desert to explain his paradoxical concept of "heteronomous experience"—experience of the absolutely other. There are, he maintains, "movements" and "attitudes" toward the other that cannot be converted into a category and a return to self; these are found in modes of goodness and work that are one-directional offerings without expectation of reciprocal return. One of his favored illustrations is the biblical Abraham's departure from his homeland of Ur contrasted to Ulysses' ultimate return home to Ithaca. As "one-directional action," such movements require a tempo-

rality and a patience which ultimately mean "to renounce being the contemporary of his accomplishments, to work without entering the promised
land." Work so oriented toward the other is work oriented toward the
future, a work for "being-beyond-my-death." This "being-*beyond*-death" is
meant, of course, to challenge Heidegger's key idea of "being-*toward*-
death." For Levinas, the triumph will come in a "time without me," a time
beyond the horizon of my time which is "eschatology without hope for self
or liberation from my own time" ("Trail" 38).

In *Totality and Infinity*, there are extensive analyses of the ways in which
works, the will, and labor also produce this kind of temporality. In brief,
works temporally separate themselves from their authors and from their
authors' wills; they are thus subject "to the designs of a foreign will," to
their own seduction and betrayal (*TI* 227). But this separation of will from
its own works is also the positive potential space of a *judgment of the will
upon itself*, and the possibility for the will also to be for-the-other. (There
are interesting parallels and applications of this idea to the form of literary
criticism known as "reception theory" and to Benjamin's idea of the "afterlife" of a work.) To be a temporal being is to be both for and against
death, for death does not simply signify nonbeing but being subject to a
foreign will. In the interval before death, the will "has time to be for the
Other, and thus to recover meaning despite death" (236).

To be temporal, then, is to "have time" as delay or postponement; and
that constitutes the very distance from the present and future which also
splits up the present "into an inexhaustible multiplicity of possibles that
suspend the instant" (238), and so can correct the instant. Maintaining
distance from the present is also patience, endurance, hope—"the passivity of undergoing and yet mastery itself." "The supreme ordeal of the will
is not death but suffering. . . . Violence does not stop Discourse; all is not
inexorable. Thus alone does violence remain endurable in patience. It is
produced only in a world where I can die *as a result of someone* and *for
someone*" (239). The for-the-other as a move beyond the ego is the mode of
a subjectivity as apology, as placing itself under a judgment "to receive the
truth from it upon its own witness," a judgment which confirms it against
death (240–41) and in its singularity. This is a judgment beyond the judgments of universal history which judge in absentia and kill the will. This
idea of the "for-the-other" triumphing over death has important parallels
to Rosenzweig's great first chapter in book 2 of *The Star of Redemption* on
"revelation"; it begins with the line from the Song of Songs 8:6, "Love is as
strong as death." The relation of the idea of witness and "dying for the
other" to Levinas's sensibility as a Holocaust survivor will be taken up in
the next chapters.

In sum, eschatology is the time of the other, and depends on the gratuitous work of the self toward the other. Levinas describes this movement
with the Greek word *liturgy*, whose original signification, he notes, includes gratuitous investment with no strings attached—liturgy without

religious connotations but as "absolutely patient action" as "the ethical itself" ("Trail" 38). In this sense, "liturgy" also quite well describes the very movement of Levinas's philosophy.

FECUNDITY

This judgment, however, also requires an "infinite time," a time beyond the visible historical time of cause-and-effect. Toward the end of *Totality and Infinity* Levinas connects the issues of history, time, metaphysics, and transcendence to eros, but again in a way quite different from that of the other French theorists. Eros, he maintains, is not consummated in the fusion of souls. The pathos of love, to the contrary, is that the two *cannot* fuse, are always separate. It is not romantic love between the sexes that produces transcendence but the ordinary phenomenon of fecundity, of relation with a *child*; there one finds an "infinite time," an "ever recommencing being" or absolute future: "Both my own and non-mine, a possibility of myself but also a possibility of the other, of the Beloved, my future does not enter into the logical essence of the possible. The relation with such a future, irreducible to the power over possibles, we shall call fecundity" (*TI* 267).

Fecundity must not be thought of as a mere biological fact, or a blind drive of self-seeking eros, "but must be set up as an ontological category" (227). Paternity can "be born by the biological life, but be lived beyond that life" (247). Fecundity, in other words, describes a relationship between same and other that escapes formal logic. "Je suis un autre" was the despairing cry of Rimbaud; but in the child, the I is another in an entirely positive sense. "Paternity remains a self-identification, but also a distinction within identification—a structure unforeseeable in formal logic" (267). The child is both same and other, a living on into the future, a renewal of time, an interruption, a discontinuity. The child lives beyond my death and establishes a relation with the absolute future, infinite time, as ever-recommencing being. Fecundity is thus a phenomenon produced within the totality which at the same time breaks up the totality. Fecundity produces and maintains the "not yet" which ruptures the closed cycles of universal history.

The renewal of fecundity is not a repetition of the same—it is difference. Levinas argues further that it ruptures the monolithic and monadic notion of being in the ancient Greek philosopher Parmenides, who defined being as what is changeless, one, and identified with thought. The Parmenidean conception is a key source of western logic which "rests on the indissoluble bond between the One and Being" (274). In fecundity, though, "Being is produced as multiple, as split into same and other; this is its ultimate structure. It is society, and hence it is time. We thus leave the philosophy of Parmenidean being" (269).

Leaving Parmenidean being also means leaving the closed circle of fate, of changeless being and cyclical, ever-repeating time: "A being capable of another fate than its own is a fecund being" (282). Paternity, then, is a mode of triumph over fate and age through the very discontinuity of the child. For the child also breaks with the parent, allows a recommencement that changes the past; in fecundity, time brings something new. It is both a "rupture of continuity and continuation across this rupture" (284).

This model of paternity of fecundity contrasts, of course, with a Freudian or Oedipal model wherein the relation of father and child is one of fated conflict and war. This rupture, conflict, and discontinuity in paternity as a negative, inexorable, and tormenting fate is the model Harold Bloom adopts in his theory of the "anxiety of influence": the later poet has to wage Oedipal war with the precursor poet to carve a poetic space of originality, to become and displace the father. (This model echoes the pathos of modernism traced in the last chapter—that quest for the entirely new and original which is nevertheless always recuperated back into the past.) Levinas is not denying the existence of psychological Oedipal phenomena, but he is refusing to give them the status of an ontological priority. For Levinas, the project to become one's own origin, to find an autonomous principle for being, is the very move of narcissistic and imperialistic reason. Against this he elicits a prior "plural reason," not a reason for itself, seeking to be its own origin, but a reason for-the-other. And among the realms in which he finds this for-the-other enacted is the plurality of sexuality and parenthood itself, in the body and production of a child.

In *Totality and Infinity*, "paternity" connotes more of a generic parenthood; in *Otherwise Than Being*, as we shall see, he will identify this radical for-the-other with *maternity*. In *The Second Sex*, Simone de Beauvoir harshly attacked Levinas's association of alterity and femininity in his *Time and the Other* (1947) as "an assertion of masculine privilege" (xix), but she neglects or misunderstands his central critique of the narcissistic logic of identity in general, and his assertion of the commanding, judging position of the other in relation to the conscious ego. Levinas seems to have anticipated by many years the recent poststructuralist feminist embrace of alterity as the undoing of the "privilege of phallogocentrism."[3] De Beauvoir's view is modeled on an existentialist paradigm of consciousness as free and for-itself caught up in a struggle for freedom vis-à-vis the hostile other. In structuralist and poststructuralist thought, this idea of a free, independent centered consciousness is abandoned.

Insofar as the discontinuity in fecundity leads away from the doomed project of an absolute self-origination, it also contains the possibility for a "freer" relation with the past than that of memory. Memory, as in the famous title Proust gave to his great novel, is "in search of lost time." Benjamin poignantly analyzed the torments of this time and memory, and the burden of the past in the works of the paradigmatic modern writers. Levinas shares with Benjamin the aim of finding a way to repair and redeem the past, but Levinas finds in fecundity as the discontinuous time-of-the-other a positive relation to the infinity of the future, something that enables a *nonnostalgic*, nonfated, nonmythical relation to the past. "Fecundity continues history without producing old age" (*TI* 268). As the very temporality of time, fecundity involves a relation to the past which contains the possibility for something entirely new, and a way to freely return to the past without being burdened by age. "This recommencement of the instant, this triumph of the time of fecundity over the becoming of the mortal and aging being, is a pardon, the very work of time" (282).

In other words, fecundity is a recommencement that has the potential to bring pardon, healing, correction of the past. Pardon is the paradox of reversal of the past and of the natural order of things. Unlike forgetting, which nullifies the past, pardon acts upon the past, repeats and purifies, but conserves the event in the present (283). This distinction between two relations to the past—"memory/forgetting" and "fecundity/pardon"— might also be used to analyze the case of Paul deMan. DeMan's analysis of the impossible aporias of modernity in terms of the opposition memory/forgetting is a way of dealing with the burden of the past which leaves no room either for judgment upon the past or for its pardon. Moreover, because alterity for deMan is never the personal "other," his deconstructions of language and history remain part of all those philosophies of the Neuter with which Levinas breaks—Heideggerian Being, or Blanchot's impersonality, or Hegel's impersonal reason. Desire in these systems is always interpreted as need "and thus bound to the essential violence of action, dismisses philosophy and is gratified only in art or politics" (298). Aesthetics and politics are indeed the poles between which current literary theory oscillates.

But philosophy for Levinas is ethics and judgment. The future which comes to Levinasian subjectivity, this time of the other, is not a succession of indifferent moments; "it comes to me across an absolute interval whose other shore the Other absolutely other—though he be my son, is alone capable of marking, and of connecting with the past." Time adds something new to being. The intervals and discontinuities of finite time are the spaces of time's renewal, a positive space, the very relation with infinity which can recommence time ever again. "It is not the finitude of being that constitutes the essence of time, as Heidegger thought, but its infinity." And this infinite existing of time is what "ensures the situation of judgement, condition of truth, behind the failure of the goodness of today" (284). Both deMan and Levinas were witnesses of that failure, that collapse of goodness in the Nazi era, and one might even say that their subsequent philosophies represent two opposite ways of coping with that failure.

The telling of truth, moreover, itself requires this infinite time, and the nature of this infinite time reconnects Levinas once more to the messianic mediations of Benjamin and Scholem. For this infinite time also puts "back in question the truth in promises." It evokes the dream of a completion, a happy eternity, a "messianic time, where the perpetual is converted into the eternal" and good is finally secured once and for all from evil (284–85). Whether this eternity is a new structure of time or "an extreme vigilance of the messianic consciousness exceeds the bounds of the book." And that reference to an exteriority and excess connected to messianism concludes the text of *Totality and Infinity* itself. The nineteen pages of the next and final section, "Conclusions," are a recapitulation and summary of the main arguments of the book. He will take up the messianic theme again in his Jewish writings, in *Difficile liberté* and in his talmudic lectures, which I shall discuss in chapters 9 and 10.

Needless to say, the idea of fecundity embodied in the structure of the family and the link of that structure to redemption is deeply rooted in Jewish tradition, from the book of Genesis onward. And despite the lack of references to Jewish thought and philosophy in *Totality and Infinity*, one can sense again the Holocaust survivor—finding in the continued power of fecundity and paternity a kind of triumph over the Nazi attempt at extermination. Levinas's idea of fecundity and infinite time as redemptive, as a corrective to historicism, parallels (without the pathos and nostalgia) the yearning of Benjamin's angel looking back at the ruins of history and trying to glimpse a healing, to see in every instant "the strait gate through which the Messiah might enter." It also has a key source in Rosenzweig's assertion of the eternity of the Jewish people as realized in the biological fecundity of ongoing Jewish generations in the third part of *The Star*. For example, Rosenzweig describes Judaism as the "community in which a linked sequence of everlasting life goes from grandfather to grandson. . . . time is not a foe that must be tamed . . . but its child and the child of its child. . . . It does not have to hire the services of the spirit; the natural propagation of the body guarantees its eternity" (298–99).

Finally, this assertion of the ontological priority of fecundity in the family is also a polemic against Hegel's position that the family is only the first stage in the dialectical progress of the Spirit toward its historical consummation in the universality of the nation-state. Levinas maintains the identity and priority of the family *outside* the state, although he grants that the state provides a framework for the family.

In sum, the infinite time of fecundity is connected to the central Levinasian theme of "infinity" and the "otherwise than being" that break up "totality" and protect the singularity of the subject from dissolution into impersonal "universal" structures: "As source of human time it permits subjectivity to place itself under a judgement while retaining speech"; fecundity is a "metaphysically ineluctable structure. . . . a relation between man and man and between the I and itself" (*TI* 306).

THE FACE, THE TRACE, AND THE ETHICAL RELATION

One reason Levinas breaks with these impersonal structures is that "they exalt the obedience which no face commands" (*TI* 298). The "face" is another key Levinasian figure connected with the alterity and infinity that guarantees subjectivity but also brings subjectivity to judgment. Yet his notion of the face is often quite ambiguous and subject to varying definitions which are more like networks of associations than any precise stipulations. Despite the connotations of the word, he maintains that "face" is *not* originally founded on any visual perception. "The face of the Other at each moment destroys and overflows the plastic image it leaves me" (50). It is not "that which appears," or is "brought to light" by the grasp of reason or consciousness.

"Face" becomes in Levinas another category of understanding, a "mode of intelligibility," a way of indicating a subject/object relation beyond/ before the formal relations of logic, or of concepts which reduce the other to the same. In both *Otherwise Than Being* and *Totality and Infinity*, the notion of the face describes a self-already-in-relation, an other-in-the-same. The "welcome of the face" is distinguished from Heideggerian "disclosure" or bringing to light. Levinas wants to insist upon a relation between the same and other that is not reducible to *knowledge* of other by the same, or even revelation of other to the same (*TI* 28). The face is prior to every question about the "what" of things, the "What is it?" The face refers to the question, "Who is it?"—the question of the other which for Levinas is already present in any question put, for the question is always *put to* someone (177).

Levinas here again follows Rosenzweig, for whom the primal philosophical error is to begin philosophy with the question of "essence," to reduce the essence of one thing back to the essence of another, whether in materialism, mysticism, ontology, or subjectivism. Nothing new or different, Rosenzweig writes, ever appears on the other side of the predicate *is*: "precisely the 'what is?' question applied to 'everything' is responsible for all the wrong answers," which are all tautological answers ("New Thinking" 191). Richard Cohen also persuasively argues that Levinas's very use of the figure "face" is inspired by Rosenzweig's evocation of the same trope to signify the apotheosis of truth at the end of *The Star of Redemption* ("Face of Truth"). In the section of *The Star* entitled "The Face of the Figure" (418–24), Rosenzweig notes that the face is composed of the most receptive organs in the body—nose, ears, eyes, mouth, and so forth. In the inner sanctum of divine truth, the human catches sight of "none other than a countenance like his own. The Star of Redemption is become countenance which glances at me and out of which I glance. Not because God is my mirror, but God's truth" (418).

"God's countenance" also signifies an above and below. "We speak in images. But the images are not arbitrary. There are essential images and coincidental ones. The irreversibility of the truth can only be enunciated in the image of a living being." Rosenzweig also uses "face" or "countenance" to signify human communion: "Nor is this brotherliness by any means identity of everything with the human countenance, but rather the harmony precisely of men of the most diverse countenances. One thing is necessary, of course, but only one: that men have a countenance at all, that they see each other" (345). The glance is also *gesture* beyond word and deed, and related to dance and poetry, to mutual recognition through processions, pageants, and carnivals: "The power to dissolve all that is rigid already inheres in the glance. . . . Once an eye has glanced at us, it will glance at us as long as we live" (372).

Yet this ultimate vision of the beyond, notes Rosenzweig in the concluding page of the entire book, is nothing but "what the word of revelation already enjoined in the midst of life" and is epitomized by the prophet Micah's words (6:2) to love justice, do mercy, and walk humbly with God. Revelation and redemption turn back into ethics; the beyond is already within experience, in life.[4]

In trying to understand further why Levinas chooses this particular figure, one could also say that the face connotes the distinctive mark of the individual human personality, unique to each person; a "face" is the opposite of impersonal, anonymous Being. The light of a "face" or "countenance" with its connotations of the human, singular, and personal is a counterterm to the abstract impersonal "light" of philosophical reason. It is also a substitute for, or displacement of, the term *phenomenon*—i.e., what appears to and is grasped by consciousness in phenomenology (the noema of a noesis), and a kind of counterpoint to a Hegelian "concrete universal" but thought outside any dialectical system. "The way in which the other presents himself, exceeding *the idea of the other in me*, we here name face. This *mode* does not consist in figuring as a theme under my gaze, in spreading itself forth as a set of qualities forming an image. . . . The face brings a notion of truth which, in contradistinction to contemporary ontology, is not the disclosure of an impersonal Neuter, but *expression*" (*TI* 50–51). And this expression of the face occurs through language in conversation as the welcome, reception, and openness to the other beyond the capacity of the I. The face is the incarnate, irreducible, immediate sign of the individual and personal. Notes Richard Cohen following Rosenzweig, it is also the place in the body with the most openings to the exterior, where the multiple organs of perception and exchange are located—the locus of sensitivity and vulnerable exposure to the world ("Face of Truth" 4). Later, in *Otherwise Than Being*, Levinas will define *subjectivity itself* precisely as *vulnerability*.

The face is the very "interface" of self and world. One sees and is seen. But why choose a term which so strongly alludes to seeing if one wants to elicit a form of relation other than the knowledge of things connected with the visual appearance of being? Perhaps because Levinas is also implicitly setting forth a critique and alternative to the brutal Hegelian "struggle for recognition" and master/slave dialectic. As Hegel outlines in his *Phenomenology* (Section IV A-3), the primordial desire by which the human self relates to the other is a desire for mastery and negation of the other. In

Hegel, the "struggle unto death" of the two warring selves results in the victory of one over the other, and it is the *recognition* by the dominated one of the victor's mastery that gives ultimate satisfaction and identity to the victor. For this reason, the master needs the slave's recognition to affirm the master's selfhood. This central Hegelian idea that the consciousness of being a self requires the recognition or "gaze of the other" is the source for many poststructuralist notions of the self; Lacan's "mirror stage" is one of the most well known examples. Needless to say, the master-slave chapter of Hegel's *Phenomenology* is also a key source for Marx's analysis of labor and the capitalist-worker relation.

In Levinas, the "face" will signify a denuding, the stripping of all "facades" and masks from the masterly ego when it is confronted with and given over to the other in the ethical relation. Like the intensely anti-Hegelian critiques of Rosenzweig and Derrida (especially in Derrida's *Glas*), Levinas is trying to expose the blindness in the panoramic impassive gaze of the philosopher who surveys and constructs the whole of knowledge and reality. This gaze is connected to and dependent upon the gaze of the dominated and defeated other in the struggle for recognition. It is just this aggressive imperial gaze that Levinas accuses; and it is precisely that defeated, wounded look in the face of the other that Levinas brings as witness and judge. He wants to position this accusation and judgment, however, *outside* any master/slave dialectic—as a witness and judge that is somehow nonviolent. The gaze of the dominator is brought to judgment "before the face" of the other. The "facing position" is the turn of the face toward me, in accusation and appeal. In sum, the face is the ethical inversion of the Hegelian gaze—the very gaze of philosophy itself.

> For the presence before a face, my orientation toward the Other, can lose the avidity proper to the gaze only by turning into generosity, incapable of approaching the other with empty hands. (*TI* 50)

> The facing position, opposition par excellence, can be only as a moral summons. This movement proceeds from the other. The idea of infinity, the infinitely more contained in the less, is concretely produced in the form of a relation with the face (196).

The Hebrew word for "face," *panim*, also has this dynamic connotation: it comes from the root *panah*, meaning "turn"—a turning to or away from. James Ponet, in his essay "Faces: A Meditation," argues that Levinas's sense of the face "is clearly biblically derived" and cites the connotations of the term especially in the Jacob stories, in the central biblical blessing of the Blessing of the Face (Num. 6:22–27), in Moses' veiling of his face (Exod. 34:29–35), in God's hiding his face (Job 12:24; Ps. 27:8–9), and so forth. This connection is strong and important, but I think that it is less a case of straight "derivation" than the characteristic way Levinas, like Rosenzweig, is "translating"—simultaneously both philosophizing a biblical figure and Judaizing philosophy, as I will analyze in more depth in later chapters. "Be*fore* the face" becomes the inversion of an autonomous reason of-and-for-itself into a *for*-the-other, i.e., ethics.

How is the trace related to the face? In *Otherwise Than Being*, the trace is described as what "lights up as the face of a neighbor, ambiguously him *before whom* (or *to whom*, without any paternalism) and him *for whom* I answer. For such is the enigma or ex-ception of a face, judge and accused" (*OTB* 12). The trace is the "passing" of the infinite as excess, the non-thematizable. Here again, the face is not an image or a representation: "a face is a trace of itself, given over to my responsibility, but to which I am wanting and faulty. It is as though I were responsible for his mortality and guilty for surviving" (91). These words in the context of Levinas's life and work cannot help but evoke again the Holocaust, although he does not explicitly mention it here or in any of his philosophical writings. The guilt of the survivor is not meant here in a psychological sense; rather, it again describes the "always already" of ethical obligation of all humans.

In another sense, Levinas is making all persons "survivors," responsible without even having decided to be so and before any voluntary act is undertaken. There is no escape. The implications in relation to the events of World War II are quite clear: there are no excuses, no "We didn't know, we didn't see, we are not responsible." All of Levinas's writing, with its difficulty and complexity, is a direct refutation of any such position or any attempt to relieve anyone of responsibility—from even such tangentially involved figures as deMan to the notorious Klaus Barbie, who at his trial for war crimes said, "I've forgotten about it. If they haven't, that's their concern." But even more, it also makes responsible everyone who excuses him- or herself precisely because he or she is not a Klaus Barbie—every one of us, even every reader of Levinas.[5]

Indeed, the very mode in which Derrida and deMan absorbed the Levinasian notion of the trace "effaced the face" and the ethical relation. For Levinas, insofar as "the face is present in its refusal to be contained" (*TI* 194) and cannot be comprehended or encompassed, it is that alterity and infinity that breaks up totality. This is the sense in which the face is a "trace" of itself, a notion which Derrida transfers to the absence-presence of linguistic signs. Yet Levinas's trace "is not a sign like any other. But it does play the role of sign, can be taken for a sign." Here Levinas make an interesting move: every sign is a trace in the sense that beyond what a given sign signifies is "the passage of the person who left the sign," who puts it forth for communication ("Trail" 44–45). As trace of the other, it "passes through" the human, the personal order.

Yet the "trace" is not synonymous with a "sign" which "reveals" the absent, or with some kind of "revelation" that still reduces alterity through the very interplay of absence and presence. The face as trace is a kind of passageway between the "beyond being" and the finite, immanent present. This beyond is beyond even "symbolic knowledge"; it is an "absence radically withdrawn from uncovering and dissimulation" ("Trail"42) but that nevertheless makes possible the coming of the "face" as a significance in "which the Other does not become the Self." The trace is an "order of which the significance remains irremediably disrupted. . . . The beyond from which the face comes signifies as trace. The face is in the trace of the Absent . . . which no introspection will be unable to discover in the Self" (43).

The "face" is also related to the time of the other, a time which is not "my time," is not synchronous with me, and so cannot be assimilated back to the self. If the face comes from the future, then the trace in the way it "signifies" is connected to an immemorial past, as a radical diachrony. For in the trace, "the relation between the signified and signification is not a correlation, but the very lack of rectitude" (43). One can see from this description written in 1963 how Levinas was a source for Derrida's critique of Saussure's definition of signification as a synchronous correlation of the signifier and signified. Derrida will use the diachrony of the trace and the "deferral of difference" to put in motion the dissemination and free play of the signifier. For Levinas, the trace as what has passed by but is not there is the "beyond being" as immemorial past, an "always already" of the Other that passes/passes by (is not captured) and disrupts the immanence of the present, and any synchronous correlation of sign and signified.

What Levinas is trying to articulate with this complex notion of face as trace is the logical paradox of "personal absence." What is "absent" is absent only in *ontological* terms, i.e., absent as "being"; but it is present-absent in the trace which passes through the personal other of human beings, and which is the very call to responsibility for the other. *The refusal of presence is converted into my presence as present for-the-other.*

Now because it is not strictly reducible to a purely linguistic sign, the Levinasian trace, like the Derridean, "signifies" in the actual sign-systems of language only through equivocation. As immemorial past, the trace indicates that radical diachrony, that temporality which is always the lapse or disruption of any self-enclosed system. But in contrast to Derrida and deMan, this "negativity" in terms of "comprehension" is an excess as positivity, and positive in its call to responsibility for the other prior to all comprehension; it is the incommensurability of the good.

Levinas describes this refusal to be wholly contained by any form or comprehension as the face's "nudity," a nakedness which "*is* by itself and not by reference to a system," i.e., which is not comprehended in a "form" that can be disclosed by illumination. This nakedness and otherness is thus at the same time its "absence" from the world or "the exiling of a being, his condition of being stranger, destitute, or proletarian." Here again is an ethical turn of the trace which Derrida does not follow. It is also the elevation of ethics over aesthetics, a kind of "prohibition against graven images" since Levinas thinks of art as that which tries to finalize and halt the elusive movements of this "infinity" in the beauty—enchanting but indifferent—of form. He will posit language and discourse over against art, as that which relates to the transcendence and nakedness of the face in its very nakedness (*TI* 74:193).

This "nudity" of the face as nonimage comes from "the emptiness of space, from space signifying emptiness, from the desert and desolate space as uninhabitable." The image of desert, of course, has strong biblical echoes, the site of the wandering of the Jewish people, the site of the giving of the Law on Sinai, the site of freedom from Egyptian oppression, and so forth. It is also a crucial metaphor for Derrida in his essay on Jabès and the relation of Judaism, postmodernism, and writing; torments of exile and emptiness become the endlessly equivocal spaces of both Judaism and language. Asks Levinas, however, is this abandoned space a nothingness completely indifferent to humanity, or is its emptiness "the trace of a passage or trace of what could not enter?"—the trace of the excess, the uncontainable, or infinite that can signify only through this ambiguity? (This question parallels that about the nature of "nothingness" in Scholem's interpretation of the void created by the *tzimtzum* and the "nothingness of revelation.") Since the trace "signifies" only in equivocation, or ambiguously, there is no "proof" or any *logical* necessity that this desert is the realm of ethics rather than an inhuman wilderness—that void which is portrayed for us in Derrida or deMan and so much other postmodern writing. There can be no "proof" that the trace is not this "nothingness"; but the surplus over pure nothingness, an infinitesimal difference, is in my non-indifference to the neighbor, where I am obedient as though to an order addressed to me" (*OTB* 91). That infinitesimal difference is all the difference as nonindifference to the other. One might also observe that Levinas's own rhetorical questions here are themselves modes of this alterity, disruptions as the space of an opening to the other, the otherwise of the logical assertions of philosophy and language.

This nonindifference, this responsibility, is then "an imperative force which is not a necessity" (93). The imperative is the force of the face in its very desolation as trace. The trace is a "non-synchronizable diachrony," not to be mistaken for the "sign of a hidden God who would impose the neighbor on me. It is a trace of itself, of an abandon where the equivocation is never dissipated." What Levinas is proposing, as the title of one of his early books well puts it, is "the humanism of the other man." It is through this human other that the "otherwise than being" passes, leaving its trace; and this trace as ethical imperative is the "very inordinateness of infinity" (94). The strangeness and destitution of the face both supplicates and demands, "deprived of everything because entitled to everything, and which one recognizes in giving. . . . To recognize the Other is to recognize a hunger. To recognize the Other is to give." Yet it is to give to one who also comes from a dimension of height (*TI* 75). In this sense, "the dimension of the divine opens forth from the human face" (78), as an absolute purged of what he calls "the violence of the sacred"—violent because in paroxysms of the "sacred," the self is obliterated, and participation in transcendence means annihilating union. Andrius Valevicius aptly observes that this position clearly contradicts that of Rudolf Otto in Otto's influential book on the phenomenology of religion, *The Idea of the Holy* (*From the Other* 125–130).

Levinas's attitude also contrasts sharply with Scholem's admiration for mysticism as the highest stage of religious consciousness and experience, and with any view of the symbol as the highest expression of a truth beyond expression. What Levinas calls "metaphysical atheism" is the position which retains the separated I in the midst of the very relation to transcendence and so which is the necessary foundation for a "faith purged of myth" and the numinous. In his Jewish writings, he will describe Judaism, especially rabbinic Judaism, as just such a demythologized, ethical faith. But here, in the philosophical work, there is no sectarian reference or labeling. As in Rosenzweig, the categories are meant to precede any theology. Revelation, similarly, is not the ecstatic dissolution of the self into the One, or an imperious crushing of the individual; it is discourse with the other. For Levinas, the face to face of the ethical relation "cuts across every relation one could call mystical" wherein discourse can be degraded into incantation, intoxication, seductive equivocation, or ritualized into a drama which manipulates persons into preassigned roles. The ethical and linguistic relations are preeminently rational, with reason defined as the nonviolent ethical relation with the other.

Another contemporary Jewish philosopher, Rabbi Joseph B. Soloveitchik, makes a similar argument for a rational approach to philosophy and religion and for not divorcing religious knowledge from temporality and sensibility. Soloveitchik, like Levinas, is haunted by the collapse of reason in Europe in World War II and the subsequent atrocities. Writing in 1944, he critiqued the historical "aftermath of epistemological anti-intellectualism rampant in European philosophy during much of this century" (*Halakhic Mind* 50–52) and its renunciation of public critical reason. He categorizes phenomenology, humanistic hermeneutics, Bergsonian biologism, and existential philosophy as forms of such nonrational intuitionism—all "romantic escapes of the theoretical man" which are similar to the medieval mysticism of Meister Eckhardt and Jacob Boehme. "It is no mere coincidence that the most celebrated philosophers of the third Reich were outstanding disciples of Husserl." They transposed Husserl's mathematical intuitionism into "emotional approaches to reality. When reason surrenders its supremacy to dark, equivocal emotions, no dam is able to stem the rising tide of the affective stream." Nietzschean "Dionysian mystic wisdom versus 'decadent' Socratism was the philosophical Armageddon of our age" (53). All the "life-affirmers" brought death and havoc instead.

Soloveitchik asserts that in European culture following World War I, the *gestalt* approach that had been "well-founded in contemporary scientific thought, was applied not only to the psyche, but also to the psycho-physical ego, both individual and collective." Despite valid intellectual possibilities,

> no concept ever degenerated to such a degree and became so powerful a weapon in the hands of fanatics as did the Gestalt. An untrammeled path led from Gestalt and group psychology through typology, philosophical anthropology and characterology (in conjunction with graphology and physiognomics) into the welter of racial theory. (54)

> All the racial theories so prominent during this century have evolved from the modern concept of "wholeness." . . . The scientific concept of Gestalt was transformed into something mythical and the idea of the structure into mystical Dionysian knowledge of "Primal Unity." (53–54)

This argument might also be applied to our discussion of the symbol and the debate over the ontologizing of the *sefirotic* configurations. It also provides an important context for the deontologized and demythologized use of *gestalt* in Rosenzweig's configurations of the "Star" of Redemption, Benjamin's "dialectical images," and Levinas's "face." In Levinas the "face" is a *gestalt* that is a critique of phenomenology, a nonphenomenon, a rupture of the wholeness of the self, or the unity of knower and known, and the supposed adequacy of intentional cognizing consciousness to its objects.

Another reason Levinas worked so intensively with the notion of the "face" might have been precisely to counter the contemporary abuses of *gestalt*, to critique them without losing the singularity of the person and ethical obligation. DeMan clearly saw the same dangers in philosophies of wholeness, but his critique appeals to impersonal and anonymous forces to rupture these totalities. "Language" becomes hypostatized as a counterterm to *gestalt*.

For Levinas, though, language is the bearer of transcendence as a "social relation," the relation of same and other; and transcendence solicits us through the very nakedness and destitution of the other, the proximity of the neighbor. Not mysticism or theology but ethics thus constitutes the relation with the metaphysical: "There can be no 'knowledge' of God separated from the relationship with men" (*TI* 78). The face of the other is the cry of naked destitution demanding response, a vulnerable nudity which itself becomes the primordial appeal/command of "Thou Shalt Not Kill." To exist for the other, to be called into question by the other, is to "dread murder more than death" (246). The very vulnerability of the face indicates a relation wherein one is captured, compelled, taken in, and exposed, but not in any kind of irrational delirium; the "nakedness of the face" is an exposure which is the "very possibility of understanding" (*DL* 21). It is the foundation of reason as the very relation with the other, a kind of "universal" which is not an impersonal abstraction or a coercive necessity of logic.

It is, rather, a command that does not negate or destroy that self to which it appeals—an ethical noncoercive reason.

Because it is not logically or physically coercive, its appeals/commands can indeed be denied: "Violence can aim only at a face." Violence is directed precisely against that which escapes all grasp and hold: the Other. Nevertheless, "the Other, in the hands of forces that break him, exposed to powers, remains unforeseeable, that is transcendent. This transcendence is not to be described negatively, but is manifested positively in the moral resistance of the face to the violence of murder. The force of the Other is already and henceforth moral" (*TI* 225). In other words, even when enduring violence, the will can yet will to be *for someone* and something else, to die for something else (238–39). In this patience and "passivity," the will affirms its triumphant freedom over violence, and enables a mode of being beyond death.

This mode of passive endurance is a counterpart to Levinas's notion of fecundity which we examined above; it is a mode of being beyond and otherwise than violence, domination, and repetition. Such an endurance of violence, though, is an exceptional and traumatic mode, whereas fecundity is a form of infinity enacted within the daily, ordinary, material finite world. Levinas will also argue that the revelation of the "face" is elsewhere enacted and accessible in the daily world—precisely in language.

LANGUAGE AND THE FACE: ROSENZWEIG'S SPEECH-THINKING

> The effort of this book is directed toward apperceiving in discourse a non-allergic relation with alterity, toward apperceiving Desire—where power, by essence murderous of the other, becomes, faced with the other and "against all good sense," the impossibility of murder, the consideration of the other, or justice. Concretely our effort consists in maintaining, within anonymous community, the society of the I with the Other—language and goodness. (*TI* 47)

In contrast to Buber and other "dialogic philosophers," in Levinas's work, the other is not in a reciprocal relation to the same (68–69). Rather, the other calls, appeals, commands from the dimensions of both height and depth. He also describes the "face" as "speech," call, expression, and appeal. What exactly is the deeper connection between the face and language? How is the nonviolent imperative of the face embodied and enacted in language?

As we have seen repeatedly, the "meta" of the metaphysical signifies for Levinas a "beyond," not as some immaterial invisible realm, or what "negates" the finite or physical, but "beyond being" as it has been classically understood as light, knowledge, representation, adequation of ideas with things. The beyond is otherness—what is other/beyond the enclosing systems of ontology, an otherness which breaches "totality"—that corollary of classical philosophical systems of knowledge and representation. "Metaphysics desires the other" (*TI* 34), but this desire does not mean union of subject and object, for that would return the other to the same. The subject of desire remains "absolutely separated," not correlated with its object.

There are extensive analyses in *Totality and Infinity*, especially in section II, of how the separate, "atheistic" I is produced—not via any Hegelian negation but from enjoyment, sensation, positivity. These analyses are beyond my scope here, but it is important to note that Levinas's emphasis on separation again strongly echoes Rosenzweig's critique of the paradigmatic move of philosophy to reduce heterogeneous reality to one principle. Rosenzweig breaks up totality—the unity of logos and being—and splits it into the *separated* existences of God, world, and humanity as "metaphysics, meta-logic, and meta-ethics." In this shattering of the All, each of the three fragments becomes a separated "All in itself" (*Star* 26), and the main effort of *The Star* is the reconfiguration, the setting up of new relations and bridges between these three isolated fragments—their reconstellation into the star of redemption, which is an entirely different kind of All.

In their first, completely separated stage, these fragments are configured as the "concealed" God, "secluded" human, and "enchanted" world of myth. Rosenzweig defines the essence of myth as "a life that knows nothing above and nothing beneath itself" and whose law is the "inner harmony of caprice and fate, a harmony that does not resound beyond itself, that constantly returns into itself" (*Star* 34). Art for Rosenzweig "is subject to the laws of the mythical world," has that self-containment, that "indifference to everything beyond itself" (38) that marks the beautiful. The classical tragic hero is isolated, silent, and defiant, buried within himself with no real bridge to the exterior, arousing our terror and pity but unable to found true community (76–80). The "language" of art, like the language of mathematical symbols, is this "speech before speech," a "speech of the unspeakable" (80), a language prior to but preparation for the living audible speech of revelation. Art is the subjective aspect of this protospeech: mathematics its objective aspect (125).

Benjamin employed this idea of the pathos, the "speechless speech" of mute creation in his early writings on language. Like Benjamin, Rosenzweig also formulated a "reception theory" of the work whereby its mute isolation is broken via the beholder to whom "it speaks" and without whom it would have no enduring effect on reality (*Star* 242). In Rosenzweig, "creation," "revelation," and "redemption" are the bridges between these self-enclosed and occulted worlds, the breakup of their mutual isolation and the opening of each to the exterior—to the other, "the turning of each to face [*sic*] each other" (115,139). There is space here for only the briefest mention of his complex analyses of these relations, but the key point is that language has an essential role in their establishment, and in linking creation and revelation. Language is simultaneously the gift of God, the common property of all humanity, and yet particular for each individual, the "seal of humanity in man." "And yet to this day there is no language of mankind; that will come to be only at the end. Real language, however, is common to all between beginning and end, and yet is a distinct one for each; it unites and divides at the same time" (110).

The individual language of today, or the language of the individual, points to and includes that end, for it is "dominated by the ideal of coming to a perfect understanding which we visualize as the language of mankind" (110). Translation is thus "the first effect of the spirit . . . to erect a bridge between man and man, between tongue and tongue"; the translation of the Bible is held equal to the original, and so "God speaks everywhere with the words of men" (366–67). For the early Benjamin, by contrast, this pure language is already *past*, lost, and we are fallen irremediably into Babel. Benjamin then sought counterparts to the ideas of revelation and redemption in the flash of dialectical images.

Both he and Rosenzweig were inspired by the central position of language in German thinkers such as Schelling and Humboldt; Rosenzweig also found precedents for his ideas about language in Feuerbach, Hermann Cohen, and his exchanges with his friend Eugen Rosenstock. Both Benjamin and Rosenzweig assaulted philosophical idealism because it had lost confidence in and become hostile to language, had tried to create the world out of pure thought and logic, and refused to recognize language itself as a form of thinking and not a mere instrument. Idealism, writes Rosenzweig, left the "divinely created Eden of language" and sought a "human Eden, a human paradise"; "Idealism, at the moment when it rejected language, apotheosized art. . . . art became for Idealism the great justification of its procedure. . . . [It] was incapable of acknowledging the word of man as answer to the word of God" (*Star* 146–47).

Rosenzweig, however, criticized this reduction of reality: art "is one limb among many. Man is more" (147), and the human becomes soul through the word of living language. Art is but the word prior to this word, what is "spoken" but not "speech," and "while there may be many languages there is but one speech" (147–48). The distinction "spoken"/ "speech" will be echoed in Levinas's distinction in his later works between the "said" and the "saying" (*le dit et le dire*). Rosenzweig coins the phrase "speech-thinking" (*Sprachdenken*) to describe the "New Thinking" which he wants to substitute for the old philosophical idealism. Unlike the solitary self-enclosed abstract thought of the idealist philosopher who wants his thought to be timeless, "speech is bound to time and nourished by time. . . . It does not know in advance just where it will end. . . . In fact, it lives by virtue of another's life, whether that other is the one who listens to a story, answers in the course of a dialogue, or joins in a chorus" ("New Thinking" 199). This is the key point for both Rosenzweig and Levinas: speech-thinking needs another person and takes time seriously—actually these two things are identical. In the old philosophy, "thinking" means thinking for no one else and speaking to no one else (and here, if you prefer, you may substitute "everyone" or the well-known "all the world" for "no one"). But "speaking" means speaking to someone and thinking for someone. And this someone is always a quite definite someone, and he has not merely ears, like "all the world," but also a mouth. (200)

This language *to* and *for* someone also becomes the meaning of "revelation" for Rosenzweig. Language "awakes to real vitality only in revelation" and is itself "the organon of revelation" (110–11). Revelation brings the mythical god out of concealment and caprice into expression, gives voice to the speechless creation, and unites the speech of God with the word of humanity. "What is redemption other than that the I learns to say Thou to the He?" (*Star* 274). The acknowledgment of the Thou external to, independent of, and freely confronting the self, the move from monologue to dialogue, makes possible the discovery "of an actual I, an I that is not self-evident," an authentic I—for both God and the human. God's question to Adam in Genesis, "Where are you?" is also this "quest for the Thou" (175).[6]

We can return to Levinas's discussion of the relation of the face and language, and its parallels with the Rosenzweigian scheme of separation and relation: "Truth arises where a being separated from the other is not engulfed in him, but speaks to him" (*TI* 62). "Without separation there would not have been truth; there would have been only being. Truth . . . does not undo 'distance,' does not result in the union of knower and known, does not issue in totality . . . [it is] epiphany at a distance" (60). It is the *separated* relation between same and other, Levinas claims, that language both maintains and bridges. Language, that is, connects but does not fuse the separated subject and other. "Language . . . does not touch the other . . . [but] reaches the other by calling upon him, or commanding him or obeying him, with all the straightforwardness of these relations." Language as conversation with the other is that which retains the separation and difference necessary for the integrity of other as "other" in a "non-allergic" relation, and thus allows the very *revelation* of the other. It does not enclose terms in a totality; it is plural truth, a non-violent plurality, and as such the very foundation of truth conceived outside the ontology which reduces all plurality to the "One" or "Identity" of Being.

This "epiphany"—truth as a relation between separated beings in discourse—is also the epiphany of the face, its "revelation" as expression of itself beyond form, beyond thematization, both direct and remote: "The face speaks. The manifestation of the face is already discourse," and not a vision accessible to the cognizing, grasping gaze of the knower. Language, then, is originally a relation to exteriority and not "an ideal essence or relation open to intellectual intuition" (66). That conception of language as some "ideal essence" is the assumption behind the many forms of structural linguistics and semiotics which Levinas here implicitly critiques. He is trying not to deny the validity of these approaches to language but to maintain the *priority* (i.e., as condition of possibility) of discourse as relation and revelation of the other; only from out of this prior situation, this relation to the other, can language as a "system of signs" itself then be constituted (73). Priority as condition of possibility is also priority as ethical inversion, not negation.

Of course, this prior discourse, this relation to the other, is itself subject to corruption, and Levinas defines rhetoric as a discourse which does not relate to exteriority but approaches the other as interlocutor through ruse and manipulation. As I shall argue in the next chapter, however, his traditional bias of the philosopher against the rhetorician is unfortunate and mistaken; for Levinas's (and Rosenzweig's) conception of the essential sociality of language as truth is inherently rhetorical.

His attack on rhetoric is meant to guard his notion of the face to face of language as justice and ethics from violence and deception. Justice is not the recognition of my *equality* with the other but "the recognition of [the other's] privilege qua Other and his mastery" (*TI* 72). Language is address, appeal to, and welcome of the other as Other and not the other as representation or category determined by my concepts. In this sense, language maintains the other and approaches the other as *teacher*: "The relation with the Other, or Conversation, is a non-allergic relation, an ethical relation; but inasmuch as it is welcomed this conversation is a teaching" (51). This is not the kind of Socratic teaching which is a remembering of what is already within the self, but a teaching coming from the "exterior," from what is outside the self and its concepts, from an other that is separated and foreign, from the "infinity" of the Other, a "traumatism of astonishment" (73). This metaphor of trauma will become central in Levinas's later theory of language in *Otherwise Than Being*.

It is a "trauma" because the relation with the other shatters the narcissistic unity of the subject and "hollows out or contracts" the I to make room for the other; but this is not accomplished through any "anonymous" function of language. The subject is decentered, displaced, traumatized as ego, but this demand of otherness is precisely a claim and demand for responsibility for the other, and leads to a metaphysical ex-cendence. Like Rosenzweig, Levinas *confirms* the singularity of the I in this incessant task of purging the I of its egoism and arbitrariness: "This is termed goodness" (*TI* 245). *"Difference" becomes non-indifference to the other.* As in other French theorists from Lacan and Barthes to Derrida and Foucault, the subject as self-enclosed, free, satisfied ego is deconstructed, made a *subject to*. In Levinas, however, this very movement also constitutes the subject as irreplaceable, a unique self who is called upon to respond to the appeal of the other—constituted as responsible for the other. "To utter 'I,' to affirm the irreducible singularity in which the apology is pursued, means to possess a privileged place with regard to responsibilities for which no one can replace me and from which no one can release me. To be unable to shirk: this is the I" (*TI* 245).

In *Otherwise Than Being*, Levinas radicalizes this idea of the subject and further defines it as the very *substituting of oneself* for the other. By this he also means something as physical as "the duty to give the other even the bread out of one's own mouth and the coat from one's shoulders" (*OTB* 55). Substitution as one-for-the-other then is seen as the basic structure of signification: A is *for* B, or A is *instead of* B. This mode of relation with the other is intended to cut across both the logic of contradiction and dialectical logic where the same "participates in" or is reconciled with (i.e., dissolves) the other in the unity of system. Here again, Rosenzweig is a key source for Levinas's central idea of the "one-for-the-other" as the relation behind all relations, that which makes relation and communication possible. Levinas writes,

> What interests Rosenzweig himself is the discovery of being as relational life. The discovery of a thought which is the very life of this being. The person no longer re-enters the system that he thinks, as with Hegel, in order to congeal there and renounce his singularity. Singularity is necessary to carry out this thought and life precisely as irreplaceable singularity. . . . ("Entre" 130)

In summary, a basic tenet of Levinas's own philosophy is that the relations between terms take precedence over their content. This primary relation to the other is not a "reflection" upon otherness (philosophy) or an imaging of otherness (aesthetics) but a lived relation to the other—ethics. One can also say of Levinas what he writes of Rosenzweig: that the relations among God, humanity, and world that Rosenzweig unifies by reconfiguration into the Star of Redemption at the end of the book are not attained by any formal, synthetic unity of a philosophical gaze which is itself exterior to these elements. "The unity of these terms is in the sense that they are for the other, when one is placed in these elements themselves. . . . *The relations between the elements are accomplished relations and not the specification of a relation in general* [italics his]. They are not specifications of a category" but a "deformalization of the notions which characterize the ensemble of modern philosophy" ("Entre" 128–29). This deformalization is the breaking down of philosophical categories and the penetration of philosophy by its other, or its "beyond."

For Levinas, the communication of communication, a sign of the giving of signs, is the ethical relation of the for-the-other. This form of "metalanguage" would be neither empty self-reflexiveness nor ideological demystification, but openness and responsibility for the other, which also defines "transcendence." This openness founds and makes possible the empirical ego who then thematizes, is conscious and cognizing. Communication would be impossible if it began with the ego as a "free subject to whom every other would only be a limitation that invites war, domination, precaution and information" (*OTB* 119).

The key point, above all, is that Levinas maintains an interhuman relation with the "other"; the subject is deconstructed but not dissolved into impersonal "systems" of signs or "discursive practices." These forms of impersonality, he claims, are as imperialistic as any other, and subordinate the ethical relation. Unlike other contemporary French theorists, he does not relocate freedom in some autonomous or anthropomorphized power of "Language"—nor is the antidote to totalizing systems the anarchic play of the signifier. While his work is a radical critique of being and philosophy, it is also "a defense of subjectivity" (*TI* 26)—the subject is dispossessed but in relation. And a subjectivity structured as the other-in-the-same is not the subjectivity of traditional philosophical "consciousness"; it is, rather, a kind of "knot," an allegiance to the other before consciousness, a responsibility which leads to the birth of consciousness (*OTB* 25); the identity of the subject comes "from the impossibility of escaping responsibility" (14).

SUBJECTIVITY AS VULNERABILITY: LANGUAGE AS GIFT AND EXPOSURE

Although language depends on a separated relation between self and other, the very dispossession of the subject also enables language to found community because "it offers things which are mine to the Other. To speak is to make the world common, to create commonplaces. Language does not refer to the generality of concepts, but lays the foundation for a possession in common. It abolishes the inalienable property of enjoyment" (*TI* 76). Levinas here is pointing to the little-discussed potential of language to be a gift, offering, and welcome of the other. In his view, this is not merely one among many potentialities of language, nor one speech act amid others; this aspect of language is precisely what *makes possible* objectivity, generality, and universality.

> The relationship with the Other is not produced outside of the world, but puts in question the world possessed. The relationship with the Other, transcendence, consists in speaking the world to the Other. . . . Generalization is a universalization . . . but universalization is not the entry of sensible things into a no man's land of the ideal . . . but is the offering of the world to the Other. Transcendence is not a vision of the Other, but a primordial donation. (*OTB* 173–74).

Just as Levinas used Descartes's notion of the "idea of the infinite," the overflow of the finite subject to ethicize the rationality of the Cartesian cogito (the "I think therefore I am"), so here, too, he does not abandon or destroy the Enlightenment ideal of universal reason but ethicizes it: the face as language is a kind of nonabstract prior universal, an "other reason" which founds and guards the "no man's land of the ideal" from inhumanity and violence. Generalization and universalization by definition require this prior receptivity of the self to what is other than its ego and needs.

Needless to say, this theory of language posits the possibility of a sincerity and disinterestedness that runs counter to many current materialist and historical theses that language is preeminently ideological and essentially complicit with games of power, dominance, and force. In Levinas, the very "detachment" characteristic of "objectivity" is made possible through language by the "hollowing out" or subjection of the subject as for-the-other. In this sense, language as the *relation between* me and the other as interlocutor presupposes every proof or symbolism—and not simply because it is necessary to agree on that symbolism or establish its conventions. The relation with the other *already* is necessary for a given phenomenon even to appear as a sign, a sign signaling a speaker, regardless of what may be signified by the sign or whether it may even be decipherable. Exposure and vulnerability then become the very conditions of communication; communication is not reducible to some manifestation of "truth," nor as in semiotic theory to a simple "intention to address a message" (*OTB* 48).

Contemporary theories of language, even those which are dialogical and social such as Bakhtin's often neglect or subordinate this essential point. Prior to cognition, there is a necessary solidarity of discourse, and that itself depends on a first dispossession of the self. For Levinas that dispossession comes not from any primary lack or negativity within the self but from the surplus of the Other, "the face of the other who calls upon the same" (*TI* 97), whom the self welcomes and receives, from whom the self is taught. Speech, then, is this very teaching; it is magisterial: "He who speaks to me and across the words proposes himself to me and retains the fundamental foreignness of the Other who judges me; our relations are never reversible. . . . The 'communication' of ideas, the reciprocity of dialogue, already hide the profound essence of language" (101).

Like Benjamin and Scholem, Levinas is maintaining that the essence of communication is not the instrumental exchange of information or signs. But for Levinas, this deepest level is not that impersonal "mystery of language beyond all meaning" evoked by Scholem, or the "pure language" of the early Benjamin which is meant for no hearer. "He who signals himself by a sign qua signifying that sign is not the 'signified' of the sign"—but delivers the sign and gives it (92). Of course, the other can and does indeed become a "theme" or object of my discourse, but the other as my interlocutor—as the one *to whom* I address myself—always upsurges behind my themes and my constructs, challenging them, remaining outside and not absorbed into the totality of the system of signs in language. Theoretical thought itself, moreover, is at bottom an *address to an other*; it must be *told to* someone. Or as Levinas writes on a personal note at the end of *Totality and Infinity*.

An interlocutor arises again behind him whom thought has just apprehended. . . . The description of the face to face which we have attempted here is told to the other, to the reader, who appears anew behind my discourse and my wisdom. Philosophy is never a wisdom, for the interlocutor whom it has just encompassed has already escaped it. Philosophy, in an essentially liturgical sense, invokes the Other to whom the "whole" is told, the master or student. (295).

This liturgy is the appeal and obligation to the other that is the very meaning of the "face" as the revelation and foundation of language, the *to whom* of every question which is prior to and makes possible the question of "what is." The "to whom" is also the face that responds, that has already addressed me, is there first, and so in turn "in discourse I expose myself to the questioning of the Other, and this urgency of response—acuteness of the present engenders me for responsibility; as responsible I am brought to my final reality" (178).

EIGHT

Parodic Play, Prophetic Reason, and Ethical Rhetoric

Derrida, Levinas, and Perelman

Levinas is reminding us that the "relationalism" of structuralism, or of any formalist theory of language which argues that meaning is a function of relations between signs rather than referents to an external reality, is inadequate. Structuralism *synchronizes* all these relations in an atemporal horizontal whole; it is another form of totalizing system, and this critique, of course, has been made by many poststructuralists as well. In Levinas, we have seen an explicit ethical cast to this critique. "Difference," diachrony, and temporality as the disruption of synchrony and system are not merely other autonomous, neutral forces, linguistic "effects," or "discursive practices." These are constituted for Levinas in the relation behind all relations: the relation with the other, and the *human* other is the place where the "other" passes, questions, and interrupts being. Signs are *given,* and Levinas takes this quite literally: before being given in impersonal systems, signs are given as offerings between interlocutors. This giving is part of the ethical nature of language as relation of same and other.

In other words, Levinas's analysis reverses the structuralist priority of *sign function* over *sign giver.* In his schema, the sign function is made possible by the primordial relation of the "face to face"—not the reverse. In much structuralist and deconstructive criticism, the phrase "Everything is mediated through language" became a way of denying connections to, or even the existence of, experiences beyond language, and nontextual referents. In an interview, however, Derrida expresses frustration at the proliferation of critical commentaries on deconstruction which teach that "there is nothing beyond language, that we are submerged in words—and other stupidities of that sort. . . . It is totally false to suggest that deconstruction is a suspension of reference. . . . The critique of logocentrism is above all else the search for the 'other' and the 'other of language' " (Kearney, *Dialogues* 123). Deconstruction really shows, he continues, not that there is no referent but that "the question of reference is more complex and problematic than traditional theories supposed. . . . I totally refuse the label of nihilism. . . . Deconstruction is not an enclosure in nothingness, but an openness towards the other. . . . My work does not destroy the subject; it simply tries to resituate it" (125).

A lucid critique of many literary critics' (mis)appropriation of Derrida is Robert Scholes's incisive chapter "Reference and Difference" in *Textual Power*. Scholes argues that Saussure's "definition of the sign as a sound-image and a concept is inadequate to describe those elements in language that depend on the relationship between concepts and objects or referents" (96). Not all signs are linguistic signs, nor are linguistic signs purely linguistic. One need not be a blind positivist to affirm that there is such a thing as "non-linguistic experience" and that "certain aspects of linguistic meaning are heavily dependent on non-linguistic forms of information" (109).

For Levinas the relation with the other is such an "experience"—an overflow of the cognitive subject, an overwhelming, a command and appeal. He remains a phenomenologist despite his strong critiques of Husserl's idealism: "What counts is the idea of the overflowing of objectifying thought by a forgotten experience from which it lives," the horizons determining but unsuspected by thought (*TI* 28). This overflow breaks up the formal structures of thought, whether of Husserlian "unintential consciousness" always defined by and adequate to its objects, or Hegelian subjectivity overcoming all difference.[1] But "the breach of totality is not an operation of thought. . . . The void that breaks the totality can be maintained against an inevitably totalizing and synoptic thought only if thought finds itself *faced* with an other refractory to categories" (40). The face as discourse, or language, is the nonviolent relation of the same to the exteriority of the other—and in this sense the metaphysical relation itself, prior to ontology. This most fundamental level of language comes before the construction of language as the system of significations grasped by consciousness. It is also beyond the ingenious playful displacements through equivocation of deconstruction: "Language is not enacted within a consciousness; it comes to me from the Other and reverberates in consciousness by putting it in question. This event is irreducible to consciousness, where everything comes about from within" (204).

In much contemporary literary theory, as a result of the influence of and (mis)appropriations of Saussure and Derrida, a reified notion of "Language" often assumes the exclusive role of the forgotten horizon. Levinas would argue that this is only the substitution of one form of self-enclosing forgetful cognition for another, for the "other," even in the most disseminated "play of signs" or most political of "discursive practices," is not the human other as "autrui"—neighbor. The irreducible and primary relation with otherness as ethical, and the structure of the object as obligated and responsible for the other is itself the *forgotten* horizon of the history of the Western philosophy of being.

Levinas may also have chosen the figure of "face" to signify the approach of the other in order to retain this sense of human ethical immediacy in signification.

It is not the mediation of the sign that forms signification, but signification (whose primordial event is the face to face) that makes the sign function possible. . . . For significations do not present themselves to theory, that is, to the constitutive freedom of a transcendental consciousness; *the being of signification consists in putting into question in an ethical relation constitutive freedom itself* [italics his]. Meaning is the face of the Other, and all recourse to words takes place already within the primordial face to face of language. . . . the essence of language is the relation with the Other. (*TI* 206–207)

Such a signification is "infinite" as an inexhaustible surplus, overflowing consciousness. Compare the famous concluding remarks of Foucault in *The Order of Things:* "As the archaeology of our thought easily shows, man is an invention of recent date. And perhaps near its end"; and if the arrangements of knowledge change, as they did at the end of the eighteenth century causing classical thought to crumble, "man would be erased, like a face [*sic*] in sand at the edge of the sea" (387).

DERRIDA'S CRITIQUE OF LEVINAS

I want here to pause and further examine some key differences between Levinas and other French poststructuralist theorists. These are highlighted in Derrida's commentary on *Totality and Infinity,* where Derrida characteristically argues that language is always violence and cannot serve as a pure realm of ethics and nonviolence. He asserts that Levinas, by using the language of traditional conceptuality and of the Greek logos, has already compromised his thought—for there is no thought before language, and to use this language is already to be contaminated by it, to remain yet within the realm of totality and ontology. There is no pure "outside" or "beyond" this realm. For instance, Derrida asks, why use the word *exteriority,* which connotes spatial relation, to describe something nonspatial? "Why is it necessary to state infinity's *excess* over totality *in* the language of totality, to state the other in the language of the same . . . to inhabit the metaphor in ruins, to dress oneself in tradition's shreds and the devils' patches."[2] There is an "irreducible complicity despite all of the philosopher's rhetorical efforts" and an "irreducible equivocality" in philosophical language, and perhaps, Derrida muses in an important passage, "philosophy must adopt it, think it and be thought in it, accommodate duplicity and difference" ("Violence" 111–12).

Yet Derrida's critique of Levinas is also an act of admiration and recognition of Levinas's contribution to Derrida's own project. Derrida is inspired by Levinas's critique of philosophy as an exhortation to a "parricide of the Greek father," something Derrida thinks a "Greek" could never resolve to do: "But will a non-Greek ever succeed in doing what a Greek in this case could not do, except by disguising himself as a Greek, by *speaking* Greek, by feigning to speak Greek in order to get near the king?" (89).

Indeed, Derrida's deconstructive strategy as it evolved after he wrote this 1964 essay (only the third he had published) was to use the language of metaphysics while undoing it, to recognize the inability to ever be "outside" that language, yet to displace it by doubling, ruse, ellipsis. If discourse is originally violent and the philosophical logos is "inhabited by war," then "language can only indefinitely tend toward justice by acknowledging and practicing the violence within it. Violence against violence," light against light (116). Derrida produces a philosophical style based not on metaphor, as is often thought, but on what he calls *catachresis,* the "violent production of meaning . . . an abuse . . . a violent writing . . . a monstrous mutation" (Kearney, *Dialogues* 123). This "violent style" involves play and parody, aggressive attack and ridicule. Derridean deconstruction is well described by the phrase he uses in his essay on Levinas: "war within discourse" occurring within history itself, not beyond history (117). Yet it is difficult to know "who will be the last victim and indeed if one can feign speaking a language" ("Violence" 89). To speak it, that is, one has to be within it. And so Derrida eventually turns for models to those literary writers and poets who press the limits of language such as Mallarmé and Blanchot, or Genet, whom he juxtaposes to Hegel in *Glas.* That, too, is why his own writing style becomes increasingly "monstrous," an off-centered mixture of philosophy, literature, seriousness, and joking.

Here is one key to the issue of parody in modern thought which Allan Megill has insightfully described in his book *Prophets of Extremity:* "Derrida is a supreme ironist: undoubtedly the most accomplished ironist of our age. He is also a parodist" (260), not the apocalyptic prophet of crisis in the high modernist vein but the very underminer of crisis thought (266). In the works after *Glas,* "comic catharsis once more becomes possible, for Derrida's is a post-ethical, aesthetic laughter that knows the limit of the thought of crisis" (267), a freer and less strained laughter than Nietzsche's, and "less bitter and hysterical" than Foucault's (266). Foucault also specifies the "parodic" as one of the Nietzschean modes to be emulated in opposing a Platonic sense of history. The new historian or "genealogist" will enjoy the masquerade of identities and push history "to its limit and prepare the great carnival of time where masks are constantly reappearing. . . . revitalizing the buffoonery of history, we adopt an identity whose unreality surpasses that of God who started the charade" ("Nietzsche" 161). Then citing Nietzsche from *Beyond Good and Evil:* " 'Perhaps, we can discover a realm where originality is again possible as parodists of history and buffoons of God.' " This would be the "parodic double" of "monumental history": "Genealogy is history in the form of a concerted carnival" (161).

One of Derrida's most interesting parodic texts is the essay "Tympan," written to introduce his collection *Margins of Philosophy.* Derrida uses the split-page format with one column explaining what it means to "tympanize philosophy." Alan Bass, the translator, notes that the word *tympaniser* is an archaic French verb meaning "to criticize, to ridicule publicly." The essay is a virtuoso performance of word play on the various meanings of *tympan,* from "to hammer on" something, to hammering on philosophy as does Nietzsche's Zarathustra, to the explanation of the hammer, anvil, and stirrup in the ear canal and the tympanic membrane—piercing the discourse of the ear. The footnotes of this essay can be seen as a parody of the traditional laborious scholarly apparatus with their references to Latin etymology, diagrams of Vitruvius's drawings of tympanum water clocks, and so on (xvii ff.).[3]

Megill makes the important connection between the strategy of the "double science," Derrida's style of repetition and difference in his readings, and parody, which also is the doubling of another text in a heightened and reflexive way. Parody, though, is by no means anarchic or nihilistic and has its own "rules," as Margaret Rose illustrates in *Parody/Meta-Fiction.* Parody is a species of imitation or quotation, a counterpart to Benjamin's theory of citation. In the etymology of the word *parody, para* means both "nearness" and "opposition." The crucial point is that unlike satire, which suppresses the target text, parody "makes the object of attack part of its own structure" (*Parody* 35). Parody is never torn away and free of the target but is closely attached. It is a kind of metalanguage, self-reflexive and self-critical, not mere "mockery" but a "refunctioning" of the target text.

Now, if the project of finding a nonsite for philosophy to appear to itself as other and to interrogate itself is central for Derrida, parody is a highly appropriate form. Derrida, like Levinas, criticizes the Hegelian dialectic as ultimately a tyranny of the logic of identity, of the same, a self-enclosed and imperial narcissism which mutes the other and always returns to itself (as in Derrida's pun on Hegel's name as "Eagle" at the beginning of *Glas*). For Derrida, it would not be enough, therefore, to criticize philosophy in its own voice, through its own reasons. Nor would it be sufficient to find a complete opposite, because the opposite would still be defined by the same, and because all discourse takes place in the space philosophical speech has created. But if one could show the *other to be already in the same,* from the beginning fissured, that would be an alterity that could not be reabsorbed. Thus Derrida has to remain extremely close and "faithful" to the text under analysis as he moves through his readings, and so his is a deeply parodic structure, incorporating the target text in the very structure of his own writing—parody as decentered mimesis. That is also why even when he is less overtly parodic, his own writing is so frustratingly off-centered, indirect, elliptical, dissimulating, digressive.

The key question, however, is precisely what and who is the "other"? As Robert Bernasconi observes, one of the central differences between Levinas and Derrida is located right at this point. Even though Derrida adopted the notion of the trace from Levinas, "for Derrida the trace is of a text and not of the Other" ("Trace of Levinas" 35). Derrida's use of the Levinasian trace to attack Saussure and Heidegger has more to do with Derrida's concern for the philosophy of presence "than to do justice to

Levinas' attack on the neutrality of philosophy" (28). One might add that poststructuralism, for all its variegated attempts to show the instability of structures—whether linguistic or political—continues to pit one form of anonymous or impersonal force against another.

Both Levinas and Derrida's ideas of the trace are attempts to formulate what Levinas calls a "third way" other than the contradictory dualisms of ontology, e.g., revelation/dissimulation or transcendence/immanence. And this "third way" cannot be a Hegelian synthesis of two opposites, for that would only lead once more to another totality, a danger which Benjamin also recognized. This non-Hegelian "third way" then leads Benjamin, Derrida, and Levinas to the borderline between philosophy and nonphilosophy.

For Derrida, parodic textual commentary becomes a key strategy to solicit alterity. In a Derridean reading, as Vincent Descombes notes, the vital point is that no synthesis is possible between the text and its parodic deconstructive critique, "no fusing into one, for the second is not the opposite of the first, but rather its counterpart, slightly phased" (*Modern* 50). Derrida's "double science" shows the duplicity of any text and enacts a duplicitous metaphysics: "It is itself as other. Every metaphysics, being double, is its own simulacrum, a slight displacement, a slight play in the reading sufficient to collapse the first into the second, the wisdom of the first into the comedy of the second." One can never quite tell, says Descombes, whether Derridean deconstruction is a tyrannicide or a game (151). I would argue that it is obviously both, a tragicomedy entitled "The Death of Philosophy."

Bakhtin has also reminded us in *The Dialogic Imagination* and his book on Rabelais that laughter and parody are among the most ancient forms of linguistic representation, and that "there never was a single strictly straightforward genre, no single type of direct discourse—artistic, rhetorical, philosophical, religious, ordinary everyday—that did not have its own parodying and travestying double, its own comic-ironic *contre-partie*" (*Dialogic* 53). We will find in Levinas's own talmudic lectures moments of a comic-ironic voice not heard in his philosophical works—not because he views the Talmud as a parody of philosophy, but rather as philosophy's other, its countervoice. In Bakhtin, parody is a "relation to another's word" (69) again involving the key question of the relation of the same and the other, the ambiguous relation between two intermixed speeches and the contest between them. The relation can be reciprocal, a dialogue, a questioning, an argument, appropriation, regeneration, or illumination, a mix of both reverence and ridicule.

Bakhtin notices that parody crosses languages with each other. The sacred parodies of the Middle Ages are both reverently accepting and paradoxically ridiculing. His analysis might be extended to some Jewish texts as well, especially to many remarks of the rabbis in the Midrash and Talmud. In Judaism, there is a special kind of dialogue between text and interpretation,

Scripture and Midrash, the words of the rabbis and the words of God. Bakthin's ideas about parody as "intentional dialogized hybrid," or relation to another's word, could extend to the other as not only person or institution but the Divine Other—the word of God. But rabbinic tradition does something else with the parodic as a "second life" or "second world." This crossing of earthly human interpretation and divine reality is reinscribed in the Book. The word *Mishnah* means "Second" Torah and refers to a second-century C.E. rabbinic compilation of oral laws not found in Scripture. The Mishnah is the basis of the commentaries of the Talmud. As the Oral Torah, it is the dialogue with God, the doubling of the divine word, the second life of the Torah as it is renewed through human reinterpretation. Yet as double, it is not merely second but a twin, and so the rabbis claim for their own interpretations the most extraordinary status: "Everything an expert disciple will say before his teacher—that too, was already given at Sinai." This illustrates a most powerful and significant difference between Bakhtin's ideas of parody, the Derridean use of language play, and the rabbinic. The rabbinic interpretive plays are seen as part of the divine imperative, the fullness of the divine word in an ever-expanding process of interpretation and renewal. They are like the second Tablets of the Law that Moses made after the first were broken. I will discuss this idea at more length in the next chapters on Levinas's talmudic lectures.

There is, in fact, an interesting Jewish undercurrent to Bakhtin's work. The preeminent philosopher of "dialogue" in our century was, of course, the Jewish thinker Martin Buber. As Joseph Frank reports, Bakhtin preserved his admiration for Buber to the very end of his life and said he thought Buber "the greatest philosopher of the twentieth century, and perhaps in this philosophically puny century, perhaps the sole philosopher on the scene. . . . I am very much indebted to him. In particular for the idea of dialogue. Of course, this is obvious to anyone who reads Buber" ("Voices" 56, n. 2). Levinas, however, strongly disagreed with Buber's idea of the other as a *symmetrical* partner, and also criticized poststructuralist theories which reduced meaning to the play and/or constraint of signifiers.[4]

Here again is a point where Derrida attacks. He tries to hold Levinas to an either/or logic by asserting that if positive infinity requires "infinite alterity, then one must renounce all language, and first of all the words *infinite* and *other*." If the other is beyond the realm of conceptuality and totalizing thought, then the other must be "unthinkable, unutterable." Levinas may call us to this unthinkable, unutterable beyond, "but it must not be possible either to think or state this call" ("Violence" 114). Unlike the practitioners of negative theology, Levinas does "not give himself the right to speak as they did, in a language resigned to its own failure" (116). What kind of language, Derrida asks, would a language which renounces being and predication be? A language which says nothing? If so, how could it ever discourse with the other? (147).

SKEPTICISM AND PHILOSOPHY

In *Otherwise Than Being* (1974) Levinas responds to many of these objections. He refines and radicalizes his idea of language and changes his emphasis from the "face" to what he calls the relation of the "saying and the said" *(le dire et le dit)*. This change is partially a response to the Derridean problem of finding or articulating the "other" of language in language. "Saying" is still a linguistic metaphor to describe this "other" realm, thus acknowledging the complexity of our access to it. Levinas then analyzes the oscillation between the saying and the said as the very alternation between skepticism and philosophy. "Saying" is a "language before language," prior to ontology, "origin," and representation, an-archic—and so unknowable, or prior to all philosophical consciousness. But this "saying" necessarily shows and "betrays itself" into the "said"—the realm of language as the set of signs which doubles being, which re-presents, synchronizes, names, designates, and which "consciousness" grasps, manipulates, thematizes, brings to light, remembers, and in which we discuss and define this "saying."

Levinas admits the methodological problem: the said is necessary, but it betrays the saying, and the otherwise than being becomes absorbed into being and thematization. But the task of philosophy becomes clear just at this crux: it is the necessity of continually *unsaying* the said: that is the role of skepticism, of philosophy as skeptical critique, or constant unsaying. Yet Levinas also recognizes that even skepticism itself repeats the very dilemma it claims to reveal. Skepticism itself *simultaneously* conveys and betrays its own statements: that is, skepticism constantly affirms "the impossibility of statement while venturing to *realize* this impossibility by the very statement of this impossibility." It affirms and denies at once and loses the diachrony of difference. (Derrida tries to deal with this methodological problem through parody, ruse, doubling, deferred meaning, digression, and more elaborate kinds of postmodernist prose [as in *Glas* and *La carte postale*].) Despite all these problems and refutations, however, skepticism continually returns, "and it always returns as philosophy's illegitimate child." And this is so because a "secret diachrony commands this ambiguous or enigmatic way of speaking, and because in general signification signifies beyond synchrony, beyond essence" (*OTB* 7).

In other words, the question has to do with the inability to *simultaneously, at the same time* (synchronously), affirm and deny. Say and unsay. But synchrony itself belongs to the order of being and totality, a mode of signification which does not admit an other, does not allow for temporal lapse, pause, or interval between the affirmation and negation, the saying and the said. This is why Derrida tries to elaborate a disruptive and nonrecuperable temporality with his notion of "deferral" in "différance." For Levinas as well, the realm of the said defined by synchrony remains enclosed within the totalizing systems of signs (e.g., Saussure), and so belongs to the conceptual idealism of Western thought which he has critiqued. But also philosophy *as* skepticism, "in its very diachrony, is the consciousness of the breakup of consciousness." Alternating or oscillating between skepticism and its refutation, philosophy both "justifies and criticizes the laws of being and of the city" (*OTB* 165). In *Totality and Infinity* Levinas did not *oppose* totality to infinity; that is why the book is entitled *Totality* and *Infinity*. In *Otherwise Than Being,* this conjunction *and* becomes the back-and-forth "oscillation" of saying and said, philosophy and skepticism, subject and other, ethics and ontology, ethics and politics.

The key point is that Levinas does not try to refute Derrida in the manner of so many of Derrida's other critics by trying to deny skepticism itself. Rather, he recognizes in the force of skepticism itself a realm of reason and intelligibility *other* than the coherent correlation of ideas. Is it fair, then, for Derrida to ask Levinas to be "coherent" in the traditional philosophical sense? When Derrida uses the binary logic of either/or to critique Levinas's positions, isn't Derrida also contradicting himself by asking Levinas to adhere to traditional formal logic? For this is precisely the logic of identity which denies the other (A = A. A cannot be other than itself. A cannot = B). In his own critique of ontology, Levinas is moving to another kind of reason where "difference," the difference between A and B, becomes the ethical nonindifference of the one to the other: A is for B in responsibility. If we set up the proposition as *"either* A *or* B," the difference between A and B can be resolved only through dissolution, conflict, war, or the violence in which one subordinates or obliterates the other.

Similarly, although traditional philosophical "reflection" may refute the contradictions of skepticism, skepticism continually returns and "follows [philosophy] like a shadow" (*OTB* 168). In Levinas's analysis, this occurs because philosophy is in fact sensitive to the other than being, to this beyond. Skepticism, then, is also the trace of what Levinas calls "illeity." *Illeity* is a neologism formed with the Latin third-person singular *il* or *ille.* (This "thirdness" also connects to the attempt to find a "third way.") It is what is outside the "I-you" relationship, "a way of concerning me without entering into conjunction with me" or as a "product of my consciousness" (13). In other words, illeity is the dimension of irreducible alterity of the other as infinitely withdrawing, remaining other, and not reducible to some image or identification or dialogue constructed by the I. This irreversibility or lack of equivalence makes the I-other relation one where the other commands, appeals, judges, and puts me in question. It is not a Buberian dialogue of equals, of I with the *thou* as my counterpart.

Alphonso Lingis, the English translator of Levinas's major works, explains: "The *ille* is indivisible and unmultipliable as infinity, and each time singular" ("Introduction," *OTB* xxxiv). *Illeity,* as this movement of infinition, is what Levinas names God. Lingis adds:

Here God figures not as compensation for us or for the wants of the universe,

nor as healer of our mortality, but as judge and as imperative which calls into
question. . . . God is not approachable through the divine, which would be his
manifestation of revelation, however ciphered or mysterious—for God is
there uniquely where manifestation or revelation is disturbed by alterity, in
the one that addresses me. (xxxiii–iv)

I shall take up the question of theology in the next two chapters; what is
important to note here is the connection Levinas makes between *skepticism and religion. Illeity,* he writes, opens onto the realm of theology or
"religion," but in a way which exceeds faith or loss of faith (*OTB* 168).
Needless to say, Levinas's philosophy clearly undermines any classical theology of God as "Being," or Being of Beings. "Theology" would belong to
the realm of the "said, which always betrays and dissimulates the saying":
"Thus theological language destroys the religious situation of transcendence. The infinite 'presents' itself anarchically, but thematization loses
the anarchy which alone can accredit it. Language about God rings false or
becomes a myth, that is, can never be taken literally" (197, fn. 25).

Just as skepticism is necessary for philosophy and shadows it, so, too,
"theology would be possible only as the contestation of the purely religious." The face is not the image of God who has passed: "Being in the
image of God does not signify being the icon of God but to find oneself in
his trace" ("Trail" 46), as in the famous chapter of Exodus 33 where God
tells Moses in verse 30, "you cannot see my face" but only "my back." The
Levinasian "face" would not then be the hidden God, nor would the trace
of infinity in the face or all the analyses of saying prior to thematization
and representation "lead to any theological thesis (*OTB* 196, fn. 19). "To
go toward [God] is not to follow the trace which is not a sign. To go toward
him is to go toward the Others who are in the trace" ("Trail" 46).

RHETORIC, SKEPTICISM, AND VIOLENCE: LEVINAS AND
CHAIM PERELMAN

We can clarify these difficult ideas by remembering that one of Levinas's
essential theses about signification is that the *orientation* of the terms takes
precedence over their content: "saying" is a preoriginal orientation, approach, nearness without abolishing distance between terms, and the relation of responsibility. This orientation, as we have seen, he takes to be the
very ability of anything to signify, to give itself, to be not only itself but
other—for something else. Despite violent appropriations of the "said" by
systems, themes, the state, prisons, or asylums (so well elaborated in the
work of Foucault), there are, Levinas maintains, forces within language
which can interrupt this violence. As in Derrida, the equivocal nature of
signification as enigma is a refusal of "simultaneity," and this interruption
is a "diachrony." But unlike many other contemporary literary theorists,
Levinas connects this diachrony with the one-for-the-other; and the ulti-

mate interruption is founded on the very essence of language as relation with another: "And I still interrupt the ultimate discourse in which all discourses are situated, in saying it to one who listens to it, and who is situated outside the said that discourse says. That is true of the discussion I am elaborating at the present moment. The reference to the interlocutor permanently breaks through the text" (*OTB* 170).

Levinas again is reminding us that in language, insofar as it is a relation *to* another and oriented *toward* another, there always remains a trace of diachrony, a breaking up of being and totality. There would be in every discourse, then, a potential for the breakup of totality; and the "permanent return of skepticism does not so much signify the breakup of structures as the fact that they are not the ultimate framework of meaning" (171).

Denomination is secondary to proclamation, or to the vocative and imperative. Adriaan Peperzak explains that the subordination of denomination is part of Levinas's critique and elaboration of Husserlian intentionality. In order for a phenomenon to appear, to be "given" or "presented to" consciousness, to emerge from the prephenomenal chaos and flux of time, it requires a kind of identification, a way of looking or positing, of taking "this as that." To mean or intend this as that "is a claim or allegiance *(pretention)* through which consciousness *intends* or . . . 'wills' the given as an appearance." This identification is a kind of *doxa,* or fable or foreword, or "already said" not yet heard or spoken, but preceding and grounding all particular historical languages and speech ("From Intentionality" 6–8).

Denomination is one aspect of language as the system of nouns which designate identities. The word identifies "this as that," and Levinas notes that this identification is not based on resemblance. Words signify things not because they are like them: rather, "identification is kerygmatical"; it is first a proclamation. "The said is not simply a sign or expression of meaning" (*OTB* 35); it proclaims and establishes "this as that" and is a kind of surplus over reflective thought. This is an aspect of what Benjamin described as the "magic" of language, and Scholem as its "mystery." Levinas, like Benjamin and Scholem, emphasizes that at this depth the word is not merely a sign or expression of meaning. Lyotard, in his long essay on Levinas, tries to compare Levinas to J. L. Austin's ideas about the "performative" in speech-act theory, but Levinas does not view language as one kind of action among others. Nor is Levinas's an-archic "saying" a contentless sacred abyss or a realm of pure and beautiful nonhuman form.

For Levinas, the consecration of "this as this . . . or that" by a saying that is also later absorbed in the said is a fiat or command *before* language signifies experiences. "It is not that a discourse, coming from one knows not where, arbitrarily arranges the phases of temporality into a 'this as that' "(37). Insofar as language is defined here as a relation to another, Levinas seems to propose an ultimately "rhetorical" theory of language. He reiterates throughout his work, however, the ancient philosophical contempt for rhetoric, which he views as the approach to the neighbor through ruse, a mode of sophistic manipulation and violence rather than search for truth. Yet Levinas's insistence on language as preeminently a call or command before it is an exchange of information is at bottom "rhetorical."

Peperzak notes that Levinas "points at the very simple fact, which surprisingly never has been taken into serious account by philosophy: *the fact that a discourse or epos (or Sage) always is said by someone to one or more others (or to oneself as listener or reader)"* [italics his] ("From Intentionality" 11). Yet Levinas is by no means the first to point to this "simple fact"; it is at the heart of Rosenzweig's critique of philosophy and furthermore has to do with the ancient debate between philosophy and rhetoric so forcefully conducted in Plato's *Phaedrus* and *Gorgias.* Rhetoric was always grounded in the social concreteness of language as an address and effect on an audience, a personal other, but Levinas follows the ancient bias of Plato in viewing rhetoricians as sophists concerned not with pure truth but only with manipulation.

In fact, Levinas's understanding of language as above all a relation to the other, a "social" relation, parallels the revival of rhetoric in recent literary and philosophical theories which assert that truth is socially constructed through language and not from any absolute, objective, or firm ontological ground. The anti-Platonism and antiontologism of theorists such as Stanley Fish, Derrida, deMan, Terry Eagleton, Richard Rorty, et al. destroys any transcendental foundation for truth, but the problem then becomes, "What defines the 'sociality' of the social relation?" Or, "What principle engenders and regulates the social relation and prevents it from dissolving into a chaotic clash of will to power, violence, and chaos?" Levinas cannot perceive how rhetoric might answer this question or be based on anything but strategic ruses of the ego and manipulation of the other—both forms of violence.

For a modern rhetorical theorist such as Chaim Perelman, however, rhetoric is by no means without foundation in rational consensus or ethical imperative. In fact, I suspect that Perelman's great masterwork, *The New Rhetoric* (1958), was written, like much of Levinas's philosophy, in response to the catastrophes and violence of World War II. Perelman was a Jew, and of Belgian nationality like Paul deMan; but Perelman was a leader of the Belgian underground resistance to the Nazis. He also had a distinguished career as a jurist. Perelman's "new rhetoric" is close in spirit and has many parallels to Levinas's philosophy; and Perelman's perspective as a jurist also has much to add to current questions about the nature of interpretation, and the relation of the literary to the political. For the juridical tradition involves modes of argumentation and interpretation other than those based solely on mathematical reasoning or the pure aesthetics of language as a world in itself apart from all practical decision and action.[5]

In fact, attempts to relate literary criticism to rabbinic texts have not yet

been able to link up their double functions of *halakhic*-legalistic deliberation and midrashic story telling and creative interpretation. This problem
is partially due to the separation of literary criticism and theory from the
kind of rhetorical theory which Perelman is proposing—a "new" rhetoric
because it returns rhetoric to its ancient *rational deliberative* functions and
away from its demotion of a "merely literary" analysis of style and tropes.

In a 1976 article on the "new rhetoric" as practical reasoning, Perelman
indeed cites the talmudic tradition as an example of the kind of deliberative rhetorical model he is propounding, in contrast to a Cartesian model
where rational self-evidence and necessary truth make it impossible for
two persons to come to opposite decisions about the same matter without
one being wrong. In the Talmud, Perelman notes, "it is accepted that opposed positions can be equally reasonable; one of them does not have to be
right." For instance, the school of the sage Hillel and the school of Sham-
mai are in constant opposition, but in a famous passage, R. Akiva is told
from above that "both are the words of the living God." ("New Rhetoric"
305).

The key point here is that there are *rational* grounds for multiple positions about truth—not that since all language is arbitrary, or all values are
relative, there are therefore multiple interpretations. Perelman's judicial
rhetoric is also close to Levinas's defense in his Jewish writings of *halakah*
and the Jewish legal tradition as the embodiment and guarantor of the
ethical nature of reason as one-for-the-other, which we shall see in the next
chapters. Both Levinas and Perelman are inspired by the Kantian notion
of practical versus theoretical reason.

Perelman's impetus for writing his masterwork was the problems he encountered in defining the nature of justice and reasoning about values, and
the difficulties in resolving questions of value on rational grounds, i.e., not
being able to draw an "ought" from an "is." Along with Lucie Olbrechts-
Tyteca, he decided to investigate the ways authors in different fields actually used arguments to reason about values—from literary to political to
philosophical texts and daily speech. He "rediscovered" the neglected heritage of Aristotle's "dialectical" (as opposed to "analytic") mode of reasoning, and rhetoric as informal, nondemonstrative reasoning (Foss, Foss, and
Trap, *Contemporary Perspectives* 102–103).

Perelman writes in the introduction to *The New Rhetoric* that his aim is
to *"break with a concept of reason and reasoning due to Descartes* [italics
his] which has set its mark on Western philosophy for the last three decades" (1). Like Levinas, Perelman's work is a critique of the limits of
formal, Cartesian reason and the attempt to constrict all reasoning to formal mathematical logic, or to self-evident ideas which constitute necessary
truths. There are many realms of human endeavor and human thought,
Perelman observes, "involving questions of a moral, social, political,
philosophical, or religious order [which] by their very nature elude the
methods of the mathematical and natural sciences" (512). Like Levinas,

Perelman devotes his whole effort to preventing the abandonment of these essential spheres of life to "irrational forces, instincts, suggestion, or even violence" (3). They share the same impulse to go beyond strictly formalistic reason without lapsing into complete irrationalism and losing all grounds for commonality and thoughtful deliberative action—to modify and expand the Enlightenment version of the universal light of reason rather than abandon it to a war of conflicting power interests and self-interested ideologies.

Levinas also notes that the questioning of reason in which he is engaged may appear to be folly from the perspective of a logic of identity and ontology. Yet the result for Levinas is *another kind of reason*—a prophetic or ethical reason, not delirium, madness, game, or will to power. The identity of the subject comes not from a free, unified ego but "from the impossibility of escaping responsibility" (*OTB* 14). The subject put in question by Levinas remains "rational," "responsible," and "inspired" even as it is "susceptible, vulnerable, wounded, traumatized, obsessed, hostage, persecuted."

Like Levinas, Perelman is struggling to find a "third way" beyond "uncompromising and irreducible philosophical opposition presented by all kinds of absolutism: dualisms of reason and imagination, of knowledge and opinion, or irrefutable self-evidence and deceptive will," universal objectivity and incommunicable subjectivity, judgments of reality and judgments of value, theory and practice (*New Rhetoric* 510). These dualisms and the "assertion that whatever is not objectively and indisputably valid belongs to the realm of the arbitrary and subjective creates an unbridgeable gulf between theoretical knowledge, which is rational, and action, for which motives would be wholly irrational" (512).

The consequences of this dualistic position would be that practice ceases to be reasonable, critical argument becomes incomprehensible, and philosophical reflection itself meaningless. *The New Rhetoric* preceded the advent of French structuralism and poststructuralism, but Perelman probably would have viewed the notion of language as an impersonal system in which human selfhood and action are but anonymous functions as yet another abdication of rational deliberative argument to distorted notions of reality—or as Levinas put it, of the primacy of formal theoretical reason. Nor do many of the poststructuralist critiques of structuralism alleviate this problem; proposing the arbitrariness of the sign and the instability of the structures of signification only replaces existentialist irrationality with linguistic irrationality. Nor does a cultural materialism which finds all structures marked by ideology, power, domination, and force provide grounds for the kind of reason which Perelman seeks.

Like Levinas, Perelman has an ethical agenda: "Only the existence of an argumentation that is neither compelling nor arbitrary can give meaning to human freedom, a state in which reasonable choice can be exercised." It also justifies "the possibility of a human community in the sphere of action when this justification cannot be based on a reality or objective truth" (514). A postmodern polemicist writer such as Lyotard, of course, would criticize Perelman's search for ongoing rational consensus as fiercely as he opposed Habermas's project. But Perelman, like Levinas, endured the effects of a massive collapse of reasonable discourse and lack of respect for individual human freedom in the violence of World War II. The embrace of what is arbitrary or nonrational or of cunningly subversive power would only be more subtle forms of absolutism and denials of the human capacity for individual choice and responsibility.

So like Levinas and Rosenzweig, Perelman instead redefines, extends, and amplifies reason to include what may not be conceptually *self*-evident, necessary, or autonomous. There are alternate forms of reasoning which require an other, depend upon the relation of address and the *noncoercive* assent of the other person through discourse. And rhetoric he defines as the art of discourse which above all is addressed to, dependent upon, and adapted to the needs of an audience. Its aim is always "to act effectively on minds" (7). Formal Cartesian reason, by contrast, is founded on the solipsistic notion of self-evident truths, clear, distinct, and necessary; there is no need for deliberation *with others,* nor any question of varying intensities of adherence to these truths or the possibility of withholding one's assent from them. Such a form of reason, like the theoretical reason of Kant, "imposes itself on every rational being," and "agreement is inevitable" (2).

The kinds of deliberations in which humans engage by addressing and appealing to each other in various particular situations, in order to secure adherence, constitute "argumentation" (rhetorical activity) as opposed to the "demonstration" of irrefutable truths. Argumentation deals not with the necessary but with the possible, the plausible, or the credible to the degree that they "elude the certainty of calculation" (1). The forms of reasoning and persuasion found in the rhetorical tradition from the Greeks onward were denigrated and neglected by Cartesian logicians and philosophers as merely ornamental, "literary," or sophistic. Yet they are the resource for what Perelman calls a "critical rationalism that transcends the duality 'judgments of reality—value judgments,' and makes both judgments of reality and value judgments dependent on the personality of the scientist or philosopher, who is responsible for his decisions in the field of knowledge as well as the field of action" (514).[6] Rhetoric is a "third way" between the compulsions of formal autonomous reason and the coercions of violence. To deliberate or argue with another

> implies that one has renounced resorting to force alone, that value is attached to gaining the adherence of one's interlocutor by means of reasoned persuasion, and that one is not regarding him as an object, but appealing to his free judgment. Recourse to argumentation assumes the establishment of a community of minds, which, while it lasts, excludes the use of violence. (55)

It is also Perelman's insight that the skeptic is not the opposite but the counterpart of the fanatic. The fanatic is one who "adheres to a disputable thesis for which no unquestionable proof can be furnished" and who refuses to submit those theses for free discussion (62), and so forecloses any argument. I take the liberty of quoting at length the following brilliant passage which concludes part 1 of *The New Rhetoric,* for it bears directly upon the situation of much contemporary literary theory:

> Equating adherence to a thesis with recognition of its absolute truth sometimes leads, not to fanaticism, but to skepticism. The man who requires that argumentation provide demonstrative proof of compelling force and will not be content with less in order to adhere to a thesis misunderstands as much as the fanatic the essential characteristic of argumentative procedure. For the very reason that argumentation aims at justifying choices, it cannot provide justifications that would tend to show there is no choice, but that only one solution is open to those examining the problem.
>
> Since rhetorical proof is never completely necessary proof, the thinking man who gives his adherence to the conclusions of an argumentation does so by an act that commits him and for which he is responsible. The fanatic accepts the commitment, but as one bowing to an absolute and irrefragable truth; the skeptic refuses the commitment, but under the pretext that he does not find it sufficiently definitive. He refuses adherence because his idea of adherence is similar to that of the fanatic: both fail to appreciate that argumentation aims at a choice among possible theses; by proposing and justifying the hierarchy of these theses, argumentation seeks to make the decision a rational one. This role of argumentation in decision making is denied by the skeptic and fanatic. In the absence of compelling reason, they both are inclined to give violence a free hand, rejecting personal commitment. (62)

This passage could provide a connection between deMan's radical skepticism and his profascist writings in World War II. Many of deMan's defenders have argued that his deconstructive skepticism was an implicit repudiation and overcoming of his earlier ideological writings, and that his postures of critical self-reflexiveness, "undecidability," and the "impossibility of reading" were intended to guard against all violent engagements. Perelman's analysis indicates that such absolute skepticism, denying the grounds for any choice between meanings, results from an overly restrictive definition of truth and knowledge. There may be no necessary, objective, stable ground for truth in a classical philosophical sense, but there are nevertheless many grounds for argument, evaluation, and deliberation. Foreclosing these in endless aporias and "undecidabilities" is an act as absolutist and open to violence as that of the fanatic, who refuses to debate because of her or his conviction of possessing that absolute truth.

The same criticism could be made of the "ideological" critic, who holds that all values are masks for self-interested power plays; or the relativist, who is intent on constantly undermining any and every claim to a firm foundation for value or truth, and who refuses to allow for any deliberative argument about the hierarchy of values or criteria for making choices. The jurist, however, faces real social external pressure and must make decisions, despite the lack of any absolute, clear, or unambiguous ground. In Perelman's view, the fanatic or skeptic relieves him- or herself of the burden of personal responsibility, action, and commitment to choices made.

Rhetorical argumentation, however, is oriented toward decision and the future: "it sets out to bring about some action or prepare the way for it by acting, by discursive methods, on the minds of the hearers" (47). Argumentation, Perelman reminds us, is not merely an intellectual exercise divorced from practical preoccupations. "Language is not only a means of communication: it is also an instrument for acting on minds, a means of persuasion" (132). That is precisely why argumentation is a substitute for the violence which attempts to obtain action by force or compulsion.

Many literary theorists, especially those influenced by linguistic poststructuralism, have neglected this aspect of rhetoric and argument. Rhetoric had been devalued by Cartesian philosophic reason, viewed as a mere set of tropes, or ornaments of language which had little to do with the logical apprehension or ordering of reality; the key move for many French structuralists and poststructuralists is to invert this order. Derrida, Lacan, Kristeva, deMan, and other French theorists in rebellion against the Cartesian tradition of rationalism have embraced rhetoric as that ancient antagonist to philosophy which thrives on and plays with the equivocations of language. They employ this notion of rhetoric to stress the inescapable metaphorical and equivocal nature of language, and so to contest the univocity of the logos. Rhetoric becomes for them an aspect of the triumph of literary language—the aesthetic—over the repressive philosophical logos.[7]

Lacan's rereading of Freud via structuralist linguistics, for example, asserts that the "unconscious is structured like a language," and that an analyst needs to understand the rhetoric of tropes to interpret these structures. Brian Vickers in the last chapter of his *In Defense of Rhetoric* lucidly explains the distortions in many of these contemporary invocations of rhetoric. In modern thought, rhetoric as a discipline has atrophied to "*elocution* alone, now detached from its expressive and persuasive functions, and brought down finally to handful of tropes" (*In Defense* 439). One sees this tendency, notes Vickers, in Vico, who in turn is the inspiration for Hayden White's tropological analysis of historical narratives; in Roman Jakobson's structural linguistics, which further reduces the tropes to only two: metaphor and metonymy; and in deMan especially, "whose actual knowledge of rhetoric as revealed in [his] essays is limited to a fundamentally misguided conception of the art, and to a few tropes, not always correctly understood. But this did not prevent him from making grand generalizations" (457).

Rhetoric becomes the "other" of philosophy for deMan et al., a kind of post-Cartesian epistemology, but rhetoric was deprived of its fundamental sense of language as an *action* or effect on a public audience. DeMan appropriated the epistemological critique of Derrida as mainly a *cognitive* problem, and so described the problem of interpretation as "undecidability" solely in epistemological terms. Perhaps for him that marked the site of the "otherness of language," and one could go no further—there is no "ex-cendence," and certainly no "good beyond being," no positivity but only ironic and impossible aporias. Rhetorical tropes in deMan are negative epistemological challenges to grammar and logic and must be separated, he writes, from "performative speech acts" and the "pragmatic banality" of psychology. (*Resistance* 19). Similarly, deMan's model for teaching is a chilling one; it is "not primarily an intersubjective relationship between people but a cognitive process in which self and other are only tangentially and contiguously involved" (3).

Levinas's philosophy reveals the violence to the other that this position implies, and Perelman's analysis reveals its covert connections with an "absolutist epistemology" (512). Perelman himself is critical of both ontology and aesthetics in linguistics and instead holds that language neither directly conforms to the objective nature of things nor is a world in itself. The problem of communication in argument is wrongly "turned into a matter of ontology and esthetics, whereas in reality the ontological order and the organic order constitute two derivations from an adaptive order. The guiding consideration in the study of order in a speech should be the needs of adaptation to the audience" (508). This refers back to the dimensions of invention and arrangement which were the preoccupation of classical rhetoric, which Perelman revives.[8] By speech, Perelman does not mean only oral discourse but any and all verbal communication, including writing.

There are many lessons here, I think, for literary criticism and theory. First, that restricting questions about meaning or the nature of the literary text to questions about the epistemological status of language is as artificial as the attempt to restrict all reasoning solely to formal logic. But the alternative is not an uncritical embrace of "politics" and the assertion that the way language acts on the world is essentially ideological and marked by relations of force, domination, and violence. In the recent reaction of many literary critics against the "ahistoricism" of deconstruction, *rhetoric* has frequently come to be used as a synonym for a social approach to language and texts which is identical with political-ideological interpretation. Perelman, like Levinas, refuses to define arguments or agreements about values solely in ideological terms as masks for a set of self-interests. Perelman makes an important distinction between a "disinterested" or "objective spectator" and an "impartial" one when it comes to judging discussions that must lead to a decision. In such discussions, "interference in a controversy whose outcome will affect a specific group may be made only by one who is a member of, or closely bound up with, the group in question": "being *impartial* is not being *objective,* it consists of belonging to the same group one is judging, without having previously decided in favor of any one of them" (60). Like Levinas, Perelman wants to preserve the possibility of "dissociating our beliefs from our interests and passions" (61).

Similarly, his analysis of epideictic oratory reveals a fundamental relation of value to action. Epideictic oratory was classically defined by Aristotle as the rhetoric concerned with praise and blame (for example, a eulogy), the beautiful or ugly. Aristotle distinguished between epideictic and the other forms of oratory: deliberative and legal oratory (counseling what is expedient; establishing what is best). Perelman points out that epideictic oratory—often considered merely ornamental or "purely literary"—cannot be separated from the functions of deliberative and legal oratory because epideictic oratory "strengthens the disposition toward action by increasing adherence to the values it lauds" (50); it thus establishes a sense of communion that is the very foundation for deliberative and legal discourse. In sum, both Perelman and Levinas expand the notion of reason to be the very ground of relation to another person in discourse, a noncoercive relation.

Perhaps the literary text could also be thought of as just such an "address to an other" in Levinas's sense of that which overflows all our philosophical cognition and conceptualization, and as human and personal speech, an opening to a "beyond" or "outside" the totality that does not dissolve into impersonal systems and games, or ideological warfare, even though these elements of the "said" certainly mark it. Perelman's idea of a "new rhetoric" or a reconceptualization of rhetoric would not allow us to isolate a literary text from the kinds of address and appeals to an audience which impel a hearer/reader toward worldly action. The reader could not be defined solely as a function of internalized linguistic codes, or as a purely individual nonrational subjectivity, or as a participant/subverter of ideological mystification. Perelman's notion of rhetoric as always connected to practical action might also legitimate literature and literary criticism as forums for deliberations about practical choices and values.

Both Levinas and Perelman would agree, however, with the emphasis in recent literary theory to take into account the social character of language. As Perelman argues, "the approaches of realism and nominalism in the linguistic field are both untenable, as they regard language either as a reflection of reality or as an arbitrary creation of an individual," whereas "all language is the language of a community." Even agreements about the conventional use of terms "no less than an agreement about the conception of reality and vision of the world" are disputable and linked to social and historical situations (513). All these forms of agreement are founded on prior sets of value judgments personally made by the scientists or philosophers or critics who construct and elaborate their various fields.

"Values," Perelman asserts, "enter, at some stage or other, into every argument" (75). They are one source of objects of agreement which influence decision toward an action and help justify choices; or they appear at the very origin, determining what rules and axiomatic principles will found a field or system. His position on the relation of judgments of value to judgments of fact parallels Levinas's assertion that ethics is not subordinate to but the very ground of metaphysics. On a broader scale, Levinas's inversion of the relation between ethics and metaphysics is similar to Perelman's reversal of the relation between rhetoric and philosophy. Perelman observes that in fact such inversions are characteristic of all advances in thought:

> Every original conceptual development in some way modifies accepted hierarchies, either by reducing a difference of order to a difference of degree or, conversely, by replacing one hierarchical system by another considered to be more fundamental. These different ways of constructing and reconstructing reality have an undeniable effect on valuations and on the way in which they are made. (349)

PHILOSOPHICAL PAIRS AND THE DISSOCIATION OF CONCEPTS

The New Rhetoric gives us a superb methodological tool with which to identify and understand these inversions: the "dissociation of concepts." The dissociation of concepts arises from "the desire to remove an incompatibility arising out of the confrontation of one proposition with others, whether one is dealing with norms, facts, or truths" (413). For example, the incompatibility between God's goodness and the existence of evil, or between human free will and divine free will is resolved by "dissociating" the concept of humanity into "man as created" and "man as fallen" (413). One of the incompatibles is dissociated, i.e., not destroyed but preserved and reordered. On a practical level, for instance within a legal system, such resolutions constitute the "compromises" made to mediate conflicting claims. On the theoretical level such dissociations remodel our very concept of reality; and "any new philosophy presupposes the working out of a conceptual apparatus, at least part of which, that which is fundamentally original, results from a dissociation of notions that enables the problems the philosopher has set himself to be solved" (414). In other words, a "dissociation" is a mode of making a distinction or definition which yields a "philosophical pair." These pairs and their relations are the characteristic objects of all philosophical inquiry. In Western philosophy, pairs such as "letter/spirit," "individual/universal," "means/end," or "subjective/objective" have had enormous influence on ordinary thought and cultural tradition. Philosophical debates and innovations generally have to do with either denying old dissociations or creating new ones, or establishing systems to relate different sets of pairs to each other.

Perelman clarifies this idea by explaining that the prototype of all philosophical dissociations is the pair "appearance/reality." Incompatibilities between various appearances need to be resolved if one presupposes a coherence to the nature of the world. That which is deceptive has to be differentiated from that which is not deceptive. So term I, "appearance," is dissociated into appearance/reality—and term II, "reality," then "provides a criterion and norm which allows us to distinguish those aspects of term I which are of value from those which are not" (416). That means preserving some aspects of term I, not denying term I completely. The relation between term I and term II is not necessarily an "either/or," or any simple opposition. The pairs are *dependent upon* and *interact with* each other. Term II does not do away with term I but helps distinguish and resolve incompatibilities within it. Although the form of a particular argument might suggest otherwise, dissociations thus always involve the work of *evaluation*.

We can better understand this idea by clarifying a distinction Perelman makes earlier in the book (sections 46 and 47) between a "logical contradiction" and an "incompatibility." In fact, the brilliance of Perelman's own method is his very ability to make innovative dissociations and construct new relations among philosophical pairs—e.g., "demonstration/argumentation," "constricted reason/enlarged reason." In his view, the absolutism which it is the central aim of his book to combat always presents "uncompromising and irreducible philosophical opposites" (510). Perelman's constant disputation of these rigid opposites through new dissociations and relations is his way of making room for human freedom and choice through argument (what a poststructuralist would call "putting into question"). He undercuts any claims to the possession of unquestionable, unarguable truth independent of the varying social and historical situations of human life.

In the realm of formal logic, terms are indeed univocal, and one cannot simultaneously assert both a proposition and its negation at the same time without contradiction to the whole system. Pointing out such contradictions is the work of skepticism. In ordinary language, however, and in the concrete problematics of human life, areas where terms are equivocal and which constitute the field of argumentation, we are faced not with logical contradictions but with "incompatibilities." An incompatibility, like a contradiction, involves "two assertions between which a choice must be made." In contrast to formal logic, with an incompatibility there is no *necessary* ground for eliminating one or the other proposition—although one still has to make a choice. For example, a political ultimatum presents its audience with an incompatibility between "the refusal to yield and the preservation of peace between two states" (196–97). Incompatibilities exist and are relative only to contingent circumstances, whereas contradictions are nontemporal and noncontingent inconsistencies within a formal system.

As Perelman notes, incompatibilities also result from the application of sacred texts to definite situations (197). Again, there is much that is useful here for interpreting rabbinic hermeneutics. The resulting "legal fictions" or apparent straining of the rabbis to tie one prooftext to another, or to relate a new position which seems to have no basis anywhere to an older one, is a way of maintaining the coherence of the legal system in the face of new situations and so to remove incompatibilities. Perelman reiterates that this is not the "coherence" of a mathematical Cartesian rationalism, but another kind of reason. In midrashic texts, it often seems as if incompatibilities are elicited to create a deeper level of coherence in order to adapt to new historical and moral problems. Perelman's assertion that rhetorical reasoning is essentially defined by ongoing adaptation to the needs of its audience rather than by revelatory self-evident truth would help explain that unique combination of skepticism and piety, freedom and discipline, worldliness and idealism in rabbinic texts.

We can now return to the main point: that the technique of "dissociation of ideas" arises to resolve incompatibilities. It is also important to distinguish Perelman's "dissociations" from the structuralist idea of formal "binary oppositions" which determine all thought. Nor is he proposing any kind of Hegelian dialectical logic between a thesis and anti-thesis. For Hegel, such a dialectic is the necessary and inherent structure of reality, but for Perelman dissociations are human adaptive responses to the concrete and contingent problems of human life and decision making, not an inherent or necessary part of the world or language.[9]

These dissociations are *con-structs* rather than inalienable *structures*. Term II in a dissociation is generated out of the need to resolve incompatibilities in term I: "it is not simply a *datum,* it is a *construction* which, during the dissociation of term I, establishes a rule that makes it possible to classify the multiple aspects of term I in a hierarchy" (416). In a dissociation, term II provides an explanatory norm which allows evaluation of the various aspects of term I. Judgments are made accordingly. From an originally undetermined status, "the dissociation into terms I and II will attach value to the aspects that correspond to term II and will lower the value of the aspects that are in opposition to it. . . . In term II, then, reality and value are closely linked. This connection is especially pronounced in all the constructions of the metaphysicians" (417).

In deconstruction, the focus is on the act of destabilizing the opposition between two terms, which is in effect another way of reordering these terms; the highest value is now the very undermining of any hierarchies themselves. In this sense, much poststructuralist thought from pragmatism to semiotics to deconstruction fits Perelman's definition of "antimetaphysical" philosophies in general: antimetaphysical philosophies are built on denying the very dissociation of appearance/reality which founds metaphysical philosophy. Now reality is defined as not coherent, and so there are no reasons to choose among the varying conceptions of reality; "reality" is no longer a term II that can serve as a norm or criterion for value or choice.

Perelman notes, however, that the problem of establishing criteria for choice and the need to resolve incompatibilities still does not disappear in antimetaphysical philosophies. Another philosophical pair or set of pairs will arise in which term II will assume the role of "reality." Often, term II itself will be founded on another term I/term II dissociation whose terms are not disputed. We do indeed find a wealth of dissociations in poststructuralist thought, pairs such as identity/alterity, speech/writing, determinacy/indeterminacy, continuity/discontinuity, hierarchy/subversion, decidability/undecidability, center/margin, power/knowledge, naive/self-reflexive, logos/dissemination, dominant/repressed, ideal/ideology, Truth/Language, presence/absence, work/text, reading/misreading, whole/fragment, metaphor/metonymy, signified/signifier, representation/signification, form/deformalization, seriousness/play, spectator/performer, structure/construct, and so on.[10]

In Levinas we have the dissociations totality/infinity, ontology/ethics, said/saying, need/desire, identity/alterity, Being/the Good, philosophy/skepticism, autonomous reason/heteronomous reason, and so forth. These pairs are attempts to resolve incompatibilities in the problematic nature of the "relationship to the other," and especially the incompatibility between violence and nonviolence in the imperative of the other. Levinas's attempt to find a realm of ultimate nonviolence to guard human relationship, action, and knowledge is born of this problem, and he ultimately has to make a dissociation between a negative ontological violence and a positive violence of the Good in order to respond to Derrida's critique that language is always violent.

In Levinas, "saying" is also the realm of equivocation in language, the relation to the other prior to thematization, representation, comprehension, and narrative (the "said"). "Saying" is also the ultimate relation to the interlocutor outside the discourse that narrates it. In this sense, "saying" is that "rhetorical" aspect of language prior to philosophy—a primary appeal to and relation with the other before any discourse can even begin. As such, it also disrupts the drive toward conclusive certainties, identities, and representations of the "said." Yet this equivocation of saying is not playful: this preoriginal saying "sets forth an order more grave than being and antecedent to being. By comparison being appears like a game . . . without responsibility where every possibility is permitted" (*OTB* 6).

In *Otherwise Than Being* Levinas radicalizes his notion of the obligation to the other in response to Derrida's critiques: this call by and to the other in responsibility now becomes a mode of "obsession, persecution, being hostage, sacrifice without reserve, wounding, trauma, denuding." The call to responsibility is an "involuntary election by the Good." These metaphors, nevertheless, are violent. Levinas asserts, however, that this violence to the narcissistic ego is the violence of the Good beyond being, and "being Good it redeems the violence of its alterity, even if the subject has to suffer through the augmentation of this ever more demeaning violence" (15).

This position leads to another critical difference with Derrida and many other poststructuralist thinkers about the heteronomy and autonomy of the subject. "One is not an irrationalist nor a mystic nor a pragmatist for questioning the identification of power and *logos*. One is not against freedom if one seeks for a justification" (*TI* 302). The aim of Levinas's work is to show that reason and freedom are founded on prior structures. As with Perelman, truth does not rest on the freedom of the autonomous, on what is self-evident, independent of all exteriority. Freedom must be justified not of itself but by and for the other. "Does not the presence of the Other put in question the naive legitimacy of freedom? Does not freedom appear to itself as a shame for itself? And, reduced to itself, as usurpation?" (303). The constraint of relation to the other is not identifiable with the heteronomy of universal reason or history; nor is the realm of the "unthought" or "unsayable" prior to philosophy a realm that is neutral, impersonal, mysterious, or monstrous as in Heidegger or Derrida.

The rupture with the egoistic realm of cognition and being in Levinas means that the relation to the other is heteronomous, a "difficult liberty," the "paradox of responsibility." But his definition of human freedom is also different from Perelman's and involves a far more exacting heteronomy: "To be free is only to do what no other person can do in my place" (*ADV* 172); "human autonomy rests on a supreme heteronomy" (*DL* 24–25). Derrida claims in his essay on Edmond Jabès that the poet (and by extension philosopher-poet) enacts an antinomian freedom, a shattering of all norms; the poet must "break the Tablets of the Law" to elicit the "other" of language, the play of the text. Poetic autonomy would thus liberate an otherness which can put philosophy in question ("Jabès" 67).

Derrida and Levinas both interrupt philosophy by soliciting its other, but they differ in defining the "call" of the other that originally engenders this putting into question, and the kind of response it requires. Derrida sees his task as eliciting alterity through the "gratuitousness" of miming, playing, dissimulation, equivocation. Levinas sees the task of philosophy as skeptical critique aimed at "unsaying" the inevitable and incessant dissimulation and betrayal of the saying into the said, for this unsaying opens to exteriority, to the transcendence of the other. Yet Levinas also recognizes the need for the said, for representation, system, thematization in order for signification to show itself; the said itself also involves a positive ethical moment. In order to have responsibility and justice, saying must retain a reference to being; there can be no justice without measurement, comparison, correlation, synchronization, representation: "Essence has its time and hour" (*OTB* 46), but "being must be understood on the basis of being's other" (16).

However, this oscillating relation of saying and said, of skepticism and philosophy, means that the "sincerity" of saying ("sincerity" as opposed to Derridean "dissimulation") will signify only through the *ambiguity* of every said (152). Ambiguity is not paralytic perplexity, dark undecidability, or an anonymous "effect of language." It is saying as the "sign given of the giving of signs" (151), the resonance of every language as inspiration, witness, and a kind of prophecy. Ambiguity here becomes the opening to the other, not an autonomous or indifferent linguistic self-reflexivity. Instead of turning on itself in the emptiness of pure formalism, signification empties itself to turn toward and substitute for the other. In other words, since by definition the "infinite" or "transcendent" or other cannot be contained in the finite, same, or said, its signification will always show itself paradoxically: it must interrupt its own demonstration to the point where it is "necessary that its pretension be exposed to derision and refutation." Such skeptical critique is also necessary especially to prevent "ideology and Sacred delirium" (152) (the twin evils for Levinas) from filling the space of this opening to the other.

So to Derrida's "language is already violence," Levinas counters with "language is already skepticism" (170). He means that language can indeed exceed thought by "suggesting, letting be understood without ever making understandable an implication of a meaning" distinct from that which comes through sign-systems or logical concepts (169–70). Skepticism itself has an ethical structure, and philosophy as critique has a double task: philosophy is both saying and said, indeed the very oscillation between them.

This oscillation between philosophy and nonphilosophy furthermore means that there is no "end" or closure of philosophical discourse, a point on which Levinas agrees with Derrida in opposition to Hegel. "Is not its interruption its only possible end?" (200), an interruption which is the continuous and renewed critique of philosophers by each other as interlocutors in the history of philosophy. But to solicit the "other" of philosophy does not mean to return to prephilosophical naivety. "Logocentric, ontotheological" philosophy may have come to an end, but speculative practice certainly has not. Levinas ironically notes: "Indeed, the whole contemporary discourse of overcoming and deconstructing metaphysics is far more speculative in many respects than is metaphysics itself. Reason is never so versatile as when it puts itself in question" (Kearney, "Dialogue" 33).

THE SAYING AND THE SAID: A SUBJECT OF FLESH AND BLOOD

In summary so far, for Levinas in *Otherwise Than Being* "saying" gives access to a realm which in Derrida's words is "before the light." Although the "saying" is nonthematizable, nonrepresentable, beyond the gatherings of history and memory, "an-archic" (i.e., in terms of ontology and phenomenology, prior to all *arche,* origins, and foundations), it is "betrayed" in the "said," in the very language one uses to speak about it. Philosophy is consigned to the "said" and "by an abuse of language, to be sure, says that of which it is but a servant, but of which it makes itself master by saying it, and then reduces its pretension in a new said" (*OTB* 126). This said nevertheless retains a "trace" of the saying. Levinas wants to remind philosophy of that which it serves, and he redefines the "phenomenological reduction" as the movement back to the saying from the said: "In it the indescribable is described" (53), a self in the accusative and put under accusation, and philosophy itself is put under accusation and subjected to the other.

Despite certain parallels to deconstruction, the realm of "saying" is ultimately antecedent to verbal signs, linguistic systems, and semantic glimmerings or any Heideggerian play of veiling and dis-closure. Levinas uses terms similar to Heidegger, such as the *unthought* of philosophy, *difference,* even the term *saying* itself, which echoes Heidegger's *sagen*—as well as *opening, sub-ject as subject to, proximity, passivity,* but he ethicizes them all by placing them under a supreme heteronomy, the obligation to the personal other. Above all, Levinas maintains in opposition to Heidegger and Derrida that this otherness, this "before/beyond" of philosophy, this "unthought" of philosophy, this language before language, is not the neuter, the impersonal, the *es gibt* of Being, the "mystery" of the holy, or the monstrosity of some strange birth. It is not, as in Heidegger or Derrida, poetic language that speaks the unspeakable; it is rather ethics as the language before language which is the "proximity of one to the other, the commitment of an approach, the one for the other, the very signifyingness of signification" (*OTB* 5).

Saying is a kind of Levinasian counterterm to *structure* or *code* in structuralist views of language—a condition of possibility of meaning. He maintains, however, that the "proximity" of saying as the relation with the other across absolute difference is "neither a structure nor an inwardness of a content in a container, nor a causality, nor even a dynamism, which still extends in a time that could be collected into a history" (70). It might seem that this "unknowable," "unrepresentable" saying is a kind of negative theology—and it is precisely complicity with ontotheology with which Derrida charges Levinas. Levinas answers that saying does not constitute a negative theology, or a language which can speak only through negation, or through speaking nothing. "Negative theology" is still ordered by being—even if it attempts to be being's negation and Levinas is trying to propose a third way between being/nonbeing. "Saying" is negative for ontology but positive for ethics as the response of the subject. Indeed, infinity cannot be "presented," but "the negation of the present and representation finds its positive form in proximity, responsibility, and substitution. This makes it different from the propositions of negative theology. The refusal of presence is converted into my presence as present, that is, as hostage, delivered over as gift to the other" (151).

We noted previously a possible source for the notion of "saying" in

Rosenzweig's contrast of the "language prior to language" of myth and art with the "speaking" of language as opening up and relation to the other in revelation. But in describing the relation of revelation to redemption, Rosenzweig writes of another speech of the speechless—the surpassing of language, a "silence which no longer has any need of the word . . . the silence of consummate understanding. One glance says everything here." "Glance" refers again to the figure of the "face": the glance shines outward, "like the face, like an eye which is eloquent without the lips having to move" (*Star* 295). This word beyond the word is found, he writes, in the communal gestures of liturgical forms, such as the silence of listening to the communal reading of Scripture. These wordless gestures anticipate the "purified lip" of redemption as an ultimate communion which needs no words; they anticipate "the way to all-embracing common unity where everyone knows everyone else and greets him wordlessly—face-to-face" (323). For Rosenzweig, this face to face is an ultimate, messianic kind of silent speech as greeting and personal relation with all others: "The very sanctification of the name occurs only so that the name might one day be muted. Beyond the word—and what is name but collective word—beyond the word there shines the silence" (383).

Yet this beyond is also *within* experience and is already anticipated and enacted in liturgical forms of today. Rosenzweig was reluctant to characterize his own "New Thinking" as another *ism,* but "the designation I would soonest accept would be that of absolute empiricism" ("New Thinking" 207). It is this same search for the "infinity" within the "totality," for a messianic "beyond" available to experience, that characterizes Levinas's thought.

Thus in *Otherwise Than Being* Levinas identifies saying not with any transcendental ontology but with the very immanence of the body, with the diachrony of aging, wrinkling, pain, the sensibility of flesh and blood itself. As Maurice Blanchot has written in an essay on Levinas:

> Jean Wahl used to say that the greatest transcendence, the transcendence of transcendence, is ultimately the immanence, or the perpetual referral, of the one to the other. Transcendence within immanence: Levinas is the first to devote himself to this strange structure (sensibility, subjectivity) and not to let himself be satisfied by the shock value of such contrarieties. ("Our Clandestine" 48)

The words *transcendence* and *immanence* come to us, of course, from the traditions of ontology and idealism. It is this "transcendental" observing "subject," the consciousness which grasps being and truth through its concepts, that Levinas critiques, the disembodied idealist consciousness that constructs the world out of its own self-reflective thought. He is trying to describe and elicit a different kind of nonegoistic sub-ject in place of the "sub-jectum" which stands behind or underlies and identifies itself with all that is. As Rosenzweig pointed out, "The monumental error of Idealism consisted in thinking that the All was really wholly contained in its 'generation' of the All" (*Star* 188).

Levinas follows Rosenzweig and proceeds to apply this critique of idealism to the latent idealisms of contemporary phenomenology and the linguistic idealisms of structuralism and poststructuralism. Like Rosenzweig, Levinas claims, "Through the suppression of the singular, through generalization, knowing is idealism" (*OTB* 87). Just as Rosenzweig shatters and fragments this All of Hegelian idealism, Levinas disrupts the "transcendental subject" of Husserl, the intentional "consciousness of" in phenomenology which grasps/constructs the world through its ideas and perceptions. He tries throughout his work to define a human self or subject which is not reducible to consciousness or self-consciousness, an "otherwise than being" that is not derived from cognition, a realm "before" being which, unlike that of Heidegger, Derrida, Bataille, et al., is not anonymous, indifferent, or lost in the enchantment of dissimulation, violence, or play, but as in Rosenzweig is personal, nonviolent, and ethical. The resulting exposed, inspired, subjected subject in Levinas is no ethereal Husserlian "consciousness"; like Bataille and Merleau-Ponty, Levinas finds in the "incarnation" of the subject, in the very *body itself*, an alterity that the subjective consciousness cannot grasp or control. The body itself is a paradigmatic example of an exteriority not constituted by my consciousness; it permanently contests the prerogatives of consciousness to "give meaning."

Against and despite our will, we are bound into bodies, "held tight in our skin," subject to lapse and loss of time in the diachrony of aging, wrinkling, exposed and vulnerable to the world, interrupted by pain and fatigue. Not some atemporal eternal order but the temporalization of time itself is where "being and time fall into ruins so as to disengage subjectivity from its essence" (*OTB* 9). There are echoes here of Benjamin's ideas about "mortification" and ruin in his theory of allegory, and Benjamin's attempt to join allegorical fragmentation with explosive moments of liberatory "messianic time" in order to disrupt the closed cycles of historicism. In Levinas, the ruin and mortification wrought by time signify an extreme sensibility and susceptibility of humanity that makes us "nonidentical" with that self-enclosed synchronizing, representing consciousness and all its constructs, systems, and narratives. This corporeal alterity unbalances the calm imperial speculative panoptical gaze of the philosopher's eye, subjecting him or her to something quite other.

But Levinas is not proposing here any philosophical or Marxist "material-ism" which would turn the idealism of Hegel on its head by reducing or redefining "reality" as a material set of economic forces, relations of production, or dialectic between the material "base" and ideological "superstructure." The materialism which Levinas is here proposing as a "locus" for a subject defined as *not* identical with itself is instead physicality as "exposure, vulnerability, passivity"—as an "other-in-the-same."

> It is as though the identity of matter resting in itself concealed a dimension in which a retreat to the hither side of immediate coincidence were possible, concealed a materiality more material than all matter—a materiality such that irritability, susceptibility, or exposedness to wounds and outrage characterizes its passivity. . . . Maternity in the complete being "for the other" which characterizes it, which is the very signifyingness of signification, is the ultimate sense of this vulnerability. (*OTB* 108)

This definition of materiality as a for-the-other rather than for-itself constitutes an implicit critique of all "materialism"—from Marxism to the contemporary cultural materialism in literary studies. The ethical or liberatory move is not, then, to reveal the material base of an ideology, or to replace or resist one form of violent consciousness or production with another. In Levinas, the "materialist" interruption of the consciousness or identity "in and for itself" is "animation" as exposure and vulnerability. The biological or material is part of a structure which inverts the "for-itself" into the "for-the-other" and that is the very definition of the ethical relation, of "saying" as giving, being bound over to the other. This for-the-other is the primary signification of the material that guides all other significations. It enacts once more the priority of ethics.

A materialism which replaces an idealist for-itself with a materialist for-itself only repeats the original violent move of idealist and ontological philosophy. (That could be seen as a problem in the newer forms of "cultural materialism" in contemporary literary theory.) For the subject is flesh and blood and not reducible to "an intersection of codes" or "effect of signifiers," and the aim of Levinas's critique, of his introducing alterity into identity, is not simply to become "more conscious"—as if to become more self-reflexive, knowing, and ironic would prevent more violence to the other. The excess of "saying" as exposure, an excess over thematizing thought, is not the excess of the purely linguistic signifier but a trauma, an alterity which obsesses, interrogates me in my very *skin*. It is not that consciousness is prior to and then afterward enters into space, and into relations of contact and mercantile exchange, but

> it is because subjectivity is sensibility—an exposure to others, a vulnerability and a responsibility in the proximity of others, the one-for-the-other, that is, signification—and because matter is the very locus of the for-the-other, the way signification shows itself before showing itself as a said in a system of synchronism, the linguistic system, that a subject is of flesh and blood, a man that is hungry and eats, entrails in a skin, and thus capable of giving bread from his mouth, or giving his skin. (*OTB* 77)

In *Totality and Infinity,* Levinas had also discussed the *body* as a mode of being in relation with another but still separate (*TI* 168), and not absorbed into Hegelian dialectics, systems, or totalities. At the end of *Totality and Infinity,* Levinas connected the erotic relation to fecundity and the family.

"Paternity" was his metaphor for the other-in-the-same: the child is a totally new and different creation, yet in-relation across difference to the parent. In *Otherwise Than Being,* it is now "maternity" and the maternal body which signify the other-in-the-same as the extreme for-the-other of ethics. Maternity is a form of sensibility as vulnerability and exposure to the other, the very

> gestation of the other, other in the same . . . the groaning of wounded entrails by those it will bear or has borne. In maternity what signifies is a responsibility for others, to the point of substitution for others and suffering from both the effect of persecution . . . [bearing] even responsibility for the persecution of the persecutor. (*OTB* 75)

Levinas is again trying to articulate a kind of signification prior to all representation, prior even to the representation of the body to consciousness—an "immediacy" prior to the free will or constituting consciousness of the subject. This kind of signification as "sensibility" would also be a "proximity" or closeness to the other without all collapse of distance. The body is a "Gordian knot" that cannot be undone, or completely constituted or controlled by consciousness and its representations or the synchronous systems of language (the "said"). The very problem of the Cartesian cogito is how to relate the conscious which thinks to the body; Levinas argues that this disjunction at the heart of the Cartesian philosophical system (or "said") indicates the "trace" of this preoriginal "saying." The animation of the body by the soul is the very one-for-the-other or other-in-the-same prior to the Cartesian consciousness which solipsistically thinks a world for-itself.

It is not just in resisting consciousness that flesh and blood signifies. This alterity of corporeal subjectivity as "the-one-for-the-other itself is the preoriginal signifyingness that gives sense, because it gives. Not because, as preoriginal, it would be more originary than the origin," but because its diachrony refers to an irrecuperable preontological past—a past which cannot be recuperated or generated out of the authoritative paternal logos but rather emanates from the maternal—the matrix of all relations (*OTB* 78).

In other words, in place of the self-enclosed Cartesian ego is the Levinasian ego disrupted, exiled from itself, contracted, exploded, but yet singular. It is now defined as a "recurring to itself" through its very assignation to the other in inescapable responsibility, "ill at ease in one's own skin," vulnerable, exposed—and thus also opened and capable of *giving.* "Maternity" characterizes this "for-the-other," and it is sensibility as signification as material "nourishing, clothing, lodging, in maternal relations, in which matter shows itself for the first time in its materiality" (77). Maternity, then would be the "matrix," the immediacy of the ethical, the very sense of "the material." In these meditations on maternity and signification,

Levinas has anticipated many of the insights of contemporary feminist theorists such as Julia Kristeva's identification of the "semiotic" with the maternal and the "symbolic" with the paternal logos (another version of "saying" and "said").[11]

This "proximity," "obsession," "trauma," "vulnerability," and wounding of the subject puts "into question the naive spontaneity of the ego" in a far more radical way than consciousness reflecting on itself (92); for even in the ultimate self-reflexiveness of the ego looking at itself, the ego still escapes, is not itself put in question. This more radical Levinasian putting in question is the accusation, obsession, and demand prior to all self-consciousness; the I is "denuded, exposed, susceptible, consumed, dislocated, delivered, exiled, emptied, persecuted, hostage," to use some of the metaphors Levinas employs.

Saying then becomes a denuding of denuding, a sign giving a sign of its very signifyingness, and an exposure prior to all dialogue or exchange of question and answer. One could almost say that Levinas proposes in *Otherwise Than Being* a "trauma theory of language and subjectivity." Sensibility becomes the *sense* of signification of the for-the-other "not in elevated feelings, in 'belles lettres,' but as in a tearing away of bread from the mouth that tastes it, to give it to the other. Such is the coring out [*dénucléation*] of enjoyment, in which the nucleus of the ego is cored out" (64). In this mode of "passivity," exposure, vulnerability, and sensibility, Levinas postulates a sincerity, frankness, and veracity beyond all dissimulation and ruse (15). This dispossession of the subject opens it for the other in a "dis-interestedness" of sincerity rather than the dissimulation of deconstruction. Play, Levinas notes, is not itself "free." It, too, has its "interests" (6). Play would still partake of the egoistic structure of being; it is not "disinterestedness"—dis-inter-*esse,* the undoing of *esse* (essence). Any game or play implies a "comic mask," and a self contemplating or expressing itself. Levinas, by contrast, tries to elicit in his "otherwise than being" and the "saying" which is its "trace," and in the face as trace which subjects the subject to the other some pure gratuitous disinterestedness, an ultimate exposure and vulnerability to the other with no protection, a responsibility to the point of becoming a substitute and hostage for the other. This complete "dis-inter-esse" is the Levinasian counterterm to "deconstruction," a kind of prophetic reason opposed to a parodic play; "nonindifference" versus Derridean "différance."

Signification here is not Barthes's "pleasure of the text" but rather pain as "pure deficit, an increase of debt in a subject that does not have a hold on itself" (55). The saying of the denuded subject would be a pure and gratuitous giving as both suffering and signification; signification as a pure giving of sign would be a kind of witness, "giving a sign of this giving of signs, expressing oneself" (15). What both Levinas and Derrida share is an idea of "gratuity" coming from a breaking up of system, and synchrony, through diachrony, disequilibrium, and disorder. But for Levinas, this is a gratuity or giving over of the self in which there is no "accounting" or "bookkeeping," i.e., no equilibrium between claim, obligation, and responsibility. (In Levinas's interpretation, this is what the biblical figure of Job did not understand.) The relation to the other is "gratuitous" in that it involves no return, no reciprocal compensation, no benefit. If there is a folly of non-sense, it is not in play but in the "non-sense" of the one-for-the-other, suffering as gratuitous giving, "folly at the confines of reason" (50).

The gratuitousness of signification as unreserved exposure and infinite responsibility means that the passivity of exposure *exposes itself* in turn. "Saying" is ultimately the holding open of its own openness, "without excuses, evasions or alibis, delivering itself without saying anything said. Saying saying itself without thematizing it, but exposing it again. . . . to exhaust oneself in exposing oneself, to make signs by making oneself a sign, without resting in one's very figure as a sign." This "extreme tension of language," the saying without the said, the sign of giving signs, is "as simple as 'hello,' but ipso facto the pure transparency of an admission, the recognition of a debt" (143). In this sense, one could say that Levinas's own repetitive rhetorical style enacts the "trace" of the saying in its own said—as if in his constant reexposure and repetition of his ideas, he enacts "saying" as radical exposure, as the holding open of openness itself—which would demand, in a way, this constant reiteration.

The key question, however, is whether this saying of saying is an infinite regress or the adventure of the infinite? On the one hand, this idea of a pure "contentless saying" parallels Scholem's elaboration of the "meaningless" word which gives birth to all meaning, and Benjamin's "pure language"—for it is the refusal to define the essence of signification with any specific content or information. But for Levinas, the saying is "outside all mysticism," and other than the play of presence and absence of the "said," or what is shown in a symbol (100). Saying would be "incommensurable" or "unassemblable" in the logos or "said"; it is already past, a past that disturbs the present without itself being present, like a "trace."

In a way, Levinas's "saying" has more in common with the later Benjamin's invocation of the fragments and ruins of allegories to critique the wholeness of the symbol. Benjamin's problem was how to open the material world to redemption without invoking either a crude Marxism or a transcendental theology. Levinas, as we have seen, critiques the foundations of both materialism and theology through the alterity of the other than being. He argues that preliminary to any quest for justice, and prior to theoretical consciousness, is the call to and dispossession of the subject which disrupts its egoism and narcissism. Without this precondition, all strivings for justice become, in their turn, other forms of oppression. The signification and embodiment of this alterity (as the holding open of signification itself) culminates not in another move of exegetical cunning but in the ethical act par excellence: "making signs by making oneself a sign" of this radical exposure to the other. This very exposure of the self does not lead to the fragmentation or unreadability of the text, or to the endlessness of signs in dissemination, or to myth and symbol, or to a pure language removed from all relation with others. Signification finally means "exposure to the other" to the very point of substitution for the other. There are obvious Dostoevskian and Tolstoyan echoes here, and indeed these writers were great influences on Levinas from his native Russian culture. One of Levinas's favorite and most oft-cited quotes is from Dostoevsky's *The Brothers Karamazov:* "Each of us is guilty before everyone for everyone, and I more than the others." Yet Levinas proposes no mystical fusion of souls, or union of subject and other; substitution is a "proximity" which retains the singularity and "separation" of the self who is called, wounded, hostage for the other.

Needless to say, the idea of gratuitous suffering for the other has strong biblical resonances, from the suffering servant of Isaiah to Pauline theology about Jesus' death as substitution and vicarious suffering for the sins of humankind. Levinas contests the latter idea, however, in that he strongly opposes any idea of suffering as "magically redemptive"; furthermore, *my* substitution for the other (in the first person as the unique, responsible "I") does not constitute in any way a reciprocal demand for the other to substitute her- or himself for me. The responsibility of the subject cannot be borne by another; no other person (or even divinity) can act as a *substitute* for me, relieve me of my responsibility and burden. It is one-way: "To say that the other has to sacrifice himself to the others would be to preach human sacrifice! . . . But it is I and no one else who am hostage" (*OTB* 126). "The self is a *sub-jectum;* it is under the weight of the universe, responsible for everything" (116).

Nor is substitution, in Levinas's schema, an act one *freely chooses* in the "will to sacrifice" (55); rather, it is prior to the realm of free choice in autonomous consciousness; as the "underside of being" it is "being emptying itself out." It would be an "obsession," not in any psychological sense but a being gripped by something despite one's will (77–78). This "underside" or "place" of saying as "proximity" to the other is not spatial; it is a kind of Levinasian equivalent to Derrida's "nonsite" thought outside ontology, cognition, and recuperable historical time. It is being gripped by the "Good beyond being," elected despite one's will, and ordered to the other. In this sense, insofar as both Levinas and Derrida elicit this nonsite, their projects are "utopian"—from the etymology of *u-topos,* i.e., "nonplace."

Yet for Levinas, this extreme situation which is seemingly so utopian is nevertheless a prehistory and *condition of possibility* for the world, just as the body is a precondition for sensibility and signification: "It is through the condition of being hostage that there can be in the world pity, compassion, pardon, and proximity—even the little there is, even the simple 'After you, sir' " (117). This relation is found in the "extraordinary and everyday event of my responsibility for the faults and misfortunes of others" prior to the realm of freedom or decision or play or subversion in the conscious, autonomous subject (10).

Prior to all foundations and philosophical principles, this proximity is an "an-archic" relation, the very "anarchy of responsibility" and "trace" of the infinite (26). This "anarchy of responsibility," this "immemorial past," intersects with the "Good beyond being" which has "chosen me before I have chosen it" and is enacted in the everyday. As responsibility for the other, it is a command, making me the other's neighbor, and so "it diverges from nothingness as well as from being." Beyond will or freedom, it is a "despite me," and this for another "is signification par excellence" (11).

All this leaves Levinas's ethics with no epistemologically certain ground: "the ethical situation is not comprehensible on the basis of ethics" (120). He gives no set of "prescriptions" but instead calls the subject to responsibility, to the other—in this world, in this body, through our language: "The transcendence of the face is not enacted outside of the world. It is not a beatific contemplation of the other. . . . Transcendence is not a vision of the other, but a primordial donation" (*TI* 172, 174).

PASSIVITY: THE SUBJECT AS LUNG

This donation, sacrifice, or deposing of self is an aspect of what Levinas so often characterizes as "passivity," a word which is quite disturbing to most contemporary Western readers. In *Otherwise Than Being*, this "passivity" is part of the "trauma" to the willing, enjoying, egoistic self. Perhaps he employs this highly unfashionable term to administer a shock to the ego of the Western reader. "Passivity" in his work means that the access to the "other than being" requires a kind of "holding back . . . breathlessness of the spirit" because being as essence is the principle of self and same as egoism—a self-expansion and filling up of everything (*OTB* 5). Although Levinas is by no means a mystic, nor does he draw his inspiration from Jewish mystical sources, there is an interesting analogy here to the kabbalistic idea of God's creation of the world through God's self-contraction—*tzimtzum*—rather than through expansion. Derrida characteristically interprets the *tzimtzum* as a duplicitous negativity in God ("Violence" 67–68, 74). For the poet Edmond Jabès, this empty space or negativity of the *tzimtzum* becomes identified with the abysses of language and the sufferings of history that torment the postmodern writer. But for Levinas, the emptying out or contraction of the subject is what opens it to the positivity of the ethical relation, not the negativity of the abyss. The term *passivity* is used to describe the subject as opened, hollowed out, traumatized, wounded, deposed, and subject to the other; the passivity of the subject is its condition of being "created," not the author of itself.[12]

The same is true of his striking metaphor "that the subject could be a lung at the bottom of its substance—all this signifies a subjectivity that suffers and offers itself before taking a foothold in being," exposed and vulnerable (*OTB* 180). In many other contemporary literary theories, the subject or self is deposed, and is no longer a self-controlling unified center of meaning; or it is "displaced" in the attack on traditional humanism. Active force is then relocated in "discursive practice" (Foucault), or the play of différance (Derrida), or the unconscious (Lacan), or the interplay of codes, "strategies of subversion," and so forth. What Levinas again tries to show is how all these terms obscure the ethical move at their base and still partake of the war of egoisms struggling with one another, whether the context is politics, psychology, sociology, or linguistics. They may capture a kind of being otherwise, but not the other than being.

Levinas also asserts that passivity is *not* that "it speaks" or that "language speaks" as in Heidegger, Saussure, Lacan, et al. He harshly criticizes all the contemporary talk in the "human sciences" about the way in which the subject is conditioned by impersonal structures. One of the aims of *Otherwise Than Being* is to critique, on the basis of the face of the other, the descriptions of the "human sciences," for these descriptions instead lead to

> the impossible indifference with regard to the human which does not succeed in dissimulating itself in the incessant discourse about the death of God, the end of man and the disintegration of the world . . . but which in the wreckage preceding the catastrophe itself, like rats abandoning the ship before the shipwreck, come to us in the already insignificant signs of a language in dissemination. (*OTB* 59)

If the human sciences are not an adequate model, what of the "hermeneutics of suspicion" taught to us by psychoanalysis, sociology, or politics? Again, it is not enough, because these forms of suspicion pertain to the realm of "knowledge," to what we can *know* about the one to whom we speak. The relation to the other as neighbor before s/he is a rational animal or individual of a genus would not be comprehended by this knowledge. Instead, the other as neighbor "is the persecuted one for whom I am responsible as hostage"—for whom no one else can substitute himself. The Levinasian critique of ontology, epistemology, and linguistics is then a defense of subjectivity as irreplaceable uniqueness: "in an unexceptionable responsibility, I posit myself deposed of sovereignty. Paradoxically, it is qua *alienus*—foreigner and other—that man is not alienated" (*OTB* 59). Rimbaud's famous tormented cry "Je est un autre" ("I am an other"), which haunts so much modern French thought and literature, is not a dark specter for Levinas but the ethical inversion, the very source of goodness, and the guardian of the personal other and singular self.

But what relation can there be between "passivity" and "politics"? In both *Totality and Infinity* and *Otherwise Than Being,* the asymmetrical relation of self and other also involves what Levinas calls the "third party," the "other of the other." This third person represents the political and social world beyond the pair of self and neighbor. Through the third party, the "whole of humanity" looks out from the destituteness of the face, appeals and commands. The ethics of ethics which Levinas has constructed here is *not* a categorical imperative, a logically necessary and abstract universal moral law. Only when "translated" into the realm of the "said," into being and system, does this passivity of substitution as for-the-other become an active law, the law of justice. For in this realm of the said, of synchronizing, of themes, of politics, of the state and impersonality, the other can be an *equal* to all others in a system of justice. Since the other is *someone else's other,* that is the other not only of myself but also of a "third person." I must also seek justice in the realm of the state, of politics, and of being. But the ethics of saying is always prior to the politics of the said.

On the very last page of *Otherwise Than Being,* Levinas defends his position against the charge of impossible utopianism. This leaving the ego, this loss of place in substitution and breakdown of essence, is needed, he asserts, so that the world "not be repelled by violence. . . . nothing less was needed for the little humanity that adorns the word":

> This relaxation of virility without cowardice is needed for the little cruelty our hands repudiate. This is the meaning . . . suggested . . . in this book concerning the passivity more passive still than any passivity, the fission of the ego unto me, its consummation for the other such that from the ashes of this consummation no act could be reborn. (185)

When Levinas writes of "passivity," or a past beyond recuperation, he is not retreating into a quietude, resignation, or political indifference. The term is used as a lever to dislodge thought and language from the ontological tradition, to force a way out of the egoism of being, the persistence of essence in its own identity—the self-assertion, as one of the epigraphs to *Otherwise Than Being* from Pascal warns, that is the very cause of violence in the world: " 'That is my place in the sun.' That is how the usurpation of the whole world began."

The important point is that this "trauma" in the passivity of the subject coincides with signification as positive "inspiration," and this "other side of being" with the discovery of the "trace" of the infinite. In other words, this access to the other than being through withholding and withdrawal is the movement of an "oscillation" like breathing—between withholding and assertion, withdrawal and expulsion, philosophy and nonphilosophy, soul and body, language and what is beyond representation and speech. This is why Levinas uses the figure of the subject as "lung" to signify that this oscillating between other and the same is like the rhythmic withholding and letting go of air in the process of breathing. And "in-spiration," he adds, is just this "breathing," the trope ("in-spire") of the body animated by the soul, or the force of alterity in me.

At the bottom of this radical critique he finds a "strange affirmation" (*OTB* 121), a positivity, "yes" prior to any consent, a yes to the very exposure which makes possible all other words. It is "more ancient than any naive spontaneity," and is a yes that makes possible the words of negativity and consciousness; it is the exposure to the other as a commitment to the Good prior even to the realm of free choice of good and evil:

> There was a time irreducible to presence, an absolute unrepresentable past. Has not the Good chosen the subject with an election recognizable in the responsibility of being hostage, to which the subject is destined, which he cannot evade . . . ? A philosopher can give to this election only the significa- tion circumscribed by responsibility for the other. This antecedence of respon- sibility to freedom would signify the Goodness of the Good: the necessity that the Good choose me first before I can be in a position to choose. . . . It is a passivity prior to all receptivity, it is transcendent. It is an antecedence prior to all representable antecedence: immemorial. The Good is before being. (122)

A philosopher can describe it only in this way, but there are discourses other than philosophy which also describe this election by the Good. As we shall see in the next chapter, discourse as relation with the other demand- ing justice for all humanity becomes "sermon, exhortation, the prophetic word" (*TI* 213). Prophetic in the classical biblical tradition of the cry for justice: "To hear his destitution which cried out for justice is not to repre- sent an image to oneself, but is to posit oneself as responsible. . . . The Other who dominates me in his transcendence is thus the stranger, the widow, and the orphan to whom I am obligated" (215). Levinas's own style at this point becomes emphatically prophetic: "Speech is not instituted in a homogenous or abstract medium, but in a world where it is necessary to aid and to give" (216). Levinas's own "showing" or exhibiting of this rela- tion to the other is also its production; his philosophy is precisely its solici- tation, his writing becomes an appeal, a prophetic appeal, a witness, a revelation, an inspiration.

To invoke, to appeal to, to solicit what always escapes; to welcome, to call and to be called to question, to justify oneself before justice, to be elected and responsible—this is metaphysics, this is philosophy. And this is Judaism.

NINE

GreekJew/JewGreek

It is not the past of the Jewish people
which forms the teaching of the Bible, but
the judgment brought upon this history.
(Levinas, *Difficile liberté* 163)

The material needs of my neighbor are
spiritual needs for me. (Rabbi Israel
Salanter)

I don't know if Judaism has articulated its
metaphysics of the spirit in the terms I
have articulated it. But I know that it has
chosen action, and that the divine word is
transmitted only as Law. Action which
doesn't attack the All in a global and magical way but lies in the particular. It doesn't
efface the problems of place, or those of
history; it is in time. History is not a perpetual test for a diploma of eternal life, but
the very element where the life of the spirit
is set. (Levinas, *Difficile liberté* 137)

Only the testimony that is maintained
through the tortures of an inquisition provides complete certainty. (Rosenzweig, *Star
of Redemption* 97)

I believe only in those stories for which the
witness would readily die. (Pascal)

In a recent and telling interview, Derrida remarked that he was fascinated
by Levinas because Levinas was "the philosopher working in phenomenology and posing the question of the 'other' to phenomenology; the Judaic
dimension remained at that stage a discrete rather than decisive reference"
(Kearney, *Dialogues* 107). The relation of "Jew" and "Greek" in Levinas's
thought is another of the main preoccupations in Derrida's essay on *Totality and Infinity,* and the last paragraph of this essay ponders a split and
double identity:

> Are we Jews? Are we Greeks? We live in the difference between the Jew and
> the Greek, which is perhaps the unity of what is called history. We live in and

of the difference, that is, in *hypocrisy,* about which Levinas so profoundly says that it is "not only a base contingent defect of man, but the underlying rending of a world attached to both the philosophers and the prophets" (*TI* 24). . . . And what is the legitimacy, what is the meaning of the *copula* in this proposition from perhaps the most Hegelian of modern novelists: "Jewgreek is greek-jew. Extremes meet." ("Violence" 153)

The Greek/Jew conflict/synthesis recapitulates the rabbi/poet conflict Derrida had written of that same year (1964) in his essay on Jabès. There he identified the conflict as "heteronomy" versus "autonomy," the poet's freedom versus the rabbi's subjection to the Law. This dichotomy two years later became the famous "two interpretations of interpretation" which Derrida postulated at the end of his essay "Structure, Sign, and Play" and which is constantly quoted by literary theorists: one interpretation nostalgically seeks origin, the other affirms free play. Most literary critics, however, have neglected Derrida's concluding statement that the two interpretations, though irreconcilable, are lived simultaneously—and that there is no possibility of choosing between them. Similarly, at the end of the Jabès essay, he writes that there will *always* be rabbis and poets and two interpretations of interpretation.

As to the location of his own thought:

> While I consider it essential to think through the copulative synthesis of Greek and Jew, I consider my own thought, paradoxically, as neither Greek nor Jewish. I often feel that the questions I attempt to formulate on the outskirts of the Greek philosophical tradition have as their "other" the model of the Jew, that is, the Jew-as-other.

His project is to find a "non-site beyond both the Jewish influence of [his] youth and the Greek philosophical heritage" of his French schooling (107). Like Rosenzweig and Levinas, Derrida seeks a "non-site, or non-philosophical site" from which to interrogate philosophy, the site from which "philosophy as such [can] appear to itself as other than itself." One of Derrida's main disagreements with Levinas, as we saw in the previous chapter, is Derrida's contention that this nonsite "cannot be defined or situated by means of philosophical language" (108). Yet in his essay on *Totality and Infinity,* Derrida had also asked how the "parricide of the Greek father" could be carried out without disguising oneself as a Greek, feigning to speak Greek to get near the king.

I would argue that Levinas's philosophy is a kind of "letter to the Gentiles" in which he "subjects the subject," puts it under accusation, and so brings the philosophy of self, consciousness, and being to trial. And this trial is a kind of prophetic indictment of Western philosophy; as Derrida himself puts it: "All the philosophical concepts interrogated by Levinas are thus dragged towards the agora, summoned to justify themselves in an ethico-political language" ("Violence" 97). But a trial is precisely *not* a parricide; it is a calling to the bar of justice, not a murder. Nor does Levinas as trial judge sentence philosophy to death, just as the indictments of the prophets were meant not to destroy but to renew and purify the remnants of the people. In Levinas's philosophy, the subject is grasped, put in question by the alterity of the other like "the restlessness of someone persecuted" (*OTB* 75), and this structure of subjectivity is itself similar to the way in which the biblical prophets, despite themselves, are gripped and inspired by a call they cannot flee, even to the point of martyrdom.

In short, Levinas seeks to fight the violence—the violence of identity and totality and history—without more violence. He speaks to the smiters in their own language to purify philosophy, to bring it to account in its own terms. Derrida does not think this is possible, and he disagrees with Levinas about whether there is an ultimate possibility—even utopian—of peace and nonviolence in language and philosophy. Perhaps this is one of the reasons why, unlike Derrida, Levinas still speaks "Greek," i.e., philosophical language, and also seeks to "translate Jewish wisdom into Greek." In an interview, he put it as follows: "The work of the 70 [referring to the Jewish tradition about the 70 elders who translated the Hebrew Bible into Greek 2,000 years ago] is not finished" (Malka, *Lire* 106); "We have a great task to articulate in Greek the principles Greece ignored. Jewish singularity awaits its philosophy" (Malka 81).

This problem of the relation of Jewish thought to Western philosophy is central in all of Levinas's works. In both his philosophical and Jewish writings, he often contrasts the figure of Abraham to Ulysses: Abraham must depart his native land and go to a land of which he knows nothing ("Trail" 37); Ulysses, on the other hand, "returns home" and symbolizes for Levinas the course of Western philosophy—the identity, sameness, and egoism of the self which is ultimately protected, not exiled, called outside, broken up.[1] I have hinted at some of the ways in which these terms in Levinas's work allude to the figure of the Jew in recent European history, and it is now time to discuss more fully Levinas's understanding of Judaism and its relation to his philosophy. One of the most important links is the latter part of *Otherwise Than Being,* where the relation of his philosophy to theology in general is made clearer. After examining that section, I will turn to Levinas's explicitly Jewish writings and examine the way in which they carry forth, inspire, and are inspired by his philosophical work.

"HERE I AM"

Despite the philosophical complexity, the terms Levinas has used to describe subjectivity and responsibility are quite disturbing: *trauma, wound, obsession, exile, dispossession.* The description of the subject in *Otherwise Than Being* culminates in the French expression *me voici:* "The word *I* means *here I am [me voici]* answering for everything and everyone" (*OTB* 114) as complete gratuitous sacrifice. Those familiar with the Hebrew Bible recognize these words as the oft-repeated Hebrew phrase *hineni,* the formulaic response of the Old Testament heroes when called by God. Abraham, for instance, uses it in Genesis 22:1 when called to sacrifice his son Isaac, and so does Jacob when God calls to him in dreams (Gen. 31:12; 46:2); Moses so responds at the burning bush (Exod. 3:4), and Isaiah says in 6:8 "Here I am! send me," and so forth.

Levinas describes the "here I am" as the "I possessed by the other," a figure of inspiration and obsession: "for the order of contemplation it is something simply demented" (*OTB* 113), "a seed of folly, already a psychosis" (142). Yet it is a "reason" or "intelligibility" beyond the cogito. Levinas is converting or translating the "I think" of the rational Cartesian cogito (which founds modern philosophy) into the biblical "here I am" of subjectivity and ethics. Levinas describes the "sickness" of this subjectivity with a quotation from a biblical text, the Song of Songs: "I am sick with love" (Song 6:8). In other words, this folly or sickness at the depth of the obligation for the other is "love"—a word Levinas has avoided using to this point. He does not want to confuse his notion of an I obligated to the other with the romantic fusion of two selves in exclusive reciprocal relationship, or with a love born of some free will or purely subjective attraction to another. The "here I am" is another kind of love that would be the most profound level of the ethical as first philosophy: "Philosophy is the wisdom of love at the service of love" (161). The etymology of the word *philo-sophy*—the "love of wisdom"—here ethically inverts into the "wisdom of love."

Although Levinas does not explicitly mention it in his philosophical works, the "here I am" and its association with love, subjectivity, and ethics also has a source in Rosenzweig, especially book 2 of part II of *The Star of Redemption,* which is entitled "Revelation or the Ever-Renewed Birth of the Soul." Scholem described this chapter of *The Star* as "one of what may be called Judaism's 'definitive statements' on religious questions" ("Rosenzweig" 36–37). In this part of *The Star,* Rosenzweig does not define "revelation" in terms of any particular legal content or dogma, and that position is compatible with Scholem's idea of the "meaningless word." When Rosenzweig subsequently reaffirms Jewish law, liturgy, and ritual later in part III of *The Star* and deemphasizes the apocalyptic and catastrophic aspects of messianism, Scholem takes issue.

Rosenzweig's chapter on revelation also begins with a quotation from the Song of Songs (8:6): "Love is as strong as death." The Song of Songs, of course, is a passionate and erotic poem describing the quest of two lovers for each other; rabbinic and patristic traditions interpreted it allegorically as an account of the relation of God and Israel, or Jesus and the Church. For Rosenzweig, the Song of Songs is the book that describes revelation "literally"; it is not an allegory or analogy but the focal book of revelation, of the I and Thou of God and humanity "where the distinction between immanence and transcendence disappears in language" because the revelation of this love is both worldly and spiritual at the same time (*Star* 199).

We remember that for Rosenzweig, the I is drawn out of its mute and isolated self-enclosure, out of the mythical, aesthetic, and pagan worlds by God's emerging from concealment and turning to the individual human self in revelation, which is now defined precisely as this "love strong as death" (156). God's question to Adam "Where are you?" (Gen. 3:9) is a quest for the "you"—and this very address is a kind of indefinite deictic which opens the possibility for an other to be constituted who can freely confront God as an "I": "The I discovers itself at the moment when it asserts the existence of the Thou by inquiring into its Where" (*Star* 175).

Yet God receives no response from Adam to this initial question; instead Adam hides himself and blames Eve and the serpent. Adam remains defiant and self-enclosed. Only when God calls out to Abraham in the vocative, in direct address, not with an indefinite "you" but with his proper name, "Abraham" (Gen. 22:1)—i.e., in all his nonconceptual particularity and individuality, and in love for his singularity—"now he answers, all unlocked, all spread-apart, all ready, all-soul: 'Here I am.' Here is the I, the individual human I, as yet wholly receptive, as yet only unlocked, only empty, without content, without nature, pure readiness, pure obedience, all ears" (*Star* 176).

For Rosenzweig, this movement of opening, this unlocking of closed self, is the very heart of revelation; he also connects this receptive "here I am" and the moment of revelation with Jewish law, whose foundation is love as command. Rosenzweig works out this connection as follows: This summons to hear is itself the preface to every commandment, and especially of the commandment which for Rosenzweig is the essence and highest of all the other commandments, to "love God with all your heart, soul, and might." Only the lover, however, can urge and command the beloved to love in return. This command is "imperative" as the very voice and urgency of love itself: "love me!" And the *present* immediacy of this imperative is different from any "declaration of love," which is always after the fact, or in the *past* tense. In contemplation of the *future,* this imperative becomes "not commandment nor order but law. . . . [But] the commandment knows only the moment" (176–77), the great "today" of revelation, spoken by the first-person "I" of God.

Redemption is connected to the command to love one's neighbor, which only the soul already beloved of God can receive as a *command:* it is not a product of the autonomous human will as in Kant. Love for the neighbor is itself the response to God's love for the human person: "Ere man can turn himself over to God's will, God must first have turned to man" (215). In other words, because God has already done what God ordains—turned to humanity in love—so, too, "the love for God is to express itself in love for one's neighbor" (214). The future redemption of the world is then bound up with enactment of the Jewish law, for "in its multiplicity and strength ordering everything, comprising everything 'external,' that is, all the life of this world . . . this law makes this world and the world to come indistinguishable" (405); it is an attempt to transform and make a *bridge between* this world and the world to come. In an essay on Rosenzweig, Levinas writes that

> it is very curious to note what is produced in response to God's love and how revelation is prolonged. God's love for selfhood is, *ipso facto,* a commandment to love. Rosenzweig thinks that one can command love . . . contrary to what Kant thought. One can command love, but it is love which commands love. And it commands in the now of its love, so that the commandment to love is repeated and renewed indefinitely in the repetition and renewal of the very love which commands love.
>
> Consequently, the Judaism in which revelation is inseparable from commandment in no wise signifies the yoke of the Law, but precisely love. The fact that Judaism was woven from commandments attests to the renewal, at all instants of God's love for man. . . . the eminent role of the mitzvah in Judaism does not signify a moral formalism but the loving presence of divine love eternally renewed. . . . Two typically Jewish ideas have appeared: the idea of commandment, as essential to the relation of love . . . and the idea of the redemptive man and not a redemptive God. Even though the redemption comes from God, it has an absolute need of this intermediary man. ("Entre" 129)

So God creates a something else, *to* whom God reveals himself; similarly, the neighbor *to* whom this love is also commanded is the turning of the human toward something else, to the world. This "turning toward," we should remember, is a prime meaning of the root of the Hebrew word for "face" *(panah, panim)* and essential in Levinas's notion of the "face." So, too, Rosenzweig's interpretation of the command to love the neighbor is an important source for the Levinasian relation to the other. For Rosenzweig, the neighbor is the nearest as "representative. He is not loved for his own sake . . . but only because he just happens to be standing there, because he happens to be nighest to me. The neighbor is the other" (*Star* 218). As such, the neighbor represents all persons and things which could potentially occupy this place or "position" of being near—in other words, everything, the entire world.

In Levinas's philosophical writings, a similar pattern or "configuration" emerges but is derived without direct exegesis of the Bible or reference to Jewish thought, even though he employs such terms as *election, creation,* and *here I am:* the subject is elected (the "chosen people"), called out of its narcissistic self-enclosure not by the traditional God of theology but by the "revelation of the face" of the other, the human other through whom the other than being "passes" or is traced. And the "subject" so elected here signifies all human beings—not only the Jews. The last page of *Otherwise Than Being* asserts that each individual of all the peoples "is virtually a chosen one, called to leave in his turn, or without awaiting his turn . . . the concept of the ego . . . to respond with responsibility: *me, that is, here I am for the others,* to lose his place radically" (*OTB* 185).

In the concluding paragraph of this book, Levinas writes that in this breakdown of the ego and of philosophy, in this turn to the other and care for the "widow, orphan, and stranger" which occurs "after the death of a certain god inhabiting the world behind the scenes," one then discovers the trace of what does not enter into any present, the "unpronounceable inscription" conveyed by the pronoun *he,* or what Levinas has called illeity. In a sense, Levinas reverses the path of *The Star;* in *The Star,* God's immediate and pressing love as "shining countenance" (157, 164) opens up and awakens the beloved human soul both to God and to the love of the neighbor. In Levinas, the immediate and pressing face of the other opens and awakens the ego, and traces the "he" of illeity which escapes all revelation. But the face is *not,* he reiterates, the image of the God who has passed: "Being in the image of God does not signify being the icon of God but to find oneself in his trace" ("Trace" 46). The God of Judaeo-Christian spirituality "preserves all the infinity of his absence which is in the personal order itself [illeity]. He does not show Himself except in his trace, as in the thirty-third chapter of Exodus. To go toward Him is not to follow the trace which is not a sign. To go toward Him is to go toward the Others who are in the trace" ("Trail" 46)[2]

In short, ontological absence means ethical presence. In Levinas's later philosophical works, this "going toward others" becomes the "here I am" as a language of the accusative, of "witness," of the "first person." The election or calling or displacement of the subject (as Abraham was elected, called, displaced) to undeclinable responsibility and sacrifice for the other means that the subject is "unique," not because of any particular attributes of the ego, or because it is loved by God, but by virtue of this undeclinable assignation. "The self without concept, unequal in identity, signifies itself in the first person, setting forth the plane of saying" (*OTB* 115). This first-person "I" is "not as a particular case of the universal, an ego belonging to concept of ego, but as I, said in the *first person*-I, unique to my genus" (139).

One must ask, then, who is the "I" that speaks in this very text of *Otherwise Than Being?* Levinas does not write his philosophy in the first person; he uses the grammatical third person, perhaps because of the necessity of speaking in "Greek," and the inevitable betrayal of the saying into the said. Perhaps he also does so because the first person of the accusative "here I am" is not a subjectivity which is the center and producer of all meanings but one emptied out for the other. Nevertheless, the repetitiveness of Levinas's writing style, its argument via the vocative and accusative, also makes it "liturgical" in the mode Levinas defined in "On the Trail of the Other"—of philosophy as liturgy.

But is the "I" who speaks in his writings a Jew or a Greek? Or both at once? Or sometimes one and sometimes another? All of Levinas's key philosophical ideas are found in his Jewish writings. To ask, then, to what extent his philosophical writings "influenced" his Jewish writings or the Jewish writings "influenced" the philosophy is probably the wrong question. They are "translations" of one into the other, or "double reading"—a term which we can borrow from Derrida. Levinas sees himself as a philosopher in his approach to the Talmud, the Bible, and the problems of modern Judaism; at the same time, his conception of philosophy as preeminently ethical and of a prophetic reason is very Jewish.

Not surprisingly, in his Jewish writings he defines the ethical appeal as the very essence of Judaism. Judaism is described as the conscience of the world, justice, witness, martyrdom,

> as if Jewish destiny were a fissure in the shell of impenetrable being, an awakening to an insomnia where the inhuman is no longer concealed and hidden by the political necessities it manufactures. . . . the prophetic moment of human reason . . . rupture of the natural and historical constantly reconstituted and, thus, Revelation always forgotten. (*ADV* 18)

Or in *Difficile liberté* he writes that the fundamental message of Jewish thought consists in

> restoring the meaning of all experience to the ethical relation between men . . . to call on the personal responsibility of man, in which he feels chosen and irreplaceable, to realize a human society where men are treated as men. This realization of the just society is *ipso facto* an elevation of man to the company with God . . . is itself the meaning of life. To the extent of saying that the meaning of the real consists in the function of ethics, this is to say the universe is sacred. But it is in an ethical sense that it is sacred. Ethics is an optical instrument to the divine. . . . The Divine can only manifest itself in relation to one's neighbor. For the Jew, incarnation is neither possible nor necessary. (*DL* 187)

Levinas does not reject philosophy for Judaism or vice versa. In his view, the modern Western Jew must approach Judaism with all the resources of Western tradition—judge and question Judaism: "resay it in the language of the university: philosophy and philology" (*DL* 75). Yet after assimilation and the collapse of European culture in the Holocaust, this philosophy and Western culture, too, must be brought to judgment and trial.

Here might be another way of answering Derrida's question of why Levinas continues to use philosophical language: Levinas is a Jew, a Jew and a Greek who lives both interpretations at once; he prophetically calls philosophy to Judaism and Judaism to philosophy. And he can do so because his call comes ultimately from the primary and irreducible interhuman relation to the other that in his view founds them both. Yet on another level, Judaism is the "other" of philosophy, and philosophy is the "other" of Judaism; the call is a call of one form of reason to "an other." He interrogates and redefines both the sacred and the secular. Like Rosenzweig, he writes neither philosophy nor theology in their traditional senses; nor is he a Greek or Jew in any simple or familiar way. Like Derrida, his work is an uncategorizable hybrid, a sometimes dissonant doubling.

In fact, he describes the interhuman relationship, the relation to the other, with a figure of doubleness: "interface." "The interhuman is thus an interface: a double axis where what is 'of the world' qua *phenomenological intelligibility* is juxtaposed with what is not 'of the world' qua *ethical responsibility*. It is in this ethical perspective that God must be thought and not in the ontological perspective. . . . as the God of alterity" (Kearney, "Dialogue" 20). Biblical thought has

> influenced my ethical reading of the interhuman, whereas Greek thought has largely determined its philosophical expression in language. . . . philosophy can be at once both Greek and non-Greek in its inspiration. These two different sources of inspiration coexist as two different tendencies in modern philosophy, and it is my own personal task to identify this dual origin of meaning—*der Ursprung der Sinnhaften*—in the interhuman relationship. (21)

The reasons for this double reading and double attachment are complex, and Levinas's thought is unique in many ways, but in its stress on the rational and ethical character of Judaism, it belongs to a main current in modern Jewish philosophy, preeminently expressed by the great neo-Kantian Hermann Cohen. As Nathan Rotenstreich notes, ethics could remain a realm unchallenged by Kant's critique, and also,

> the ethical interpretation of Judaism makes possible a further, more radical interpretation, that the ethical teaching of Judaism may be meaningful and binding apart from religious attachment. Thus the ethical interpretation can be placed historically on the borderline of the religious attitude and the secular transformation of Judaism. (*Philosophy* 3–4)

THE WITNESS AND THE HOLOCAUST

Like Hermann Cohen, Levinas took the legacy of Kant quite seriously, but Levinas also had to contend with other new voices in German and French philosophy. His "translation into Greek" used the language of contemporary phenomenology, of Heidegger and Husserl. Moreover, unlike Cohen, who died in 1918, and Rosenzweig, who finally succumbed to his illness in 1929, Levinas witnessed the rise of Nazism and the collapse of German philosophy and culture in World War II. Cohen had thought that the prophetic message of Judaism was harmonious with the spirit of modern German culture; the modern nation-state would be a step forward on the path toward a larger world federation, an ultimate universalism and unity of all peoples. From Cohen's perspective, the exile of the Jews and their lack of a state were necessary to fulfill their messianic mission as a "light to the nations." They were the example of a people detached from local community and land, who thus signaled and embodied that messianic future.

Needless to say, the Holocaust brought those assumptions into question. How could German culture now be compatible with prophetic Judaism, and how could the lack of a state be a blessing to the Jews when it was precisely that German culture and that stateless vulnerability of the Jews which wrought their destruction? World War II, during which Levinas was held in a detention camp and lost much of his family in Russia, forced a new turn in his thought. In *Existence and Existents,* a book he worked on while in captivity and published right after the war, he wrote of his "profound need to leave the climate of that [Heidegger's] philosophy" (19). He not only turned the language of phenomenology back upon itself in philosophical critique, but he also began to translate it into "Hebrew," to recall to it what it had forgotten or repressed. Yet even in this project there remains a strong vision of some "compatibility" or a relation between Greek and Hebrew—not, however, as a reciprocal brotherhood but as ethical order and demand. We have seen in previous chapters how Levinas redefines the very notions of "universal" and "reason" to mean precisely obligation to the other.

But the language he uses in his philosophical works becomes unusually charged. The bearing witness of the accusative "here I am" is a witness *before* any content as "thematized said" or "truth of representation": "It is the meaning of language, before language scatters into words . . . and dissimulating in the said the openness of the saying exposed like a bleeding wound" (*OTB* 151). The "bearing witness of itself to the other" (119) is the "sign bearing witness of the giving of signs" an ultimate exposure as the condition for all communication. To put it even more strongly, "signification is witness or martyrdom. It is intelligibility before the light" (77–78). The imagery of wounding describes the way obsession by the other puts the self in question as a radical denuding and shattering of egoism, so that the self is now "like a stranger, hunted down even in one's home, contested in one's identity . . . it is always to empty oneself anew of oneself . . . like in a hemophiliac's hemorrhage" (92). I cannot help but hear in the voice behind this voice, and in these images of bleeding wounds, the "witness" of the Holocaust survivor, even though that event is never explicitly evoked. Levinas describes the self as "shattered, hunted, persecuted, hemorrhaging," and the image of the Jew as exile, homeless, hunted, bleeding hovers behind these descriptions—like a saying behind the said, leaving only its traces.

One could say that in Levinas, the witness of the Holocaust now enters into the "reason" of philosophy. I would also argue that the "force" of Levinas's argument has its source in the appeal of Levinas's own "face,"

Levinas in the first person as well as Levinas the philosopher; it is Levinas's own "here I am" not only as witness of the horror and catastrophe of this century, but as his prophetic appeal and imperative to the reader. At the same time, this rhetoric of witness is indirect, for he does not explicitly invoke either his personal experiences or specific historical events within his philosophical work. The most profound signification of these events for him is not their specificity for any one nation or group. In the preface to *Existence and Existents,* for example, he writes: "These studies begun before the war were continued and written down for the most part in captivity. The stalag is evoked here not as a guarantee of profundity nor a claim to indulgence, but as an explanation for the absence of any consideration of those philosophical works published with so much impact, between 1940 and 1945." The latter alludes especially to Sartre's *Being and Nothingness,* which was published in 1943.

This obliqueness may also be an inevitable part of the language of the survivor, one who comes from the "other" side indeed—who must bring the indescribable to description, who tries to say the unsayable, who speaks for the impossible and says the unthinkable by speaking his own vulnerability and exposure. In Levinas's sense, witness is not "confession," a witness *of the self,* but a testimony *for the other.* And the Holocaust is also that extraordinary event that one is forced to witness, bear, and "say," even though any "thematization or representation" of it is torturous and finally impossible. The Holocaust is almost a kind of "negative" of Levinas's idea of the glory of the infinite—the obverse side, the negative excess brought about precisely by the assertion of the same over the other.

So Levinas will "not make a graven image" or icon of these wounds as some kind of holy stigmata upon which we should fixate in horror. The task instead is to move back from these images and themes—from the said—to the saying, and that is the very task of philosophy as Levinas has defined it. In that move, these traumas become the foundation and guarantor of language and ethics; the negative becomes positive in the for-the-other opened up by these wounds. "Hebrew" reminds, calls to, founds "Greek" not by losing its specificity or being sublated (to use the Hegelian term) into the "universality" of Greek reason, but by being witness to the ethical relation to the other, in a prophetic call to all human beings.

Of course, the themes of exile, homelessness, emptiness are quite familiar in the modern literature of alienation. But alienation can be thought only in terms of "identity," and Levinas's point is precisely not to let us rest in identity, even in "identity betrayed," which would be only another form of gazing narcissistically at our own wounds rather than being opened to and for another in a responsibility in which the I is unique and irreplaceable: "I exist through the other and for the other, but without this being alienation: I am inspired. This inspiration is the psyche" (*OTB* 114).

It is almost "as if" (to use a favored Levinasian locution) this notion of signification as martyrdom is a kind of secular or philosophical equivalent of the Jewish notion of *kiddush ha-shem*—the "sanctification of the name of God" that Jewish tradition ascribes to the death of a Jew murdered for his or her faith. As if Levinas is attempting to sanctify and redeem the deaths of those murdered in the Holocaust, that event which above all expressed the hatred and intolerance for the other. Or as if he is making it impossible for the persecutors to escape responsibility, to forget, deny their involvement.[3] As if he is making the victimizer recognize and inhabit the skin of the victims, and more, for he expands his notion of substitution to an extreme responsibility that makes even "the persecuted one liable to answer for the persecutor" (*OTB* 111). As if the very outrage of persecution itself inverted into a grounds of solidarity as expiation rather than violence.

One can see why this becomes an almost "unsayable" position. It also has strong Christian echoes and moves beyond Jewish tradition. Andrius Valevicius quite rightly points out in these Dostoevskian and Tolstoyan themes of suffering for the other Levinas's Russian background and the connection of even his most mature philosophy to Slavic as well as Jewish thought (*From the Other* 146–55). In classical Jewish law, however, one is *not* supposed to actively seek martyrdom; the only cases in which one must allow oneself to be killed are if one is ordered upon penalty of death to commit adultery, idolatry, or murder. In these cases, one is required to choose death rather than commit one of those three sins. In other cases, such as for self-defense, the Talmud says, "If one arises to kill you, arise and kill him first." One does not always give one's life for the other.

There is another similar famous talmudic discussion about the meaning of the verse Leviticus 25:36, which is a directive not to take interest when one lends money to sustain "your brother who has become poor" but to "fear your God; that thy brother may live with you." What, ask the rabbis, is the meaning of "that thy brother may live with you"?

> That is what Ben-Patura expounded: Two men are journeying through the desert, and one of them has a single pitcher of water. If one of them drinks it, he (alone) will get back to civilization. But if both of them drink it, both of them will die. Ben Patura taught that they should both drink and die, as it said "That your brother may live with you." Said Rabbi Akiba to him: "That thy brother may *live with you.*" Your own life comes before the life of your fellow-man. (*Sifra, Behar* 5:3; cf. *B. Metzia* 62a)[4]

This is the same R. Akiba who also propounded that the fundamental principle of the Torah was "You shall love your neighbor as yourself."

But as Robert Gibbs writes, Levinas's work would also require a Christian thinker to recast Christology, for

> is not the other in the me, the other person, and not the absolute You of God? . . . Is not the truth of incarnation that we are incarnate, vulnerable in our naked skin? That we are persecuted and so expiation for others, and not that

some divinity is expiation for us? I make expiation and suffer for him: not "You or even He make expiation for me." . . . but then perhaps we would no longer need to worry whether it was Jewish or Christian. ("Substitution" 14)

Or perhaps we could say it is a "translation" of Jewish wisdom into "Christian," which is another form of "Greek." But that makes for an unusual and unstable hybrid, certainly not any "orthodox theology."

THE HOLOCAUST: TO LOVE THE TORAH MORE THAN GOD

One essay in which Levinas does write directly and poignantly about the Holocaust and the difference between the Jewish and Christian attitudes toward suffering is "To Love the Torah More Than God" in *Difficile liberté*. This title is taken from a midrash (Lam Rab. Intro. ch. 2; also Yer. Hagigah 1:7) which attributes to God the words *Halevai oti azavu v'et Torati shamaru*—"Would that you forsake me, but keep my Torah." Levinas uses this midrash to comment on a fictional story that had been published anonymously in an Israeli journal and translated in a Parisian Zionist periodical: "Yossel ben Yossel Rakover of Tarnopol Speaks to God." The story is the account of a Jew who has lost his family, endured the horrors of the Warsaw ghetto, and writes during its final hours of resistance. Writes Levinas, "Certainly it is literary fiction, but fiction where the life of each of us who has survived recognizes itself with dizzying clarity."[5]

> We are not going to recount all of it, even though the world has learned nothing and forgotten everything. We refuse to make an exhibition of the Passion of Passions or to extract any petty vanity as the author or producer of these inhumanities. They echo inextinguishably throughout eternities. Let us listen only to the thought which is articulated in them. ("To Love the Torah" 217)

In the darkness where God seems to have withdrawn from the world and hidden his face, where Yossel is alone, "it is to feel all the responsibilities of God on his shoulders," and precisely "there is the moment of atheism necessary for a true monotheism." Such an "adult God manifests himself through the emptiness of a childish heaven" (218). At this moment, the just person is completely vulnerable, unprotected by any institution and without external recourse or even the assurance of God's presence. This very "vulnerability," as in Levinas's philosophical writings, itself becomes the foundation of the self. In such complete vulnerability and aloneness, "the individual can triumph only in his own conscience—that is—necessarily, in suffering." This is not suffering as a mystic expiation of sin but a specifically Jewish mode: "The position of victims in a world in chaos, that is, a world where goodness does not triumph, is suffering" (218).

The phrase "a world where goodness does not triumph" is all the more poignant in the text of a thinker who so earnestly solicits the "good being" in his philosophical writings—who tries to define subjectivity as a being given over to the other, as goodness. Could it have been the personal witness during the war of that impenetrably dark and vicious world where goodness did not triumph that impelled him to seek the "Good beyond being," to try to find an "elsewhere" that might judge and redeem that world? Or at least give some meaning to the deaths of those murdered, some kind of *kiddush ha-shem*?

This "elsewhere" or "outside" for both Jew and philosopher becomes the very responsibility for the good that one must take upon oneself, to which one is bound without any choice. "Suffering reveals a God who, in renouncing all beneficial manifestations, thus appeals to the full maturity of an entirely responsible man." The God who conceals his face (a Being behind beings) is not that "outside" to which one can have recourse. But the distant God who "abandons the just to their justice without triumph . . . comes from within" in an intense intimacy "which coincides, for the conscience with the pride of being Jewish, concretely, historically, and yet incomprehensibly. . . . The suffering of the just for a justice without triumph is lived as Judaism. Israel, historical and physical, becomes again the religious category" (218).

The important point here is that the Jew for Levinas is no abstract allegory, or a symbol for the "other" or for "otherness" in general. Rather, as in Rosenzweig's philosophy, physical, historical Israel itself in all its lived experience is a "category"—an independent structure of understanding reality. In Levinas's view, one of the key accomplishments of Rosenzweig's *Star* was that it no longer defined Judaism as a teaching whose propositions may be true or false; instead, it maintains that *"Jewish existence itself is an essential event of being; Jewish existence is a category of being"* [italics his] ("Entre" 122). Levinas's refusal to view the Jew as an allegory, trope, metaphor, or figure depends on this notion of Jewish existence as a "category of being," and not just a matter of faith, emotion, or dogma. As such, Jewish existence and Jewish texts, in all their corporeality and history, can and must be understood "philosophically." And this philosophical approach does not negate or surmount but affirms what is "particular" about Judaism. Rosenzweig helps Levinas in Levinas's project of finding a non-Hegelian "concrete universal" and a modus vivendi of Jew and Greek. As category, Israel is affirmed in all its particularity as a people of flesh, a people in history whose very experience and witness of that history becomes the judgment on that history. This category constitutes an "outside" that is also an "inside," immediate and accessible.

In Levinas's analysis of the story of Yossel Rakover, the divine is preserved insofar as the Jewish people carry forth the moral principles of Torah; their persecution itself testifies to their opposition to the crassness and cruelty of a world given over to its basest instincts. Writes Yossel in the story: "Now I know that you are my God, because You would not know how to be the God of those whose acts are militantly the most horrible expression of an absence of God." This image of Judaism alternately engaging and disengaging from the world, of the Jew as living in history and beyond history, parallels Levinas's idea of the oscillation of saying/said in the philosophical works, and of course again echoes Rosenzweig. What makes possible that alternation is a lapse, a diachrony; or, as he writes elsewhere, "Judaism is a noncoincidence with its time, in the coincidence: in the radical sense of the term, an *anachronism*" (*DL* 237). Anachronism would be an aspect of the judgment of history, or its messianic or ethical reversal. Judaism for Levinas is simultaneously young, attentive to change, and old, having endured all, all the while simultaneously engaging/disengaging with history defined as the war of impersonal power and force of the unredeemed world.

Many of the seemingly strange and willful anachronisms in midrashic or rabbinic interpretation could be fruitfully understood via this Levinasian insight. Anachronism, instead of being viewed as the quaint naive piety of the rabbis' "withdrawing" into a world of texts to evade the chaos and violence of history, would instead be the possibility of redemptive action *in* history. And this position has everything to do with the way the Bible is interpreted. Or as Levinas writes, "For us, the world of the Bible is not a world of figures, but of faces. They are entirely there and in relation with us." Whereas the "figurative" reading of the Bible subsumes the lives and actions of its characters to another world, the "face" marks the passing of transcendence as the ethical call to responsibility, not to withdrawal from action. The Bible demands not "interior meditation but action—in the very impurity of the world," in history (*DL* 170).

This action, however, is not the self-reflexive "passion" of suffering in and for itself; action means breaking out of interiority and self-reflexive consciousness. So for Levinas, the intimacy and immanence of God comes to the Jew not as "a sentimental communion in love of an incarnate God, but a relation between spirits, through the intermediary of a teaching, the Torah. It is precisely a discourse, *not* embodied in God, that assures us of a living God among us" ("To Love the Torah" 219). This discourse is the Torah, of which Yossel says, citing the midrash of the essay's title, "I love Him, but I love His Torah even more . . . and even if I were disappointed by him and downtrodden, I would nonetheless observe the precepts of the Torah."

Not suffering as irrational, or "fear and trembling" before the sacred, or blind faith connects humanity and God: "the spiritual does not present itself as a tenable substance but, rather, through its absence; God is made real, not through incarnation, but rather, through the Law" (219). Just as Torah or "teaching" is the discourse which mediates between humanity and God—not any incarnation—similarly, in the philosophical works the other is described as the first "teaching," the call to responsibility.

God conceals himself "in order to demand of man—superhumanly—

everything," and that, in turn, is the great gift to and dignity of the human, that she or he "is capable of responding, capable of grappling with his God, in the role of creditor and not always a debtor" (219). This creditor retains faith in the debtor but will not let the debtor evade his debts. Such would be an adult faith, and a love of humanity for God despite what God does. It is consequently a difficult faith, a "difficult freedom," and a dangerous stance. For "religious life" also does require some unveiling of God, and ultimately "it is necessary that justice and power be rejoined"—earthly institutions must guarantee this: "But only the man who has recognized God obscured can demand this unveiling," and in the tension of this relation, a mode of equality is established between humanity and God, "a full and austere humanism, bound to a burdensome adoration." And so "to love the Torah more than God: it is precisely this which means access to a personal God against whom one may revolt—for whom one can die" (220).

Like the biblical book of Job, this essay is a kind of affirmation through accusation, a piety on the border of blasphemy, a trial of God with Israel as accuser, prosecutor, and witness. An Israel which, in the absence and delay of judgment, will love the Torah more than God and retain the ethical imperative in a world given over to immorality.[6] As in his philosophical works, Levinas tries to convert the absence of God or justice into ethical positivity. The tension between this absence and the ethics it engenders is a key to the "utopian or messianic" structure of Levinas's thought. The judgment of history and responsible action within history necessitate the refusal to be immersed in history's implacable and cruel currents. The moment of self-conscious critique by itself is not enough to combat history's cruelties; one must also "keep a foot in the Eternal." The contemporary crisis of Judaism, in Levinas's view, is the potential loss of this "liberty to judge history in place of letting oneself be judged by it" (*DL* 249). This liberty comes only from a distance, an interval, a patience, in the midst of the necessary engagement.

Like Rosenzweig, Levinas finds this disengagement amid engagement, this ability to judge history, effected not through any dogma about the End of Days but through the concrete forms of Jewish life. Jewish law and the Jewish prescription for study as a mode of life, the study of the Torah, are a "permanent reopening, renewal of the content of revelation where all situations that traverse the human adventure are judged." And that for Levinas is the essence of revelation. The "necessary categories" to apprehend all historical and future phenomena "are already at the disposition of monotheism. It is the eternal anteriority of wisdom over science and history" (*DL* 238), a patient wisdom which also detects false prophecy and false and premature messianism.

AMBIGUOUS REVELATION AS ETHICAL POSITIVITY

In Levinas's philosophical writings, which are addressed to a nontheological and nonsectarian audience, the concrete forms of Jewish life and law are not mentioned. Here, too, the judgment of history, the perspective of eschatology, and the call to responsibility are derived not from any dogma but from a kind of "witness." The "accusative," the very voice of the "here I am" in responsibility for the other, is the positive way infinity "passes" the finite. It is not that the witness witnesses to some "evidence" or representation of the infinite. "One is tempted to call this plot religious," Levinas writes, but "it is not stated in terms of certainty or uncertainty, and does not rest on any positive theology" (*OTB* 147). As the sincerity of the for-the-other, "the Infinite then has glory only through subjectivity, in the human adventure of the approach of the other, through the substitution for the other, by the expiation for the other" (148).

The "said" does not testify to some dogmatic content of language. As we have seen repeatedly, one of Levinas's key tenets is that language is not merely instrumental or cognitive, but coordinates me with another to whom I speak and signifies from the face of the other as a call to responsibility. "Saying" coincides with what he calls the *prophetic dignity of language,* "inspiration" as the "more in the less." Inspiration would be the very fact that language can say more than it says. At the hour of its ethical truth, language is prophecy, not prophecy as some type of individual genius or frenzied possession but an "ability of human speech in overflowing the first intentions which bear it"—the very spirituality of the spirit (*ADV* 141). Inspiration as this "otherness" or other sense (the "tearing of the Same by the Other" [138, n. 11]) is also the ethical beyond of conscience; in "theological terms," it would be called "revelation."

The critical point here is that for Levinas (as for Rosenzweig), saying as "revelation" is *without* any "organized content." Its content is the "meaning of meaning" as the awakening of the listener to the proximity of the other. Levinas is trying to formulate a way in which the exteriority of the In-finite becomes in-ward, but not in any secret or psychological sense. He defines the "here I am" as the "voice" of saying "which orders me by my own voice," where the "command is stated by the mouth of him it commands" (*OTB* 147). In other words, the voice which says "here I am" itself produces *by this very saying* the "infinition of the Infinite," or its "glory"; that is how the Infinite "passes" the finite. And as in *Totality and Infinity* Levinas is trying here to maintain a *relation* between what is separated and disjunctive, the subject and other, the finite and Infinite, without either fusing or entirely severing the terms. This is a kind of philosophical equivalent to (or "translation" of) his notion of monotheism as requiring a prior atheism, an absolute separation of God and humanity to the point of God's withdrawing his "presence"—to the point that the just suffer in history for a justice "without triumph."

As in Rosenzweig, the relation that bridges self and other, or finite and infinite, cannot be defined by the correlations of ontology or the synchronies of signifier/signified, all of which ultimately efface the other. That is why he uses terms such as *passes,* or *passes itself* [*se passer*], and *trace.* In other words, "transcendence" does not "appear" in a vision; nor is it heard in a literal revelation. "Saying" as exposure to the other is itself inspiration and the passing or "production" of transcendence. Although it is a relation to the other, it is not a voice coming from a "you" as a dialogue partner; that is why Levinas calls the infinite illeity, the "third person." Not a "you" but a "he"—"in" a personal relation but also "withdrawn" from that relation.

This "third way" of the passing and production of transcendence sets up a different relation between finite and infinite, inside and outside, autonomy and heteronomy—outside an either/or logic. Levinas is also attempting here to reconcile heteronomy and autonomy, and perhaps Jew and Greek. The sign given over to the other as witness and the acceptance of responsibility constitute an "obedience prior to hearing any command," prior to representation, the said, consciousness, and so forth. "The possibility of finding, anachronously, the order in the obedience itself, and of receiving the order out of oneself, this reverting of heteronomy into autonomy, is the very way the Infinite passes itself" (*OTB* 148).

In this sense, the order to the neighbor is found "in my response itself," a nonphenomenal order which cannot dominate but which is heard in my own saying. "Authority is not somewhere, where a look could go see it, like an idol, or assume it like a logos." Outside of all intuition and symbolism, "it is the pure trace of a 'wandering cause,' inscribed in me" (150). As the realm of saying, as signification, this movement is diachronic and ambiguous, anarchic and anachronistic; but it is also thus the possibility of inspiration, "of being the author of what had been breathed in unbeknownst to me. . . . In the responsibility for the other we are at the heart of the ambiguity of inspiration" (148–49).

So there can be no "proof" about what this ambiguity ultimately signifies, no way to "demonstrate" logically that ambiguity is the trace of the glory of the infinite. There can be no logical certainty or necessity that this alterity is transcendence instead of nihilism, or the call of the Good as opposed to an anonymous play of forces. Lyotard or Derrida's positions are just as possible here: the cunning play of strategic moves in the game, a dry laughter. Is the comedy divine, diabolic, or cruelly indifferent? Is it Benjamin's deceptive chess game with the hunchback theology manipulating the puppet of materialism? Or is it perhaps that seemingly cruel wager that opens the Book of Job where the just suffer because of an arbitrary game played between God and Satan? In Levinas's schema, transcendence "shows" itself only by interrupting itself: "Its voice has to be silent as soon as one listens for its message. It is necessary that its pretension be exposed to derision and refutation, to the point of suspecting in the 'here I am' that attests to it a cry or slip of a sick subjectivity. But of a subjectivity responsible for the other!" (*OTB* 152).

The interruption, the exposure to questioning, the derision, and refutation become a "contestation of the Infinite," and this contestation makes "everything incumbent on me," assures me of no assistance in my responsibility. There are, of course, echoes here of postwar existentialist philosophy. In a figure such as Sartre, this ultimate responsibility comes from God's death; I am "condemned to freedom," which is, however, a freedom "for myself [*pour soi*]" always entangled in a sadomasochistic struggle with the other who looks at and contests me. In Levinas, by contrast, the death of the God of ontology results in responsibility for-the-other, whose glance and face draws me out of myself and into the Good beyond being. This is "the enigma of a God speaking in man and of man not counting on any god," "the very pivot of revelation, of its blinking light" (154). The witness of the "here I am" culminates as

> "here I am in the name of God" without referring myself directly to his presence. "Here I am," just that! The word God is still absent from the phrase in which God is for the first time involved in words. It does not at all state "I believe in God." To bear witness to God is precisely not to state this extraordinary word, as though glory would be lodged in a theme or converted into being's essence. As a sign given to the other of this very signification, the "here I am" signifies me in the name of God, at the service of men that look at me, without having anything to identify myself with anything but the sound of my own voice or the figure of my gesture—the saying itself. (149)

These words echo the well-known prohibition in Jewish tradition against pronouncing the holiest of the names of God—except on the holiest day of the year, Yom Kippur, by the High Priest in the ancient Temple in the inner precinct of the Holy of Holies. In another important essay, "The Name of God According to Some Talmudic Texts," Levinas analyzes the "Name of God" in the context of divine imperative and command instead of theosophy; this analysis makes an interesting contrast to Scholem and Benjamin's reflections on the linguistics of naming. Levinas notes that the mere pronunciation of the names of God in prayer or reading does not constitute for Judaism intimacy with God, nor does the *knowledge* which would seek the essence behind these names (*ADV* 144). Over and above speculation on "the *meaning* of the Name of God is a completely other relation with the One who is named" (145).

As in his philosophical works, Levinas is stressing that there is a *relation* prior to knowing, and that relation as response to command, as a practice and obligation, is the very condition of knowing. In theological terms, this relation to God is an adherence or prior allegiance and the greatest *proximity to* God. These comments coincidentally parallel Idel's critique of Scholem's overemphasis on kabbalistic theosophical speculation and neglect of kabbalistic practice as a relation to divine command and search for union with God. Levinas observes that for the Talmud, all reading, writing, and studying of the Name of God is done as a result of *mitzvah,* a command from the text itself "in the Name of God." Reflection as *knowing* for the Talmud is inseparable from reflection on *practice:* "To reflect on God by reflecting on his commandments is certainly an intellectual act of an order other than philosophical thematization of God," but it is neverthe-less related to philosophy (145).

In the talmudic commentaries, Levinas notes that the rabbis often refer to God as simply *Ha-Shem,* which translates as "The Name." "The Name" itself is the generic name, of which the other names are particulars. Nor does the Talmud use the word *God* as we do in English, or as the Germans use *Gott;* instead it uses the idiom "The Holy One Blessed Be He" *(ha kodesh baruch-hu),* thus referring to God by the attribute of holiness. Holi-ness indicates separation; the term *Name–Ha-shem*—then is quite remark-able: it is a "mode of being or an *au-delà,* a beyond being rather than quiddity." Similarly, all the other names used for God in the Talmud such as "Master of the Universe" or "Father in Heaven" are above all "terms which express relations and not essence" (ADV 148). Levinas argues that in the Kabbalah, by contrast, names constitute an objective sphere of the manifestation of an inaccessible, nonthematizable God, a world of names and letters which offer their own dimension and order to thought, whereas "in the Talmud, the names of God acquire a sense in relation to the situa-tions of the one who invokes them" (150, n. 6).

He illustrates his point with a remarkable example where effacing the tetragrammaton, the holiest Name of God (normally a forbidden act), be-comes an *obligation* as part of a religious ritual. The situation is that of the *sotah,* the woman suspected of adultery (Num. 5:11–29). As part of her biblically prescribed ritual of interrogation, the priest is to write the tetra-grammaton, this holiest Name of God, and efface it in the "bitter waters" which she must then drink. The ritual is part of a test to prove either her guilt or innocence. If she is innocent, she is reconciled with her husband and blessed. Comments Levinas, the Talmud here affirms a remarkable new idea: "the effacement of the Name is the reconciliation of humans"; and this is a paradigmatic affirmation. In characteristic style, he then frames his next assertion in the form of a question and asks, isn't "the transcendence of the Name of God in relation to every thematization the effacement, and isn't this effacement the very command which obliges me in relation to the other man?" (*ADV* 153).

INSPIRATION, REVELATION, AND EXEGESIS

But what further is the relation of this "otherwise than being" to the Jew-ish idea of "revelation"? And what is the relation of this "beyond" to secular literature and its interpretation? In fact, Levinas chooses the French word for beyond, *au-delà,* for the title of his 1982 collection of Jewish writings, *L'au-delà du verset,* "The Beyond of the Verse." Through-out these essays, the "beyond" of the verse in Jewish hermeneutics intersects with the *au-delà* of the "beyond/other than" being in the philo-sophical works.

For Levinas as for Rosenzweig, "the very fact itself—metaphysical—

called Revelation . . . is also the first and primary revealed content of all revelation" (*ADV* 158). The question of revelation is not any set of apologetics or polemics about the contents of the various revealed religions, but the core issue is the same as in Levinas's philosophical writings—how to rupture totality but retain reason, another reason which is practical reason as ethics and is the very beginning of philosophy and at the same time the primordial prescriptive or commanding character of revelation (even of its narrative aspects). The negation of Hegel which permeates so much of Rosenzweig and Levinas's writing helps account for this definition of revelation as the irruption of the Other into the Same, or as "the possibility of rupture, of an opening in the closed order of totality, of the world, or of the self-sufficiency of its correlative reason; a rupture which would be owed to a movement coming from the outside, but a rupture which, paradoxically, would not alienate this rational self-sufficiency" (176). Revelation is "not a question of deducing the concrete contents of the Bible, Moses, and the prophets. It is a question of formulating the possibility of a heteronomy excluding enslavement, a rational ear, an obedience which doesn't alienate the one who listens, and of recognizing in the ethical model of the Bible the transcendence of understanding . . . opening an irreducible transcendence" (177). He is once more Judaizing philosophy and philosophizing Judaism. Levinas's understanding of this *prescriptive aspect* of language ought to be a critical addition to literary study of the Bible and rabbinic texts. Current literary studies of this material tend to separate the "legal" and prescriptive portions from the so-called nonlegal narratives, and most historicist, formalist, or poststructuralist theories often neglect the imperative and ethical senses of language when applied to classical Jewish texts. As Levinas insists, the word of God is commandment as much as narration, and this imperative is the very "beginning of language" (174). To readapt the British speech-act theorist J. L. Austin's terms, language is "performative," but it is performative in a prescriptive or a prophetic manner. Or prescriptive *as* prophetic.

Levinas's philosophical works express the idea that language as such is prophetic because it can "contain more than it contains," can bear meanings "other" than those intended in its use as instrument for transmitting thoughts or information. In his Jewish writings, this idea is further extended: there is an inherent "prophetic dignity of language, always capable of meaning more than it says . . . where already the human word is Scripture" (*ADV* 7). Such is also his interpretation of the line in Deuteronomy 4:15 reminding the Jews that "you saw no shape when the Lord your God spoke to you at Horeb out of the fire." The rabbis interpreted this verse to mean that there was no mediation, that all the Israelites present at the foot of Sinai were "prophets." Levinas comments that this idea "suggests that in principle the human spirit such as it is opens to inspiration, that the human as such is possibly prophetic . . . isn't subjectivity, by its possibility of hearing, that is to say obeying, the very rupture of immanence?" (174).

In a famous talmudic statement, R. Ishmael claims that "the Torah speaks in the language of humanity." Comments Levinas, on one level this means that one need not look for metaphysical meanings behind all the terms of biblical discourse; but the deeper concept is that "the Word of God can be held in the language which created beings use among themselves"—which is a "marvelous contraction of the Infinite in the Finite" (7). This "more inhabiting the less" is also a surplus or excess that makes Scripture enigmatic and exegesis necessary and inexhaustible.

What is "prophetic," "inspired," "more" is possible within language because language is not a self-enclosed, autonomous entity but the very site of alterity, of the interhuman relation, of sociality. Levinasian philosophical "transcendence," as we have seen again and again, is no Platonic ideality but the Other passing through the human finite other. Similarly, human language would already have "Scripture" within it *before* the actual writing down of any holy texts on material parchment, an idea which parallels the "language prior to language" as the relation of saying and said of Levinas's philosophical works. This is a "literature before the letter," the inspired essence of language which itself "institutes and commands an 'ontological' order" (8). "Writing before the Letter" is also the title Derrida gave to the first part of his *Grammatology* in order to enable a move beyond the "book" and the Western conceptuality of linguistic meaning. But for Levinas, following Rosenzweig, a move beyond the book, as the move toward the other, is "religion." And, Levinas argues, this "religious" relation of humanity to the book has not really been thought through, but it constitutes a modality or philosophical category as essential and irreducible as "language itself" or "thought" or "technological activity." The fact that meaning comes to us precisely through the book, even in secular literature, "attests its biblical essence" (137). In this sense, the interpretation of national and secular literary texts would be affirmed by and in some way always directed toward this "biblical inspiration."

All this implies that the activity of exegesis itself, of *any* reading "beyond the verse," comes from an inherent spirituality in all language; that in *all* language the Word of God is heard; and in all language, though muffled, the prophetic call resounds. At the end of his essay on the linguistic theory of the Kabbalah, Scholem had ascribed only to the poets the ability to hear these echoes of the divine word and implied that their prescriptive character as command has become undecipherable. Like Scholem and Benjamin, Levinas is again searching for that aspect of language beyond its use as instrument, finding there an otherness which is marked by and marks the beyond. But this "beyond" of language as the ethical relation to the other means that such "writing is always prescriptive and ethics, word of God which commands me and dedicates me to the other, holy writing before being sacred text" (9). His idea also parallels or perhaps "translates" the rabbinic description of the nature of the Torah which "preexisted" the creation of world; prior to its physical embodiment in parchment and ink, the Torah was written, say the rabbis, with letters of "white fire on black fire."

The nature of this "preexistent" Torah has been subject to much speculation in the kabbalistic tradition. One kabbalist wrote, "The form of the written Torah is that of the colors of white fire, and the form of the oral Torah [the rabbinic interpretations] has the colored forms of black fire." Moshe Idel notes that Scholem interpreted this statement to mean that the real "written Torah" is the white background to the black letters; the black letters paradoxically form the "oral Torah," thus inverting our usual sense of the relation of text and interpretation, and lending a metaphysical primacy to the emptiness of the blank spaces as in Mallarmé's poetry (Idel, "Infinities of Torah" 145). In Levinas, this empty space or beyond is precisely not poetic but ethical command as saying.

Levinas wants to claim that "literature before the letter" (like "saying") is not containable in the traditional orders of history, ideality, or interiority but is the very "religious essence of language, the place where prophecy would make the Holy Scriptures surge forth, but that all literature awaits or commemorates, celebrates or profanes." In other words, this prophetic saying makes possible both the Book and the books. These books with a small *b*—works such as Shakespeare, Molière, Dante, Cervantes, Goethe, Pushkin—would thus play "an eminent role in the very anthropology of the human" beyond their significance as cultural artifacts or emblems of national literatures (*ADV* 8). Insofar as they signify "beyond" their obvious sense and invite exegesis—no matter how tortured or complex—they partake of "spiritual life."

As in Levinas's philosophical work, inspiration would signify to our understanding not as any "thematized" concrete content but as ethics, the one-for-the-other. Ethics would be the resonance of this other voice as the "beyond" and the "message of the message" as the awakening of the listener to the face and proximity of the other. In "theological" terms, this opening would be called "revelation"; it is a disturbance of being, a beyond, an *au-delà*. The inspiration or "transcendent" sense of the Bible itself in its status as the "Book of Books" would come precisely from the way it embodies this sense of the ethical, and the way its message ceaselessly breaks forth (*ADV* 138); "Inspiration . . . is the exercise of reason itself" of an already prophetic logos (141).

The critical result of this position is that in both "sacred" and "secular" scripture the *prophetic* moment is inextricably tied to the *exegetical* moment; for they both elicit the "beyond" or otherwise than being. The book as "said" retains the trace and call of saying. So if inspiration is one pole of the irruption of the other into being, or the "said," or language or text, exegesis is its counterpart. Exegesis opens the text to the other voice; in Levinasian terms it is also the "ethical" *self-exposure* of the text, analogous to the way subjectivity is defined in the philosophical works as traumatized, broken up, vulnerable, exposed, and opened to the other.

This idea has interesting connections to current debates in literary theory about what can be said to be "inside" or "outside" the "text itself." Levinas's model of exegesis as the self-exposure of the text (of the text-in-relation to the other) would negate the idea of the text as "enclosed container where meaning is fully inside" or as some blank slate upon which the reader arbitrarily projects her or his own willful meanings, or as a cultural artifact which essentially reflects the contest of ideologies. Levinas's idea of interpretation rests on his notion of language as *already* opened to the other, an idea parallel to the idea of subjectivity as vulnerability and exposure in his philosophical works. The "said" or book retains an "other voice, a second sonority" in the verses and letters and is the very modality which opens and "exposes itself to exegesis and solicits it, and where meaning, immobilized in the characters, already tears the texture which conceals and encloses it" (*ADV* 136–37). Exegesis is thus the very locus, the place where the text takes on its "transcendent" or inspired sense, just as the human other is the site where the other than being passes. And such exegetical reading of the Bible then becomes "the original figure of the beyond liberated from the mythology of the afterworld." In this sense, the very ideas of transcendence and God come to us from the interpretation of Scripture, which for a modern is not a difficult or subversive idea (141).

Levinas's strong critique of idealism means a constant refusal to define these terms (*revelation, subjectivity, transcendence,* etc.) as abstract conceptions of mind. As in Rosenzweig, they become *relational* terms, each *bound* to each. Any theory which proposes to found itself on something other than "being or essence"—be it deconstruction or semiotics or pragmatism—tends to define its terms relationally, for there is no ultimate solid, "ontological ground" on which to rest. In Levinas, the *relation,* as we have seen throughout, is an ethical "binding to the other," a heteronomy, a difficult liberty. Language carries and enacts this relation: it is both inspired and mundane, human and "divine," material and spiritual at once. What constitutes a logical paradox or ontological impossibility becomes possible as practical reason, modeled on the nonindifference for the other.

Similarly, a "God beyond being," a God defined relationally and not as a "thematized essence," would also be "constituted" or "God" *in relation to human response and action.* This would be one meaning of a well-known midrash on the verse from Isaiah 43:10 "You are my witnesses, says the Lord." According to the midrash, this means: "If you are my witnesses, I am God, but if you are not my witnesses, I am not God" (*Sifre,* Deut. 346; *Pesikta* 102b; *Yalkut Shimoni* 455). Relation without ontology is relation without mutual identification in some essence; it is, rather, a religion which both bridges and maintains utter separation of the terms.

For Levinas, this nonontological relation across distance is a philosophic equivalent (or "translation") of Jewish monotheism. God is utterly separated and transcendent, and yet in relation with humanity not through incarnation but through teaching, command, and law. (A Levinasian form of rhetoric, then, would be quite distinct from that of Kenneth Burke, for whom "identification and participation" are key aspects of symbolic expression and rhetorical persuasion—thus marking a different theology underlying Burke's schema, a far more Christian one.) This distance or separation as a "rupture of being" redefines the relation of God, world, and humanity: "Humanity is also the irruption of God in being or the breaking out of being toward God: humanity is the rupture of being where giving is produced, full hands instead of battles and rapes" (*ADV* 172).

In both rabbinic hermeneutics and literary criticism, author, text, and interpreter would be in a mutually defining interrelation. There is no isolated text-in-itself or text as "verbal icon." The Levinas-Rosenzweig perspective would locate the idea of pure text in isolation from its reader or creator with that primal pagan configuration of the All where God, world, and humanity are unrelated, separated, autonomous. The creator is concealed, the tragic hero of art is mute, and the cosmos is self-existent and indifferent. The corollary in literary criticism would be a text independent of its author, its readers, or the world, as, for example, in the New Criticism or indeed any type of autonomous formalism such as structuralism. To briefly highlight a few of Rosenzweig's analyses of art which accompany each of the three main sections of *The Star:* In part I of *The Star,* he first connects all art to the pagan world of myth. "Even today, all art is subject to the laws of the mythical world. A work of art must have that self-containedness unto itself, that indifference to everything beyond itself, that independence of higher laws, that freedom from base duties . . . peculiar to the world of myth" (38). Yet the work of art creates a kind of speechless speech, "a speech of the unspeakable, a first, speechless, mutual comprehension, for all time indispensable beneath and besides actual speech. . . . The life aroused in the beholder does not arouse the beheld to life; it at once turns inward the beholder himself" (81). The self nurtured by art is the "wholly solitary, individual self; art nowhere creates a real plurality of selves," and though it produces the possibility for such awakening, in art "self" never becomes "soul." That requires revelation and another kind of language (81). Art prepares the way for revelation, but "art itself is only the language of the unspeakable, the language as long as there is no language, the language of the protocosmos" (147). This indifferent "speech of the unspeakable" has striking parallels to certain forms of modernist aesthetics, e.g., Heidegger, Blanchot, Bataille, Derrida, and so forth.

In part II of *The Star,* revelation breaks open the self-enclosed God, human, and world and turns each to and for the other. Language is the bridge coming from both without and within. Here "art is the Spoken, not the speech" (191). Here also seems to be a source for Levinas's "saying and said."

In part III, Rosenzweig identifies art as the temporal form which helps Christianity prepare to celebrate its festivals of redemption in contrast to the celebrations of the closed circle of Jewish liturgical time (370). Art is also that which competes with the cross within the Christian soul for a way of salvation that will overcome contradiction and suffering (376). Finally, in the conclusion, Rosenzweig writes that "paganism will live on to the eternal end in its eternal gods, the state and art, the former the idol of the realists, the latter of the individualists" (421).

In sum, in a Levinasian-Rosenzwegian schema, revelation is the opening of each to each: "and" becomes "for"; art becomes Scripture as ethics, love, command. Interpretation becomes the for-the-other, text-for-reader; but reader is also no longer the willful, isolated, heroic pagan self but in turn hollowed out, opened, called by and obligated to the text and author in responsibility and command. The "reader" would not be an arbitrary, willful misreader bent on power and domination over the text.

In Levinas's own description of this interrelation of inspiration, revelation, and exegesis, "prophecy" would therefore exist not only in the words of the one who speaks the revelation but also in the one who hears it, "as if the Revelation were a system of signs to be interpreted by the hearer, and in this sense already delivered to him" (*ADV* 175). Such would be one of the meanings of the famous talmudic statement that "the Torah is no longer in heaven" (*B. Metzia* 59b). Indeed, in Hebrew the word for "tradition," *masorah,* comes from the root *massar,* meaning "to give over, to surrender, to deliver."[7] There is a surrender, a relinquishing, a giving over as binding to the other on the part of God as well as humanity. Humanity, then, is not only the passive receiver of sublime information but "at the same time, the one to whom the word is said, but also the one for whom there is Revelation. Humanity would be the place where transcendence passes. . . . Perhaps the entire status of subjectivity and reason must be revised in light of this situation" (*ADV* 175).

As in Rosenzweig, the "to whom" becomes the "for whom." In short, the very "structure of revelation is the call to exegesis," and revelation is not mystification but transcendence heard as the "invitation to intelligence" (160, 162). Levinas comments here on the strange ambiguities in the Hebrew sacred texts and the "polysemy of the Hebrew syntax": "the words coexist in place of coordinating and subordinating immediately with each other" (161). Thus to ascertain even the "literal meaning" or original intent of the text requires searching and inquiry. The word *drash,* the root of the Hebrew word *midrash,* means precisely "to search or inquire." Each word opens a whole unsuspected world. In his felicitous wording, the rabbis read the letters as if they were "the folded wings of the Spirit—all the horizons that the flight of the Spirit could encompass." The text is extended on the amplifications of the tradition "like the strings on the wood of a violin." Enigma and ambiguity become pretexts for new profundity, renewal of meaning: the "mystery" of revelation is "not a mystery which evades clarity, but which calls it to increased intensity" (162).

Exegesis is "already the participation of the reader in Revelation, in

Scripture, making the reader a kind of scribe." Again, this position does not assert that the reader arbitrarily constructs the text or that a predetermined dogmatic content founds revelation. Levinas is trying to maintain that revelation comes at once from "outside" and "inside," inhabiting the one who receives it like the crossing or intersection of Other and other (*autre* and *autrui*) in his philosophical work. This inhabiting is not an ontological identification but retains the distance between God and humanity while yet binding them in a relation for-the-other.

Furthermore, just as the depth of language is a sociality of the "face" and a relation which is not anonymous, so, too, the unsaid of the text must be solicited by persons. The call for exegesis is the call for the particular significations that only each individual can bring forth. It is as if "the very multiplicity of persons is the condition of the plenitude of the absolute truth," a nondogmatic truth sought through the intelligence (*ADV* 163). As in Rosenzweig, revelation calls to the unique in me.

As we have also seen in Levinas's philosophical works, though, this "personal" self is not the self of substantial identity but the very rupture of that identity, and that very rupture makes possible a message coming from without:

> All comes about as if the multiplicity of persons—wouldn't this be the very sense of the personal?—were the condition of the plenitude of the "absolute truth," as if each person, by his unicity, assured the revelation of a unique aspect of truth, and certain of its facets would never be revealed if a certain person were missing in humanity.

The "totality" of truth is not an ideality beyond persons or history, or one which denies multiplicity. Nor does multiplicity mean an anonymous collective. On the contrary, this irreducible multiplicity of persons is necessary to the very meaning of truth; "the multiple meanings, these are the multiple persons" (*ADV* 163). Such would be the Levinasian interpretation of the well-known statement from Jewish mysticism that there are "600,000 faces to the Torah."

Multiplicity of meaning, rupture of totality, the necessity of difference, difference as a condition of identity are the common themes of poststructuralism. Levinas, however, deconstructs the subject but saves the person. The radical heterogeneity of truth in most poststructuralist theories is not personal, and fiercely resists any form of unity or coherence. Levinas not only saves the person, he maintains a continuity across rupture—just as he maintains a relation across the absolute difference between God and humanity, or infinite and finite. In his version of Jewish hermeneutics, the ambiguity of revelation as the necessity of exegesis and the multiplicity of truth is also the fount of a *unity of the Word* across time. The very colloquy of rabbis and interpreters across the generations (a relation across separation without ontology but through history and language) constitutes this plurality of truth. The message depends on each messenger and reader, and expands through this plurality across the generations in commentary, and commentary upon commentary unto the present.

He notes that even the style of the oral law, which came to be written down belatedly, retains its reference to oral teaching, to the discussion of master and student embodied in question and response, debate, dialogue, argument, and the disagreement among colleagues—all of which remain open to its readers. "The religious act of hearing the revealed word is thus identified with the discussion that is meant to be opened in all the audacity of its problematics" (*ADV* 167). Revelation is not then only a source of wisdom or way of deliverance "but also nourishes this life and the very joy of knowing" (168). This destiny of the inspired word enables the richness of the unsaid to be said, and to renew the said. In this sense is Israel the people of the Book as the Continuing Revelation—and reading becomes the "highest liturgy" (136).

In other words, this "second sonority" of texts, this inspired saying, is not some ethereal inaccessible realm of pure thought; it lives through the life of those who hear, understand, and interpret them. In the next chapter, we shall examine at length one of Levinas's own interpretations of a talmudic text and the way his reading attempts to *enact* this relation of revelation and interpretation, and to take his place in this ongoing life.

THE RETURN OF HISTORY

This ongoing life is what embeds the text in history. History, and each person in her or his unique historicity, is a necessary part of revelation. But this kind of history is neither mystical theosophy (the life of God) nor is it the Hegelian theater of war or dialectic of the Spirit, nor the site of anonymous ruptures and power struggles. It is another kind of continuity through the lived generations, and their commentaries. This form of non-Parmenidean unity parallels Levinas's meditations on fecundity at the end of *Totality and Infinity* as a continuity across rupture through ongoing generations. This idea also echoes Rosenzweig's emphasis in the third part of *The Star* on the coherence of living communities of the Jewish people, of the "eternal life" which Jews already possess through their ongoing biological generations. The Jew is a Jew simply by birth, not by any professed dogma, while the Christian must be "reborn" (397). Rosenzweig writes, "Only a community based on common blood feels the warrant of eternity in its veins even now. For such a community, time is not a foe that must be tamed, a foe it may or may not defeat—though it hopes it may!—but its child and the child of its child" (*Star* 298–99). The Jewish people, in distinction to all the other peoples, roots itself not in the earth or soil or land but in its own "blood," i.e., its own biological generations or "peoplehood": "We have struck root in ourselves. We do not root in earth and so we are eternal wanderers, but deeply rooted in our own body and blood.

And it is this rooting in ourselves, and in nothing but ourselves, that vouchsafes eternity" (305). Rosenzweig contrasts this eternity with that won by nations and states through wars and revolutions in world history (334–35).

For both Levinas and Rosenzweig, the Jew is not the abstract or allegorical "other" as a figure of modern fragmentation, but retains a binding power across rupture. Claims Levinas, the mysterious and powerful unity of Israel across historical time, despite dispersal among the nations, is "without doubt the originality of Israel and of its relation to Revelation" (*ADV* 158). The rupture as revelation is ethical *binding,* and the actuality of Israel is a living collective and not just a philosophical allegory. Levinas argues that this "living actuality" of Israel as a community that founds itself on the Bible, even in the midst of persecution, temptation, apostasy, and weakness, also opposes any transfiguration of revelation into a "myth." Through their relation to revelation, however, the sufferings of Israel in profane history become chapters in the "sacred history" begun with the Bible. The Holocaust, the condemnation of nations become part of the "passion of Israel" as these events are referred back to the Bible, and to the revelation through interpretation (159).

Again, like Rosenzweig, Levinas is asserting that in the Jewish experience the idea and value of history itself is redefined. Just as the very act of interpreting the text "constitutes" God's nonontological transcendence, so, too, does the ongoing history of these interpretations in the life of Israel: the history of Israel from Egypt to Auschwitz "is not only that of an encounter between humanity and the Absolute, and of a faith—but it is, if one dares to say it, constitutive of the very existence of God." This assertion comes from no logical or theoretical syllogism or "proof," but it is "as if the meaning of this existence, the meaning of the verb 'being, existence' applied to God, could not be approached or understood outside of this sacred History, through its contradictions, depths and heights, sacrifices and doubts, faiths and denials; as if the history of Israel were the 'divine comedy' or the 'divine ontology' itself" (*ADV* 20).

The phrasing of these statements is crucial: "as if" but not "is." History is not the actual "ontological life of God"; "history" is not reified as some autonomous impersonal power but is the site of relation, where human action for the other in itself is proximity to God. History returns, not as some ultimate ground of understanding, as some Hegelian Absolute, as a Marxist material inversion of Hegel, or as Foucaultian struggle of power/ knowledge. It is "sacred" not in any mystical sense but sanctified as human action for the other. In a critique of a work by Paul Claudel in *Difficile liberté,* Levinas defines a "sacred history" which is not to be understood "figuratively," i.e., in the Christian tradition of typological interpretation of the Hebrew Bible. This history is not a "prefiguration" of some thesis but "the articulation of human liberty in a real life" (*DL* 153). History is not a theater in which we receive prefigured, rigid "roles" from

God but a world where we receive commands for action as personal agents. In this context, Levinas affirms the efficacy of the acting subject, and "passivity" is not a virtue.

Levinas opposes a mythical notion of history as theosophy, but his concept of human ethical history as "the sociality where the other than being passes" connotes a kind of "life of God" that might help illumine some of the rhetoric of kabbalistic texts. The issue, as we remember, has to do with to what extent the kabbalists understood their own images and tropes to be metaphorical. The "as if" is the crucial word, and the "as if" is all the difference—for it maintains the difference between God, humanity, and world but keeps them in relation as "for-the-other." At almost all the crucial points of Levinas's argument, the possibility or construction of the signification "otherwise" rests on the "as though." "As though" is an opening of signification, a kind of mode of "revelation" within philosophical thought itself, like the questioning of skepticism or the equivocal nature of language. "As though" in Levinas parallels Benjamin's attempt to construct constellations of meaning and relation without ontology; it is an "as if" which is the ability to envision utopia, or redeem history. "As though" as a key structure in Levinas would also make his thought "allegorical" in Benjamin's sense. "As though" is the "other meaning" of an allegoresis which ruins, strips, fragments its object, which intervenes and disrupts the smooth continuities of meaning and representation, truth and its immanent manifestations. "As though" points to the gap, the noncoincidence of truth and representation, and the diachrony of time as the interruption of nature through history. Or in Levinas's case, an immemorial past, beyond even the conscious gatherings of history and memory.

This "as though" is connected to Levinas's central idea of Infinity as that which breaks up totality. The idea of the Infinite "put into" thought is not a formal or abstract negation of the finite but signifies the "Infinite in me. . . . as though [sic] . . . the in of the Infinite were to signify both the non and the within" ("God and Philosophy" 160). (The birth of "negation," Levinas adds in a footnote, would not be then in subjectivity, as Hegel proposed, but in this Idea of the Infinite.) This "in" of the "Infinite" signifies the exposure or opening that Levinas defined in *Otherwise Than Being* as the ethical essence of signification.

The phrase "as if the history of Israel were the . . . 'divine ontology' itself" then means that in the very sociality of society lies the proximity of God (*ADV* 20). But this history is itself a "counterhistory," an "other history," and is lived by the Jews as an awakening, "a fissure in the shell of impenetrable being," "a refusal of the violence of so-called historical and political necessity." This social bond is produced by and produces an "incessant rupture of the natural and historical," an "original dissidence . . . resistance to the pure force of things," and its paradigm is the liberation from slavery in Egypt (18). Revelation is both rupture and relation, the personal and political. Or to phrase it in philosophical terms, rupture of

Hegelian universal history and Heideggerian being culminate in revelation as ethical metaphysics and prophetic messianic politics.

THE RETURN OF THE LAW

As in Rosenzweig, Jewish life, ritual, and law are defined by their very resistance to immersion and dissolution in the anonymous flow and warfare of Hegelian universal history. For Rosenzweig, the law is that which ties the *future* of redemption to the *present* of revelation, ordering the life of this world in the image of the world to come:

> Jewish feeling takes only this world for unfinished, while it takes for finished and unalterable the law that it presumes to impose on this world so that it might be transformed into the world to come. Even if the law appears in the highly modern garb of some contemporary Utopianism the law then stands in sharp contrast to the Christian lack of law which can and wants to be taken by surprise, which still distinguishes the Christian-turned-politician from the Jew-turned-Utopian and which endows the latter with the greater power to shake up, the former with the greater readiness to attain. The Jew always thinks that what counts is only to turn his legal doctrine this way and that; sooner or later it would turn out to have "everything in it." . . . The idea of the transition from this world into the world to come, the idea of the messianic age which is suspended over life as a Today that is ever to be awaited, this idea coalesces here and becomes an everyday object as the Law. . . . (*Star* 406)

Another of Rosenzweig's central anti-Hegelian ideas was that Jewish history defies secular history and its expansionism. "Power is the basic concept of history because in Christianity revelation began to spread over the word"; that was its mandate, and every other expansionist urge, even the most secular, "became the unconscious servant of this expansionist movement." Rosenzweig views the Jewish people as the archetypal survivors of the ravages of history, the prophetic "remnant" which will always remain, apart, outside, alone, maintaining itself by "subtraction, contraction, by the formation of ever new remnants." Even while externally assimilating, Judaism continually divests itself of un-Jewish elements to set itself apart on the inside (*Star* 404).

For Levinas, too, this separation from the flow of history is *not* the mark of a moment of alienation or antithesis in the life of the Spirit, as Hegel had claimed. Instead, Jewish law is positive; it embodies the moment of arrest, the separation from the immediacies of nature, and the resistance to myth and to the violent anonymity of history. In Jewish ritual, "there is nothing numinous, no idolatry; it is a distance taken *in* nature *in relation to* nature, and perhaps thus precisely the waiting for the Most High which is a relation—or, if one prefers, a deference—to Him, a deference to the beyond which here engenders the very concept of the beyond or of the to-God [*à-Dieu*]" (*ADV* 173).

This position is a polemic against any sense of Jewish law as somehow magically effective. For Levinas, it is in not an ontological but an ethical sense that Jewish law and ritual enact and engender the *au-delà,* the beyond. "Beyond" means here, as in the philosophical works, distance as "what does not enter into the present, nature, immanence" and is distinct from any theosophic or mystical sense. And distance is the principle of holiness—as separation. Indeed, "separation" is the root meaning of the Hebrew word for holiness—*kedusha.* Jewish law is not the apostle Paul's "Yoke of the Law . . . not resented as a stigma of some sort of slavery. . . . [Rather, it] effects the unity of Judaism and is quite distinct, on the religious level, from any doctrinal unity whatever. . . . It is the practice which engenders the unity of the Jewish people" (170). This holds true, Levinas claims, even when the law is not fully observed. Nor does obedience to these commandments arrest the intellectual dialectic involved in establishing these practices. The continuous discussion of the motives of *halakah* involves "all of thought," and the discussion goes beyond [*au-delà*] the initial problem; the legal decision isn't a final conclusion.

Levinas understands these laws and rituals as the very bridge between daily material and spiritual life. When Moses, the greatest of the prophets, has his most direct vision of God "face to face" (Exod. 33:11; 23), he sees no image but only the "backside" of God. The rabbis interpreted "backside" as a reference to the knot formed by the straps of the phylacteries on the nape of the neck. (Wearing *tefillin*—phylacteries—during daily morning prayer is a religious obligation of all Jewish men.) This extraordinary image of God wearing phylacteries is no crude anthropomorphism, writes Levinas, but rather indicates the *prescriptive* nature of the revelation—that it is always tied to daily ritual conduct. This tie does not reflect mindless rabbinic legalism; rather, this daily conduct is meant to "arrest" one's immediate absorption into nature and the blind spontaneity of one's desires. It thus conditions the ethical relation with the other person: once more God is welcomed in the face to face with the other and in obligation (*ADV* 174–75).

Spiritual life is not, then, the "interiority of the beautiful soul" but "exteriority," i.e., the opening to the other. "Torah and the liturgical significance it confers on material acts of life outside their natural finality . . . is the surest safeguard of the ethics of Israel, the most faithful memory" (*ADV* 23). There is also in Jewish spirituality, he claims, the feeling of a passive belonging apart from any initiative, the awareness of an irremediable participation, of a responsibility to sacred history, as if one were seized—even when one forgets the commandments. Logically and formally, this "seizure" is a subordination; but it is also the "difficult liberty" of Judaism, and "it is just herein that God is God—and not by a logical term; and that the biblical ontology of the person departs from the subjectivity of the idealist subject" (24). Once more, a concrete heteronomy assures an autonomy.

Just as he defines the "saying" in terms of the corporeality of the body, its vulnerability, and self-exposure, the giving of bread from one's very mouth, he interprets the focus of Jewish law on the material aspects of life not as a sign of blindness to grand notions of spirit (of which it is accused by Christianity) or "the tribute paid to our material nature": "Our material nature, on the contrary, is the very accomplishment of our solidarity in being. It does not prefigure anything. Economic life is the ontological site where the creature is transformed into spirit, or if one desires a more suggestive terminology, where the flesh opens to the verb" (*DL* 159). This materiality is not an "incarnation of the spirit" in any Christian or Hegelian sense but signifies a material relation to the *other,* an acting for-the-other, as justice in this world.

Like Rosenzweig, Levinas neither allegorizes nor historicizes Jewish law. Its "literal" or "carnal" meanings are not "spiritualized" away. But the "dis-inter-esse" or dis-interestedness which Jewish law accomplishes also does mean a *déracinement,* an uprooting from attachments to the material locality of place in the violence of nationalism: "Every word is an uprooting. Every rational institution is uprooting. The constitution of a true society is uprooting" (165). Uprooting here again means the uprooting of the self from itself and its interiority, in contrast to "paganism," which is defined as the rootedness of narcissistic self-enclosure, and is also enclosure in a local place.

Levinas's discussion draws once again from Rosenzweig's conception of the pagan world as self-enclosed and mute, a world prior to the opening of revelation; but it also strongly alludes to Heidegger, especially in his contrast of the "desert" to the "forest"—the forest representing "interiority," "rootedness," "being there," the place where trees push their roots into the ground to nourish themselves. Heidegger, of course, not only retreated to the Black Forest to write his philosophy but entitled his later works "wood paths"—*holzweigs.* Warns Levinas, one should not be "duped by the peace of the woods" (165); one finds there the paganism of a "prehuman humanity." This attachment to and mystification of "place" is far more dangerous than all of Heidegger's worries about "technology"; for to make rootedness of primary importance separates humanity in effect into "natives" and "strangers." The stranger as "other" then becomes metaphysically tainted, abnormal.

For Levinas, it is not in the forest but "in the arid sun of the desert, where nothing is fixed, that the true spirit descends in a text in order to accomplish itself universally." Needless to say, the desert was the biblical site of the revelation of Sinai, the advent of law and Scripture. Scripture does not "subordinate spirit to the letter. . . . The spirit is free in the letter and enchained in the root" (165). This "emptiness" of the desert signifies the potential for universality, i.e., is an open space where all can enter. In Derrida's essay on Jabès, this emptiness of the desert and its shifting sands are the tropes for the shifting meanings of the text where one wanders eternally. This anguish of ancient and eternal wandering in language, of eternal questioning, becomes for Jabès the condition of both the postmodern writer and the Jew. In the desert of Derrida and Jabès, however, the Scripture that is given has no law, only unanswered questions which are the "torments of an ancient word." Here again Levinas veers away from the poststructuralist emphasis on endless equivocation, wandering meaning, and antinomian subversion: "It is not a question of returning to a nomadism that is equally incapable of sedentary existence." Judaism, he notes, has its own form of attachment to place, but only to one Holy Land, a land one can dwell in only under certain conditions—a land which, as the Bible says, "vomits out the unjust." (He aptly illustrates this point with some rabbinic commentary on a story from Genesis. In Genesis, Abraham plants a tree which in Hebrew is called a *tamar*. The rabbis interpreted the word to be an acronym for the Hebrew words for "food, drink, and lodging"—the three necessities of human life. Or, in Levinasian terms, "what man offers to man. The earth is for that. Man is its master to serve man" [258].)

The "nonsite" or desert or "saying" is an opening up as an exposure to the *outside*—to the other. While this opening is a hollowing out and hemorrhaging of the self, he sharply distinguishes it from "existential alienation" or the dissolution of self in a mystical abyss, or any fusion with the godhead, or any kind of "otherworldliness." There is nothing "mystical" in "saying"; it is the ultimate openness and exposure to the other as ethics and responsibility for the other. Saying is not a "secret or hidden" language, or the deepest "interior" of speech or self, but the reversal out: "The openness of the ego exposed to the other is the breakup or turning inside out of inwardness. Sincerity is the name of this extra-version" ("God and Philosophy" 169). This, of course, becomes the excess of debt and obligation. The "here I am" is the self at the service of others "without having anything to identify myself with, but the sound of my own voice or the figure of my gesture—the saying itself" (*OTB* 149). In terms of the said, it appears as a "speaking nothing," but as a sign of the giving of signs " 'as simple as hello,' but ipso facto the pure transparency of an admission, the recognition of a debt," it is a bearing witness and inspiration (143). In this context, the word *God* is an extraordinary word that "unsays itself without vanishing into nothingness . . . a unique said not inclined exactly to logical rules" (151).

This redefinition of subjectivity by reversal to the outside aligns Levinas with semiotics, deconstruction, and much poststructuralist theory in contrast to traditional "hermeneutics." The latter tries to penetrate to the *interior* of a self or a text in order to find some hidden essence to then unveil. In the former, alterity is solicited by turning a text over and around, fracturing it by a play with its seams and surfaces, and the category "inside/outside" is itself put in question. For thinkers such as Derrida or Foucault, there is no "sincerity of saying" in this extraversion.

In summary, in his philosophical writings, Levinas associates "history" with the realm of totalizing Hegelian idealism, which he then disrupts with notions of the trace, infinity, fecundity, saying, passivity, the time of an irrecuperable past "beyond all history and memory." In *Totality and Infinity* and *Otherwise Than Being,* his accent was on the withholding, the breathlessness of the Spirit, the vulnerability, susceptibility, and disengagement of the subject from the egoisms of ontology. But in his Jewish writings, this emphasis on "passivity" is replaced by a call to activity, especially action as sanctified and disciplined by Jewish law, an activity that revalorizes engagement with history and brings to history the beyond of ethical judgment. History itself becomes the arena for spiritual life. The Bible, Talmud, and Jewish law offer Levinas models for a *positive entry into history,* a way of being in history that might avoid the violence into which philosophical thought has fallen through systems of ontology, totality, and idealism. The Bible, he observes, does not begin like Plato's *Republic,* with the abstract construction of an ideal city; it instead "takes humanity in its savagely real situation" of war, slavery, sacrifices, crimes, jealousy, hatred, killing, places itself in the interior of these situations in order to be able to surmount them: "To recognize the necessity of a law—this is to recognize that humanity cannot save itself straightaway, by magically denying its own conditions" (*DL* 328).

Yet Levinas describes Jewish law by using the key terms from his philosophical works: this law defines a relation among human persons as "faces," a relation which accomplishes the *"dis-inter-esse-ment,"* the undoing of the imperialistic essence or being of the ego. In the vast and detailed *halakhic* discussion of all matters of economic and social life, Levinas finds the transformation of action from the self-interested strategies of the general violence and war of "being" to a "disinterestedness." Jewish law elevates all the material, commercial, and economic transactions which it adjudicates "from interested acts to the order of justice": "There something new is produced in the middle of the universal war" (*DL* 159). Here, of course, Levinas's thought runs counter to that extreme antipathy to "the law" which one finds in almost all other poststructuralist writers from Derrida to Barthes to Kristeva to Foucault, who associate law with domination, exclusion, and repression. We earlier traced this antipathy to the law back to the Protestant antinomianism of Kant and Hegel. Rosenzweig and Levinas, unlike Scholem, Benjamin, and Buber, refused to accept this hostile attitude toward the law.[8]

LEVINAS AND SCHOLEM: MYSTICISM, MYTH, AND LAW

Let us now clarify and summarize the similarities and differences between Levinas's position and that of Scholem on revelation, interpretation, and law. For Scholem, Benjamin, and Levinas, the deepest level of language is that beyond instrumentality and communication, a level at which a positive content of communication is extinguished. But Levinas strongly asserts that this realm of saying as the openness to the other than being, as witness and inspiration, is "outside of any mysticism" (*OTB* 115). The critical difference between this idea and Benjamin's "pure language" or Scholem's "abyss of language" as the ultimate and infinite "meaningless word" is that Levinas makes this lack of content as openness coincide with the personal accusative, a bearing witness of a self which is inescapably called and disrupted—"here I am."

Scholem described the mystical meaning of revelation as that which emanates from the "ultimate meaningless word," the abyss in language, the unknown and anarchic; and he viewed this anarchic realm in a highly romantic sense as the arena of teeming formlessness and creative vitality which the pharisaic tradition of Talmud, law, and ethics had rigidified and ossified. Anarchy for Levinas, by contrast, means the "anarchy of responsibility"—saying as bearing witness in gratuitous self-sacrifice. To put it another way, anarchy in Scholem represents a kind of vitalizing "freedom" and anti-*halakhism;* an-archy in Levinas is what is prior to all "arche" or ontological origins—the subjectivity called, elected, hostage, beyond freedom/nonfreedom. Levinas finds in *halakah* the very concretion and safeguarding of this call.

For Scholem, it seems, ethical positivity was found in politics through Zionism and the rebuilding of Palestine, and through a new historiography of Jewish history, and this he carefully separated from mystical messianism. To confuse the anarchic realms of mystical and apocalyptic messianism with politics, he warned, would lead only to disastrous violence. Claims Levinas, without the prophetic and ethical witness of saying, *all* politics turns to violence. Perhaps it was also this vision of ethical positivity as the solidarity of relation to the other that Benjamin tried to find in Marxism as he oscillated between theology and materialism—as if that dualism constituted his own "saying" and "said."

Despite their uncovering of various "others," the "other" underground tradition of mysticism or the "other" of philosophy or counterhistory, Scholem and Levinas do not abandon reason and rational inquiry; what they recognized—like Freud—were the ways in which classical reason is penetrated by and must respect "an other reason." To Scholem, as to Levinas, Benjamin, Freud, and other Jews of this generation, the German university, despite its antisemitism, bureaucracy, and pomposity, had also imparted an ethic of rigorous and self-abnegating search for truth. Ernest Wallwork reminds us that the German term *Wissenschaft,* used by Freud when he identified psychoanalysis with the "scientific world view,"

> is considerably richer than what is conveyed by the English word "science."
> . . . [It] points to a "this-worldly" rationalism, in that it includes such rationalistic disciplines as ethics and law as well as such interpretive disciplines in the humanities as history and clinical psychotherapy. As Freud says of his

perspective, it includes the "intellectual working-over" of carefully scrutinized observations, but these may be gleaned from a variety of sources, many of them previously suspect, such as dreams and fantasies. (Wallwork and Wallwork, "Psychoanalysis" 164–65)

The term *Wissenschaft,* of course, was also used by the creators of the modern "Science of Judaism" to describe their enterprise.

Yet there is also a Jewish component in what Levinas calls the characteristic intellectualism of Jewish spirituality, its "non-Luciferian pride in reason . . . the dignity of the responsible being" (*DL* 29). For the Jew, the way in which the intellect must be applied to revelation broadens the concept of Torah "to comprehend all essential knowledge"; "human existence, despite its inferior ontological position—and because of this inferiority, its torment, critique, and unquiet—is the true place where the divine word meets the intellect and loses the rest of its supposedly mystical virtues" (30).

For Levinas, anarchy, ambiguity, ambivalence, oscillation, skepticism are not assaults on reason but calls to the reason behind reason, to the very "first" philosophy, to "reason before the thematization of signification by a thinking subject . . . a pre-original reason . . . anarchic reason" (*OTB* 166): "Reason is the one-for-the-other! . . . To intelligibility as impersonal logos is opposed intelligibility as proximity" (167). But Levinas also perceives the dangers of a "contentless revelation," of the ambiguity or anarchy of the infinite, of the "nakedness of the face" or the overflow of inspiration: transcendence can be distorted into "ideology" or "sacred delirium" (152). Both of these alternatives must be circumvented, he warns—the first by linguistics, sociology, psychology, the second by philosophy. Like Scholem, he is wary of any contemporary attempts to claim *direct* access to the sacred or to mystical intuition; philological criticism and commentary are indeed necessary, but one does not stop there. The movement or "passing" of transcendence is "from prophecy to philology and transcending philology toward prophetic signification" (152). Reason as prophetic signification is the ethical for-the-other and justice. Levinas does not seek that "mystical totality of truth" of which Scholem hoped to catch a glimpse through that "misty wall of history" hanging about the mountain. Philology, scientific scholarship, politics, mysticism, and aesthetics must all be grounded in saying as the ethical a priori, as both the "before" and the "beyond."

Levinas finds the "echoes of the divine word of creation" in philosophers rather than in Scholem's poets, because for Levinas rabbis and philosophers share the common task of *demythologizing* the said, disenchanting the myths, passions, symbols, and "-ologies" of theology. Just as monotheism demystified the pagan gods, the task of philosophy is to reduce the dissimulation and "sophism with which philosophy begins," a demystification prior to any of the various contemporary "hermeneutics of suspicion" such as psychoanalysis or Marxism (151). Indeed, the ethical imperative of "saying," he argues, is itself the very foundation of the modern critique of philosophy as ideology, for this critique "draws its force from elsewhere. It begins in a cry of ethical revolt, bearing witness to responsibility; it begins in prophecy" ("God and Philosophy" 171–72). The turn toward politics would express, in a way, this urge to be responsible to the other, to solicit alterity as a subversive force against the oppressive force of domination. The Levinasian position would maintain, however, that without the priority of the "face" of the other, as the passing of the infinite and ethics of saying as obligation, political liberation degenerates into the construction of new prisons.

This antimystical and antimythical strain figures prominently in almost all of Levinas's writings about Judaism, especially *Difficile liberté*. Judaism is described as an "adult religion" whose aim "is to understand the holiness of God in a sense which severs it from the numinous meaning of the term" (*DL* 28)—a religion of demystification, idol-smashing, and disenchantment. "Fear and trembling" before the sacred or enthusiastic frenzies of poetic delirium are identified as forms of violence, for they empty and crush the separate self without maintaining and binding it to the other in the ethical relation (e.g., Kierkegaard's "teleological suspension of the ethical"). As in Levinas's philosophical thought, reason and language bear the spiritual order. "Enthusiasm is, after all, possession by a god. Jews don't want to be possessed but responsible. Their God is the Lord of justice" (78). Scholem, however, would make the same objections to Levinas's position as he made to Hermann Cohen's—that this rationalism was too hostile to myth and mysticism, still too tied to an Enlightenment ideal of reason. In fact, Scholem is purported to have once said of Levinas, "He is more of a Litvak than he thinks" (Malka 52, n. 1). This is a reference to the highly intellectual character of the Lithuanian Jewish culture from which Levinas came, which intensely cultivated talmudic learning, gave birth to the ethical sobriety of the *mussar* movement, and was a bastion of resistance to Hassidism.

Scholem, we remember, argued that in Jewish mysticism, myth had penetrated into and revitalized the heart of monotheism; Levinas claims that Judaism "calls to a humanity without myth" (*DL* 70), because he associates myth with identification and participation in Being, i.e., with the entire tradition of ontology and totality he has critiqued as violent: "Myth, even if sublime, introduces into the soul this troubling element, this impure element of magic and sorcery, and this drunkenness of the sacred and war, which prolongs the animal in the civilized" (71). The remnants of these impurities in so-called spiritual exaltations lead to cruelty; authentic spirituality has nothing to do with the supernatural or even with concern for one's own "salvation," which is but another form of self-love (69). Spirituality, instead, is determined by the ethical relation to the other, a relation of the most concrete kind: "To be attached to the sacred is infinitely more materialistic than to proclaim the value—incontestable—of bread and meat in human life" (19). This statement echoes a famous saying of the great originator of the Lithuanian *mussar* movement, R. Israel Salanter (1810–1883): "The material needs of my neighbor are spiritual needs for me."[9]

In Levinas's philosophical works, the other than being culminates in transcendence to the point of absence. Here, too, Levinas admits that to destroy the numinous conception of the sacred risks atheism, but that risk must be taken for humanity to "rise to a spiritual notion of the Transcendent" (30). To abjure the ecstasies of ontological "participation" in the divine means to maintain separation—also an essential theme in Levinas's philosophical construction of the subject. Monotheism, as a shattering of the idols, also requires this separation from the "sacred"; and it "is impossible to one who has not reached the age of doubt, solitude, revolt." Monotheism then would *share* the path of Western philosophy, for one "can ask if the Western spirit, if philosophy, isn't in the last analysis the possibility of a humanity which accepts the risk of atheism that it is necessary to run, but surmounts it" (31).

That, too, was the philosophical path which Rosenzweig followed, shattering the identity of logos and being; maintaining the separated, atheistic, self in its isolation; and then surmounting that isolation not through any collapse of identity but through the call of revelation, the "here I am" as response to both God and neighbor, and the reconfiguration of the relations among God, world, and humanity into the Star of Redemption, a unity across separation.

Scholem, though, thought that Judaism in Rosenzweig took on a "strangely churchlike aspect . . . [whereas] Apocalypticism, as a doubtlessly anarchic element, provided some fresh air in the house of Judaism; it provided a recognition of the catastrophic potential of all historical order in an unredeemed world" (*Mess Idea* 324). Rosenzweig erred in trying to tame this liberating destructive force and render it "harmless." The issue again involves Scholem's own philosophy of history and language and his objections to the "concretions" of traditional Jewish law, to revelation as meaning a specific commanding word, or personal subjective immediacy. Scholem had argued that revelation as linguistic phenomenon signifies the varying human historical interpretations of Judaism which have struggled to "translate" the Absolute Word. But this Word spawns an endless plurality of meanings because its "Absolute" is located not so much in any "commanding presence" of God but in pure language as the opening into the very abysses of language.

For Scholem, moreover, counterhistory was a dialectical phenomenon which incorporated those "fresh breezes of anarchism," myth, and the nonrational, all of which he thought he found in Kabbalah. "Catastrophe" becomes an essential interpretive category in his historiography; he views the catastrophe of the expulsion of the Jews from Spain as the propelling factor in the development of Lurianic Kabbalah; "catastrophe" even becomes for him the central trope of the Lurianic theory of creation.

In short, for Scholem the "anarchic breezes" of mysticism blowing through the closed house of Judaism were a covert source of its endurance and creative vitality; for Levinas Jewish law and ritual practices are the vital sources and preserving forces of Judaism, and embodiments of its mission in the world. He vigorously defends Jewish ritual law as the "rigorous discipline which leads toward this justice" for the other and so brings one close to God (*DL* 35). The task of *halakah,* like the task of philosophy and monotheism, is to demystify the world through submitting the violent and irrational forces to numerous prohibitions. The naive, spontaneous, or natural ego is arbitrary, dominating, and violent, and in order to know the face of the other, one must "impose severe rules on one's own nature" (34).

This affirmation of the discipline of Jewish law is the analogue of Levinas's accusation and trial of philosophy's cognizing consciousness—a consciousness which makes the self, the *soi-même,* the "entrance to the Kingdom of the absolute." As in his philosophy, the relation with the other puts the self in question, questions its right to appropriate, dominate, encroach, usurp; and this relation with the other is the way I am in relation with God (31). Transcendence is the ethical relation, the contact with God through the relation with the other person: "Ethics is not the corollary of the vision of God, but that vision itself." Knowledge of God is not to be found in rapturous "visions" or in the philosophical cognition of some "essence." Following Maimonides, the preeminent Jewish rationalist philosopher, Levinas writes that to know God's "attributes" means to know God's "ways or actions": " 'God is merciful' signifies 'Be merciful like him.' The attributes of God are given not in the indicative, but in the imperative. The knowledge of God comes to us as a commandment, as a *mitzvah.* To know God is to know what it is necessary to do" (33).

So Levinas also adamantly opposes Scholem's implicit affirmation of the mystical-mythical rationales for Jewish law by maintaining that "at no moment does it [ritual law] have the value of a sacrament. No intrinsic power is given to ritual gestures" (34).[10] In any case, supernatural or mystical rituals, he argues, cannot erase evil: evil is "an offense that man does to man. No one, not even God, can substitute for the victim" (37). A theology of all-powerful pardon is inhuman, and this emphasis on human effort, conscience, and law again affirms a classically Jewish position, in contrast to a Christian theology of grace or redemption through vicarious sacrifice. The soul comes close to God because ritual and law lead it back to humanity, through self-discipline, self-abnegation, self-education. "Its greatness is in its daily regularity," and for Levinas this arduous effort requires a courage and calm "greater than that of the warrior" (34).

On the whole, one can say that for all these Jewish thinkers—Scholem, Benjamin, Levinas, Rosenzweig—there was no direct "immediate" reconnection with Jewish tradition, no simple acceptance of all its "concrete expressions" as laid down by past authorities. The breach opened by the Enlightenment and emancipation could not be denied. If, however, one could locate some opening *within* the tradition itself, perhaps one could reconnect with, revitalize, and re-create tradition. The openings each found within Jewish tradition then were turned back to enact a judgment upon the legacy of that Western culture which had opened the breach to begin with. But Scholem, Benjamin, Levinas, and Rosenzweig each described the nature of the openings they found quite differently.

ETHICS VERSUS AESTHETICS

Allan Megill has well described how our modern "prophets of extremity," Nietzsche, Foucault, Heidegger, and Derrida, all turn to the aesthetic rather than the ethical as the ultimate way out of the crisis of modernism and post-Enlightenment reason. Since Kant had split practical, aesthetic, and theoretical reason apart and maintained the "autonomy" of the aesthetic and ethical realms, the aesthetic principle itself became one post-Enlightenment "reason or rationale" that might replace lost transcendence. This Kantian legacy had played a large role in the philosophies of Benjamin and Scholem in the early stage of their relationship, as each struggled to find an alternative to the restricted domains of Kantian reason. For Scholem, the path back to the "mountain" around which clung the misty wall of history had to follow the circuitous and arduous routes of philology and critical scholarship. There was no direct access to the "mystical totality of truth." Scholem, though, replaced the loss of one kind of immediacy with another: he accepted the German romantic definition of the "symbol" as that which paradoxically can express the inexpressible, unite the universal and particular, overcome alienation.[11] But for the romantics, art was the realm where this was accomplished, and art took the place of religion.

Levinas and Rosenzweig contest this move toward myth and the aesthetic; instead, the ethical is the relation which founds all relations (aesthetic or political) as the for-the-other, immediate and proximate, and the foundation for action in the world. For Levinas, even theology—like all "ide-ologies" including the "ideologies" of politics, "art," or "literature"—inevitably betrays this "saying" into the said. Despite his close friendships with writers such as Blanchot, Levinas has always been reserved about the function of art, especially the plastic visual arts, in soliciting the other than being. He views art in Rosenzweigian terms as a plastic form that can dangerously "freeze" the saying in the forms of the said and so tempt toward idolatry. (This is a kind of philosophical translation of the biblical ban on making images of God.) He sees danger insofar as the movement beyond being and ontology can be halted in both theology and the "idolatry of the beautiful" where "a work of art substitutes itself for

God" (*OTB* 199, fn. 21). To seek authority elsewhere is to set up an idol—
even if it is in the logos or the "symbol."

But if philosophy is the "wisdom of love," and saying is the sign given of
the signification of signs as proximity, exposure, and substitution for the
other, then it "also delineates the trope of lyricism: to love by telling one's
love to the beloved—love songs, the possibility of poetry, of art" (199, fn.
10). Poetry and art could then emanate from the ethics of saying, but they
do not define or engender it. The possibility for inspiration "is laid bare in
the poetic said and the interpretation it calls for ad infinitum. It is shown
in the prophetic said, scorning its conditions in a sort of levitation" (170).

If inspiration—both poetic and prophetic—is the continuous opening
up of the same to the other as the ethics of saying, then inspiration also
coincides with the continuous exegesis of the said, opening it up, interrupting it in the act of interpretation. Writing belongs to the realm of the said
in Levinas's schema: "books have their fate; they belong to a world they do
not include, but recognize by being written and printed, by being prefaced,
and getting themselves preceded with forewords. They are interrupted, and
call for other books and in the end are interpreted in a saying distinct from
the said" (171).

This applies to both sacred and secular writings, but the central question
is the site from which those interruptions and interpretations come—from
the saying as the nonhuman abyss at the source of language, or the otherwise than being that coincides with the face as ethical imperative and
messianic disruption. Levinas shares certain poststructuralist notions of
alterity and the equivocations of signification, but he maintains that the
multiplicity of meaning does not imply subjectivism without any authority; the subject is never entirely free but always obliged to the other. Similarly, the pluralism and personalism of rabbinic interpretations are not
arbitrary, and the historical continuity of Jewish commentary on sacred
texts becomes a kind of touchstone for anchoring and evaluating interpretations. "Inspiration" does not come directly from the text but is mediated
by tradition, which means that history is necessary for revelation. What
helps one to distinguish between pure subjective fantasy and authentic
originality in the interpretation of Scripture is this "necessary reference of
the subjective to the historical continuity of the reading, that is the tradition of commentaries that one can't ignore" (*ADV* 164). No "renewal," he
argues, can evade or avoid these references to the Oral Law. Given
Levinas's idea of a nondogmatic revelation, however, the "reference" to
the tradition of commentary and law would be another form of "difficult
liberty," or heteronomous autonomy.

His own talmudic lectures attempt to enact this hermeneutic, and his
claim that the reading of a prophetic text is itself prophetic. But the prophetic word, as he reminds us, is already a command to the other and
coincides with the urgent demand for justice, political as well as personal.
Wouldn't that demand for justice, he asks, "be equivalent to the spiritual-

ity of the Spirit and the proximity of God?" (*ADV* 18), a scorning of both myth and the terror of the Machiavellian state, but also the knowledge that "nothing is superior to the approach of the neighbor, to the care for 'the orphan, the widow, the stranger.' . . . It is on earth among humans that the adventure of the Spirit unfolds" (172).

What, then, is the relation of this prophetic reading to messianic disruption? Scholem argued that as long as the messianic hope is placed in a distant future, no conflict with rabbinic law ensues; when, however, the desire to bring about the End by direct activity occurs, this conflict is awakened. Let us finally turn to Levinas's talmudic lecture on messianism, to examine his hermeneutic in practice, and to observe the way in which his differences with Scholem about the meaning of language, knowledge, and history change the entire interpretation of the messianic idea in Judaism.

TEN

Talmudic Messianism

To be Jewish, this is to believe in the intelligence of the Pharisees and their teachers. Through the intellect of the Talmud, to reach the faith in the Bible. (Levinas, *Difficile liberté* 164)

Hegel wanted to judge peoples by anonymous history. Rosenzweig's contribution has consisted in recalling that the roles are reversed. To want to be Jewish in our time, prior to believing in Moses and the prophets, is to insist on this right to judge history, that is to say, to insist on the position of a consciousness which posits itself unconditionally, to be a member of the eternal people. Only, in the final analysis, this consciousness is perhaps not possible without Moses and the prophets. (Levinas, "Franz Rosenzweig" 220)

Levinas's first collection of essays on Judaism, *Difficile liberté*, was published in 1963, two years after the appearance of *Totality and Infinity*. *Difficile liberté* also contains two of his early talmudic lectures, whose subject is the nature of the Messiah and the messianic era. Messianism was a central preoccupation for both Benjamin and Scholem, and Levinas's version of it contrasts sharply with theirs. Through a close reading of his two talmudic lectures on messianism, we can highlight the differences among these three thinkers' conceptions of the nature of language, history, selfhood, reason, myth, violence, art, and hermeneutics, and finally consider some implications for contemporary theological and literary thought.

The talmudic commentaries in *Difficile liberté* focus on the messianic speculations at the end of the talmudic tractate *Sanhedrin*. The central questions which occupy Levinas in his intricate analyses of these passages again involve the relation of history to a realm "beyond" it: (1) Does messianism mean a complete end to history, a pure spirituality *beyond* all politics, a fully delivered humanity, or a continuing struggle *within* history for a just politics, economics, and morality? (2) Does the power to bring about a messianic era come through human struggle and effort, or can redemption from political violence come only from an objective principle, a "beyond"? (3) Is history negative and corrupt, or does it have a positive sense?

These two talmudic lectures are long and complex, composed of two of Levinas's first talks on the Talmud to the Colloquium of French-Jewish Intellectuals. The colloquium was begun in 1957 and has been sponsored annually by the World Jewish Congress. Each year, a theme is preselected, generally some pressing contemporary issue, upon which the speakers then base their presentations. This setting and audience constitute the forum for all of Levinas's subsequent talmudic commentaries. The two lectures on talmudic messianism were delivered at the third and fourth colloquia in 1960 and 1961 to elaborate upon issues raised in Levinas's talk on Rosenzweig at the second colloquium—"Entre deux mondes," which I have liberally cited in previous chapters—and especially his discussion of Rosenzweig's position that the Jew exists "outside" history.[1] Before examining this commentary on messianism in detail, we first need to discuss his particular mode of interpreting these texts.

LEVINAS'S TALMUDIC LECTURES: INTERPRETIVE METHODOLOGY

Levinas writes in the introduction to the first volume of his collected talmudic lectures, *Quatre lectures talmudiques* (1968), that although he was well instructed in Hebrew and the Bible as a child, he came to talmudic studies very late "and in the margin of purely philosophical studies" (*QLT* 22). He usually prefaces each talmudic lecture with expressions of modesty before the "spiritual and intellectual greatness of the Talmud," and confessions of his own lack of "professional expertise" in this area. Talmudic interpretation, he avers, cannot be taken up as some kind of hobby; one needs an entire life to master the Talmud, and "it is always a question of a world spiritually infinitely more complex and refined than that of our awkward analyses" (25).

As Annette Aronowicz observes in her introduction to her translation of nine of the lectures, these demurrals are also meant to express "the *necessary* presupposition of the text's power to teach" (xxvi) and of its infinite meaning and status as "other." This otherness is analogous to that of the "other" in Levinas's philosophical works: that before which we are judged. Although his commentaries relate the talmudic texts to the concerns of the present, they also maintain the authority of those texts to judge the present as well, a judgment which represents the "beyond" of history and the politics of power, referring back to the Rosenzweigian theme.

Levinas ascribes the awakening of his interest in the Talmud to an extraordinary teacher he met in Paris after the war, an enigmatic figure named Mordechai Shushani, whom he often mentions in the talmudic lectures and in the various interviews he has given about his life and philosophy. Shushani was also Elie Wiesel's teacher during this time (1946–47) and is memorably described by Wiesel as the "Wandering Jew" in Wiesel's *Legends of Our Time* and in a eulogy, "The Death of My Teacher," in *One Generation After*. Both Wiesel and Levinas portray Shushani as a mysterious figure, a brilliant man with the appearance of a hobo who had no fixed home, appeared and disappeared without notice, lived in various countries throughout the world, and refused to reveal any of his own personal history. Shushani left Paris abruptly, disappeared for many years, and died in

Montevideo in Uruguay in 1968 just as *Quatre lectures talmudiques* was
being published. Writes Levinas, Shushani

> has shown us what can be the true method. For us, he made forever impossible
> a purely dogmatic or even theological approach to the Talmud. Our attempt
> must attest this search for freedom, although it is a conquered freedom. To
> this freedom, it would invite other seekers. Without it, the sovereign exercise
> of intelligence which is imprinted in the pages of the Talmud can itself as well
> turn into a litany and pious murmuring. . . . (*QLT* 22)

For Levinas, this right of intellectual research is essential to the Talmud
and links it to philosophy. Although he recognizes that the Talmud is not
philosophy per se in the Greek or Western sense, and that the Talmud has a
special style which distinguishes it from philosophical discourse (*ADV*
143), he maintains that it has "philosophical content" and is an "eminent
source of experiences which nourish philosophy" (*QLT* 13). This reliance
of the philosophical on the nonphilosophical is a theme we have noted
throughout Levinas's work. He also restricts his talmudic commentaries to
aggadic passages, claiming to lack the professional expertise necessary for
analysis of the intricacies of the legal portions: "The *halakah* requires
a muscularity of spirit which is not given to all. I cannot pretend to it"
(22, 70).

Nevertheless, his readings are not religious exercises, for he maintains
that the thought of the Talmud not only is meant to be "pious" but is an
"intellectual combat and a bold opening on questions—even the most irritating" (13). As the record and codification of oral discussion and debates,
the Talmud is a "dialogical and polemical life where multiple meanings—
although not arbitrary"—arise in every saying. The rabbis of the Talmud
were audacious and inventive yet rigorous and "hypercritical spirits" demanding an equal boldness on the part of the reader. Consequently, the
codification of these texts cannot be explained "either by the piety of the
authors or the credulity of the public" (14).

But neither is Levinas interested in viewing them as "ethnographic or
archeological curiosities," or using them for "homiletic or apologetic
purposes (despite the inevitable part apology plays in all discourse)."
He wants instead to "distinguish a philosophical option . . . extricate a
thought running through the multiple meanings" (*ADV* 144). To accomplish this aim, one cannot stop at the "theological language": "My effort
consists in extricating from this theological language meanings which address themselves to reason" (*QLT* 33). By reason or rationalism, Levinas
adds, he does not mean to replace God by concepts such as Nature, Supreme Being, or "Jews of the Working Class." In other words, "meanings
which address themselves to reason" does not mean self-enclosed logical
rationalism but reason as the for-the-other defined in his philosophical
works. In sum, he is dissatisfied with the options contemporary thought

has offered for a free, nondogmatic exegesis—options such as historicism, sociology, philology, or formalistic analyses. He aims, instead, to read these texts as "teachings," and not merely remnants of ancient mythologies. One could say that in this sense, he returns to the fundamental assumptions of the rabbis themselves about the power of the text to instruct us, but he comes to this position independently of any dogmatic authority. The "other as teacher" is the fundamental presupposition of all his work.

Yet the language and method of his talmudic readings are quite different from his style in his philosophical works. In the latter, he uses the language and conventions of philosophy and speaks "Greek" to critique Greek; in the former he intentionally bases his readings on the Talmud's *own* conventions and assumptions. But just as his philosophical "Greek" has a strong Hebrew accent, here, too, his Hebrew is tinged with Greek. (To use Bakhtin's terms, it is almost as if he speaks a dialogized hybrid.) Levinas calls this language "translation": the aim is for a reading "limited neither to philology, nor piety in relation to a 'dear but outmoded past,' nor to a religious act of adoration" (*QLT* 23), but a reading in quest of problems and truths that also "translates" the meanings of these texts into modern language. "Translation" is interpretation in terms of the problems which a modern Western Jew exposed to sources other than Judaism can understand, a mode of "universalization and interiorization" (15).

This goal for the translation of Jewish wisdom into Greek strongly echoes some of Rosenzweig's ideas about his own translations of the Bible into German and his reflections on the question of translation in general. Annette Aronowicz astutely cites a comment of Rosenzweig's in a letter to Rudolf Ehrenberg as the epigraph to her introduction of the talmudic lectures:

> The true goal of the mind is translating: only when a thing has been translated does it become truly vocal, no longer to be done away with. Only in the Septuagint has revelation come to be at home in the world, and so long as Homer did not speak Latin he was not a fact. The same holds good for translating man to man. (In Glatzer, *Rosenzweig* 62–63)

In this sense, the translation of Jewish wisdom into Greek would be a necessity as much for the Jew as for the Greek—for the continuing reinterpretation and life of Judaism in the world. This relation of Hebrew and Greek would also parallel Levinas's idea of the relation of the saying and the said, or the oscillation between skepticism and philosophy. The said, the realm of conceptualization, abstraction, thematization (Greek), is necessary for a just state, for political life, but it must be founded on the priority of saying—the extreme exposure and obligation to the other of the ethical relation (Hebrew). Likewise, skepticism constantly returns to shadow and interrupt philosophy and remind philosophy of its limits. "Translation" as the relation between two languages would be part of this

oscillation of saying and said, or Jew and Greek, or other and same. Rosenzweig also writes:

> The translator makes himself a mouthpiece for an alien voice and transmits it
> across the chasm of space or time. If this alien voice has something to commu-
> nicate, the language will be different from what it was before. This is the
> criterion for conscientious translating. . . . The language will be rejuvenated
> by the translator as surely as if a genius had arisen in the language itself. (In
> Glatzer 253)

The "whole heritage of the spirit" of the original's language will be brought
to the new language, and so renew it. In this sense, "Greek" would be
renewed and transformed by "Hebrew," that "prior" language which
Greek ignored.

Rosenzweig maintains that the phenomenon of one language being renewed through another presupposes an "essential oneness of all languages." Translation is based on the "command springing from that
oneness that there shall be communication among all men" (254). Translation, in other words, reflects the very essence of language as relation, as
bridge among persons, and can be found in the everyday event of simply
speaking, listening to, and trying to understand another. This notion of
translation as essence of speech and as bridge is a key to Levinas's project
of translating Hebrew into Greek. As in Rosenzweig, that "translation"
also helps form a "bridge" between theology and philosophy, heteronomy
and autonomy, in which the prophetic goal of "light to the nations," the
universalization of the Jewish message, is realized. Suffice it to cite here
one of Levinas's comments from the talmudic lectures:

> I have it from an eminent master: each time Israel is mentioned in the Tal-
> mud, one is free, certainly, to understand by it a particular ethnic group which
> probably really did fulfill an incomparable destiny. But to interpret in this
> manner would diminish the general aspect of the idea enunciated in the tal-
> mudic passage, would be to forget that Israel means a people who has received
> the Law and as a result, a human nature which has arrived at the fullness of its
> responsibilities and of its self-consciousness. The descendants of Abraham,
> Isaac and Jacob—that is a human nature which is no longer childish. (*DSS* 18)

(The talmudic master referred to here is Shushani. Levinas elsewhere
writes that it was Shushani who taught him to read the meaning of Israel
[*ADV* 152]: "The notion of Israel in the Talmud, as my teacher taught me,
must be separated from all particularism, except that of election. But election signifies a surplus of duties, confirming the formula in Amos 3:2.")

Of course, the audience for the talmudic lectures is composed of largely
secularized Jewish intellectuals, and the purpose of these colloquia is
precisely this "translation" of Jewish thought into "Greek," to address
contemporary Western problems. In a deeper sense, *translation*, as in Ben-

jamin and Scholem, is the "literary term" for the deeper sociological and philosophical problems of post-Enlightenment and assimilated Jews. The larger question is, to what extent can this translation be completely successful, and what would constitute the criteria of that success? Is Rosenzweig's optimism warranted? Is Levinas's translation of Hebrew into Greek ultimately as impossible a project as Benjamin's translation of theology into materialism? To what extent does translation as another kind of "betrayal of the saying into the said" require its own unsaying?

Robert Gibbs notes that Levinas makes distinctions between "Greek wisdom and Greek language," and means by the latter not the literal tongue but a philosophical and academic style "which is universal, conceptual, anti-metaphorical . . . the language of the university . . . the common language of the West" (" 'Greek' in the 'Hebrew' " 120). By contrast, "Hebrew" in the classical Jewish writings such as the Bible or Talmud represents a mode of thought which is basically "social, spoken, practical and above all, always ethical" (121). The "universalism" which Levinas intends in his "translation" of the Talmud into Greek is not the "Greek" conceptual universalism which coincides with the politics of totality and domination, assimilates the other back to the same, and denies the individual and the ethical relation. "Hebrew" represents what Gibbs calls a "second politics and a second universal" (123). (Gibbs's distinction here is an example of what Chaim Perelman calls the rhetorical "dissociation of concepts" discussed earlier in chapter 8. Term I, "universal," is dissociated into two terms, a "first" and a "second reason," with term II now used as a criterion by which to evaluate term I.) Levinas does not reject universalism but only

> the universal that violates the individual. . . . In its place is a universalism, which for Levinas is Messianism proper, which is bound to my unique responsibility for an other person. "Hebrew" universalism is bound to particularism intrinsically. . . . Obligation is universal, and any other whom I meet I am bound to, but I and no one else, I as unique and irreplaceable. (124)

The talmudic lecture I will discuss in this chapter examines that connection of ethical obligation to the idea of messianism. Needless to say, this notion of obligation and relation to the other is the "reason prior to reason" that permeates all Levinas's philosophical works and makes possible philosophy. Gibbs argues that the philosophical "language" which could solicit this reason prior to reason and enable it to speak and appeal to all would be the genius of "Greek," a language of purity, clarity, rigor, demystification, a "universal" discourse "only in so far as it is taken in a practical and non-technical sense." Moreover, "Levinas had to re-discover a positive 'Greek' in order to justify writing so much in 'Greek,' " i.e., his own philosophical works. In a sense, then, his own "Greek" philosophical writings become "translations" of "Hebrew" modes of thought, and his

"Hebrew" talmudic commentaries become "translations" into "Greek" (128–29)—a kind of prophetical appeal, as we noted in the previous chapters, of a wisdom and ethics the "Greeks" have glimpsed but not attended.

Gibbs makes an astute and important point, but this distinction between "wisdom" and "language or style" or "conceptual content" and "nontechnical style" does not hold up consistently throughout Levinas's works. Nor does Levinas think this distinction out particularly well or with much rigor, especially compared to his other carefully articulated ideas about the relation between the "face" and language in the early works, and the saying and the said in the later ones. One could also ask: given his notion of language as preeminently relation to an other before it is a formal system of signs, could the use of "Greek" ever be taken only in a "practical and nontechnical sense"? I would also add that Levinas's philosophical style, even in his "Greek" works, is by no means that pure, nonmetaphorical, conceptual, abstract language. It is instead a highly rhetorical style in the evocative mode, a language of "witness" which overflows and intrudes on the language of Greek at all the key points of the philosophical critique— for example, where "infinity" breaks up totality, ethics ruptures ontology, the saying undoes the said, the face disrupts the ego.

Gibbs notes another problem in Levinas's attempt at "universalization" and "translation into Greek." If, as Levinas often argues, philosophy is based on prior "prephilosophical" experiences, are not these experiences available equally to both Hebrew and Greek? And if translation could be completed, the "Hebrew" would also lose its uniqueness, be subordinate to the clarity and appeal of Greek "universal expression," unless there were some untranslatable core content. One could then ask, "Isn't the development of a universal, ethical Judaism merely a reduction of what is unique in Judaism into a Greek concept?" (139).

If sustained, this objection would be similar to the one which Scholem makes against the rational philosophers of Judaism. Scholem does so, however, in order to bring the mystical tradition to the fore and to assert the primacy of historical development in Judaism over any attempt to define its "essence." What is prephilosophical for Levinas, however, is the "reason prior to reason" as ethics, not mystical experience or symbolic apprehension. This "rational" approach makes Levinas wary of trying to find in these texts any theosophical information about the "life of God." Any esoteric references to such things in talmudic literature interest him only insofar as they relate "to the life of man and for his life," "the moral experience of humanity." That, he argues, is the very context in which these statements are made in the talmudic texts: "We know since Maimonides that all that is said of God in Judaism *signifies* through human *praxis*" [italics his]. Whatever God's inner essence might be, God appears to human consciousness and in Jewish experience already " 'clothed' in values," and this is certainly a part of God's nature as well (*QLT* 33).

In the Talmud, he maintains, religious experience is not prior to moral experience. Philosophically, the word "God is the most obscure notion," but it could be *philosophically* clarified "from the ethical situations of the human that the talmudic texts describe." A "theosophy" which begins from "pretentious familiarity with the 'psychology' of God and God's 'behavior' " would not be philosophy: "Theosophy is the very negation of philosophy" (71). Levinas is objecting to the notion of mystical theosophy as a system of autonomous symbolism (as favored by Scholem), and to descriptions of the life of God unrelated to any ethical domain, but as some kind of impersonal realm apart from all human relation. (Idel's critique of Scholem's detachment of Kabbalah from its practical applications and its connections to divine commands might, however, reconnect Levinasian philosophical rationalism with Jewish mysticism.) Levinas adds that he does not intend to exclude the religious significance talmudic texts might have for a mystic, theologian, or naive believer, but "we begin always from the idea that this meaning is not only translatable into philosophical language, but that it itself refers to philosophical problems. The thought of the scholars of the Talmud proceeds from a reflection which is radical enough to also satisfy the requirements of philosophy. This is the rational signification which is the object of our research" (*DL* 95).

Annette Aronowicz has another perspective on the relation of Greek and Hebrew, philosophy and Judaism in Levinas. She points out that Levinas's meditations on Greek and Jew are also rooted in his early childhood experiences with both the Hebrew Bible and the Russian classics, as well as his later philosophical training. But it was the shattering experience of the Holocaust which made him question his previous "Enlightenment" assumptions about the coincidence of Western European and Jewish values:

> For Levinas, the rethinking of the relation of Jewish to "Greek" sources would have to include the vision of *universality*, of *one* mankind in which all related as equals and in which all participated responsibly, the ideals of the Alliance. The difference now was that in order for this *one* mankind to come into being, Western sources of spirituality, Western wisdom, would no longer suffice. In order for a genuine human community to emerge, it was *Jewish* wisdom, the *Jewish* vision of the human being, which must be understood and made available to everyone else. ("Intro" xiii)

> Each essay . . . addresses the following question: what teachings about the human being do the Rabbis convey that cannot be found anywhere else but here which apply to the entire world? (xv)

This phrasing recalls Levinas's own descriptions of Rosenzweig: that what renders Rosenzweig's life and work "so close to us" is that it "goes to Judaism starting from the universal and the human" ("Entre" 122); Rosenzweig's questions about the nature, destiny, and redemption of humanity were "of a universal nature; the answer is Jewish" ("Une pensée" 209).

Furthermore, "Greek" and "Hebrew" not only are stylistic modes of expression or representations of certain philosophical contents but also signify *modes of reading and commentary.* Whereas Gibbs writes that Levinas's mode of reading classical Jewish sources does not imitate the very hermeneutic of those texts but is itself "philosophical and Greek," Aronowicz argues that the very hermeneutic Levinas develops to comment on the rabbinic texts "is also a living embodiment of what Levinas feels to be the specific content of the Jewish tradition, as conveyed through the Talmud" (xxi). Levinas's hermeneutic in these lectures reveals that "learning *how* to read a rabbinic source is already learning what the sources prescribe. The order can also be reversed. Learning what these sources prescribe also teaches the proper approach for deriving this teaching" (xxvii).[2] Levinas's "translating" is not just a question of style but itself a hermeneutic which embodies and enacts the content of what is being translated. The content unalterably affects the expression; language is not an empty container but already a relation to another, a hermeneutic.

Anyone familiar with Levinas's philosophical texts is indeed struck by the difference in tone, style, and language of the talmudic lectures. The conceptual themes and key terms of the philosophy ("face," "one-for-the-other," language and violence, and so forth) are clearly identifiable. Here, though, they emerge from a line-by-line scrutiny of a talmudic passage, after the fashion of classical rabbinic textual commentary and teaching, which atomistically takes a text word by word and expands the immediate context by reference to larger wholes. Levinas constantly reiterates what he apparently came to see with the help of Shushani: that understanding the Bible and the specificity of Jewish wisdom must begin through understanding the Talmud and comprehending the Talmud's mode of interpretation and discourse. In other words, Jewish wisdom is inseparable from Jewish hermeneutics. He retains, even in the printed versions of the talmudic lectures, the cadences and informality of oral exposition, and makes no attempt to convert the ideas into the rhetorical form of the philosophical treatise. Like the style of the Talmud itself, these talks have not been rewritten into essays but retain the dialogic features of the colloquium; they contain unexpurgated references to previous speakers, to people in the audience, to events of the conference.

Aronowicz also perceptively notes that in contrast to the intense seriousness of the philosophical writing, the talmudic commentaries are often touched with humor, a humor which indicates a certain kind of "subjectivity" and is meant to foreground the relation between the "objective authority" of the material and the subjectivity of the person who is conveying this material: "It is a sudden catapulting to the fore of his subjectivity, often in the form of irony, which reveals the distance, the heterogeneity between the text and its interpreter at the same time as it reveals the relationship between the two" (xv). This intentional juxtaposition of modern and ancient draws attention to their disjunction and connection, and to the very process of interpretation itself. Levinas continually makes self-reflexive references to the very problem of how he is interpreting the texts, of how to "solicit" them, of how he might be "imposing" a meaning upon them in his interpretive struggles, and whether or not they themselves cry out for such aggressive reading. I would further note that one does not find this personal self-reflexiveness, hesitancy, or humor when he writes about the texts of Hegel, Husserl, or Heidegger.

This intentional drawing of attention to Levinas's own subjectivity, Aronowicz argues, is also meant to show that the "text does not mean by itself but requires the specific person of the interpreter to bring this meaning to light" (xvi); that is another aspect of the "infinity" of the text, its inexhaustible capacity to reveal new meanings. These meanings depend, however, on the plurality of persons who come to interpret it, each in his or her own uniqueness.[3]

Needless to say, this idea accords with Levinas's view of language as above all interpersonal, an act of witness, a coordination with an other before it is any kind of abstract process of formal signification. Yet the personhood of the interpreter here is not that hemorrhaging, bleeding, wounded, and emptied subjectivity described in the later philosophical writings. It is as if the talmudic text as teacher endows the subjectivity of the interpreter-student with a new kind of purified joyful independent subjectivity. In the philosophical works, the separate, joyful, "atheistic" subjectivity had first to be broken open, made vulnerable, emptied, and judged by the other, and then reconstructed through the very binding of itself over in ethical obligation—in expiation, sacrifice, maternity, giving the very bread from its mouth, and so forth. In the talmudic lectures, the disciple-interpreter, bound over to the world of the text and its teaching, attains a "difficile liberté," an arduous freedom that reconstructs that self, that makes adherence to the Talmud's teachings coincide with the responsibility to struggle with and for its meanings, and connect that text back to the world—an autonomy in the heteronomy.

ANACHRONISM AND HISTORICISM

In summary, Levinas finds in the Talmud a concrete mode of ethical philosophy paralleling the model he sets forth in his philosophical works. The other, transcendence, infinity, cross/pass through the human—as ethical call and obligation. And this concreteness has another methodological corollary: it means that one can understand the laconic expressions, allusions, and images of the Talmud only "if one approaches them from the concrete problems and situations of existence without worrying about the apparent anachronisms one thus commits." Such an "anachronistic" approach can only "shock fanatics of the historical method who profess that *it is forbidden for brilliant thought to anticipate the meaning of all experience*" [italics his] (*DL* 95), and that certain words and thoughts may not be pronounced or thought before a certain time.

Levinas assumes that the rabbis were brilliant thinkers situated in the "absolute of thought," and in their fashion already considered the most profound issues; this philosophic reference justifies reading the texts in light of "contemporary" issues. But there is, I think, a further relation between the "anachronism" of this exegetical method and the concept of diachrony in Levinas's own philosophical works where "philosophy" itself has a special meaning. Philosophy was there defined as the oscillation between saying and said, being and the other than being—an other than being that is not captured in the synchronies of time, in any correlation or causality of past and present. The "order" of this otherwise than being comes from a disruptive diachrony, and is thus "heard" as an anachronism. By extension, one could also say that the reflections of this "otherness" in both philosophical and talmudic texts requires, in turn, a kind of "anachronistic" reading.

Levinas argues, moreover, that without this "anachronistic" approach, Judaism, whose content is principally made up of these talmudic texts, would be "reduced to folklore or anecdotes about Jewish history and would not justify its own history, would not be worth the pain of being continued" (*DL* 96). This position differs from the dominant methods of academic study of the Talmud conducted over the past century using the methodologies of "scientific" historicism, philology, form criticism, text editing, anthropology, folklore, and linguistics. Some might accuse Levinas of an "apologetic" approach, but for Levinas on the deepest philosophical level, *all* thought is apologetic; that is, all thought is a thought for-the-other and must justify itself and its history, must be brought to judgment.

The nineteenth-century historical scientific schools of Judaism in his view were "naively respectful of the scientism of the period": "To spiritualize religion does not consist in judging its experiences in light of scientific results of the hour, but to understand its experiences even as relations between intelligences, minds, situated in the bright full day of consciousness and language" (*DL* 19). He avows that his aim is not to contest the value of the historical method or the importance of the perspective it opens; yet if one remains content to stay within its boundaries, the truths which made Judaism live "are transformed into incident, small local history." And even if these truths were determined by now-forgotten local historical circumstances and conflicts, the words of the rabbis "establish intellectual structures and categories which are situated in the absolute of thought" (96). Perhaps, he admits, his confidence in the wisdom of the sages is itself a faith, but certainly, he adds, one that it isn't necessary to hide—given the other kinds of faith so immodestly propounded in public.

Levinas's anachronisms, like Rosenzweig's and Benjamin's, are in service of that ethical judgment of history from a realm "exterior" to its violence. He deals further with the problem of historical method by distinguishing two aspects to the past: one has a mythological dimension and is indeed intelligible only through critical historiography; the other belongs to a more recent epoch, and more immediately joins itself to current events and to the present. The latter is a "living tradition" and so "defines a past which can be said to be modern" (*QLT* 17). But Levinas ascribes the Bible to the *first* type of past and the Talmud to the *second*, arguing that for the modern person, any *immediate* access to the Bible other than that of faith has to come through perceiving biblical narrative as "myth." To separate myth and fact, one *does* need to use the historical method. Critical history then is justified as a demythologizing process, and that is quite in accord with his overall program for demystification of the "sacred" for the sake of ethics.

In an essay on Claudel, Levinas asserts that one does not attain proper interpretation of the Bible through instantaneous "allegorical" or "symbolic" readings; instead the Bible contains an "absolute thought in rigorous expression demanding rigorous study" and master teachers (*DL* 155). This ideal is embodied by the Pharisees, the oft-maligned creators of talmudic Judaism. The Pharisees are not blind idolaters of the literal meaning but those who "retain the dignity of the word as word," not a "word made flesh" as in the Logos of John's Gospel, but a word which can "adapt to rock or parchment," thus alone "sustaining a spiritual relation in an intelligence," liberating moral action, and the pure élan of love (156). This is the "freedom engraved on the rocks," the engraved writing of the law as freedom or freedom in the heteronomy of law—a "difficile liberté," a "difficult freedom." This is an allusion to the famous rabbinic word play from the Mishnah, *Pirke Avot* 6:2, about the "freedom written on the rocks," which he also uses as the epigraph to the entire volume *Difficile liberté*. The context of *Pirke Avot* 6:2 has to do with study of the Torah: "And it is further stated [Exod. 32:16]: 'The tablets were the work of God, and the writing was the writing of God, *harut* [engraved] on the Tablets.' Do not read *harut* [engraved] but *herut* [freedom], for there is no free person except one who is occupied in the study of the Torah."

This pharisaic rationalism and continuous study which constitute the essence of the Talmud belong then to the "modern history of Judaism," for this tradition allows one to *directly* engage in a dialogue with it. The continuity of this dialogic tradition is accomplished in part through that self-consciously critical and rational spirit of the Talmud, especially in its approach to the Bible. Here is "without doubt, the originality of Judaism: the existence of an uninterrupted tradition precisely through the transmission and commentary of talmudic texts, commentary astride commentary" (*QLT* 18).

To what extent that tradition is uninterrupted, of course, is *the* question for modern Judaism. Benjamin and Scholem in their writings on Kafka had meditated on the "sickness of tradition," the "lost consistency of truth." They felt painfully the ruptures in Jewish tradition caused by the Enlightenment and modernism—like Kafka's assistants described by Benjamin as the "sextons who have lost their house of prayer . . . pupils who have lost their Holy Writ." The critical point was whether revelation had become an endless series of mediations behind which the divine word had vanished, and whether commentary, history, and exegesis were ultimately "parables" like those of Kafka—which, while seeming "to lie at the feet of doctrine" and assume the burden of transmitting truth, also inevitably raised a paw against it.

Levinas, Benjamin, and Scholem each struggled to find a way to live with those ruptures, to find a mode of commentary, a relation to the past that speaks both from *within* and *to* those ruptures. In this sense, Levinas's "anachronistic" critique of historicism parallels Scholem and Benjamin's attempts at different constructions of the past. His "translation into Greek" creates a commentary that attempts to maintain the continuity of that living transmission of "Hebrew" wisdom, but that Hebrew wisdom also in turn judges the present and ruptures "Greek." Or, it is a rupture seen from one side but a continuity from another—like Levinas's image of the blinking light of revelation which as "said" is ambiguous but as saying is ethical binding to the other. His *aggadah*, unlike Kafka's, does not rise up against the *halakah*. He follows Rosenzweig's vision of the Jewish mode of surviving the tumultuous course of history: externally assimilating elements from the cultures into which the Jews have been thrown ("translation into Greek") but internally divesting them of their non-Jewish elements to save the living Jewish core and remnant.

For Benjamin as for Levinas, the historicist method was an evasion, a defensive distancing of the past—in Benjamin's charged rhetoric, the "whore called 'Once upon a time' in historicism's bordello." Benjamin, with his mixture of messianism and materialism, sought like his horrified "angel of history" for a redemptive construction of the past, a past that would not be constituted of homogeneous empty time. "Historicism gives the 'eternal' image of the past; historical materialism supplies a unique experience with the past" (*Illum* 262). Flashing dialectical images, constellations formed between the present and previous eras, might have revolutionary potential to judge and blast open the continuum of history, and "only a redeemed mankind receives the fullness of its past" (254). But this redemption required a materialist revolution.

For Scholem, "dialectic," "catastrophe," and "myth" countered linear progressive narratives of the Jewish past. Yet despite Scholem's harsh critique of the "Science of Judaism," it was almost as if the rigor of this philological-historical method was some kind of dam to the explosive forces within the mystical texts he sought to restore to modern Jewish thought—a kind of "hedge for the Torah." Unlike Levinas, he could not make any immediate dialogical link to the Jewish past through engagement with talmudic texts, nor could he find there the secret sustaining life of Judaism, or the potential to continue it across the ruptures it had suffered through engagement with the modern world and the subsequent stilling of the divine voice.

For Levinas, a living and direct relation to classical talmudic texts is precisely what modern Judaism needs to flourish, and a purely "historical" approach to these texts would be essentially meaningless for contemporary Jewish life. Unlike Scholem, he connects the very essence and function of Zionism to the study and continuity of talmudic tradition. An understanding of the Talmud is as necessary for maintaining Jewish self-awareness in the modern world, he claims, as is the project of political independence in Israel—and necessary for *both* Zionist and Diaspora Jews (those living in as well as those living outside the land of Israel). Even further, "a modern form of talmudic wisdom" must also be accessible to the inquiries of a "cultivated humanity." This he sees as among the highest tasks of the Hebrew University in Jerusalem, not the academic intricacies of philological and textual study which can be accomplished elsewhere but this "translation into modernity of the wisdom of the Talmud, to confront it with the issues of our time." That would be the "Torah coming from Jerusalem"—and that is the noblest essence of Zionism itself: "Zionism makes possible *everywhere*, a western Jew, Jew and Greek" (*QLT* 24).

In sum, in the talmudic lectures, Levinas defends the inspiration and grandeur of what had been denigrated as ossified, pharisaic legalism by Scholem and others. Here in the Talmud and its commentaries rather than the esoteric tracts of Kabbalah, he finds the living source. For it is this very philosophical and ethical rationalism of the rabbis that enables the Jew to judge history, to transform and redeem it, and that is the very topic of the talmudic passages he comments on in *Difficile liberté*. Because of space limitations, I will here only paraphrase some of the highlights, logically ordering and stating the ideas, and so sacrificing much of the suspense, the drama, the asides, ironies, and intimacies of the original.

TALMUDIC MESSIANISM

Talmudic texts, *Sanhedrin 99a:*

> R. Hiyya b. Abba said in R. Yochanan's name: All the prophets prophesied [all the good things] only in respect of the Messianic era; but as for the World to Come, "no eye has seen it beside you O God, who acts for those who await you" [Isa. 64:3]. Now, he disagrees with Shmuel, who said: There is no difference between the present time and the Messianic era except the subjugation of Israel to the nations.
>
> R. Hiyya b. Abba also said in R. Yochanan's name: All the prophets prophesied only for repentant sinners; but as for the perfectly righteous [who had never sinned at all], "no eye has seen it beside you O God, who acts for those who await you." Now he differs from R. Abbahu, who said: The place occupied by repentant sinners cannot be attained even by the completely righteous, for it is written, "Peace, peace, to him that is far off, and to him that is near" [Isa. 57:19], thus first he that is "far off," then he that is "near." Now what is meant by "far off"?—*originally* far off; and what is meant by

"near"?—originally near [and still so]. But R. Yochanan interprets: "him that is far off"—that is [and has been] far from sin; "him that is near"—that was near to sin, but is now far off.

R. Hiyya b. Abba also said in R. Yochanan's name: All the prophets prophesied only in respect of him who marries his daughter to a scholar, or engages in business on behalf of a scholar, or benefits a scholar with his possessions; but as for scholars themselves—"no eye has seen but you, O God etc." What does "no eye has seen" refer to? R. Yehoshua b. Levi said: To the wine that has been kept [maturing] with its grapes since the six days of Creation. Resh Lakish said: To Eden, which no eye has ever seen. And should you demur, Where then did Adam live? In the garden. And should you object, the garden and Eden are one: therefore Scripture teaches, "And a river issued from Eden to water the garden."

Sanhedrin 97b–98a:

Rav said: All the predestined dates [for redemption] have passed, and the matter [now] depends only on repentance and good deeds. But Shmuel maintained: The one who is in mourning has had enough of his bereavement. This matter is disputed by Tannaim: R. Eliezer said: If Israel repent, they will be redeemed; if not, they will not be redeemed. R. Yehoshua said to him, If they do not repent, will they not be redeemed! But the Holy One, blessed be He, will set up a king over them, whose decrees shall be as cruel as Haman's, whereby Israel shall engage in repentance, and he will thus bring them back to the right path. Another [Baraitha] taught: R. Eliezer said: If Israel repent, they will be redeemed, as it is written, "Return, you backsliding children, and I will heal your backslidings" [Jer. 3:2]. R. Yehoshua said to him, But is it not written, "you have sold yourselves for nought; and you shall be redeemed without money"? [Isa. 52:3]. "You have sold yourselves for nought," for idolatry; and "you shall be redeemed without money"—without repentance and good deeds. R. Eliezer retorted to R. Yehoshua, But is it not written, "Return unto me, and I will return unto you"? [Mal. 3:7]. R. Yehoshua rejoined, But is it not written, "For I am master over you: and I will take you one of a city, and two of a family, and I will bring you to Zion"? [Jer. 3:14]. R. Eliezer replied, But it is written, "In returning and rest shall you be saved" [Isa. 30:15]. R. Yehoshua replied, But is it not written, "Thus says the Lord, The Redeemer of Israel, and his Holy One, to him whom man despises, to him whom the nations abhor, to a servant of rulers, Kings shall see and arise, princes also shall worship"? [Isa. 49:7]. R. Eliezer countered, But is it not written, "If you will return, O Israel, says the Lord, return unto me"? [Jer. 4:1]. R. Yehoshua answered, But it is elsewhere written, "And I heard the man clothed in linen, which was upon the waters of the river, when he held up his right hand and his left hand unto heaven, and swore by him that lives for ever that it shall be for a time, times and a half; and when he shall have accomplished to scatter the power of the holy people, all these things shall be finished" [Dan. 12:7]. At this R. Eliezer remained silent.

Sanhedrin 98b–99a:

R. Giddal said in Rav's name: The Jews are destined to eat [their fill] in the days of the Messiah. R. Yosef demurred: Is this not obvious; who else then should eat, Hilik and Bilik? This was said in opposition to R. Hillel, who maintained that there will be no Messiah for Israel, since they have already enjoyed him during the reign of Hezekiah.

Rav said: The world was created only on David's account. Shmuel said: On Moses' account; R. Yochanan said: For the sake of the Messiah. What is his [the Messiah's] name? The School of R. Shila said: His name is Shiloh, for it is written, "until Shiloh come" [Gen. 49:10]. The School of R. Yannai said: His name is Yinnon, for it is written, "His name shall endure for ever: e'er the sun was, his name is Yinnon" [Ps. 72:17]. The School of R. Haninah maintained: His name is Haninah, as it is written, "Where I will not give you Haninah" [Jer. 16:13]. Others say: His name is Menahem the son of Hezekiah, for it is written, "Because Menahem ['the comforter'], that would relieve my soul, is far" [Lam. 1:16]. The Rabbis said: His name is "the leper scholar," as it is written, "Surely he has borne our griefs, and carried our sorrows: yet we did esteem him a leper, smitten of God, and afflicted" [Isa. 53:4].

R. Nahman said: If he [the Messiah] is among those living [today], it might be one like myself, as it is written, "His chieftain shall be one of his own, His rule shall come from his midst" [Jer. 30:21]. Rav said: If he is of the living, it would be our holy Master [R. Yehuda ha Nassi]; if of the dead, it would have been Daniel the most desirable man. Rav Judah said in Rav's name: The Holy One, blessed be He, will raise up another David for us, as it is written, "But they shall serve the Lord their God, and David their king, whom I will raise up unto them" [Jer. 30:9] not "I raised up," but "I will raise up" is said. R. Papa said to Abaye: And thus a *min* said to R. Abbahu: "When will the Messiah come?" He replied, "When darkness covers those people." "You curse me," he exclaimed. He retorted, "It is but a verse: "Behold! Darkness shall cover the earth, and gross darkness the peoples; but upon you the Lord will shine, and his glory shall be seen upon you" [Isa. 60:2].[4]

There is an important prefatory footnote to his commentary in which Levinas distinguishes his reading of these messianic texts from Scholem's in Scholem's essay "Towards an Understanding of the Messianic Idea in Judaism." Levinas refers to the first version of this essay, which had appeared in the *Eranos Jahrbuch* in 1959, a year before Levinas presented his first lecture on the messianic passages of these tractates from *Sanhedrin*. Scholem's essay was reprinted in English as the first chapter to his collection *The Messianic Idea in Judaism*. In this essay, Scholem differentiates between a largely popular apocalyptic messianism and a rabbinic rationalistic messianism. While Levinas praises Scholem's combination of historical science and his "remarkable intuition of the systematic meaning of the texts studied," "All has not, however, been said—as it seems sometimes Scholem would have us believe—when one affirms the rationalistic character of this Messianism. As if rationalism signified only the negation of the supernatural. . . . It is the positive meaning of the Messianism of the rabbis which I would like to show in my commentary" (*DL* 83).

Levinas begins by warning that the popular concept of the Messiah as a person who miraculously appears and puts an end to violence and injustice does not at all correspond to the complexity of the idea in these talmudic texts. Instead, the Talmud contains several alternative and unresolved perspectives on the nature and identity of the Messiah. The first strand of the debate asks whether there is a difference between the "Future World" [*Olam ha-ba* or "World to Come"] and the "messianic era." In other words, is the messianic era a turning point and bridge between two different epochs—this world and the Future World—or *itself* an end to history?

The position taken by R. Hiyya and R. Yochanan is that the messianic era signifies the fulfillment of the promises of the prophets for a delivered and redeemed humanity; that is, redemption in political and social terms is an end to political violence and social injustice. But if that is the case, what then is the meaning of the "Future World"? The Talmud contextually cites Isaiah 64:3, which the rabbis "liberally" translate as "No eye has seen it outside of you, O God, who acts for those who await you," interpreting the pronoun *it* as an allusion to the "Future World." This seemingly distorted translation, comments Levinas, is actually intended to open a new perspective, to give access to another dimension of the text. The "Future World" is for "those who await you," and this Levinas takes to mean a personal and intimate order of things (*DL* 86), an order outside the collective accomplishments of human history and destiny. This order would signify a direct relation between God and the individual apart from the objective institutions of Judaism, the synagogue, the public order, the mechanisms of social justice, and so forth; it is this personal order which "no one has seen or prophesied."

Shmuel, however, holds a quite different opinion: "There is no difference between the present time and the messianic era except the subjugation of Israel to the nations." In this view, political power is taken most seriously, and messianism would essentially mean an end to political violence, a time when politics no longer contradicts the moral enterprise of humanity. That *in itself* would be the messianic era, the goal and conclusion of history.

Asks Levinas, however, would the end of *political* violence also mean the end of *social* violence? For in a parallel text (a *baraitha*), Shmuel also cites the famous line from Deuteronomy 15:11: "The poor will not disappear from the earth." To Levinas, the significance of the difference between R. Yochanan and Shmuel is that for R. Yochanan, the messianic era resolves all political contradictions and economic inequalities and so inaugurates a contemplative or "nonalienated" active life, artistic, philosophical, or communitarian. This would be a life *beyond* that of politics, for politics would be disarmed. But Shmuel in citing "The poor will not disappear . . . " means to say that on the contrary, spiritual life as such is *inseparable* from economic solidarity with the other. Such material giving to the other is in some way the original movement of spiritual life, the source of greatest joy and purity, and messianic consummation would not suppress it. This issue of the relation of politics to ethics, of course, is at the core of Levinas's philosophical works.

POLITICAL LIFE OR MORAL LIFE; REDEMPTION VIA HUMAN OR NONHUMAN ACTION?

Obviously, Levinas continues, the poor do not exist in order for the rich to have messianic fulfillment, and Shmuel's citation of the verse about the poor requires a more radical interpretation: it means that "the other is always the poor; poverty defines him inasmuch as he is other, and the relation with the other will always be offering and gift, never an approach with 'empty hands' " (*DL* 88). (Needless to say, this is the grand Levinasian philosophical theme of "the other," and a paradigmatic example of the confluence of Levinas the philosopher and Levinas the Jew.) So understood, the relation to the other as always "poor" means that spiritual life is essentially *moral* life and is located in the economic realm. Shmuel would thus conceive messianic life to be inseparable from moral difficulties and struggles. R. Yochanan, by contrast, would view messianism as a pure spiritual life, a life freed of the heavy burden of concrete economic woes, a life of direct relation with the other who does not appear as poor but as a friend. The other as "friend" is an ideal of a harmonious disincarnated spirit, analogous to the Hegelian idealism of an "absolute spirit" (87); there is also an unspoken allusion here to Buber's "I-Thou" relation. But Shmuel would be an "anti-Hegelian" for whom spiritual life is perpetual struggle and never consummated.

At first glance it would seem that Shmuel's view accords with (or is being reinterpreted to accord with) the positions Levinas sets forth in his own philosophical writings, and that he would implicitly affirm Shmuel's position. Levinas goes on to say, though, that the opposition between R. Yochanan and Shmuel is characteristic of rabbinic conflicts in general; they reflect two positions between which thought always oscillates in some eternal fashion. Does spirit mean a quasi-divine life released from all the limitations of the human condition, *or* does the very human condition, its limits and its drama, articulate the life of the spirit? These two conceptions emerge from Jewish thought because these two conceptions express humanity (90). (In a sense, Benjamin's combination of messianism and materialism itself combines the two strands of this debate.)

The talmudic discussion continues with the question of the extent to which the enjoyment of the messianic era depends on one's individual merits. For R. Yochanan, it does; in his view, the political and social problems are resolved simultaneously, and this requires human moral power, freedom, and moral action. From Shmuel's perspective, the coming of the messianic era could not depend solely on the moral perfection of individuals. In his darker view, political violence is an overwhelming obstacle between human freedom and the accomplishment of good, and it is this very political violence which must be overcome by the messianic event. Levinas understands Shmuel's position to imply that something utterly alien to individual morality exists and must be suppressed in order for the Messiah to come.

Messianism, in other words, would require some nonrational element, something not dependent on humanity, something coming from the "outside," or some outcome of all the political contradictions. This "outside" is the interesting category to Levinas (like "exteriority" in his philosophical works); here it must be either the action of God or a political revolution *separate* from morality.

The next part of the talmudic text deals with R. Yochanan's explanation of precisely what it is that the righteous will enjoy in the unknown "World to Come" which "no eye has seen." Says R. Yochanan, "It is the wine hidden in the grapes since the six days of Creation." Levinas interprets this enigmatic image of a pure, unadulterated wine as a kind of metaphor for the *act of interpretation itself.* The enjoyment of this wine is the "promise" of perhaps overcoming the frustrations of trying to understand an ancient text, with its multiple interpretations, ambiguities of every word, and historical distance. The Future World, that is, might be the possibility of recovering the primordial, ultimate sense of words. The image of the wine conserved in the grapes "promises the original meaning of Scripture beyond all commentaries and all the history which changes it," and that also implies the promise of a new understanding of all human language: "it announces a new Logos, thus another humanity. The image undoes the tragic knot of the history of the world" (*DL* 93).

Characteristically, however, there is another opinion about the meaning of this Future World for the righteous. R. Levi maintains that what "no eye has ever seen" is "Eden." As is well known, Adam lived in the garden, but, R. Levi argues, the "garden" and "Eden" are not necessarily the *same* place. The proof? R. Levi cites Genesis (2:10): "And a stream flowed out of Eden to water the garden." Conclusion: Eden and the garden are therefore separate! Comments Levinas, although the argument is specious, R. Levi's position teaches that the Future World does not simply equal a return to a lost paradise. That lost paradise itself was watered by a source "no eye has seen," which will be found at the "end"; paradise, that is, was *not* the source. Levinas understands R. Levi's position to imply a positive *affirmation of history* and the future; history in this view is not a corrupt fall from an immobile eternity. This interpretation parallels his discussion at the end of *Totality and Infinity* where he philosophically locates an "unpredictable fecundity" as the positivity in time. Here, too, he reads the talmudic text to mean that although the future instant is entirely new, "it requires history and time for its appearance" (*DL* 94). This fecundity will bring about a perfection and happiness even greater than that of Adam and Eve's paradise.

THE CONDITIONS FOR THE MESSIAH: WHEN IS
THE END OF HISTORY?

Shmuel and Rav then argue over the times and conditions for the Messiah. Rav says that all the time limits have expired, and that redemption depends only on repentance and good deeds; Shmuel says, "The one who is in mourning has had enough of his bereavement." Comments Levinas somewhat ironically, one need not have waited for Hegel's "phenomenology of the Spirit" for the notion of the end of history. Rav already thinks that all the objective conditions for deliverance have been met. "History" is ended; everything is ripe; only humanity's good action is lacking. The implication: moral action now as the *"work of the individual"* [his underlining] is not alienated from history, and one need not detour through the ugly necessities of politics. "Good actions are efficacious. The Messiah—is that" (*DL* 97). But for Shmuel, political realities are crucial. Only a messianism which is itself distinct from individual human efforts would be able to foil the destructive effects of politics on moral life. The messianic deliverance cannot ensue from individual effort.

What does Shmuel mean, then, when he says, "The one who is in mourning has had enough of his bereavement"? The Talmud's own commentaries offer three opinions about the identity of this "one who is in mourning": God, Israel, or the Messiah. In Levinas's reading, these alternatives reveal a philosophical meaning. The first, that "God is in mourning," means "in another language [translation into 'Greek']: the objective will which directs history is in mourning. God is in mourning and has had enough of his mourning. *The objective order of things cannot rest eternally on failure*" [italics his], on a state of disorder. In other words, the messianic era does not need to wait for the efforts of the individual; rather, the individual's effort itself depends on the rational arrangement of things, on the majestic course of history. God has had enough of his "mourning," his suffering from human deficiency: i.e., regardless of what happens, the "will guiding history" will resolve history's contradictions and failures (*DL* 97–98). (This is a kind of Hegelian option.) Moreover, this necessary objective arrangement of history is required for religion as well; it is not solely a rationalist requirement.

In the Talmud's second interpretation, the sufferer is not God or history but Israel; and this suffering as a part of Israel's repentance will bring about its salvation. Again, the contrast is between the necessity of human moral effort and the objectivity of deliverance. Levinas includes here the suffering Israel has endured throughout the millennia, even the innocent suffering of martyrdom which is thus given a dignity and a place in moral life.

The Talmud's third option is to identify the one who is in mourning with the Messiah himself. Levinas cites the well-known story of R. Yehoshua ben Levi's encounter with the prophet Elijah wherein R. Yehoshua took the opportunity to ask Elijah when the Messiah would come, and was told to go ask the Messiah himself. When R. Yehoshua asked where the Messiah could be found, Elijah answered: "At the gates of Rome, among the just who suffer, among the beggars, all covered with bandages." R. Yehoshua locates the Messiah there just as described, tending his own wounds. When he asks him, "When will you come?" the Messiah answers, "Today!" Returning to Elijah, R. Yehoshua asks whether this answer isn't false and is reminded that the word *today* comes from the verse in Psalm 95: "Today if you will listen to my voice." Comments Levinas, this implies that the Messiah suffers, but his suffering alone does not bring salvation: though history has run its course, though the times are fulfilled and the Messiah is ready to come, all depends on humanity. All the suffering of the Messiah for humanity, and even that of humanity itself, is not enough to save humanity.

Levinas now clarifies the critical difference between Rav and Shmuel: "They witness to a fundamental alternative: is it morality, i.e., the effort of humans as masters of their intentions and acts which will save the world, or will an objective event be necessary, one which goes beyond morality and all the good will of individuals?" (*DL* 100). Does salvation depend on humanity, on a moral condition, or is deliverance in the end unconditional, requiring a gratuitousness which exceeds all human effort (103)?

The notion of the gratuitous as the "excess" of ethical alterity and the site where the ego and totality are broken and transcendence or infinity passes is familiar from Levinas's philosophical works. The corollary is the call or obligation to the other, and the priority of this responsibility to any free consciousness. In his commentary on this text, the arguments of the rabbis come to represent two philosophical positions concerning freedom and morality. Is one of the eternal requirements of morality a total reciprocity between free persons and thus a relation with God as an equal partner? Or "doesn't freedom presuppose a preliminary engagement with the being in relation to which one posits oneself as free?" (105). Are God and humanity like fiancées freely deciding upon their union and always able to refuse it, or are they already attached by a bond as in marriage? Can one accept or refuse God as a partner, or does freedom in general presuppose a preliminary agreement/obligation?

There is not enough space here to discuss Levinas's analyses of the war of prooftexts through which R. Eliezer and R. Yehoshua support their positions. But one of the most interesting deals with the prophetic verse cited near the end of the debate by R. Eliezer to buttress his argument that redemption depends on human moral initiative: "If you will return to Me," God says, "I will return to you." Comments Levinas: The "if" implies that absolute morality requires an absolute freedom, "and consequently a possibility of immorality" (*DL* 106). In other words, if humanity does not return to God, there never will be any redemption; the Messiah will never come, and the world will be given over to the wicked. The moral requirement of absolute freedom involves "the possibility of an immoral world, that is to say, the end of morality: the possibility of an immoral world is thus found to be included in the conditions for morality" (107). That is why, Levinas argues, in the end R. Eliezer is silenced by R. Yehoshua's last argument, the quotation from Daniel 12:7 which signifies an unconditional deliverance at a fixed date, whether humanity merits it or not. Rabbi Eliezer is silenced because

> this time the requirements of morality result in a situation where in the name of morality itself, they negate God—that is to say, the absolute certainty of the defeat of Evil. There is no morality without God; without God morality is not preserved against immorality. God emerges here in his purest essence, far from every imagery of incarnation, through the very adventure of human morality. God here is the very principle of the triumph of the good. If you do not believe in that, if you do not believe that *in some way* [italics his] the Messiah will come, you do not believe any longer in God.

Yet, even as R. Eliezer is silenced, his thesis is not abandoned; it reappears in the debate between Rav and Shmuel, "and it is still living. Judaism adores its God in the acute consciousness of all reason—even the reason of atheism" (107).

UNIVERSAL HISTORY AND ITS RUPTURES

Certain Hegelian philosophical issues again frame Levinas's interpretation of the next section, where the question is asked: exactly who in the future will enjoy the messianic era? R. Guidel says "Israel," but R. Yosef objects, asking if that would mean including even "Hilik or Bilik," i.e., "every Tom, Dick, and Harry." The underlying question is whether one must be somehow "worthy" to enjoy the messianic era. If so, messianism would differ from the end of history, where objective events liberate the whole world and everyone fortunate enough simply to exist at that moment.

There are other interpretations in the Talmud's commentaries about who is signified by the names "Hilik and Bilik." Hilik and Bilik could mean two magistrates, those from the wicked city of Sodom. But is the messianic era then made for the judges of Sodom? Or, as Levinas puts it, perhaps magistrates of "Sodom" are those who, insofar as they are magistrates, "place their actions under the sign of the universal" (*DL* 111); they are people who know political life and the state. According to the theoreticians of the end of history (Hegelians, etc.), such men, acting under the sign of the universal, would be considered just for their epoch, for "all politics—by virtue of the universality of its intention—is moral and all universal intention is oriented toward the end of history" (112). R. Joseph's objection would then teach that acting in accord with the "universal" does *not* qualify one for the messianic era, and that messianic time does *not* correspond solely to the universality born in the Law or a human ideal. Again, the allusions are to Hegel, Kant, and Marx, and the German philosophical traditions Levinas has critiqued in his other work.

This critique is also close to Benjamin's concept of a messianism that explodes the time of universal history, and makes every moment of the past susceptible to redemption. Indeed, continues Levinas, Hilik and Bilik are not judged according to their historical situation: "They are at every moment ripe for absolute judgment. No historical relativism to excuse man! Evil can take universal forms, and the very sense of messianic hope consists, perhaps, in admitting that by itself, evil can dress itself in universal forms, make itself *state*, but that a supreme will prevent its triumph" (112). This critique of the state as a closed and repressive totality in the guise of a universal is familiar to us from *Totality and Infinity*.

The Talmud then discusses a radical statement by Rabbi Hillel (a different figure from the other famous sage also named Hillel): "There is no longer a Messiah for Israel—he was Hezekiah." Although the majority of sages reject this gloomy opinion, it remains an important pole of the debate. To Levinas, Rabbi Hillel's statement means not only that the Messiah had already come in the historical figure of King Hezekiah, but that the *idea itself is obsolete*, and that there is a higher mode of deliverance than via a Messiah—deliverance by God himself. In other words, if the moral order by definition is unceasing, unremitting, always on the move, then a "conclusion" to morality is immoral. One cannot immobilize time, or ever accomplish an end or closure of history. "Deliverance by God would coincide with the sovereignty of a living morality, open on infinite progress" (114). Infinity, as in the philosophical works, breaks up totality.

But if the text is referring only to Israel as the object of this deliverance, it would be open to accusations of narrow nationalism. Levinas intervenes with another explanation of the debt his interpretations owe to his "prestigious teacher" Shushani: "It consists in never giving to the word 'Israel' uniquely an ethnic sense. . . . The notion of Israel designates an elite, certainly, but an open elite, and an elite which defines itself by certain properties that concretely have been attributed to the Jewish people." In our talmudic passage, that attribute would be the "excellence of being delivered by God himself." To interpret it this way would enlarge and open entirely new perspectives on the talmudic texts and "release us, once and for all, from the strictly nationalist character given to the particularism of Israel. This particularism exists, but it has in no way a nationalistic sense. A certain notion of universality is expressed in Jewish particularism" (114).

This admonition about nationalism returns us to the Jew/Greek issue, the relation of Judaism and philosophy, and the Levinasian concept of a non-Greek universal, especially one which would not be confounded with the nation-state as in Hegel. The very fate of the Jews in Hegel's system was to have their stubborn particularity superseded by the higher dialectical unity of Christianity. Levinas, however, validates Israel's own history in and of itself as the locus of moral struggle. The thrust of his commentary on this entire talmudic passage is the relation of this struggle within history to the judgment upon history.

As we have seen earlier, for Levinas translation of the Talmud into "Greek" does not mean abandoning the concrete rituals, commands, or ceremonies of a Jewish law, which for Enlightenment reason had little "universal ethical or rational content." He instead redefines or "Hebraicizes" reason itself. The "translation of the wisdom of the Talmud 'into Greek' " (*QLT* 24) is not a denial of Jewish particularism; it employs an altered concept of the "universal," a "universal" which is inherently bound and obligated to the other, the particular. In this sense, Israel as a "concrete universal" fulfills its mission as "light to the nations," as the light that illumines the human "face"—itself the site where the infinite passes the finite.

Yet one could also ask whether Levinas isn't somehow "allegorizing" the Talmud in these philosophical readings. Or ask the same question of his philosophical works: what is the difference between the *au-delà*, the "beyond" or "otherwise than being," and the other-ness of alle-goresis, "other-speaking"? One would have to answer by recalling his strong critique of idealist philosophy. The Levinasian "for-the-other" is an ethical and material "one-for-the-other" which destructures the subjectivity and ego, and to which (as he writes on the last page of *Otherwise Than Being*) all human beings are elected and called, chosen. We might better understand his concept of Israel's "universal particularism" in this context. Israel's particularism is related to its universalism by this structure of the for-the-other, a "standing-for" as an ethical opening rather than an allegorical substitution or negation of one *ontological* realm for another (a literal meaning for a spiritual meaning, the ideal forms, the Absolute, etc.). The ethical opening is an otherwise than identity, totality, or the dialectical negations that guarantee identity and totality. Enacting this opening also opens the possibility of this ethical relation for all others to enact as well. It does not "represent" this meaning as a static particular to be sublated into some other higher or more abstract universal system.

Scholem, by contrast, found a "concrete universal" in a more romantic mythos of "the symbol" which was linked to a kind of quasi-Hegelian dialectical reason as the key to spirit and history. And so the mystical symbol becomes in Scholem's schema the vivifying life force that Jewish mysticism brings to the "dry legalism" of the rabbis. For Levinas, the "second universal" or the "concrete universal" is both concrete and universal only as an appeal to and material responsibility for the other, and that is a moral possibility and obligation for all humanity—and as this talmudic lecture will assert, an essential meaning of messianism. The preface to *Quatre lectures talmudiques* also contains a somewhat lengthy discussion of the relation of letter and spirit in the Talmud. There Levinas has recourse to a quasi-hermeneutic idea of the "symbol" which is somewhat unclear. Problems with his text here may have to do with the limits of "translation into Greek," for he employs the notion of "symbol" while trying to retain a specifically "Hebrew" use of it, and in other essays decries symbolic interpretation. Just as he could use the term *universal* only by redefining it ethically in terms of obligation to the other, he attempts to do the same here with the textual symbol, though less successfully. The stubborn concreteness and particularity of the "literal" meaning, and its guiding priority, is what he wants to preserve—as a counterpart, I think, to the ethical idea of the irreducible otherness of the other person, and as a guard against all "spiritualizing" interpretations which have sought freedom not as graven in the tablets but in breaking and shattering the Tablets of the Law.[5]

On the one hand, Levinas's idea of the "universal" is rooted in a biblical prophetic "universalism," but it also shares the vocabulary of European Jewish Enlightenment thinkers who sought a modern Jewish identity which defused ethnicity and particularism. Yet Levinas, like Rosenzweig, is also a "post-Enlightenment and post-assimilated" Jew, and his Jewish universalism is not aimed at dissolving Jewish particularity to make Jews wholly assimilable and acceptable to European culture, or to legitimate their acceptance as national citizens in the European nation-states, the kind of move Scholem also detested. Like Rosenzweig, Levinas views Israel, its life, liturgy, and law, as enacting this judgment upon history, as a rupture with immanent, universal history. By remaining faithful and enclosed in its own particular life (the fire at the heart of the burning "Star of Redemption"), it becomes a prophetic "universal" call to all humanity, and a critique of inherently violent political nationalisms and the claim of those nationalisms to priority in defining identity and universality.

How does Levinas then affirm the legitimacy of the Zionist dream for a Jewish national homeland? The function of this homeland in his view is precisely a "universal one": "Zionism makes possible *everywhere*, a western Jew, Jew and Greek." In this sense, his view is close to Scholem's: the political and cultural autonomy Zionism confers upon the Jews provides a way out of the destructive dilemma of having to choose to be *either* a Jew who is enclosed in a ghetto, defenseless and subject to extermination, *or* a Jew who disappears as Jew for the opposite reason: complete assimilation into Western culture.

WHO IS THE MESSIAH?

The talmudic text from Sanhedrin also considers the question of what form the political existence of Israel will take. It cites the dispute of the ancient Israelites with the prophet Samuel. The people clamored for a king, and Samuel reproached them for desiring a political existence like that of all the other nations. He would retain "God" as their king; i.e., each

individual would enjoy a direct relation to God without political mediation. This signifies, comments Levinas, an option entirely other than political messianism, and expresses another fundamental possibility for
Judaism. Even though God finally does order Samuel to accede to the
people's wishes, the prophet Samuel and Rabbi Hillel (who said there was
no longer a Messiah) represent another ideal which is significant because it
shows that "the messianic idea does not exhaust the meaning of human
history for all the sages of Israel" (*DL* 116).

The question remains as to the exact identity of the Messiah, and in the
next section the sages offer different possible names for him: Shilo, Yinnon,
Menahem. These are the names of masters of the rabbinical schools, and the
names are given by their students. Levinas finds an extraordinary implication here: that the relation between student and teacher—rigorously intellectual—reveals an aspect of the messianic experience and can confirm the
grand promises of the prophetic texts. The prooftexts which support the
names Shilo and Yinnon signify peace, justice, and pity. Menahem means
"comforter" and is announced outside the order of teaching. This would
define the messianic relation between the individual and the collective as an
"epoch where the individual attains a personal recognition beyond that
which he acquires by belonging to the humanity of the state. It is not in his
rights that he is recognized, but in his person, in his strict individuality.
Persons do not disappear in the generality of an entity" (*DL* 119). Truth
keeps its personal accent, and salvation by God is direct.

The conflict between personal and political messianism continues
through discussion of the next extraordinary passage about the name of the
Messiah: "His name is 'the leper scholar.' Or 'If he is of the living, it would
be our holy Master; if of the dead, it would have been Daniel.' " Levinas
interprets these statements to signify a transcendence of the "mythical notion of a Messiah presenting himself at the end of history, in order to
conceive of messianism as a personal vocation of men" (*DL* 120). The
options of "the leprous" and "Daniel" signify that the Messiah is no longer
conceived in terms of his relation with us, but in his own essence. The
Messiah is the man who suffers—the leprous, or Daniel, who suffered un-
justly from Nebuchadnezzar. But the suffering itself is not any kind of
expiatory power, only a "sign of fidelity and vigilance of conscience." As
the talmudic tractate *Bava Metzia* 84b tells us: "Each era has a Messiah."

But what is one to make of the extraordinary statement of Rav Nachman: "If he is among those living, it might be one like myself, as it is
written, 'His chieftain shall be one of his own, His rule shall come from his
midst' " (Jer. 30:21). The rabbinic commentator known as the Maharsha
tries to explain this prooftext by saying that Nachman was a literal descen-
dent of David. David was the political ruler, and his was the royal line
from which the Messiah was prophesied to descend. Taken this way, this
text would refer to a time when political sovereignty will return to Israel,
and so according to Levinas would mean that

> the Messiah is the prince who governs in a manner that no longer alienates the sovereignty of Israel. He is the absolute interiority of government. Does there exist an interiority more radical than that where the I commands itself? Nonalienation par excellence—this is *ipseity*. The Messiah is the King who no longer commands from the exterior. (*DL* 122)

Taking another point of view, Levinas draws the extraordinary conclusion from Nachman's statement that "the Messiah is me, to be me is to be the Messiah." "The Messiah is me" would refer to "the just who suffers, who has taken on himself the suffering of others." Not to evade "the responsibility that the suffering of others imposes defines *ipseity* [selfhood] itself. Everyone is the Messiah" (122). In other words, "the Messiah is me" is like the "here I am" in Levinas's philosophical works, and, as in the great theme of *Otherwise Than Being*, the ego (or "ipseity") is hostage and wounded, given over, responsible, and suffering for the other. In taking on itself the suffering of the world, the self appropriates that role to

> the point of responding before the appeal even calls—that precisely is being the self [*Moi*]. . . . he can only say "me" in the measure that he has already taken on this suffering. Messianism—isn't it this very apogee in being, the torsion of the self—of the Me? And concretely that signifies that each one must act as if he were the Messiah. (122)

Messianism in this sense does not mean any certainty about the coming of a person who brings an end to history. Instead, it would be "my power to bear the suffering of all. It is the instant where I recognize this power and my universal responsibility" (123).

HISTORY, HISTORICISM, AND PHILOSOPHY

The final part of the talmudic text speculates about the relation of King David to the Messiah. Ask the rabbis: does the prophecy asserting that David will reign in the messianic future refer to the King David of old—or to an entirely new David? One interpretation attempts to resolve the issue by proposing that the ancient King David of Israel will be the "viceroy," or "Vice-Messiah," to the new David of the future.

Levinas analyzes this strange text by reflecting on the relation of messianic history to the conception of history embodied in the modern historical method. For the latter, the freedom the Talmud takes with historical personages and its blatant anachronisms are irritating. In the Talmud and Midrash, for instance, David the great warrior is transformed into David a "rabbi" who studies Torah and is concerned with the details of ritual law. In Levinas's view, the dual Davids signify a rabbinic understanding of history in which the

> David of history is only second to his proper double; the meaning assumed by

David beyond his own time, commands the real David. The ancient David is only the viceroy of this other David, "who I will establish for them" and who is the real David, the new David, nonhistorical. No historical person exists who is not doubled in this suprahistorical phenomenon. Each historical event transcends itself, acquires a metaphorical meaning which guides its literal signification. The metaphorical sense commands the local and literal sense of the events and ideas. And in this sense, human history is spiritual work. (*DL* 124)

Levinas finds in this conception of history a clue to rabbinic exegesis: it is not that the rabbis are crudely anachronistic, or obstinately dogmatic, or simplistically naive, or arbitrary and willful. Rather, the key is their conception of time and the very meaning of history. The very "spirituality" of history is the way in which the literal is guided by the metaphorical—the metaphorical as the "beyond." There is here again a parallel with Benjamin's idea of the "afterlife" of a text; and the underlying issues once more are the definitions of history itself, the tension between history and what is "beyond" history, history and judgment, politics and ethics.

Yet how does this position relate to Levinas's objections against "allegorical" readings of the Bible? Is this "metaphorical" or doubled meaning another mode of allegorical reading? I would argue that the confusion is due to his use of "Greek" terminology. His concept of the "metaphorical" here actually means *judgment* of/in history, not a reference to an otherworldly symbolic meaning. This judgment is made possible by an outside/exterior to immanent universal history, but the Levinasian "beyond" is not the beyond of some eternal, other world, as we have so often noted. The anachronistic doubling of the historical figures is another aspect of that diachronic break with totality and universal history. "Anachronistic" because it reads history not only forward but backward (as in Benjamin's images of history), and this backward reading is ethical judgment of history, a history which cannot be left to judge itself.

Toward the end of his commentary, Levinas again takes up the themes of messianism and universalism in relation to the Talmud's discussion about the "obscurity or darkness" that will accompany the arrival of the messianic era. One of the prooftexts used is the famous line from Isaiah 60:2: "Behold! Darkness shall cover the earth, and gross darkness the peoples; but upon you the Lord will shine, and his glory shall be seen upon you."

What mode of universality is this? asks Levinas. Characteristically, he searches for the context of the prooftext. In context, R. Abbahu is first trying to answer the question of a heretic (*min* in Hebrew—possibly a Christian) about when the Messiah will come. R. Abbahu responds: "When darkness covers those people." Retorts the schismatic: "You come to curse me." R. Abbahu only then quotes Isaiah 60:2. At first glance, this seems to mean that the obscurity of one people is necessary for the light of the other—not a "universal" vision at all. However, the succeeding verse stating that all "nations and kings" will walk in this light implies that all humanity will be carried along in this political future. Levinas suspects that R. Abbahu here cites Isaiah to describe a "noncatholic" messianic universalism in which "the messianic order is not universal like a law in a modern state and doesn't result in a political development" (*DL* 127). The classical march toward universality in the political order is defined by "comparing multiple beliefs—a multiplicity of coherent discourses—in order to seek a coherent discourse which encompasses them all, and which is precisely the universal order" (127–28). For Levinas, this also constitutes the beginning of philosophy: when someone who has remained within the enclosure of a particular coherent discourse begins to be concerned with the internal coherence of discourse other than his own in order to surpass his own particularity that opens upon the universal—indeed it opens philosophy itself.

Of course, he has certain kinds of philosophy in mind, which he then identifies with *all* philosophy, or what he considers to be the essential gestures of all Western philosophy. Here he follows Rosenzweig again: Hegel is the paradigmatic Western philosopher, the culmination of the tradition from Ionia to Jena. So Levinas argues here that the logic and destiny of Western philosophy are recognized in a political condition: the point where the full expression of truth and the constitution of the universal state coincide. The flashes of individual conflict and combat, wars and wounds, are dialectically absorbed and become one in the universal light of reason, of ultimate truth, just as the end of history embraces all histories.

But in one of the most telling passages of the entire talmudic lecture, in fact of all his talmudic lectures, Levinas implicitly contrasts the anguish of Jewish history (and, I think, of his own personal history) with philosophical universal history:

> Suppose for an instant that political life did not appear as a dialectical adjustment of each person to the other, but as an infernal cycle of violence and unreason; suppose for an instant that the moral ends which politics claims to realize—but that it amends and limits in the process of this very realization—that these ends appear lost in the immorality which pretends to support them; suppose, in other words, that you have lost the sense of politics and the awareness of its grandeur—that the nonsense or the non-value of the political world was your first certainty, that you were a people apart from the peoples. . . . a people capable of diaspora, capable of maintaining itself outside, alone and abandoned, and you would have a completely different vision of universality. (*DL* 128–29)

In such a case, the light would be produced when (referring now back to the passage in Isaiah) "darkness covered the people," that is, when these violent political teachings would be silenced, and their prestige diminished. "At the moment when the political temptation of the light 'of the others' is surmounted, my responsibility is the most irreplaceable. The true light then can shine. Then the true universality is affirmed—noncatholic—

which consists of serving the universe. One calls it messianism" (129). This is a universalism of *serving all* as opposed to *comprehending all* in cognition or discourse.

I find this to be one of the most poignant and revelatory passages in all of Levinas's writings. It is the vision of Rosenzweig, but it is also the vision of a man marked by the Holocaust, and close to the vision of Walter Benjamin's sad angel of history, who also sees only "an infernal cycle of violence," catastrophe upon catastrophe piling up at his feet—even as his wings are caught in the winds blowing from paradise and caught in the violent storms of progress. The pathos of Benjamin's image expresses how deeply anguished Benjamin was in the end about politics and the ability of a political revolution "to open the strait gate for the Messiah." Scholem, similarly, despaired of the confusion between politics and religion in Benjamin and in contemporary Zionist thought. The political state of Israel, in his view, was not to be identified with apocalyptic messianism. Levinas recognizes that this final talmudic conception of messianism is also "dangerous": the lack of a universal discourse entails the danger of each promoting his or her own truth, unwilling to compromise. Perhaps, though, this conception moves well beyond primitive subjectivism, for it knows the danger of politicizing truth and morality: "Jewish universalism . . . signifies above all that Israel doesn't measure its morality by politics—that its universality is messianism itself" (*DL* 129).

THE POSSIBILITY OF A MODERN MESSIANISM

Levinas concludes the talmudic lecture with the most crucial contemporary political question: Are Jews still capable of messianism after emancipation? When freed from the medieval ghettoes, given rights within the modern political state and power to act in secular history, "can we still consider history to have no sense, to manifest no rationality?" (*DL* 129). Jewish historical experience from talmudic to medieval times often led rabbinic thinkers to view the secular political world as arbitrary and irrational. The seeming historical confusions and anachronisms of the Talmud "do not proceed from ignorance, but attest the refusal to take these events seriously" in an attempt to mitigate the nature of history's infernal violence and crime. Since the emancipation, however, "we can no longer so radically separate reason and history. Perhaps because since the eighteenth century, reason has penetrated history." In other words, a modern Jew cannot so easily deny meaning and truth to political life. Emancipation was not only the welcome of the Jew to the company of the nations, or a juridical reform within Judaism: "The emancipation was for Judaism itself an opening—not onto humanity for which he always felt responsible—but onto the political forms of this humanity, the taking seriously of its history" (130).

The question, then, is whether this new attitude and participation in modern political life compromises messianism in its strongest sense. How can one reconcile prophetic values with the values of the surrounding secular world, without either becoming a hypocrite or losing the messianic sensibility of the absurdities of history? One could say that this question impels almost all of Levinas's *oeuvre*. These comments also help illumine his defense of "reason" in his own writings on religion, and his refusal to wholly condemn Enlightenment rationalism. The enemy is the "reason" of Hegel, not Kant. It is necessary to enter into history and politics but with a purified reason, a messianic reason—ethical metaphysics.

At this point Levinas again turns to Zionism:

> The messianic sensibility inseparable from the consciousness of election (which perhaps, after all, is the very subjectivity of the subject) would be irremediably lost if the solution of the State of Israel didn't represent an attempt to reunite the already irreversible acceptance of universal history, and a necessarily particularist messianism. (*DL* 130)

This "particularist universalism" of Zionism is not, he warns again, the "concrete universal" of Hegel. Zionism does recognize and collaborate with history, but this collaboration begins with a movement of "retreat"— that is, withdrawal from history as the arena of assimilation of the Jews. (This image of "retreat" echoes Scholem's elegant description of Zionism as the "utopian retreat of the Jews into their own history.") The importance of Zionism for the history of Israel, Levinas argues, is precisely in preserving this particularist universalism in the very womb of history. One cannot believe oneself to be outside history and yet hypocritically to benefit from it; only in the times of persecution was it permitted for the victims to remain "outside" history. Israeli Judaism in the State of Israel has to accept the danger and risks of living in history.

Conclusion

Before and beyond the Book

I do not know how far metaphysicians are correct; perhaps somewhere there is a particularly compelling metaphysical system or fragment. But I do know that metaphysicians are usually impressed only to the smallest degree by what men suffer. (Max Horkheimer)

There are three categories of philosophers: one group hears the heartbeat of things, a second only that of human beings, a third only that of concepts; a fourth group, the philosophy professors, hears only the heart of the literature. (Georg Simmel)

Our life is living testimony that it is more than a mere book. . . . A mere book would easily fall victim to the arts of allegorical exegesis. Had the Jews of the Old Testament disappeared from the earth like Christ, they would [now] denote the idea of the People, and Zion the idea of the Center of the World, just as Christ denotes the idea of Man. But the stalwart, undeniable vitality of the Jewish people, attested in the very hatred of the Jews, resists such "idealizing." Whether Christ is more than an idea—no Christian can know it. But that Israel is more than an idea, that he knows, that he sees. For we live. We are eternal not as an idea may be eternal: if we are eternal it is in full reality. For the Christian we are thus the really indubitable. (Rosenzweig, *The Star of Redemption* 414–15)

REVELATION AND MESSIANIC KNOWLEDGE

Of Rosenzweig's concept of truth, a truth ultimately attained not in contemplation but in verification through one's very life, Levinas wrote: "*Human truth is a testimony borne by a life* [italics his] of the divine truth of the end of time. Rosenzweig called this theory of truth the 'theory of messianic knowledge' " ("Entre deux mondes" 132). This phrase, "messianic knowledge," links together Levinas, Rosenzweig, Benjamin, and Scholem; for despite their differences, they each confronted and reworked this "messianism" in the face of the challenges of modern secular thought—idealism, materialism, Marxism, modernism, historicism, nationalism, philology, phenomenology, structuralism, and poststructuralism.

In a sense, the life of each also bore testimony to the truths he sought. Rosenzweig chose to leave the university and later courageously struggled with increasing paralysis and approaching death. Benjamin lived as an exile and took his own life in flight from the Nazis, bearing his manuscripts to the very end. Scholem left Europe, emigrated to Palestine, and created a new field of academic study. Levinas survived the Holocaust, became director of the Parisian school of the Alliance Israélite, and taught philosophy in French universities. In all these thinkers, a kind of "messianism" exists as the pulling of thought toward its other, toward some interruptive force that can break through the violence and cruelty of immanent history—a search for some way of being otherwise, whether through political revolution, Zionism, mystical reinterpretation, philosophical critique, or ethics.

For Rosenzweig, "religion" as a category of being or "the ultimate sense of the real" is already that eschatological time which is the other of a Hegelian universal history filled with war and violence. As Stéphane Mosès puts it, "This history outside of history, this temporality without becoming, this sociality without wars or revolutions, defines for Rosenzweig the ideal space which is that of the Jewish people" ("Hegel pris au mot" 334). Scholem and Benjamin also elicited a counterhistory but differed as to what constituted its contents, and what generated its life. They both saw redemptive historical possibilities in the very forces of catastrophe and destruction. Scholem devalued Rosenzweig's "well-ordered house" of *halakhic* and liturgical community, and instead examined the upsurges of the anarchic and apocalyptic temperament in Jewish thought. In his work, catastrophe and disruption became fulcrums on which to construct a revisionary history, to unmask the ideology of the "lifeless" rationalistic "Science of Judaism" and its narrative of the evolutionary, progressive development of Jewish history.

Nevertheless, Scholem, Benjamin, Rosenzweig, and Levinas are united in their anti-Hegelianism —their opposition to the identification of reason and history—despite the different paths each took in his critique. And like Scholem, Levinas and Rosenzweig also recognized that the secularization of Jewish life since the emancipation meant a Jewish "return to history" that had to be taken very seriously. Mosès again perceptively observes that it is not accurate to say that for Rosenzweig the Jewish people are entirely "outside" all history: "its nonhistoricity is relative; it designates the place of an absence within universal history, or rather within the consciousness which the West has forged of this history" ("Hegel" 334). Rosenzweig's definition of the "metahistorical" vocation and spiritual essence of the Jewish people thus "should be understood not as the theory of a political practice—precisely that of the Jews' nonparticipation in their own history—but as a regulative idea, that of the 'limit imposed on all politics' " (337–38).

This analysis could be aptly applied to Levinas's "messianism" or "utopianism." *Utopianism* is probably the wrong word to use, though, for Levinas asserts that utopianism is "vain" and "dangerous" if it signifies the desire and dream of the solitary soul refusing the effort of creating a just world; "it is to forget that the soul is not a demand for immortality but the impossibility of killing—and consequently, the spirit is the concern for a just society" (*DL* 139). The "Good beyond being," "subjectivity as the one-for-the-other," "the face," "infinity and exteriority," "saying and unsaying" function in his thought as "regulative" ideas: history, totality, interiority, and politics are not negated but critiqued from a certain "outside"; Jewish existence as a disjunction within history and being also opens up an interval of distance and time, a diachrony, an anachronism, a space and time of the other as judgment and ethical witness. The space of this opening as a "sociality without wars or revolutions" is meant as a possibility for all humanity, and so at the end of *Otherwise Than Being* Levinas reminds his readers that all the peoples are called to the "here I am," elected.

Rosenzweig and Levinas also deny Hegel's identification of the Jew with the purely "negative" moment of the dialectic, as some representation of an "unhappy consciousness" subject to the merciless and impossible rigors of the Law. Jewish existence, consciousness, and law as an "outside," otherness, or diachrony are positive expressions of rupture-as-relation; the Jew as other, and ordered by the other, traces the positivity of transcendence. Levinas's Abraham, unlike Hegel or Kierkegaard's Abraham, is not epitomized by the stark, tormented figure of Genesis 22, knife in hand, ready to sacrifice his son Isaac at the command of God. Levinas's Abraham is the figure of Genesis 18 who welcomes strangers to his tent and exerts himself for them in an excess of hospitality. Unbeknownst to him, the men are "angels" appearing in human form as three strangers. As Abraham welcomes them in Genesis 18:3, he calls them *Adonai*, "My Lord," pronouncing one of the names of God. Thus, comments Levinas, the welcome of the other is the very welcome and intimacy with God, and this Abraham is the forerunner of an awakened humanity (*ADV* 153).

The negative Hegelian Jew-as-other, however, has a poststructuralist counterpart in Derrida or Jabès, where the Jew becomes the allegory of the wandering "trace" or tortured exile, or of "difference and otherness" in general, which then are identified with the condition of "writing" and signification. The very possibility of an "outside" that could also be "within" was questioned by Derrida in his critique of Levinas's relation of infinity to totality; Derrida did not think that a nonviolent sociality was possible. The Derridean moment of disruptive time is the moment of delay and difference, but this disruptive diachrony is removed from "eschatological" notions and, insofar as it takes place in language, is already subject to the violence and the entrapping systems of Western metaphysics. In Derrida's *Glas*, Hegel, the imperial "eagle" who is the subject of Derrida's meditations, is juxtaposed not to a Jewish counterhistory but to Genet; "literature" becomes the site where "philosophy" is to be contested.

For Derrida, the poet represents the "shattered Tablets" of the Law, a breaking up of meaning which subverts Judaic heteronomy and moves toward a "writing" outside the book. The poet (and by extension the philosopher-poet, or critic) needs to "break the Tablets of the Law" to elicit the "other" of language, the play of the text; poetic autonomy thus liberates an otherness which can put philosophy in question. But for Levinas, the act of breakup is instead the rupture with the egoistic realm of cognition and being. This is a trauma which comes from the relation to the other, the other as heteronomous, and constitutes a "difficult liberty" which does not shatter the tablets but which engraves the Law on the very stones: "Do not read *harut* [engraved] but *herut* [freedom], for there is no free person except one who is occupied in the study of the Torah." This very "awakening by the other of the same" is finally "revelation" and opening to transcendence. For Derrida, as he writes in his essay on Levinas in "Violence and Metaphysics," the opening is the play of meaning *within* difference; difference produces history, meaning, and God himself. As in Levinas, the opening of difference does not lead to any psychological or hermeneutic "interiority," but in Derrida neither does it lead to the other than being as "the glory of the Infinite." Derrida's moves are horizontal. Difference is dissimulation, and if there can be no consistent ground for identity, there can also be no "sincerity"—how could there be anything but indirection and ruse? Even God himself is ruse, as he writes in his essay on Jabès. For Derrida, the negativity of the kabbalistic *tzimtzum* or self-contraction of God is the "question within God" as the ruse of God.[1]

Yet Derrida also writes that we are both "rabbis" and "poets," free and unfree, caught always between philosophy and its other. We live both interpretations simultaneously. For Levinas, Judaism and philosophy are the pair that put each other in question; for Derrida, that pair is "literature" and philosophy. Both Derrida and Levinas interrupt philosophy by soliciting its other. But they differ in defining the "call" that originally engenders this putting into question—and the kind of response it requires.

And Levinas asks, now sounding Derridean, isn't revelation of the other, more than any received knowledge, precisely "to think this awakening. . . .

to put in question the rationality of reason and even the possibility of the question?" This is revelation as an "incessant questioning of quietude and priority of the Same like the burning without consummation of an inextinguishable flame. . . . Isn't the prescription of Jewish revelation in its priceless obligation this very modality?" (*ADV* 180). That, however, is the way transcendence is described in the "said." "But can such a transcendence be converted into responses without being lost in this mutation in response? And the question which is also a putting in question, isn't it the very characteristic of the voice which commands from beyond?" (181).

In sum, the rupture for Levinas is ethics, and ethics is the beyond of saying, the for-the-other prior to and beyond philosophy, prior to and beyond the book, but enacted in the daily world, in the flesh and blood. Levinas's conclusion has not been to deny philosophy and freedom but to bind them to their "other." For Levinas, philosophy is ultimately the servant of the nonphilosophical, of this Good beyond being. Yet Levinas remains a philosopher, for the truth is found in neither philosophy nor its refusal, but in the alternation or oscillation of "concept and refusal of concept" (*OTB* 126); this oscillation as ambiguity is the opening of the other, and is in time and the body, in life.

Rosenzweig also concludes *The Star* with the words "to life," and Rosenzweig's connection of the book to life, and to the "end of philosophy," is a critical influence of Levinas's own conception of truth as an oscillation in and out of philosophy. Levinas notes that for Rosenzweig, writing *The Star* was "an *essential moment of his relation with life* [italics his], a book which opens the doors of life. Life stretches beyond the book but supposes a passage across it"; as Rosenzweig wrote in "The New Thinking," the justification for the book, for philosophy, "is accomplished in everyday life" ("Entre" 124). The key point is the way Rosenzweig accomplishes this move beyond the book, and beyond the totalities of philosophy: "the way in which in the general economy of being the union of absolutely irreducible and heterogeneous elements can be produced—the unity of what cannot be united—is *life and time*" (127).

So there is indeed a shattering, a shattering of the tablets of philosophy, but then also a reconfiguration of these fragments in a new constellation. This is unity *after* the book, not attained by the philosopher's panoptical gaze, or by the formal categories of logic, or by any play of textuality or discursive practices—indeed an "outside the text." Levinas finds in Rosenzweig the key recognition that what follows the end of philosophy is not aesthetics or politics, the idolatry of the beautiful, or the fatal immersion in the anonymous stream of history, but "religion." This, however, is not a naive, premodern, or prephilosophical religion. For Rosenzweig—and for Levinas following him—religion is understood not primarily as a set of dogmatic beliefs or social institutions but as an original "ontological" level, "*the very way in which being is*" [italics his] (125). That is why Rosenzweig's concept of "religion," Levinas adds, is not the version against which secularists struggle, nor does it have anything to do with mindless piety, mysticism, or any clerical notions. What *The Star* makes possible is an ontology of religious truth which is as philosophically sovereign as the rest of Western thought from Thales on. And that, too, has been Levinas's project. In Rosenzweig, "theological experience is neither incommunicable mystical experience nor recourse to the 'content' of revelation, but the objective existence of religious communities, the totality of significations which articulate their very being, a religious existence as ancient as history" ("Une pensée" 211).

Jewish life, through its collective social practices which embody the End within time, is "eternal." Eternal not in any abstract, idealistic sense but as the judgment of history at every moment of time. Levinas retells a midrashic commentary on the story of Hagar's expulsion from the house of Abraham (Gen. 21). Wandering in the desert, Hagar finally runs out of water, and retreats in despair at the imminent death of her child. God hears the child's cries, opens Hagar's eyes, and shows her a well of water. According to the midrash, the angels protest this action because Ishmael's descendants will become bitter and destructive enemies of Israel. God answers, "What do tomorrows matter; I judge each at the hour when he lives. Today Ishmael is without fault." Comments Levinas:

> Israel's eternity is thus in its independence with regard to History, and in its capacity to recognize men as at every moment ripe for judgment, without waiting for what the end of History surrenders to us as their allegedly final meaning. And Israel, beyond carnal Israel, includes all persons who refuse the purely authoritarian verdict of History. ("Une pensée" 221)

This "every moment ripe for judgment," extracted from the linear stream of ongoing history, is also what Benjamin called a "now-time," a "Messianic cessation of happening, or, to put it differently, a revolutionary chance in the fight for the oppressed past" (*Illum* 263). Benjamin's brand of "historical materialism" made each instant "the strait gate through which the Messiah might enter," where "a redeemed mankind receives the fullness of its past. . . . Each moment it has lived becomes a *citation à l'ordre du jour*—and that day is Judgment Day" (254).

REPAIRING THE BROKEN TABLETS

Rosenzweig and Levinas finally take us beyond the book. The shattered fragments of philosophy and the broken Tablets of the Law have been reconfigured. The other has been drawn out of the realm of myth, aesthetics, and politics, and into ethics, religion, life. The unique self has been broken open and called to the neighbor. Rupture has become human relation and messianic hope. Perhaps it is fitting, then, that I conclude this book with the rabbinic commentary on the words which conclude the last book of the Pentateuch. The final words come after the description of the death of Moses:

> Never again did there arise in Israel a prophet like Moses, whom the Lord knew face to face; in all the signs and wonders, which the Lord sent him to do in the land of Egypt, to Pharaoh, and to all his servants, and to all his land; and in all the great might, and in all the awesome power which Moses wrought before the eyes of all Israel. (Deut. 34:10)

Rashi (R. Shlomo Yitzhaki [1040–1105]) is the French-Jewish medieval exegete acknowledged as the greatest of all Jewish commentators. His is the first commentary learned by all Jewish schoolchildren, and it is continuously studied by the most advanced scholar. Rashi often reiterates that his commentary is intended only to explain the plain meaning of the text (the *peshat*), not the homiletic or allegorical or mystical meanings. Yet in his comments on the end of the book of Deuteronomy, we find him referring to an extraordinary midrash. Rashi cites the final phrase of the Deuteronomy text, "Before the eyes of all Israel," and writes: "His heart inspired him to break the Tablets before their eyes as it is stated in Deut. 9:17, 'And I broke them before your eyes.'" Then come Rashi's final words on Deuteronomy, which he takes from a midrashic passage in the Talmud (*Shabb.* 87): "And the opinion of the Holy One blessed be He was in agreement with his opinion, as it is stated in Ex. 34, 'Which you broke' [*asher shibbarta*]—may your strength be firm for having broken them [*yishar cokhahka she-shibbarta*]."

Rashi is implicitly asking to what the final verse refers. What was the great might and awesome power which Moses wrought before the eyes of all Israel? Answer: the breaking of the tablets. The "proof" is twenty-five verses earlier in Deuteronomy 9:17, where Moses, in recounting the event, says, "And I broke them *before your eyes*." "Before your eyes" [*le'eynekhem*] here echoes the last words of the verse in Deuteronomy 34:10, *le eynei kol Israel*—"before the eyes of all Israel." And what is the proof that God agreed to this? God said in Exodus 34:1, "Hew two tablets of stone like the first; and I will write upon the tablets the words which were on the first tablets which you broke." The phrase picked up here is "which you broke"—in Hebrew *asher shibbarta*. In the midrash Rashi is citing, the ancient rabbi Reish Lakish is playing on the word *asher*, or "which," in Hebrew, substituting the letter *yud* for the letter *aleph*, thus transforming it into the *yishar* of the idiomatic phrase *yishar cohahkh*, which roughly means "Congratulations, good work!" The last words of the Pentateuch, "which Moses wrought before the eyes of all Israel," are now read as a reference to the breaking of the tablets—the moment of anger, catastrophe, and threat to the whole enterprise, the moment when Moses saw the Golden Calf and broke the divine writing in the eyes of all Israel.

The Talmud also explains that there were only three major actions that

Moses chose to do on his own, and breaking the tablets was one of them. It was a human decision with which God agreed. Reish Lakish, the ancient sage who made the extraordinary word play on *asher* and *yishar*, also says in another part of the Talmud: "At times the abolition of the Torah is its founding" (*Menahot 96 a & b*).

But what is the meaning of this potential catastrophe and rupture? What does the "end" of the book mean as either destruction or completion? In Derrida and Jabès, the moment of shattering itself becomes the "Law"—a continuous play with abyss and negativity. Writes Jabès:

> The Hebrew people gave Moses a crucial lesson in reading when they forced him to break the tablets of the law. Because they were not able to accept a word without origins, the word of God. It was necessary for Moses to break the book in order for the book to become human. . . . This gesture on the part of the Hebrew people was necessary before they could accept the book. This is exactly what we do as well. We destroy the book when we read it to make it into another book. The book is always born from a broken book. And the word, too, is born from a broken word. . . . (Auster, "Interview" 23)

> "God" as the extreme Name of the abyss. "Jew" as the figure of exile, wandering, strangeness, and separation, a condition which is also that of the writer. "Book" as the impossibility of the book, or as the place and non-place of all possibility of constructing the book. "Name" as the unpronounceability of the Name as canceling of all names, the silent Name of God, of the Invisible. (*Le soupçon* 85)[2]

For Benjamin and Scholem, this shattering also signifies a ruse or absence of God. But a messianic hope remains, in the "beyond" of mystical otherness, in the void or force of catastrophe itself, or in the material reconstruction of a national homeland, or a revolutionary society.

In the rabbinic commentary, however, God has remained to congratulate Moses, has handed over the divine writing to Moses, "withdrawn" only to give over authority to humanity as part of the convenantal relationship. Levinas and Rosenzweig find in this very moment of shattering the ethical imperatives entailed in this relation. There is a community to be nurtured; there is a need not only to survive but to reconstruct the Second Tablets, and to receive them anew.

Is there any model here for contemporary literacy criticism? Perhaps another midrash on that most cynical of all biblical books, another book to end all books, Ecclesiastes, has one answer. The last chapter of Ecclesiastes contains the words "The words of the wise are as spurs" (12:11). In Hebrew the word for spurs is *darban*, or in the pural *darbanot*. *Ki* means "like" or "as," and in Hebrew grammar, the preposition is affixed to the word. So the verse reads: *Divrei hakhamim ka-darbanot*. The midrash proceeds to break the word down into two new different compounds: *kadur* and *banot*. *Kadur* in Hebrew means "ball;" "*banot*" means "girls." Reread this way, the phrase "like spurs" now means "the ball of girls."

Continues the midrash, "As a ball is flung by hand without falling, so Moses received the Torah at Sinai and transmitted it to Joshua, Joshua to the elders, the elders to the prophets, and the prophets to the men of the Great Assembly." The verb used here for "transmission" or "delivery" is *massar*, which also connotes "surrender."[3] In other words, God's withdrawal and giving over the word is like the tossing of a ball in the play of girls. Could literary interpretation take something from this image in the midrash—tradition, transmission, and interpretation not always as an indifferent language game, a violent war of discourse, or a struggle for power but an ethical or covenantal relationship between author-text-reader? An act of bequest, generosity, affectionate play, but a play that is not indifferent to the human face, to the vulnerable young girl? An imperative which would bring to judgment the violence of history and war?

While writing these sentences, I came upon a newspaper story about a document written in the midst of the catastrophic violence of World War II, *The Diary of Anne Frank*. The article noted that the house and hiding place in which that diary was written are visited by half a million people a year. Anne Frank was but a girl—like one of those girls in the midrashic image of interpretation and transmission as a game of *kadur banot*, the ball tossed back and forth by girls. Her testament, with all its tortured images of hope, its belief still in the essential goodness of people, is another form of "messianic knowledge," an enduring judgment upon her murderers, a book which, despite the death of the author, opens into life.

Notes

PREFACE

1. Since much of Benjamin's great work of "cultural criticism," the Arcades project, was never seen by Scholem and has only recently been reconstructed, I do not deal with it at length here. For an excellent in-depth analysis, see Susan Buck-Morss, *The Dialectics of Seeing: Walter Benjamin and the Arcades Project.*

INTRODUCTION. THE STORY OF A FRIENDSHIP

1. A moving account of those days is given by the woman who guided Benjamin's party over the mountains, Lisa Fittko, in her book *Mein Weg über die Pyrenäen* (Munich and Vienna: Carl Hanser Verlag, 1985), part of which is translated as "The Last Days of Walter Benjamin" in *Orim* 1 (1986): 48–59.

2. The standard scholarly edition of Benjamin's works, the *Gesammelte Schriften* by Rolf Tiedemann, was begun in 1972 and now amounts to six volumes with recent additions of the Arcades project.

3. The historian David Biale has done pioneering work in his book *Gershom Scholem: Kabbalah and Counter-History*, an analysis of Scholem as a modern Jewish thinker, philosopher of history, and theologian—and not just a philologist, bibliographer, and historian of Jewish mysticism. Some of Scholem's disciples, however, have taken offense at this view. See, for example, the works by Joseph Dan listed in my bibliography. Others such as the philosopher Eliezer Schweid and Moshe Idel have written critical appraisals of Scholem's underlying assumptions about religion, history, theology, and philosophy. Scholem's essay attacking the "Science of Judaism" is found in his *The Messianic Idea in Judaism*, pp. 304–13.

4. I use here the translation of Leigh Hafrey and Richard Sieburth from Gary Smith's 1989 collection *Benjamin: Philosophy, Aesthetics, History*. The numbers and letters in brackets represent Rolf Tiedemann's system for organizing the fragments and various strata of the folios which constitute this text.

5. David Biale has done the best work so far on the relation of Benjamin's linguistic theory to Scholem. He has suggested, contrary to other critics, that it was not Scholem who influenced Benjamin's "mystical theories of language," but vice versa. Biale, however, writes as a historian of ideas, and not from the perspective of contemporary literary criticism.

On the relation between Benjamin, Scholem, and philosophy of language, Michael Jennings, in his book on Benjamin *Dialectical Images*, writes as a specialist in German literature and criticism; he argues that Benjamin's early "mystical" theories of language preceded Scholem's and came instead from "a twentieth-century continuation of the eighteenth-century debate on the origins of language" and the "linguistic speculations of German Romanticism" (94–95).

6. The history of this period has been aptly told by scholars such as Jacob Katz, Michael Meyer, Jehuda Reinharz,Ismar Schorsch, Marsha Rozenblit, Paula Hyman, et al.

7. The rest of this extraordinary quotation reads: "(since the despair could not be assuaged by writing, was hostile to both life and writing; writing is only an expedi-

ent, as for someone who is writing his will shortly before he hangs himself—an expedient that may well last a whole life). Thus what resulted was a literature impossible in all respects, a gypsy literature which had stolen the German child out of its cradle and in great haste put it through some kind of training, for someone has to dance on the tightrope. (But it wasn't even a German child, it was nothing; people merely said that someone was dancing.)" (289).

8. The massive critical debate surrounding Benjamin is aptly summed up in the first chapter of Jennings's *Dialectical Images*.

1. LANGUAGE AND REDEMPTION

1. Another elegant description and analysis of this period is Carl Schorske's *Fin-de-Siècle Vienna*.

2. See the extraordinary letter of Scholem to Benjamin of August 1, 1931 (*SF* 169–74).

3. See the particularly intense exchange of letters between him and Adorno about his methodology in *Aesthetics and Politics*, pp. 110–41.

4. See especially Scholem's famous essay "Martin Buber's Idea of Judaism" in *On Jews and Judaism in Crisis*. Biale explains quite well the contemporary debates in Jewish theology that are the background for many of Benjamin and Scholem's comments in his chapter "Theology, Language, and History." Jennings, however, gives an excellent account of the non-Jewish German literary and linguistic history behind these arguments. Richard Wolin's first chapter of his book on Benjamin has an excellent summary of the atmosphere surrounding the German youth movements and Benjamin's disillusionment with them.

5. For some contemporary appraisals of Hamann on language and religion, see Stephen Dunning, *The Tongues of Men* (Missoula, Mont.: Scholars P, 1979), and Terence German, *Hamann on Language and Religion* (Oxford: Oxford UP, 1981). Humboldt's writing on language, *On Language*, has been edited and introduced by Hans Aarsleff.

6. Stéphane Mosès's essay "Walter Benjamin and Franz Rosenzweig" is a lucid study of the relation of these thinkers. Mosès traces every reference to Rosenzweig in Benjamin's works and describes what ideas Benjamin took from Rosenzweig (especially Rosenzweig's notion of the meta-ethical self and silent hero of Greek tragedy) as well as those of his ideas which anticipated Rosenzweig.

7. Rosen notes that Benjamin also introduced new and very different elements into the mystical theories he used: "The symbolic aspect of the word has not been perceived until its representation has been constructed," and this emphasis on representation distinguishes Benjamin from Heidegger, of whom Benjamin intended to write a strong critique ("Ruins" 158). For an explanation of this, see my discussion below of the preface to *The Origin of German Tragic Drama*.

Richard Wolin tends to present a highly theological view of Benjamin less marked by the ambivalence and nihilism critics such as Jennings, Biale, deMan, and Jacobs find. While Wolin argues that Benjamin's theory of language was influenced by discussions with Scholem, and especially their conversation about the kabbalist Abulafia, Wolin also reports in a footnote that Scholem wrote Wolin a letter in 1980 suggesting that Hamann was an important source for Benjamin's philosophy of language. Wolin notes, however, that Hamann's own ideas about language as expressive and not communicative were influenced by kabbalistic sources (Wolin, *Benjamin* 37–43; n. 35). However, Wolin's interpretation, like most others, understands kabbalistic sources through Scholem without questioning to what extent Scholem's own philosophy of language colored his interpretations of Kabbalah.

Biale and Schweid, however, convincingly explicate the ways in which Scholem's presentation of Kabbalah was often filtered through his own anarchistic tendencies, but they connect this more to the role of Scholem's politics, his Zionism as a radical rejection of the culture of European Judaism in all its forms. Biale focuses on Scholem's dialectical philosophy of history as Scholem's way of rejecting what he viewed as the apologetic and hyperrationalism of the "Science of Judaism."

8. See Biale pp. 72–73, where the importance of Benjamin for this decision and Scholem's proposed topic of the linguistic theory of the Kabbalah are discussed, as well as pp. 103–108, where he argues that Benjamin's philosophy of language was one of Scholem's predominant sources; Benjamin's "linguistic theory bears a remarkable resemblance to that which Scholem ascribes to the Kabbalah," especially Benjamin's 1916 essay "On Language" (103).

9. See Rosenzweig's essay "The Function of Translation" in Glatzer's anthology of his works (pp. 252–61). For the historical and philosophical background and debate surrounding the Buber-Rosenzweig translation, see Martin Jay's essay "Politics of Translation" and Edward Greenstein, "Theories of Modern Bible Translation."

10. See George Steiner's *After Babel: Aspects of Language and Translation* for a magisterial overview of the history and philosophy of translation, and Joseph Graham's *Difference in Translation* for poststructuralist views of the linguistics of translation. Graham's book contains an essay by Derrida with extensive commentary on Benjamin's essay on translation.

11. For an explanation of "God-terms" see Burke's *A Rhetoric of Motives* (298–301). Writes Matthew Arnold, creeds and dogmas are now all questionable, traditions are dissolving:

> The strongest part of our religion today is its unconscious poetry. . . . More and more mankind will discover that we have to turn to poetry to interpret life for us, to console us, to sustain us. Without poetry, our science will appear incomplete; and philosophy will be replaced by poetry. It is literary criticism which will now teach us "the best that is known and thought in the world."

Matthew Arnold, "The Study of Poetry," in Hazard Adams, ed., *Critical Theory since Plato* (New York: Harcourt Brace, 1971), p. 596.

12. The literature of and on the New Historicism is by now immense, and it is not my intention here to enter into the complicated theoretical debates about the methodological claims and problems of its various practitioners. A good overall introduction to these issues is H. Aram Veeser's collection *The New Historicism*. The footnotes to Louis Montrose's essay in this volume cogently summarize all the writings of the key New Historicists.

13. Compare Scholem's famous essay "Revelation and Tradition as Religious Categories in Judaism" in *Messianic Idea*, pp. 282–303, on the relation of divine revelation to the historical tradition of commentaries about it.

14. Another deconstructive reading is furnished by J. Hillis Miller in the last chapter of his book *The Ethics of Reading*. Benjamin's "pure language" is a form of "undecidability or unreadability": "There is an almost irresistible temptation to think of the thing, matter, law or force latent in the text as some kind of religious or metaphysical entity, the 'Absolute' as transcendent spirit. There is no reason, in the sense of 'ground,' for doing that, rather the reverse, no reason to think we are encountering anything other than a law of language, not an ontological law, and yet the temptation to ontologize is almost irresistible." This type of unreadability is "the impossibility of distinguishing clearly between a linguistic reading and an ontological one. What is only a linguistic necessity or imperative is infallibly misread as a transcendental one" (122).

15. The debate over deMan surfaced a few years after his death when, in 1987, a

set of his writings for the collaborationist Belgian newspaper *Le Soir* from 1940–42 were discovered. See the volume of these writings translated into English by Ortwin de Graef, *Wartime Journalism, 1939–1943*, ed. Werner Hamacher et al. (Lincoln: U of Nebraska P, 1988), and the companion volume by the same editors, *Responses: On Paul DeMan's Wartime Journalism* (1989). For the extensive debate on this subject, see also the two special issues of *Critical Inquiry*, vol. 14 (Spring 1988) and vol. 15 (Summer 1989).

16. For an excellent perspective on Kafka's Jewishness, see Ernst Pawell's biography of Kafka, *The Nightmare of Reason*.

17. Schwarzschild adds that "Kant's *Critique of Judgment* had laid a new foundation for art. Whatever Romanticism and Absolute idealism made of it, Kant's third *Critique* analyzed art to the effect here proposed—as the actualization of the ideal (otherwise, a theoretical impossibility), as the asymptotic embodiment of human, rational, ethical values, and as the glory of the conception of infinity and the pain of human inadequacy to that conception under the judgment of 'sublimity' " ("Aesthetics" 5).

18. Schwarzschild writes, translating into Kantian terminology, that the eschatological doctrine makes

> statements that are synthetic a prioris—i.e., they are judgments which cannot themselves be empirically verified but which are, in the first place, logically, analytically true, and which also, as regulatives, make other statements that are a posteriori, synthetically, empirically true logically possible. In other words we are dealing with "transcendentals" or with "possible worlds" theorizing. Thus here statements about life in the messianic era or in the world-to-come are not logically self-contradictory or morally counter-productive and, in addition, produce this-worldly ethical injunctions which can function empirically and be approved of morally. ("On Eschatology" 187–88)

See also the end of Schwarzschild's essay on Rav Hutner and Levinas, where he discusses the critical influence of the philosopher Hermann Cohen on this entire discussion.

19. See the excellent essay by Hans Mayer "Walter Benjamin and Franz Kafka: Report on a Constellation" in Gary Smith, ed., *On Walter Benjamin*, for a historical account of Benjamin's Kafka writing and Benjamin's and Scholem's discussions. Mayer thinks that Benjamin's interest in the motifs of deferment and postponement in Kafka also have to do with Benjamin's own "deferment and postponement of a conceivable decision between Scholem and Brecht" (196).

20. Cited in Biale, *Scholem*, p. 129. In an earlier letter (*Corr* 28) of February 28, 1933, Benjamin had also cited this statement by Scholem, "The absolutely concrete can never be fulfilled at all," as a definition of revelation that Benjamin "held in high esteem." Scholem notes in a footnote to this letter that "thirty years later I incorporated these remarks—with small modification—into an Eranos lecture," his now-famous "Revelation and Tradition as Religious Categories in Judaism." There the passage reads: "Theologians have described the word of God as the 'absolutely concrete.' But the absolutely concrete is, at the same time, the simply unfulfillable—it is that which in no way can be put into practice" (*Mess Idea* 296). See Biale pp. 127–31 for a lucid presentation of the debate between Scholem and Schoeps.

21. Eliezer Schweid writes in his critique of Scholem's ideas that despite the centrality of the idea of "Torah from Heaven" in Scholem's schema, Scholem sees the "*halakah* that bases itself on the myth of Sinaitic revelation as nothing other than instrumental framework, external, not a life-content that encompasses a religious experience with its own distinct essence" (40). Nor does Scholem view Jewish

philosophy as opposed to Jewish *mysticism* as a genuinely useful mode of coping with the crises of Jewish belief. Thus he implicitly denigrates the attempt to decipher and adhere to God's will through systematic knowledge, rationality, and the comprehension of the natural order as grounded in divine wisdom (41). Schweid's critique of Scholem also is a defense of the Jewish philosophy and *halakhic* discourse—but he does not do it through the issue of philosophy of language. For other modern philosophical defenses of *halakah* see, for example, the works of David Hartman and R. Joseph Soleveitchik.

22. See here the entire exchange of letters which contains one of Rosenzweig's most brilliant expositions of the meaning of the Law, the letter-essay "The Builders." See also part II of *The Star of Redemption* (pp. 156–85), in which revelation and commandment are discussed in terms of the relation between lover and beloved paradigmatically expressed in the Song of Songs.

23. Biale also cites a letter Rosenzweig wrote in 1922 to Rudolf Hallo where he describes Scholem as a nihilist in Rosenzweig's *Briefe*, 431. Qtd. in Biale, p. 196, n. 79.

24. Eliezer Schweid makes a similar argument: "Kabbalists do not apply their method of scriptural interpretation to the realm of *halakah*. Halakhic deliberation is a non-mystical activity; mystical creativity in the area of *halakah* manifests itself in clarifications of the rationale underlying the divine commandments (*mitzvot*)" (32). Schweid argues contrary to Scholem that mysticism traditionally played the role of secondary support to "normative Judaism," especially for the spiritual elite, but it was not, as Scholem asserted, the secret source of Judaism's vitality. In fact, Schweid thinks that it was precisely when mysticism deviated from its secondary role that catastrophe ensued (78).

2. SUSPENDED OVER THE ABYSS

1. Aarsleff notes that Bréal was a French Jew born in 1832. In 1852, after the coup d'état, Bréal was one of several Jewish students expelled from the Ecole Normale in the reaction (321 n. 7). Aarsleff connects Bréal's attack on Germanic philology to his desire to undermine its racist elements; the romantic strain in comparative philology stressed that the various linguistic forms expressed the spiritual or cultural natures of the peoples who spoke them. One could then "evaluate" the varying levels and merits of these forms. By asserting that language was not "natural and organic," not attached to the life of a people and their spirit, but was rather human and conventional and a function of universal human mental activity, these pernicious distinctions between different forms could not be made (306–307).

2. For an example of Aarsleff's criticisms of contemporary literary theorists' misreadings of the history of linguistics, see especially his p. 366 n. 9, where he argues that Fredric Jameson in *The Prison-House of Language* does not understand the tradition of Locke.

3. *Literary Notebooks* (1797–1801), Fragment 1989, qtd. in Rosen, "Ruins," p. 169.

4. In the thirteenth century Nachmanides, an early Spanish kabbalist, wrote in his famous introduction to his commentary on the Torah that all the secrets of creation were taught to Moses by God, and everything that was transmitted to him "was written in the Torah explicitly or by implication in words, in the numerical value of the letters or in the form of the letters." He continues, "We have yet another mystic tradition that the whole Torah is comprised of Names of the Holy One, blessed be He, and that the letters of the words separate themselves into Divine Names when divided in a different manner. . . . this principle applies like-

wise to the entire Torah, aside from the combinations and the numerical equivalents of the Holy Names."

For this reason, the law exists that a scroll of the Torah in which only one letter is missing is disqualified. Nachmanides thus explains an enigmatic talmudic statement about the way Torah existed before the creation of the world. The Talmud (*Yer* Shek. 13b) says that this preexistent Torah was "written with letters of black fire upon a background of white fire." This means, continues Nachmanides, "that the writing was continuous, without break of words, which made it possible for it to be read by way of Divine Names and also by way of our normal reading which makes explicit the Torah and the commandment." Moses received orally the rendition in which it is read as Divine Names. Thus, too, does the *Zohar* also say, "The Torah is a unique holy and mystic name." *Zohar*, III 36a; II 87b; III 80b, 176 a (qtd. in "Linguistic Theory" 75–79).

For an interesting alternative explanation of kabbalistic theories of language (which, unlike Scholem's, do not depend on the legacy of German romanticism), see the contemporary Israeli talmudic scholar and kabbalist Adin Steinsaltz's *The Sustaining Utterance*.

5. See Scholem's historical study *Sabbatai Sevi*, and his essay "Redemption through Sin" in *The Messianic Idea*, 78–141.

6. The foundation of all this is Scholem's Benjaminian analysis of the meaning of the "Name of God," and his continual assertion that it "has nothing to do with rational understanding of possible communicative and social functions of a name" (79). To conceive of the Torah as a text woven of the names of God means that the Torah

> represents a mysterious unity the purpose of which is not primarily to convey a specific sense, to "mean" something, but rather to give expression to that creative power itself which is concentrated in the name of God and which is present on all creation as its secret signature in one or another variation. . . . The word of God must contain an infinite richness, which is communicated by it. This communication, however—and here lies the core of the Kabbalistic concept of Revelation—is unintelligible. Its purpose is not a communication that is easily intelligible. Only after it has passed through numerous media can such a message, originally but an expression of the Being itself, become communication as well. (*JJC* 268)

3. THE LEGACY OF GERMAN IDEALISM

1. See also Jürgen Habermas's eloquent commentary in an address he gave in 1978 in honor of Scholem's eightieth birthday, "The Torah in Disguise," in *Philosophical-Political Profiles*.

2. See, for example, Derrida's essay on Jabès in *Writing and Difference*.

3. I have sought to describe elsewhere the differences between a relational metaphysic and a static one, and between rabbinic and other modes of philosophical thought, in my book *The Slayers of Moses* (1982).

4. The great Jewish philosopher Hermann Cohen, a leader of the neo-Kantian movement (Marburg School), tried to illustrate, as the title of one of his great works indicates, the *Religion of Reason out of the Sources of Judaism*. Although Scholem and Benjamin found Cohen to be a great but disappointing thinker (*SR* 58–60), Cohen was to be an important influence on Rosenzweig and Levinas, who were impressed by the ethical implications of his thought, especially the role the consciousness of the other person plays in Cohen's work and his view of the stranger as the mediating concept in the concept of man (Rotenstreich, *Jews and German* 61).

5. See, for example, Hegel's 1827 lectures on the philosophy of religion, especially "The Religion of Sublimity, or Jewish Religion" (357–74). Hegel thinks that Judaism is limited insofar as the Jewish God is only a "national God"; that Judaism does not grasp God in universal thought, and does "not yet include God's development"; and that its attachment to God's laws as absolute authority is an expression of a "servile consciousness" and "fanaticism of stubbornness" (371–73).

For an excellent interpretation of the relation of Jewish philosophy to the challenge to German philosophy, see Emil Fackenheim, *Encounters between Judaism and Modern Philosophy*. Fackenheim argues in a highly Rosenzweigian manner that Kant did not understand the authentic nature of revealed morality in Judaism because "it is outside the realm of both autonomous and heteronomous morality. . . . the source and life of the revealed morality of Judaism lies precisely in the togetherness of a divine commanding Presence that never dissipates itself into irrelevance, and a human response that freely appropriates what it receives" (44). The key is this very simultaneous "togetherness."

One might add that the "commanding Presence" is what both Benjamin and Scholem leave out; their accounts of language have little room for imperative or rhetorical modes, the interhuman communicative relation, or the triadic relation of God, humanity, and neighbor. As we shall see, this is exactly what Levinas, following Rosenzweig, will stress.

6. David Miles notes that the triadic schemes of German idealism had a correspondent aesthetic in which ancient Greece represented a unified consciousness and community, modern "lyric" time was fragmented, and a future time would unify consciousness on a higher level. All this presupposed the romantic idea of some "totality" or "organic unity of being" ("Portrait").

7. See especially the work of Marcus Bullock in his *Romanticism and Marxism* for Benjamin's relation to Schlegel. Jennings also notes that Heidegger "used Benjamin's ideas unabashedly in his essays on Hölderlin" (*Dialectical* 124).

8. The definition and meaning of romanticism is a topic of endless scholarly controversy, in which Abrams himself has been embroiled. I cite Abrams here simply because of his interest in some of the important relations between romantic theory and theology. However, there are important different accounts of romanticism. See, for example, Jerome McGann's *The Romantic Ideology*, a book which critiques Abrams and much of the scholarship on romanticism as itself being under the domination of a "Romantic ideology, by an uncritical absorption in Romanticism's own self-representations" (1). McGann takes issue with Abrams's Christian Protestant model for understanding romanticism and for depoliticizing romanticism and masking its tensions and contradictions.

Hans Aarsleff also takes Abrams to task in *From Locke to Saussure*, where he argues contra Abrams that Wordsworth built his poetic practice on eighteenth-century theories of language. See also the special issue of *South Atlantic Review* titled *Contemporary Perspectives on Romanticism* ([88]: 1989) and *Rethinking Romanticism: Critical Readings in Romantic History* (Blackwell, 1989), which contain essays by the best recent critics of romanticism and consider the field in light of poststructuralist literary theory.

9. There are obviously also Neo-Platonic and esoteric elements in Hegel's vision and the subterranean influence of Kabbalah itself as mediated through the Christian Kabbalah and thinkers such as Bruno and Jacob Boehme. Abrams has argued that the biblical paradigm of history was transformed by pietist and mystical movements into an inner drama in the life of the individual soul, and romantic writers transformed it once again into an inner drama of the psyche: "Faith in an apocalypse by revelation had been replaced by faith in an apocalypse by revolution, and this now gave way to faith in an apocalypse by imagination or cognition" (334).

10. Miles writes that the notion behind the romantic myth of a lost primordial unity or concrete "totality" is Platonic: "It assumes that the world, when it was first made, was a 'totality' on a mystical order. . . . In fact, the concept of 'totality' in the Marxist thinker Lukács derives philosophically from the romantic belief—active in Hegel, Hölderlin, and Schelling—in the existence of an ultimate unity or mystical *en kai pan* ('one and all')" (28). The nostalgia for unmediated and organic existence is a large problem stemming from Plato and Aristotle "on down through Schiller, Hegel, T. S. Eliot's 'dissociation of sensibility,' Heidegger's 'Being' and to the agrarianism of the Southern New Critics" (35, n. 22).

11. Scholem's idea of the "transparency" or "translucence" of the symbol is close to Coleridge's definition. Coleridge was also one of the main contributors to the romantic elevation of symbol over allegory. See Angus Fletcher's *Allegory: The Theory of a Symbolic Mode*, pp. 14–20.

12. In other words, in ecstatic as opposed to theosophic Kabbalah, symbolism and symbolic experience as defined by Scholem are absent (Idel, *Kabbalah* 201). Abulafia is a central figure in the ecstatic Kabbalah, and Idel notes that he rejected the theosophic-symbolic mode for a "linguistic-allegorical" Kabbalah. Idel, however, seems to accept the conventional notion of allegory in his own descriptions. He writes that the unitive experiences sought in this other type of Kabbalah were obtained and described in nonsymbolic language, for in these experiences, the corporeal had to be utterly transcended; the material realm only inhibited one's attempt to "ascend" directly to the supernal realms. Similarly, the literal or "corporeal" meaning of the text was perceived negatively, and "Abulafia's hermeneutics culminated in a text-destroying exegesis that focused on separate letters understood as divine names" (208). This method sharply contrasted with theosophic Kabbalah, where the literal and material shared a common structure with the spiritual world, which was mediated through the *sefirot*; and here the word and sentence were the basic units of interpretation. In the ecstatic Kabbalah, however, the esoteric meanings of the text were elicited by atomizing or disintegrating the words into individual letters, discrete monads. But for Abulafia this was to culminate in prophetic and ecstatic experience.

Schweid has also argued that despite their construction of a rich "dictionary" of symbols, the kabbalists use these symbols "in a distinctly allegorical way" (126). They interpret the plain meaning of texts in a highly mechanical and arbitrary way, one which requires a mediating conceptual network between the symbol and the higher spiritual meaning. And that mediating network was "found neither in the uninterpreted text nor in its explication," but "in the scholastic tradition that shapes the interpretive mode of thought" (127).

This distinction Schweid makes is important because it reminds us that unlike the romantic poet, artist, or philosopher, the kabbalists had to attach their symbols as *commentary* to an already existing sacred scripture. They could not construct a completely autonomous, self-contained, self-generating symbolic system as could the romantic poets and philosophers.

13. Thus Goldman argues that while Judaism was less "naive" toward the symbol, this attitude was less motivating for the development of science than the Christian position. The same holds true for Islam and its aniconic attitude toward images which halted in the twelfth century the progress Islamic science had made until then, and also for the Taoist influence on Chinese thought—preventing taking partial, idealized models of the world for the whole (19–20). I would add that perhaps this lack of ontologizing or less intense attitude toward symbols was also one factor in the development of Jewish irony, that lack of ultimate seriousness about our constructions of reality—a counterpart to aniconic skepticism.

14. The problem of symbolism is epistemological—how to bridge the gap between consciousness and sublime object. "In theurgy, the question is somewhat

different: how to change the object whose structural contour is already known." In the theurgical approach, humanity is a source of power; the relation of epistemology/action has to be inverted. "The symbolical process now serves not contemplation but action" (Idel, *Kabbalah* 176). In Judaism, humanity is given extraordinary power and responsibility not only to repair the world but to repair the divine glory itself. This emphasis on action over thought and responsibility for the entire cosmos means that "no speculation of faith can change exterior reality, which must be rescued from its fallen state" (179).

15. Another one of Scholem's central theses which Idel strongly challenges is that Kabbalah was essentially an infusion of gnostic ideas into Judaism. Recent research has indicated that gnosticism itself might have been influenced by ancient Judaism. Although there are some structural similarities, Idel proposes that gnosticism "can be seen as a type of theosophy that severed itself from the ritualistic—eventually theurgic—backgrounds that had sustained and motivated it, one of which was Jewish." This separation of speculation from practice led to some of its unbalanced and esoteric ideas, which ultimately separated it from a larger public: "bizarre theosophies are commonly the patrimony of elites," writes Idel (*Kabbalah* 262). This analysis also helps explain again why Scholem's work has had so much appeal for many contemporary writers and critics who are alienated from the realm of Jewish law and practice yet attracted to a highly speculative, theosophical-hermeneutic image of Judaism.

4. ALLEGORY AND REDEMPTION

1. This notion was quite inadequate from an orthodox Marxist point of view, for Benjamin had no adequate theory of "mediation" between the material "base" and the cultural "superstructure." Jennings points out that the links between base and superstructure made through "constellations" of dialectical images were more like the Freudian dream mechanisms of displacement, condensation, and transference (32).

2. Biale goes so far as to argue that Scholem's historiography itself was a product of his anarchistic theology. Although the kabbalists were not anarchists but adherents of traditional Jewish law, the latent anarchism Scholem claimed to find in their understanding of revelation made them a kind of precursor for Scholem's secular historiography. Kabbalah, like all Jewish tradition, presents itself as a *commentary* on revelation, and the secularized commentaries of modern historiography then become a kind of counterpart of theology (*Scholem* 102). As Biale and others have noted, Scholem clearly had a strong affinity with his kabbalistic sources, and the similarities between Scholem's own philological and "theological formulations and those he ascribes to Kabbalah seem too striking to be coincidental" (101).

3. See Steven Schwarzschild's astute essay on Jewish aesthetics, where he relates the Second Commandment against making "images" and representations of God (Exod. 20:4, Deut. 4:16–18; 5–8) to the history of Jewish art and aesthetics. According to Jewish law, it is permissible, however, to show the "absence of spirit" in physical representations. This evolves into what Schwarzchild calls the "theology of the slashed nose," splitting the nose to emphasize that what one could see did not really represent the spiritual object. This same principle of "incompleteness," he notes, is a critical component in modernist art, and part of its "Jewishness" ("Aesthetics" 3–4).

4. See Menninghaus's essay on Benjamin's theory of myth for more on the relation of Creuzer to Benjamin, and the relation of allegory, symbol, and myth throughout Benjamin's work. Menninghaus argues that

what Benjamin's early essay on language abstractly introduced (concrete and abstract linguistic elements, name and word, symbol and allegory), and what the subsequent essays on literature divided into the analysis of differing poles (myth and symbolism in the *Elective Affinities* essay versus anti-mythical allegory in the *trauerspiel* book), are finally reunited on an advanced level in the *Passagen-work*: this work deals with both the mythical symbolism of the technical thing worlds . . . *and* with the anti-mythical allegory in Baudelaire's poetry. . . . Benjamin's intentions were not realized in the mere destruction of myth, but in its reconciling redemption. (314)

5. In a 1921 essay on Goethe's *Elective Affinites*, Benjamin formulated a distinction between two aspects of criticism, "critique" and "commentary": "Critique seeks the truth content of a work of art, commentary its material content." The truth content is bound to the material content, and the greater the work, the more inward and inconspicuous is this binding. The truth content lies "hidden" in the material content, but a separation occurs over time, and so "that which is real in the work will reveal itself all the more clearly to the observer as, in the course of its life, the work gradually dies." There is again no *Lebensphilosophie* here—no immediate access to the springs of vital life. There is no immediate access to the truth content, but "increasingly, the interpretation of the striking and strange—of the material content—becomes the precondition for every later critic" (*GS* I: 125).

Commentary, which analyzes the material content, is not only traditional philology. In a characteristically brilliant metaphor, Benjamin compares the growing work, that is, the work as it lives through historical time, to a "flaming pyre . . . the commentator stands before it like the chemist, the critic like the alchemist. Whereas for the former wood and ashes remain the objects of analysis, the flame alone remains for the latter a riddle: that of the living. Thus the critic asks after truth, whose living flame burns on over the ponderous failure of what has been and the light ashes of experience" (*GS* I: 126). The interpretation of this figure is as complicated a task as that of the image of the vessel in fragments in the translation essay. For there is also the "burning pyre" of Benjamin's own work, "whose living flame burns on over the ponderous failure of what has been." Fire is destructive, transforming material to ashes. Traditional philological criticism examines these remnants, ashes, ruins; criticism sees the flame as another form of transmutation, like the alchemist who attempts to convert base matter into gold. Flame as truth and/or as destructive apocalypse? as redemptive self-sacrifice and/or negative death wish? Benjamin's theology and/or Benjamin's materialism, and/or Benjamin's nihilism?

6. See also deMan's reliance on Benjamin's theory of allegory in his critique of Jauss's phenomenology of reading in "Reading and History," in *The Resistance to Theory*.

7. I shall also discuss this comic-ironic temperament of deconstruction in the next part of this book when I compare Levinas's critique of ontology, representation, and signification to that of Derrida as the difference between "prophetic reason" and "parodic play."

8. On a visit with Scholem to Ernest Lewy (a philologist and one of the teachers with whom Benjamin had studied Humboldt's work on language), "there developed a long conversation about the Jews' relationship to language" and a heated debate about Karl Kraus. Writes Scholem: "I had for a long time reflected on the derivation of Kraus's style from the Hebrew prose and poetry of medieval Jewry— the language of the great *halakhists* and of the 'mosaic style,' the poetic prose in which linguistic scraps of sacred texts are whirled around kaleidoscope like and are journalistically, polemically, descriptively, and even erotically profaned" (*SF* 107).

5. MEMORY IS THE SECRET OF REDEMPTION

1. For more on historiography and the interpretation of Midrash, see my essay "Fragments of the Rock: Contemporary Literary Theory and the Study of Rabbinic Texts."

2. Roskies describes how his own book emerged from a personal preoccupation with the question of how a modern Jew can respond to the catastrophe of the Holocaust: "How, then, does one mourn effectively when there is no way back and the ruins will never be rebuilt? Perhaps the answer lies in the question itself: by that which is most sacred, most fraught with meaning, and demolishing it with the force of the Holocaust, the mourner-survivor approximates the actions of the enemy and thus arrives at a permanent break which leaves a few sacred shards while shattering the vessel for all time. . . . by invoking His Name, even in vain, I was reaching out for meaning, . . . by subjecting the ancient texts to violence I was merely doing what my ancestors had done since the beginning. The memory of sacrilege and murder was always channeled back into the sources of greatest holiness" (*Against* 8–9). Roskies's method parallels the constellations of Benjamin's dialectical images in a moment of shock.

3. See also Michael Walzer's *Exodus and Revolution* for a discussion of the influence on the Puritan revolutionaries in England of the biblical Exodus narratives, and Norman Cohn's *The Pursuit of the Millennium* for the relation of biblical messianism to medieval and reformation chiliastic and political movements, and to modern totalitarianism.

4. One of Scholem's most cogent expositions of Lurianic theory and its relation to Jewish history is his introduction to his book on Sabbatai Sevi. Lurianic ideas became transformed by the Sabbatians, however, into heretical antinomians. See also Scholem's discussion in "Redemption through Sin" in *The Messianic Idea*, and the chapters on Luria and "Sabbatianism and Mystical Heresy" in *Major Trends*.

5. Paul Mendes-Flohr connects this negative definition of truth in Benjamin and the Frankfurt School to the Jewish prescription of forbidding images of God, and defining God as entirely other. Horkheimer, a leading member of the Frankfurt School, also made the association ("To Brush History" 633–36).

6. On the relation between Benjamin and Nietzsche's philosophy of history, and their mutual disgust for traditional academic life, see Irving Wohlfarth's "Resentment Begins at Home," in Smith, *On Walter Benjamin*.

7. I have also discussed the relation of Bloom's literary theory to Scholem and Kabbalah in my book *The Slayers of Moses*.

8. See the letter of Scholem to Benjamin of September 19, 1933, for the complete text of Scholem's poem (*Corr* 79–80). Scholem found this will only in 1966, in the Benjamin archives in Potsdam, East Germany. Benjamin had made it out when he was seriously contemplating suicide. He bequeathed all the manuscripts in his estate to Scholem for deposit in the library of the Hebrew University, and also ceded him the rights for publication of his writings (*SF* 187–88).

9. In one of his books, Scholem describes some of the kabbalistic interpretations of the rituals of *tikkun hatzoth*, the midnight lamentation over the destruction of the Temple. The *Zohar* relates that "at midnight God enters Paradise to rejoice with the righteous. All the trees in Paradise burst into hymns. A wind rises from the north, a spark flies from the power of the north, the fire in God, which is the fire of the power of judgment, and strikes the Archangel Gabriel (who himself sprang from this power in God) under his wings. His cry awakens all the cocks at midnight. . . . Then it is time for the pious to arise. . . . " And at midnight, God himself remembers the destruction and breaks into lamentations which shake all the worlds, and halts the songs of praise of the angels (*KS* 148).

10. According to Benjamin's notes, "Remembrance" is the "quintessence of the Jews' theological conception of history" (*GS* I, 3: 1252). "Memory," he writes in his essay "The Storyteller," "creates the chain of tradition which passes a happening on from generation to generation" (*Illum* 98); that is, it creates the future.

Benjamin also emphasizes the power of memory in his conversations with Brecht about Kafka's story "The Next Village": "the true measure of life is remembrance. Retrospectively, it traverses life with the speed of lightning. As quickly as one turns back a few pages, it has gone back from the next village to the point where the rider decided to set off. He whose life has turned into writing, like old people's, likes to read this writing only backward. Only so does he meet himself, and only so—in flight from the present—can his life be understood" (*Refl* 209–10).

6. THE RUPTURE OF THE GOOD

1. One of the best sources for biographical material on Levinas is the series of recent interviews with François Poirié *Emmanuel Levinas: Qui êtes-vous?* See also the interviews with Philippe Nemo published in English as *Ethics and Infinity*, and Annette Aronowicz's excellent introduction to her translation of Levinas's talmudic lectures.

2. See Andre Chouraqui's study *L'Alliance Israélite Universelle et la renaissance juive contemporaine.*

3. The most complete bibliography of Levinas has been compiled by Roger Burggraeve, *Emmanuel Levinas: Une bibliographie primaire et secondaire (1925–1985)*, published by the Center for Metaphysics and Philosophy of God (Leuven, Belgium, 1986). It lists approximately four hundred items by Levinas himself and about eight hundred more essays and books written about him over the past fifty years. A recent collection in his honor, *Textes pour Emmanuel Levinas* (1982), contains Derrida's second major essay on Levinas, along with contributions by Blanchot, Jabès, Lyotard, Ricoeur, and others. Edith Wyschogrod wrote the first major study of Levinas in English. See her book for an excellent explication of Levinas's work up to *Totality and Infinity* in the context of Husserl, Heidegger, and the problems of philosophy.

4. For Levinas's evaluation of Blanchot's thought, see his *Sur Maurice Blanchot* (Paris: Fata Morgana, 1975). For Blanchot on Levinas, see his *L'entretien infini* (Paris: Gallimard, 1969).

5. I am indebted to Annette Aronowicz for this insight about repetition as an aspect of the idea of infinity in Levinas's style (personal interview, July 7, 1987).

6. For a literary analysis of the Bible that is congruent with the Levinasian view of language as ethical bond, see Harold Fisch's *Poetry with a Purpose.*

7. In another interview with Salomon Malka, Levinas says that it is Rosenzweig's critique of the idea of totality in *The Star* "that I have purely and simply taken over" (Malka 105). Hermann Cohen, the great neo-Kantian and founder of the Marburg School, is another key influence on Levinas as he also was on Rosenzweig. For an exposition of the relation between Levinas and Cohen, see the forthcoming book on Levinas by Robert Gibbs, who has generously shared with me his lucid discussions of this relation in his unpublished talk to the Association for Jewish Studies, December 1988, "The Unique Other: Hermann Cohen and Emmanuel Levinas," and his essay "The Limits of Thought: Rosenzweig, Schelling, and Cohen," forthcoming in *Zeitschrift für philosophische Forschung*. See also Edith Wyschogrod's excellent essay "The Moral Self: Emmanuel Levinas and Hermann Cohen."

8. For an excellent exposition of Rosenzweig's idea of "meta," see Nathan Rotenstreich, "Rosenzweig's Notion of Metaethics," in Mendes-Flohr, *The Philosophy of Franz Rosenzweig.*

9. See especially Levinas's talmudic lecture "The Temptation of Temptation" in *Quatre lectures talmudiques*, where he defines the temptation of philosophy in Rosenzweigian terms and contrasts it with a Jewish mode of knowing and the idea of revelation.

10. See the excellent anthology *After Philosophy: End or Transformation*, ed. K. Baynes et al., for an in-depth examination of these issues.

11. See, for example, Miller's *The Ethics of Reading*, Booth's *The Company We Keep*, and Tobin Siebers's *The Ethics of Criticism*.

12. See, for example, the statement of Louis Montrose, one of the most well known exponents of the New Historicism:

> Our most important work as teachers and scholars . . . [is] to interrogate the legacy we are charged (and paid) to transmit. It is by construing literature as an unstable and agonistic field of verbal and social practices—rather than as the trans-historical residence of what Bennett calls "great works, ideas, and minds"—that literary criticism rearticulates itself as a site of intellectually and socially significant work in the historical present. If, by the ways in which we choose to read Renaissance texts, we bring to our students and to ourselves a sense of our own historicity, an apprehension of our own positionings within ideology, then we are at the same time demonstrating the limited but nevertheless tangible possibility of contesting the regime of power and knowledge that at once sustains and constrains us. ("Professing the Renaissance" 30–31)

For a critique of the rhetoric and logic of the New Historicist view of the impersonality of "textual functions," see Richard Levin's "The Poetics and Politics of Bardicide."

13. See Abraham Kaplan's excellent essay on this topic, "The Jewish Argument with God," *Commentary*, October 1980: 43–47.

14. This idea about the respective roles Judaism and Christianity play in bringing about the redemption of history is one of Rosenzweig's most well known and controversial notions. It is elaborated at length in part III of *The Star*. For him, the collective "we" of each community represents different ways Eternity comes into Time, the "eternal way" as contrasted with the "eternal life." Part III of *The Star* contains extensive phenomenological analyses of the liturgical structures of each religion, and the ways in which "religious time" relates to the historical existence of each religion. As Levinas writes, the *collective* and *communal* nature of this Eternity in time protects Rosenzweig against "the mystique and hallucinations of subjectivity" ("Une pensée" 217) while at the same guarding the singularity of the individual. I will address this topic more in later chapters. For more on the analysis of intersubjectivity in Rosenzweig and Levinas, see Richard Cohen, "Non-indifference in the Thought of Emmanuel Levinas and Franz Rosenzweig."

15. See *Star*, part III, book 1, "The Peoples of the World: Messianic Politics."

7. THE TRACE, THE FACE, AND THE WORD OF THE OTHER

1. See Levinas's *Time and the Other* for more on this subject.

2. See also Fredric Jameson's comments about "The Dialectic of Utopia and Ideology" in the conclusion to his *The Political Unconscious* for a rendering of this problem in terms of contemporary Marxism.

3. For an extended reading of Levinas in relation to contemporary French feminism, see Catherine Chalier, *Figures du féminin*.

4. See also Maimonides's discussion of the meaning of the trope "face" in *The Guide for the Perplexed*, part I, section 37. Among the biblical significations Maimonides enumerates for "face" (*panim*) are "the presence and existence of a per-

son," "the hearing of a voice without seeing any similitude," i.e., the inability to comprehend God's true existence as such, and "attention or regard" for the other person. All these meanings are taken up by Levinas as well.

5. The elaborate attempts by many literary theorists to disentangle deMan from his profascist early writings and to see deMan's later development of deconstruction as a form of purifying skepticism that would prevent all such violence reminds one of the warning of Trollope's old Duke of Omnium: "There is such a thing as a conscience with so fine an edge that it will allow a man to do nothing."

6. See especially Rosenzweig's brilliant close reading of Genesis 1, in *The Star* (151–55).

8. PARODIC PLAY, PROPHETIC REASON, AND ETHICAL RHETORIC

1. For a particularly lucid explanation of the relation of Levinas's philosophy of language to Husserlian and Heideggerian phenomenology, see Adriaan Peperzak's essay "From Intentionality to Responsibility" in Dallery and Scott, *The Question of the Other.*

2. I do not have space here to discuss Derrida's intricate analyses of Levinas in this piece. Moreover, this has already been done superbly by Robert Bernasconi in his essays "The Trace of Levinas in Derrida" and "Deconstruction and the Possibility of Ethics." I agree with Bernasconi's conclusion that "the question remains whether Derrida in being deaf to the ethical voice of saying, does not fail to do justice to all the possibilities of language to which Levinas has introduced us and does not therefore ultimately fail in his description of the necessities governing Levinas's language" ("Trace of Levinas" 40).

3. See also David Hoy's essay "Foucault: Modern or Postmodern?" in *After Foucault.* Hoy here contrasts the "lightheartedness" of postmodernism and its attraction to parody and pastiche to the more ponderous seriousness of modernism. (I also cannot resist mentioning here that the SpellCheck function of my word processor consistently offered *deride* whenever it came to the name "Derrida.")

4. See, for example, Levinas's essay "Martin Buber et la théorie de la Conaissance" in his collection *Noms propres,* translated into English as "Martin Buber and the Theory of Knowledge" in *The Philosophy of Martin Buber.*

5. Levinas and Perelman have shown me an important dimension to the literary approach to rabbinic hermeneutics that I neglected in my *The Slayers of Moses*— the ethical and juridical

6. I am grateful to my colleague Jeanne Fahnestock for introducing me to and helping explicate Perelman's work. *The New Rhetoric* is a lengthy and complex book, and I only briefly touch upon it here. The central portion of the book is an extensive set of philosophical and technical analyses of the various techniques of argumentation, rhetorical strategies, and tropes. Perelman also directly addresses the problem of rhetoric used deceptively to manipulate, of propaganda and ruse in his idea of the "universal audience" (section 7), his discussion of the "audience as a construction of the speaker" (section 4), and the "adaptation of the speaker to the audience" (section 5). The speaker is not obligated to persuade an audience if that audience can be persuaded only by repugant means. As Quintilian said, rhetoric is *scientia bien dicendi*: speaking well means also speaking what is ethically good (25). For an excellent analysis of the notion of the "universal audience," see Allen Scult, "Perelman's Universal Audience," p. 176.

7. See, for example, the oft-cited essay by deMan "Semiology and Rhetoric," in *Textual Strategies,* ed. J. Harari, and Derrida's "White Metaphor: Metaphor in the Text of Philosophy," in *Margins of Philosophy.*

8. I am indebted to Jeanne Fahnestock for this observation.

9. In fact, Perelman describes "Hegelian realism"—Hegel's assertion that the

real is the rational and the rational the real—as a kind of "pragmatic argument." A pragmatic argument is defined as one which "permits the evaluation of an act or event in terms of its favorable or unfavorable consequences . . . allows a thing to be judged in terms of its present or its future consequences" (266–67). This kind of argument is often found in historicist modes of thinking; "Hegelian realism . . . sanctifies history by conferring on it the role of ultimate judge. It is this bias which makes reality a guarantee of values and causes what has been born, has developed and survived, to represent itself as success, as a promise of future success, as a proof of rationality and objectivity" (268).

10. Ihab Hassan, one of the best explicators of "postmodernism," provides many more of these pairs and classifications in his *The Postmodern Turn*; see especially the list on pp. 91–92.

11. Another prominent French feminist, Luce Irigaray, responded to his earlier writing on eros in *Totality and Infinity*; see her essay "The Fecundity of the Caress" in Cohen, *Face to Face.*

12. There is another deep link here to Rosenzweig's transformation of the relations between the independent shattered fragments of the All (God-humanity-world) to creation, revelation, and redemption. The pagan world of the self-subsistent opens to God as a "creation," God opens to humanity in revelation, and humanity opens to the world in the act of redemption.

9. GREEKJEW/JEWGREEK

1. See especially Levinas's talmudic lecture "The Temptation of Temptation," in *Quatre lectures talmudiques,* where he defines the temptation of philosophy in Rosenzweigian terms and contrasts it with a Jewish mode of knowing. The "temptation of temptation" is the desire for complete experimentation, for exploring every possibility, for feeling, testing, and knowing everything like Ulysses or Don Juan. To know and try everything is again the theme of totality. But as Levinas adds, the "all" includes everything, evil as well as good, and awakened evil may threaten to overturn and destroy everything. Yet the self which desires and is tempted thinks it can remain untouched, whole, immune to the destruction that might ensue from pursuing all, that it can remain secure and ultimately return home as did Ulysses after his long voyages.

This is the very temptation of knowledge, for "knowledge" means to hold oneself in a way "beyond good and evil," or to think that one could somehow explore evil without being tainted oneself, that one could test the world without being tested oneself, without committing one's very self in the endeavor, without having to choose, or limit oneself. This "temptation of temptation" he then identifies as philosophy:

> Philosophy can be defined as the subordination of every act to the knowledge that one can have of this act, knowledge being precisely this merciless demand to remain at a distance, to surmount the congenital narrowness of the pure act and to thus cure its dangerous generosity. The priority of knowledge is the temptation of temptation. (*QLT* 76)

The pure naiveté of faith is not a sufficient alternative, and one needs to avoid an either/or dilemma of spontaneous, naive engagement versus theoretical exploration, and find a "third way" beyond either an innocent *doing* which is beautiful and generous but childish and a *doing* which is a pure praxis, cut off from theoretical problems and complexities. Levinas locates in the talmudic passage which discusses the way the Jews received the revelation at Sinai, the paradigmatic Jewish idea of knowledge and revelation and an alternative to philosophy. When they are about to receive the Torah, the Jews make the statement: "We will do and we will understand"—*na'aseh ve-nishmah*. This statement reverses the order of "I will know, and then do"; and Levinas interprets this mode of reception as a mode of knowing "Otherwise than being"—another order where the opposition engagement/disengagement or theory/praxis "is no longer determinative." It is, rather, an order which "precedes"—or even conditions—these notions" (*QLT* 78–79). Revelation here is an order more ancient than that of "the temptation of temptation" philosophy, although from the viewpoint of Western thought, he adds, revelation would consist only of that which reason could not discover and so be defined as an area of blind faith where one risks being duped. His aim here is to show a different relation between being and knowing which itself is important for philosophy.

2. See Levinas's essay "God and Philosophy" (1973) in his *Collected Philosophical Papers.* Here he attempts to clarify the relationship between philosophy and religion, and define his notion of a religion that not only exceeds theology but is not even founded on "religious experience" or faith and the loss of faith. The key question of this essay is, Can God be expressed in a rational discourse which would be neither ontology or faith? He traces the connections between Western philosophy and Western spirituality which share a notion of truth defined as manifestation of being, and he posits another knowing, a "knowing otherwise" where consciousness is conscience and insomnia, not enlightenment and effectivity. This knowing otherwise is reflected in a religious discourse in which God does not signify to begin with as a theme, or object of a dogma.

God is not the "wholly other" or "first other" but "other than the otherwise, other with an alterity prior to the alterity of the other, prior to the ethical bond with the other and different from every neighbor, transcendent to the point of absence, to the point of a possible confusion with the stirring of the *there is*" (165–66). The God of the Bible, argues Levinas, signifies this "beyond being" and is beyond the philosophies of being where truth is manifestation or disclosure (159).

The "birth of religion" prior to any "religious experiences," emotions, or voices is the sound resounding out of the stillness of the mute appeal from the misery and nakedness of the other. To hear or understand this cry is the very critique and "disturbance of being." And so, subjectivity is consumed in this responsibility on the model of Abraham, who says, "I am dust and ashes" (Gen. 18:27), and Moses, who says, "What are we?" (Exod. 16:7) when he intercedes for the evildoers of Sodom.

3. See his talmudic lecture "Towards the Other" in *Quatre lectures talmudiques,* which analyzes the nature of forgiveness. In another essay, he writes that the trials and death of the righteous, those who die for Judaism, for what is called the "Sanctification of the Name" [*kiddush ha-Shem*], constitute in this sense a life stronger than death, a concrete experience of the eternity of the Divine, and "belong to the semiotics of the word God" (*ADV* 20). As the rabbis say, when Israel was exiled, God went into exile with them.

4. See Abner Weiss's discussion of these issues in relation to Levinas in Fox, *Modern Jewish Ethics,* pp. 139–52. See also David Roskies's *Against the Apocalypse* for the typology of the historical Jewish responses to suffering.

5. The essay has been translated by Richard Sugarman and Helen Stephenson, and I use their version.

6. For an excellent survey of the literature and philosophy of the "Jewish argument with God," see Abraham Kaplan's 1980 essay by the same title.

7. See the brilliant work of the rabbinics scholar José Faur on the Jewish notion of transmission and interpretation of Torah, its relation to the legal and midrashic modes of exegesis and to contemporary semiotic theory, in his book *Golden Doves with Silver Dots.*

8. See the excellent article by Paul Mendes-Flohr, "Rosenzweig and Kant: Two

Views of Ritual and Religion," for an elaboration of Rosenzweig's relation to Kant-ian ethical theory.

9. For a good introduction and overview of the thought of Rabbi Salanter, see Immanuel Etkes, "Rabbi Israel Salanter and His Psychology of Mussar."

10. See especially Scholem's essay "Tradition and New Creation in the Ritual of the Kabbalists," in *On the Kabbalah and Its Symbolism,* 118–57.

11. As outlined in the first part of this book, Scholem proposed a Hegelian three-stage mode of religion, where a stage of innocent and immediate connection of humanity and God through myth was followed by a second stage of alienation, doubt, and distance from God due to disparity between the religious myth and reality (religion of law and priests). This is reconciled in a third stage—that of mysticism, which overcomes this alienation by self-consciously revitalizing the old myth.

10. TALMUDIC MESSIANISM

1. At the time of my writing this chapter, the two lectures on messianism from *Difficile liberté* were not translated into English. They appeared after the comple-tion of this manuscript. I have decided nevertheless to quote from the original texts at length to ensure the clarity of my exposition, and also to provide some commen-tary. Edith Wyschogrod considers them at length in chapter 7 of her book on Levinas. See also the superb introduction and translation by Annette Aronowicz of several other talmudic lectures from Levinas's collections *Quatre lectures talmudi-ques* and *Du sacré au saint.* I use Annette Aronowicz's translations wherever I cite from the talmudic lectures from *Quatre lectures talmudiques* and *Du sacré au saint*; all other translations from *Difficile liberté* and *l'au-delà du verset* are my own. Aronowicz also points out that in 1946, when Levinas became the director of the École Normale Israélite Orientale, the school of the Alliance Israélite Universelle in Paris which trains teachers for the Alliance's network of schools, he took charge of giving the talmudic lesson himself.

2. She adds that "the hermeneutic required, as we recall, that the word 'God' be understood on the basis of the context, the human interactions, in which it appears in the text. But that is also how the presence of God is to be glimpsed in daily life, itself in the exchange between people. In both cases, it is the *embodied* truth—the truth in action—that conveys meaning. In both cases, it is a fight against a merely abstract knowledge, a desire to penetrate reality through the concrete and particu-lar, through the *act.* The hermeneutic is, once again, symbolic of the very content of the tradition it searches to understand" (xxiii).

3. See especially his elaboration of this issue in his essays "La Révélation dans la tradition juive" and "De la lecture juive des Ecritures," in the collection *L'au-delà du verset.*

4. This translation generally follows that of the Soncino English version of the Babylonian Talmud, ed. I. Epstein. I have made some minor changes.

5. Like Benjamin, Levinas wants to protect the integrity of historical meanings; he claims that precisely through the rabbinic commentary, the symbol itself is enriched by its many *concrete* historical meanings. The light of talmudic thought "reawakens" their symbolizing power, but the spirit also awakens from the letter. The "symbols" are "realities and often concrete forms and people" and "are given meanings they themselves have helped bring out." This movement back and forth between concrete objects and their illumination as commentary is "unceasing." In Levinas's estimation, the "scientific" historical method of understanding the Tal-mud lacks precisely this continuous dialectic. It "risks attaching itself to the origin of the symbols that have long ago gone beyond the meaning they had at the time of their birth." That impoverishes these symbols by restricting and enclosing them in

anecdotes or the local events from which they originated. Above all, these "possibilities of signifying tied to a concrete object freed from its history" constitute a "paradigmatic method of thought" (*QLT* 21). This notion somewhat parallels Benjamin's idea of blasting a historical moment out of its historicist continuum while retaining all its concreteness.

But for Levinas, although in each generation the rabbinic commentaries begin again from this inexhaustible plenitude, they do not plunge in arbitrarily; they are "opened to those possibilities by the defined outline of these object-signs." Moreover, one can understand the Talmud and these "signs" only from "the experience of life itself." These "signs" as concrete realities signify "according to the context of the life lived." By "signs," Levinas means biblical verses, objects, persons, situations, rituals, etc., which function nevertheless as "perfect signs" because despite the changes that "the passages of time introduces into their visible texture, they keep their privilege of revealing the same meanings or new aspects of these same meanings." In this sense they are "irreplaceable" and "sacred" in a hermeneutical sense.

In another essay in *L'au-delà du verset,* Levinas argues that the Talmud is a distinctive mode of reading the bible, different from Christianity, science, history, philosophy. While this mode of interpretation is often mistakenly thought to be literal, it "consists perhaps in reality in maintaining each particular text in the context of the whole." Needless to say, this notion of the "whole," like Rosenzweig's, is a non-Hegelian whole, not a unified ontological identity but a constellation of independent relations. What appears to be a literal relation to the verses "represents in fact an effort to make the verses resonate in 'harmonies' with other verses." And this mode maintains the contact between more "spiritual, interior" verses with cruder, more material ones—to extract from the former their truth and, obversely, to "relate generous spirits to hard realities" (*ADV* 166).

CONCLUSION

1. As Richard Cohen notes, Derrida's idea of the play of meaning in his differential theory of signs lays waste both transcendence and immanence ("Privilege of Reason and Play" 245), and in Cohen's view the reason/play opposition is too simple. The answer to the crisis of philosophy is not the opposition between play and reason, he argues, but a recognition of the bond uniting them; they are both forms of privilege. The privilege of reason is not the metaphysical privilege of presence "which is rightfully subverted by play, but rather the privileging exigency of *responsibility.*" Reason is not solely the rational but a form of responsibility, and "play is reason's necessary companion if reason is to remain reasonable. Reason has a sense of humor," and play is responsive to this (251).

2. See Berel Lang's essay "Writing-the-Holocaust: Jabès and the Measure of History" and Peter Cole's "Edmond Jabès and the Excuses of Exile" for perceptive critiques of Jabès's position.

3. José Faur notes the legal implications of this connotation of the word *massar* in Jewish law. *Massar* is used to denote the legal status of a document which is surrendered by the legal holder to the court. The court is then given the right to interpret it independent of the author of the document's intentions (*Golden Doves* 88, 109, 123–24).

Works Consulted

Aarsleff, Hans, ed. *From Locke to Saussure: Essays on the Study of Language and Intellectual History.* Minneapolis: U of Minnesota P, 1982.

Abrams, M. H. *Natural Supernaturalism: Tradition and Revolution in Romantic Literature.* New York: W. W. Norton, 1971.

Adorno, Theodor. *Minima Moralia: Reflections from a Damaged Life.* 1951; London: Verso, 1971.

——. *Prisms.* Trans. Samuel and Shierry Weber. 1967; Cambridge: MIT P, 1981.

Aesthetics and Politics: Theodor Adorno, Walter Benjamin, Ernst Bloch, Bertolt Brecht, Georg Lukacs. London: Verso NLB, 1977.

Alter, Robert. *Defenses of the Imagination.* Philadelphia: Jewish Publication Society, 1977.

Arendt, Hannah. Introduction. *Illuminations.* By Water Benjamin. Trans. Harry Zohn. 1955; New York: Schocken, 1969. 1–55.

Aronowicz, Annette. "Translator's Introduction." *Nine Talmudic Readings by Emmanuel Levinas.* Bloomington: Indiana UP, 1990. ix–xxix.

Auster, Paul. "An Interview with Edmond Jabès." *The Sin of the Book: Edmond Jabès.* Ed. Eric Gould. Lincoln: U of Nebraska P, 1985. 3–25.

Austin, J. L. *How to Do Things with Words.* Ed. J. O. Urmson and Marina Sbisa. 2nd ed. Cambridge: Harvard UP, 1975.

Baeck, Leo. *The Essence of Judaism.* Trans. Irving Howe and Victor Grubweiser. 2nd ed. New York: Schocken, 1961.

Bahti, Timothy. "History as Rhetorical Enactment: Walter Benjamin's Theses 'On the Concept of History.'" *Diacritics* 9.3 (1979): 2–17.

Bakhtin, M. M. *The Dialogic Imagination.* Ed. Michael Holquist. Trans. Caryl Emerson. Austin: U of Texas P, 1981.

——. *Rabelais and His World.* Trans. Helene Iswolsky. Bloomington: Indiana UP, 1984.

Baynes, Kenneth, James Bohman, and Thomas McCarthy, eds. *After Philosophy: End or Transformation.* Cambridge: MIT Press, 1987.

Benjamin, Walter. *Briefe.* Ed. Gershom Scholem and Theodor Adorno. 2 vols. Frankfurt: Suhrkamp, 1966.

——. *Charles Baudelaire: A Lyric Poet in the Era of High Capitalism.* Trans. Harry Zohn. London: NLB, 1973.

——. "Doctrine of the Similar." Trans. Knut Tarnowski. *New German Critique* 17 (1979): 65–69.

——. *Gesammelte Schriften.* Ed. Rolf Tiedemann and Hermann Schweppenhauser. 7 vols. Frankfurt: Suhrkamp Verlag, 1972–89.

——. *Illuminations.* Ed. Hannah Arendt. 1955; New York: Schocken, 1969.

——. *Moscow Diary.* Cambridge: Harvard UP, 1986.

——. "N [Re the Theory of Knowledge, Theory of Progress]." Trans. Leigh Hafrey and Richard Sieburth. *Benjamin: Philosophy, History, Aesthetics.* Ed. Gary Smith. Chicago: U of Chicago P, 1989. 43–83.

——. *One-Way Street and Other Writings.* Trans. Edmund Jephcott and Kingsley Shorter. London: NLB, 1979.

——. *The Origin of German Tragic Drama.* Trans. John Osborne. 1963; London: NLB, 1977.

———. "Program of the Coming Philosophy." Trans. Mark Ritter. *Philosophical Forum* 15.1–2 (1983): 41–51.

———. *Reflections: Essays, Aphorisms, Autobiographical Writings.* Ed. Peter Demetz. Trans. Edmund Jephcott. New York: Harcourt Brace, 1978.

———. *Understanding Brecht.* Trans. Anna Bostock. London: NLB, 1973.

Bernasconi, Robert. "Deconstruction and the Possibility of Ethics." *Deconstruction and Philosophy.* Ed. John Sallis. Chicago: U of Chicago P, 1987. 122–39.

———. "Levinas Face to Face—with Hegel." *Journal of the British Society for Phenomenology* 13 (1982): 267–76.

———. "The Trace of Levinas in Derrida." *Derrida and Difference.* Ed. D. Wood and R. Bernasconi. Coventry, England: Parousia P, U of Warwick, 1986. 17–44.

Biale, David. "Gershom Scholem's Ten Unhistorical Aphorisms on Kabbalah: Text and Commentary." *Modern Judaism* 5 (1985): 67–93.

———. *Gershom Scholem: Kabbalah and Counter-History.* Cambridge: Harvard UP, 1979.

———. Rev. of *Walter Benjamin: The Story of a Friendship,* by Gershom Scholem. *Association for Jewish Studies Newsletter* 34 (1983): 19–20.

Bialik, Hayim Nachman. *Halachah and Aggadah.* Trans. Sir Leon Simon. London: Press Printers, 1944.

———. *Halakah and Aggadah. Modern Jewish Thought: A Source Reader.* Ed. Nahman Glatzer. 1917; New York: Schocken, 1977. 55–64.

Blanchot, Maurice. "Être Juif." *L'entretien infini.* Paris: Gallimard. 181–91.

———. "Our Clandestine Companion." *Face to Face with Levinas.* Ed. Richard A. Cohen. Albany: State U of New York P, 1986. 41–52.

Bloom, Harold. *Agon: Towards a Theory of Revisionism.* New York: Oxford UP, 1982.

———. "The Masks of the Normative." *Orim: A Jewish Journal at Yale* 1 (1985): 9–25.

———. "A Speculation upon American Jewish Culture." *Judaism* 31 (1982): 266–73.

Booth, Wayne C. *The Company We Keep: An Ethics of Fiction.* Berkeley: U of California P, 1988.

Brewster, Philip, and Carl Howard. "Language and Critique: Jürgen Habermas on Walter Benjamin." *New German Critique* 17 (1979): 15–29. Special Issue on Benjamin.

Bruns, Gerald. "Midrash and Allegory." *The Literary Guide to the Bible.* Ed. Robert Alter and Frank Kermode. Cambridge: Harvard UP, 1987. 625–46.

———. *Modern Poetry and the Idea of Language: A Critical and Historical Study.* New Haven: Yale UP, 1974.

Buck-Morss, Susan. *The Dialectics of Seeing: Walter Benjamin and the Arcades Project.* Cambridge: MIT P, 1989.

———. *The Origin of Negative Dialectics: Theodor Adorno, Walter Benjamin, and the Frankfort Institute.* New York: Free P, 1977.

Bullock, Marcus. *Romanticism and Marxism: The Philosophical Development of Literary Theory and Literary History in Walter Benjamin and Friedrich Schlegel.* New York: Peter Lang, 1987.

Burggraeve, Robert. *Emmanuel Levinas: Une bibliographie primaire et secondaire (1925–1985).* Leuven, Belgium: Center for Metaphysics and Philosophy of God, 1986.

Burke, Kenneth. *A Rhetoric of Motives.* 1950; Berkeley: U of California P, 1969.

Calinescu, Matei. *Faces of Modernity: Avant-Garde, Decadence, Kitsch.* Bloomington: Indiana UP, 1977.

Campbell, Colin. "The Tyranny of the Yale Critics." *New York Times Magazine* Feb. 1986: 20–48.

Chalier, Catherine. *Figures du féminin: Lecture d' Emmanuel Levinas.* Paris: La Nuit Surveillée, 1982.

Chouraqui, Andre. *L'Alliance Israélite Universelle et la renaissance juive contemporaine.* Paris, 1965.

Ciaramelli, Fabio. "Le rôle du Judaisme dans l'oeuvre de Levinas." *Revue Philosophique de Louvain* 81.52 (1983): 580–600.

Cohen, Arthur. "A Short, Rich and Tortured Life." Rev. of *Walter Benjamin: The Story of a Friendship,* by Benjamin Scholem. *New York Times Book Review* 16 May 1982: 12, 32–35.

Cohen, Arthur, and Paul Mendes-Flohr, eds. *Contemporary Jewish Religious Thought.* New York: Scribner, 1987.

Cohen, Gershon. "German Jewry as a Mirror of Modernity." *Leo Baeck Institute Yearbook* 20 (1975): 9–22.

Cohen, Richard A. "The Face of Truth in Rosenzweig, Levinas, and Jewish Mysticism." *Phenomenology of the Truth Proper to Religion.* Ed. Daniel Guerrière, Albany: State U of New York P, 1990.

————. "Levinas, Rosenzweig, and the Phenomenologies of Husserl and Heidegger." *Philosophy Today* 32.2 (1988): 165–78.

————. "Non-in-difference in the Thought of Emmanuel Levinas and Franz Rosenzweig." Forthcoming in *Graduate Faculty Philosophy Journal.*

————. "The Privilege of Reason and Play: Levinas and Derrida." *Tijdschrift voor Filosofie* 45.2 (1983): 242–55.

————. "Rosenzweig's Critique of Nietzsche in *The Star of Redemption.*" Forthcoming in *Nietzsche-Studien* 19 (1989).

Cohen, Richard A., ed. *Face to Face with Levinas.* Albany: State U of New York P, 1986.

Cohn, Norman. *The Pursuit of the Millennium: Revolutionary Messianism in Medieval and Reformation England and Its Bearing on Modern Totalitarian Movements.* New York: Harper & Row, 1957.

Cole, Peter. "Edmond Jabès and the Excuses of Exile." *Tikkun* 5.4 (1990): 39–42.

Corngold, Stanley, and Michael Jennings. "Walter Benjamin/Gershom Scholem." *Interpretation* 12 (1984): 357–66.

Cowan, Bainard. "Walter Benjamin's Theory of Allegory." *New German Critique* 22 (1981): 109–22.

Dallery, Arleen, and Charles E. Scott, eds. *The Question of the Other: Essays in Contemporary Continental Philosophy.* Albany: State U of New York P, 1989.

Dan, Joseph. *Gershom Scholem and the Mystical Dimensions of Jewish History.* New York: New York UP, 1987.

————. *Gershom Scholem: Between History and Historiosophy.* Trans. Roberta Bell-Kligler. Binah: Jewish Civilization University Series. Jerusalem: International Center for University Teaching of Jewish Civilization, n.d. *Jerusalem Studies in Jewish Thought* 3 (1983–84).

De Beauvoir, Simone. *The Second Sex.* Trans. H. M. Parshley. 1949; New York: Vintage, 1974.

DeMan, Paul. *Allegories of Reading: Figural Language in Rousseau, Nietzsche, Rilke, and Proust.* Minneapolis: U of Minnesota P, 1979.

————. *The Resistance to Theory.* Minneapolis: U of Minnesota P, 1986.

————. *Blindness and Insight: Essays in the Rhetoric of Contemporary Criticism.* 2nd ed. Minneapolis: U of Minnesota P, 1983.

————. "Semiology and Rhetoric." *Textual Strategies: Perspectives in Post-Structuralist Criticism.* Ed. Josué Harari. Ithaca: Cornell UP, 1979. 121–40.

Demetz, Peter. Introduction. *Reflections*. By Walter Benjamin. New York: Harcourt Brace, 1978. vii–xliii.

Derrida, Jacques. "Edmond Jabès and the Question of the Book." *Writing and Difference*. Trans. Alan Bass. Chicago: U of Chicago P, 1978. 64–78.

——. "En ce moment même dans cet ouvrage me voici." *Textes pour Emmanuel Levinas*. Ed. François Laruelle. Paris: Editions Jean-Michel Place, 1980. 21–60.

——. *Glas*. Trans. J. P. Leavey and R. A. Rand. 1974; Lincoln: U of Nebraska P, 1986.

——. *Margins of Philosophy*. Trans. Alan Bass. 1972; Chicago: U of Chicago P, 1982.

——. "Violence and Metaphysics: An Essay on the Thought of Emmanuel Levinas." *Writing and Difference*. Trans. Alan Bass. Chicago: U of Chicago P, 79–153.

——. *Of Grammatology*. Trans. Gayatri Spivak. 1967; Baltimore: Johns Hopkins UP, 1976.

Descombes, Vincent. *Modern French Philosophy*. Trans. J.-M. Scott-Fox and J.-M. Harding. 1979; Cambridge: Cambridge UP, 1980.

Durfee, Harold. "Emmanuel Levinas' Philosophy of Language." *Explanation: New Directions in Philosophy*. Ed. B. Blose, H. A. Durfee, and D. F. T. Rodier. The Hague: Martinus Nijhoff, 1973. 89–120.

——. "War, Politics, and Radical Pluralism." *Philosophy and Phenomenological Research* 35 (1975): 549–58.

Eagleton, Terry, ed. *Walter Benjamin, or Towards a Revolutionary Criticism*. London: NLB, 1981.

Epstein, I., ed. *The Babylonian Talmud*. London: Soncino, 1938.

Etkes, Immanuel. "Rabbi Israel Salanter and His Psychology of Mussar." *Jewish Spirituality from the Sixteenth-Century Revival to the Present*. Ed. Arthur Green. New York: Crossroad, 1987. 206–44.

Fackenheim, Emil. *Encounters between Judaism and Modern Philosophy: A Preface to Future Jewish Thought*. 1973; New York: Schocken, 1980.

Faur, José. *Golden Doves with Silver Dots: Semiotics and Textuality in Rabbinic Tradition*. Bloomington: Indiana UP, 1986.

Fisch, Harold. *Poetry with a Purpose: Biblical Poetics and Interpretation*. Bloomington: Indiana UP, 1988.

Fittko, Lisa. "The Last Days of Walter Benjamin." *Orim: A Jewish Journal at Yale* 1 (1986): 48–59.

Fletcher, Angus. *Allegory: The Theory of a Symbolic Mode*. Ithaca: Cornell UP, 1964.

Foss, Sonja K., Robert Foss, and Robert Trapp. *Contemporary Perspectives on Rhetoric*. Prospect Heights, Ill.: Waveland Press, 1985.

Foucault, Michel. "Nietzsche, Genealogy, History." *Language, Counter-Memory, Practice: Selected Essays and Interviews*. Ed. Donald F. Bouchard. Trans. Donald F. Bouchard and Sherry Simon. Ithaca: Cornell UP, 1977. 139–64.

——. *The Order of Things: An Archaeology of the Human Sciences*. 1966; New York: Vintage, 1973.

Fox, Marvin, ed. *Modern Jewish Ethics: Theory and Practice*. Columbus: Ohio State UP, 1975.

Frank, Joseph. "The Voices of Mikhail Bakhtin." *New York Review of Books* 23 Oct. 1986: 56–60.

Frisby, David. *Fragments of Modernity: Theories of Modernity in the Work of Simmel, Kracauer and Benjamin*. Cambridge: MIT Press, 1986.

Gay, Peter. *Freud, Jews and Other Germans: Masters and Victims in Modernist Culture*. New York: Oxford UP, 1978.

Gibbs, Robert. " 'Greek' in the 'Hebrew' Writings of Emmanual Levinas." *Papers from the Academy for Jewish Philosophy Conference 1987.* Philadelphia: Academy for Jewish Philosophy, 1987. 119–43.

――――. "A Jewish Context for the Social Ethics of Marx and Levinas." *Autonomy and Judaism: Papers from the Academy for Jewish Philosophy Conference 1989.* Philadelphia: Academy for Jewish Philosophy, 1987. 89–114.

――――. "The Limits of Thought: Rosenzweig, Schelling, and Cohen." *Zeitschrift für philosophische Forschung* (1990). Forthcoming.

――――. "Substitution: Marcel and Levinas." Unpublished lecture.

――――. "The Unique Other: Hermann Cohen and Emmanuel Levinas." Unpublished lecture delivered 20 December 1988 at the Association for Jewish Studies.

Glatzer, Nahum. *Franz Rosenzweig: His Life and Thought.* 1953; New York: Schocken, 1961.

Goldman, Steven Louis. "On the Interpretation of Symbols and the Christian Origins of Modern Science." *Journal of Religion* 62.1 (1982): 1–20.

Gould, Eric, ed. *The Sin of the Book: Essays on the Writings of Edmond Jabès.* Lincoln: U of Nebraska P, 1985.

Graham, Joseph, ed. *Difference in Translation.* Ithaca: Cornell UP, 1985.

Green, Kenneth Hart. "The Notion of Truth in Franz Rosenzweig's *The Star of Redemption*: A Philosophical Inquiry." *Modern Judaism* 7 (1987): 297–323.

Greenstein, Edward. "Theories of Modern Bible Translation." *Prooftexts* 3 (1983): 9–40.

Grunfeld, Fredric V. *Prophets without Honor: A Background to Freud, Kafka, Einstein and Their World.* New York: Holt Rinehart, 1979.

Habermas, Jürgen. "Consciousness-Raising or Redemptive Criticism—The Contemporaneity of Walter Benjamin." *New German Critique* 17 (1979): 30–59.

――――. "Modernity versus Postmodernity." *New German Critique* 22 (1981): 3–14.

――――. *Philosophical-Political Profiles.* Trans. Frederick Lawrence. 1971; Cambridge: MIT Press, 1983.

Handelman, Susan A. " 'Everything Is in It': Rabbinic Interpretation and Modern Literary Criticism." *Judaism* 35 (1986): 429–40.

――――. "Fragments of the Rock: Contemporary Literary Theory and the Study of Rabbinic Texts." *Prooftexts* 5 (1985): 75–95.

――――. "Parodic Play and Prophetic Reason: Two Interpretations of Interpretation." *Poetics Today* 9:2 (1988): 396–423.

――――. *The Slayers of Moses: The Emergence of Rabbinic Interpretation in Modern Literary Theory.* Albany: State U of New York P, 1982.

――――. "Torments of an Ancient Word: Edmond Jabès and the Rabbinic Tradition." *The Sin of the Book: Essays on the Writing of Edmond Jabès.* Ed. Eric Gould. Lincoln: U of Nebraska P, 1983. 55–91.

Harari, Josúe, ed. *Textual Strategies: Perspectives in Post-Structuralist Criticism.* Ithaca: Cornell UP, 1979.

Hartman, David. *The Living Covenant: The Innovative Spirit in Traditional Judaism.* New York: Free P, 1985.

Hartman, Geoffrey. *Criticism in the Wilderness: The Study of Literature Today.* New Haven: Yale UP, 1980.

Hartman, Geoffrey, and Sanford Budick, eds. *Midrash and Literature.* New Haven: Yale UP, 1986.

Hassan, Ihab. *The Postmodern Turn: Essays in Postmodern Theory and Culture.* 1987 ed. Columbus: Ohio State UP.

Hegel, G. W. F. *Lectures on the Philosophy of Religion: One Volume Edition. The Lectures of 1827.* Ed. Peter Hodgson. Berkeley: U of California P, 1988.

_____. *The Phenomenology of Mind.* Trans. J. B. Baillie. London: Macmillan, 1910. New York: Harper & Row, 1967.

Heinemann, F. H. "Jewish Contributions to German Philosophy." *Leo Baeck Institute Yearbook* 9 (1964): 161–77.

Hertzberg, Arthur. "Gershom Scholem as Zionist and Believer." *Modern Judaism* 5 (1985): 3–19.

Howe, Irving, and Eliezer Greenberg, eds. *A Treasury of Yiddish Stories.* 1953; New York: Schocken, 1973.

Hoy, David. "Foucault: Modern or Postmodern?" *After Foucault: Humanistic Knowledge, Postmodern Challenges.* Ed. Jonathan Arac. New Brunswick: Rutgers UP, 1988.

Humboldt, Wilhelm von. *On Language: The Diversity of Human Language-Structure and Its Influence on the Mental Development of Mankind.* Trans. Peter Heath. 1836: Cambridge: Cambridge UP, 1988.

Idel, Moshe. "Infinities of Torah in Kabbalah." *Midrash and Literature.* Ed. Geoffrey Hartman and Sanford Budick. New Haven: Yale UP, 1986. 141–57.

_____. *Kabbalah: New Perspectives.* New Haven: Yale UP, 1988.

Jabès, Edmond. *.(El, Ou Le Dernier Livre)* Paris: Gallimard, 1973.

_____. *The Book of Questions.* Trans. Rosemarie Waldrop. 7 vols. Middletown: Wesleyan UP, 1976–84.

_____. "The Key." *Midrash and Literature.* Ed. Geoffrey Hartman and Sanford Budick. New Haven: Yale UP, 1986. 349–62.

_____. *Le Livre des ressemblances.* Paris: Gallimard, 1976.

_____. *Le Livre des questions.* Paris: Gallimard, 1963.

_____. *Le Retour au livre.* 3 vols. Paris: Gallimard, 1965, 1965–72.

_____. *Le Soupçon, le désert.* Paris: Gallimard, 1978.

Jacobs, Carol. "The Monstrosity of Translation." *Modern Language Notes* 90 (1975): 765–66.

Jameson, Fredric. *Marxism and Form: Twentieth Century Dialectical Theories of Literature.* Princeton: Princeton UP, 1971.

_____. *The Political Unconscious: Narrative as a Socially Symbolic Act.* Ithaca: Cornell UP, 1981.

Janik, Allan, and Stephen Toulmin. *Wittgenstein's Vienna.* New York: Simon & Schuster, 1973.

Jay, Martin. *The Dialectical Imagination: A History of the Frankfurt School and the Institute for Social Research, 1923–1950.* Boston: Little, Brown, 1973.

_____. "The Frankfurt School and the Genesis of Critical Theory." *The Unknown Dimension: European Marxism since Lenin.* Ed. Dick Howard and Karl Klare. New York: Basic Books, 1972. 224–27.

_____. "The Politics of Translation: Siegfried Kracauer and Walter Benjamin on the Buber-Rosenzweig Bible." *Leo Baeck Institute Yearbook* 21 (1976): 3–24.

Jennings, Michael. *Dialectical Images: Walter Benjamin's Theory of Literary Criticism.* Ithaca: Cornell UP, 1987.

Kafka, Franz. *Briefe, 1902–1924.* Ed. Max Brod. New York: Schocken, 1958.

_____. *Letter to His Father.* Trans. Ernst Kaiser and Eithne Wilkins. 1919; New York: Schocken, 1953.

_____. *Letters to Friends, Family, and Editors.* Trans. Richard and Clara Winston. 1958; New York: Schocken, 1977.

Kant, Immanuel. *Philosophical Writings.* Ed. Ernst Behler. The German Library vol. 13. New York: Continuum, 1986.

Kaplan, Abraham. "The Jewish Argument with God." *Commentary* Oct. 1980: 43–47.

Katz, Jacob. *Out of the Ghetto: The Social Background of Jewish Emancipation, 1770–1870.* 1973; New York: Schocken, 1978.

Kearney, Richard. "Dialogue with Emmanuel Levinas." *Face to Face with Levinas.* Ed. Richard A. Cohen. Albany: State U of New York P, 1986. 13–25.

―――. "Emmanuel Levinas: On the Revelation of the Other." Diss. McGill U, 1976.

―――. "Jacques Derrida." *Dialogues with Contemporary Continental Thinkers: The Phenomenological Heritage.* Manchester: Manchester UP, 1984. 105–26.

Klein, Dennis. "Assimilation and Dissimilation: Peter Gay's *Freud, Jews and Other Germans: Masters and Victims in Modernist Culture.*" *New German Critique* 19 (1979): 151–67.

Lacoue-Labarthe, Philippe, and Jean-Luc Nancy. *The Literary Absolute: A Theory of Literature in German Romanticism.* Trans. Philip Barnard and Cheryl Lester. 1978; Albany: State U of New York P, 1988.

Lang, Berel. "Writing-the-Holocaust: Jabès and the Measure of History." *The Sin of the Book: Edmond Jabès.* Ed. Eric Gould. Lincoln: U of Nebraska P, 1985. 191–206.

Laruelle, François, ed. *Textes pour Emmanuel Levinas.* Paris: Éditions Jean-Michel Place, 1980.

Levin, Richard. "The Poetics and Politics of Bardicide." *PMLA* 105.3 (1990): 491–504.

Levinas, Emmanuel. *Collected Philosophical Papers.* Trans. Alphonso Lingis. Dordrecht: Martinus Nijhoff, 1987.

―――. "The Contemporary Criticism of the Idea of Value and the Prospects for Humanism." *Value and Values in Evolution.* Ed. Edward Maziarz. New York: Gordon & Breach, 1979. 178–88.

―――. *Difficile liberté: Essais sur le judaisme.* Paris: Éditions Albin Michel, 1963.

―――. *Du sacré au saint: Cinq nouvelles lectures talmudiques.* Paris: Éditions de Minuit, 1977.

―――. "Entre deux mondes (biographie spirituelle de Franz Rosenzweig)." *La conscience juive: Données et débats (textes des trois premieres Colloques d'Intellectuels Juifs de Langue Française).* Ed. Amado Lévy-Valensi and Jean Halperin. Paris: Presses Universitaires de France, 1963. 121–49.

―――. *Ethics and Infinity: Conversations with Philippe Nemo.* Trans. Richard A. Cohen. Pittsburgh: Duquesne UP, 1985.

―――. *Existence and Existents.* Trans. Alphonso Lingis. 1947; The Hague: Martinus Nijhoff, 1978.

―――. "Franz Rosenzweig." Trans. Richard A. Cohen. *Midstream* 29.9 (1983): 33–40.

―――. "Franz Rosenzweig: une pensée juive moderne." *Revue de theologie et de philosophie* 98 (1965): 208–21.

―――. "God and Philosophy." *Collected Philosophical Papers.* Trans. Alphonso Lingis. Dordrecht: Martinus Nijhoff, 1987.

―――. "Ideology and Idealism." *Modern Jewish Ethics.* Ed. Marvin Fox. Columbus: Ohio State UP, 1975. 121–38.

―――. "Judaism and the Feminine Element." Trans. Edith Wyschogrod. *Judaism* 18 (1969): 30–38.

―――. *L'au-delà du verset: Lectures et discours talmudiques.* Paris: Éditions de Minuit, 1982.

―――. "Martin Buber and the Theory of Knowledge." *The Philosophy of Martin Buber.* Ed. Paul Schilpp and Maurice Friedman. La Salle, Ill.: Open Court Pub., 1967. 133–50.

————. *Nine Talmudic Readings by Emmanuel Levinas*. Trans. Annette Aronowicz. Bloomington: Indiana UP, 1990.

————. "On the Trail of the Other." Trans. Daniel Hoy. *Philosophy Today* 10
(1966): 34–36.

————. *Otherwise Than Being, or Beyond Essence*. Trans. Alphonso Lingis. 1974;
The Hague: Martinus Nijhoff, 1981.

————. *Quatre lectures talmudiques*. Paris: Éditions de Minuit, 1968.

————. "Signature." Ed. and Trans. Adriaan Peperzak. *Research in Phenomenology* 8 (1978): 175–89.

————. Préface. *Système et Révelation: La philosophie de Franz Rosenzweig*. By
Stéphane Mosès. Paris, 1987. 1–16.

————. *The Theory of Intuition in Husserl's Phenomenology*. Trans. Andre Ori-
anne. Evanston: Northwestern UP, 1973.

————. *Time and the Other: And Additional Esays*. Trans. Richard A. Cohen. Pittsburgh: Duquesne UP, 1987.

————. "To Love the Torah More Than God." Trans. Richard Sugarman and
Helen Stephenson. *Judaism* 28 (1979): 217–22.

————. *Totality and Infinity: An Essay on Exteriority*. Trans. Alphonso Lingis.
1961; Pittsburgh: Duquesne UP, 1969.

————. "Transcendance et hauteur." *Bulletin de la Societé française de Philosophie*
56 (1962): 89–101.

Levinas, Emmanuel, and Richard Kearney. "Dialogue with Emmanuel Levinas."
Face to Face with Levinas. Ed. Richard A. Cohen. Albany: State U of New
York P, 1986. 13–34.

Lewis, Philip. "The Post-Structuralist Condition." *Diacritics* 12 (1982): 2–24.

Lingis, Alphonso. *Libido: The French Existentialist Theories*. Bloomington: Indiana UP, 1985.

Lowy, Michael. "Jewish Messianism and Libertarian Utopia in Central Europe
(1900–1933)." *New German Critique* 20 (1980): 105–16.

Lyotard, Jean-François. *The Postmodern Condition: A Report on Knowledge*. Trans.
Geoff Bennington and Brian Massum. 1979; Minneapolis: U of Minnesota
P, 1984.

Maimonides, Moses. *The Guide for the Perplexed*. Trans. M. Friedlander. 2nd ed.
New York: Dover, 1956.

Malka, Solomon. *Lire Levinas*. Paris: Éditions du Cerf, 1984.

McBride, James. "Marooned in the Realm of the Profane: Walter Benjamin's Synthesis of Kabbalah and Communism." *Journal of the American Academy of
Religion* 57 (1989): 241–66.

McGann, Jerome. *The Romantic Ideology: A Critical Investigation*. Chicago: U of
Chicago P, 1983.

Megill, Allan. *Prophets of Extremity: Nietzsche, Heidegger, Foucault, Derrida*.
Berkeley: U of California P, 1985.

Mendes-Flohr, Paul. "Rosenzweig and Kant: Two Views of Ritual and Religion."
*Mystics, Philosophers, and Politicians: Essays in Jewish Intellectual History
in Honor of Alexander Altmann*. Ed. Jehuda Reinharz and Daniel Swetchin-
ski. Durham: Duke UP, 1982. 315–42.

————. "The Study of the Jewish-Intellectual: Some Methodological Proposals."
Essays in Modern Jewish History. Ed. Frances Malino. Cranbury, N.J.: Associated University Presses, 1981.

————. "The Study of the Modern Jewish Intellectual: Some Methodological Proposals." *Essays in Modern Jewish History*. Ed. Frances Malino. Cranbury,
N.J.: Associated University Presses, 1982. 142–72.

————. "The Throes of Assimilation: Self-Hatred and the Jewish Revolutionary."
European Judaism 12 (1978): 34–39.

———. " 'To Brush History against the Grain': The Eschatology of the Frankfurt School and Ernst Bloch." *Journal of the American Academy of Religion* 51 (1983): 631–50.

Mendes-Flohr, Paul, ed. *The Philosophy of Franz Rosenzweig.* Hanover: UP of New England, 1988.

Menninghaus, Winfried. "Walter Benjamin's Theory of Myth." *On Walter Benjamin: Critical Essays and Recollections.* Ed. Gary Smith. Cambridge: MIT Press, 1988. 292–325.

Meyer, Michael. *The Origins of the Modern Jew: Jewish Identity and European Culture in Germany, 1749–1824.* Detroit: Wayne State UP, 1967.

Miles, David. "Portrait of the Marxist as a Young Hegelian: Lukacs' *Theory of the Novel."* PMLA (1979): 22–35.

Miller, J. Hillis. *The Ethics of Reading: Kant, DeMan, Eliot, Trollope, James, and Benjamin.* New York: Columbia UP, 1987.

———. "Presidential Address, 1986: 'The Triumph of Theory, the Resistance to Reading, and the Question of the Material Base.' " *PMLA* 102 (1987): 281–91.

Modern Judaism 5.1 (1985). Gershom Scholem Memorial Issue.

Montrose, Louis A. "Professing the Renaissance: The Poetics and Politics of Culture." *The New Historicism.* Ed. H. Aram Veeser. New York: Routledge, 1989. 15–36.

Mosès, Stéphane. *Système et Révelation: La philosophie de Franz Rosenzweig.* Paris: Éditions du Seil, 1982.

———. "Hegel pris au mot: La critique d'histoire chez Franz Rosenzweig." *Revue de metaphysique et de morale* 31 (1985): 328–40.

———. "Walter Benjamin and Franz Rosenzweig." *The Philosophical Forum* 15.1–2 (1983): 188–205.

Nägele, Rainer. "Benjamin's Ground." *Studies in Twentieth Century Literature* 11.1 (1986): 5–24. Special Issue on Walter Benjamin.

Nietzsche, Friedrich. *The Use and Abuse of History.* Trans. Adrian Collins. Indianapolis: Bobbs-Merril, 1957.

Pawell, Ernst. *The Nightmare of Reason: A Life of Franz Kafka.* New York: Farrar Straus, 1984.

Peperzak, Adriaan. "From Intentionality to Responsibility: On Levinas' Philosophy of Language." *The Question of the Other: Essays in Contemporary Continental Philosophy.* Ed. Arleen Dallery and Charles Scott. Albany: State U of New York P, 1989, 3–22.

Perelman, Chaim. "The New Rhetoric: A Theory of Practical Reasoning." *The Rhetoric of Western Thought.* Ed. J. Golden. Dubuque: Kendall Hunt, 1976. 298–317.

Perelman, Chaim, and Olbrechts-Tyteca, L. *The New Rhetoric: A Treatise on Argumentation.* Trans. J. Wilkinson and P. Weaver. 1958; Notre Dame: U of Notre Dame P, 1969.

Pöggeler, Otto. "Between Enlightenment and Romanticism: Rosenzweig and Hegel." *The Philosophy of Franz Rosenzweig.* Ed. Paul Mendes-Flohr. Hanover: UP of New England, 1988. 107–23.

Poirié, François. *Emmanuel Levinas: Qui êtes vous?* Lyons: La Manufacture, 1987.

Ponet, James. "Faces: A Meditation." *Orim: A Jewish Journal at Yale* 1 (1985): 58–76.

Rabinbach, Anson. "Between Enlightenment and Apocalypse: Benjamin, Bloch and Modern German Jewish Messianism." *New German Critique* 34 (1985): 78–125.

———. "Critique and Commentary/Alchemy and Chemistry: Some Remarks on

Walter Benjamin and This Special Issue." *New German Critique* 17 (1979): 3–14.

———. "Introductions to Walter Benjamin's Doctrine of the Similar." *New German Critique* 17 (1979): 60–69.

Rajchman, John, and Cornel West, eds. *Post-Analytic Philosophy.* New York: Columbia, UP, 1985.

Raschke, Carl, ed. *Deconstruction and Theology.* New York: Crossroad, 1982.

Reinharz, Jehuda. *Fatherland or Promised Land: The Dilemma of the German Jews, 1893–1914.* Ann Arbor: U of Michigan P, 1975.

———, ed. *Mystics, Philosophers, and Politicians: Essays in Jewish Intellectual History in Honor of Alexander Altmann.* Durham: Duke UP, 1982.

Reinharz, Jehuda, and Walter Schatzberg, eds. *The Jewish Response to German Culture: From the Enlightenment to the Second World War.* Hanover: UP of New England, 1985.

Roberts, Julian. *Walter Benjamin.* London: Macmillan, 1982.

Rose, Margaret. *Parody/Meta-Fiction: An Analysis of Parody as a Critical Mirror to the Writing and Reception of Fiction.* London: Croom Helm, 1979.

Rosen, Charles. "The Ruins of Walter Benjamin." *On Walter Benjamin: Critical Essays and Recollections.* Ed. Gary Smith. Cambridge: MIT P, 1988. 129–75.

Rosenzweig, Franz. "The New Thinking." *Franz Rosenzweig: His Life and Thought.* Ed. Nahum Glatzer. 2nd ed. New York: Schocken, 1961. 179–213.

———. *On Jewish Learning.* Ed. Nahum Glatzer. 1955; New York: Schocken, 1965.

———. *The Star of Redemption.* 2nd ed., 1930. Trans. William Hallo. New York: Holt Rinehart, 1970. Notre Dame: Notre Dame UP, 1985.

Roskies, David. *Against the Apocalypse: Responses to Catastrophe in Modern Jewish Culture.* Cambridge: Harvard UP, 1984.

———, ed. *The Literature of Destruction: Jewish Responses to Catastrophe.* Philadelphia: Jewish Publication Society, 1988.

Rotenstreich, Nathan. *Jewish Philosophy in Modern Times: From Mendelssohn to Rosenzweig.* New York: Holt Rinehart, 1968.

———. *Jews and German Philosophy: The Polemics of Emancipation.* New York: Schocken, 1984.

———. "Symbolism and Transcendence: On Some Philosophical Aspects of Gershom Scholem's Opus." *Review of Metaphysics* 31 (1977): 604–14.

Rozenblit, Marsha. *The Jews of Vienna, 1867–1914: Assimilation and Identity.* Albany: State U of New York P, 1983.

Scholem, Gershom. *Devarim Be-Go.* 2 vols. Tel Aviv: Am Oved, 1976.

———. "Franz Rosenzweig and His Book *The Star of Redemption.*" *The Philosophy of Franz Rosenzweig.* Ed. Paul Mendes-Flohr. Hanover: UP of New England, 1988. 20–41.

———. *From Berlin to Jerusalem: Memories of My Youth.* Trans. Harry Zohn. 1977; New York: Schocken, 1980.

———. *Jewish Gnosticism, Merkabah Mysticism, and Talmudic Tradition.* 2nd ed. New York: Jewish Theological Seminary, 1965.

———. *Kabbalah.* Jerusalem: Keter, 1974. New York: NAL, 1978.

———. *Major Trends in Jewish Mysticism.* 1946; New York: Schocken, 1961.

———. *The Messianic Idea in Judaism and Other Essays on Jewish Spirituality.* New York: Schocken, 1971.

———. "The Name of God and the Linguistic Theory of the Kabbalah." *Diogenes* 79 (1972): 59–80.

———. "The Name of God and the Linguistic Theory of the Kabbalah." *Diogenes* 80 (1972): 165–94.

_____. *On Jews and Judaism in Crisis: Selected Essays.* Ed. Werner J. Dannhauser. New York: Schocken, 1976.

_____. *On the Kabbalah and Its Symbolism.* Trans. Ralph Mannheim. 1960; New York: Schocken, 1974.

_____. *Origins of the Kabbalah.* Ed. R. J. Werblowsky. Trans. Allan Arkush. Berlin: Walter De Gruyter & Co., 1962. Philadelphia: Jewish Publication Society and Princeton UP, 1987.

_____. "Reflections on the Possibility of Jewish Mysticism in Our Times." *Ariel* 26 (1970): 43–52.

_____. *Sabbatai Sevi: The Mystical Messiah, 1626–1676.* Bollingen Series 93. 1957; Princeton: Princeton UP, 1973.

_____. *Walter Benjamin: The Story of a Friendship.* Trans. Harry Zohn. 1975; Philadelphia: Jewish Publication Society, 1981.

Scholem, Gershom, ed. *The Correspondence of Walter Benjamin and Gershom Scholem, 1932–1940.* Trans. Gary Smith and Andre Lefevere. 1980; New York: Schocken, 1989.

Scholes, Robert. *Textual Power: Literary Theory and the Teaching of English.* New Haven: Yale UP, 1985.

Schorske, Carl E. *Fin-de-Siècle Vienna: Politics and Culture.* 1961; New York: Vintage, 1981.

Schwarzschild, Steven. "Aesthetics." *Contemporary Jewish Religious Thought.* Ed. Arthur Cohen and Paul Mendes-Flohr. New York: Scribner's, 1987. 1–6.

_____. "An Introduction to the Thought of R. Isaac Hutner." *Modern Judaism* 5 (1985): 235–77.

_____. "On Jewish Eschatology." *The Human Condition in the Jewish and Christian Traditions.* Ed. Frederick Greenspahn. Hoboken: Ktav, 1986. 171–211.

Schweid, Eliezer. *Judaism and Mysticism According to Gershom Scholem: A Critical Analysis and Programmatic Discussion.* Trans. David Weiner. Jerusalem: Magnes P, 1983. Atlanta: Scholars P, 1985.

Scult, Allen. "Perelman's Universal Audience: One Perspective." *Central States Speech Journal* 27 (1976): 176–80.

Siebers, Tobin. *The Ethics of Criticism.* Ithaca: Cornell UP, 1986.

Simpson, David, ed. *German Aesthetic and Literary Criticism: Kant, Fichte, Schelling, Schopenhauer.* Cambridge: Cambridge UP, 1984.

Smith, Gary. "The Images of Philosophy: Editor's Introduction." *Philosophical Forum* 15.1–2 (1983): i–ix.

Smith, Gary, ed. *Benjamin: Philosophy, Aesthetics, History.* Chicago: U of Chicago P, 1989.

_____. *On Walter Benjamin: Critical Essays and Recollections.* Cambridge: MIT P, 1988.

Smith, Joseph, and Susan A. Handelman, eds. *Psychoanalysis and Religion.* Psychiatry and the Humanities 11. Baltimore: Johns Hopkins UP, 1990.

Soloveitchik, Rabbi Joseph B. *The Halakhic Mind: An Essay on Jewish Tradition and Modern Thought.* 1944; New York: Free P, 1986.

Steiner, George. *After Babel: Aspects of Language and Translation.* New York: Oxford UP, 1975.

_____. "Heidegger, Again." *Salmagundi* 82–83 (1989): 31–55.

Steinsaltz, Adin. *The Sustaining Utterance: Discourses on Chassidic Thought.* Northvale, N.J.: Jason Aronson, 1989.

Sugarman, Richard, and Helen Stephenson, trans. "To Love the Torah More Than God." *Judaism* 28 (1979): 217–22.

Szondi, Peter. "Hope in the Past: On Walter Benjamin." *Critical Inquiry* 4 (1978): 491–505.

Taylor, Mark C. *Altarity.* Chicago: U of Chicago P, 1987.

Todorov, Tzvetan. *Theories of the Symbol.* Trans. Catherine Porter. Paris: Éditions du Seuil, 1977. Ithaca: Cornell UP, 1982.

Valevicius, Andrius. *From the Other to the Totally Other: The Religious Philosophy of Emmanuel Levinas.* New York: Peter Lang, 1988.

Veeser, H. Aram, ed. *The New Historicism.* New York: Routledge, 1989.

Vickers, Brian. *In Defense of Rhetoric.* Oxford: Clarendon Press, 1988.

Wallwork, Ernest, and Shere Anne Wallwork. "Psychoanalysis and Religion: Current Status of a Historical Antagonism." *Psychoanalysis and Religion.* Ed. Joseph M. Smith and Susan A. Handelman. Baltimore: Johns Hopkins UP, 1990. 160–73.

Walzer, Michael. *Exodus and Revolution.* New York: Basic Books, 1985.

Weaver, Richard. *The Ethics of Rhetoric.* Davis, Calif.: Hermagoras Press, 1985.

——. "Language Is Sermonic." *Contemporary Theories of Rhetoric.* Ed. R. Johanneson. New York: Harper & Row, 1971. 163–83.

White, Hayden. *Metahistory: The Historical Imagination in Nineteenth Century Europe.* Baltimore: Johns Hopkins UP, 1973.

Wiesel, Elie. *Legends of Our Time.* New York: Avon, 1968.

——. *One Generation After.* New York: Random House, 1970.

Wohlfarth, Irving. "Et Cetera? The Historian as Chiffonier." *New German Critique* 39 (1986): 143–68.

——. "History, Literature and the Text: The Case of Walter Benjamin." *Modern Language Notes* 96 (1981): 1002–14.

——. "No-Man's Land: On Walter Benjamin's 'Destructive Character.' " *Diacritics* 8 (1978): 47–65.

——. "On Some Jewish Motifs in Walter Benjamin." Unpublished translation by the author of "Quelques motifs juifs dans l'oeuvre de Walter Benjamin." *Walter Benjamin et Paris.* Ed. Heinz Wismann. Paris: Éditions du Cerf, 1986.

——. "On The Messianic Structure of Walter Benjamin's Last Reflections." *Glyph 3.* Baltimore: Johns Hopkins UP, 1978: 148–212.

——. "Re-fusing Theology." *New German Critique* 39 (1986): 142–68. Second Special Issue on Walter Benjamin.

——. "Walter Benjamin's Image of Interpretation." *New German Critique* 17 (1979): 70–97.

Wolin, Richard. "An Aesthetic of Redemption: Benjamin's Path to Trauerspiel." *Telos* 43 (1980): 61–90.

——. "From Messianism to Materialism: The Later Aesthetics of Walter Benjamin." *New German Critique* 22 (1981): 81–108.

——. *Walter Benjamin: An Aesthetic of Redemption.* New York: Columbia UP, 1982.

Wyschogrod, Edith. "Doing before Hearing: On The Primacy of Touch." *Textes pour Emmanuel Levinas.* Ed. François Laruelle. Paris: Éditions Jean-Michel Place, 1980. 179–202.

——. *Emmanuel Levinas: The Problem of Ethical Metaphysics.* The Hague: Martinus Nijhoff, 1974.

——. "The Moral Self: Emmanuel Levinas and Hermann Cohen." *Da'at* 4 (1980): 35–58.

Yerushalmi, Yosef Haim. *Zakhor: Jewish History and Jewish Memory.* Seattle: U of Washington P, 1982.

Index

SUSAN A. HANDELMAN, Professor of English at the University of Maryland, is author of *The Slayers of Moses: The Emergence of Rabbinic Interpretation in Modern Literary Theory* and coeditor of *Psychoanalysis and Religion*.